THE GENTLE ART
OF PHILOSOPHICAL POLEMICS

THE GENTLE
ART OF PHILOSOPHICAL
POLEMICS:

selected reviews and comments
by
Joseph Agassi

OPEN  COURT

La Salle, Illinois

OPEN COURT and the above logo are registered in the U.S. Patent and Trademark Office.

© 1988 by Open Court Publishing Company

First printing 1988

Printed and bound in the United States of America.

Library of Congress Cataloging-in-Publication Data

Agassi, Joseph.
  The gentle art of philosophical polemics: selected reviews and comments / by Joseph Agassi.
    p.   cm.
  Includes bibliographies and index.
  ISBN 0-912050-63-2: $45.95. ISBN 0-8126-9036-2 (pbk.): $19.95 1. Philosophy
—Book reviews. I. Title.
  B73.A43   1988   88–19000
  100—dc19   CIP

*For Judith with love,
gratitude and appreciation*

Contents

PREFACE

The following selection of reviews and comments is presented to the reader for three distinct purposes. The first is to promote the new standards of criticism, of hard-hitting yet appreciative assaults on worthy opponents. Voltaire ascribed this attitude to the English, with obvious envy and appreciation, and as he confided this to his diary one may assume that he was sincere in his expression. This attitude is described by Karl Popper as friendly-hostile co-operation and declared essential for science. It is still not very popular. Even today too few intellectuals welcome criticism. More on this in the preface to Part I—as well as *passim*.

The second purpose is to promote critical surveys of fields of study or problem-situations from several distinct points of view, in the hope that each field will repeatedly receive attention from competing points of view. Part I is an attempt at a critical survey of philosophy of science (and, much more cursorily, of fields) from a more or less coherent point of view, the 'Popperian' or—as the German philosophers call it—the 'criticalist' school.

The third purpose is to give a picture of this school, increasingly influential yet insufficiently familiar as it is. Part II begins with a review of two works by non-members regarding the Popper school, but the rest is from the inside, so to speak, ending with my own attempt to offer a rounded picture of Popper's contribution to philosophy.

Some of the chapters appearing here were written in order to fill gaps in the picture. That is not to say that any claim for completeness is made, only that an attempt was made to offer a rounded impression.

This merits a small *aperçu* as to the progress we have witnessed in a field so often accused of barrenness. Not so long ago, reviewers of Karl Popper's *The Open Society and Its Enemies*, first edition (1945) and second edition (1950), complained that the author's own views are not clearly expounded, as he spends most of his pages criticizing other authors. These days such a complaint sounds less convincing. This is a measure of progress. It can be consolidated by the institution and extension of the practice of expressing ideas in review-essays and surveys, which can grow to the point where scholars will generally welcome criticism and will naturally endorse the critical style of learning. This work is an attempt to contribute to that salutary process.

Finally, the essays reprinted here have undergone minor corrections, which do not change any of the arguments advanced. I do not mean to imply that I would today endorse every statement I have published over the last 30 years. I hope, however, that regardless of agreement or disagreement they are still of interest.

J. A.

ACKNOWLEDGMENTS

As it is customary not to make the usual acknowledgment to colleagues who help in the preparation or in the writing of an essay when that essay is a comment or a review, this is an occasion to make some acknowledgments belatedly. Yet I find overwhelming the thought of mentioning all the teachers, colleagues, and friends who have had a hand in many of the enclosed essays which cover a period of thirty years. With apologies to most of them, I should mention only three. First, Karl Popper worked with me with unbelievable generosity over the earliest essays included here, from 1956 to 1960. He also kindly spent a few hours discussing with me my planned review of his *Objective Knowledge* in 1974. This was, to my loss and profound regret, our last intellectual exchange: he met the uncompromising harshness of my review with a similar attitude towards the very possibility of our having valuable exchanges. I would also like to mention here Judith Buber Agassi and I. C. Jarvie who regularly read parts of my output with pencil in hand. And I could not have written the closing essay—the Popper retrospect—without their help, as well as that of Gerd Fleischmann, Jagdish Hattiangadi, Nathaniel Laor, and John Wettersten. The idea that, since methodology was never taken to be strictly an algorithm, there can be no sharp divide between a method and a heuristic, seems to me to be of great importance as it opens new avenues of research, and I cannot claim priority for it. I learned it from discussion with all of them over a long period of time.

I also owe a debt of gratitude to all the editors and publishers who have given me permission to republish the essays here reproduced, and to the authors of the responses here reproduced, namely Gunnar Andersson and Paul K. Feyerabend.

PART I

CASTING DOWN GAUNTLETS

INTRODUCTION TO PART I

When an editor, whose permission to republish was requested, learned that the present collection was to be titled *The Gentle Art of Philosophical Polemics*, he responded that of course the title is meant to be ironic. Well, yes. It is taken from the painter, James Whistler, whose title* was doubtless meant in irony. Yet irony, as distinct from sheer parody, satire, sarcasm or farce, is always to be taken literally as well. Otherwise, the greatest master of irony, the Socrates of Plato's early dialogues, will be utterly misunderstood. And, indeed, he is misunderstood by every commentator who cannot agree with ironic statements in Plato's texts taken literally.

The trouble begins with the idea that disagreement entails disrespect, which idea follows the demand that we all produce proofs of the truth of our assertions. For, had we followed this demand properly, disagreement would be bound to vanish.

Yet I feel I am dodging the observation of my learned friend about the irony of my title. I will return to the idea of friendly dissent and criticism. Here I must admit that this is an ideal, one not shared by most of my peers, who consequently are all too often justified in taking my critical stance as a mark of my wild aggressive impulse which is but a regrettable personality trait.

No amount of justification of an action may allow us to ignore the pain it causes, and to the extent that my criticisms—whether ones reproduced here or others—have caused pain, I do sincerely express genuine regret. Was I in error causing the pain I have caused? Was it avoidable? I do not know.

Criticism fundamentally differs from polemics, which is the Greek for war and the English for verbal war, namely for public criticism. Criticism

---

*James Abbott McNeill Whistler, *The Gentle Art of Making Enemies*, London, 1890.

resembles a sporting contest in private, while polemics is like a similar contest on public display. They seem essentially the same, as they supposedly follow the same rules; in practice they differ, and the chief difference is not in the game or in the playing of it, but in the very setting.

The rule for the setting of a critical debate, like the rule for the setting of any private contest, is very simple: all parties to the game are there due to their own free decision. Therefore, whether a party gets hurt or not, whether a party decides to continue despite damage—to body or to proud ego—all this is private, not in the public arena.

The rules for setting a public debate are as complex as the rules for setting any other public contest. And a party may wish to avoid it but be in no position to do so, and then the blows come down and the contestant may be hurt and defenseless. This is never pleasant. Harry S Truman said: if you can't stand the heat, stay out of the kitchen. This is very sound advice, but one may be unable to heed it, and for all sorts of reasons, one of which may be that one has entered the kitchen when conditions were quite different and is trapped there now. One may have entered the wrong kitchen by some oversight and be trapped there.

The most painful critical piece in my whole career may illustrate this. I had no idea at the time what game I was playing and what was the arena. I was a young beginner and a temporary teacher in the London School of Economics, under the tutelage of Karl Popper, my former thesis adviser and close friend. He naturally hoped that I would expound and commend his ideas, as I admired them so, which I gladly did—and still do. Whenever I published, later on, a review which did not do that, he took it as an affront—always, except when I wrote a review of a book by Jorge Luis Borges (not reproduced here), which he presumably considered too remote from his own work. When I published a highly unfavorable critical review of his *Objective Knowledge* (reproduced here in Part II), he broke off relations with me for good. Yet I am telling of a review written in my earliest days when we were still close. It was a brief review of *Minnesota Studies in the Philosophy of Science*, Volume II (reproduced here), which appeared in *Mind* in 1958. It was almost an accident that I did it, yet it was very significant in my career. I was given the opportunity by Gilbert Ryle whom I met then for the first time and who kindly befriended me. He gave me the book to review, evidently desiring to help me launch a career. Unfortunately the book was very poor even by the standard accepted then in the philosophical world. Paul Feyerabend was a friend of the editors and much later he kindly reported to me that one of them confessed to him that the volume was prepared in haste and not carefully enough. I did not know that then. I could not suspect how important it was for them just then to receive favorable reviews, but such was the case: the Minnesota Center was up for the renewal of its grant, I am told. I am a fast worker and so my review appeared soon and, by a series of further accidents, it was a trend-setter.

Herbert Feigl, the head of the Center and chief editor of the book, was deeply hurt. He wrote Popper a long plaintive letter, asking him why he could not control that young colt—meaning me. Popper was impressed and passed the complaint on to me. I was truly amazed. At the period in question I was just emerging from my status as his research assistant, which permitted me a close co-operation with him. (He made me a very handsome acknowledgment in the preface to his *Postscript*.) It seemed very natural to me that he should see the draft of my review of that book, which was deeply indebted to his ideas, and that I should seek his help in its completion. When I received the proofs I wanted to make some small changes, and, still unsure of myself, I went to the nearest public phone booth (I had no private phone then) and rang him to consult him on the changes. I do not know why, but he actually scoffed at me. I was used to his shouting at me when I was his assistant: he was the only person I allowed this privilege, and I did not resent it since it was my own choice to stay with him—an obviously wise choice it was.

The reviewer of Volume III of *Minnesota Studies* that appeared in *Mind* began his report by an attack on my review of Volume II. I still think this is not according to the rules. There are proper ways to attack a reviewer, but this is not one of them. I met Herbert Feigl many times later on. He rejected my offers of friendship out of hand. He claimed I hadn't read the book I had condemned. He said that the only way I could make amends and gain his good will would be for me to praise his ideas on induction. I am afraid I never did. I was regularly penalized, and in many ways, by those of his admirers who were in positions of power. I am glad to say that I did make friends with some of them later on—but only on a personal basis. On the professional level they still think the profession better off without a fellow like me and they behave accordingly.

I do not mean to single out one case: it is, doubtless, unusual; but it is not unique—since no group has a monopoly over the dislike of criticism. I should mention, though only in passing, that the late Maurice Freedman, who commissioned my review of Popper's *Conjectures and Refutations*—reprinted here—concluded that we Popperians are a crazy lot, after he stood up against an aggressive demand from the late Imre Lakatos to suppress that review. And Lakatos did manage to suppress some of my work when editors less brave than Freedman were involved, but that is another story.

All this is not meant as a complaint: I do consider my career, as far as my own ambition is concerned, a stupendous success, both in my own assessment of my own attainment and in the public recognition I was fortunate to acquire. I am only comparing my success with my ambition; let me repeat myself: I have no objective standards. Sociologists say many things about achievement but they offer me no help, as they never question their own supposition that intellectual achievement is properly measurable by public acclaim; and this despite the truism that acclaim may radically alter one way or another. This supposition could be relied upon only if information were very easily accessible, at least in the world of learning, and if scholars were honest about their own assessments of their colleagues.

In my youth I thought Karl Popper was amazingly underestimated. When I was in Jerusalem, a young graduate in physics seeking a place to study the philosophy of science, I inquired about possible teachers, particularly in England. I asked friends who were studying in London; I consulted teachers; I went to official information offices. After all this I came upon Popper's name when I was already in London, and by accident. Although I still think Popper was underestimated at the time, I think he was better known than the literature of the time would lead us to surmise. In other words, his ideas were better appreciated by the knowledgeable than they let on to the general public.

Such intellectual success as I have enjoyed is almost entirely thanks to my work under Popper's tutelage. Sociologists, by the way, not only identify intellectual achievement with intellectual prestige; they equate the two with teaching achievement. This, too, is amply refuted. Popper's success as a teacher is rooted in his utter dedication to his work and to his utterly egalitarian attitude toward his students in all intellectual exchanges. Unfortunately, he has limited his intellectual exchanges with all of us to private encounters; his expressions of disagreement with any of us in public are, as far as I know, brief, *ad hominem*, and worthless at best. Even his constant admonition to us to be fair to our opponents is not one for which he is a model: I think John Watkins is, and the little I have of this ability I have acquired from him.

Yet my worldly success, my first lucky break, came when J. O. Wisdom, editor of the *British Journal for the Philosophy of Science* at the peak of its intellectual achievement, offered me the chance to publish there an essay-review on Pierre Duhem's *Aim and Structure of Physical Theory*—republished here—and other essay reviews, despite the crudeness of my scholarship and the poor control I had of my pen and my struggles with the English tongue. These reviews established me at once, and other editors invited me to write other reviews.

I mention all this not only as an expression of gratitude to Popper and his associates, but also as an encouragement to ambitious young colleagues to attempt to publish ambitious and honest reviews. No doubt this may cause some hostility, but it also brings about much friendship. And much of my success I owe to my friends. Among them are some targets of my sharp criticism who never felt hurt by it, or who never resented the hurt. I am particularly grateful to those—Gunnar Andersson, and Paul Feyerabend—who kindly permitted me to republish their replies. I am sorry that Feyerabend has not permitted me to republish his reply to my last attack on him, which is republished here regrettably without his response. His reasons, he assures me, are not personal. I also regret my requests from others to grant me the opportunity to incorporate their responses here did not meet with success. Especially regrettable, may I repeat, I find Popper's reluctance to respond to criticisms I have offered against his views. I have a constant sense of failure due to my inability to sustain reasonably good relations with the person to whom I am most deeply indebted, both intellectually and personally.

To return to Whistler, it mattered to him very little that a presumptuous, pompous critic should think his work a piece of fraud; and the fact that the critic in question was a famous thinker, John Ruskin by name, mattered to him less. But the write-up hurt his reputation and was false on matters of fact as well as supercilious in matters of taste. So there was room for complaint; and complain Whistler did—and in a fashion he won in court.* To return to my review of *Minnesota Studies*, Volume II, I did not discuss its preparation, only the final product, and I declared it poor. I stand by the details of my judgment and expect no one to challenge them, simply because they are now shared by all concerned. The overall judgment, however, is still open to contest—if anyone is still willing to defend that volume.

Nevertheless, it is painful to see one's work dismissed as of little value. If one is well-trained, and I am proud to say I am, one is not pained by being so dismissed, not even by so being dismissed by the Establishment year in and year out, yet decidedly it is much more enjoyable to have the fruits of one's labor appreciated by some people rather than totally ignored or dismissed.

And here comes the most important philosophic point, made by Plato (*Gorgias*) and by Martin Buber (*I and Thou*): any criticism is better than a dismissal or an oversight. Yet philosophers, no less than other intellectuals, take criticism as harsh dismissal and as worse than oversight. Nothing is worse, we all know, than faint praise and backhanded compliment. Yet those who practice this vicious art always get away with it. This situation calls for more than a correction of a personal error: it calls for some institutional reform. We have to find ways to rehabilitate the word 'polemics', which, to repeat, is the Greek for war and the English for verbal war. The pen, we all agree, is indeed mightier than the sword. Also, of course, it is ever so much cleaner. Yet this important dynamic and moral superiority is neither here nor there. The injustice we show in our usual contempt for polemics stems from an intellectual error: Who needs polemics? we wonder, and conclude that, since there is no intellectual need for polemics, polemics merely satisfy personal needs, and are therefore petty, perhaps demagogic, misrepresentational, and thus sheer irresponsibility. This conclusion verifies itself: one finds one's involvement in polemics irritating and responds in irritation and in moral indignation.

It must be seen that polemics is a ramification, in public, of criticism which may very well be offered in private. I report that many a time I had

---

*The case was complicated, chiefly by Ruskin's mental illness. Whistler won one farthing in damages.

occasion to criticize publicly and did so privately—with the resultant gratitude, at times indicated or hinted at, at times expressed quite explicitly. I can also report that Popper's enormous annoyance at my public criticism of his ideas is rooted in his opinion that I should have offered him that criticism in private, since he is so very open to criticism and ready, even eager, to accept it, so that my criticizing him in public is evidently rooted in my ambition to be one up on him.

Let me say that, though I find Popper's view of the public display of criticism not the last word on the topic, I admire his Socratic view of the importance of criticism as such, of the wisdom of taking it seriously. One need not be a great philosopher to see this point. Who needs criticism? boldly asked James Blish, the celebrated science-fiction author and critic. Everybody! he boldly answered his own question. And criticism means: fault-finding, whether moral or intellectual or artistic; when moral it is preaching, and when intellectual it is polemics, and when artistic it is art criticism.

When discussing this with young friends I often praised polemics, and used words like 'war', 'attack', and 'quarrel'. The use of these words in this way causes displeasure all too often. So, to avoid this displeasure, especially in initial stages of contacts with new young friends, I now prefer 'discussion' or 'debate'. I have thus made a psycho-linguistic empirical discovery the like of which I have found nowhere in the literature, except in the works of the famous anthropologist John M. Roberts, whose researches may have alerted me to this discovery. When I use the word 'discussion' favorably, I am advised to use the word 'debate' instead, and *vice versa*, and the advice is accompanied by the explanation that the one word has positive overtones, while those of the other are negative. Clearly, then, both words carry both overtones, thus indicating the neurotic or ambivalent attitude toward polemics inherent in our culture—not as a psychological component but as a philosophic confusion.

I never attack a person, only a doctrine, said Friedrich Nietzsche, meaning that his attacks were intellectual and not personal, not petty. But this is not good enough: criticism is a sign of appreciation, says Karl Popper. This is better: it is a sign of appreciation of ideas and thus of their bearers. Even when a critic chooses a target for no better reason than the target's popularity, the choice bespeaks some appreciation, though regrettably more political-intellectual than strictly intellectual.

So much for criticism. If criticism is a sign of appreciation, why is there so much more dislike for its public display than for offering it in private? The most important answer is that people hate criticism, that even if they are ready to take it, it is bitter medicine: criticism is finding fault and error and we can very well do without them!

This metaphor is obstructive rather than enlightening. Medicine is at times very pleasant and at times very unpleasant; it may hurt, but it never hurts the ego. Why does criticism hurt the ego? Because one wants to be above all error. Why? Because one wants to be accepted, loved, appreciated. Hence the appropriateness of George Bernard Shaw's astute observation (in his preface to *St. Joan*): one who achieves the high position of being ever so often more right than one's peers is forced to drink hemlock, or is crucified, or is burned at the stake. Why do we feel that in order to be acceptable we must be right? Because our teachers and parents say so throughout our childhood, and because we have to do our jobs well, and popular prejudice accepts the norms of our society as beyond question, so that to do the job well is to be right. This does not hold for intellectuals, and so they suffer. Their suffering shows every time they are challenged. The hostility to criticism, especially polemics, is often enough rooted in sheer confusion and self-rejection.

Yet before I leave the general matter and plunge to the material at hand I should observe one more detail. Ever so often the accepted norms are known to be in need of improvement, yet it is taken for granted that they should be heeded until they are replaced. (This is known as the idea of constructive criticism: we know that our system is not perfect, so we do not want to hear your remarks which merely put it down: if you want to be useful, work out a viable alternative. And when you have one, we will ignore your strictures and attack your alternative.) One of the fictions accepted in many societies is that office-holders hold their office by right, and by the right of their having proved themselves superior to their competitors. When a lecture given by a big fellow contains errors it should not contain, the errors must be overlooked by the same fiction. When a young impetuous colleague goes to great lengths to embarrass the big fellow publicly, then the young colleague is in error in simply playing the right game at the wrong time. If a lecturer makes silly mistakes yet the lecture is given not as a ceremony but as the real thing, then he is fair game and the complaint that the young colleague has embarrassed the august lecturer is no complaint at all, and penalizing the young then, for example by denying them tenure, is an impediment to learning and the betrayal of a trust.

This is not to say that such matters are or are not daily occurrences. It is to say that they will become rare if we see to it that public polemics be properly performed and in the right spirit and with no ego punctured. And this invites discourses on the gentle art of polemics, which in turn invites the publication and examination of scholarly polemical literature.

What we need, let me emphasize, is not a new art, nor the development of an existing art, but institutions to safeguard it. Let me speak of my own experiences, if I may. As a fairly well-known critic, I am usually judged too eager to slaughter opponents in public, with no concern for personal feelings, for reputations, for anything. This would make me utterly friendless. Yet my success, such as it is, must be ascribed to a large extent to the good will of ever so many friendly colleagues, some of whom I encountered during polemical sessions of one sort or another. I can report that some moderators behaved quite abominably and protectively when I, as a young

commentator, had too easy a job pricking bubbles of some famous, allegedly able, intellectual leaders. Once, I remember, a second commentator commented on the excesses of my first comments rather than on the speaker's
talk, even though he agreed with my strictures. And the moderator did not
intervene! Yet ever so many cases I remember of decent moderators and of
decent speakers who took my comments in the right spirit; and they remained friends for life. One such was H. L. A. Hart, the leading legal
philosopher, whom I had never met before he chaired a philosophical
gathering in London which I happened to attend. The speaker complained
about my conduct in the question period but the chair stuck to the rules. I
had an occasion to meet Hart again only a quarter-of-a-century later. He
spoke to me as to an old friend, and I was deeply touched. The speaker on
that old occasion, too, incidentally, is a friend. England is where the gentle
art of polemics is traditional, and it aroused the just admiration of Voltaire.
Nevertheless, even there experience is not always happy. The leadership of
the profession has to be forced by popular demand to institute safeguards
similar to those which exist in public sporting contests.

Publishing a collection of critical reviews is not common—at least I
know of no instance of it, though quite a few recent collections of essays include review essays. Conspicuous examples are Collingwood's critical
review of Croce, and Einstein's contribution to *The Philosophy of Bertrand
Russell*. The review essay is a recent arrival, and it does signify a welcome
change in public attitudes towards criticism. Recently that *éminence grise* of
philosophy, Sidney Hook, told a story concerning his beloved teacher, Morris
Raphael Cohen, who showed incredible hostility to anyone inclined to criticize his work in public. Hook meant such peculiar hostility to seem idiosyncratic. In fact, it was standard in Europe for centuries and until World War
II, if not to date. Yet there is a change in the climate of opinion on this, as exemplified by the recent demand of eminent physicist and philosopher, John
Ziman, FRS, for more critical surveys and critical essays. The reviews and
review-essays republished here are offered to the reader in the new spirit of
polemics: they were not written lightly or aggressively, and whenever their
forthrightness sounds aggressive, I hope the reader will take it as a failure
on my part: my intention in presenting this volume is to help the reader to
gain a truer picture of the present situation in the philosophy of science, not
to discharge hostility.

Let these essays, then, be taken as tributes to their targets, of the variety
of tributes at one's disposal when engaged in combat and in the heat of a
public contest. Even a complaint that someone has broken the rules may be
taken as a compliment: we cannot possibly record all instances of breaking
the rules. We can notice only the most significant cases—always in the hope
that thus the general level of performance, public and private, will improve,
and in ever so many ways.

— 1 —

ON BACON

father of modern radicalism

The case of Sir Francis Bacon is as colorful as it is puzzling. He was a trained lawyer and a professional politician of note in Elizabethan England—especially for a most unusual eloquence and rhetorical force. His story is vividly told in a classic essay written by one of the best and most imaginative English historians ever, Lord Macaulay (1837), who portrayed him as a corrupt politician and a traitor to his friends. This essay led an admirer of Bacon, James Spedding, to write a defense of Bacon, *Conversations with a Reviewer* (1848), which is a few times longer than Macaulay's essay, tortured, and typical of the unending and apologetic literature devoted to this extraordinarily colorful person. Macaulay's judgment is still the received opinion; the importance of Spedding's work is chiefly in that it drew the attention of Robert Leslie Ellis to its author, who thus became the chief editor of the standard edition of Bacon's works in one of the strangest stories of modern scholarship.

Ellis was a genius who died of consumption in early middle age over a hundred years ago. He was a mathematician and a biologist, but mainly a classical scholar. He was fascinated with Bacon and decided to edit his works. He did much of the editing, but on his deathbed he passed the material unpublished to Spedding, including his translations of some of the Latin works, his classic general preface to Bacon's *Works*, and his preface to the *Novum Organum* and a few more prefaces. To these Spedding has added the missing prefaces; classic amongst these are those to Bacon's *The Wisdom of the Ancients* and to *The New Atlantis* as well as a moving life of Bacon. The result was the still-standard edition by Spedding, Ellis, and

This review of James Stephens, *Francis Bacon and the Style of Science* (Chicago: University of Chicago Press, 1976) appeared in *Philosophy and Rhetoric*, 9, 1976.

Heath (who specialized on Bacon's legal works), of 14 volumes (1857–74). The prefaces reveal a breathtaking picture of the collapse of an intellectual house of cards.

Bacon was revered in the 18th century as the father of modern science. Paul Hazard tells us that his name was then the only one mentionable in one breath with Newton's without blasphemy. Ellis, naturally, approached his subject with awe. He found Bacon's egalitarian idea that scientific method equalizes intellects, just as ruler and compass equalize draftsmen, both marvelous and historically very influential. But all promises notwithstanding, Bacon offered no method and said almost nothing about induction. The method of science advocated by Newton and accepted by Ellis, namely that of induction by generalization, Bacon had attacked as childish. Bacon's six-volume *Great Instauration* was only sketched. Its major work, the *Novum Organum*, which advocates avoiding all guesses and sticking only to certainties, breaks down at the crucial moment, where Bacon, in lieu of his promised example of induction, offers a conjecture. The scant scientific works he offers are crude plagiarisms at best, often from people whom he derided (in particular, William Gilbert, whose manuscripts on diverse topics he plagiarized while insinuating that Gilbert wrote only on magnets because magnets became his monomania). What was new in Bacon? Why was he important?

Bacon said, I am first, I follow no one. Ellis was impressed, even though he knew how conceited Bacon could be. Recently R. F. Jones showed that this claim was in the style of the time; Lynn Thorndike published a classic essay with a string of doubtful, boastful claims for utter novelty. Ellis felt at least Bacon's rendering of the myth of Cupid was new and intriguing. Ellis was an incredibly learned scholar, but here he showed ignorance of one, rather insignificant mystic author, Natale Conti. Recently C. W. Lemmi has shown Bacon's passage on Cupid to have been lifted from Conti. No matter. Spedding accepted Ellis's views *en bloc* and concluded, anyway, that they are damning enough. He also showed that Bacon was naive enough to really believe his own myths and fables. No matter. Bacon had suggested a new method of science: that of collecting innumerable data with no hypothesis to put any order into them, in the hope that these would lead straight to certain knowledge. This had not been tried and Spedding said it should. William Whewell, the greatest nineteenth-century philosopher of science, reviewed Spedding and said, naval meteorological records are Baconian and no good. The *coup de grâce* came soon after: the most damning all-round attack on Bacon was a very learned and very contemptuous essay by a great scientist, Justus von Liebig (English trans., *Macmillan's Magazine*, 8, 1863). Bacon's only claim to fame, he said, is his *Essays*.

Yet Bacon's influence was immense. His theory that all hypotheses are prejudices to be eschewed (even the word 'prejudice' is his), inconsistent though it is (being a prejudice by its very own light), had a great impact.

His demand that facts be reported as they are can only be met, as he noted, by abolishing most current language, which cannot be done. Yet he encouraged scientists to report facts clearly, and this is a great merit. His rules concerning style are still imposed on writers for many periodicals in the social and life sciences, where facts unexplained are presented for no apparent reason in the first and longest part of each paper; physicists—Faraday and Einstein, in particular—have since developed a much better style. Bacon's venomous attack on all his predecessors and on the universities, though unjust, put an end to the tedious scholarly style of his day and led to writing with almost no acknowledgments, and to educational reforms as well. In short, he was the father of modern radicalism and thus the greatest modern influence on most of the philosophers of the succeeding generations, from Descartes to the Philosophes.

The title of the present volume is exciting. It attempts to combine—correctly, I think—Bacon's views on science with his views on rhetoric. But the author dismisses Macaulay as a historian-in-inverted-commas, accepts Bacon's inconsistent views as true, describes him as an elitist, as the originator of the true scientific method, as a profound psychologist, as a serious scholar and an original natural scientist, and so on. Back to the drawing board.

Bacon declared that science must be kept pure and free from all error, hence free also from all rhetorical devices. But since the prejudiced are convinced of the truth of their prejudice and so not given to rational dissuasion, he may well be tackled by rhetoric. Bacon incredibly combines two opposite classical rhetorical devices here: he (1) confides in his readers about (2) cheating them: he tells his readers that they are prejudiced and thus unfit for science and he tells his (one?) reader that he is going to deceive his (other?) reader so as to make good (i.e., Baconian) scientists out of (both of) them.

This is all that matters on Bacon, on science, and on rhetoric proper; as to Bacon on scientific nonrhetorical style and on nonscientific style—rhetorical and nonrhetorical—there is a vast topic here. Bacon's influence was so vast that it even led to the misinterpretation of Shakespeare by classic critics too sane even to suggest any link between the two. But I am not competent to survey the modern literature on Renaissance works on rhetoric and style, general European or English, and Bacon's place there. The author of the present volume offers a glimpse at the literature, but I for one am unenlightened. All in all I found perusing the present volume rather painful as these pages seem to me apologetic, elitist, pro-myth, narrow, out-of-date, and unscholarly. But I may be in serious error: it may well be but the style of a genre or of a literature with which I am simply unaccustomed.

2

ANALOGIES AS GENERALIZATIONS

either ad hoc or fallacious

I

Traditionally, analogies have been recognized as a proper part of inductive procedures, akin to generalizations. Seldom, however, have they been presented as superior to generalizations in the attainability of a higher degree of certitude for their conclusions or in other respects. Though Bacon definitely preferred analogy to generalization,[1] the tradition seems to me to go the other way—until the publication of works by R. Harré ([1] pp. 23–28 and *passim*) and by Mary B. Hesse ([2] pp. 21–28 and *passim*).

I shall now argue the following two points. First, generalizations proper are preferable to predictions from past observations to a single future observation, since the latter are *ad hoc*. Second, analogies are either generalizations proper—perhaps higher-level ones—or *ad hoc*. In any case, they are not more certain than generalizations, but they are still equally legitimate.

II

Traditionally, extensions of known observation-reports to unknown cases are of two kinds: from the sample to the whole ensemble—generalizations proper—and from the sample to the next case to be observed. Of course, all intermediate cases between these two extremes are possible, but inductive philosophers have hardly paid any attention to them. The reason may be this: the principle of paucity of assumptions leads us to reject the generalization, i.e., the extension of an observation-report about the observed sample to the whole ensemble, in favour of a less bold extension. The least bold extension is not to extend the report at all (the conventionalist twist); but as this will not do, the extension to the next case to be observed is advocated as a secondbest. In my

---

This first appeared in *Philosophy of Science*, 31, 1964.

opinion, this mode of thinking is erroneous. Our assertion about the next case should be interpreted in the following way: the next case to be observed will agree with the sample on the basis of the hypothesis that the sample is representative; otherwise, we claim, in effect, that the next case to be observed is somehow more closely linked to our sample than to the ensemble as a whole.

Take the standard example of induction concerning the whiteness of swans. The next swan is going to be white, we assert. We may so assert because we think all swans are white. Alternatively, we may think that all swans in our neighbourhood are white. This is not different at all from the previous case, except in the choice of ensemble—swans-in-our-neighbourhood instead of swans. Alternatively, we may expect to be lucky and avoid on the next occasion encountering any of the existing non-white swans. The next swan we meet may be white even though all unobserved swans in the universe except that one are non-white, or even though only one quarter of the unobserved swans in the universe are white, or one-half, or three-quarters, etc. In other words, the hypothesis that the next swan to be observed will be white is not an extension from the existing sample, but rather a disjunction among (infinitely) many conjunctions about all unobserved swans in the universe and about our luck with the next observation (see *Appendix*). *If we do not claim that all unobserved swans in the universe are white, and if we deny that our next encounter with a swan is of any special cosmic significance, then we cannot but ascribe the whiteness of the next swan to mere chance.* The assumption that no matter what the distribution of swans in the universe, the chances are that the next swan to be observed will be white *because* all swans so far observed were white, seems to be a way out. But it is merely the well-known gambler's fallacy, as has been proved by Popper.[2] This exhausts all possibilities, as well as explaining why we refuse to consider seriously the theory 'since all observed swans are white the swan that Tom will observe next is white but the swan that Dick will observe next is not'. It is too arbitrary; it gives *ad hoc*, or with no reason, a special significance to Tom's observation.[3]

III

And now to analogy. Take the assertion that since Tom possesses the property *P* and the property *Q*, so Dick, who possesses the property *P*, also by analogy possesses the property *Q*. Suppose that Harry also possesses the property *P*; either (*a*) by the same analogy Harry also possesses the property *Q*, or (*b*) we arbitrarily discriminate between Dick and Harry, or else (*c*) we give reasons for discriminating—by differentiating between Dick and Harry. Case (*a*) is obviously an argument by analogy which is the same as a generalization; case (*b*) must be dismissed like all *ad hoc* hypotheses. Take, then, case (*c*). Differentiating between Dick and Harry amounts to the claim that the one but not the other possesses the property R. This property R is either (C_1) possessed by Tom as well, or (C_2). Case (C_1) is:

	Known			Assumed
Tom	P	Q	R	
Dick	P		R	Q
Harry	P	$\sim Q$	$\sim R$	

The argument here is by analogy not from P to Q as had first been stated, but from P and R to Q (or perhaps even from R to Q). Either it applies to all who possess P and R, or it is *ad hoc*, or it is not from P and R but from P, R, and S. And so on, until we exhaust all the characteristics shared by Tom and Dick. Case (C_2) is:

	Known		Assumed
Tom	P	$Q \sim R$	
Dick	P	R	Q
Harry	$P \sim Q \sim R$		

Here we see no argument by analogy at all; it is merely the hypothesis that Dick posesses the property Q.

This discussion, then, shows conclusively that the analogy from Tom to Dick is either a generalization or *ad hoc*.

IV

In the literature, the label 'analogy' is usually employed when the names 'Tom', 'Dick', etc. are universal names. This does not alter the above discussion; it merely presents analogy as a higher-level generalization which, being based on lower-level ones, cannot be more reliable, or less open to objection, than the lower-level ones.[4]

Also, in the literature, more often than not, the word 'analogy' is used when Dick or his possession of the property Q is unobservable (rather than not yet observed). Examples are Ampère's (alleged) analogy from the existence of currents in electromagnets to the existence of currents in magnets proper, or the (alleged) analogies concerning the elastic properties of the luminous ether. Here, again, the previous discussion remains applicable, and unobservability surely does not add to the reliability of a mode of argument or detract from the objections raised against it.

A generalization is often claimed to be more reliable when certain conditions are met to a higher degree. The conditions stated differ from author to author. Yet on the whole I have the feeling that three conditions are traditional: (*a*) that the sample should be random, (*b*) that it be (relatively) large,

(c) that the ensemble or population be characterized by a stringent set of properties. Quite possibly when condition (b) is met we tend to speak more of a generalization, and when condition (c) is met we tend to speak more of an analogy (we can never know that condition (a) has been met). But this is an intuitive matter, and one can construct examples which intuitively go either way. In any case the form of a generalization which meets condition (b) more readily than (c) is the same as the form of one which goes the other way. Hence one cannot ascribe more reliability to the one or the other, and objections validly applicable to one are equally validly applicable to the other.

As both Hesse ([2] p. 25) and Harré ([1] p. 26) have noticed, statements like 'atoms are round and hard like billiard balls' are, strictly speaking, not analogies: they are metaphors, to use these authors' terminology. Metaphors are easy to construct to elucidate any theory, but they go no further. Statements like 'nerves conduct electricity like telegraphs' are analogies proper: nerves and telegraphs both transmit information and, we claim, both transmit electricity. But the analogy is *ad hoc*: no one dreams of applying it to any other information channel. The analogy perhaps was fruitful in suggesting a theory—nerves transmit electricity—but we then consider the theory on its own merit, ignoring the analogy altogether (unless as teachers we wish to employ it as a metaphor or as historians of science we wish to investigate whether it was originally the trigger of a new idea). Analogies which are non-*ad hoc* are easy to construct but one scarcely finds them in science textbooks; usually they are stated as generalizations proper. An author concerned with the inductive mode of presentation may, for instance, explain that element *x* whose atomic number is not a whole number has isotopes and then suggest, by analogy, that element *y*, whose atomic number is not a whole number, also has isotopes. In this case the author has in mind a modern variant of Prout's hypothesis, and will soon state it. Most authors, however, prefer to approach the same hypotheses with protons and neutrons, and come to the table of chemical elements later on, in the proper deductive order.

V

Hesse seems to suggest that analogies are significant in science because they enable us to explain the meanings of abstract terms and theories, even though this necessarily makes the analogy (from the more concrete to the more abstract) imperfect. In this case analogies are admittedly *ad hoc* analogies, so that one can hardly see the difference between analogy and metaphor (or analogy and "dead metaphor" to quote the author). Harré's view is more traditional: confirming analogies is, in his view, "a character-

istic move in the advanced sciences" ([1] p. 25). He gives an example of a hypothetical protective 'skin' which prevents aluminum from corrosion, which has actually been peeled off pieces of aluminum ([1] p. 26). I fail to see any analogy here at all; there is here a metaphor and one which is completely redundant, as we can speak of a thin layer of oxydized aluminum instead of a skin since nobody has claimed that just as the human body is protected from corrosion and has a thin layer so is aluminum. There was a problem: as aluminum is combustible, what prevents aluminum from bursting into flames like sodium or kalium? And the answer was that it is protected by a thin layer. The analogy, incidentally, between sodium and aluminum, as all analogies concerning the table of chemical elements, is a proper analogy, and not *ad hoc* at all—it is a generalization.

To conclude, I have contended here that arguments from existing knowledge to single predictions, or from one known case to another by analogy, are either *ad hoc* or fallacious; but I have argued neither against generalizations proper nor against analogies proper. I have merely contended that their logic is the same and that hence they are equally reliable or unreliable. For my own part, I think that all hypotheses are welcome, be they generalizations or not. I am not concerned with reliability, nor do I object to either generalization or analogy, but rather to the *ad hoc* character of some analogies, or, more particularly, to their being advocated as in compliance with the (allegedly) reliable methods of science.

APPENDIX

Consider a set of statements d_1, d_2, d_3 $\cdots$ of all possible occurrences of the properties 'white' and 'non-white' in a finite population ('state-descriptions'), such that,

for every i $p(d_i) \neq 0$;
for every different i and j $p(d_i d_j) = 0$;

$$\Sigma_i p(d_i) = 1.$$

For any statement a, obviously,

$$p(a) = p(a \ U_i d_i) = \Sigma_i p(a, d_i) p(d_i).$$

If a is the assertion that the next swan to be observed is white and the population described by the various d_i-s is of swans, then the above formula provides the disjunction of conjunctions discussed in the text above. (The element of luck in finding a to be true is $1 - p(a)$.)

The contention in the text above is

$$p(a) = p(a, b),$$

where a is the prediction about the next swan to be observed and b is an observation-report. It can easily be proved if the d_i-s refer to the population of unobserved swans. The inductive contention is that by considering the d_i-s as referring to the whole population of swans—observed and unobserved, we shall obtain a different result, because in such a case b is incompatible with some d_i-s and entailed by others. Let us work this out slowly. When the d_i-s refer to the whole swan population,

$$p(a, b) = p(aU_i d_i, b) = \Sigma_i p(ad_i, b) = \Sigma_i p(a, d_i b) p(d_i, b).$$

Now, when d_i is inconsistent with b,

$$p(d_i, b) = 0$$

and hence,

$$p(a, d_i b) p(d_i, b) = p(a, d_i) p(d_i, b);$$

when d_i entails b the same holds since in this case

$$p(a, d_i b) = p(a, d_i).$$

Hence,

$$p(a, b) = \Sigma_i p(a, d_i) p(d_i, b)$$

whereas

$$p(a) = \Sigma_i p(a, d_i) p(d_i).$$

Assume now that all d_i-s are equiprobable, so that the (*apriori*) probability of whiteness is $1/2$; we can esily see that $p(d_i, b)$ equals twice $p(d_i)$ for one half of the d_i-s and zero for the rest, so that

$$\Sigma_i p(a, d_i) p(d_i, b) = \Sigma_i p(a, d_i) p(d_i),$$

and hence,

$$p(a, b) = p(a).$$

This case has been extensively discussed by Carnap who, on the basis of the contention that inductive learning is possible, has rejected the hypothesis of equiprobability of the d_i-s.

The same proof can very easily be generalized to the case of the probability of whiteness being $1/n$ where there exist n alternative possible colors. Obviously the only way round the difficulty is to deny that the d_i-s are equiprobable, and this will render cases in which $p(a) \neq p(a, b)$. It would be a hypothesis, however, which may be empirically refuted. We can postulate, to take an extreme but easy instance, that all swans are of the same colour, where there are n possible colors and where $p(d_i) = 1/n$ or $p(d_i) = 0$; in this case, $p(a) = 1/n$ but $p(a, b) = 0$ or $p(a, b) = 1$ in all cases of b being an observation-report consistent with our postulate. In this case, then, $p(a) \neq p(a, b)$ is desired. But the postulate may be refuted by many observation reports, such as the report of having observed one white and one green swan. This is the gist of the criticism of Carnap's *Continuum of Inductive Methods* (a 'continuum' of possibilities of ascribing weights to the d_i-s) first presented by Popper [4]: the 'continuum' is not of methods but of falsifiable hypotheses.

NOTES

1. Bacon's opposition to generalization—induction by simple enumeration—on the basis of their uncertainty which rests on the smallness of the sample as compared with the ensemble (*Novum Organum*, I. Aph. 105) is well-known, and so

is Ellis's discussion of it in his introduction to that work. Bacon's advocacy of analogy (II, Aph. 42) is well-known too. One should stress, however, in all fairness, that he was not unaware of its problematic character. He says that analogy "is doubtless useful, but is less certain, and should therefore be applied with some judgment." As usual, he is ambiguous wherever he senses a difficulty.

2. This part of the discussion rephrases works by K. R. Popper: ([3] pp. 69–73), [4], [5], [6]. A more formal statement of the argument is in the appendix to this note.

3. We can easily give a special significance to the next observation in a game of chance; we can first select the object of observation but refrain from observing it, and then calculate the probability of its having a certain property, as Popper does when building a model complying with Laplace's rule of succession. This means that the application of Laplace's rule to science implicitly assumes the intervention of providence, a hypothesis which Laplace said he did not need.

4. This invalidates the following contention of Harré ([1] p. 27): '(Here, by the way, is a part, and a vital part, of science to which the pure Popper rejection account does not apply; for complete and final verification is possible, at each descending order or mechanism.)'. By 'descending order' Harré means order of increasing depth, which seems to be the same as level of generalization, though I cannot be sure. By 'mechanism' he means analogy which is later verified.

REFERENCES

[1] Harré, R. *Theories and Things*, London and New York, 1961.
[2] Hesse, Mary B. *Forces and Fields*, Nelsons, 1961.
[3] Popper, K. R. 'On Carnap's Version of Laplace's Rule of Succession', *Mind*, LXXI, 1962.
[4] Popper, K. R. 'The Demarcation of Science', P. A. Schilpp (ed.), *The Philosophy of Rudolf Carnap*, Open Court, La Salle, 1963.
[5] Popper, K. R. *Conjectures and Refutations*.
[6] Popper, K. R. *Logic of Scientific Discovery*, relevant new appendices.

— 3 —

MACH ON THE LOGIC OF ENQUIRY

taste maker philosopher of science

It is no easy matter to review Mach's newly translated *Knowledge and Error*, especially for one who, like myself, defends the cause of speculative metaphysics proper in the face of Machian anti-metaphysical prejudices. There are so many approaches a reviewer might, perhaps should, employ when presenting such a book to the reader; and both the book and its author present a challenging wealth of material that simply cannot be ignored.

I confess I approached this book with the mixture of the excitement of coming to an ancestral monument, and the dullness of a *déjà vu*. In a sense Mach is an old bore of a strict empiricist turned conventionalist-instrumentalist, like William James and Karl Pearson and Judge Stallo and many other lesser lights. Of these one can only say ruefully that they fall between the stools of the inductivist and the instrumentalist approach, and wonder if the British empiricists proper, perhaps the heirs of John Stuart Mill, perhaps the heirs of Dr. William Whewell, are not better off in their naive hope of solving the problem of induction; or else whether the instrumentalists are not better off, Duhem, Poincaré, and Eddington for my money, who decided to live in a sophisticated world with no induction and no vexation about it. For, after all, inductivism is one form of justification, conventionalism plus instrumentalism another: either we prove our theories by empirically founding them on facts or we present them as mere definitions and justify their adoption pragmatically. The only other justification possible, apriorism, is justly passé. What can a Pearson or a Mach possibly gain by playing on both the inductivist and the pragmatist justifications? They are incompatible with each other, they cannot possibly complement each other as justifications, and they have no other role to play!

This review of Ernst Mach's *Knowledge and Error: Sketches on the Psychology of Enquiry*, translated by Paul Foulkes (Dordrecht: Reidel, 1976) appeared in *Philosophia*, 8, 1978.

I want to drive the last point home with as much plea for personal good faith as possible. For better or worse, I cannot see anyone taking inductivism or instrumentalism to be a model, a Weberian model, of the scientist; nobody says, that in fact the dictator dictates, the bureaucrat spins red tape, the capitalist transacts, and the scientist makes induction—or instruments. No philosopher has started by taking induction to be a fact, and only then a justification, or pragmatism to be a fact and then a justification. It is of course impossible that one and the same research project be conducted both on the inductive model and on the pragmatic model; and yet it is easy to see that both models claim universality. Suppose you agreed with an inductivist that some research is inductive, some not. He will at once understand you to say, some research is not scientific, not proper, prejudiced, and evil in some of its consequences. Tell an inductivist that some very proper research is not inductive, and at best he will find it a very special and peculiar case that does not invalidate the rule. So the rule must be quite universal or else it is rather questionable!

Yet this is only partly so. Take any other rules for success—in making money, love, or anything else. Surely there is nothing there about universality: if one way succeeds perhaps other ways succeed too, perhaps sheer luck too, perhaps the right way is also not foolproof—it really does not matter in the least. This is, precisely, why instrumentalism is more lax a standard than inductivism: for the instrumentalist some pragmatic success will do, even if there is no doubt that if two theories apply in a given domain and one of them is true, then that one applies in a wider domain, and is thus better by the pragmatist standard of the size of the area of practical applicability. Hence, if and when inductive verification is possible, pragmatism must give way to inductivism by its own light, and as Ernst Mach accepted the method of crucial experiment as a method of verification, he could not be a consistent instrumentalist but a mixture of inductivist and instrumentalist (it is no wonder that Duhem denied verification by crucial experiment in a justly celebrated passage of his [Pierre Duhem, *The Aim and Structure of Physical Theory*, Part I, Chapter VI, Section 3 'A "Crucial Experiment" is Impossible in Physics.']).

This point is extremely vexing—at least I always found it so. Some insist on taking one side clearly and driving home all of its consequences that are significant, palatable and unpalatable alike. They are all for ruthless logic. Others are more hesitant: when they find a dichotomy that is a dilemma yet cannot explode it, they shamelessly use one horn at a time and are happy enough as long as they are progressing and leave it to foundationists to ground their new ideas on a new basis which defies the dichotomy. The paradigm for this will probably remain for a long time Sir William Bragg who has allowed light to be waves on the odd days of the week and particles on the even days.

Mach defies this dichotomy. On the one hand he is a juggler, as I say, like Pearson and others, who uses inductivist ideas and instrumentalist ideas very freely. On the other hand he is doggedly logical and takes his sensationalism—the element common to both schools (see my 'Sensationalism', *Mind*, 1966, reprinted in my *Science in Flux*, 1975) logically to its bitter end. First, the world consists of nothing but elements of sensation and whatever else they tell us exists; second, the principle of induction fails to elicit from the existence of these elements of sensation any other existence.

This view, expressed in the last sentence, is known as phenomenalism or as neutral monism, and it grants elements of sensation objective independent existence: they *are* the facts. But terminology is a bit confused. Those who label, by definition, any denial of materialism by the label "idealism" will regard phenomenalism as a brand of idealism. For my part, I think it better to use 'materialism' to denote the theory that only matter exists, 'idealism' that only minds exist, 'dualism' that both exist, and 'neutral monism' that neither exists—I would prefer the word 'nihilism' but it is preempted. Thus, phenomenalism is a verson of neutral monism; was there any neutral monist who was not a phenomenalist? I cannot say. In a sense Heraclitus's view can be called phenomenalism because he says that there is no reality, only appearances—only phenomena. In a sense he cannot be called a phenomenalist since he never tried to decompose the world of phenomena to isolated items, whether to elementary observed facts or to sensa (or sense-data or elements of sensation); on the contrary, he was more concerned with emphasizing inconstancy, change, or flux.

An added terminological point. The reason the name "neutral monism" caught on is the theory that elementary items of the world of appearance, elementary facts as Wittgenstein referred to them, are both facts of sensation and thus the foundation of psychology, and facts of the objective world and thus the foundation of physics. Neutral monism: neutral between psychology and physics, not between materialism and idealism.

Back to Mach. His mixture of foundationism and eclecticism, if I may so label the two approaches each of which has its own merit, makes him a very hard target of criticism. The foundationist calls for a very different form of critical assessment than an eclectic, and I for one do not know which canon to apply to Mach; or rather I do not know which canon to apply to him in which case, since clearly at times he calls for this canon, at times for that. But I have a simple rule: when Mach handles a problem in a manner which is aimed at producing a detailed result I use the eclectic criterion: is the result interesting, worthwhile, etc.? When performing a general broad task that is far from new or idiosyncratic, I use the criterion of success or failure: Did he manage better than his predecessors? Did he succeed?

But this is not all. The dichotomy cannot be nicely balanced to the very end. When Mach takes the world to consist of nothing but elementary facts, we can see his foundationism at work. When he combats speculative metaphysics one wonders on what ground he does what. Even if one says he ought to oppose that speculative metaphysics that postulates the existence of substances on top of elementary facts, even then we could easily expect Mach to tolerate speculative metaphysics with no substance, or *as if* with substance, or outside science (as Duhem advocated). But he was an inductivist at heart; his instrumentalism was a mere make-shift, a mere substitute for a solution to the problem of induction. His opposition to all speculation was, with him, as fundamental as with Sir Francis Bacon and all his followers: all speculations are prejudices and superstitions!

And so, again, inductivism should count with him as a justification, not as a model of scientific thinking. Yet he also approached matters differently. He was a psychologist who asked, how do we erect our space-time manifold from elements of sensation?

Here Mach was a poor foundationist but an excellent eclecticist. I think the best way to see this is through the examination of his mature works, *Analysis of the Sensations* and *Knowledge and Error* (Leipzig, 1905), the latter being the richer and more intriguing of the two. I find even his subtitle for the latter exciting: *Sketches on the Psychology of Enquiry*. Moreover, it was based on his lecture on *the logic and psychology of enquiry* (preface to first edition). We see here Mach as the first modern philosopher of science, the veritable predecessor of both the Vienna Circle and its official opposition, Karl Popper, author of his famous *Logic of Enquiry*, 1935. (*Logic of Scientific Discovery*, 1959.)

But I shall let the allusions chime by themselves and perhaps comment on some of them later. Here I wish to offer a summary of the book: it has 25 chapters of 362 densely packed pages, and I shall try to present their contents with minimal comment. A classic, says Mark Twain in an unforgettable aphorism, is a book one wishes one has read. This is on the first level, so to speak. On the second level, a classic is a book one wishes to have time to read or to reread for instruction and pleasure. The following summary is an attempt to please on both levels: to satisfy those who cannot find the leisure to go through the whole thing, and to whet the appetite of those who might. I do not think I shall mislead anyone, anyway: I did aim at interest rather than balance and tried not to overlook anything piquant—but I cannot possibly mention all that I think might arouse the reader's curiosity. For that, nothing short of the full text would do.

Here, then, is my summary. I shall return to my discussion after it is finished.

Preface to first edition: Speculative and transcendental philosophy feed on pseudo-problems. Mach is no philosopher but a scientist, concerned with the growth of knowledge. "Above all, there is no Machian philosophy, but at best scientific methodology and cognitive psychology and both are provisional, imperfect attempts, like all scientific theories" (p. xxxiii, n2).

Preface to second edition: The author has learned that other authors have similar views: W. Jerusalem, A. Stöhr, and particularly P. Duhem, whose book complements Mach's, especially on the difference between science and common sense.

Chapter 1: Philosophy equals the toality of science; any specific scientific endeavor suffers from some arbitrariness that is removed when the totality is observed. The value of a synoptic view is in its removal of prejudices and of pseudo-problems (p. 9).

Chapter 2. We have as elements of experience sensations, memories, and their fabric, called ideas (p. 16). Affects and moods are decomposable (p. 17). The only real, irreducible elements are sensations, which are both physical and mental. Men are only more complex than other organisms, not essentially different: we are all automata (p. 20).

Chapter 3. We have inborn reflexes plus associations. Both memory and fantasy are associations—involuntary or voluntary, unconscious or conscious, purposeless or purposeful (especially in the arts and sciences). An amusing and revealing final note: "Psychological observation can reveal the existence of physical processes that we should not so readily come to know by way of physics."

Chapter 4. Are insects "reflex machines" or do they have "a full mental life"? "We need not take sides" (p. 40). That is, we can either deny mental life, or see it as an aspect of physical life. Will and ego are decomposable to sensations; "boundary between ego and world is difficult to maintain and is somewhat arbitrary." [Presumably Federn's discovery of the existence of boundary feelings and images would have delighted Mach. It is interesting to query how much Mach influenced Freud's and Federn's theories of the ego.]

Chapter 5. Needs cause mental functions, such as curiosity, that survive their causes (p. 53). [This seems to make Mach's inductivism hopeless, but he feels no difficulty here.] No qualitative difference between men's and other animals' mental lives. An interesting note on Joseph Popper: let the fundamental needs of the individual be safeguarded, and only the secondary ones subject to democratic decisions. A final note: the Greek slaves had no time to think and their masters no experience to think about; it is thus "in a large measure clear why ancient science has a streak of naive and dreamlike vagueness. Only rarely . . . Archimedes . . . ."

Chapter 6. Too much imagination is bad: magic, ghosts, superstition and prejudice, social maladjustment, religion. Child and savage have a charming curiosity—regrettably unchecked. Even scientists at times regrettably speculate. A delightful note: "Up to the age of four or five I continued to hear the sun hiss as it seemed to dive into a big pond and was mocked for it by adults. Still, I greatly value the memory."

Chapter 7. Darwinism. Obviously, knowledge has survival value; error may be fatal. "Knowledge and error flow from the same mental sources, only success can tell the one from the other. A clearly recognized error, by way of corrective, can benefit knowledge just as a positive piece of knowledge can" (p. 84). "The same mental functions, operating under the same rules, in one case lead to knowledge and in another to error; from the latter, only repeated and exhaustive examination can protect us" (p. 90). [Explosively anti-Machian, or the real Mach seeping through?]

Chapter 8 rejects realism, nominalism, as well as conceptualism. Concepts are durable and grow to meet practical or scientific needs; their meaning is their proper, effective use (p. 95); they are forced by abstraction (p. 96). Concepts, like scientific theories, are economic means of amassing and retaining knowledge.

Chapter 9. Sensations, intuitions, and fantasy, are objective since given to examination and manipulation. Sensations are primary and when pressed hard enliven the imagination: after days of experimenting with spiders, Mach saw spiders in horror dreams and, after feeding sparrows with grasshoppers for days, a man-size grasshopper came to him to complain. Fantasy is a recombination of memories; memory is partly fantasy, partly a complex of intuitions; intuition is a complex of sensations. Science requires fantasy. [All these reductions are presented as partly circular, yet, it seems, with the feeling that the circularity can be reduced on an earlier level.] The law of association cannot cope with all psychology, but associations may be built on earlier ones—the charm in art is often in simple yet clever variations on earlier art (p. 116)—depending on amounts of energy and concentration and other configurations. Abstract concepts must be revitalized with intuition. For example, written history is 3,600 years old—not a very intuitive concept; if we imagine a man who was born at the dawn of history, was 60 years of age when he had a son who at sixty had a son and so on, then we intuitively see that 60 such generations bring us from the dawn of history to date; no wonder we are still such barbarians! The need to translate between concepts and sensations and back is the need to stay unprejudiced. [This chapter is crucial for and the weakest link in Mach's psychologism.]

Chapter 10. Thought adapts to facts, and vice versa—sense illusion is corrected by thinking. The existence of sense illusion led the Eleatics to apriorism and sophists "in the bad sense" to distort morality. But we are no longer worried by sophisms and clever arguments like the liar, which "have already been settled by our forebears" (p. 123). [Here we see how easy it is to declare a solution satisfactory quite uncritically: it happens all the time, and psychologically indicates that the contrary is disturbing. We had better learn the psychological disposition to take delight in intellectual disturbance!]

Adaptation can be *ad hoc*: the ancient and Renaissance idea that the weight of smoke equals the weight of the combustile minus the weight of the ashes is an *ad hoc* adjustment of the law of conservation of mass to the facts of combustion (p. 124). Adaptation of theory is illustrated by the history of science, e.g., the change of—from?—the caloric theory by its transformation to the energy theory. [This seems facile, and perhaps it is; yet it is shared by Duhem and others. The idea of a rejected scientific theory is 20th-century; before that it seemed a contradictory idea, and so the idea of the alterability of a scientific theory already sounded daring.]

Adaptation is economy, harmony, richness. The rule is: avoid contradictions. It is easy to reword Euclidean geometry in terms of Aristotelian logic. [Again, Mach goofs badly, and at times sounds apologetic.]

Two asides that through a strange line of thought offer insights in Mach's character. Note 3: "The quiet happiness experienced by those who had found their way into the narrow closed circle of scholastic ideas cannot be concealed even by the '*Epistulae obscurorum virorum*', however fierce the caricature." Note 11: Duhem describes the English national character as narrow and ridicules it; yet we can congratulate ourselves on the intellectual division of labor between nations.

Chapter 11. The simplest and oldest experiments are not planned but randomly and freely executed, and favorable results remembered. Better experiments must be planned, and when complex and well planned, e.g., novels, they are thought-experiments. The most important thought-experiment is that which reveals contradictions (p. 139); but also that which removes paradox signifies (p. 143). For example, J. Müller's work on sense illusions seemingly contradicts associationism, but it does not.[1]

Since thought-experiment is largely logical, not surprisingly its natural place is mathematics. Thus, "the great apparent gap between experiment and deduction does not in fact exist. It is always a matter of attunement of thoughts with fact and with each other." Refutations may disappoint engineers but are welcome for scientists as they "can lead to new clarifications and discoveries." (p. 145) [This is an amazing passage: deduction and experiment are one; hence, theory merely restates facts; hence, the only thing that may trouble us is inaccurate reflection. This, then, is Mach's theory of error: error is the margin of knowledge. Mach writes on *Knowledge and Error* because he dimly notices a difficulty: *Associationism leaves no room for error; we do err; hence associationism is false.* Yet he defends it against Müller's criticism all the same and finds room for error within associationism, *ad hoc*, and as merely marginal.]

Chapter 12. Experience begins with chance but develops into a deliberate thought-experiment that is then tried out, by the methods of variation, substitution, compensation, composition, etc., etc. [All this, I think, is really poor. As already Whewell said, and Duhem and Mach agree, experiment tests a theory in any way possible, and that is all that matters.]

Chapter 13, on analogy, consists of a series of (poor) examples.

Chapter 14. Hypotheses are modifications of commonsense views which stem by degree from sensation. Newton's "hypotheses non fingo", his strict inductivism, is impossible, and is due to a mere "euphoric mood" (p. 175). No matter: a "sharp distinction in principle between . . . definitely established knowledge and mere surmise . . . is found everywhere in Newton. Errors in detail are an important. . . ."—[Clearly all of Mach's defense of tentativity did not prevent him from expressing old-fashioned verificationism even while he rejects it. Even though in his general view he agrees with Duhem and Poincaré], he still speaks (e.g., p. 179) of "the ideas we have formed on the basis of our observations". [The more one goes into Mach's philosophy, the more one feels his naive good will and desire to be both an inductivist and a conventionalist.] The chapter on hypotheses slides into old-fashioned views and (on p. 181) echoes Sir John Herschel's chapter on hypotheses in his *Preliminary Discourse* of 1831: "in its self-destroying function, a hypothesis in the end leads up to the conceptual expression of facts." [This is Mach's clearest statement of the verification principle, yet it does not quite exclude conventionalism.]

Chapter 15. There are three methods [of attacking problems?]: the analytic or inductive or empirical or from the detail to the generality; the synthetic or deductive or apriori; and the dialectical or critical, or, as it is often misnamed, the reductio. [In my opinion, decidedly opposed to Mach's, only the dialectic method is problem-oriented proper. The inductive method must exclude problems as Bacon knew, and the deductive method leads to series of deductions all equally valid yet some, *post hoc*, more interesting than others.]

In science, says Mach, one method is that of the elimination of prejudice and of the elimination of paradox. [What this has to do with problems I find unclear.] Some problems are pseudo-problems (p. 194). Mach is now ready to side with the analytic method (p. 197). I am not clear on things here, except that the analytic method somehow allows, it seems, for "the function of hypotheses" (p. 198) [which makes it rather obvious that Mach confuses the analytic method with the dialectical method].

Chapter 16. We presuppose causality, but the presupposition is now leaving science: causes give way to descriptive equations. So causality, and with it determinism, can be overlooked, but not some degree of stability in the world of fact (p. 209). Fact, function, variation; these are the prerequisites of research.

Aside; note 6. "I have read somewhere that I am leading a 'bitter struggle' against the concept of cause. Not so, for I am no founder of religions .... I neither can, nor wish to, convert anybody to my views ... mixture of humor and tolerance. . . . Our successors will one day be amazed at the things we quarrel about and even more at how excited we grew in doing so" (p. 210). [I think this prediction has come true. I think people have expressed surprise at Mach's fear that his ideas are ascribed to Kirchhoff. Is it an accident that the next chapter begins by quoting Kirchhoff (1874), Mach (1872), and Grassmann (1894), to the same effect?]

Chapter 17. A series of anecdotes: I cannot summarize it.

Chapter 18. "Inductive results must later be justified by deduction", i.e., by passing tests successfully (p. 235). [Here, as already in Whewell's *Novum Organum Renovatum*, we find Hans Reichenbach's point that the context of discovery differs from the context of justification. I think the clearest exposition on this matter is still Whewell's.]

Aside; note 23; "next to Kant I think Schopenhauer best appreciated the importance of intuition." I do not propose to understand this: Kepler and Whewell and Müller and Liebig occupy the next four notes, and as ones who knew about intuition too; how does Mach measure appreciation?

Chapter 19. On number and measure; in physics and elsewhere.

Chapter 20. Physiological space is different from geometrical space, but we fail to observe it due to too much knowledge. Also two personal asides on Mach's childhood and illness memories.

Chapter 21. A chapter of over 30 pages devoted to illustrating the intuitive way to Euclidean geometry. We cannot measure our perception of space but can create situations where perception yields quantitative results. [Mach never doubted Euclideanism; whether it was with him inductive or conventional (certainly not apriori) I cannot say. That so much of his geometry rests on the axiom that we can move a rod sideways or along its length and arrive at the simplest Euclidean results is amazing in view of the rise, at the very same time, of the absolute differential calculus of Ricci and Levi-Civita, where the same operations were allowed different results in accord with already known results of metric geometry of Riemann and others.][2]

Chapter 22. Again a long one of 30 pages, on geometry as a part of physics. [In fact it is a history of non-Euclidean geometry, coupled with a dogmatic commitment to Euclid (p. 323). Anyone familiar with Russell's *Foundations of Geometry* of 1896 should not be surprised: everyone was Euclidean then, even the greatest and most daring travellers into the non-Euclidean outer spaces.]

The chapter ends with a paragraph which has an air alien to the book: contemptuous of the critics of the great non-Euclideans. True, he says of them, they too "are liable to error, but even errors of some men are often more fruitful in their consequences than the discoveries of others." True. But the consequences of this remark are different from what Mach takes them to be.

Chapter 23. Physiological time is not physical time.

Chapter 24. "Our intuitions of space and time form the most important foundations of our sensory view of the world and as such cannot be eliminated. However, this does not prevent us from trying to reduce the manifold of qualities" of space and time sensations; and the physiological manifold need not be a continuum (p. 349).

Chapter 25. Natural laws are unbreakable, so an error proves to be only a pretender to the status; tentativity prevents us, then, from ever using the term in this sense. Natural laws may be, however, no more than "prescriptions for an observer's expectations. . . . Thus we have not been mistaken in postulating the uniformity of nature, even if, because our experience is inexhaustible, we shall never be able to prove . . . it will remain an ideal" (p. 358).

*   *   *

Much of what I present here, rather one-sidedly no doubt, speaks for itself—or for myself. But I wish to make a few observations to round things off, since I confess I was much more moved than I expected to be by careful reading of Mach now, after years during which I had little or no patience for him.

I will not dwell on Mach's beautiful character and humanism that shine through every crack in his writings; nor on the fact that the cracks are irreparable. Rather, I was impressed by the fact that the cracks are caused by a wealth of new ideas, which indicate a wealth of interesting problems; it is simply that the new ideas burst the old vessels.

This is not all. It is now time to start assessing the undoubted import of Mach's philosophy in the history of our culture, and I wish to make my minor contribution to this here. I was long puzzled by Freud's sloppy reductionism that enabled him to break away from his own strict materialism under a thin associationist-reductionist mask, under the confusion or pretension of one act as another—the act of presenting A as anchored genetically in B, as if it were the act of a reduction proper. I supposed this had something to do with Freud's Darwinism; I am now of the opinion that it was Freud's Machianism.

Mach's Darwinism enabled him to give error a respectable place and even make it permanent, though only on the margin of knowledge. He presented the ego as built by layers of associations. He presented associations as *Gestalten* and so was really not in the least associationist, though in adopting neutral monism he did stay an associationist to the bitter end. He was worried about it. He accepted Kant's transcendental aesthetics, but was loath to admit it as synthetic apriori. He was led, thus, to a quasi-Darwinian way of building space-time intuitions from sensations by quasi-associations in a process of trial and error.

The process was self-defeating. "In its self-destroying function [Mach's] hypothesis in the end leads to a conceptual expression of facts" and yet the facts do not accord with Mach's hypothesis. The more elaborate his hypothesis, moreover, the more suspect it becomes. The very conception of the logic and psychology of research was either a breakdown of a justification collapsing under its own weight, or the end of justificationism, as Bartley saw in the views of Popper who dared break the bond between the logic of enquiry and the psychology of enquiry.

Mach's vacillation between the systemic and the eclectic is his version of higher-level eclecticism: it is the transition from the justificationist to the critical way of being systemic. It is no accident that the period following Mach, thanks to Mach and to Külpe and others perhaps, gave birth to intense activity in psychology where trial-and-error won an increasingly important role. *Knowledge and Error*, then, is the highest expression of the view half-way between theory of knowledge proper and trial-and-error proper. It is similar to Mach's criticism of Newtonianism that did not sway him to oppose Newtonianism, but did sway Einstein; and to Mach's critique of associationism that helped open the road to modern psychology. Mach was no doubt a brave thinker and a trail-blazer in spite of his confusion of instrumentalist and inductivist ingredients. He wanted to be known as the father of an idea that is neither new nor impressive, yet his advocacy of it was of a monumental historical import as it was the (Kantian) idea of taking no side in any philosophical dispute.

Our standards of acknowledgment are inductivist in origin; though they never were purely inductivist, they were sufficiently of that ilk to distort history and to raise problems. We still abide by them, after many adjustments and patch-up jobs. We recognize Mach's discoveries—of the Mach bands and Mach numbers; we even recognize Mach's Principle, be it true or false. But it is time to recognize novelty and contribution by better standards. [3] For me, reading Mach was strong medicine: it is still hard for me to say why exactly, despite myself, I find him so admirable.

The volume comes out in the *Vienna Circle Collection*. It is well translated and edited, and is handsomely produced, with a Mach bibliography and a bibliography of works cited, which could also have served, with a touch of extra work, as an index of works cited too; this, and a subject index should really be added in the next reprint. Still, it is a lovely production.

NOTES

1. Mach was here plainly apologetic; sense illusions are quite impossible if associationism is true. Yet later philosophers of the analytic persuasion, from Moore to Ayer, are more persistent. See the doubly anachronistic collection of Robert H. Swartz, ed., *Perceiving, Sensing, and Knowing* (Anchor, 1965), in which a refuted psychology is defended as a philosophy. The analytic philosophers, Mach included, thus commit what they traditionally declare the philosopher's prime crime!

2. I recommend to the reader R. S. Cohen and R. J. Seeger, eds., *Ernst Mach: Physicist and Philosopher* (*Boston Studies in the Philosophy of Science*, Vol. 6, Reidel and Humanities, Dordrecht and New York, 1970), and Mach's own *Analysis of Sensations*.

3. (Added in the reprint, 1988.) Mach's most significant follower in methodology was P. W. Bridgman, whose critique of Mach's principle, written after his change of heart, is a classic, published posthumously in the Popper *Festschrift*, edited by Mario Bunge, 1964.

Mach's principle is a concretization of the principle of inertia—as is his observation that when the eye rests on a point in a stream it sees the bank flow backwards. Concretization was a part of his methodology. His attempts to apply insights to both cosmology and experimental perception psychology led to triumphs of his neutral monism and to the above-mentioned impossibility of his secret power and charm: his systemism saved him from the danger of ecclecticism, which is shallowness leading to triviality: and his ecclecticism saved him from the danger of systemism, which is dogmatism leading to barrenness. In a sense he fell prey to both, but for a time he overcame both in a tour de force—and won our lasting gratitude.

—4—

HEMPEL'S PARADOX

the ravens pose no riddle

The controversy concerning Carl G. Hempel's paradox of the ravens is going strong. Yet its purpose is not clear. What Hempel has shown is this. Assume the theory of confirmation by satisfaction or instantiation (e.g., "all ravens are black" is confirmed by "at such and such time and place there was a black raven"). Assume further the principle of equivalence of confirmation (all logically equivalent hypotheses are equally confirmed by a given observation). These two lead to a somewhat surprising result according to which practically any non-disconfirming evidence is confirming evidence (e.g., a red herring, which is a non-raven-like, non-black thing, confirms "all non-black things are non-raven-like" and thus its equivalent "all ravens are black"). It is assumed by all writers on the subject that this result calls for some further thinking, but it is seldom clear what kind of thinking, or to what end. It is not clear, to be precise, what is the problem to be solved. Hempel did not try to solve a problem but to resolve a paradox; this, it may be assumed, is in keeping with the analytic approach. Paradoxically, because Hempel followed this approach he fell prey to the confusion which this approach seeks to expose; because he did not pose a problem he could use the words 'resolve', 'paradox', and 'confirmation' in senses wavering between the technical and the ordinary. (The previous statement is an application of a general point concerning analytic philosophy made by Popper in the new preface to his *Logic of Scientific Discovery*.) Let me explain in detail.

I

Being no authority on ordinary English, I looked for a paradigm case before posing an instance to my liking. I am assured that Gilbert and

---

Philosophy of Science, 33, 1966; previously published under the title, 'The Mystery of the Ravens'.

Sullivan excel both in their Englishness and in their ordinariness. So I have chosen my first instance from the *Pirates of Penzance*, where it is declared to be very much of a paradox that a twenty-four year old fellow should have had but six birthdays. My second choice is the paradoxical fact—or theory—that at present the American economy would improve as the outcome of increased consumption, even though, or particularly if, this is achieved largely by borrowing money. Paradoxically, the national economy will improve if consumers borrow in order to consume luxuries.

What is to be done about a paradox? About many paradoxes we do nothing; some of us record them and use them as witticisms. Some of us want to explain paradoxical phenomena, but this is nothing peculiar to paradoxes: someone wants to explain this, someone that. However, someone may want the paradox explained in order to be relieved of the sense of paradoxicality; some people feel that only puzzling phenomena should be explained, particularly paradoxes. Often puzzling or paradoxical phenomena are counter-examples to deeply seated and widely accepted views. Those particularly irked (rather than enchanted) by paradoxes are of two kinds. They may be dogmatists who look for an auxiliary hypothesis which reconciles their pet theories with the paradox which is a *seeming* counter-example. Alternatively, they may be neurotics who cannot stand the feeling of paradoxicalness. In either case the explanation of the paradox—by the theory of the leap-year or by Keynesian economics, in our instances—may be of little avail for such people. Treatment may help; explanation surely will not.

What problems are involved here it is difficult to list. Do we wish to find the source of the sense of paradoxicalness, or the means of overcoming it, or do we wish to determine whether it is at all desirable to overcome it, or how to overcome other difficulties it gives rise to? To take an instance, we may wish to know how borrowing for the sake of buying luxuries leads to a boom; or we may wish to know why people deny this claim. We may assume, in reply to the latter question, that the public denies this because it holds a primitive theory of wealth and value, a view that entails that consumption is loss and debt is poverty. These popular prejudices are a nuisance to economic planners who may have the problem how best to get rid of such nuisances. The solution may be to teach people Keynesian economics—a solution attempted by President Kennedy in a television talk to the nation. That solution, perhaps because of the death of Kennedy, did not work fast enough; nor would advertising for easily available loans. So one might conceive of more ingenious solutions, such as, to create the illusion in many people that their income-tax is much smaller than it is in fact. The federal government of the United States has tried this solution, with a fair measure of success, but of a kind which cannot be lasting: the illusion was corrected so painfully that it will not be readily repeated.

So much for paradoxes in the ordinary sense of this word, and for the diversity of problems which they may ordinarily raise. The one problem that is common to all of them is, whether intuition, which causes our feeling of paradoxicalness, is not thereby proven fallible. Further, if intuition is fallible, should it not be dismissed? This is precisely what formalists of all sorts and other kinds of anti-intuitionists often allege. Intuitionists, however, contend that intuition can only be misled by intellectual juggling, conjuring, or sleight-of-hand. Intuition may be misled, they admit, by creating conditions under which a perfectly intuitive idea looks counter-intuitive, or else by deducing an idea from premises which are only tacitly assumed so that the idea looks counter-intuitive. Let us discuss this point in some detail.

Philosophical intuitionism is the doctrine (associated with the name of Descartes) according to which by the use of our mental eye we can see with assuredness the truth of certain ideas; it is analogous to philosophical sensationalism, the doctrine (associated with the name of Bacon) according to which by the use of our physical eye we can see with assurance the truth of certain factual information. Taken literally both of these doctrines as formulated above may be viewed as having been refuted by paradoxes and sense illusions respectively. But the doctrines can easily be saved by the claim that under certain conditions we can avoid such errors, that certain conditions guarantee the absence of paradoxes or sense-illusions. One may now try to formulate a theory concerning these conditions and submit that theory for critical examination. One may also try to formulate a theory concerning the causes of the paradoxes or sense-illusions and how these can be avoided. Here one may go into detail and suggest how to avoid such errors from the start and how to rectify such errors after they have been committed. For instance, one may suggest that though a slow and cautious progress may prevent the error in question, the elimination of the error requires more than caution. It may be claimed that to eliminate a paradox one must see how it was created, by what default or sleight-of-hand.

One may claim that Hempel's study is an instance of this kind of elimination of paradox: by laying bare all the elements which go into causing us the feeling of paradoxicalness he has expelled that feeling. If so, then the very existence of a literature on the paradox of the ravens is empirical evidence for his failure to expel the feeling of paradoxicalness, and so an empirical refutation of the intuitionist thesis under examination. One may, however, insist on the intuitionist thesis and reject the thesis that Hempel has succeeded in laying bare all the ingredients which have led to the sense of paradoxicalness.

This may be true. Moreover, however many unsuccessful attempts were made to expel the sense of paradoxicalness by trying to lay bare the ingredients that gave rise to it, one may still blame the attempts rather than the intuitionist thesis. One may stick to that thesis and propose it as a criterion for success: we may say that one has found all the ingredients which went into the making of a paradox, if and only if one has thereby succeeded in eliminating the sense of paradoxicalness in question.

But such a policy is somewhat dangerous, since the intuitionist view may be false while the policy leads us to uphold it in spite of any number of failures. Indeed, Michael Polanyi has proposed in his *Personal Knowledge* just this characteristic of a policy as a mark of its being pseudo-scientific. Any procedure is pseudo-scientific, he suggests, when and only when failures of its application are automatically viewed as the results of shortcomings of those who apply it, never as the possible results of the shortcomings of the procedure itself. Polanyi's characterization is very much in the spirit of Popper's view of science.

This seems to be an obvious argument against the policy of viewing every failed attempt to dispel the sense of paradoxicalness as a failure to reveal all the ingredients which make the paradox rather than as evidence that intuitionism is false. Still, there is one good reason for the persistence of that policy, and it is the unsatisfactoriness of the view opposed to intuitionism—namely formalism. As Jacques Hadamard has shown empirically in his *The Psychology of Invention in the Mathematical Field*, we need our intuitions badly, if not to judge truths, at least for heuristic purposes. But whenever two opposite views are unsatisfactory the obvious policy is to try and invent a new one, as William James and John Dewey have so amply stressed. Indeed, a new theory of intuition has developed recently, though it was adumbrated already in Bertrand Russell's *Mysticism and Logic*. It is as follows. We need our intuition not for the purpose of judging truths but for heuristic purposes. Therefore, we have to improve our intuitions so as to come to a stage where what once was felt to be paradoxical is felt as paradoxical no longer. Imre Lakatos is a notable proponent of this view amongst our contemporaries, especially in his already classic, though quite recent, *Proofs and Refutations*. [1]

The suggestion that intuition may be in error but is capable of improvement, is rather common sense; and the view that it is indeed useful to improve it is not striking either. Yet some philosophers have often claimed that some intuition is the final authority. Even Russell, who endorses the view that intuition can and should always be improved, accepts one intuition as final, namely the *a priori* intuition we have of the principle of induction. As Hume had argued before and as Russell has argued in his 'The Limits of Empiricism' and other works, the principle of induction cannot itself be based on experience without appeal to a (higher level) principle of induction. And so he has advocated the principle on the authority of an *a priori* intuition. The only other alternative is to claim that the principle of induction belongs to logic (Rudolf Carnap, *Logical Foundations of Probability*). Hempel, it seems, vacillates between the intuitionist and the logical view of the foundation of the principle of induction. If he is intuitionist, then his use of 'paradox' in the ordinary sense of the word is adequate; if he holds that the principle of induction belongs to logic, he may well have to use the word in the logician's technical sense which I shall now present.

II

Though the word 'paradox' belongs to ordinary English, the expression 'to resolve a paradox' does not. Intelligent non-philosophers usually interpret this expression to mean 'to remove the sense of paradoxicalness', but confess not to have encountered it before (this is an empirical finding of mine). When asked how a paradox is resolved people scarcely know how to answer this question, even if they are philosophers (this is also an empirical finding of mine). This is not to say that the expression 'to resolve a paradox' is meaningless or that there is no established procedure of sorts by which to resolve a paradox: indeed, logicians understand all this with no great difficulty as long as they do not confuse 'paradox' in their technical sense with 'paradox' in the ordinary sense.

In the technical sense a paradox is an antinomy, a proven contradiction. When we prove that the normal class is normal and also that the normal class is non-normal, we have a paradox—Russell's paradox—on our hands; and we must resolve it. 'Resolve' is here used, as elsewhere in mathematics, to mean, 'solve the problem posed by'. The paradigm case is 'to resolve an equation'; it means, to solve the problem, what is the value of the unknown in that given equation? Since 'resolve' is often used by the ignorant as a synonym for 'solve' it must be stressed that this is a misuse of that word; an equation cannot properly be solved since it is not a problem, nor can a problem be properly resolved. Since to resolve something (whether an equation or a conflict or anything else) is to solve the problem posed by that thing, there is ample room for ambiguity here. Since a paradox in the ordinary sense of this word may pose many problems, or no problem at all, the application of the verb 'resolve' in such a context would be intolerably ambiguous. The problem raised by a paradox in the technical sense of the word, that is to say by an antinomy, is one very clear-cut and very urgent problem: It is: how can we eliminate it at minimal cost? The verb 'resolve' may be used here with no fear of ambiguity.

The problem raised by a logical paradox has nothing to do with intuition: it is a matter of formal logic. The resolution of the paradox, indeed, may be highly counter-intuitive. In particular, the attempts to eliminate the paradoxes of set-theory, such as Cantor's or Russell's paradox, may lead to the highly counter-intuitive result that we cannot speak of a class-complement in the abstract: when we speak of non-ravens it is no more automatically clear what we mean. Thus, non-ravens may be all birds other than ravens, or all animals other than ravens, or all numbers other than ravens, depending on what is known as the universe of discourse (that is to say, the context).

Though logicians are at present pretty much agreed about logical paradoxes in general, this is no reason to accept their view. In particular, one may endorse the view proposed by Ludwig Wittgenstein (in his *Tractatus*). Wittgenstein denied that there exist any philosophical problems, and he claims that what may give us a sense of a problem or of puzzlement or of paradox (in the ordinary sense) is a confusion which has to be dispelled, and with it the seeming problem would dissolve. As instances of such pseudo-problems Wittgenstein presented both traditional philosophical material and new logical material, including Russell's paradox. Thus, according to Wittgenstein we should not resolve a (logical) paradox but dissolve it. It is of some importance here, if confusion is to be avoided, to note that, properly and rigorously speaking, we can resolve a logical paradox only if we think it poses a genuine problem; if we share Wittgenstein's view according to which the logical paradoxes are not genuine antinomies but merely paradoxical—i.e., seemingly counter-intuitive results rooted in confusions—then we cannot resolve them though we can dissolve them. As a genuine antinomy a paradox is to be resolved, and as a mere puzzle or a pseudo-problem it is to be dissolved.

Does Hempel try to dissolve the paradox of confirmation or does he try to resolve it? Does he think that it poses a seeming problem which results from the fact that our intuition is misled? Or does he think that there is an antinomy here to be eliminated and does he try to solve the problem how to eliminate it at minimum cost? It is hard to say. In some places ('Inductive Inconsistencies') he may be thinking of paradoxicalness in the logician's sense, in some he may be thinking of paradoxicalness in the ordinary sense. We must first find out what he means by "confirmation."

Let me first briefly show that confirmation in its ordinary sense is different from confirmation in its technical sense, the sense so well captured by Whewell and by Popper. In the ordinary sense of the word one may be legitimately confirmed in one's belief by reassurances of friends and acquaintances, or at the very least by assurances from experts. If experts are confirmed in their beliefs by other experts, then confirmation is very different from what scientists in the modern world call confirmation or empirical confirmation. Also, the conditions for empirical confirmation in the ordinary use of the term are much more lax than the conditions for empirical confirmation in the technical sense. Scientists are able and ready to doubt doctrines amply confirmed by ordinary criteria, and these facts are reflected in usages. To take one instance, we are confirmed in our belief in our doctor since many of his patients recover, whereas—according to the *Consumers Report*—expert students of medical practices in the USA are very skeptical of all private practioners there, and of many who practice in clinics, because their practices do not compare favorably in any way with those which take place in hospitals, especially hospitals attached to medical schools. Thus, common people are more credulous than expert examiners; their conditions for confirmation are more lax.

Now when Hempel resolves the paradox of confirmation he sometimes argues as if once we see where our intuition went wrong it will be rectified all by itself. Our intuition, he says, goes wrong when we feel it paradoxical that a red herring confirms the hypothesis that all ravens are black because we know too much; we may see a red thing and, wishing to test the hypothesis, we may wish to know if it is not a red raven. In this case, obviously, says Hempel, the red herring is a confirming instance; but if we are told in advance that the red thing is a herring which, as we already know, is very different from any raven, we feel the difference to be the reason for the felt irrelevance of the evidence.

I agree with this point. Suppose I told you that all black things are ravens. You will want to know what about my shoe, which happens to look black; and if it turns out to be a raven, or not-black after all, you will be impressed. That is to say, you will be ready to consider the non-blackness of my shoe, or its being made of a raven, as confirmation. (A better example is present in modern physics: all black surfaces are carbonic.)

Now Hempel uses the example of testing a hypothesis as support for his theory of confirmation as instantiation. He thereby confuses the technical (test) and the ordinary (instance) senses of confirmation; he does so because of his analytic or linguistic approach which leads him to search for a linguistic or analytic criterion of confirmation. If in one case—the test case—the statement 'Here is a red herring' confirms the hypothesis 'All herrings are red' or the hypothesis 'All ravens are black', then it does so in all cases, since the criterion depends on the logical relation between propositions and not on the cases. And the logical relation between these propositions is that of instantiation. Thus the analytic approach imposes on us the acceptance of the lax and ordinary sense of confirmation and the rejection of the technical scientific sense.

To conclude with a clear and concise presentation of Hempel's view as I understand it: There is a contradiction between the scientific theory of confirmation as the result of examination and the analytic theory of confirmation as a result of finding an instance of the hypothesis. Not noticing this we are baffled. Once we notice this we shall be baffled no more. All this may be viewed as Hempel's dissolution of a seeming problem, his elimination of an inconsistency which results from confusing two incompatible theories; or it may be viewed as his elimination of a sense of counter-intuitiveness. For my part, I agree that the causes of the uneasiness or the sense of paradoxicalness result from confusing the idea of confirmation as applied in science and the analytic theory of confirmation. But I neither endorse his preference for the analytic theory, nor do I think that this theory can be rendered intuitive. The counter-intuitiveness of the analytic theory, or rather of the corollary to it that a red herring confirms 'All ravens are black', may pose a problem for the dogmatist or for the neurotic. Others may find cause here for relinquishing—at least temporarily—the analytic approach. If they would, they might reject the task of dissolving a paradox (as meaningless) and pose instead clear-cut problems to be solved.

Nelson Goodman's view (*Fact, Fiction, and Forecast*) is somewhat similar to Hempel's, equally convincing as far as it goes, and breaks down when stretched further than permissible due to the desire to have a formal criterion of confirmation. Rather than speaking of tests, Goodman speaks of a special case of testing, crucial experiments. A red herring does not serve as a crucial experiment, say, between 'All ravens are black' and 'All ravens are non-black', so we feel it is no confirmation of the one vis-à-vis the other. Had Goodman said that confirmations only occur as results of crucial experiments, he would be offering rather too stringent a condition for confirmation; but this cannot be, because this condition is not formal. The search for a formal criterion, then, is what stands behind much of the present discussion.

III

Is the analytic requirement for a formal criterion, rather than a material criterion, so very intuitive that intuitionists must endorse it? The statement that intuition supports the requirement for a formal criterion of confirmation is not in accord with facts (this is another empirical finding of mine). Yet Hempel and Goodman, who are intuitionists of sorts, do endorse it. They endorse it, I suppose, because it leads to the satisfaction or instantiation theory of confirmation (a black raven confirms 'All ravens are black'), which is intuitive, even though this latter theory leads to the counter-intuitive results. Intuitionists, therefore, wish to show that the intuitive theory does not lead to counter-intuitive results. To show this they (both Hempel and Goodman) describe material circumstances under which the paradoxical results do not seem paradoxical. These circumstances only show the theory to be intuitively comfortably applicable in some circumstances. Were the intuitionist thesis true, and were the requirement for a formal criterion intuitive, the paradox would disappear. It does not. Hence at least one of these theses is mistaken. Indeed, one is empirically refuted and the other has no leg to stand on.

There was one further suggestion, which has been adumbrated in a paper by H. G. Alexander (and already by Goodman, in a way), which has been repeated by others, and which ascribes the counter-intuitiveness of Hempel's result (a red herring confirms 'All ravens are black') to the smallness of the confirmation provided by a red herring as compared with the one provided by a black raven. The relative paucity of ravens and of black things makes a black raven so much more of a rare phenomenon than a non-raven non-black; and this makes the former so much more of a confirmation than the latter, that the latter is negligible by comparison and we tend to forget it. The counter-intuitiveness of Hempel's result, in other words, is the same as we have when we notice that a drop of water is something, yet compared with Niagara Falls it is nothing. Let us examine this contention by a simple substitution. Ravens and blacks are rare indeed; let us replace them by common things and see what happens. Instead of black we take opaque, whose complement is transparent; intuitively, most things seem to be opaque. Instead of ravens let us take inorganic things. We shall have 'All inorganic things are opaque' as confirmed by the opaque inorganic thing my wrist-watch, and disconfirmed by the transparent inorganic thing the glass cover of my wrist-watch; also, it is confirmed by the opaque organic thing myself, as well as by a transparent organic thing like a jelly-fish. People feel that it is counter-intuitive that a transparent jelly-fish confirms 'all inorganic things are opaque' (this is an empirical finding). So, the argument from the rarity of black ravens must be rejected.

Moreover, it may look from Hempel's study—and some have so claimed—that the cause of the defect is in his presenting the ravens hypothesis as a conditional, or in our having forgotten the way to contrapposit a conditional. If this were so, biconditionals would be unproblematic. Take the theory 'All and only amorphous (i..e, non-crystalline) carbonic surfaces are black' which is declared by physicists to be true. Everything is black if and only if its surface is sooty. What is black is sooty, and what is sooty is black. Ask your intuitions these questions. Will black soot confirm this? I think the answer is yes. Will a seemingly black but really gray blackboard? I think it is yes again. Will a very seemingly black, but still gray, crystalline carbon (graphite)? I think the answer is, emphatically, yes. Will a red herring? Hardly. But a red herring is a non-black non-soot. The biconditional is paradoxical. But take another instance of a biconditional: 'All and only Americans are wise' which is the same as 'All and only non-Americans are unwise.' Here the counter-intuitiveness, or the sense of paradox, totally disappears, no matter who is commoner, the American or the non-American, the wise or the unwise.

The reason for this variance between the two biconditionals is in the implicit choice of a proper universe of discourse. When Hempel takes the hypothesis '(x) Raven $(x) \supset$ Black (x)' he does not dwell on 'x'. If x ranges over atoms, think how highly confirmed the hypothesis is. But let us take 'x' to be spatio-temporal regions and reformulate 'all ravens are black' to say 'No spatio-temporal region contains any unblack-raven,' and upon careful experimentation you will find it difficult to decide what confirmation is counter-intuitive and what is not. The logical schema is now

$$\text{'}(x) \text{ something } (x)\text{'}$$
$$\text{or}$$
$$\text{'}\sim(\exists x) \ \sim\text{something } (x)\text{'}$$

etc. This enables us to include biconditionals, and even equations. Take Boyle's Law of gases: 'No spatio-temporal region contains a non-ideal gas', where gasses are ideal if and only if they obey the equation $PV = RT$. The law may be a conjunction of instances, in series: spatio-temporal region a contains no non-ideal gas, spatio-temporal region b contains no non-ideal gas, etc. Similarly, consider 'no spatio-temporal region contains a perpetual-motion machine', 'no spatio-temporal region contains elementary electric charges different from that of the electron', etc., etc. Remembering that almost all spatio-temporal regions are empty, it follows that they do not contain non-ideal gases, or perpetual-motion machines, or flying horses, and so there is an *a priori* high degree of confirmation—indeed near 1—to Boyle's law and to other laws as so stated and understood. Similarly, there is an *a priori* high degree of confirmation to the contrary of each of these laws. This, I think, is a powerful generalization of Hempel's result and I would love to claim the authorship of it, but the fact is, it is in Popper's *Logik der Forschung*, which preceded even Hempel's and Goodman's works by some years. It is a pity that the discussion has centered on black ravens and not on the more powerful examples above. As long as our intuition hankers after the popular doctrine of confirmation by satisfaction or instantiation, or after the analytic doctrine of confirmation as a formal relation between statements, we will not escape the sense of paradox.

---

1. See Chapter 34 below.

DUHEM VERSUS GALILEO

*an instrumentalist counterattack
on essentialism*

The idea that a question has no meaning unless the truth of the answer to it can be decided by observation is current both among physicists and among philosophers. It is also customary to view this idea as novel and revolutionary, both in philosophy and in physics. The recent publication[1] of English translations of two great works by two people who excelled both in philosophy and in physics may at least help to dispel the myth concerning the novelty of this idea.

The idea that statements make no sense—or no 'empirical sense', as the ultra-modern terminology goes—unless they refer to observable facts suggests that the main function of science is to describe the observable world; that is to say, that it is the sole function of the scientist to organize known information and to predict future events. This idea is attributed to Scholasticism by both its adherent Duhem and its opponent Galileo. The Scholastics did believe in a metaphysical theory concerning the unobservable world, the hidden reality behind the appearances. But on these matters their views were fixed; and they interpreted the changes in astronomy since antiquity as bearing on appearances only, and not on the hidden reality behind them. A more modern trend, deriving from Berkeley and Hume, shares with Scholasticism the view that science must confine itself to appearances but denies the existence of a corresponding reality behind these appearances. The point at issue between Galileo and Duhem is whether science merely describes observable facts and is therefore simply an *instrument* for classification and prediction, or whether it should not attempt to describe the hidden reality—the *essence* of things, as it were.

The controversy between *essentialism* and *instrumentalism* (if I may follow Popper's terminology) was topical in the time of Galileo, and again

The British Journal for the Philosophy of Science 8, 1957.

in that of Duhem. The declared problem discussed in the *Dialogue* is whether Copernicanism is true. But its main problem is whether the Copernican system is a meaningless mathematical instrument, merely useful for prediction, as Galileo's Scholastic opponents had it. The problem arose again in the time of Duhem, for reasons which I shall discuss below.

Galileo's declared aim in the *Dialogue* is to present all the arguments for and against the two world systems, the Ptolemaic and the Copernican. The value of these arguments is mainly historical. But the work contains much which is of a wider interest. I cannot discuss here the great artistic beauty of the book, the influences of ancient philosophers, and especially of Plato, the similarity to Descartes, and many other interesting points. But I shall discuss the major idea in the background of the *Dialogue*—the view that science should be separated from faith.

The story of Galileo is sometimes told with the tacit implication that Galileo was anti-clerical. In his interesting Introduction to his edition of the *Dialogue* Giorgio de Santillana argues vehemently against this approach—an approach which misjudges the power of Galileo's religious feelings, and which amounts to saying that Galileo was a weak person broken by the Inquisition rather than an ardent Catholic who sincerely wished to co-operate with the Church as far as his conscience permitted him.

Santillana's presentation also brings out a problem which must still be considered as open. Why did the Church encourage Galileo to write the *Dialogue*, permit him to publish it, and then persecute him without being able to produce any evidence that he had sinned?

The usual answer to his problem is that the Pope was offended when it was suggested to him that Simplicius of the *Dialogue* was intended as a portrait of the Pope himself. This explanation (though not the identification of the Pope and Simplicius) is amply refuted by Santillana. The Pope had discussed the plan of the *Dialogue* with Galileo and the work had been given the *imprimatur* after it had been read by a whole array of chief censors. Moreover, the affair of the publication and of the persecution of Galileo was too important a matter to be motivated by the personal feelings of the Pope, who also was a friend and admirer of Galileo. In addition, Simplicius is a most mature and charming interlocutor. He takes a keen interest, he takes his defeats in good grace, and he is not offended by unfair remarks by his Copernican friends.

Why then was Galileo persecuted?[2]

My conjecture is that the Church wished to embrace Copernicus' system, in order to retain its intellectual hegemony; that it wanted to make the transition from Aristotelianism as smooth as possible; and that Galileo was supposed to help in this transition. This would explain why the Pope took so much interest in the preparation of the book. The long delay due to censorship shows that Galileo did not entirely satisfy the censors. His book satisfied their expectations in various ways, but he had been unwilling to compromise on questions of principle. Salviati, the author's mouthpiece, rebukes Sagredo, the enthusiastic layman, for committing himself to Copernicanism before the Pope had decided the matter. He also admonished him to be more polite to Simplicius. Sagredo admits his error and recants. This incident recurs several times. The Church's attitude is presented as pro-Aristotelian but also as undogmatic. 'I do not doubt your rationality', says Salviati to Simplicius. One of the censors admitted that he had read some of Salviati's statements with tears of joy; which shows how near Galileo had come to establishing a compromise. Yet Galileo had made it clear that the Church's authority in science was unacceptable, even though he himself had sincerely waited for the Pope to decide the issue in favor of Copernicanism before committing himself. Salviati criticizes the acceptance of Aristotle's authority, and the existing method of reconciling his works with new discoveries, but does not attribute these faults to the Church, and he says almost nothing about the analogous approach to the Bible. He makes statements which are unfavorable to the Church in a very brief manner, and even repeats some of the official views of the Church, although in a non-committal way and often with irony, for which Simplicius criticises him in a friendly way.

In short, though I do not think that Galileo would have written the *Dialogue* as he did if he had been more free to speak his mind, I do think that throughout the *Dialogue* he meant what he said and that the constrictions he accepted were those he freely chose as a religious person. It seems to me that the Church was ready to grant more freedom to scientists provided it could save its face, and that Galileo, the ardent Catholic and leading scientist, was eager to help.

Why then did the plan misfire? Because, I suggest, of the enthusiastic reception of the book: the Copernicans took the permission to publish the *Dialogue* as the Church's admission of failure. This is why the Pope decided to proceed against Galileo at once.

The First Day of the *Dialogue* is devoted to the criticism of the old system and the theory of truth behind it. Simplicius argues that truth is manifest,[3] both through observations and through common sense. Salviati contests this attitude. The senses do mislead us. Walking in the street we can see the moon following us like a cat on the roof-tops. Common sense does not object to inconsistent theories if the contradictions in them are not obvious and if we do not think very carefully. Attacking the theory that truth is obvious Salviati concludes the First Day by declaring himself a Socratic, and Sceptic.

On the Third Day the Copernican theory is propounded. Now Simplicius tries to show that nothing compels us to accept the Copernican system in spite of its by now admitted merits: truth is now hidden for him, beyond the reach of human reason and simple observation. Salviati attacks this attitude as dogmatic. 'In playing with you', he tells Simplicius, 'a man shall never win but be always on the losing hand.' The method of accepting a theory merely because it does its job is uncritical and leads to stagnation. The fault with the Aristotelians is that they took seriously only that part or aspect of a theory which was known to have direct observational consequences. This allowed them to stick to most untenable theories. And it is also the reason why they never tested their theories. Tests are difficult to find, and only after we have deduced a testable statement from a theory can we be certain that this can be done. To look for no more than what we have already observed, in judging a theory, means in effect to exclude *new* tests. Moreover, the demand that the theory should merely agree with observation is too easily fulfilled. The Ptolemaic system satisfied this demand, yet Copernicus felt that truth must be simpler than the Ptolemaic system. Thus it was the fact that he regarded the theory as something which can be true or false, and not merely as a convenient instrument (a 'hypothesis' as his opponents used the word, meant a 'mere instrument', as was pointed out by Popper[4]) which led him to try a better idea. Furthermore, Simplicius' idea would be bound to arrest science, for it requires any theory to accept what we 'see', but what we see is, in its turn, dependent upon our beliefs. We cannot start, and should not attempt to start, with observation, but rather with reasoning.

Galileo insists that we must emphasize every problem in our theoretical system and argue about it until we can solve it. Galileo's only criticism of Copernicus is that he did not emphasize sufficiently a certain problem which he (and Galileo too) could not solve. If we wish to attain the truth we must break away from scholastic apologetics and stress, on the contrary, our difficulties. And only after all these difficulties have been overcome, and our theory stated with the utmost simplicity, only then will truth be manifest.

Simplicity is the keynote of Copernicanism. Copernicus did not invent the heliocentric system but he succeeded in simplifying it. And although the simplicity of his calculations was understood only by the few, the intellectuals became enthusiastic about the heliocentric system because of the prospect of having a system simple enough to be comprehensible to all. Galileo tells us how surprised he was to find that the greatest scholars were those who wanted to shift the emphasis from scholarship to comprehensibility. He tells us that, when he was young, he did not bother to go to listen to a Copernican visiting lecturer because he considered him a crank or a madman, but that he was carried away by the enthusiasm of those who went to the lecture. The enthusiasm was shared by people who knew very little about astronomy but who now saw some hope that they would be able to understand it.

Galileo offers alternative theories, and his views are tentative. But he argues from a position of strength. He is convinced that truth is simple, and that we can create simple geometrical models of the universe and argue about them until we have found the truth.

I have tried to focus upon those aspects of Galileo's philosophy of science which show most sharply the contrast between his views and those of Pierre Duhem (1861-1916). For Duhem was not only one of the most distinguished instrumenalist philosophers of all time—he also was the only instrumentalist philosopher who answered Galileo's challenge. Instrumentalists have argued very little against essentialism, and none of them except Duhem has attempted to answer Galileo's criticism. Duhem's answer to Galileo is that not instrumentalism, but essentialism, is the view of science which leads to obscurantism.

The history of science was written almost entirely by essentialists. This is one of the reasons why medieval science was almost totally neglected. Duhem undertook vast and most interesting researches in pre-Copernican physics. He tried hard to show that there was continuity of progress towards Copernicanism, attributing, for example, the invention of the law of inertia to a scholastic of the 13th century. (By the way, Galileo did not claim priority for the law which he puts in Simplicius' mouth; Salviati induces him to admit that it follows from some of his own assertions, and to agree that this invalidates an important objection to Copernicanism.) Duhem's thesis is that if physics is viewed as an instrument, then its history becomes coherent and organic—a history of ideas constantly developed and improved by people who often were conscious instrumentlists, and who always acted according to the instrumentalist theory. But if physics is viewed as the discovery of the esence of the physical world, it becomes dependent on metaphysics with the consequence that the continuity of its history breaks down, and is replaced by a chronology of arbitrary and conflicting metaphysical dogmas.

Duhem wrote at a time when the field theory had succeeded in shaking the confidence of some leading Newtonians who started (in the manner of Simplicius) to argue that they did not really or literally mean what they said. Duhem was impressed by the fact that Helmholtz accepted the field theory while insisting that it is a mere mathematical fiction and that the field does not really exist; and he was also impressed by Poincaré's insistence that the Newtonian principles are implicit definitions and cannot tell us anything about the world. He saw in all clarity that this was a break with the traditional rationalistic approach, and he hoped that the disturbing conflict between science and the Church (which, he felt, was a mere misunderstanding) was now ripe for a negotiated settlement.

Duhem made no secret of the fact that his passionate interest in the problem was connected with his religious views. (He was an orthodox Roman Catholic.) But he was deeply convinced that his arguments were in no way biased. Yet his approach was very different from that of Poincaré or Mach, whom he was proud to view as his allies. For unlike Mach he was not much interested in the difficulties inherent in Newton's theory of gravity and unlike Poincaré he never saw the point of Maxwell's theory. On the contrary, among the three he was the most ardent Newtonian. Although he argued that Newton's theory is fictitious—a mere instrument—and although he contested Poincaré's assertion that it is preferable to stick to Newtonianism under any circumstances, he stuck to his Newtonian views until the end. He derided the enthusiasm for Einstein as a 'frantic and hectic race in pursuit of a novel idea [which] has upset the whole domain of physical theories, and has turned it into a real chaos where logic loses its way and common sense runs away frightened'. (He did not ever bother to name the 'novel idea'; but this attack, placed in the preface to the second edition of the present work, which appeared in 1914, is quite unambiguous.) Indeed the 'novel idea' did 'upset the whole domain of physical theories', but why should a progressivist object?

The answer may be found in the first part of the present volume which was first published as an independent essay. It consists of four chapters. The first two chapters present the two views on the aim of science, which I label here (following Popper) as 'essentialism' and 'instrumentalism'. The third chapter is about the history of these views. Here we learn that Kepler was naive and that Descartes was proud and confident. As to Galileo we are only told that his judges were right in deciding that he only pretended to be an instrumentalist, and that they were right in their philosophical judgment, too. (This is far-fetched: they did not bother about philosophy.) The fourth chapter is psychological: it classifies mind into two categories, the concrete and the abstract, or the English and the French. Here he pours out all his hatred of English inductivism and scientific realism. He is as unfair as he is cheap. He ridicules the English method of writing vectorial formulae (which was later improved by Continental scientists and is now universal) and he attributes Green's discoveries to Cauchy. He attributes the idea of abstract electrostatic fields to all the continental physicists and he alleges that it is a notorious fact that, by contrast, Faraday invented a mechanical model of electrostatic action (regrettably he gives no reference to this alleged 'fact'). Inductivism being essentially English, he considers that the Continental inductivism can only be a 'diffusion of the English methods'. The craze for a mechanical model is also typically English; and while Galileo's and Descartes' interest in mechanical models is explained as a reaction to scholastism, he has no excuse for these unimaginative Englishmen, Kelvin and Maxwell (of course, 'English' in French usage even more than in English-speaking countries often denotes also Scottish).

Duhem does not make explicit the point of this farrago—but it does have a point, and a very interesting one too. Duhem identifies 'abstract' with 'imaginative' and therefore with 'fictitious'. It follows, then, that 'real' is identical with 'concrete'. Hence, as Faraday insisted that the electromagnetic field is real, it follows that he must have thought of the field as something concrete like a piece of rubber. Realism is a psychologically explicable error, similar to sense illusion: it is an attempt to deceive oneself

that the abstract is concrete. That is why unimaginative people are attracted to realism. And that is why realists believe in mechanism. But this realism is dangerously dogmatic. While there can be no room for a display of the imagination in matters of concrete facts, our theories can and should be abstract, bold, and imaginative.

Let it be quite clear that this attempt of mine to connect the fourth chapter with the previous three is not unobjectionable. It is difficult to reconcile Duhem's statement that scientific theories 'enjoy universal consent' (p. 10) with his Galilean appeal for freely imagined abstract theories. But the demand that we should imagine theories freely is explicitly made in the second part of the work, and the argument that scientific theories 'enjoy universal consent' cannot be taken seriously anyhow, not so much because it is, historically, palpably false, as because, within Duhem's own philosophy it does not signify: we neither can assent to nor dissent from a string of words which has no independent meaning.

The great controversy over Einstein's theory was raging during the interval between the two original editions of the present work. It did not at all fit into the way in which Duhem was used to seeing things. If he was not prepared to change his view, he could only ignore all this as yet another little incident of minor importance. 'They', Duhem tells us scornfully, speaking of 'certain schools', 'they think they can run all the more easily and quickly from one discovery to another . . . .' while they merely evict logic and common sense.

It is a bit difficult to understand these accusations. As to common sense, Duhem's leading idea was that all theories, save that of Aristotle's, are abstract, fictitious, and counter to common sense. From which he should have concluded that if common sense and science never went together, then 'certain schools' could not evict common sense. As to logic, it does not seem to me that Duhem had any right to speak in its name in this context. An instrumentalist has no reason to demand that his various 'fictitious' theories cohere: they are all instruments, and logical coherence between them is unnecessary, since they do not aspire to be true. For example, the fact that Newton's theory did not cohere with electrodynamics did not prevent Duhem from accepting them both. (Yet he condemned Maxwell for having two alternative theories of the dielectric; which is a strange, but not necessarily an unfair condemnation if Duhem had in mind that Maxwell was not an instrumentalist but an English realist and thus had no excuse for this incoherence.)

Duhem said quite clearly that an instrumentalist has no need to be coherent in this way; and if he nevertheless hoped for coherence, he admitted (p. 220) that his only ground for this hope was 'an intuition we are powerless to justify.'

Now it is this intuition which is essential to the interest and fascination of Duhem, and especially of his history of science. It alone makes this history coherent, and progressive. The admission that he could not justify his intuitive demand of universal consistency therefore amounts to a declaration of bankruptcy as far as his analysis of science is concerned. And Duhem's intuitive demand for universal coherence between theories is of course equivalent to a demand for realism. And he knows this, for he hopes and believes that science will approach something like a *natural classification* of the real essence—on the order of Aristotle's physics (Appendix I, 9). (De Broglie also comments on the strangeness of this retreat to realism in his provocative preface to the book, written from a realistic viewpoint.)

Duhem, however, proposed very strong arguments in favor of his thesis that if we are really sceptical and open-minded we must accept his instrumentalism. He tried to show that there can be only two views of science. And he tried to show that his view is the only alternative to the theory that science has acquired the happy state of near-perfection, that we have achieved the truth, if not totally then at least essentially. If we are realists, we must be essentialists, we must believe that we have found the essence of reality. And thus, he concluded, we must become dogmatists.

Duhem's argument may be presented in this way. We must admit that we do not know everything, that there is room for improvement. The way to show that our theories are not yet perfect is to refute them, to find a fact which is contrary to a prediction based on them. This means that our theories are likely to be false unless we possess the ultimate truth. One cannot even say that a part of our theories, say, mechanics, is absolutely true while other parts, say, electrodynamics, are tentative. The distinction between these two branches is ours, and we cannot even fully mark it, because we know too little of electrodynamics. The distinction between the two branches is a part of *our* theory which is open to refutations [and which indeed was refuted by Einstein]. If we take the history of physics between the 15th and the 19th centuries, we see clearly that there was great progress, though strictly speaking the 19th century's theories are false. This progress, then, cannot have been towards truth. The realist thinker is tempted to say that it was progress towards truth because the later theories, even though false, are 'essentially' true. Thus, Duhem explains (and, I think, very convincingly) why realists tend to fall back on essentialism. But, Duhem argues, to say that we are ready to learn, to accept criticism, while insisting that we are essentially right, is both naive and hypocritical; in addition, it is the fallacy of mixing physics with metaphysics (to use Bacon's idiom). I think it would be preferable to argue that this is a bad and obscurantist metaphysics. But Duhem could not say this since in metaphysics he is essentialist too: he insists that the Aristotelian system of 'natural classification' is essentially right in spite of all the mishaps and refutations which it had to suffer.

Let us, however, leave Duhem's metaphysics and return to his criticism of scientific dogmatism. He gives in the last chapter of the present work a specimen of his vast historical research—and it is a superb piece of research—to show that physics has progressed gradually, by small changes, now in this respect, now in that, so that it is absurd to declare that at a certain stage physics got hold of the essence of truth and since then has only eliminated minor errors. If we forget essentialism then we are faced either with the problem of how physics approaches truth by transitions from one false theory to another, or with the admission that the immediate aim of physics, the one we observe to be partially attainable, is not truth (as he suggests, unless he remembers his 'natural classification') but utility.

This is Duhem's strongest argument. We cannot attain truth by a series of false theories. Truth remains the *unattainable* ideal, the regulative idea (to use Kant's idiom). Therefore in each stage our theories are, most likely, false. (They may include, perhaps, some true statements, but since they are tested as wholes, they are, in all likelihood, false as wholes.) In what sense, then, can it be said that we did progress, if our theories are false?

In the second part of the present work Duhem offers as a solution a new theory of truth, or rather, a new theory of meaning. A physical theory is *true*, according to Duhem, if it agrees with all *known* facts, all *observed* facts. It has no other *meaning* than the total meaning of all the *known* statements of fact which can be deduced from it and which were verified by observation. We can of course deduce new statements of fact from it and thus test them; but then the verification will change, and enrich, the meaning of the theory. It may of course be said that if the result of the test is negative the theory is refuted. But this 'refutation' would not be one in the sense of the realist, but a 'refutation' in a purely pragmatic sense of finding a limit to its applicability. Now we can see how science may progress from a useful to a still more useful theory. *There are no degrees of truth in the ordinary sense of the word, but there are degrees of pragmatic 'truth'—of usefulness.*

Duhem's theory of meaning (or rather of empirical meaning) is the best of its kind. Duhem showed that it is preferable to Poincaré's theory of meaning. For Poincaré scientific assertions are everyday assertions of observed facts put in a compact manner. 'Here runs a current' means for him, for example, the statement of brute fact like 'The needle of the galvanometer moves'. Duhem argued that it *also* means 'Gas bubbles appear in the battery' and *also* 'Whenever the needle of the galvanometer moves there appear gas bubbles in the battery'. Poincaré's reply was that the language of scientific theories is such that these observed effects are all said in one sentence—that science is a sort of a shorthand. To this Duhem replied that, if knowing the meaning of a theory meant knowing all the verifications of its consequences, then we could not test it any further.

Duhem's theory of empirical meaning is not, however, his whole theory of meaning. It is only the theory of 'meaning in physics'. There can be also a mathematical meaning (here Duhem refers to Hadamard) and a metaphysical meaning. This enables him to say that the same statement may be meaningless in physics and meaningful in metaphysics. He tried to show that this is necessarily so. Yet even if it were necessary and convincingly so, to me it would remain a repugnant idea. It deprives science of its value (except its pragmatic value which is but of little interest); it thereby vulgarizes science, and it makes metaphysics a kind of religion—or part of religion.

Fortunately the idea is most unconvincing. (1) From the pragmatist point of view, we are not interested in logic or in history or in hairsplitting arguments. (2) From the epistemological point of view Duhem cannot explain how some purely fictitious ideas enable us to predict future events. Indeed he admits that they have a kernel of theoretical truth in them. But to the extent to which he admits this, he is a realist, and implies that scientific ideas are not purely fictitious. (3) From the point of view of historiography Duhem's interpretation is defective. It entirely ignores the terrific impact that purely metaphysical doctrines had on the history of science, the great inspiration which science drew from purely metaphysical doctrines like the indestructibility of matter, the soul of nature, or atomism. (The adverse effect of Duhem the epistemologist upon Duhem the historian may be illustrated by his derision of Gassendi: here he is no longer a historian but a partisan.) (4) It ignores the impact of science on metaphysics (whose importance might be shown by the history of determinism). (5) It detaches science from humanism and is (meant to be used as) an instrument for ousting the great tradition we inherited from the Renaissance.

However, Duhem's arguments against scientific realism are too strong to be ignored or to be left unanswered. He is very convincing both in his attack on essentialism, and in his argument that the choice is between essentialism and instrumentalism. Indeed we have only to remember that Galileo, in spite of his professed scepticism, fell back on essentialism when arguing against the philosophy of Duhem's predecessors. But somewhere there lies an error. Both Galileo and Duhem (when remembering his 'natural classification') would agree with what has become a commonplace since Einstein—that *we approach the truth by a series of approximations.* This is the genuine form of the sceptical attitude which Duhem wishes to adopt since it admits that there is always room for improvement. Yet neither of these two theories accounts satisfactorily for this situation. The essentialist view asserts that truth, if not at hand, is round the corner. The pragmatist view asserts that the progress is purely technical, not intellectual. We must therefore find a third view which will explain more satisfactorily how we can progress while holding only tentative conjectures which we hope will be superseded. And for the sake of doing so we must find the error in the argument, common to Galileo and Duhem, in favour of the assertion that there can be only two views concerning human knowledge, or science. The starting point must be that Galileo's scientific realism is the better of the two views. Galileo's arguments against instrumentalism were never answered; this should be borne in mind even though we have to admit that his essentialist theory of scientific realism is unsatisfactory. He made a brave attempt, and if he failed he was still right, 'essentially', and in what matters most: his case for intellectual independence needs no advocacy.

Perhaps I might say at this stage that my criticism of the 'two views' is an adaptation of Popper's criticism in his 'Three Views Concerning Human Knowledge',[5] and that his third view seems to answer the question without falling into the same difficulties as the previous traditional views. But let me first reformulate the problem—the *problem of knowledge*. I wish to pose it in a form which, though alluding to Kant, is new, I think: *how is partial theoretical knowledge possible?*

Popper's simple answer to this question is that we learn something about the truth (although not the whole truth itself) by learning from our mistakes. In this way we can make discoveries. In his *Logic of Scientific Discovery* Popper describes theories as questions put to nature. And even though we may argue that our fundamental questions about the nature of the physical world and about our place in it are never answered, it cannot be denied that we can pose more and more intelligent questions. The more intelligent the question the more we can learn from negative replies to it. The statement that Newton's theory is false is both true and *theoretically more informative* than the statement that Kepler's theory is false. There is no room for deriding science because its theories are refuted or likely to be false. The only rational manner of discussion is to try to refute the present theory by concrete argument. By a concrete empirical argument, by a refutation, we transcend the limits of our knowledge and open new horizons for a better theory, for a better-formulated question. When Simplicius argues vehemently against Copernicanism, Salviati encourages him and asserts that he does not doubt his rationality, but when Simplicius accepts the Copernican system as useful though probably false, Salviati reproaches him for being an irrationalist. Likewise, Duhem's fault was not that he opposed Maxwell and Einstein, but that he condemned Einstein on general grounds instead of arguing to the point.

Popper's philosophy of critical discussion need not be confined to physics. It distinguishes between physics and metaphysics by characterizing physics as a discussion which involves experimental arguments (to use Faraday's idiom). It thus explains the development of metaphysical doctrines into scientific ones, and the fact that science does influence our metaphysical beliefs if we do not create an iron curtain between the two. Galileo's chief thesis was that the new science had to reshape our metaphysical beliefs. He argued that the acceptance of Copernicanism *together with an attitude of searching for a more comprehensive picture of the world* was revolutionary—more revolutionary than the acceptance of Copernicus' theory. Galileo tried to show what the Copernican way of thinking could mean if we re-interpret all the known facts with its help. He tells us (in the Fourth Day) that his attempt to have a theory of the tides which will fit his picture of the world nearly drove him mad. We may smile[6] at Galileo's attempt to explain everything by a law of inertia. But even though his idea that such assumptions must be essential and ultimate was uncritical, his brave attempt to take them as ultimate and to argue for them scientifically was not only fruitful, but necessary: someone had to make the attempt to find out how far we could proceed with a minimum of assumptions. Science cannot proceed without a metaphysical hankering after the secret of the world, even though it is quite naive to believe that the interest is satiable. As Einstein has put it:[7] 'there exists a passion for comprehension, just as there exists a passion for music . . . . Without this passion there could be neither mathematics nor natural science. Time and again the passion for understanding had led to the illusion that man is able to comprehend the world . . . by metaphysics. I believe that every true theorist is a kind of a tame metaphysicist . . . .'

NOTES

1. *Dialogue on the Great World Systems*. Galileo Galilei, Salusbury's translation revised and annotated and with an Introduction by Giorgio de Santillana. Chicago University Press, 1953, pp. lviii + 506.

The Aim and Structure of Physical Theory, by Pierre Duhem, trans. by Phillip P. Wiener. Foreword by Louis de Broglie. Princeton University Press and Geoffrey Cumberlege, 1954, pp. xxii + 344. (The first edition was published in 1905, and the second edition in 1914.)

2. For more details, see my 'On Explaining the Trial of Galileo', which is a review of Arthur Koestler's *The Sleepwalkers*, republished in my *Science and Society*, Dordrecht, 1981.

3. For the discussion of the theory that truth is manifest see K. R. Popper, 'Die öffentliche Meinung im Lichte der Grundsätze des Liberalismus', *Ordo*, 1956, namely his 'Public Opinion and Liberal Principles', Chapter 17 of his *Conjectures and Refutations*, London, 1963.

4. See K. R. Popper. 'A Note on Berkeley as a Precursor of Mach', in Chapter 6 of his *Conjectures and Refutations*.

5. Chapter 3 of his *Conjectures and Refutations*.

6. Santillana subscribes to the description of Galileo's theory of the tides as 'Galileo's folly'. This is too harsh. His ultimate model of the tides was very ingenious, and its refutation encouraged the return to dynamical theories of celestial action. Thus his failure is not less important than his success.

7. 'On the Generalized Theory of Gravitation', *Scientific American*, 1950, 182, reprinted in his *Ideas and Opinions*, 1954.

6

THE FUTURE OF BERKELEY'S INSTRUMENTALISM

just terrific as a self-observer

I got tremendous kicks out of reading *Berkeley's Philosophy of Science*, yet I am already impatient to see the next book on the topic that ought to make it obsolete. Indeed, anybody who wants to make a killing can do so by simply rewriting this volume sans three cardinal defects. Yet I wish, before discussing the book and its defects, to sincerely praise it, as the pioneering comprehensive critical study of the topic, and as the work which forces us to clarify our views on instrumentalism and its history. Yet the author himself seems to me to be anything but clear on this. He would have been clearer had he defined his position as against those of his predecessors, but he does not. Consequently he is prone to ascribe to Berkeley confusions which, in my opinion, are his own. I shall now offer a view of instrumentalism and its history, a view of Berkeley in history, a view of Berkeley today, and finally a review of Brook's book. It is my compliment to the book that I find that reviewing it demands so much preparation.

1. THE PARASITIC NATURE OF INSTRUMENTALISM.

One who is concerned solely with facts and with predictions may use all sorts of formulas which fit his facts, modify them, or invent new ones. One may have no concern with anything except one's successful use of the formulas. One behaves, then, in the manner in which the instrumentalists say scientists behave even if one is not consciously an instrumentalist. One may even partially adopt the instrumentalist viewpoint while being, on the whole, decidedly an anti-instrumentalist. For example, the debate on the

This review of Richard J. Brook's *Berkeley's Philosophy of Science* (The Hague: Nijhoff, 1973) appeared in *International Studies in Philosophy*, 7, 1975.

question, is heat a substance or a mere quality of a system, such as its inner motion, makes no scientific sense to the instrumentalist. Rumford and Davy said that, since friction generates unlimited quantities of heat, heat does not conserve, and hence is not a substance. The materialists, of course, claimed that friction only transports heat, it does not generate it, since a substance cannot be generated. And so Sadi Carnot studied heat transport (or entropy, to use the Greek word), and Joseph Fourier studied heat conduction. Fourier presented his theory as phenomenological, as neutral to the debate, in quite an instrumental fashion; yet, as it was instrumental to a scientific controversy on the nature of heat, it was anti-instrumentalist at heart.

The story brings home, I hope, the point that neither a concern with phenomena alone, nor a limited phenomenological approach, are properly instrumentalist; proper instrumentalism is the view of science as a whole—the view of science as concerned with nothing but the phenomena.

Now what is there to say for the instrumentalist view? There are two or three classic defenses of instrumentalism, plus combinations of some of them. First, phenomenalism. Phenomenalism is the view that there are no substances, no things, except their appearances; the world is made up of elements of perception. If we limit our study to physics alone, then Berkeley, Hume, and Mach are all phenomenalists; if we permit psychology to enter as well, then Berkeley drops out of the list: whereas he thought tables and trees in the park are mere phenomena, he thought people were both phenomena and reality. Hume and Mach denied reality or substantiality even to people. Anyway, a phenomenalist will either demand that science center only on the phenomena or denounce it as postulating all sorts of fictitious substances, whether the matter of fire (phlogiston) or of electricity (electric charges), or of magnetism (magnetic charges and later magnetic fields), or of chemistry (atoms). Since, undoubtedly, science does postulate all sorts of unobservable substances, and since it is too useful to dispense with, the phenomenalist resorts to the famous 'as if' clause: science postulates the existence of unobserved entities as if they were real, but this is merely a *façon de parler*.

No one, to my knowledge, took phenomenalism to be the reason for adopting instrumentalism. Not even Hume, who was not really an instrumentalist proper, nor Berkeley and Mach who were. On the contrary, they were driven both to phenomenalism and to instrumentalism by methodological considerations. (Berkeley, no doubt, had religious reasons as well; but I shall ignore those now.) Briefly, they said we can never ascertain anything except about the phenomena, and in science we only allow what we can ascertain. I shall return to this argument later; here I only wish to stress that it is the crucial argument of all instrumentalists.

Of course, we can find ulterior motives here. Pierre Duhem, to my mind the greatest instrumentalist of them all, confessed he believed in Aristotelianism because he was a good Roman Catholic and so he could not accept modern science taken literally. But he insisted that this was his private prejudice and that his public stand was totally free of it. And, I am of the deepest conviction that we must grant Duhem this freedom, and take him at his word (even though I too have a private prejudice to confess: I do think his reactionary metaphysics was more pervasive than he cared to admit).

The reason Duhem did not use his own metaphysics as an argument in favor of instrumentalism is obvious: it is too arbitrary unless he could offer arguments in defense of his metaphysics—metaphysical arguments or any other. Some philosophers, Roman Catholic or not, do offer metaphysical views for which they argue, cogently or not. And when they notice that their views clash with science when taken literally, they advise against taking science literally and thus advocate instrumentalism usually as a mere afterthought.

We have, then, three kinds of defense of instrumentalism: from phenomenalism, which, however, was never taken as a starting point and so was never used; from methodology of science, which is always used by philosophers of science; and from metaphysics, which is never used by philosophers of science, even when applicable, but is often used by metaphysicians. I should stress the difference between the two because, I shall later indicate, Berkeley was considered a metaphysician until recently, when he was claimed by philosophers of science to be one of them—no minor revolution, this.

Throughout the history of science realists claimed that the simplicity, or the non-*ad hoc* character, of their theories guaranteed their realistic status. This is deeply entrenched in tradition: nature is simple, appearances are not. Ptolemy offered his eccentrics or epicycles (mathematically they go together) as *ad hoc* and so as mere instruments for storing and predicting phenomena, whereas for reality he preserved the perfect circles. Copernicus hoped to have an epicycle-free heliocentric system in order to justify his realistic claims for it. And so did Galileo. Newton claimed reality for his forces—they were no occult qualities, he protested—on account of the simplicity of his theory as a whole. Einstein protested similar sentiments. How do instrumentalists respond to this?

A huge and surreptitious change in instrumentalism was effected by Andreas Osiander, the author of the fake preface to Copernicus's posthumous major work, *De Revolutionibus*, and his follower, St. Robert, Cardinal Bellarmine, the chief opponent to Galileo who is to blame for the legal murder of Giordano Bruno. Against the whole tradition from Ptolemy to Einstein, and with no argument, they denied that the simplicity, or the non-*ad hoc* character, of a theory proves it to be true; and on this they were quite right. Indeed they denied that scientific theories are ever provable. And relying on the false but traditional (Platonic or Aristotelian) view that (true) theories about reality are provable, they denied realistic status to any scientific theory. Bellarmine declared Copernicanism philosophically (i.e., taken literally) false, but nonetheless a decent mathematical hypothesis (i.e., a mere instrument, taken to be a piece of fiction, as if saying what it does). Indeed, instrumentalists soon took simplicity to be one of the (instrumentalist) requirements of a good scientific theory (thus deviating surreptitiously yet sharply from Ptolemy).

This tacit change has caused much confusion in all sorts of discussion and even befuddles contemporary debate. I shall mention one confusion that has been cleared up only in recent years. Ernst Mach opposed atomism, and his opposition was viewed as rooted in his phenomenalism. This would have made him a metaphysician rather than a philosopher of science, we may remember, and a metaphysician espousing phenomenalism. In truth his phenomenalism was rooted in methodology; it was his methodology, then, which barred all atomism as a realistic theory. On this he was quite adamant, and this regardless of the details of the scientific controversy over atomism in which he took a lively part. His scientific objection was not to atomism realistically taken, but rather to atomism as a mere instrument, to 'as if' atomism. It was 'as if' atomism which he rejected, on the specific ground that it was not simple enough; and on this he was quite open-minded.

In this respect instrumentalists were much more demanding than realists. Both parties demanded simplicity, but the realists were quite willing and ready to grant the status of a good instrument to a theory not simple enough to graduate as really scientific. This is how the Cartesians viewed Newtonianism, and this is how the Newtonians viewed field theory, etc. For realists, instrumentality was a mere consolation prize, and they gladly offered it to runners-up; whereas for instrumentalists instrumentality was granted to the winner as first prize.

Here, then, lies the greatest strength and the greatest weakness of all instrumentalism. We can use both the best theory and the second best, as we find convenient. Instrumentalism allows for this, and hence its strength. But it can hardly distinguish, then, the second best from the best, and hence its weakness. (Did Mach allow atomism as second best, perhaps?) Yet as long as both realists and instrumentalists viewed the second best as a mere instrument the point was obscure, and instrumentalism was allowed, confusedly, to both demand from every theory as much simplicity as possible, and to allow scope for the less simple ones.

Nowadays the scene has radically changed: we view, or try to view when we can, the second best as the approximation to the best. This breaks away from the ancient dichotomy between reality and appearance; it breaks away from the dichotomy between classical realism and classical phenomenalism and instrumentalism. For now we can take a scientific theory literally, as a putative truth which, however, may turn out to be a mere approximation to the truth—something between appearance and reality. I think this is very widely accepted due to the authority of Einstein, and used increasingly in the philosophic garb given by Popper and utilized in the present paragraph.

Before concluding this section I wish to say the Einstein-Popper view just presented may need some liberalization: it does not matter, I think, how we explain the merit of the runner-up in terms of the winner, be it as an approximation or in any other way. All that matters is that we do offer some explanation. Let me offer examples to show that the liberalization just offered is not vacuous. In 1967 Robin Horton claimed that the fact that witch-doctors use the ancestor-worship systems of thought of their cultures is not so objectionable as it sounds since ancestor-worship is, naturally, linked to social stratification, and under certain conditions of poverty and ignorance social stratification may be a significant factor in the distribution of disease. Older explanations of the same facts referred either to the gullibility of preliterate people or to the symbolic value of magic. Clearly, methodology should not prescribe any decision between these three views of the matter, but rather lay conditions for any empirical study designed to help such a decision.

For another example I should mention G. J. Warnock's explanation of Berkeley's advocacy of tar-water as a cure-all (*Berkeley*, 1953, p. 231): "It is possible that tar-water was, in fact, not entirely useless; . . . in the then state of medical knowledge [his] excited zeal was at least excusable. Tar-water became for a short time immensely fashionable: and it retained until quite recent years a place on the shelves of the more traditional medical practitioners."

It will take me too long properly to analyze this quotation, and perhaps it raises the question, how come a leading British philosopher can be so silly; yet I check myself. I must allow that perhaps I am the silly party. Let me only notice that traditionally it was Berkeley's silly excursion into medicine—allegedly silly or truly so—which reinforced the view that he was a metaphysician, not a philosopher of science of any sort. This brings me to a closer look at Berkeley and his place in history.

To conclude this section, then, the greatest weakness of all instrumentalism is that it cannot allow us to explain the big success of one given scientific theory and the small success of another, since it forbids science from explaining anything anyway on the pretext that science ought to confine itself to mere phenomena.

2. BERKELEY IN HISTORY

Berkeley's idealism was viewed as a scandal in philosophy—not only by Kant, who used this expression, but also by Diderot, who declared the refutation of Berkeley a major and urgent task—and by many others. Idealism, they all agreed, is unrefuted yet ought to be refuted. This view is reflected even in Jack London's futuristic novel, *The Iron Heel*, written in the early 20th century.

In the 18th and 19th centuries, when scientific theories were deemed provable and often proven, e.g., Newtonian mechanics, the falsity of idealism had to be accepted as deducible from proven theories and hence proven. Somehow, nevertheless, the need was felt for a direct disproof, for a disproof not resting on any specific example from science. Evidently, this can only mean that it was known that either idealism calls into question the very nature of scientific proof, or else leads to paradox. For, clearly, an idealist can accept any scientific theory as proven, yet deny the literal reading of it: Newtonianism need not mean to refer to heavenly bodies; it may be understood to refer to appearances. Alternatively, if we do have proof of the existence of heavenly bodies, as well as (idealistic) proofs of their unknowability, then we land in paradox.

Kant's position on this issue is both very important and very subtle, since his concept of proof, of substance, of anything else, is so greatly different, though transformed, from the traditional concepts. Thus, first of all, he split the traditional concept of substance which is the real as well as the permanent and self-contained or active, into the real (which is unknowable though thinkable) and the permanent and active. The first he called *das Ding-an-sich*, the thing-in-itself, which is real as opposed to the apparent (*Critique of Pure Reason* A 576 B 604) and the second he called the category of substance which, like all categories, is a pure concept of synthesis, namely a means of putting order into the world of appearances. And so, when relating to idealism, clearly, Kant has to take issue on two fronts, and perhaps relate these. He does so in the first edition of the *Critique* (A 366–380) but only briefly refers to it in the second (B 275–6). And so, he both refuted Berkeley's idealism to his own satisfaction and felt it was a scandal in philosophy that he had not.

Kant even put his finger on matters when he contrasted Descartes's 'skeptical' or tentative idealism and Berkeley's 'dogmatic' or definite one. For he felt the one was justified, but not the other; not Berkeley's. Yet this does not resolve the difficulty in comprehending Kant. For, as he insisted, *das Ding-an-sich* was a mere "transcendental ideal" and so its existence not demonstrated (see note 24 to my 'Unity and Diversity in Science', reprinted in my *Science in Flux, Boston Studies in the Philosophy of Science*, 1975), but were Berkeley's idealism refuted, the existence of *das Ding-an-sich* would be demonstrated contrary to its being a mere transcendental ideal. Hence, Kant's requirement for disproof of Berkeley's idealism cannot be the requirement for a proof of the negation of idealism; what he wanted was at most a proof of undecidability and at least the discovery of a defect in Berkeley's proof of the truth of idealism.

Exactly this kind of disproof has been found, anyway, and by Bertrand Russell. In his early *Problems of Philosophy*, in his *Inquiry*, and in his very latest philosophic essay, he said, Berkeley only proved idealism consistent, not true (*Inquiry*, 1940, chapter 20, Pelican edition, p. 269): "The argument from epistemology, which unlike that from logic, is as powerful as it ever was, does not attempt to show that [realism] is false, but only that it is gratuitous, in the sense that it sins against Occam's razor by assuming the existence of unnecessary entities." And, on page 270: "At this point there is danger of a fallacy, so simple that it ought to be easy to avoid, but nevertheless not always avoided. A man may say: 'everything that I have ever perceived was perceived; therefore there is inductive evidence that everything is perceived' ".* This fallacy, like all fallacies, can be replaced by an explicit added premiss: (in principle) everything there is is knowable. It is what Popper has labelled the theory of manifest truth. And, as Popper has argued, the theory of manifest truth was widely held throughout the Age of Reason.

Berkeley not only declared appearances to constitute hard data; he took it for granted that any proven theory which can be taken literally must be based on hard data by induction. And induction, he said, cannot establish Newtonianism taken literally; it can at most establish a physical theory of a Cartesian sort, and hardly even that. Today, however, we can easily take literally even an unproven theory, to view it as a genuine hypothesis. In Berkeley's day, as in Copernicus's day, there were theories proven and taken literally—those whose status can be viewed as realistic—and there were mathematical hypotheses—as if realistic, or mere instruments. The ancient Greek dichotomy into nature and convention, reality and appearance, truth and falsity, ensures the existence of only two kinds of theories and no more. This is why the third view, of scientific theory as hypothetical and as an approximation, is a break with the time-honored dichotomy and much more of a revolution than it seems.

This explains the scandal in philosophy: what could not be done for centuries could not be done for good and deep-seated limitations. It can now be done because the limitations are removed. And so, when Berkeley proved that no induction from the facts to Newton's theory is possible, the rest was almost an easy exercise in deduction and elaboration.

Traditionally, then, the scandal persisted. Berkeley's argument from perception, induction, quest for certitude, and Occam's razor, were absorbed into the tradition as very convincing yet impossible to endorse. The intolerable thing about it was not so much his ideas already mentioned, but his metaphysics. Whereas Descartes presented a picture of the physical world as a huge clock-work, with hidden cogs and wheels, and whereas

---

*This fallacy Sir Karl Popper labelled the Agassi paradox of inductive confirmation—much to my regret—and he reported that Nelson Goodman has claimed that it is the same as his famous grue paradox. It is of course Russell's and not mine; and, oddly, its distinctness from Goodman's is provable; R. Carnap proves in his *Logical Foundations of Probability* that the system presented in that book is impregnable to Goodman's paradox, and Popper proves in his *Conjectures and Refutations* that Carnap's system is hit by Russell's (which Popper calls Agassi's).

Newton replaced this picture by another, where attraction between particles, forces acting at a distance, replace the cogs pushing each other, for Berkeley the physical world was all appearance and no reality. This flat world was repugnant: "substance, as I understand the word," says George Santayana (*Skepticism and Animal Faith*, ch. 20, p. 209 of the Dover edition), "is nothing of the sort. It is not metaphysical but simply whatever physical substance may be which is found in things or between them. . . . It helps us to explain. . . . If they were detached facts, not forms regularly taken on by enduring and pervasive substances, there would be no knowing when, where, of what sort, or in what numbers they would not assault me; and my life would not seem life in a tractable world, but an inexplicable nightmare."

Berkeley knew of this sort of objection. He protested (*Principles*, Sec. 35 et seq.) that the objection was unfair; that, on the contrary, his philosophy is commonsense since it leaves things as they are, including their observed durability such as it is; whereas others, the realists, hypostatize things by giving them some metaphysical durability, indeed utter indestructibility, above and beyond the observed durabilities.

There is a sublte distinction here. Common sense is the way we see things not necessarily things as they are. Also, common sense takes things superficially enough but it does not insist on superficiality, as Berkeley's philosophy does. But let us ignore that, since Berkeley is not at all the only philosopher who, objecting to all hypostasis, hypostatizes common sense.

The most revealing traditional view of Berkeley can be found in G. J. Warnock's *Berkeley* of 1953, where, in the chapter on Berkeley's account of language (p. 59), we read: "Berkeley enunciates with vigour and clarity a view of philosophical enquiry which would be widely accepted today, and which is a fact sometimes taken to be wholly modern. He argues that a large number (at least) of the philosophical difficulties in which we find ourselves entangled are really *our own fault*, problems of our own making. . . . He goes on to contend, still anticipating contemporary views, that the dust we raise (and thus block our own vision) is the dust of linguistic confusion . . . ." In his postscript the author makes it abundantly clear that sense data and clear expressions are the central concern of both Berkeley and his successors. There is, in Warnock's book, a chapter on science, where the question is raised, is Berkeley's philosophy not opposed to science, and is answered, for Berkeley, by saying that science can be viewed as merely predictive.

It is hard for me to decide whether Warnock himself agrees with Berkeley, and to what extent; I suppose they both are, essentially, staunch defenders of common sense. I cannot see more than this either in his book on Berkeley or in his *English Philosophy since 1900*, which is his book on his own school of philosophy—analytic philosophy, so-called. The postscript to his *Berkeley* presents Berkeley's concern with perception, with our knowledge of the external world, as perennial in philosophy, and proceeds with a discussion about language and concept, as well as common sense. His *English Philosophy since 1900* presents Berkeley as an instrumentalist philosopher of science, but not relating to Berkeley's metaphysics. Between these two books, it seems, quite a change in viewpoint took place.

There is no doubt that Berkeley does qualify, both as a metaphysician and as a philosopher of science. There is no doubt that as a metaphysician he discusses substance; yet as his chief argument for his stand against physical substance is methodological, he is more in a class with, say, Hans Reichenbach of *The Philosophical Foundations of Quantum Mechanics* than with, say, Bradley of *Appearance and Reality*.

3. BERKELEY TODAY

The new attitude to Berkeley can be properly assessed only by comparing it to the hostility which philosophers, especially those favorably disposed towards science, have traditionally shown him. His criticism of the calculus, in particular, was taken to be nit-picking, until J. O. Wisdom, in 1939 and 1941 (in *Hermathene*), argued that the criticism was (a) valid and (b) fruitful. The great philosophic import of Wisdom's view has not been sufficiently assessed and it fits Lakatos's philosophy of mathematics. Being critical, it is obvious his philosophy is akin to Popper's, and it is no surprise to learn that soon afterwards he became his disciple, as did Lakatos for a while.

In 1953 Wisdom, as editor of *The British Journal for the Philosophy of Science*, dedicated a bicentenary issue to Berkeley as a philosopher of science. That remarkable issue contains two papers that serve Brook well, M. H. Pirenne, 'Physiological Mechanisms in the Perception of Distance by Sight and Berkeley's Theory of Vision' and Karl Popper, 'A Note on Berkeley as a Precursor to Mach and Einstein' (reprinted in his *Conjectures and Refutations*, 1963). Berkeley's critique of Newtonianism, says Popper, foreshadowed Mach's to a large extent, even to the point of suggesting Mach's Principle.

Now, Berkeley's critique was, of course, largely epistemological, not scientific, and in this it differed from his critique of the calculus; and, of course, it was not only ineffective, it was totally overlooked. The reason for the oversight of Berkeley's instrumentalism is complicated, but largely it has to do with the scientific success of Newtonianism and so with inductivism, not to mention the instrumentalism of Cardinal Bellarmine who was the *bête noire* of the Age of Reason. Only when Helmholtz endorsed field theory as a mere instrument did the tide turn the other way and Mach could combine instrumentalism with progressivism so successfully that Duhem could piously declare he was proud to be Mach's ally as evidence that he was not selling instrumentalism and Roman Catholicism in a package deal. In the meantime Berkeley's critique was forgotten. Historians of philosophy went in the wake of Hegel, the pioneer modern historian of philosophy. And for Hegel each important philosopher either had a system or did not count; in particular, Berkeley had a system. Also for Hegel science had little or nothing to do with philosophy. I should only mention one point made by Popper in this respect: "As far as I know", he says (n3), "there does not exist an English translation of [Berkeley's *De Motu*] which succeeds in making clear what Berkeley meant to say; and the Editor of the latest edition of the *Works* [of George Berkeley] even goes out of his way to belittle the significance of this highly original and in many ways unique essay." I do not know how typical this is, though: Gerard Hinrich has a paper on 'The Logical Positivism of *De Motu*' in *Review of Metaphysics*, 3, 1950, and Warnock, whose book on Berkeley of 1953 is conventional—with the longest chapter on perception and existence, and the next-longest on language—has three pages devoted to *De Motu* (from a traditional viewpoint, though).

The modern view of Berkeley (or anyone else) as a philosopher of science, begins with an exposition—from his viewpoint, of course—of the problems that science presents, both as a system of knowledge in general and as a specific system whose specific content needs to be examined. No doubt, Berkeley's peculiarity is that he took Locke's philosophy as given and claimed to be doing hardly more than straightening out certain faults within it. Therefore it makes hardly any sense to view Berkeley as a philosopher of science unless and until we do the same for Locke. It so happens, however, that this is hardly novel. Locke was the leading philosopher of the Enlightenment or the Age of Reason, and for him science, "natural philosophy" to use his words, was always central and the paradigm of rationality.

This being so, it is puzzling that Berkeley ever ceased to be viewed as a philosopher of science. No matter how we view him, no one ever overlooked his claim to be a Lockean and a commentator on Locke's system. There are two possible solutions to the puzzle. First, it is quite possible that though Berkeley viewed himself as a Lockean, his modification made little of Locke's taste for science. In a sense this can be said of all commonsense philosophers, such as the analytic philosophers, including the old Wittgenstein: though they followed Locke and Russell and the young Wittgenstein, they lost contact with science in general and with physics and mathematics in particular (contrast Wittgenstein's mathematically oriented *Tractatus Logico-Philosophicus* with his opposite *Remarks on the Foundations of Mathematics*).

This may be true, yet it can be only a part of the story. Let me present, anyway, the second solution to the puzzle (why was Berkeley not viewed as a philosopher of science even though he was a follower of Locke?), which, I think, is true: we are facing an apologetic attitude of the defenders of science: they could not see a critic of Newton, an instrumentalist, as a person passionately concerned with science; they could not admit that the severest critic of Newton was also one of his greatest admirers. (See, for example, Dr. Thomas Thomson's *History of the Royal Society*.) But this, I hope, is now largely past history.

4. BROOK ON BERKELEY

Brook does Berkeley the honor of treating him as one who offers a viable philosophy to be critically examined. "Historical considerations are, of course, important" he admits on page two; "nevertheless", he adds on page three, what matters is Berkeley's view of science in general rather than of Newtonian forces in particular: for Berkeley "the proper object of science . . . is not to disclose efficient causes—the latter is properly the object of metaphysics (or theology)—but rather to disclose the uniformities among the phenomena of nature." This is to say, Berkeley offers instrumentalism and Brook intends to gloss over historical considerations as much as reasonable and examine critically Berkeley's case for instrumentalism. "We will not spend much time in criticism of the metaphysical doctrine of 'immaterialism' ", namely Berkeley's phenomenalism (which is but one version of immaterialism, I should add, and scientifically the least interesting).

Brook's plan is to present Berkeley's theories of (a) meaning, (b) vision, (c) physics, and (d) mathematics. The order of the first three chapters seems intuitive and can easily be defended. (As it happens, I think it is problematic; see below.) His chapter on mathematics seems to me quite out of place: his discussion of arithmetic concerns meaning and should go in the first chapter; his discussion of geometry belongs in the second chapter, since Berkeley's concern was to identify the space of physics with visual space; his discussion of the calculus belongs with the discussion of physics, since Berkeley's denial of the existence of the infinitely small is part and parcel of his instrumentalism. In particular, one can say, insofar as Berkeley does have a philosophy of mathematics, or even of logic, I am afraid it is totally left out of this volume. The author offers his own view of the "ultimate clarification of the concepts" of mathematics which, he thinks (p. 192) "to some extent vindicated Berkeley". I am at a loss to see the "vindication", not to mention the "ultimate" quality of clarity of concepts. I shall therefore say no more on this than that he could be more explicit both about Berkeley and about Wisdom, whose view he both generously declares "interesting" and enigmatically dismisses as "an exaggeration" (p. 192).

(a) Let us proceed, then, to Berkeley's theory of meaning. Clearly, what he wanted to achieve is a theory which enables us to speak of perceived things, of the two substances which he recognized, i.e., human souls and God, but not of material substances, atoms, forces, etc. Also, it is obvious, he did not wish anyone to stop talking about non-existent, fictitious entities such as atoms, forces, infinitesimals.

This is not easy to do, as any modern student of logic knows. Moreover, the very fact that Brook can ascribe to Berkeley the view that a concept inconsistently defined is meaningless (p. 11), even if exegesis may show him in error, suffices to convince any logician that Berkeley is hopelessly out of date. For, certainly, we do wish both disjunction and complementation to be freely usable, so that any adjective can be used to create a tautologous adjective x-or-non-x; and, by added complementation, an inconsistent yet meaningful adjective should be constructible from it. The question is, can we gloss over the inaccuracies of Berkeley's theory of meaning and reconstruct a modern version of it? Certainly Brook's preface imposes on him this question, but I do not see that he notices it. Certainly the question, Can there be a satisfactory modern theory of meaning akin to Berkeley's? is highly controversial. One of the latest papers that Rudolf Carnap wrote was in this vein, in the first volume of the *Minnesota Studies in the Philosophy of Science* series. Even his barest sketch or outline was so very unsatisfactory: he wanted the language of physics to include the statement that the speed of light is maximal as a mere tautology, regardless of the partly empirical content of this statement. One can easily sympathize with Ludwig Wittgenstein giving up all hope of building a formal system of this kind.

Clearly, Berkeley had no idea of the size of the task he was undertaking. His starting point was Locke's theory of meaning which he thought he had simplified and much improved upon. No doubt Hume had a similar objective, and he had better reason to think he had simplified Locke's system. But they were both very mistaken.

Perhaps the worst of all this is the view that causes or forces cannot be seen and therefore cannot exist and therefore the terms 'cause' and 'force' are meaningless: it is thus both meaningless and false to speak of causes.

Brook offers a very sophisticated reading of Berkeley, who had both syntax and semantics, and who viewed the abstract theories of physics, causal theories, to be one of the languages of God: God tells us what to do by showing us facts, by talking to us through our sense-organs, and his speech follows certain grammatical rules. Science, then, is "the grammar of nature". This is less odd in its historical context, where the Book of Nature was put on a par with the Bible, as God's two messages to Man. It is also less odd in a period when the meaningful was so often confused with the true, or at least the meaningless with the logically impossible (p. 11).

I find it very puzzling that Brook does criticize Berkeley's language of nature since nature cannot utter a falsehood, but not Berkeley's view that 'square-circle' is meaningless. I also cannot but say this. Let us view seriously both Berkeley's theory of vision as a theory of 'visual language' (this is a title of a book by Berkeley) and his theory of science as 'the grammar of nature', and thus identify his philosophy of science as well as his metaphysics with his theory of meaning. Let us also agree that Berkeley's theory of meaning is antiquated and confused. This, in itself, will put an end to his philosophy as a serious contender. But Brook's program was to start with his philosophy of science, and as a candidate to be seriously considered and rejected only after due criticism! I confess I find quite fascinating the historical Berkeley that forces himself from these pages as against Brook's declared intention.

I shall go further, and add a point of my own, to which, however, I am indebted to Brook. In Locke's *Essay*, Bk. IV, Ch. II, §14, idealism is presented and dismissed: the world is not a dream since men act. It is perhaps no accident that Berkeley made action the center of his philosophy: both science and religion guide our actions.

b) I will not go into Berkeley's work on vision; it is doubtlessly a valid critique of previously accepted views as it is a challenge to pursue further empirical researches; it also put on the map the discovery of Molyneux that we learn to perceive distances; it made it clear that whether or not objective space exists, there are, on top of this, the visual subjective space and the tactile one. Berkeley raised both the question, how do we map the two spaces on each other, and whether it makes empirical difference to say that these spaces are Euclidean or not; for better or worse—and I think matters go both ways—these are questions that are still very much with us.

What puzzles me about all this is the fact that whereas Locke connected by induction parts of tactile and of visual space into given objects, Berkeley probed more deeply, asking about the mapping of the two spaces as such. He had no right to ask: any question like that is answered by a theory and every theory will be fictitious. For, whereas there are, in the phenomenal world, both portions of tactile space and portions of visual space, these spaces are not parts of the phenomena. In Berkeley's philosophy there was the world of the phenomena, and the mere correlations of them by induction or by laws of nature that are, strictly speaking, empty of all content and merely serve us in the forming and storing inductive generalizations. Hence, whereas the claim that my table both looks and feels like a table is accepted by induction, the theory of mapping between the visual and the tactile spaces should have the status of Euclidean geometry or Newtonian mechanics, not as Berkeley wants them to be, i.e., God's medium for His message to Man. Brook discusses at length the arguments Berkeley offers in order to distinguish visual space from Euclidean space, and he says a lot about the mapping of visual and tactile spaces without, however, raising the question of the status of the mapping. I find this a severe defect.

c) This brings me to the last point, the chapter on physics (since I shall not comment on the final chapter on mathematics). This, after all, is the central issue of the book, according to the introduction. I find commenting on it the hardest. And it is because of a simple question that has to be answered. Does Brook think that Berkeley was an instrumentalist proper? He admits Berkeley denied realistic status to Newtonianism (pp. 81–84, 91, 93, 95, 96, 100, 103, 114, 126, 131, 145, *et passim*), he ascribes to Berkeley the notion of "mathematical fictions" (pp. 3, 189, 190), of "mathematical hypotheses" (pp. 13, 100, 133–34), instrumentalism (p. 16, perhaps also 189), "fictionalism" (p. 190), "conventionalism" (pp. 141–42, 198, perhaps also 189)—the reader may appreciate my frustration with the absence of an index; a scholarly work without an index is like a triple-fugue without a stretto—yet he always manages to qualify these ascriptions. I shall only name two kinds of qualification, both invalid: one, that Berkeley was often not so successful in his execution of his program as Brook finds desirable, and the other that he finds Berkeley's demand for non-*ad hoc* hypotheses a break from instrumentalism.

As to the non-*ad hoc* nature of scientific theory, I cannot blame Brook for a confusion, since I have already said that the instrumentalists themselves allow for it, both in demanding avoidance of the *ad hoc*, as well as relaxing that demand. Yet, I am very unhappy to see Brook amplify it. He is puzzled that Berkeley accepts the view that light is corpuscular (p. 98 and note), yet critical of Popper's claim (p. 99) that Berkeley rejects it. He says that "Berkeley himself . . . is not clear about the distinction" between force in a realist sense and force in an instrumentalist sense (p. 105)—I hope I understand him correctly. And there are other alleged confusions (pp. 117–18, 68, 188, 134, 142). And he is even unable to evaluate Berkeley's view of Newtonian gravitation as a mere inductive generalization (p. 119) except by ascribing to Berkeley a confusion (p. 120) between the two different views of force. Clearly, Brook could have ascribed less confusion to Berkeley had he noted that he (Berkeley) rejects and accepts the same views on different levels, yet he (Berkeley) is a bit arbitrary about it all. "Though a case can be made for the thesis [Popper's] that Berkeley, like Mach, views mechanics as fundamentally a kinematics, or a mathematical description of motion", concludes Brook, "the case is flawed by Berkeley's failure . . .". Not only was Mach's attempt a failure, too; it is a severe historiographic error to deny an author an intention because of any failure to execute it: most authors fail. Moreover, I think Brook is bound to tell us how else can an instrumentalist view Newton's mechanics, or how else can Berkeley, an anti-materialist, have viewed Newtonian mechanics than by holding an instrumentalist view. There may be a subtlety here that has evaded me; all I can say is, I tried to find it in the book and failed.

d) I have skipped much that Brook discusses, e.g., Berkeley on mathematics, or on the mind-body problem. Let me finish with a minor point of learning psychology which is very pertinent. Inductivists—and all instrumentalists, I have explained, are inductivists who accept the Berkeley-Hume argument against induction from effects to causes—take it for granted that we perceive sensa and that we generalize. (Only A. J. Ayer has said, suffice it if the world were such that our knowledge can be construed as if it were so accumulated. I find Ayer's suggestion hilarious and cannot be surprised that it has been ignored.) What is amazing is that most inductivists take it for granted that we remember how in childhood we learned. It is to Piaget that we owe the empirical evidence that we do not. And it is Claude Lévi-Strauss who raised a very interesting question here: is child learning primitive or scientific? For, in his conclusion of *The Savage Mind* he says, whereas in science the distinction between the symbol and the symbolized is essential, in preliterate thinking it is non-existent. In Berkeley we have a middle system where every thing can be a symbol for everything, by association, conscious or not. This explains why he is so prone to confuse the meaningless with the false (pp. 38–39, 117–18, 134, 142). This is also why Berkeley can take vision to represent tactile sensation while hardly noticing the translation (p. 56). As Brook explains, looking at a musical score we do not 'see' the music; but, of course, the expert musician does. Lévi-Strauss's distinction between the savage and the scientist is a matter of degree of familiarity, as well as, I should think, the ability to reflect and to avoid the deception due to that familiarity.

I think Berkeley's greatness lies just here. He was just terrific as a self-observer, as one who knew what subtle tricks familiarity can play, and who used this knowledge to build his philosophy. Yet his philosophy had no room for such subtleties. Brook's book presents Berkeley, contrary to his intention, as a metaphysician of hidden signals, of meaning everywhere, conscious and unconscious. This should lead us to a reexamination of J. O. Wisdom's important and scandalously neglected book on Berkeley. But that is another story.

7

THE SECRET OF CARNAP

excellence in mediocrity

I

The Romantic view of fame says, you may win real fame only after you die. Stendhal was upset by early fame, lest it foreshadow oblivion. The rationalist view of fame says, on the contrary, now or never: just discovery leads to an almost immediate recognition by peers. Both views are false, and reassessments of artists and scientists and philosophers go on all the time. The volume at hand, *Rudolf Carnap, Logical Empiricist, Materials and Perspectives*, is the latest monument to Carnap, edited by Jaakko Hintikka, who is one of Carnap's heirs and successors. It is an invitation for such a reassessment and is on the side of the angels, thus suggesting to the reviewer the possibility of playing fairly the role of devil's advocate. It is as reasonable a defense as one may expect. A few of the essays included here were written specifically for this volume to fill the gap in a solid selection from respectable sources intended to offer the reader the best of and about Carnap's kaleidoscopic career. I shall now review each item separately, in an attempt to show that they add up to disappointingly little.

The first 50 pages are eulogies by famous philosophers. Read in the Boston Philosophy of Science conference and published in its proceedings in the *Boston Studies in the Philosophy of Science* volume dedicated to his memory, they are now given added import. As a devil's advocate I am called to comment on them, yet as a reasonable reader I must make allowances. Fortunately, one of them is by Quine and he invites no allowance. I will therefore pay him the compliment of a detailed—though severe—review and add a little about other, less sincere eulogies.

This review of *Rudolf Carnap, Logical Empiricist, Materials and Perspectives*, edited by Jaakko Hintikka (Dordrecht and Boston: Reidel, 1975) appeared in *Philosophia*, 10, 1981.

Quine's homage is, on the whole, just terrific; it portrays a beautiful teacher, beautiful encounters, *joie de vivre* and *amor dei intellectualis*. It calls Carnap the heir of Russell (p. xxiv), and "my greatest teacher" (p. xxv). I wish to take it for granted that Carnap was a person of great quality. Nor is this irrelevant: on this I do not agree with Imre Lakatos. When he wanted to give full expression to his deep contempt for Rudolf Carnap he used to say, with devilish mock-sincerity, "I am quite sure he is an excellent *pater-familias*". Though I own that some kindly people are not important thinkers and some important thinkers [e.g., Lakatos himself], are not kind, this is not the end of the story. On the contrary, I constantly look for connections between a person's character and his production. Back to Quine. I wish to accept as much of his praise of Carnap as I can, personal as well as intellectual. But Quine praises not only Carnap's openness to him, "We moved with Carnap as henchmen" says Quine (p. xxvii) of himself, Goodman, and others, "through the metaphysicians' camp" that the American Philosophical Association's Baltimore meeting of the year 1935 was. "We beamed with pride when he countered a diatribe of Arthur Lovejoy's in his characteristically reasonable way, explaining that if Lovejoy meant *A* then *p*, and if he meant *B* then *q*. I had yet to learn how unsatisfying this way of Carnap's could sometimes be." Quine goes on to list the occasions of which he met Carnap, ending with the 1965 congress which Lakatos organized, single-handed, in order to establish the Popper school, and to which Quine refers as "Popper's colloquium in London" (p. xxvii). "When Popper confronted him on induction his defense was masterly. It carried me back to his confrontation of [i.e., with] Lovejoy thirty years before. It was the same old Carnap. His tragic death," etc. Popper, like Lovejoy, in the "metaphysicians' camp"? And has Quine again "beamed with pride when he (Carnap) countered a diatribe of" Popper's? Or do I read too much into an allusion? I do not know. It is possible that Quine still feels that neither Lovejoy nor Popper have made any contribution to philosophy. Then he is the last of the Mohicans and I should let him be. He praises three books of Carnap's (p. xxv). First his *Aufbau* (though a failure, he admits), for its "rigor and explicitness" and for its instrumentalism. He also praises *Logical Syntax* as "the embodiment of logical positivism, logical empiricism, the Vienna Circle." No admission of any failure: the last of the Mohicans for sure. Finally he praises *Logical Foundations of Probability* as "a monument to his unwavering concern with the logic of science." As a teacher I, too, have to pay somewhat vacuous compliments, especially when I have to dish out poor grades; but I do so more openly, and in the line of my paid duty.

Trying to ignore the eulogies of Carnap that are so non-specific that with suitable biographical alterations they might apply to any esteemed intellectual, let me briefly notice those by Feigl and Hempel.

Feigl calls him "one of the greatest logicians and philosophers of science of our century" (p. xiii). What does this signify? What theorem did he discover, what proof did he invent, what has earned him this epithet? The only tangible thing Feigl says is that Gödel used Carnap's meta-linguistic technique in his famous proof, which seems to me sheer fancy, and that Carnap was the first philosopher to recognize the significance of Gödel, which is no doubt true and of a significance to be judged later on. Hempel's eulogy seems to me just about right. It praises qualities that are laudable, like clarity, and speaks of him less as a philosopher and more as a teacher and a person. He only mentions his earliest philosophy which at the time sounded so terrific, and which, I understand, Hempel now judges differently, though he stresses Carnap's devotion as a teacher and his proverbial open-mindedness.

Abner Shimony, his former student (yet not disciple) (p. xvii): though a metaphysician, he found talk with Carnap useful. Not very surprisingly, then, Shimony sees Carnap as "a great systematic philosopher, who had a coherent approach to nearly the whole range of classical philosophical problems." This, for a philosopher who held the view that "the whole range of classical philosophical problems" was stuff and nonsense, is intriguing. Shimony does not elaborate. Bar-Hillel, the most devoted of disciples, is frank and touching. Carnap always complained of weak memory, he says, and gains corroboration from Stegmüller (p. lxvi). Shimony says his memory was most extraordinary and he, too, gains corroboration from Maria Reichenbach (p. lii).

I suppose I must mention Stegmüller's lengthy contribution, as it is part homage and part summary of Carnap's contributions. I find it singularly unimpressive, and I wish to describe some of my reactions which I later on decide to disqualify (as explained in the next paragraph). For example, Stegmüller speaks of Carnap's contributions to the theory of subjective probability—a theory I deem a total loss at best anyway. He calls (p. lxiv) "unique" Carnap's combination of originality "insightful and absolute precision together with patience" etc., and I find this meaningless, not knowing what combination is unique, what not. He characterizes (p. lxv) Popper's disputes with Carnap as "a small internal family quarrel," on account of their common "affirmative attitude to a rational philosophy." Will no quarrel between any two rationalistic philosophers ever be more than "a small internal family quarrel"? Do Locke's criticism of Descartes and Kant's of his predecessors, too, qualify as small family quarrels? If Stegmüller means what he says, he should say, Yes. I suspect his view will then be entertained by very few serious philosophers. I should turn this question round and attack myself no less fiercely. Do I admit some quarrels to be family quarrels, some not, some small quarrels, some not, some small family quarrels, some not? How do I view matters? What do I deem the common sense that Stegmüller so violates that I judge him so severely and so harshly? Am I not very unfair?

To repeat, I find not serious the view that all quarrels between rationalists are small family quarrels. But how can I ascribe this view to Stegmüller? Only on account that he adds to his verdict nothing but the claim that the two contestants were both rationalists. This may be too flimsy on his part, and then also on my part. Therefore, I modify my remarks: the obituary by Stegmüller is either not serious or its wording is flimsy. But I must confess: any view of Carnap's disagreement with Popper as a small family quarrel makes Carnap an important thinker, and it is my self-appointed task as a devil's advocate that forces me to deny this view. And so, I disqualify myself as a judge, and address myself against arguments in favor of this view. Stegmüller offers none. Was Carnap an important thinker?

Before reviewing the remaining 395 pages of this volume, I wish to launch a few complaints. Except for the eulogies and the final essay by Shimony, the volume consists of three parts: the first concerns the problem of analyticity; I do not know what the second part concerns, but I will come to that; the last part concerns the problem of induction. The problem of analyticity is related to Quine's objection to the dichotomy, analytic/synthetic, on the ground that "all bachelors are unmarried" is unlike "all bachelors are young" on the one hand and unlike "all bachelors are bachelors" on the other. But how? The simple guess is, the problem of analyticity is, how, if at all, can we restore the dichotomy? But this is not true. For why should we bother? The problem, then, is different. I cannot quite say what it is. This is my first complaint. If the editor could not find and include a suitable paper that states the problem, I think he ought to have done the job himself, or assign it to an able person.

Complaint number two. The papers contain a lot of very high-powered material—I do not profess to understand it all—which is hastily explained and whose service is questionable. There are more problems than I can list, but an example might do. I choose the paper of P. M. Williams 'On the Conservative Extension of Semantical Systems: A Contribution to the Problem of Analyticity' (p. 123–41), since in another paper (p. 100) in this volume it is declared "incisive" and "elegant" and treated there as a classic of sorts—though it appeared only in 1973.

Williams defines "conservative extension" (p. 127): a semantic system is a conservative extension of another if it contains all its logically valid formulae as logically valid, its possible worlds as possible, and its true statements as true. This seems sufficiently straightforward and easy even if before he can say so Williams uses a whole page to define entities from a novel theory and a couple of pages to define a semantic system. The length, one hopes, insures precision which may come in handy later on. (Honestly, I am in no position to judge.) And yet, no sooner has the feat been performed in all its exactitude, when Williams adds (p. 127–28): "A conservative extension is one in which new expressions are introduced but the original expressions retain their meanings." Now the first half, "new expressions are introduced" is just fine: the definition does not say how the extension is made, and any addition may be considered an extension, be it a proper name, a class name, a sentence, or any other linguistic items permissible. But the second half, "the original expressions retain their meanings" has such an obvious refutation that I am sure I have misunderstood Williams. Here it is. Take the positive part of the normal calculus of statements and extend it by adding the negation which normally belongs to that calculus. The definition cited above tells us that the addition is a conservative extension; yet, as is well-known, the meaning of the expression "if . . . then . . ." is altered—extended, indeed, by the addition. Suppose we demand, in addition to Williams's long, detailed, and precise set of requirements, that the extension will not be of the logic of the system. I will then take the ordinary lower functional calculus and add to it, as is done by so many authors, Peano's axioms. Surely this will be a paradigm of what Williams means by an extension. But let us do so—as he almost explicitly permits—in two steps, the first including the whole system sans the axiom of induction; or the ZF system minus the axiom of choice and then that axiom; or projective geometry for the plane minus Desargue, etc. There is no doubt that the literature, scarcely agreed on anything regarding meaning, agrees that the terms introduced half-cocked are "open-ended" and their meanings are completed when the missing axioms are added. If readers will push harder and deny me the right to use examples from axiomatic mathematics, I would invite them to construct examples from axiomatic physics. I wish to stress: I see nothing fundamental here, but an "incisive and elegant" paper presenting a simple definition in three technical pages and missing an obvious point.

Perhaps I am finicky. But I do not think so. For, the main concern of those who contribute here to the problem of analyticity is what prescribes the rules of their game. Their concern is to build a language which is free of metaphysics. Perhaps they should say, why. Anyway, metaphysics constitutes sets of propositions, whether about normal things or about metaphysical things. As Popper has proven in his paper on that topic in the Carnap volume in The Library of Living Philosophers series, the elimination of metaphysics is of both propositions and other expressions, whether names of deities, proper descriptions of them, etc. What is at stake here is nonetheless the elimination of metaphysical statements: a deity which has a name that cannot enter a proper statement is much less bothersome than the unnamed undescribed intervener who is alleged by some metaphysical statement or other to have every event happen just so as to suit a certain unnamed undescribed design. Clearly, then, what we need is to see whether a system which includes some metaphysical statements is not an extension of a purely empirical one. And to this end we need to see, first, whether or not a system with only empirical statements and tautologies is at all possible. This is how analyticity is dragged in. That is, suppose we have such a system; can we build into it a metaphysical statement while adding neither to its semantics nor to its expressions-other-than-statements? If we can, then the game is up; if we cannot, then we can try the same while adding metaphysical expressions-other-than-statements. If we still cannot, then metaphysics is at long last successfully eliminated. Popper, to repeat, destroyed all hopes in that line. Williams is nonetheless persistent in his search for a series of extensions of the observation language. Now that language includes, Carnap says, words like 'red', 'hot', etc. I assume Williams concurs, though I cannot say. Now, if this means that observation reports should be accepted as true regardless of the growth of science, then I, for one, cannot concur. Nor can I concur that the very meanings of words such as 'red' or 'hot' remain unchanged through scientific progress. The designation of 'hot' has altered: Robert Boyle still thought pepper hot (and opium cold). The content of an observation report is not confined to what has been observed: it contains dispositional terms and thus it may entail new tests (Popper, 1935). The flavor of redness, and of heat too, has altered with the advent of modern technology, as any reader of anti-scientific literature or of science-fiction knows all too well.

What are they talking about? Why do they use such high-powered logical techniques? Why does Wojcicki, for another example, mention the difference between entailment and (effective) deductibility and then say nothing explicitly about it?

So much for my two preliminary complaints. My first complaint was that the editor did not have the problem of analyticity explained. My second was that too much idling powerful machinery was put on show. I suspect that the two complaints are related thus. The real problem at hand is, how to eliminate metaphysics? Carnap's attempts were bogged down by a few snags, including some that relate to the dichotomy between analytic and synthetic statements. All the high-powered machinery is exhibited in the hope of having some use for it.

At least that much is common knowledge: Carnap's own attempts at the elimination of metaphysics have led nowhere. And in order to show this I need not go into Carnap's elimination of metaphysics. Its latest version, included here, has been refuted with ease by David Kaplan in a paper which is also included here. With the end of this lengthy preliminary I can now start.

II

The first paper in this volume is by Hempel, and on Carnap. Hempel explains the value of Carnap's effort in the fight against metaphysics. Carnap's first attempt to eliminate metaphysics is his famous *Logical Structure of the World*—his *Aufbau* (his earliest opus) as a reduction of all knowledge, *à la* Russell's *Our Knowledge of the External World*, but a precise one, namely to (a) a number of phenomenological terms, and (b) the single term, x, remembers partial similarity between y and z, as a primitive term, plus (c) a few axioms. I know of very few people who have studied it. Hempel quotes Quine's admiration of this work, and Quine, we remember, hints at it as an exercise in instrumentalism. Indeed, already Popper has argued that Carnap could just as well execute his program by replacing or defining any property by the list of things known to possess it. Yet this would make any true ascription of a property to a thing verifiable by the definition of that property (that is, by finding that thing's name on the list defining that property) and so a tautology, and it would likewise make any non-tautologous ascription a contradiction. Carnap himself, in his auto-biography, avoids final assessment of his *Aufbau* and instead expresses his delight and surprise at the fact that Nelson Goodman took up his *Aufbau* in his own phenomenological study (which seems to me no more than a variant of it). Neither Carnap nor Goodman led a trend of research in the wake of these works. Phenomenalism is really neither here nor there, imprecise or precise, and that is the end of Carnap's *Aufbau* one way or another: a lost labor of love. In his early *Pseudo-problems* already Carnap says he is neutral between phenomenalism and its competitors, and so has transcend-ed the *Aufbau*. In the preface to the English translation of the *Aufbau* Car-nap denounces it, as Hempel notes (p. 3).

What is common to Carnap's earliest *Aufbau* and Carnap's middle period—his work of his Vienna Circle years—is verificationism, from which he moved through his first American opus, his *Testability and Meaning* of 1936, to probability as his verification surrogate. Hempel uses this to gloss completely over the Vienna Circle years, with the mere statement of the residue of these years that stayed with Carnap to the end: the essence of the teaching of the Circle was their meaning theory: the meaning of a proposi-tion, said Schlick, is its method of verification. But what the Circle was after is a definition of the empirical character of science that will make metaphysics nonsense, or 'not cognitively significant' or 'empirically mean-ingless'. To the end of his life, Carnap continued to hope—a metaphysical hope, need I say—that such a definition would be found. Popper's proof of its impossibility never even dented his faith. I suppose I should join the chorus of those who praise him as exceptionally open-minded, since he never claimed success.

Hempel praises Carnap's predilection for precision and argues that precision was prevented from imposing dogmas—on the world of philosophy or on the commonwealth of learning at large—since Carnap maintained a principle of tolerance. Now the principle of tolerance pertains to the choice of a formal language. Hence, either tolerance means we can present with precision difficult metaphysical doctrines so as to debate them well, or that in spite of tolerance no metaphysical doctrine will survive any attempt to formulate it in any precise language. Carnap held the second view, even though, to repeat, it was mere pious hope with him. Instead of discussing his hope, he constructed a few fragments of a few possible exact languages. "Carnap often stressed that these studies are intended only as the first stage in the development of more comprehensive theories . . . ." (p. 10). Rather pathetic, wouldn't you say?

Anders Wedberg's 39-page essay is the second in this volume. It is on the *Aufbau*; his aim is primarily exegetic, not critical. He admits from the start (p. 16) that the *Aufbau* is solipsistic. That is enough for me, not so much because solipsism is a ludicrous metaphysics or an outdated methodology; rather because, as Wedberg observes (*loc. cit.*), it is an introspectionist psychology. We do not need to deny introspection, even as a tool for research, to note the fact that as psychology introspectionism (as distinct from introspection) was defunct by the time he wrote the *Aufbau*. Carnap was behind science, then. This Wedberg notices obliquely on p. 46, where Carnap's sensationalism is declared a *façon de parler*. This is scholasticism: first we deemed utterly certain and final our sensational fund of knowledge—which Carnap designated '*erl*'—and we tried to base scientific theories on it; when we failed we were pleased to retain our scientific theories even if as no more than a *façon de parler*, since the fund of experiences still seemed to us to be the rock of our certitude; now it—Carnap's '*erl*'—is declared a *façon de parler*. Why? Why not simply overthrow it and be done with sensationalism once and for all as a refuted scientific theory? If '*erl*' is a mere *façon de parler* then scientific theories no longer are! So better realistic science than fictional Carnap.

Finally, Popper's criticism of the *Aufbau* mentioned above, that in it all truths are true by definition, is circumvented implicitly on p. 48 by declaring the definitions in it to be hypotheses; which makes Carnap's definitions proper not definitions at all, but a "daring (if not absurd) second-order hypothesis that each scientific concept *a* has such a correlated *Aufbau* notion *b*" that some day science will be able to establish as the first-order hypothesis that *a* is *b* and thereby, posthumously, justify the *Aufbau*'s definition $a = b$. Will that save the *Aufbau* from the status of fiction? Or is this mere fiction itself, mere pious hope, mere *façon de parler*?

Rolf A. Eberle has a 19-page improvement on a point in the *Aufbau*. I am afraid I must skip it. After over 50 pages on the *Aufbau*, Carnap's earliest attempt to eliminate metaphysics with rigor, we come to his latest effort in this direction; the elimination of metaphysics with the aid of the division of a formal language into observational and theoretical. The classic paper on this is his contribution to the first volume of *Minnesota Studies in the Philosophy of Science* of 1956. The editor reproduces here a translation of a short variant of it of 1958. The topic occupies pp. 75–160 of this volume, with the obvious result that it is, as it always was, a *cul-de-sac*.

The central idea, says Carnap, is Hilbert's procedure: we construct theoretical systems as uninterpreted calculi and formulas on the one hand, and add interpretations on the other. The interpretations, says Carnap—following Ramsey or other positivists—correlate theoretical terms (e.g., 'electromagnetic-fields') and empirical terms (e.g., 'blue'). There are two claims that Carnap makes here. First, this procedure gives partial meaning to theoretical terms. (Hence, his latest 1956 view replaces his celebrated 1936 theory of reduction sentences; oh, how I wish he said so in a few words!) Second, this procedure permits the analytic-synthetic distinction to hold within the resultant interpreted system. But first, what made him choose this procedure?

Perhaps Carnap's reason for adopting this procedure is the same reason as Hilbert's; and this may be good enough. Why then did Hilbert take Euclid's geometry as an utterly uninterpreted system? I do not know, except that he was worried about mathematics, not about science; he never worried about how we interpret. Clearly, very few people did. It did not matter to Hilbert, so no one can be angry with him.

We may assume that physicists care more about interpretations than mathematicians. How do they interpret? It was Einstein who boldly declared this problem not soluble, not even amenable to rational analysis! We do infer from a scientific system some conclusions which we check empirically, he said, but the final step, the link between observation and a decision whether observation agrees with prediction or not—this link is intuitive, given as an unanalyzable unit. Carnap's view seems to indicate that he never left the sensationalism of his *Aufbau*, but I cannot say. Clearly, he suggested, we all see blue, or red, and say 'I see blue' or 'I see red', and that is all there is to it. They both agreed that the observation of a hard white thing is not given to analysis and so there is no disagreement here, then, though there is still a profound disagreement between sensationalists like Carnap and non-sensationalist empiricists like Einstein. It lies precisely in the fact that for the sensationalist there is a finite set of sensations given *a priori*, among them blueness, hardness, and coldness, but not electric polarization. Their names are the observation terms of the language and the word designating electric polarization is a theoretical term. For non-sensationalist empiricists things stand quite differently. They perceive levels of abstractness, and in testing a theory they go one level down, or two, perhaps more, but they do not pretend that any level reached is the lowest level. So for them there are levels of abstractness, not two kinds of entities, concrete and abstract. Hence, as the psychologist James Gibson repeatedly stressed, the amount of information in one act of perception is not a given, and certainly there is no given finite list of all possible sensations. But was Carnap a sensationalist to the end? As long as Carnap sticks to sticks and stones and their coldness and hardness, I can suspect him of sensationalism. When he takes 'Zurich' (p. 76) to be an observation term, I am baffled, since if Zurich is denoted by an observation term, may we also have the same for the turmoil in which Zurich was during the Reformation? If not, why not? If yes, then all terms are observational, as a number of philosophers have indeed concluded one way or another.

But I must return to Carnap's 1958 paper, even though it seems I cannot properly follow it. Take a formal system which contains only logic and mathematics. Call it L. Add to L a few theoretical terms (like temperature) and you obtain L_1, a theoretical language, in which you can formulate theories outside logic and mathematics. Or, instead, you can add observation terms, in which case you get L_0. What we really want, of course, is more than a language which joins the two, one which also makes a combined use of the two, which makes combined statements, ones that include both theoretical and observation terms. Now, the Ramsey theory says, all we need are a few correspondence rules, to wit, a few key statements in which, by definition, both observational and theoretical terms are presented in a particular way: they are not "operational definitions" says Carnap, yet "operational" they are all the same (p. 79). I do not think the expression is meaningful. I think it highly misleading. What is an operational statement? Can we have an example for it other than a correspondence rule? Can we have an example of a correspondence rule? We have Hilbert's example of Euclidean geometry. Yet perhaps it is mathematical even after we give it the standard interpretation. No: this is impossible. Under the standard intended interpretation, Carnap thinks Euclid's geometry is false, yet he says all mathematics is L-true. What, then, will be the correspondence rules for the interpretation of Euclid? I do not know. Carnap gives the rule stating that warmer bodies have higher temperatures, but he offers us no uninterpreted formal system of thermodynamics whatsoever which can be thus given the standard interpretation, let alone an "operational" interpretation. The more detailed example Carnap offers (pp. 80–81) relates to the mass of a body which can be placed in a four-co-ordinate system. In such a way, clearly, a mass field can be described within a discrete system, but with arbitrarily small intervals. The mass field thus described is observational, but when the limit is reached and a field proper—a continuous field, that is—is thereby described, it is not observational and hence it is theoretical. What we can learn from this example, then, is that Carnap demands that the number of observables be finite or denumerable (p. 80). This is unproblematic, to be sure, but no answer to any of the questions posed in this paragraph which badly want answers.

We might seek them in the paper by David Kaplan on significance and analyticity, a 1959 paper, which refutes Carnap's theory of 1956 and which "might have curiosity value" (p. 94); it does indeed have this for Carnap's fans. Anyway, I do agree with Kaplan that even if we can separate empirical concepts from non-empirical ones, we can re-introduce the latter by the aid of definitions. The reason is that we can deduce from an empirical hypothesis a weak non-empirical statement, as Popper has shown in 1935 (*Logik der Forschung*, secs. 15 and 16; see also secs. 17 and 19). So, though Kaplan is right, a significantly stronger thesis was established with much greater ease than he or others he cites have managed to produce, and established it roughly when he was born. Ryszard Wojcicki on the factual content of empirical theories should also touch upon this. Instead he shuns this altogether and centers on the distinction between "factual and conventional (analytic) truth" (p. 94), thus lumping from the start the scientific or empirical with the metaphysical or untestable under the rubric of the factual; yet he is concerned with the empirical, not the factual-yet-unempirical.

I cannot help wondering. Wojcicki is really thoughtful and careful. Thus, he explicitly says of "an empirical theory", that the "set of all sentences asserted within" it "we do not require (of it) to be deductively closed" (p. 102). Yet he would not say why; he only shows that the deductive closure and the empirical content of any empirical theory are not identical even if we ignore the analytical part of the system. So he knows he lumps together two different kinds of statements, yet his paper gets too complicated because he would not say that factual content equals an empirical plus non-empirical parts, as Popper showed in 1935 (see above reference). Rather, he exploits the fact that the non-empirical factual part is non-empty in order to deduce that the analytic-synthetic dichotomy is not sharp. Since the simplest non-empirical yet factual statement is a purely existential statement which follows from an observation report, clearly the inference concerning the analytic-synthetic dichotomy is a paralogism (see Assertion 7 on page 115; notice also that on page 111 Wojcicki endorses Popper's theory of content as improbability without reference; it is now commonly accepted).

P. M. Williams's paper comes next, and complements its predecessor. It explicitly states on page 137 that there may be a theory which can be divided into two parts, one falsifiable (and false), and the other (true and) unfalsifiable The unfalsifiable part, Popper (not I) will say, is redundant and better omitted. For, he stipulates, though when removing that part we reduce a theory's content, we also thereby increase its empirical content and so its refutability. And he (not I) advises that refutability should be maximized. The question is, can an omission like that always be effected? No, says Popper, since from observation statements (at place and time x there is a y) follow purely existential statements (there exists at least one y)—factual but irrefutable. And so the closure of the system under deduction guarantees the inclusion of some irrefutable elements. Or, to take a more abstract example, "there exists at least one magnetic monopole" belongs to Dirac's theory and has testable consequences in Dirac's system ("all electronic monopoles are of the same electric charge") but not in isolation; the same hypothesis can be added say, to Poisson's theory, where it has no testable consequences. Hence, such matters cannot be decided generally or a priori. Williams does not discuss examples and uses high-powered tools of up-to-date logic and mathematics. Quite redundantly, as this paragraph fully demonstrates.

Next comes a paper by John A. Winnie who refutes Carnap's last solution to the problem of theoretical analyticity (p. 143). I do not know what this problem is. He does point out a difficulty posed by Hempel (p. 145), which seems to relate to the role of interpretative statements. Indeed, it is a difficulty that led Hempel, at least for a time but probably for good, to relinquish the idea that scientific theory is a set of formulas plus their interpretations. The difficulty stems from the following question, What is the status of an interpretation? It cannot have empirical content or else, like a scientific theory, it should be split into formulas plus interpretations. And not having content it is a tautology. If the formulas uninterpreted are tautologies, and if interpretations are too, how does fusing them bring forth empirical content?

I do not mean to suggest that Hempel does not know that rules of interpretation are meta-linguistic. I am reporting here Winnie's reading of Hempel. I think the idea is simply that if Carnap wants the whole empirical content of a theory to reside in the observational part and also to be siphoned by correspondence rules to the theoretical side, then the correspondence rules themselves—object-linguistic or meta-linguistic—will be problematic. I cannot really go into all the subtleties of the matter, but will draw the reader's attention to the fact, and a very strange fact it is, that in Carnap's central and last paper on the topic, the already-mentioned classic of 1956, Carnap suggest that the proposition asserting the existence of a fundamental maximal velocity in the world—clearly a synthetic one—be construed as analytic. How come?

In Hilbert's system the non-logic words are given within a set of axioms and are allowed any interpretation which renders the axioms true. In other words, the axioms are matrices, or axiom-schemata: they are neither true nor false, but stipulating the existence of an unspecified interpretation we treat them as true; treating them as true is making a promissory note, and one which we may be unable to redeem. Now comes the interpretation. There are two distinct ways of doing so. The form of the statements offering the interpretation can simply be, 'point is point', 'line is line', 'between is between', which look tautologous because they are presented as if they were written in one object language (but as such the last instance is ungrammatical). But either they are in the meta-language and referring to one object language, and so would better be written as, "the word 'point' denotes any point" or else in the meta-language referring to two object languages and offer translations: "The word 'point' in Hilbertian means the same as 'point' in ordinary English." Once so translated, we have the legitimacy of the resultant interpretation contingent on the truth of Euclidean geometry, which truth is merely putative: Euclidean geometry is a hypothesis (and happens to be false). Quine made it amply clear that his famous thesis—the distinction analytic/synthetic is neither sharp nor exhaustive—is within a reasonable framework for language theory equivalent to his thesis about translatability between languages or within one language (i.e., synonymity): perfect translatability (synonymity) is impossible. The above presentation makes this amply obvious: Hilbert's correspondence rules are both perfect translations and the sharp division between uninterpreted analytic character and interpreted synthetic character.

Also Hempel's problem is dissolved: Hilbert's system is not tautologous unless implicit definitions are allowed, and then the very interpretations, the correspondence rules so-called, are legitimized on the basis of a hypothesis or constitute a hypothesis, or its equivalent on the meta-level. This is not really peculiar to Hilbert's system: when we say something like, 'Homer is the author of the *Iliad*' to mean, traditionally, that name is the name given him, it is akin to tautology, yet when we say 'Homer was a blind Greek individual who lived somewhere in the eighth century B.C.', we further identify the author, thereby making the implicit hypothesis that there was one person who wrote or at least put together the canonic form, or the almost canonic form, of the *Iliad*. Hempel's difficulty which he could not solve thus dissolves. The reason he could not solve it is obvious: within the framework in which it arose it is, indeed, quite insoluble. He was thus right to relinquish that framework: the approach presented here alludes to hypotheses proper, whereas the Carnapian system avoids all hypotheses as it gives theories only that much content as experience already fully warrants.

III

The next topic of this volume is not clear to me, and looks like an odd collection of flotsam and jetsam. I will take each paper in the order in which it appears, as I have done thus far.

Anders Wedberg contributes a review of an essay by Carnap that finally became a part of his famous *Meaning and Necessity*. In that essay Carnap tried to exorcize ontology: what Carnap tries to exclude is, for example, the truth or the falsity of any existence theorem in mathematics understood in a crass, simple way. But whereas usually what one thinks exists depends on one's theory of the universe, often called metaphysics or ontology, Carnap wants what he thinks exists to depend on science, not on metaphysics. This, in itself, seems to me a reasonable choice except that science comprises bits and pieces of theories that cannot be put together without some interpretation. For example, the continuity postulated by general relativity must be reinterpreted if it is to be adjoined to quantum theory with consistency and the reinterpretation is metaphysical though generative of a research program that may lead to the generation of some testable theories, e.g., those resulting from the quantization of the relativist theory of black holes by viewing black holes as black cavities. What I have just said may be false, I cannot judge. But it is a center of an ongoing discussion in the philosophy of science that is quite free of the issues involved here.

Back to Anders Wedberg. Carnap's formalist, pseudo-Hilbertian approach led him to see mathematics as the prime framework of science, and he began by trying to explain away the existence postulates and theorems of mathematics: his ontology or his metaphysics (which he refused to view as ontology or as metaphysics, but this is neither here nor there), denies existence to mathematical entities like the real numbers, or the natural numbers. Wedberg finds it hard to follow Carnap since he failed to comprehend his concept of acceptance. He concludes that Carnap was a nominalist *malgré lui*.

Wedberg's is the first paper in this volume that is exoteric in that it exhibits a sense of proportion and a sense of purpose, and is quite straightforward and unencumbered. It is also well written. The snag it hits from the start is Carnap's concept of confirmation. Carnap apologists may suggest that for this one has to consult later works of Carnap's on inductive logic. This, however, will not do. First, were Carnap to have published a theory of confirmation that satisfied him, it would still behoove his followers to see how well it fit his earlier works. Second, already in earlier works that have no theory of confirmation, that theory is foreshadowed and so one can discuss the foreshadow in lieu of the real thing; what is legit for Carnap is legit for his critic.

The ideal is to have all and only true statements accepted, and the question is, How well does the foreshadowed theory capture the ideal or any part of it? Carnap admits, and Wedberg quotes him in full (p. 167), that the acceptance of the rules of a language "although itself not of a cognitive nature, will nevertheless usually be influenced by theoretical knowledge", yet he insists that the choice is free "because it does imply a belief or assertion". When I meet the cavalier dismissal of an admitted criticism that to my judgment looks deadly, I simply gasp. It seems to be obvious (and so also to Herbert Bohnert in his contribution which I shall discuss next) that if knowledge influences language then language influences knowledge (since knowledge proper prior to language is impossible) and so goodbye to empiricism. (But I shall not elaborate; see Alan Musgrave's enlightening and already classic 'Logicism Revisited', *The British Journal for the Philosophy of Science*, 1977.) Wedberg stresses that since rules of language prescribe the acceptance of some sentences as true, the acceptance of the rules must be debatable (he says "justified"). And particularly if the metaphysics one wishes to endorse come not as explicit metaphysics but as rules absorbed into the language, then the acceptance of the rules ought to be debatable. I agree. The idea, adumbrated by Russell and practiced by both Wittgenstein (unsuccessfully) and Popper (with limited success), does smack of the very dogmatism (hypostatization) it was intended to circumvent. I have discussed this at length in my 'Between Metaphysics and Methodology' (*Poznań Studies in the Philosophy of Science and Humanities*, 1974, reprinted in my *Science and Society*, 1981) and I will not elaborate here. Wedberg's concluding sentence is shattering: "The kind of vague, schematic assertions with which Carnap's essay abounds are, I feel, far removed from any genuine and philosophically clarifying study of those diverse phenomena in our world that can be subsumed under the two (vague and not necessarily exclusive) titles 'ontology' and 'science'.''

Next comes Herbert G. Bohnert, 'Carnap's Logicism'; over 30 pages long. It is apologetic beyond the limit usually accepted in the commonwealth of learning. Bohnert distinguishes in Carnap four incompatible philosophies of logic but inexplicably refers to them as phases, saying (note 5) that "it will be more convenient" to describe them as "phases" than as different "attitudes". His discussion does not warrant this. But at least he promises on his opening page to describe the fourth phase/attitude as "an emergent, overall viewpoint in which a certain, underlying, long-held pragmatist-experimental attitude provided a unifying setting . . . ." and he wishes to "argue for its basic viability and value." (I have changed the order of the above quotes and in this way I may have misread Bohnert. What can we do with interpreters who need interpreters for their interpretations?) Here, then, is a direct promise in the opening of the paper. It becomes a "closing suggestion" at the last sentence—a suggestion not to ask whether Carnap's logicism is true, but to ask whether it can be *made* true and, if so, whether the effort is worth it. I confess, I find reading Bohnert's text rather vexing. Thus, we read on page 184 the following: Carnap's first phase is "strong logicism", i.e., the view of mathematics as analytic or as a set of empty tautologies; this view "was weakened by the concession that the axioms of infinity and choice" are not analytic; and so "Carnap treated them, as *Principia Mathematica* already did, as hypotheses." Nevertheless, in that very phase, and still on page 184, Carnap "never shared Russell's shifts between a viewing of a system of logic as . . . (2) a hypothesis, or (3) a body of factually empty tautology . . ." But he always stuck to (3). When I read such profundities I usually move on to the next item on the agenda, but now I am the devil's advocate and must go on, even if my task is made too easy by an editor who should impose a minimum standard, but fails here.

I shall skip Bohnert's description of the move of logicism to "if-then-ism"; anyone interested should look up the already mentioned careful and thoughtful 'Logicism Revisited' by Alan Musgrave. I barely need mention Church's classic 'Mathematics and Logic' of 1962, except to say I cannot share Bohnert's views of it, at least until he leaves his cryptic wording (notes 6 and 8) and attains the degree of clarity required by most editors. Carnap's first phase is logicist; his second "seemed a 'surrender to formalism' " (p. 185), and, indeed, "there was reason for such an impression" (still p. 185), the reason being that the impression is true (but not before we have reached p. 186); traces of logicism are still in evidence in phase two.

Phase two: formalism (pp. 186–87). Analyticity was then viewed as (1) determinable by syntax alone, and as (2) empirical or factual vacuity. The word 'determinable' is here vague, meaning perhaps decidable, and if so, contrary to Gödel. Certainly Carnap, following Wittgenstein and Schlick, demanded decidability; but he also was the first philosopher to champion Gödel nonetheless. On page 187 Bohnert apologetically covers up for this development, thus missing a chance to praise the Master for his celebrated open-mindedness. Instead he tries to explain what Gödel has done in a passage (p. 187) which is not only presentationally inadequate—seven lines is too little for the novice and too much for the adept—but also funny, since it speaks of the "syntax of P M-plus-Peano (or, equivalently, plus PM's infinity axiom)" which is rather amusing. If he thinks he can explain it in a purely syntactical system of a purely formalist nature, then he should say so. I am open-minded too. But perhaps he does not mean to say this. Perhaps he explains on p. 188 why Gödel has embarrassed (Bohnert's word) both logicists and formalists. I cannot follow him.

Third phase: semantics of course. The idea of analyticity as that of truth by virtue of the rules of logic alone, with semantic rules now included. All of a sudden the essay turns out to concern itself with the problem of analyticity in the various phases. Anyway, Bohnert claims for Carnap (what previously Popper had claimed for himself) that he was always a semanticist at heart but had hesitated, had a fear of metaphysics, and was now reassured by Tarski, and so came out of the closet. All this is on page 198. Page 199 tells another story. Semantics, we are now told, enable one to question the logical status of Peano's axioms, of any definitions, in fact, as was discovered by Quine. *A fortiori*, then, we may question the logical status of Carnap's somewhat fantastic meaning postulates, the ones for which he demanded the status of analyticity. And so Carnap slid in his third phase to his first one on occasion, or buffered his third with bits and pieces of the first. A crucial paragraph, pages 201–02, makes the proposal that should rescue the analyticity of all the definitions which serve as abbreviations. That in general this is possible is freely conceded by Quine at his most austere; the question is of advisability or propriety of seeing bachelorhood as mere shorthand for unmarried masculinity—no joke intended, but rather a slight accent on the problem of universals—and on this the author makes judgments involving both Carnap's theory of intentionality and someone's theory of possible worlds—he forgets his name, I suppose—and model theory to boot; it will take a book to explicate this paragraph. Weird.

"Turning now to the problem of non-definitional meaning postulates", we are told (p. 202), with no information about what are these postulates and with no statement of the problem—the problem seems to be, how can we force them into the analytic mold? But as the problem is not stated the author has to be excused for not telling us what relief its solution brings. "We see" (that is a slight exaggeration) "that although the ploy of keeping definitions extra-systematic is no longer available" (I can't say why), "the technique of requiring of a logical-analytic truth only that it be true under all the appropriate assignment of extensions *which make a given set of sentences true*", namely that of viewing axioms as implicit definitions, "is still available." At what cost, he doesn't say. "It is appealing on grounds very similar to those mentioned." They are not mentioned. "But it raises difficult questions as to when the limitation of apparent logical space is merely appropriate to meaning and when it forecloses genuine possibility." In other words, when we state a meaning postulate we may thereby transform a given uninterpreted axiom system into a hypothesis; and we may thereby transform it into a set of tautologies proper. Bohnert says in Gobbledygook that he cannot say *a priori* which is which. "Much useful work has been done on the assumption that the borderline," i.e., the sharp borderline between the analytic-logical and the synthetic, "can be drawn, and many persuasive arguments have been offered" and the author refers us to the literature. Solzhenitsyn tells of a prisoner who boasted to the authorities that he had a plan to improve a torpedo boat and asked for help from all sorts of experts; other prisoners, each with one required expertise, were dragged from all over the Gulag and placed at his disposal. "Gentlemen," he said to them, "I will not presume to issue any instructions to such august company; act as you think fit," and went away leaving them to their travails.

Still, a couple of interesting examples are given by Bohnert (p. 203). First, identity. Is it a logical sign? I do not know why he does not mention Tarski's proof that it is not. Suppose identity is logical, then the sentence saying every two things are identical contains only logical signs (two variables, two universal quantifiers to bind them, and the identity sign between them) and so must be either true in all substitutions (as there are none) and so logically true, or likewise, logically false; yet it is true for all and only those universes with at most one object in them. Q.E.D. Second, the Boolean inclusion. Is it purely logical? Is it short-hand for some symbol from quantification theory even if Boolean algebra historically preceded quantification theory? What an intriguing question relating logical priority to a historical one. Still, on this much hinges. Quine says he is no logicist, since abstract set membership and inclusion is no matter of mere logic. This is the death of all logicism, to be sure, and then the devil may take the problem of analyticity. But at least Boolean inclusion is rescued since, Quine says, the sign of inclusion is redundant in Boolean algebra proper: AB may just as well mean all As are Bs, and so on. Perhaps this is what allows our author to speak of "a certain naturalness" of a certain approach to inclusion; he describes it too briefly for me to feel confident that I comprehend. Yet his hope (p. 204) of having a "purely extentional abstraction from the original prediction" to fulfill the meaning of class inclusion sounds to me more monstrous than the *Aufbau* ever could be: it would make the concept of inclusion logical, but at the cost of having no possible categorical synthetic statement in the language so constructed. But, anyway, it matters not: even if it is impossible to make the concept of inclusion fully logical, phase four will absorb the shock.

Phase four. Carnap wanted sharp and clear-cut rules that could be endorsed by intuition and pass the test of formal double-check. Since empirical science influences our full interpretation of our mathematics, we must also formalize science, and have observation language and all that. Theoretical statements will then have only partial meanings derived from observation statements. Theoretical science will then include no hypotheses. Yet there is a problem here: we have no semantics for partially meaningful sentences, let alone a formal one. And so, in the absence of semantics to take him all the way, wouldn't you have guessed, Carnap reverts to syntax again, yet the syntax is supposed to offer an underlying structure upon which semantic concepts hover. I cannot make sense of Bohnert's pages 208–09 and can praise in them only the frankness of their author's mysticism. Before he died, Carnap personally confessed to Bohnert his fidelity to logicism, one which is a naive and intentionally superficial view of naive set theory (sans the axiom of choice?) whose "axioms seemed analytic, in the informal sense of true-in-virtue-of-meaning," and that was that. (Yes, it must be sans the axiom of choice since that axiom asserts existence. Or will an intuitionistic variant of it do?)

We have now passed the middle of this book and are arriving at the slalom. Jaakko Hintikka, editor of this volume, contributes an essay on 'Carnap's Heritage in Logical Semantics'. Much of "recent work in semantics is, appearances notwithstanding, an outgrowth of Carnap's ideas or consists of attempts to solve the important problems Carnap raised in semantics" (p. 217). For Quine's just criticism of *Meaning and Necessity* led to "developments which serve to solve Carnap's difficulties to an incomparably greater extent than the critics, and the philosophical community at large, have so far acknowledged" (p. 219), even though at the expense of transcending Carnap's original framework "so as to widen this framework essentially." I am not sure I understand this "widen essentially" business, but I like the spirit, and hope my task as a devil's advocate may now begin in earnest. So where was the essential widening? "Carnap was . . . the first and foremost herald of a new epoch of possible-worlds semantics" (p. 219), we are told. It is a very difficult task to show that Carnap's was the seminal idea behind this trend, and no less so to show this trend as more than trendy, let alone that it heralds a new epoch: only time can tell. So any reasonable effort should count as success, of course. What, then, is Hintikka's strategy? Very simple. Carnap is unconvincing due to the lack of a framework within which to couch his arguments. Possible-worlds semantics is such a framework. Ergo, etc. (pp. 219–20). So much for the situational logic. As for history, Carnap came tantalizingly close to "the basic ideas of possible worlds semantics, and yet" missed (p. 220). That is, Carnap's theory of state-descriptions is a stone's throw from possible-worlds. Carnap worked whole logical systems on them, with L-truth, L-equivalence, and such. Carnap said in his *Meaning and Necessity* that his state-descriptions represent Leibniz's possible worlds, and he also said Leibniz's possible worlds have guided him in his search for the demarcation of logical truths. "What was missing is thus apparently [*sic*] only an insight into the possibility of using these possible worlds for the purpose of analyzing the intentional objects which Carnap in fact leaves unanalyzed in *Meaning and Necessity*" (p. 220). I cannot agree, but will not quarrel. I can only report that Hintikka does not even mention Tarski's contribution to the beginning and growth of model theory, Henkin's famous completeness proof of 1949, and Abraham Robinson's contributions, which together put model theory on the map with no help from Carnap. The history of possible-worlds semantic theory will be written if that semantic theory proves at all as promising as they say it will. Only then will we be able to judge Carnap's state-descriptions' contributions to this outgrowth. In the meantime the question remains, is the enthusiasm which possible-worlds semantics generates at all just?

The idea that fires Hintikka so is Carnap's claim that the range of a proposition is the set of possible-worlds/state-descriptions in which it obtains. I am at a loss. In Popper's *Logik der Forschung* of 1935, section 37, on Logical Ranges, first note, I find that the idea is quite traditional; it names von Kries (1886), Bolzano, Waismann, and even Keynes. But I really think it is as traditional as the theory of games of chance and of insurance, i.e., of probability; what Carnap did, I think, is first to invent universes or languages that are so poor that in them one can hardly say of Socrates that he is a biped, and then apply it rigorously there. I honestly do not see the merit of Carnap's technique of applying such severe and fantastic restrictions. The main point about Carnap's state-description technique is that it enables us to describe exhaustively every one of a complete list of possible universes—when the word 'universe' is either used to describe a non-existent baby universe, or used to denote small sectors of one, such as the simultaneous toss of three coins, and so the word 'universe' is used in an incredibly Pickwickian sense. It may sound funny, but the very restriction that every single thing in the Carnapian universe has a name is already so far-reaching as to make state-descriptions too fantastic (see Popper, 'On Carnap's Version of Laplace's Rule of Succession', *Mind*, 1962). In Carnap's own lecture notes, published in *Synthese* and reproduced in this volume, Carnap notices that much. "In simple languages" he says (page 295), "every model is describable by a state-description. In richer languages this is not possible."

Hintikka concludes by arguing that Quine's critique of Carnap's *Meaning and Necessity* does not hold for possible-world semantics. This, to my mind, proves the distinctness of the two doctrines; to Hintikka's mind things look like the vindication of Carnap. It is like saying, though Olber's paradox hits Newton's cosmology, since it does not hit Einstein's, the latter vindicates the former.

Barbara Hall Partee, in 'The Semantics of Belief Sentences', asserts of both Carnap's attempt to analyze belief sentences, and Chomsky's attempt that they are inadequate. She suggests an alternative. The problem is Russell's puzzle: two equivalent expressions (names, sentences, etc.), even logically equivalent ones, need not be substitutable *salva veritatis* in statements expressing belief, knowledge, etc., in sentences usually known as opaque for this very reason. Now, in all natural languages the opacity of some opaque sentences is a fact that the formulator of their rules of grammar must acknowledge. The problem in dealing with natural languages is thus to demarcate opacity. It is inherently different from the problem of one wishing to translate opaque sentences into a transparent formal system under some specified adequacy conditions for translation. What all the adequacy conditions are I cannot say, but one of them is that intensional equivalence, however rough, must be kept between an original natural opaque sentence and the formal sentence that is its alleged translation. Carnap wanted to translate belief-sentences to expressed-beliefs-sentences on some behavioristic theory of belief. This ensures violation of the condition just stated. I can therefore skip Partee's discussion of Carnap. Her discussion of Chomsky is utterly unclear to me: what does she try to do? To cite an objection from Quine to a move by Chomsky (p. 263) seems to me *a priori* a howler, since Quine opposes every move of Chomsky, since Chomsky looks for rules transforming sentences to their synonyms whereas Quine denies all synonymity.

Next come Asa Kasher's 'Pragmatic Representations and Language Games: Beyond Intensions and Extensions'. Carnap showed little interest in pragmatics since he saw no general framework for it, but Kasher does. And so Carnap drops out of the picture at once. Kasher begins with the statement that a lady desires to marry the mayor. Her desire may hinge on her love for a man who happens to be the mayor, or alternatively, on her determination to be the town's first lady. In the first case, substituting the mayor's name in the statement about the lady's desire will yield a true statement; in the second, not. (This is an instance of referential opacity, of course.) Kasher wants to offer rules for the distinction between the two cases. For my part I cannot see the need. Perhaps the desired distinction will clarify matters. No doubt the statement is ambiguous and, like all ambiguous statements, it requires clarification. But then rather than seek a criterion we may want clarification either in the form of added statements, e.g., one reporting her not knowing who the mayor is but guessing he is a bachelor, or from rewording the statement—e.g., to say that she desires so-and-so who happens to be the mayor. Or perhaps Kasher wants the ambiguity explained rather than rectified. Kasher discusses the situation in terms of possible worlds, and this raises in me a question I never contemplated before: can I desire to be nice to my wife in all possible-but-not-actual-worlds-in-which-I-am-a-mayor and nasty to her in all others? Of course my wish, if it be possible, is not possible to gratify, both on account of its referring to all and only possible-but-not-actual worlds, and on account that there simply must exist a possible-but-not-actual world in which my wish is not granted. But then I may replace the possible-but-not-actual worlds with possible worlds and the fact that I am actually not a mayor. Also Freud has shown the existence, indeed the prevalence, of wishes that are not possible, i.e., impossible-but-actual wishes and even inconsistent ones. And so, perhaps my wish to have such a wish may be granted. And so, Kasher's framework for his discussion may not be adequate for clarifying, though in a strange way may explain the ambiguity as a kind of inbuilt Freudian ambivalence. Kasher goes on. What if the lady desires to marry a mayor? The ambiguities still abound: no clarification is complete. He selects a complicated set of rules invented by Hintikka and at best applicable to very stringent cross-examinations that clear such ambiguities in no time. Here the distance from Carnap is so big that I feel exempt from a comment apart from observing that Carnap really believed all such discussions unnecessary since he thought that soon utter clarity will reign supreme.

IV

So much for the second part, chiefly odds and ends. The third part is on probability and induction.

We begin with Carnap's lecture notes on probability and induction, 1955. They are, except for a few additions, fairly close abstracts from his *Logical Foundations of Probability* and *The Continuum of Inductive Methods*, with a minor elegant improvement due to Shimony. Regrettably, a few theorems of probability theory are here transcribed straight into confirmation theory, thereby hardly making any sense. For example, Bernoulli's theorem, in which the sufficiently long series becomes sufficiently large sample, and to no avail (a sample need not be ordered), quite apart from the somewhat odd concept of infinitely large sample, or evidence, or what-have-you. This should ring a bell somewhere, since Carnap's innovation was the idea that confirmation explicates probability, yet here probability seems clearer and broader than confirmation! Also, how can there be relative frequency with no randomness or some substitute for it, such as a measure theory? I am baffled. I suppose Carnap took the theory of fair bets (in Shimony's formulation) to be such a substitute, and under some fairly obvious conditions I suppose this is so, but there is a bothering lacuna here. Towards the end of the notes (of about 30 pages), richer languages, with more than one place predicate, are introduced. This raises the problem of consistency and makes calculations exceedingly complex. I did not check the derivations and suppose some Carnap addicts will. The mind boggles at the complexity of the situation where more than one place predicate is permitted. Some say it cannot be done, but I know it can: there is no magic formula to stop increasing complexity. The only question is, is the game worth the candle? The amazing thing is that all this tremendous complexity has not yet reached the level of inductive generalization that Piaget ascribed to five-year-olds, and that it comes to explicate—make us see with greater clarity—concepts that were clearer before. In the whole paper printed here I found nothing about the end at hand except a principle of learning from experience (p. 309f), which is declared intuitive, and says that, other things (which? of what range?) being equal, the more frequently an event has been observed, the more probable is its future occurrence. The frequency here, I presume, is not of an event in a given series, but the total number of occurrences in the abstract; in life experience of an individual or of a community? And so I do not know if the principle's formal equivalent, the axiom of instantial relevance, as Carnap christens it, has to do with given sequences or not, and if yes, which. The whole text on this matter is baffling; and so the question of randomness and all that again raises its ugly head.

But I check myself. I have fallen into the Carnapian magic circle and started asking Carnapian questions hoping for more clarification. But the real issue lies elsewhere. What does the probability of a future event have to do with learning from experience? We will grant that a gambler may learn from experience that a die is loaded and hence expect . . . , etc. We may also grant that a citizen may learn to expect the bureaucrat to procrastinate once more. In these and similar experiences all cultures are equal. But in the world of learning we learn different things from our contemplation of experience; we learn about the stuff the moon is made of and about new sources of energy and about the means for putting brakes on the trade-cycle and about extinct species and cultures and about the dark recesses of the soul. What does the learning of these new phenomena as learning from experience, have to do with the learning from experience which allegedly constitutes the probability of future events depending on their past frequency? I asked Bar-Hillel (a Carnap devotee, if ever there was one), to tell me the answer to this question. He liked the question. He said there are two kinds of learning from experience—à la Carnap and à la Popper. I waited for him to say so in print. But he first left Carnap and then went to a better world. I suppose I have to learn from experience, but I somehow fail. God knows how frequently I come upon a Carnapian text, full of tortured, complicated formulas that offer statements too trite ever to be applicable to the world as we know it, and always evading the most obvious questions.

To begin with, I do not mean only the *raison d'être* of the whole study. I also mean the most obvious objection to a given research program. Thus, ever since the middle of the last century, with the studies of John Stuart Mill and of Robert Leslie Ellis, or at the very least since it was proven by Keynes and Jeffreys, the initial probability of a universal law in a universe possibly infinite (in space or in time—either will do), is zero and therefore also its ordinary posterior probability. Both Keynes and Jeffreys offered solutions to these difficulties, and of necessity by favoring some hypotheses *a priori*. This *a priorism* may be innocuous if experience soon relegates it to the background, but it does not. (See my 'Subjectivism: From Infantile Illness to Chronic Disease', reprinted here as Chapter 12.) Also, it does no good to decide to favor some unspecified hypotheses *a priori*—they have to be singled out; and they are not. Carnap knew of course of this trouble when he started his venture, yet he went on, seemingly heedlessly, and hit the expected snare at the very end of his bulky *Logical Foundations of Probability* where, as a seeming stop-gap, he pulled out of his sleeve a new concept, called instant confirmation. When Popper thundered that it was a blunder since it was not a probability function proper of its explicit argument, Bar-Hillel said, but it is a probability function in some sense. In some sense even Popper's confirmation is. In Carnap's lecture notes here reproduced instant confirmation is dropped, and even the problem is evaded: the last line defines the confirmation function for infinite domains to be the limit of the confirmation function for the finite domain whose membership increases indefinitely; even the corollary is not stated that the limit function is zero and so no confirmation in the infinite domain raises probability from zero (see p. 365). Not raising a problem may be read in diverse fashions, of course. Professor Kasher tells me that there are new solutions to surmount this difficulty, some by Hintikka. Perhaps they should have been surveyed in this volume—or at least mentioned.

Next, Richard C. Jeffreys, 'Carnap's inductive Logic'. Carnap prescribed credence in hypotheses in accord with a probability theory that is both non-factual and intuitively congenial, he says. I wonder if this ought to hold for arithmetic too. Does one have to believe arithmetic and does it have to be intuitive? If not, I ask Jeffreys, Why the difference between the two, and does it not render probability synthetic *a priori* knowledge? If yes, then I ask Jeffreys, What does it mean for analyticity to abide by intuition? But I know he is mathematically sufficiently well informed to be able to recall jolts in his intuition received from analyticity. Hobbes here is the paradigm. I find Jeffreys's point intolerable and hopeless. I am familiar enough with Jeffreys and his work to ask, if my question has occurred to him why did he conceal it? If not, how come the sensitive and critically minded thinker that he is failed to do the obvious and examine the situation before moving on? But his remark on Carnap (p. 329), "at times he sounds Kantian", his remark, in his conclusion, about Carnap's program requiring to create rather than discover intuitions, and other hints, makes me think that Jeffreys knows more than he says. Pity.

Now as to Risto Hilpinen's 'Carnap's New System of Inductive Logic': Since the intuitive background to a theory is both important and insufficient, Carnap proposed early in his career rules of explication, so-called, namely adequacy criteria for explication proper. There are three concepts to handle: the classificatory concept (the 'yes-or-no', e.g., hot or not, confirmed or not;); the comparative concept (e.g., hotter, more confirmed); and the numerical concept (e.g., temperature, the degree of confirmation).

In general, we shall have a property P, its comparative cognate MP (read 'more P'), and its quantitative cognate, p. The rules relate the three concepts thus:

    I. $P(a)$ & $MP(b, a) \rightarrow P(b)$;

    II. $P(a) \leftrightarrow p(a) \geq min$;

    III. $MP(a, b) \leftrightarrow p(a) \geq p(b)$;

That is to say,

    I. If a is P and if b is more P than a, than b is P;

    II. a is P if and only if the numerical value of p is above fixed minimum;

    III. a is more P than b if and only if its numerical value is higher.

Now, when P is probability of h by e, Carnap introduced an added concept, of positive relevance, and in rather a customary manner: (PR) e is positively (negatively) relevant to h if and only if e raises (lowers) its probability. Carnap then said, (1) e confirms h if and only if the probability of h given e exceeds a given minimum; and (2) e confirms h if and only if e is positively relevant to h. Popper has shown that (1) and (2) lead to (3) there exist distinct e, h_1 and h_2 such that by (1), e confirms h_1 but not h_2; and by (2), e confirms h_2 but not h_1. (For details one can look up Popper's celebrated paper on degree of confirmation, reprinted in his *Logic of Scientific Discovery*, and his debate with Bar-Hillel in *The British Journal for the Philosophy of Science* in the 50s. Intuitively, Popper showed, Carnap relied once on the intuition (α) that confirmation is high probability, and once on the intuition (β) that confirmation raises probability. And whereas on the whole Carnap endorsed (α) and only occasionally and quite inconsistently endorsed (β), Popper systematically rejects (α) and occasionally or systematically endorses (β). So much for Popper. Risto Hilpinen reports all this at a greater length and less clarity and ascribes confusion to Popper.

There are three more short technical papers on inductive logic which I think I can safely skip. There remains one grand finale, Abner Shimony's preface to Carnap's posthumous two essays on entropy. The problem is very simple and straightforward: since entropy is characteristic of an objective physical system, it cannot represent our knowledge of the system; since probability is a matter of knowledge and belief it has no place within science. What, then, is the probability of statistical dynamics? The problem is not as simple as it looks since our knowledge of kinds of order may be operative. Thus, if we know something about, say, spin, and find all spins of a given set of particles ordered the same way, we can exploit this fact to direct the energy flow by destroying that order. Shimony's solution is equally elegant: entropy is not an absolute quality of a system as such, but a characterization of the distribution of given characteristics; relative to different characteristics the same system may be assigned different entropy functions with no inconsistency. Still, what is, objectively speaking, the concept of order involved? This is a matter of the improbability of a system to be in given sets of states. To this the propensity interpretation—Peirce, Popper—seems natural but is not the last word. This is a mere sketch of Shimony's interesting and enlightening preliminary to a sketch concerning Carnap's enquiry as to how free entropy is from arbitrariness. In his conclusion Shimony notices how unrelated all this study of probability in science is to Carnap's inductive probability. The reason is obvious: the one concern is for freedom from subjectivity, the other is frankly subjectivist.

V

Considered as a whole, the book seems to me something of a shambles. Some of its defects are no doubt due to mere human frailty; some are due to the state of flux of the field, especially of the part that Carnap was deeply concerned with, philosophical logic, particularly foundations of mathematics; some are due to backwardness in the field of the philosophy of science in which so many philosophers are still seeking the principle of induction and are still ignorant of recent developments, particularly in the field of the history of science and its relevance to science itself.

There is a story, maybe a myth, that Alexandre Koyré read his 'Galileo Platonist' in Chicago in Carnap's presence. Carnap is said to have contributed one sentence to the ensuing discussion in which he allegedly reported his failure to find one sentence with cognitive meaning in Koyré's paper. So much the worse for cognitive meaning. What is left of Carnap's contribution to cognitive meaning theory? No more than that theory itself; i.e., no more than nothing. What is left of his logicism, formalism, etc.? Shambles, along with the rest of the philosophy of mathematics, since it is almost entirely foundationist, i.e., justificationist, with all the magnificent foundation programs now admittedly defunct. What is left of his inductive studies? Nothing. There are aspirations. Most of them as poor as what inspired them. What is the memory of Carnap's teaching? Logic proves that philosophy is meaningless. Carnap's *Scheinprobleme* has no better flavor than Ayer's *Language, Truth and Logic*; whereof one cannot speak thereof one must keep silent. Must! Hush!

I met many people who spoke appreciatively, even tenderly, of Carnap, contemporaries like Church, Quine, Feigl, Hempel, and Popper; younger admirers, no less sincere, like Bar-Hillel, Montague, Shimony, and Jeffreys. I pumped them all as best I could, but got little that is even possibly inspiring. Now Hintikka has assembled a volume of testimonies to his inspiration, to which Hintikka himself has contributed a paper full of panegyric, spiced with epithets like the somebody-Carnap theory, or even the Carnap-somebody theory, dropping in vain such a big name as Frege. I must have a blind spot. Carnap developed a style of philosophizing. His books are full of formulas; his philosophy is incidental to his formulas. Take his *Logical*

Foundations of Probability; it contains a moral injunction, formulated five times in increasingly satisfactory wording. Its last wording, R5, still tells businessmen to follow inductive probability's predictions so as to maximize profits in the long run. I mention this fact since I have no doubt that Carnap was a socialist, a deeply sensitive and a truly brave one; yet he wrote a funny line like that. Evidently it mattered little to him. Not *what* but *how* to do philosophy is what inspired him as well as those whom he influenced. Even his incredible clumsiness was an asset as it was at least seemingly deliberate and so it encouraged the blind and the lame to try their hand too. I mean this with no sarcasm; I sincerely appreciate it.

I appreciate, but I do not approve. I think formulas are fine when they help, but Carnap's influence was not limited to the improvement of technical dexterity. His carelessness about essentials encouraged an in-group contempt for true philosophical rigor, substituting for the genuine article an illusion founded on pointless exactitudes. Within that in-group, the same old anti-philosophy still reigns supreme, not as a theory but as a practice. And so the best intentions—spreading the techniques of logic, destroying all philosophic cliques—has led to hell, to a closed Carnap clique. And so my personal search for Carnap and my present self-appointed task as a devil's advocate, must both end on an inconclusive note. I do appreciate his faith in logic, his willingness to develop technical paraphernalia even if in a clumsy preliminary manner. But I cannot overlook his lasting contempt for philosophy, his genuine lack of a sense of proportion rather than its mere temporary suspension, his ending one volume with a promise to come to the point in the next and in the next. Yehoshua Bar-Hillel, his avid and leading disciple, told me he was led by the nose, and quite willingly, from the mid-thirties to the end of Carnap's career. He told very movingly about his pilgrimage to Los Angeles after the Master had died, to look at his latest contributions to inductive philosophy, to see how the Master came to the point on his dying day. He did not, according to Bar-Hillel, who said he saw at once that Carnap's last papers were a mess. And then something snapped, and Bar-Hillel went looking for a worthier Master.

In a way, the tragedy that was Bar-Hillel's odyssey reflected Carnap's own. Robert S. Cohen, one of the many whom I have interrogated, tells me Carnap was unassuming, and only accepted people's verdict of him as a great philosopher because in his humility he could not contradict so many senior philosophers. I do not doubt this story, a pragmatic paradox though it be. Yet the verdict echoes in my ears: logic tells us, said Carnap, many a time and never retracted, that philosophy is meaningless. Later and under pressure he softened his wording of his view: he said he still believed—believed!—that it is possible to construct a language of science that excludes all metaphysics. Finally, what I feel made him such a leading philosopher was his excellence in mediocrity, his simplistic view of the universe, of science, of rationality, his everlasting hope that however clumsy and limited his formal tools were, a slight improvement would render them quite adequate. It is particularly impressive that this clumsy technician seems a master and a wizard to most of the leading masters and the true masters in the field.

I do not think that any of his doctrines are going to be cited for long: he said nothing original. I do not think any of the techniques he invented, his modal logic, his state-descriptions, his (already forgotton, but once so topical) reduction-sentences, his theoretical and observational languages, his inductive system, his c functions, his lambda and the continuum of inductive methods—all these are already museum-pieces and they never worked. Still, I think he should be remembered for his tireless attempts to build formal systems, to use logic instead of philosophy, to clarify. His failure may be our failure, and his life may stand as a moral of sorts; but, above all, let us not emulate him too closely: no matter how understandable was his neglect of essentials in favor of technicalities, it is time to restore some sense of proportion and some sense of purpose.

Finally, a word on the editing of the present volume. I have little quarrel with the editorial policy as expressed in the editor's brief preface, though I do think quite erroneous his view, say, of Kasher's paper as not only transcending Carnap, but in a way also in the Carnap tradition/vein/mold. I would like to concede this point as I concede and admire Russell's point that non-Euclidean geometry transcends Kant and owes its very existence to Kant. Kasher's work on pragmatics has roots in many non-Carnapian traditions and in the innovations of Bar-Hillel that strangely owe nothing to Carnap. For more details see Kasher's other works, as well as Bar-Hillel's contribution to the *Carnap* volume in the Library of Living Philosophers series.

But I also wonder if the editor has selected the most representative at its best. He rightly refrained from reprinting, for example, essays from the *Carnap* volume in the Library of Living Philosophers; but he could have selected an old *Erkenntnis* Carnap paper, an old Bar-Hillel or even Arthur Pap, and thus be more historical and less concerned with prospects. But I am biased of course, not so much because he thinks the growth prospects of the Carnap school are excellent (and I deem this a slight exaggeration), but because I am a social historian at heart.

In conclusion, should papers be reprinted unretouched? Arguments go hither and thither and compromise requires editorial insertions at least for cross-reference. For example, Hintikka's essay contains a reference to Montague's report of a private conversation in which Carnap identifies state-descriptions with models. Such reports mean little as they may refer to anything from a passing thought to a *leitmotif*. In this same volume Carnap says more: state-descriptions can be viewed as models for baby universes, not for decent fully-fledged worlds (p. 295). With no subject-index published, shouldn't the editor at least make a note here? And similarly for other resolved difficulties, and for difficulties proven unresolvable. Strangely, all of Carnap's concerns seem, in retrospect, either to have been proven easily resolvable or unresolvable in principle. Perhaps this should not sound surprising, at least not to those who view him as a teacher and a logician. And what else could a person be whose motto was, logic provides a proof that there is no philosophy, and whose life-work was the vain search for that proof?

EXEGETES OF WITTGENSTEIN

appalling intellectual poverty

Though I am grateful to Godfrey Vesey and his collaborators for their *Understanding Wittgenstein*, I hesitate to recommend it. The fifteen lectures in this volume are each very technical and tough going, so that each is at least one hour's concentrated reading, and at the generous pace of 10–15 pages an hour its 267 pages should require at least 18 hours of hard work—even if one skips the Foreword. Still, if one is expert—really expert, I mean—one can make do with a few hours of careful study of the Foreword which is an excellent essay, though a misleading or at least partial summary of the whole book.

The reasons I hesitate to recommend investing so much work in this book are two: (1) it is exegetic; (2) it is poor. I know there is enough room for exegesis of any number of authors. The wish to make sense of a given remark of a given author may so engage a given exegete that he may feel rewarded even if his search is futile. And this is fine for both the exegete and his avowed readers, who may perhaps exegize on his exegesis. But shall I recommend all this to my readers? Perhaps I should apply here the Golden Rule. Well, then. Would I myself be happy if someone spent much enjoyable but intellectually worthless time dissecting a passage from my pen? No. I shudder at the thought. And so I propose, before undertaking an exegesis, or a review of an exegetic volume like the present, to declare my hand and explain what I plan to do and what I hope to achieve.

There is an infectious habit of doing something instead of explaining it and what it is about. It is well known that Wittgenstein and all whom he infected were averse to discussing their philosophic activities and preferred,

---

This review of *Understanding Wittgenstein*, edited by Godfrey Vesey *et al* (Ithaca: Cornell University Press, 1974; Cornell paperback, 1976) appeared in *Erkenntnis*, 13, 1978. It was first published under the title 'Wittgenstein's Heritage'. Copyright 1978 by D. Reidel Publishing Company, Dordrecht, Holland.

indeed insisted on, plunging right into them. When I came to England as a graduate student and Wittgenstein's first mature publication appeared—it was his *Philosophical Investigations,* but this is quite immaterial—I could not make head or tail of it, and only from not knowing what it was all about. I also could make no sense whatsoever of G. E. M. Anscombe's B.B.C. lectures on him, and for the same reason. Though the B.B.C. Third Programme had high aspirations, it was still directed to the general public, to non-professionals; I felt that as a graduate student I should not be so ill-equipped as to have fully missed its content; but I did. I remember to this day her voice, that sounded as if it were, and I assumed then without hesitation that indeed it was, simply choked with tears. I remember to this day that she was supposed to talk about Wittgenstein's philosophy but instead seemed to me to be talking exclusively about the intellectual responses of ordinary Westerners to events from Western everyday life; and they were all intellectually unchallenging events. For example, looking at one's wristwatch and surmising some information from what one sees; not even the slightly more baffling case of hearing a halting voice and surmising that its owner is choked with tears. What was it all about? Until I read this book I never found out, though the Lord knows I tried.

Perhaps some readers know the secret already, and so may wonder whether to go on reading this essay. I wonder if they felt this way when reading earlier essays in the same vein, e.g., Bouwsma's review of the Colored Books (Blue and Brown) in the *Journal of Philosophy* or the anonymous review of Anscombe's and David Pole's exegeses in the *Times Literary Supplement.* For the question is very far from being new: Wittgenstein's incomprehensibility is a fixture of the Wittgensteinian lore from its very inception—from the time Ramsey went all the way from Cambridge to Trachtenbach to ask him to explain what he had meant in a certain passage in his celebrated *Tractatus Logico-Philosophicus* and he said he had forgotten. What is new is the answer. But before we hear the answer we may ask, Do we care about the question? If so, why? Those who do care about the question and not about why they care about it may proceed. What should others do?

Why for over 20 years did I wish to know why others care about Wittgenstein at all? Because they were there. If only he were there, but not the hordes of his followers, I would not be more interested in him than in Nostradamus. Of course, I do sometimes care about neglected writers, such as Hans Christian Oersted, and not about admired ones, such as Martin Heidegger. But when one finds many intelligent and able people exegizing, one wonders why. In the case of Marx, the answer is easy to come by; in the case of Wittgenstein, it is not so easy. These are facts, and generally admitted ones.

Once the search for a thinker is justified in a reasonable manner, facile solutions to it are *a priori* excluded, and solutions that present him as facile are *prima facie a priori* excluded; a serious following *prima facie* presumes a serious thinker, though on good evidence he may nevertheless be branded a confidence man, pretentious, seemingly interesting but merely a paradoxer, promising to resolve difficulties but only hinting at possible solutions, seemingly offering a way out of the thicket but in fact more lost than his followers, etc., etc. All these solutions are *prima facie* unsatisfactory and always more problematic than the situations they come to relieve.

The simplest way to find a solution to the question, How and why did a given thinker stimulate many intelligent people? is to try and find their own answers to this question. If this seems baffling too, it may be advisable to read the way they compare him with other thinkers. In this volume we have little or no opportunity for that: the short name index here is indicative. In this context we should ignore the dummy references, i.e., proper names which are used (metaphorically) as name-variables, e.g., in a sentence reporting that a certain famous philosopher is a non-robot (p. 209) and that a certain famous composer's music is noise to the ears of members of a certain alien culture (p. 266); ignoring these we come up then with almost nothing. The little that is left I shall try to report. (Should dummy references be recorded in a name index?)

Since there is no reference that can provide the clue to the answer, I cannot but surmise. Nor will the surmise be good, or else the answer is as good as explicitly given in the body of the book. And so the reviewer is on a sticky wicket: if he does not surmise the point of a book he had better not review it or at least declare it pointless; if he does, he bases much criticism on a mere surmise and so seems unkind. Moreover, there may be a snag. There always is in a problematic case.

The snag is a seeming gestalt-switch, one without which the surmise cannot stand and would mean little anyway. And the question is, Assuming the switch is there, why is it not openly declared? Perhaps because the editor and contributors were determined to avoid interpretational controversy.

Let me, then, briefly report the history of a switch that appears to me in retrospect from the present volume, then report at some length the editor's preface, before dealing with each of the fifteen contributions separately and bringing this essay to a close.

The most important change concerns the idea that all philosophy is nonsense, an idea once so very popular and now to be eschewed. This idea enraged some people: to say that philosophy is nonsense is nonsense! was the resounding verdict of Frederick Waismann. When I read this in the mid-fifties I considered Waismann a renegade from the Wittgenstein camp. But here, on p. 13, he is quoted, recording in short-hand, Wittgenstein saying in the Intertestamental period, something like (I do not pretend that my translation can convey the original flavor), "What, you dirty dog, you will speak no nonsense? Do speak nonsense; it doesn't matter!" Whatever happened to the famous commandment to be silent, in its famous whereof and thereof, that Wittgenstein said (in the end of his preface to his *Tractatus*) was his chief point? No matter.

It was not easy to effect a switch when Waismann kindly let nonsense be. The old reading said philosophy was nonsense; the new one was hardly available, particularly since Wittgenstein did not publish much in his lifetime. It was G. J. Warnock who began the new reading. First, he said contemporary English philosophy is almost identical with Berkeley's—or so he seemed to say—and both exorcize nonsense relentlessly. Then in his *English Philosophy Since 1900* he said, contemporary—anti-nonsense or commonsense—English philosophy was following G. E. Moore, not Ludwig Wittgenstein. (In this volume, the only real reference to Moore is that of Ayer; of which more later.) Reviewers barely bothered to refute Warnock at the time. Judging from the present volume, by now he has won.

How, then, could I, an outsider, trust Warnock? In his book he (1) ascribed logical atomism to Bertrand Russell, yet I had assumed he knew Russell had always ascribed it to Wittgenstein; and (2) criticized the theory, offering no reference. When a historian says something without offering a reference, it may be a mark of humility or of ignorance, yet I had assumed Warnock knew that the source was Russell. So it appeared that Warnock turned Russell from successful critic to victim of obvious criticism. Not nice. The criticism of logical atomism that Russell has fathered and Warnock has reproduced is exceedingly simple: the fact that the list of atomic facts (or propositons) is complete (or not) is neither atomic nor composite of atomic ones. This refutes not only logical atomism but also the picture theory of language, so-called; perhaps even the two theories are one, or fused into one.

Now, as one reads Wittgenstein's famous dictum, "whereof one cannot speak thereof one must be silent", as anti-nonsense, I cannot consider an author such as Warnock convincing. There must be a critical debate of alternative readings of this dictum first. The alternatives themselves, perhaps variants of one alternative, came between Warnock's volume and the present one. And so here we are. What was Wittgenstein's dictum if not anti-nonsense?

Our editor, Godfrey Vesey, offers the answer right off the bat (p. xiv). I shall split it into different components so as to facilitate both comprehension and critical discussion. The point as he puts it is this: "the possibility of a language game" ". . . is conditioned by our *not calling in question* certain facts." I have to apologize for the composite quotation, but things are exceedingly complicated—and with no excuse except the hagiographic attitude prevailing in this volume beyond any reasonable limit. To a sentence of Wittgenstein (from his intolerably confusing *On Certainty*) which says, "the possibility of a language-game is conditioned by certain facts"; or rather, "does it not seem obvious that", etc. Vesey adds, "I take him to mean", etc. It is amazing that what Wittgenstein says seems obvious is viewed as being in need of reinterpretation without the slightest hint of unease!

There is here, to come to the point, a new transcendental proof: if certainty were not possible, then science/language/reason (choose your favorite) would be impossible; but the latter exists, hence is possible, hence we have certainty. I think all transcendental proofs, from Kant's days on, have the same defect: they are only seemingly obvious. Kant's claim that science exists is in a sense obvious, but not in the sense it was used in his proof. Languages exist, and so, after many a fashion, language games; but the language-games described by Wittgenstein, I think simply do not exist. Also, Kant's claim that only his transcendental aesthetics and all that make science possible is questionable: the "only" included in his claim is the moot point. Similarly, the claim that the possibility that language is conditioned by certain facts is too vague, and that it is conditional on us not questioning some assumptions is questionable. For example, whatever Vesey says we do not question, I now do question. In sheer defiance.

Of course, he says I cannot. For here is the other innovation: we cannot follow the Cartesian program of doubting everything and also (here is an item all too often overlooked) of not admitting any item that is in doubt until and unless proven.

This claim, that we cannot start afresh, that we must take something upon faith, the ground for the *tu quoque* of the irrationalists, is certainly correct, and the *tu quoque* is certainly valid. I do not know who was the first to make it; and certainly in our own century a few Catholic thinkers, such as Etienne Gilson and Jacques Maritain, have made it in response to Descartes's program; and others, such as E. E. Evans-Pritchard and Michael Polanyi, have made it in response to the claim of science to utter universality and validity.

This claim, the *tu quoque*, is meant to be a defense of irrationalism by way of criticizing rationalism. It raises the question: are we rationalists still, and if so how do we respond to it; do we riposte, or admit a defeat and try to mend our fences, or what?

Suppose we admit the claim. Suppose we agree that rational debate should go on, yet it rests on a presupposition. Is this presupposition one common to people engaged (properly) in one given debate or in all debates? In other words, is the same presupposition behind all language-games that have to do with rationality? If yes, the proof is transcendental; if not, we are dealing with the myth of the framework and a *tu quoque*!

Here seems to me to be the unstated concern of this book, and thereby the answer to my query; Wittgenstein is the proclaimed new Kant who is saving rationality from the *tu quoque* argument, and so all efforts required for understanding him are worth it. Except that this is my interpretation of the interpreters who, coming to clarify matters, only compound confusions. For example, they say nothing about earlier claims, e.g., Kai Nielsen's, that Wittgenstein was a fideist.

I confess I am very uneasy. It is no accident that Wittenstein's "is conditioned by certain facts" is interpreted from the start by the editor as "is conditioned by our *not calling in question* certain facts". It is a factual claim made by practically all psychologists that any activity can be hampered by the actors' stopping too often to ask whether they are doing the right thing. For example, Gilbert Ryle once complained, rather bitterly, that certain philosophers were good at wondering whether they understood so many words of their interlocutors that they managed to slow down any conversation they did not like. (Find an echo of this in his 'Ordinary Language', *Philosophical Review*, 62, 1953, reprinted in Charles Caton's *Philosophy and Ordinary Language*, pp. 110 and 126.) Now, let us call the activity of one who constantly raises doubts 'skeptical pestering'. Is skeptical pestering the same as "calling into question certain facts"? If so, then the claim Vesey ascribes to Wittgenstein is commonplace. Both Sextus and Bayle have noted that critics of skepticism say it forces its holder to act impossibly since it leads to skeptical pestering. From the fact that skeptics are not always engaged in skeptical pestering two different conclusions are drawn: the anti-skeptics conclude that skeptics are not sincere, and the skeptics that skepticism need not cause skeptical pestering. I think Wittgenstein does not speak of "our *not calling in question* certain facts" because he is familiar with this dispute and knows that logically Sextus and Bayle are in the right even though philosophically he combats them. He says, I think, that society exists because skepticism is false, not that Bayle is an insincere skeptic because he is not just a skeptical pest. The situation, of course, quickly gets involved. The claim that any game rests on presuppositions is a standard anti-rationalistic ploy. Yet the very same claim, when made regarding language-games, is problematic since it involves a fine point: making a language-game possible may be viewed as making a set of propositions have truth value; the presupposition which makes the language-game possible is equivalent to the assertion that the same presupposition is true; and thus Wittgenstein's claim "that the possibility of a language-game is conditioned by certain facts" may be read to say "the very truth value of some proposition is conditioned by the truth of another". The second paper here, by R. M. White, is entitled, 'Can Whether One Proposition Makes Sense Depend on the Truth of Another? (*Tractatus* (2.0211-2)'. So there. Following Professor Vesey's Foreword we can now survey all the essays in this volume and see how they treat this point, the question of the presuppositions to all rational response. The result is disappointing. So I may be in error; but I hope I have now presented to my reader some concern that may easily be recognized. Professor Vesey's Foreword does not. And with this I leave the Foreword and proceed to assay the 15 lectures of the present volume.

One. Anthony Kenny, 'The Ghost of the Tractatus': Wittgenstein distorted history, especially when renouncing his first book. All his life he held the picture theory of language *sans* logical atomism (i.e., all real propositions are contingent; so, sense is prior to truth; every facet of the world corresponds to one of two contradictory propositions). Whereas he earlier thought that language mirrors the world, he later thought our world mirrors our language and so what we can see depends on our language, which is given. To maintain this we must avoid both nominalism and realism; but Wittgenstein probably failed to avoid these. Anyway, clearly, for Wittgenstein thus presented, we must add that all presuppositions must remain either tentative or ineffable [see R. G. Collingwood's *Essay on Metaphysics*, Regnery-Gateway reprint, 1972].

Supposing this to be the case, what of it? A view of logically necessary and of logically impossible propositions as propositions 'by courtesy only' is one we cannot take seriously without further ado; here there is no inducement to take it seriously, and much inducement to take it as a mere historical curiosity. What does it do here in this volume? Mainly bring closer together the early and the late Wittgenstein, no doubt.

Two. R. M. White, 'Can Whether One Proposition Makes Sense Depend on the Truth of Another? (*Tractatus*, 2.0211–2)': Logical atomism is fragmentary and bizarre. Young Wittgenstein then, with Leibniz and Spinoza, are "in a sense . . . prehistoric monsters . . . curiosities of human thought . . . ." "And yet paradoxically it is this . . . which makes [each of them] a constant stimulus to further reflection on a wide range of the most fundamental questions . . . [if] we do not approach them with crude philistinism or mere dilettante aesthetic curiosity . . . ." This is a laudable sentiment, but not a well thought-out attitude; not well worded either.

Wittgenstein's *Tractatus*, we are told, draws bizarre conclusions from widely accepted views about a proposition's sense, truth-value, and negation: to understand a proposition equals to know its sense equals to know what is the case if it is true, and what is the case if it is false, and to see that it is the same proposition whether it is true or whether it is false.

Now all this is fine, except that it conflicts with Strawson's theory of definite descriptions, according to which truth value can be denied to a proposition if some conditions are violated. If we use a proper name in a subject-predicate sentence of a simple sort, we understand it, we can see what it would be for it to be true, and likewise to be false; yet if the proper name designates nothing, it has no truth value. Thus spake Strawson.

It is this kind of chit-chat that gives all the philosophers of the Wittgenstein-Moore circle(s) their bad reputation. The question of the truth value of a proposition concerning a nonexistent individual can be decided one way or another in this formal system or that, with this or that cost or benefit. Outside formal systems, in ordinary parlance, we usually do not employ proper names unless we assume they denote specifiable individuals, and when our assumption to that effect is refuted we modify what we say—e.g., replace the proper name by another, or by a class name etc., or delete the whole discourse as erroneous without bothering about the question where to pin the error. In other words, ordinary discourse is not complete—why should it be?—and may be completed in diverse ways in accord with decision and the sense of adequacy of the speakers.

All this is really too far from the interesting problems discussed earlier when the paper at hand was mentioned. If Wittgenstein exegeses must continue—for want of ability to do anything else or for any other reason—then the public may reasonably expect some progress, and not the endless repetition of well-criticized errors.

I do not mean to oppose Strawson the way some writers have, and I for one do not see much harm in deciding that, say, propositions about a fictitious character may be true to that character or not yet neither true nor false, if I may echo Leonard Linsky. Russell and the early Wittgenstein, perhaps also Frege, could not accept this, as they were committed to the idea that meaning is welded to truth-value; I do agree that we may wish to try different views of meaning that may offer cases of meaning without truth-value. From this to the exegesis of Wittgenstein there is a great distance; what is Strawson to Wittgenstein that he should care about him?

Three. Rush Rhees, 'Question on Logical Inference'. I had to invest some effort to read it without skipping. It makes no coherent sense to me at all, though there is no difficulty reading each sentence, even the most elusive ones, which repeatedly tell us that proofs are enlightening in some sense, and useful in some sense, or something to that effect. I would not usually mind if an author treats some propositions as rules and some rules as propositions. But a commentator on the philosopher famous for the view that all propositions are meaningful and all rules are meaningless, who comments on that philosopher's views concerning rules of inference, should not be allowed by the editor to get away with such a confusing usage. Rhees reports Tarski's view of inference and says, it reminds him of Wittgenstein's criticism of Russell's theory of numbers, e.g., "his remark" that the claim that 'there are as many chairs here as there' is no answer to the query, How many? I may be dense, but I see no criticism in this "remark", at least not of Russell's theory of numbers. And even if I could, should I also see how this can be used to criticize Tarski? Rhees omits to report what question Tarski asks, yet seems to say Tarski fails to answer the/his own/Wittgenstein's/Rhees's (delete the inapplicable) question.

Rhees ends thus: "What is it that makes a transition from one proposition (or a set of propositions) to another a logical inference? We cannot give a simple or formal answer. In any case no such answer could help a man who had asked that question. We can answer by giving examples; like . . . Wittgenstein . . . . And the discussion can go on from there." This is confusing and seemingly an expression of irrationalism; also an insult to the reader's intelligence, perhaps.

Four. Brian McGuinness, 'The *Grundgedanke* of the *Tractatus*'. This is a moving essay, a part of a subtle rational reconstruction of the period of close cooperation between Russell and Wittgenstein (with Frege in the background), showing how Russell's wrestling with his paradox and his temporary solution of it with the idea that there are no classes, linked logic and ontology-in-the-making and led Wittgenstein to his logical atomism, his quaint metaphysics, his *Tractatus*. At the end of his lecture McGuinness cites Wittgenstein's *Notebooks* (p. 79), "My work has broadened out from the foundations of logic to the essence of the world", in his own translation, as the theme of his lecture, and he thinks his analysis explains why Wittgenstein's *Tractatus* is rather about the unsayable than the sayable. He ends the lecture with Russell's anecdote which tells of Wittgenstein's answer with "both" to the question whether he was thinking of logic or of his sins. The joke is terrific on all levels, from his switch from an exclusive to an inclusive disjunction, to the fact that the final entry in his *Notebooks* a few years later contains the idea of 'elementary sin' (in parallel with 'elementary proposition'?). The concern of the *Notebooks* with ethics and aesthetics, its broad Spinozist outlook, must open to readers of his *Tractatus* new avenues of approach to it—as a broad outline to a future philosophy, or as the shambles of a brilliant prospect, or as something undecided which way to go (the decisive tone of its preface notwithstanding). It is all very fascinating and makes one wonder whether after publication of his first-and-last book Wittgenstein had any choice but to go into exile. I find this very moving.

There was a period during which among most English-speaking philosophers the phrase "this sounds odd" suggested severe consternation, if not downright censure. We forget how odd were both logic and philosophical logic in the early 20th century—McGuinness reminds us that the heuristics of both went hand-in-hand—at least until Wittgenstein decreed 'the puzzle' out of existence. Proper names 'stand for' individual people and numerals for numbers: start there, and feel troubled by a few blind or not-blind avenues of exit from your bother, and one of them might be, the world is the totality of facts. Pow! If so, then who is God? Says Wittgenstein, "How things stand, is God." Hence, "the world itself is neither good nor evil . . . but the willing subject" is. Let us look then at this. "How can man be happy at all . . . ? Through the life of knowledge." (*Notebooks*, pp. 79 and 81). When I first read the pages here quoted I could not see in them the author of the *Tractatus Logico-philosophicus*. Yet between these two pages comes the one cited by McGuinness about the study of logic leading young Wittgenstein to the discovery of the essence of the world. The Spinozist ideals of the *Notebooks*, he says, still stood behind the *Tractatus*, but as unsayable. Very interesting.

Five. Guy Stock. 'Wittgenstein on Russell's Theory of Judgment'. Since we must identify an object before we can have a judgment about it, we cannot use judgments to identify an object. How then can we identify anything? Russell's variant of logical atomism postulates the existence of incorrigible perceptions and so must give a perfect answer to the question; yet it cannot. Wittgenstein's variant in principle does away with all objects to begin with, and with the judging subject as well. (Not, remember, that they categorically do not exist, but that their possible existence and qualities transcend language.) This seems to be too evasive, but then the psychological theory of Russell (at the time) was rejected as a theory of judgment in the philosophic realm (though admittedly it was allowed reentry in the realm of psychology). Why did Russell view judgment and perception as philosophical? So as to make science possible? This is the question for Guy Stock to answer. He reports, correctly, that Wittgenstein required (*Tractatus* 2.0123) that we know an object's "internal qualities". What it means is that since sense is truth or falsity, and since understanding or making sense is prior to (empirical) judgment, we must have all possible worlds before our eyes in order to judge which of these happens to be the real world. This is "internal" in a rather Pickwickian sense, which Stock tries to defend by making it sound less odd. He need not take the trouble.

Six. Bernard Williams, 'Wittgenstein and Idealism'. I am stuck here. To an extent this lecture is an exegesis on an exegesis, and I will not go with it. It introduces the perilous term "private language" (on p. 80) with the innocence of one who talks about dragons or unicorns, as if we all know precisely enough what one is talking about, and he dismisses phenomenalism there as a philosophy that can be (satisfactorily) criticized "by undermining a private language". I am not able either to defend phenomenalism or to endorse such a cavalier attitude to it. Williams is perhaps a little considerate in allowing phenomenalists to protest that they are not idealists, but in a historical note of four lines he pulls the carpet from under their feet. Mach knew all that Williams alludes to and honestly tried to handle it; we may ignore phenomenalism altogether and we may treat it with respect, as we wish; but respect requires allowing Mach to have his say.

Was Wittgenstein's *Tractatus* a treatise in phenomenalism? Was it the dismissal of all transcendental object and the insistence that all that there is are facts? I am not competent to judge and will not explicate an exegesis on an exegesis that is not even presented as having any useful purpose. Was Carnap of the *Logische Aufbau* a phenomenalist? I suppose he was, and here I accept Williams's view (p. 81). Is phenomenalism identical with neutral monism? Crudely, it seems so; finally, I cannot judge and lose interest. Is the 'two language' theory likewise the same? I give this the same answer; Williams refers me to Austin. He could likewise refer me to Wittgenstein and be done with it. Myself, I comprehend neither of them.

Verdict: "phenomenalism is one or another form of idealism" (p. 82). I protest. For the phenomenalists deny or ignore all substance, idealists deny (and transcendental idealists ignore) material substance; but whereas idealists affirm existence of mental substance (and transcendental idealists affirm some substance), phenomenalists hold all substance in equal contempt. Professor Bernard Williams manages to discuss Wittgenstein's refutation of both kinds of idealism, believe it or not, with no reference to substance at all. What was Wittgenstein, an anti-idealist, a materialist, or a dualist, or what? Is it not clear that within any philosophy-without-the-concept-of-substance all substance-philosophies (idealism, materialist, and all their alternatives) are meaningless and in any philosophy-that-denies-the-existence-of-substance they are all false? Either kind of philosophy permits phenomenalism, the former tacitly and the latter explicitly, and then it may, but need not, affirm or deny it, the former tacitly (Young Wittgenstein affirms it tacitly) and the latter explicitly (Old Wittgenstein à la Bernard Williams, perhaps; I read him entirely contrary to the way the editor reads him, I fear; but I am not sure I read the editor's reading right!). For in Williams's view, "implicit in some of Wittgenstein's later work" (p. 83), is that when the 'I' of the idealist is replaced by 'we', so as to replace private language with language proper, their case collapses. This, of course, is in itself neither here nor there unless and until all this is related to substance. Moreover, Williams seems to withdraw his case.

Things do not get better. Williams notices "the curious use that Wittgenstein makes of 'we' ", and the "preposterousness" of his use of 'forms of life' (pp. 85–86), and yet he does not ask, Why bother with all these? Rather, he tries to compare Wittgenstein to an imaginary Whorfian who (like Benjamin Lee Whorf and many many others) thinks natural languages are imbued with metaphysical presuppositions and who (unlike Whorf) is a relativist on matters of truth. But relativism turns out to be a red herring (p. 92). The main point is that Wittgenstein clings to justificationism by the use of a transcendental proof resting on the existence of language. I have elucidated the point above once, and will leave it at that.

Williams's paper is at best too obscure to be considered even as useful exegesis. Its obscurity is at times seemingly studied, e.g, in his promising to introduce a neologism and then referring to the promise as if it were its own execution. He does this twice.

Seven. A. Phillips Griffiths, 'Wittgenstein, Schopenhauer, and Ethics'. This is an exegetic paper in a more traditional sense, and it is also poetic. It discusses the young Wittgenstein. The most illuminating point, perhaps, is the quote from Schopenhauer about goodness as expressible not in words but only in deeds. (Wittgenstein's famous dictum, Philosophy is an activity, incidentally, may be viewed in its light as a shyly concealed self-compliment.) There can be no proper exegesis of Schopenhauer without some disputing of his misreading of Spinoza; doing so would bring the three together—to my surprise—more than ever suspected. But I doubt it is worth the bother. The trouble Griffiths has with Young Wittgenstein, namely (1) that the world is meaningless and (2) any will is impotent, is only partly met by the intellectual love of God (p. 110); Griffiths could go further had he noticed and used Wittgenstein's *Tractatus*, 6.342, where he says, our physics tell nothing about the world, but its definiteness and completeness do. For we may conclude that meaning is there all right, though it is ineffable. Since *Tractatus* 6.3 rejects all claims for regularity in the world—an unpopular remark that seems taboo to quote (Popper cited it in his presidential address to the Aristotelian Society and he thereby elicited and met, I regret to report, with a somewhat unphilosophic unfriendliness)—

and since *Tractatus* 6.341 endorses Newtonianism and so seems most impolite to quote; and since it and the paragraph next to it are instrumentalist and so debatable philosophy of science rather than language analysis proper . . . . Oh, never mind.

Eight. Renford Bambrough, 'How to Read Wittgenstein'. The Master is always right though what he says is always wrong because both a proposition and its negation may be false since, to quote Anthony Powell [*sic*], language is so limited we cannot have a true description of anything [*sic*]. The editor sums up this paper generously by claiming it says that everything Wittgenstein says needs "immediate qualification" (p. xix), because his thought "strains" language. I read here something very different. In his *Tractatus* Wittgenstein admits that what he says is unsayable and hence, strictly speaking, meaningless. To say, with all traditional mystics, oriental and other, that I cannot say my message and so, in struggle, I say both that which is false and its negation which is likewise false, is very different from the *Tractatus*'s claim to be uttering "profound nonsense" (Popper's expression). What is common to both is the claim that words are mere means, that once the message is conveyed, they become superfluous and are better shed. I am willing to admit this. But they also share the claim that the wordless message is true. Which is both dogmatism and irrationalism (Russell, 'Mysticism and Logic'). Bambrough complains (p. 115) that his view is unjustly called "this Wittgenstein poison". This is indeed unjust as his view is neither Wittgenstein nor poison; we have survived it before and may be immune to it by now.

Nine. Jenny Teichman, 'Wittgenstein on Persons and Human Beings'. Why did the Master use the word "person" somewhere in the Colored Books but not in his later books? The question runs, it seems to me, contrary to the canons of interpretation: the Colored Books were published posthumously and so cannot be viewed as the author's definite publications. Moreover, as she notices (p. 133), the Colored Books, but not what she compares them with, were written in English. Oh, there is no rule against examining the most fleeting expression of a writer, of course; but there the aim is to catch his thought in transit, not to weigh mature opinion. Moreover, the topic at hand is personal identity, and the expression "the same person"; what matters is not the English expression that happens to have served best one who studied the problem, but why he left it so soon.

The problem is ascribed by Aristotle to Thales and the solution is declared by him to be the very start of philosophy: behind changing appearances lies the unchanging reality (essence, character, substance, substratum, nature, form, being). Since, we have heard repeatedly, for Wittgenstein any talk of reality is but "transcendental fog", one may wonder what he does with the question, particularly since it is a real obstacle to every Schopenhauerian (see the end of Jorge Luis Borges's 'Borges and I'). Teichman shows that Wittgenstein's view of personal identity is poor.

Yet she goes on to speak of the ordinary use of the word 'person' (p. 137), thus evoking in me memories of the 'fifties. Referring to the *Oxford English Dictionary*'s item 'fairy' she says (*loc. cit.*), "since fairies are small they must have bodies, so *supernatural* does not in this context imply the beings in question are spirits." Why not look in the dictionary while it is still in hand, under the item "supernatural"? If this is the way to *Understanding Wittgenstein* then we are a long way from our target: we must first study the ordinary use of small and of large apparitions, it seems.

Teichman interprets the later Wittgenstein to say that thought presupposes language, and language a life form, i.e., a human community. Not surprising, nor controversial, except for her added claim that the dependence of language on a community is logical! She cites in her Postscript a statement by Wittgenstein against this added claim and dismisses it as conflicting with the rest of his work. Incidentally, I have split her claim into two to show she has done a poor exegetic job. But I do not know that her error matters: I do not know that there is any point to it all, anyway.

Ten. Godfrey Vesey, 'Other Minds'. The problem of other minds is, in my opinion, a straw man. Whoever said, 'I know I have a mind but I am not sure about you'? No one that I ever heard of. If 'mind' denotes substance, then how do I know I have a mind? If not, then we all safely and commonsensically have each his own (Hume).

Vesey starts by claiming that saying that 'it is afternoon now' we presuppose some facts of nature, yet the presuppositions get into grammar: afternoon means sun above zenith. The natural fact presupposed is of the earth's diurnal motion, he says. He may not have met pre-Copernican people, perhaps; but he must have read some. They also said, it is afternoon. Did Copernicus alter language? I do not know. If yes, it is interesting to examine to what extent. But he has not altered the afternoon as yet. I wish to report that I have met pre-Copernican people and spoke with them about all sorts of things with no difficulty, until I told them about the Copernican hypothesis.

Am I pedantic? Does it matter that 20th-century English is still possibly pre-Copernican about the afternoon? Does language always retain some archaisms? God knows it does often enough, but we can show that no item has a guaranteed survival. Vesey moves then to space travel, and so his science fiction literature should tell him that the question, how plausible a transfer of terms can be, depends much on the author's ingenuity. But he trusts his own limited scope too much. He says, we can, indeed, have an afternoon on Mars. But not on the sun. He imagines someone trying to extend the phrase to the sun and failing ridiculously. But the failure is Vesey's! On the sun one sees the Milky Way—the whole galaxy almost (since the sun is near the edge of the galaxy). And so the proximate center of the galaxy when on the zenith as viewed from a place on the sun makes it noon there!

I loathe the previous two paragraphs. They take seriously some three pointless pages and argue against them as if they signify. But we have here nearly three hundred pages, most of which are of this level and below. I am sorry.

Vesey ascribes to Descartes the view that pain is mental. The only mental attribute that I have found in Descartes is thought; even memory is for Descartes and the Cartesians not mental, but animal! No classical philosopher could be blamed for the pseudo-problem of other minds; it has been created by those whose declared business it is to destroy, not create, pseudo-problems.

The moral Vesey draws from his brilliant analysis, however, is correct and pre-Wittgensteinian: language is a part of human life; words need not denote objects; pain is not an object (pp. 159–60). Also 'facts of nature' refer to nature *sans* man; the residue is called 'form of life' (p. 160): forms of life are "facts of human nature". This seems to me to be metaphysical fog. Decidedly un-Wittgensteinian, too.

Eleven. Ilham Dilman, 'Wittgenstein on the Soul'. Straight to the point, at long last. Wittgenstein did assume/postulate/assert/teach/think/believe that the soul/mind exists; but not as substance. Or rather, he believed it is unavoidable to believe, etc., because it is a part of everybody's frame of reference (p. 163). Or rather—I start emulating those who repeatedly qualify themselves, I see—Wittgenstein believed or taught or said that one's having a soul is not a matter of another's opinion of one but of another's attitude towards one, and attitudes belong to frameworks; they are "prototypes of ways of thinking", whatever this means; I take Dilman to do the job of explicating backward, by solving the problem of what "prototypes" etc. means by telling us they are attitudes that belong to a framework; "attitudes" is Wittgenstein's, "frameworks" is probably not; these Wittgensteinians have to learn how properly to present an exegesis. And going backward, but fast, Dilman arrives after a mere three pages at the skeptic. Speaking of our "natural reaction" to pain he accuses the skeptic of holding that "unless such a reaction is based on reason and can be justified, it is irrational." The justification in question, as far as I know, never referred to attitudes but always to theories, statements, opinions, beliefs, and such. Perhaps Wittgenstein seems to cover these too: for, Dilman says, "Wittgenstein would say that if that [as usual, Wittgenstein's followers tend to misuse the indicator; I do not know what this 'that' points at] stands in need of justification then none of our beliefs and conjectures about our friends and acquaintances can be justified." This, the consequent of the sentence ascribed to Wittgenstein, is, indeed, true: none of our beliefs and conjectures can be justified. To Dilman this consequent seems so unreasonable that he does not bother with it. Rather he goes on to say, "we see that there is no direct way of stating or affirming the reality of the soul." By "we" he means he and his friends, not the reviewer, who has a way, and uses it, and asserts directly that the soul is real. The author means, I conjecture, the claim is a part of the framework and hence it is never made or affirmed within the framework. This profound claim (empirically easily refutable) about people never reaffirming their framework or parts within it seems to be the commonest assumption in the present volume. What is so outrageous about it is that it is coupled with another common trait: some people also deny the accepted framework, and then they are denounced here as confused by philosophy. Dilman himself picks on Watson's denunciation of the soul. Why call him confused? Just in order to dismiss his very existence so as to be able to denounce the skeptic's questioning of the framework as unreasonable? But then, by the same token the skeptic too does not exist!

A computer, continues Dilman, does not compute. Is this debatable? If yes, then Wittgenstein's consecration of the framework as a matter of course must go; if not, then why does Dilman try so hard to convince us (pp. 165–76)? One paragraph on p. 169 dismisses the idea of the soul as a substance; Descartes's substantive soul clashes with common usage and Plato's agrees with common usage: Plato's picture of the soul is commended for being "not a *philosopher's* picture." Words defy me.

Still, I am delighted at the gush of spiritualism a Wittgensteinian permits himself, when citing Plato, and Dostoevsky, and Kierkegaard, and more. The mind boggles to meet Sonia and Calicles and their friends all in one framework: one wonders what exchanges would occur if they could converse. I am afraid I must skip these pages, merely acknowledging that Dilman has found a meaning at long last to the celebrated kingdom of God that is within you, and even in a way that is harmonized with Wittgenstein. For sheer joy! Sonia, Christ, Antigone, and Kierkegaard share with Simone Weil most of the remaining space so that Plato's frivolous distinction between knowledge and opinion must be consigned to a passing brief footnote (p. 181). In the end all falls into place. Wittgenstein scolds Frazer for his spiritual poverty and expresses a solemn promise never never to ridicule those who seek the ultimate meaning of life. Dilman says, for himself only or also as a mouthpiece for Wittgenstein (I cannot say which), that "the most talented" may break out of the framework when having something to say there; otherwise one should stay silent, as Wittgenstein chose to do "out of philosophical integrity and also religious humility" (pp. 190–91). I do not see. Did Wittgenstein have "something to say there"? If no, he had to use for his celebrated integrity and all that in order to "stay silent". If he had "something to say there", then, we know from Malcolm and others, his integrity forced him to speak up. So he simply had nothing to say and the medals for integrity and humility are mere embellishments, it seems. No need for these.

Twelve. Les Halborow, 'The Prejudice in Favor of Psychophysical Parallelism'. Wittgenstein favored emergentism and non-reductionism to the point of suggesting that certain things need not be explained. This was his prejudice, since attempts at explaining can always be made. Yet Halborow sympathizes with Wittgenstein. First, his subtlety. Take the most obviously physical part of our mental life: our memory banks (we may remember that Descartes, the great dualist, declared them physical already). Even there, it is unclear whether activating them is purely physical; and remembering, unlike dreaming, is the awareness of memory as such. And awareness, of course, is the nub of it. Now some hard-line parallelists, I wish to add, may follow Marvin Minsky and his friends in viewing awareness as nothing other than one subsystem (computer or human) monitoring another. Halborow does not like this: it shows that in a sense all parallelism is today epiphenomenalist, and epiphenominalism is a threat to human autonomy. I am very sympathetic but regret that Halborow spends too much time on exegeses on Wittgenstein, whose contribution to the study is almost nil, and no time on facing the real issues he outlines in his last page.

Thirteen. Roger Squires, 'Silent Soliloquy'. The title seems to allude to Watson's theory of thought as silent larynx movements, which are notoriously not there, and the notorious possibility of replacing the larynx with some other material part or parts. Beyond that I cannot say much. The paper makes wild allegations about codes and about monitoring and about the mental processes of calculating and of introspecting and of self-monitoring that would be tedious to report and correct, and he offers some expressions of unfriendly feelings toward writers he cites that seem to me not exactly unavoidable but serve the author as a mere introduction to "It is an enormous merit of Wittgenstein's *Philosophical Investigations* that it begins to emancipate us from this traditional view and to forge alternative answers to the question whether such items of knowledge about a person as that he thinks such-and-such are also items of knowledge for that person" (p. 216). Notice that this is a yes-or-no question. Since the traditional answer is yes/no (delete the mistaken option), I make some mental calculation and come up with the conjecture that the "alternative answers [*sic!*] to the question" which "it is an enormous merit of Wittgenstein's *Philosophical Investigations* that it begins . . . to forge", is no/yes (ditto).

Squires denies (or at least questions) the existence of some goings on that constitute silent soliloquy, whether in the body or in the spirit. This may be the denial of any necessary goings on, or the assertion of their presence elsewhere, or something else. The paper ends just when it becomes possibly interesting.

Fourteen. A. J. Ayer 'Wittgenstein on Certainty'. Sir Alfred is surely the lion in this pack, both in position and in age: he is the only survival among them of the heroic age which they are studying. Here he offers a review of Wittgenstein's *On Certainty* (published in 1967), so as neither to join the exegesis nor to stand apart, I suppose. As usual, Ayer manages to use the English language well, even masterly; and, as usual, he argues cogently (which is not to say that I endorse his views). In this volume he stands out more than ever in these respects.

Moore proved the existence of the external world. Was he right? Wittgenstein sides with Moore, but reluctantly: not that Moore's answers to his own questions (about his own possible knowledge, etc.) are false, but that the question "does not seriously arise" (p. 227). The novelty, may I interject, the last-ditch effort by Wittgenstein, is hidden in the innocuous word 'seriously'. By what standard of seriousness? For, surely, questions of standards of seriousness do regularly seriously arise! I shall come back to this soon.

Were Wittgenstein and Moore of the same mind or not? Surely, Moore would not have minded being told he should not have raised the questions he was asking. He said in his autobiography he was never puzzled except when reading philosophy, and he often made it clear that he was not shocked by Hume's consignment of purely metaphysical books to the flames (as not books at all, of course). But here we see also a difference in attitude: whereas Moore was so placid and at peace that he annoyed even his friend Russell a bit, it was the other way with Russell's other friend Wittgenstein, who annoyed Russell by walking up and down Russell's rooms nights thinking long about logic, sin, and "the essence of the world".

Can these two attitudes equally support Wittgenstein's running theme and lifelong thesis, that "the puzzle does not exist"? I do not think so; I think it was wishful thinking, a Wittgenstein or a Tolstoy wishing he were a Moore or a peasant. For Moore was blessed in that he was both an intellectual and a peasant—the dream of all those made sick of reason, perhaps also (as they assume) by reason: Pascal, Tolstoy and Wittgenstein alike. (There are other names on the list, but I stick with those singled out by Russell in his *Portraits from Memory*.)

The difference between Moore and Wittgenstein is drawn by Ayer at once: Moore is certain, and that is fine; but to know is more than to be certain, it is to be justified. In other words, Wittgenstein, but not Moore, knows that Moore has not "*shown* that no mistake is possible" (*loc. cit.*). (To the end Wittgenstein could not shake the habit of italicizing "*show*".)

Ayer seems to me to force an issue first: it is all right to say no one raises the question and no answer is therefore required. But what if a philosopher does? Wittgenstein has an answer: the peculiarity of the philosopher's doubt is that its object is the "frame of reference", whereas ordinary thinking is within the frame. Thus, not the historical accident of the discovery of skepticism is at issue, but the logical difference between doubt about a given framework, and doubt about an item within it (p. 233). What is the frame and where does it come from? No clear answer is forthcoming (p. 234). Wittgenstein himself is more concerned to fend off the skeptic's doubt about the frame: it is futile (pp. 240–41). For it to be serious, doubt must be resolvable (p. 240).

And Ayer is right. It really is exasperating to find that wherever you turn the crux of Wittgenstein's idea is good old positivist impatience; be it the verification principle or the myth of the framework, they all share the idea that a question that keeps bothering us for centuries must be an offender. This is stuff and nonsense. Wittgenstein has promised, we remember, not to ridicule the quest for the meaning of the universe; he clearly would like to join the quest himself; yet repeatedly he ends up with (self-)contempt.

Back to Ayer. Speaking of Berkeley as he does, he touches upon the theory of substance; he stresses that Berkeley opposes material substance, not commonsense objects, and "Consequently, Moore's and Wittgenstein's certainty does not touch him" (p. 242). These are strong words. The rest of Ayer's lecture is an honest—and not very successful—attempt to mollify: reasonable or not, language and life are there, and so must be accepted. But I, the present reviewer, am at liberty to choose between competing frameworks, between alternative ways of life. How? Answer! Answer!

Fifteen. Christopher Coope, 'Wittgenstein's Theory of Knowledge'. Some false views/beliefs/utterances a person advances are avoidable (say by further checking), some not. Hence, says Coope, says Wittgenstein, they are not mistakes—meaning, not culpable (p. 251). Correct, of course.

"To what extent can we rationally discuss disagreements with those who radically differ from us in background belief?" (p. 262). Just at its end the book almost comes to its point: is Wittgenstein's theory that of a commitment to some one framework or is it a Kantian frame common to all humans that Wittgenstein postulates? It is a retreat to commitment (Bartley's phrase) (p. 262), akin to that of Evans-Pritchard in his book on the Azande (of 1937!) (p. 263). Nevertheless, we can use extra-rational criteria of choice between frameworks, e.g., "pragmatic considerations" (p. 264). Again, words defy me.

That's it. *Understanding Wittgenstein* reveals the appalling intellectual poverty of those who still wish to cash in on his ideas, so much so that the editor's summaries are more in the nature of a cover-up than exposure. Yet something shines through, the glorious days when budding youthful Wittgenstein walked tall among the giants as an equal among equals and knew a happy moment, fleeting though it was. Tolstoy said, in his story of the two brothers, a moment of glory leaves behind forever the treasure of its memory. Dante was of a different opinion. There is no greater suffering, he said, than the remembrance of times of happiness when in misery. Some lives substantiate Tolstoy's view, some Dante's; one way or another, I feel that here, in this pathetic volume, is the very key to the intriguing mystery, to understanding Wittgenstein in a sympathetic vein.

KUHN ON REVOLUTIONS

demarcation by textbook

This is, generally, a very interesting and stimulating volume, full of information and ideas. The chief problem it sets out to solve is the problem of the demarcation of science, which came to Kuhn's notice in two striking facts that greatly impressed him. First, when he became familiar with the history of science he had to reject most of the ideas about science which he had uncritically and unnoticingly absorbed from his environment as a student of physics. Second, when he was established as a historian of science he started mixing with social scientists and was struck by their frequent use of the words "scientific" and "unscientific", which words he had seldom heard physicists use. Whereas the practitioners of an established science like physics seldom bother to notice the problem of the demarcation of science, he noted, practitioners of a pre-science like sociology or psychology are quite obsessed with it. Especially since physicists hold as a matter of course an easily criticizable view of the nature of science, it is remarkable that they can ignore the question: What is the nature of science? This, Kuhn explains, is rooted in the fact that they regularly see a living example, though definitely not a case history, of a science. A science proper has a standard textbook; a pre-science does not.

Kuhn does not refer to the history of the problem of demarcation or to others' studies of it; he does not stress that he is demarcating science from pre-science rather than from superstition (Bacon), from unscientific metaphysics (Kant), or from pseudo-science (Whewell, Popper). The problem of demarcating science from pre-science has a prehistory in the works of Frazer and of his followers in both anthropology and the prehistory of science, Yet, to my knowledge, this is the first explicit, direct, and full presentation of the problem, at least as it appears when one compares

This review of Thomas S. Kuhn's *The Structure of Scientific Revolutions* (Chicago: University of Chicago Press, 1962) appeared in *Journal of the History of Philosophy*, 4, 1966.

established science with modern pre-science. Unfortunately, however, Kuhn returns to the discussion of the demarcation of science from pre-science only when he wants to present a concrete example of the demarcation of science from non-science in general. Sometimes he gives the impression that he confuses pre-science with non-science, much as others have identified non-science with superstitition or with metaphysics or with pseudo-science, and much as the positivists have confused non-science with nonsense. To make this clear, let me elaborate.

According to Kuhn, whereas a pre-science does not have a standard textbook, every branch of science does have one. This is admirably clear cut and simple; one may now ask certain questions about the textbook and how it comes to be written, but these questions are secondary: the demarcation between pre-science and science has already been made, and discussing such questions would only elucidate it. This demarcation, however, will not work between science and petrified science (like contemporary phrenology or astrology). For this, another demarcation can easily be set, very much in the spirit of the present volume: Whereas the textbook of a petrified science is unchangeable, the science textbook is always alterable. (Indeed, yesterday's science textbook, if it survives, becomes today's pseudo-science, superstition, and/or petrified science; at least this holds for Marxist economic theory, astrology, and phrenology.) One may now ask again how a science textbook is changeable, and when does it have to undergo a change in order to escape becoming petrified? This question is subsidiary to the question of demarcating science from petrified science.

Can we demarcate science as such? Can we, in other words, demarcate science from all other intellectual activities, or theoretical systems, or whatever else? I do not know; following Popper's teaching, I would suggest that this cannot be achieved (as it would amount to finding the essence of science). But I would be less than fair to the author if I pretended that when demarcating science from pseudo-science Popper avoids the same pitfalls: I think all authors thus far have either identified or confused the *general* problem of demarcating science from everything else intellectual with the *special* problem of demarcating science from one of its neighbors which they would study—be it dogma, metaphysics, pseudo-science, or pre-science.

Kuhn demarcates science as such by describing one full cycle of its development from one given standard textbook to the next. As we have already noted, a science evolves with the evolution of its textbook. First, the textbook changes in small steps, by small modifications; and, by some process similar to Hegel's first law of dialectics, when the quantity of the minor modifications increases sufficiently to change the quality of the standard textbook from elegance to messiness, time is ripe for the development of a new textbook: this is the time of crisis. Following the crisis emerges the next textbook.

All this is not in the least to my liking, but it is a very popular theory of science, and one which gained popularity even among serious students of the philosophy of science when Duhem's views became popular; it is a view already foreshadowed by Duhem, though with him it is not half as central and elaborated as with Kuhn. And so I think it a great step forward that he has given it a careful presentation and as strong a defense as a critical scholar can. I think the fact that the present volume has been dismissed by a few commentators is not very happy, since they have failed to point out the popularity of this view in its less well-presented versions, or that Kuhn's version is an improvement on Duhem's view. Moreover, there is a kernel of truth in Kuhn's thesis, which I wish to discuss now.

The reasons against the thesis of the present volume are of a kind that can even be found toward the end of the volume itself: in many, if not most, cases there is no standard textbook to be found. Even in physics, it is difficult to find standard textbooks. Newton's mechanics between about 1700 and 1900, and his optics between 1700 and 1820, may easily count as standard textbooks. So might Coulomb's theory be viewed between, roughly, 1790 and 1820, and Maxwell's theory in some rather unspecified modification, say, between 1890 and 1920. Kuhn also mentions Lavoisier's and Dalton's theories, which are dubious examples. If Lavoisier's theory ever enjoyed universal acceptance, it did so for no more than twenty years, between Richard Kirwan's capitulation to Lavoisier and Davy's overthrow of his doctrine. Dalton's theory was refuted and modified scores of times in his own lifetime already, and opposition to it had a tradition beginning with Davy and ending with Mach and Oswald. By 1905, Dalton's atomism may have won, but long after its demise. Yet something is wrong here: excluding the last fifty years or so, and looking at the remaining three centuries or more of modern science, with its fast proliferation, one may be struck by the paucity of examples of standard textbooks or of widely accepted theories in the various fields of scientific endeavor. Certainly, we know that there is a body of knowledge in scientific fields, today at least. When did the change take place? Can we say that by and large science has just come of age? Surely this is rather preposterous.

There is a small but significant incongruity here. Admittedly, physics contains a body of knowledge: One who does not know the major assumption and certain central theorems of, say, Newtonian mechanics, or of Schrödinger's wave mechanics, will not count as a physicist anywhere in the Western world. But that does not mean that one has to accept them. On the contrary, one will not find a scientist believing these theories anywhere. The less established sciences are those where beliefs matter more and knowledge less. Sociology has scarcely a definite body of knowledge: will, for instance, one's claim that one is a sociologist be rejected if one is ignorant of Auguste Comte's sociology or of Georg Simmel's sociology of religion? Empirically, I wish to make the observation that this is not the case. Psychology fares even worse. In some universities in the United States people graduate in psychology after having acquired no more than a nodding acquaintance with that pseudo-scientist, Freud; in other universities, Freud's theory is so scientific, it is all that graduates really have to know. Even in economics, which is nearer to having a body of established theoretical background, how much of Marx's economics is accepted as belonging to that background is not yet entirely determined by the tradition of that field. But it is established that believing Marx is a Bad Thing, as it is established in sociology that believing Durkheim is a Good Thing.

In other words, though there is no such thing as a standard textbook of any science, the more established sciences have a standard introductory text which contains a standard body of theories—most, if not all of them, belong to the historical background of science and are by now superseded— and no standard accepted theory. This is an empirical observation which can easily be tested: We can intuitively list sciences in the order of their respectability, beginning, I suppose, with celestial mechanics and going through colloidal and bio-chemistry to economics and the other social sciences; one may then take a sample of introductory textbooks in these fields, on various levels, sophomore or higher level, and measure the degree of overlap between them by any reasonable rule of thumb: the more established sciences will show a higher degree of overlap in their introductory theory. This is not much of a test, but better than the test which Kuhn's theory fails to pass; so the present theory explains some observations, however few and crude.

The error Kuhn makes, thus, is in taking the standard body of knowledge to be the body of theory acquiesced in by practitioners of science. But acquiescence is not characteristic of science; rather, as many have stressed occasionally, and as Popper has declared to be the core of scientific philosophy, what characterizes science is a sense of criticism. A sense of criticism does involve some acquiescence—not to the truth of an idea, however, but to its significance.

Let me mention one instance which Kuhn himself refers to. Certainly, matrix quantum mechanics is part and parcel of the introductory text to science; but is it, or was it ever, a part of the standard text? Was it, in other words, ever accepted by physicists? "To be sure it does not supply the solution to the riddle," said Wolfgang Pauli a few months after its invention, "but I believe it is again possible to march forward." Marching forward, thus, is finding worthwhile ideas and examining them critically; not incorporating them in the standard scientific dogma of the day. The quotation from Pauli appears in the present volume. Yet it is used either as a support of the author's view, or, at most, as a qualification of his own theory: matrix quantum mechanics was not the standard text but the embryo of the standard text. This, I think, is but a mystification. If the text has an embryo, if after birth it changes, when exactly is its moment of birth?

The difference between a standard textbook of Kuhn's suggestion and a standard introductory text as envisaged here in a Popperian manner, is not merely, or even chiefly, a matter of characterizing science, but rather what is important in research. The fact reported by Kuhn is that, in a mature science, research is properly conducted without its practitioners' great knowledge of its rules. He seems to explain this strange fact by reference to the standard text: The method of inquiry is learned in each period from that period's standard text. The rise of the standard text, thus, not only is, but must remain, in Kuhn's theory, quite a mystery: the method of research is prescribed by different texts differently, and so one text is judged favorably by the method it prescribes, but unfavorably judged by others; thus it is no accident that, on the authority of science, Kuhn becomes plainly a collectivist (p. 167). Popper's answer to Kuhn's question: How does science develop without public knowledge of its rules? is answered in a much simpler manner: in the West most modern scholars know enough about criticism to keep things moving. Popper's characterization, however, is more constructive. Popper's proposal is that a (scientific?) discipline develops when enough people are sufficiently interested in a set of problems and are sufficiently agreed on what sort of solutions to them deserve critical examination. When the process of critical examination is sufficiently elaborate to bring in new empirical examination, that activity becomes part of empirical science. Yet, I think, all this also shows that Popper's demarcation of empirical science is somewhat deficient: empirical criticism of the Book of Genesis does not make that book a part of science; it is not merely empirical criticism, but a chain, a tradition, of criticism. Discrepancies of Popper's view can be smoothed out by putting greater emphasis on the social character of science—much in accord with his own suggestions, and with a modified version of Kuhn's. It is regrettable, in my opinion, that in the present volume Kuhn entirely ignores Popper; it is lamentable that he conceals this defect behind a page or so devoted to criticism of sorts of Popper's view; that page does not at all measure up to the high standard of clarity, accuracy, and interest manifest in most of the rest of the book.

In this brief note I centered only on the main issues of the volume. Let me stress that it contains quite a number of interesting arguments; the reader will benefit from examining them critically. Let me add that it discusses in a very intriguing way a number of allied topics. I can only mention here one striking example: Kuhn's theory of the continuity in the development of science goes much further than Duhem's. He boldly proposes that there is no clear-cut point in the history of science in which it may be claimed that a factual discovery came into being; discoveries never appear fully fledged in one go. This, if true, must lead us to serious reconsiderations of our views of a variety of topics, beginning with the history of discovery and ending with present-day rewards of individual discoverers. It is easier to dismiss Kunn's view as fantastic than to criticize it. I confess I find the idea refreshingly novel and fantastic, and it is with much regret that I cannot claim that it is thus far the best solution to the problem of demarcation of new facts. Indeed, Kuhn hardly presents any case for which his strikingly novel and interesting view proves satisfactory. The problem is too involved to be discussed here; I can only state briefly that Kuhn's view is a solution to the problem of criterion of novelty of facts, that no previous solution to this problem fits Duhem's theory of continuity, and that Duhem himself has entirely ignored this problem. Kuhn is braver and more consistent than Duhem. This point alone, I think, makes the present work significant to students of scientific method who take Duhem seriously—others do not really count. I hope that Kuhn will consider his own work no more final than the standard textbook of science, and I look forward to more interesting surprises from his elegant pen.

— 10 —

COHEN CONTRA KUHN

clues hidden in many details

Bernard Cohen's *Revolutions in Science*, (Cambridge: Harvard University Press, 1987) is dazzling in its breadth. An amazingly wide scope of detailed studies of an enormous diversity is packed into 20 pages of preface plus 472 large pages of text plus 100 pages of supplements, of odds-and-ends which do not quite fit, 49 pages of dense notes, 54 pages of bibliography and 34 pages of an index. The book reads easily and includes many delightful observations; some of them are amazingly thought-provoking. Is it a mere similarity, for example, of expressions in Friedrich Engels and Pierre Duhem, or did the famous revolutionary influence that great conservative? No answer. Much of the detailed discussion, consisting largely of analogies and comparisons, either merely titilates or raises problems, rather than offering new ideas. But the book has a thesis, "based on historical evidence": there are four criteria which, when satisfied, point at a scientific revolution (opening paragraph). After two chapters, one on scientific and political revolutions and one on Cohen's criteria, we have the data marshalled in centuries, from the 17th to the 20th, ending with a brief presentation of conversion, in the religious sense, as a feature of scientific revolutions.

The nuggets, perhaps, are the supplements. An essay by two modern writers on David Hume as a revolutionary social scientist, an essay on Ludwig Boltzmann or on Ernst Mach, or Claude Bernard on science and scientific revolutions, Engels on science, the Electra complex, and more. Each is an informative essay in its own right. What ties them together is loosely something to do with revolutions. But the accent seems to be on the word 'loosely'. The looseness of Cohen's presentation is reflected in the reader's inability to see the relevance of many details, the choice of these details, and

Not previously published.

so on. It looks as if the author hurls at the reader's head any handy detail. But I am side-tracked. Let me return.

The historical details, we are told in the opening paragraph, substantiate the author's four criteria for a scientific revolution. We can show at once that this is questionable, since the author seems to agree too much and praise too highly the ideas on the matter of all of his esteemed colleagues, incuding Henry Guerlac, Alexandre Koyré, Karl Popper, and to an extent even Thomas S. Kuhn. There was a rabbi who once agreed with both litigants who were appearing before his court; when he was told that he could not do so, he agreed yet again.

Just for fun, however, let us examine Cohen's "set of criteria . . . for the occurrence of a scientific revolution":

C_1: The originator of a revolution knows that it is a revolution and says so.
C_2: The revolutionary idea then floods the literature in a gush.
C_3: Historians say it was a revolution.
C_4: Scientists say so too.
Let us now stipulate a few abbreviations:

p = x is a revolution;
q = x satisfies all the conditions of C_1 to C_4;
r = x satisfies at least one of the conditions C_1 to C_4
T_1: if p then q;
T_2: if q then p;
$T_3 = T_1 + T_2$.
T_4: if r then p;
T_5: if p then r;
$T_6 = T_4 + T_5$.

We can now observe the following two points:

(1)   The content of q or r may increase or decrease, depending on the stringency of the application of the criteria;
(2)   when the content of q or r increases then the content of T_1 or of T_4 respectively increases and the content of T_2 or T_5 respectively decreases.

The reader is invited to check whether Cohen applies his criteria stringently or loosely and which T he has in mind. If anyone finds the answer, I will be pleased to learn what it is. In the meantime we should notice that Cohen's criteria may be much too weak and much too strong. Finally, the book discusses the possibility of revolutions of different sizes and kinds, so that we have many additional possible readings.

All this is perhaps neither here nor there, except that it is a comment on the only theoretical point in the book.

The criteria mentioned are intentionally external, presented in an attempt to apply them to known cases of true or alleged revolutions. Cohen stresses that the true concern with scientific revolutions is intellectual: they are new solutions or new techniques or other significant novelties which severely affect our ways of thinking. In other words, we have to apply the external and the internal criteria and try to match them.

What then are the internal criteria? What novelties are revolutions?

There are competing answers to this question, but the most famous is known as radicalism. The radicalist criterion holds that a revolution is not a new idea but the act which obliterates the past and presents us with a clean slate to develop solid science on.

This very important criterion has led to two or three very important theories of scientific revolutions: Bacon's, Duhem's and variants on Bacon, all false but still very important.

Bacon demanded that a scientific revolution be effected, that all preconceived notions be set aside, and that science begin anew and on solid foundations. Clearly, in his view only one scientific revolution can occur, since it wipes out all past developments as worthless, including past revolutions. (Bacon says explicitly that the victory of Aristotle over all his predecessors is quite worthless.)

The obvious variant on Bacon's radicalism is the one taken by Hume, Lavoisier, and lesser lights, including, in our century, J. B. Watson (p. 375). Quite intuitively, and as if unproblematically, they all divided science into many fields of study and allowed as many revolutions—one in each field.

This attitude is what caused the ceremonial burning of a magnificent book by Georg Ernst Stahl at an appropriate occasion in Laviosier's home. This same attitude is what caused Henry Guerlac to invest a highly productive lifetime in the worthless distortion of Lavoisier's work to prove that everything he said as a scientist still holds today in science. (The reader is invited to check in Cohen's book and see that Cohen is aware of the fact, rejects Baconianism and Guerlac's Baconian history of science and will not say so.)

Opposed to radicalism is the continuity theory of Pierre Duhem. Science cannot start fresh, and hence there is no scientific revolution by the radicalist criterion. There never was a cleaning of the slate.

This attitude is what caused Duhem, and his followers, most of them orthodox Roman Catholics like himself, to revive medieval science. Scholars impressed with a Duhemian or post-Duhemian text which presents medieval science should consult some medieval texts. They will see that whereas the modern presentation is made of hard steel and transparent glass, the medieval original is a flamboyantly Gothic mixture of snippets of religion, metaphysics, superstition, and some undigested ideas, usually ancient. Yet the Duhemian opponents to radicalism may retort, rightly I think, that many modernist works are just as medieval, such as those of Paracelsus and even Kepler. The enormous similarity between *De Revolutionibus* of Copernicus and the *Almagest* of Ptolemy is stressed in Derek J. de Solla Price's classic 'Contra-Copernicus'. The debt of Bacon to his medieval predecessors is by now well known, but the debt of Descartes to his predecessors is less well-known, even though both Alexandre Koyré and Etienne Gilson have shown it, and this is mentioned in Edmund Husserl's important *Cartesian Meditations*. Yet Descartes's style is modern, whereas Bacon is the peak of the flamboyant.

Duhem lived in the midst of the revolution in which field theories replaced action-at-a-distance theories. He wanted scientific progress, but only if its revolutionary detonators could be safely defused. To that end he went back to Bellarmine's attack on Galileo, sided with Bellarmine, and hoped for a rapprochement between science and religion. The series of revolutions in science are not revolutions in the radicalist sense, and so they must be reinterpreted, Duhem taught. And this has an enormous appeal—especially for anyone who has begun as a radicalist but will not give up classical science as a whole. Duhem offers to such a disturbed soul a new view of things and an entry to religion as a by-product. How irresistible! (The reader is invited to check in Cohen's book and see that Cohen is aware of the validity of Duhem's critique of radicalism, that he is appalled by Duhem's conservative hostility to field theory, that he rejects Duhem's continuity theory and will not say so.)

Having disposed of the two crystal-clear extremist views which share the definition of a scientific revolution as a clean start, we must now ask, what alternative view of scientific revolutions we have.

The simplest is the view—offered by Sir Karl Popper—of a revolution as an overthrow, with the overthrow of a minor idea as a minor revolution and of a major one as a major one. The overthrow, says Popper, opens new intellectual vistas. This invites a confusion: in the radicalist sense of the word overthrow is the burning of books. And so, many people object to viewing Newton's ideas as overthrown—just because the thought of burning Newton's book makes them shudder. These people should take a good look at themselves and ask themselves if they shudder at the idea of the burning of Stahl's books; if they do not mind the burning of Stahl's book, then they should be ashamed of themselves. Stahl's book is not half as exciting as Newton's, but it is admirable all the same.

The idea that revolutions are overthrows which do not lead to the burning of books has led some writers, such as Robert Schoffield and myself, to attempt to rehabilitate phlogistonism: it is absurd to consider the great precursors of Lavoisier, especially Black, Priestley and Cavendish, merely prejudiced and superstitious. Guerlac once tried hard to present Black as a non-phlogistonist. It is better to see why individuals like John Kirwan marvelled at the fact that phlogistonism was once so admired and then so despised (see p. 236): it was the radicalism of the age that made it look so. Now we know better.

The reader is invited to check and see that Cohen is familiar with all that and, indeed, expressed as much agreement with Popper as he can without outright committing himself to the endorsement of his view and the rejection of its competitors. His presentation of the rise of quanta in pages 425-29 is as Popperian as I have ever seen.

The view offered by Popper presents scientific research as autonomous. It agrees that a researcher may be inspired by extra-scientific factors, even by metaphysics, namely by intellectual frameworks widespread at the time. Yet science, Popper said, is not concerned with the origin of ideas, only with their empirical testability and empirical tests.

Alexandre Koyré, and under his influence I. Bernard Cohen, approached matters differently, and viewed revolutions as the changes of intellectual frameworks. Following Gaston Bachelard, they accepted both trial-and-error and scientific revolutions as given. This is really not such a great insight after Einstein. Indeed, Cohen quotes a personal report from Guerlac about Koyré's observation that he was [also] influenced quite significantly by E. A. Burtt (p. 613 n3—somehow not in the index under Burtt). I once asked Burtt if he was influenced by Einstein. He smiled and said pensively, "Perhaps, quite possibly." After all, could one speak of the tyranny of Newtonianism so openly before it was exposed as not-the-last-word?

Cohen's classic *Newton and Franklin* shows Franklin's work as within the Newtonian intellectual framework of action at a distance. Einstein's relativity theories are field theories. They signal a revolution both in the empirical overthrow of one scientific theory through its replacement by another, and the replacement of one intellectual framework by another. And, of course, at the same time a new framework was forged, of quantum mechanics (especially of relativistic quantum mechanics).

One need not check to learn that Cohen knows that a theory exists which says that scientific revolutions, genuine, far-reaching ones, are those where frameworks are changed with the overthrow of detailed items. It is his.

Cohen shows subtlety here, and subtlety which will be lost on the ingenuous reader. It is the fact that revolutions can even go further than the change of intellectual framework: there are changes of religious ideologies as well, whatever an ideology is. And here Cohen explicitly sides with Popper: such a change of ideology is really a revolution, but never a scientific one, even when inspired by science: except when the ideology is that of science, of course; and what is that ideology?

There still is one important theory—that of Thomas S. Kuhn, author of *The Structure of Scientific Revolutions*—that says, a scientific revolution is a change of paradigm. What is a paradigm? It does not matter much, says Kuhn. Pity.

Cohen observes that and adds, "But Kuhn's analysis has the solid merit of reminding us that the occurrence of revolution is a regular feature of scientific change and that a revolution in science has a social component—the acceptance of the new paradigm by the scientific community" (p. 27). This highly laudatory-sounding sentence is an insult: reminding us is all that Kuhn has ever done. And so we really need not endorse his views (pp. 40, 403, 559, 578). Why, then is he so influential (pp. 23, 371, 389)? First and foremost, he seems simplistic (p. 27), yet only because details of his views are not elaborately checked (pp. 309, 578, 584 n3; the last item not in the index). Second, because he presents revolutions as religious conversions, which is often true enough and understandable, yet so impressive (p. 105, 379, 464, 468 and 467–72, which last is the concluding chapter). Yet conversion is more to be associated with non-science, pseudo-science and pseudo-revolutions (pp. 31ff.). On page 378 Cohen views Kuhn's ideas as a repeat of Eddington's. Pages 387–88 of Cohen's book are simply aggressive against Kuhn. Peter Medawar is quoted there to say that the assent Kuhn receives from scientists is but a symptom of their lack of interest in "what they think of as philosophizing". Cohen adds to this the conjecture that by now many scientists simply show hostility to Kuhn because his description of typical scientists is unflattering. All this is not serious, at least not more serious than Kuhn's work. Anyone who has studied the case empirically has to agree that as a first approximation scientists approve of Kuhn because he staunchly supports the establishment of science and approves of revolutions in science no more than an American political conservative does who approves of the American Revolution. Cohen reports hostility on the part of scientists against his writing a book on revolutions. Such hostility shows more ambivalence among contemporary intellectuals than anything more specific, I think. Finally, Kuhn is popular because he encourages and justifies the disposition, so popular among scientists, to ignore history and yield to peer pressure (p. 397). To this one can add Kuhn's luck in publishing his book on scientific revolutions coincidentally with the plate tectonic revolution (pp. 448 and 563–69).

All this is intriguing and question-begging. Cohen disarmingly declares he has only begun the study. Cohen's book is vastly informative, and hardly any reader, however erudite, can be expected to have even heard of every author cited in it. Yet there are conspicuous omissions. Derek J. de Solla Price on Copernicus, Lane Cooper on Galileo, Vasco Ronchi, not to mention the critics of Bacon as excessive in his revolutionary claims (such as Robert Leslie Ellis and R. F. Jones, no less!); and the critics of the Royal Society of London as excessive in its revolutionary claims (Hobbes, Henry Moore, and Henry Stubbes). It is clear that often Cohen cites authors whom he disagrees with or even disapproves of. The reticence concerning some relevant works, then, seems to be a special form of severe censure. Perhaps. One way or another, it is impossible not to ascribe to Cohen's book a certain obvious imbalance, even by current standards, not to mention the more reasonable standard which requires the mention of some commentators on Darwinism who are usually ignored by the Establishment, such as Samuel Butler and even George Bernard Shaw, not to mention Kropotkin. I should also say, with no false modesty, that Cohen's remarks on Faraday and Maxwell are pallid by comparison with my study which he knows but prefers not to mention—perhaps because I have argued, contrary to his criterion 1, that Faraday was conservative in disposition. But we must return to Kuhn. Cohen agrees with Kuhn that the institutions of science have to be more carefully considered than hitherto noticed; he even notices Ian Hacking's generalization of some "implied suggestion" of Kuhn (pp. 95, 101) to say that every "big" scientific revolution is concomitant with an institutional reform. He evidently finds this fascinating. Or does he pull our legs?

What does all this amount to? Perhaps I do not see it fall into pattern because I have been too selective in my presentation. But what can I do with a book so full of so many details and no clear-cut clues? The background information about the intellectual aspects of scientific revolutions offered here may be mistaken; the question, how good is it as a representation of Cohen's book cannot be studied without much tedious textual analysis of this obviously untidy book which is written much too diplomatically to be clear. Yet we do have Cohen's external criteria, and the historical evidence on which he says it is based. How? How can one decide about criteria, internal or external, by historical evidence? I think Cohen owes us just a little explanation.

Historical evidence can refute Bacon, Duhem, Kuhn too, perhaps (depending on how much of Kuhn we take at face value). We hardly need historical evidence to learn that science is a social venture, that some of it is unsavory, some of it is of little value and some of it is the best we ever had. How are we going to investigate all this? Can we put empirical hypotheses and test them? What hypotheses does Cohen offer in this book?

I do not know. I have a conjecture. I think it is all an elaborate ruse, a cloud of lovely but half-relevant and irrelevant material surrounding the core of criticisms of Kuhn, and some allusions to more criticisms. Let me stress this, and put it side-by-side with Cohen's own disclaimer, which he has put in a prominent place in his book (conclusion of his preface). As historians are able to see through declared intents of authors and find, or claim to find, the intents that transpire through their books, it is permissible for commentators on them to do the same. This is not to deny Cohen's disclaimer, nor to endorse it; this is not to analyze Cohen's state of mind; and this is certainly as remote from questioning his veracity as to his motive. Clearly, he means to say his work should not be read as a [mere] critique of Kuhn but "as an attempt to examine the subject of revolution in science from a new and strictly historical viewpoint". We may, then, look at the disclaimer as presented in a fine ambiguity: Kuhn may be said to have been left sideways and he may be said to have been left way behind. This kind of ambiguity is very common, especially in the scientific literature of the 18th century. It is an out-dated form of politeness. But Cohen's intent, whatever it is, clearly clashes with the way his book looks to his contemporaries. My conjecture that Cohen's aim is a concealed critique of Kuhn, by the way, has been aired by other commentators on this book already. Suppose this conjecture is true. What can one say about it?

Circumlocution was introduced into the tradition of science by Robert Boyle, who said explicit criticism of a hypothesis only discourages its originator and so ought to be avoided. Boyle warned individuals he considered outsiders that he would explicitly criticize them if they continued saying unsavory things about certain insiders! Even Robert Boyle was not perfect. Were his successor someone other than the hyper-neurotic and superb scientist Sir Isaac Newton, Boyle's folly could be corrected. But Newton became, as E. A. Burtt observes, an authority much superior to Aristotle. It is no accident that the scientific revolution in optics, usually dated 1818, is not mentioned in this book, nor Thomas Young, nor Fresnel except, explicitly, in the 1820s (p. 95). In brief, the revolution in optics was suppressed because the great Newton allegedly could not be mistaken. William Whewell's classic critical discussion of Newton's optics is not alluded to either. Cohen is presumably aware of my claim that the refutation of Newton's optics was an earthquake. But he overlooks it. Why? And he mentions Popper's claim that Einstein has brought about a methodological revolution—but he does not explain that Einstein made us see that revolutions are a part of science, a fact that Kuhn had to remind us of, as Cohen says, we may remember. Why? Because these conflict with his criteria?

Although Einstein refuted the views of science current at the time, and although for a while scientists forgot their diplomacy—E. T. Whittaker cited in his 1913 talk to the British Association, the popular, robust saying, 'if the ink has dried on it, it's already out-of-date'—the good manners instilled in the scientific tradition by Boyle and Newton prevailed. And historians of science, especially Henry Guerlac, kept consciously and systemtically distorting history in a Baconian fashion as if Einstein had not existed.

What shall we have, blunt truthfulness or circumlocution? Why is diplomacy needed? Why all the tacit understanding? Are scientists still as discouraged when their errors are exposed as in the 17th century? Even though we now recognize that some ideas are excellent though they need rectification?

On one point Cohen agrees with Kuhn—and they are both right. When a revolutionary idea is employed, it takes a large mopping-up operation to bring older and lesser ideas in line with it. When relativity is accepted in physics, a lot of specific ideas in physics have to be relativized. When radicalism is overthrown, likewise, many institutions of science have to be remodelled. This remodelling will enable Cohen to rewrite his book in a ready and easily comprehensible manner. The time will come when explicit criticism will be taken not as a put-down but rather as a sign of appreciation. Certainly this is the way my criticism of Cohen is offered: as a sign of appreciation.

— 11 —

GOODFIELD ON THE HISTORY OF BIOLOGY

continuity in dissent

June Goodfield's paper on the recent history of genetic theory contains new and interesting ideas cast in an old and vulnerable philosophical framework. In an effort toward making a just comment on her valuable paper, I offer the following constructive criticism.

The question, Does a certain theoretical entity exist? is nowadays very fashionable. What it really means is very hard to understand. Indeed, I have the suspicion that its being hard to understand is viewed as its chief asset. Take the question, Do atoms exist? which, folklore has it, has been affirmatively answered with Einstein's study of Brownian motion of 1905. This question-and-answer, this myth, almost assuredly will fend off any self-respecting critic since the critic's first move must be that contemptible and bothersome ploy: "It all depends on what you mean by 'atoms'." Indeed, if atoms are what old Democritus had meant, then surely, we can say, Democritean atoms are not declared to exist by anyone. Come to think of it, even atoms as conceived by Einstein in the first decade of the century, prior to Rutherford and Bohr, cannot be said to exist. Now, perhaps this last claim is less obvious than the previous one: Democritean atoms more obviously do not exist than 1905-Einsteinian atoms do not exist. But to be clearer we have to explain what exactly is the theoretical entity, '1905-Einsteinian atom' and what exactly do we claim when we say that it exists. Hence, when we say, atoms exist as Einstein showed in 1905, as Goodfield says, the unclarity of the claim is almost painful.

This was a comment from the floor to June Goodfield's 'Theories and Hypotheses in Biology: Theoretical Entities and Functional Explanations'; both were published in *Boston Studies in the Philosophy of Science*, 5, 1969. The original title was 'Theoretical Entities versus Theories'. Copyright 1969 by D. Reidel Publishing Company, Dordrecht, Holland.

Let us say 'Democritean atoms exist' is true if and only if Democritus's theory is true in the ordinary correspondence sense of 'true'; '1905-Einsteinian atoms exist' is true if and only if the theory Einstein expounded in his 1905 paper on Brownian motion is true; etc. This strict interpretation clarifies all claims for existence of theoretical entities very much—to the point of making them utterly redundant and replaceable by claims for the truth of the theories regarding these entities. Let us toy with this interpretation for a while and see why, though it lurks behind, it is never explicitly endorsed or rejected.

In the strict interpretation offered here, we may easily claim existence for 1905-Einsteinian atoms, even though they are endowed with indivisibility (which was implicitly given all atoms in 1905), simply because indivisibility happens to be irrelevant to the theory of Brownian motion. Not so the organizer: in the strict interpretation here offered, organizers do not exist since the organizer theory has been superseded. Goodfield feels that this is not as easily said as, for example, that the crystal spheres of the planets, as postulated by so many ancient astronomers, do not exist. And she is right. I only wish she had articulated and explained this point.

The idea that the history of science is a graveyard for defunct theories is somehow disturbing to most scientists, philosophers, and historians of science. Yet, Goodfield shows, such is a segment of history—German biology of the inter-war period, the famous organizer theory. Let me not enlarge again, à la Popper, my view that rejected theories are a part of our heritage, and that therefore there is nothing disturbing about rejection so-called, namely about correction of error. I have done so elsewhere. Rather, let me say, there are a few different views concerning history to meet the disturbing fact that the history of science is a graveyard. The first is Whewell's, in retrospect a Darwinian view: we must invent many hypotheses because only few of them survive tests and these are the ones that matter, the hard core around which research develops.

Goodfield's study shows that this view is somehow unsatisfactory here: it makes us reject a chunk of history which we can forget only reluctantly: intuitively we find the history of the organizer theory so interesting and stimulating, and full of a life of its own and even a logic of its own.

Two alternatives to Whewell's view concerning continuity in history, or perhaps three, are offered in the literature. The first is to introduce some ambiguity into Whewell's view: not, only those theories count which are literally true, but also the *essentially* true: history may show the need to modify a theory here or tinker with it there, especially to replace a working or an auxiliary hypothesis. Indeed, such ambiguity, it may transpire, is none other than the one we began with: a concept, to signify, must denote an essence, and the view I am adumbrating here is that some theories are significant though they are not literally true: they are, however, in essence right.

A more sophisticated view is Duhem's theory of continuity: all theories undergo modification, but slow modification and not all at once, so that a certain stability is always retained.

A third, and more daring view, is due to E. A. Burtt and Alexandre Koyré, according to whom certain broad—metaphysical—hypotheses are accepted by a whole tradition of scientific research, thus providing unity over time and through varieties of changes, in the form of research programs, or, as Gerald Holton calls them, themes, or, as Kuhn calls them, paradigms.

Whether a theme is an essence, a metaphysics, or a transient similarity emerging from slow changes, there is a difficulty in applying the idea of a theme to the history of *Entwicklungsmechanik* or ontogenesis of the first half of the century. There is some continuity, no doubt, between the pre-war organizer theory and the post-war nucleic-acid theories. And yet the war, so extraneous to biology, caused a visible fault, a real break!

The coincidence between the termination of research along a blind alley and the start of World War II permits the raising of a few problems. Could it be that discontinuity is there all the time but that usually we bridge it *post hoc*, with exceptions like wars? Was there a metaphysics common to the German inter-war researchers and the RNA Anglo-American post-war students? If so, is it not the case that metaphysical connections do not explain it all? In particular, is not our view of the history of science too much colored by the views of the actors in the historical events?

For my part, I think a mode of continuity still sadly overlooked by historians is that of disagreement with, and criticism of, our predecessors. And, indeed, later geneticists certainly did not ignore their predecessors but rather responded to their failures. There is continuity in disagreement.

SUBJECTIVISM—FROM INFANTILE DISEASE TO CHRONIC ILLNESS

the Red King and the Bayesians

The classic distinction which I was taught in all my undergraduate philosophy courses equates objectivism with realism with materialism, and contrasts the three with subjectivism which is identified with idealism. I have discussed the distinction between materialism and realism in my book on Faraday, an anti-materialist realist. Here I wish to discuss the difference between subjectivism and idealism, not on account of Hegel's objectivist idealism, which is justly dismissed as confused, but both to show that idealism is usually objectivist, and in an attempt to place on a clear map the modern subjectivist school of induction, the Bayesian school so-called. I shall try to place all subjectivism within the epistemological error of empiricism and verificationism combined. I shall argue that Bayesianism can only gain its vindication from objectivist, not subjectivist, arguments, and that it is bogged down in subjectivism only because the vindication does not deliver the goods. In brief, as a stage in an argument or an intellectual development subjectivism is understandable; fixed subjectivism is simply the outcome of getting stuck early in the game and showing too much inflexibility to extricate oneself.

1. SUBJECTIVISM VERSUS ONTOLOGY

Subjectivity can be opposed in two ways: to reality and to intersubjectivity: the subjective can be opposed to the real and to the common. The word 'objective', incidentally, may signify at times the real and at times the common (common to several subjects). Compare the expressions 'objective fact', and 'objective estimation' in the given situation.

Synthese, 30, 1975. Copyright 1975 by D. Reidel Publishing Company, Dordrecht, Holland.

We are witnesses here to a systematic confusion which I think is intentional, and it is the confusion of the real with the common. There is nothing simpler to overcome than a confusion: once articulated a confusion becomes a doctrine, be that doctrine true or false. The doctrine here is called naive realism and it was articulated at least as early as Heraclitus, who said: the dream is private, the common real. Plato had already noted that if the whole community lives in the same cave, then all its members may share the same illusion.

And so, although Plato agreed with Heraclitus about the subjective, he was troubled about the objective. The private opinion, the *doxa*, may be a sheer whim, a private individual caprice. This does not imply that the view shared by a whole community is no caprice: on the contrary, the mob is fickle and it may follow the whim of any individual. Plato wanted *epistēmē*, true knowledge, to ensure that his views were objective, real, true. Kant gave up all hope for objectivity and settled once and for all for the intersubjective, for that which is given neither to the whim of an individual nor to the whim of a single community, but which all thinking beings as such must share.

Let us ignore for a moment the intersubjective altogether; let us ignore subjectivism as well. We may center on the pure object, on the real, and ask what it is made of. Strangely enough, almost any noun can serve as an answer to the question: what is the world made of? We can say, green cheese: the world is made of green cheese. Or we can say, sheer hysteria: the world is made of sheer hysteria. This may puzzle the naive onlooker. To say the world is made of green cheese is silly not only because we have in the world chalk and cheese, red and green, but also because the answer simply raises the question, what is green cheese made of, and then we are back where we started.

Let this be so. It follows, simply, that 'green cheese' is not a good answer to 'what is the world made of?' But an answer it remains, though it is, no doubt, a bad answer. Now, of course, we do have questions to which 'green cheese' is no answer at all, good or bad, such as all yes-or-no questions, all how-much questions, indeed all how questions, all who-done-it questions, etc. Assume, then, that green cheese is something the world can be made of, as a matter of grammar, at least. By contrast, there are things which the world cannot be made of, such as numbers, and even for reasons of grammar alone, the long and venerable Pythagorean tradition notwithstanding. I am speaking of the grammar of Russell's *Principia*, of course. According to this grammar, numbers are classes of classes of things (things being objects or events) and the principle of stratification, then, precludes numbers themselves from being things. This is so, mark you, according to any definition of number we have, and so we must take the Pythagorean 'all is number' metaphorically—which we do anyway. But the world can be made of classes of events and we can declare all objects to be loving—as a matter of grammar. This result is counter-intuitive not because we all feel very strongly that stones are objects devoid of the ability to love, or to suffer pain. It is counter-intuitive because we often feel that it does not make sense to say such things of stones, and that stones must be declared objects proper, so that grammar rules out answers like 'all things are made of love'.

As ever so often with commonsense intuitions, they are expressions of old and rejected theories. We have an intuition about grammar, according to which thinking, or willing, or suffering, or walking, implies the existence of a thinking or willing or walking object. It is the grammar of Aristotle, which was out-of-date already when published, 25 centuries ago. That Aristotle is behind this kind of thinking transpires clearly from the Descartes-Hobbes debate. Hobbes asked why 'I think, therefore, I exist'? Why not, 'I walk therefore I exist'? And Descartes saw the point and allowed that indeed if I walk then of necessity I exist; but, he said: I am not sure I walk; I am sure I think; and this is why I prefer 'I think therefore I exist', to 'I walk therefore I exist'. He did not doubt the validity of the inference, 'I walk therefore I exist', only the assumption, 'I walk'. More clearly this is shown in Lichtenberg's modification of Descartes's argument which Heine adopted when criticizing Fichte, which shows a clear awareness of the dependence of the argument on the subject-predicate logic. 'I think', says Lichtenberg, smuggles in a hidden assumption about the subject. We can put the subject more vaguely, as in the expression 'it rains'. 'It thinks, therefore, it exists'—it being the thinking thing. For Fichte, however, the subject has to be an actor proper. And so, in his *Human Destiny* he begins not with thinking but with I, and with 'am I free'? And he says, since the world is *my* dream I control it and so it does not control *me*. It is this, a difference within the same logic, which makes any version of Cartesian idealism—only thinking things exist—objectivist, and Fichte's idealism both subjectivist and an incredibly silly expression of hubris or megalomania.*

And so we see that idealism is naturally objectivist, not subjectivist. It is no accident that whereas idealism is the most popular philosophy all over the civilized world, subjectivism is a very peculiar western phenomenon. Also, if we grant that the classical western idealistic views, ancient and modern, are more often objectivist than subjectivist, if we grant that Descartes's 'I think therefore I exist' does actually mean, as Lichtenberg and Heine seem to suggest, that something thinks therefore it exists, then we must agree that even the Cartesian idealism which Descartes rejects

---

*Professor Roberto Torretti tells me that I misrepresent Fichte. Perhaps I even misrepresent his *Human Destiny*. The argument here does not hinge on this matter, especially since I correctly represent Heine.

ultimately is objectivist. Subjectivism was invented in the West by Bishop Berkeley and further developed by Fichte.

I first distinguished the two opposites to the subjective, namely, the real and the intersubjective, and then I discussed the question of what is real. I concluded that possibly the real is the will or the thinking entity, thus arguing that idealism is realistic, not subjectivist. In other words, I was engaging in an exercise pertaining to ontology, and I said, when an ideal or mental ontology is postulated we have before us an objectivist idealism. The question one could ask at once is 'What does a subjectivist ontology look like?' The answer, I am afraid, is very shaky. The answer can be, perhaps, something like solipsism: only I exist, whatever I am. This, however, is fairly objectivist: Spinoza was an objectivist who said only God exists, and Fichte was, perhaps, an objectivist who said only Fichte exists. But what earned him the label 'subjectivist' is, we saw, his claim that the world does not exist, that it was only his dream. The philosopher who best understood this point—that subjectivism is not an ontology but an anti-ontology—was Lewis Carroll, who said: the world is the Red King's dream; wake him up and poof! we all vanish.

But even Lewis Carroll's perspicacious and perspicuous invention, subjectivist though it surely is, is objectivist enough: it declares that we, Alice, you and I do not exist, but that at least the Red King does.

In a last-ditch effort I may try out the idea: nothing exists, everything is but a dream (including the Red King who is a work of fiction). This sounds logically faulty, as a dream may imply a real dreamer. But this is not so, as we saw, and as was proven by Quine as rigorously as any philosophical point was ever proven. So quite possibly nothing exists. Call this nihilism, and ascribe it to Kratyllos. Nihilism clearly is objectivist and not in the least subjectivist; indeed, it dismisses out of hand my strong subjective conviction of my own very existence.

Here, then, subjective is that which clashes with ontology. Any perusal, even a slight one, of the philosophic literature, including Hegel's texts, will reveal that 'subjective' means at times simply 'a false intuition'. At times, also, by extension, it means 'unfounded'. If my ontology is proven, by the way, then your ontology must be unfounded and false. But whereas I may claim mine to be proven and so objective, you may claim the same. And so you will claim mine subjective and I, likewise, yours.

A source of terrible confusion has now entered. I said: if my ontology is proven then it is objective. By now 'objective' means 'true because proven' or may so mean. And soon 'objective' may mean 'proven'. But this might be quite objectionable. The word 'proven', unlike the word 'true', holds aspects of two different traditional areas of inquiry, ontology and epistemology. Let me first sum up my claim: there is no subjectivist ontology; the subjective may be contrasted with ontology as such. 'I have a subjective feeling that you are my enemy but I do not say that you are' is the paradigm. Once my feeling is proven, then you also are, but you may be my enemy without my having proof, or even subjective feelings. Your being my enemy in fact is ontology, my feeling of it is subjective, and my proof of it is epistemology. To epistemology, then.

2. SUBJECTIVISM VERSUS EPISTEMOLOGY

We begin with the parallel subjective-objective and subjective-intersubjective. The most obvious intersubjective will be proof and so we can replace subjective-intersubjective, tentatively at least, with *doxa-epistēmē* or opinion-knowledge. We may then say, *doxa* is arbitrary and so subjective; each to his *doxa*; but *epistēmē* is compelling and so common, and pertains to the true common, to the necessarily common, which is the real. It follows at once, that just as subjectivism was not an ontology but extra-ontological, subjectivism now turns out to be not an epistemology but extra-epistemological. I confess I like that enormously.

Let me here insert a warning. Just as I am no idealist yet I tolerate idealism, so I am no epistemologist yet here I tolerate epistemology. That is to say, supposing some knowledge of the world possible, I wish to say that the subjective has nothing to do with knowledge; whether what I say or think or feel or fancy or perceive, is either purely subjective, i.e., unproven, or also intersubjective, i.e., proven, i.e., objective. The purely subjective is that which is not also proven and which is not also intersubjective.

Whereas the proven is intersubjective, we made the hypothesis that the intersubjective is also the proven; but even without this hypothesis the conclusion we had just arrived at holds, namely that the purely subjective is that which is not also proven and which is not also intersubjective.

This was the case until the mid-18th century when Berkeley invented the impossible, namely subjectivist epistemology. For, clearly, whatever is proven is real, and so subjectivist epistemology now becomes also an ontology! What this amounts to, of course, is nothing but absurdity. But I shall take it slowly, step by step, and explain the confusing situation.

The idea that Berkeley's subjective idealism or subjectivism or subjectivist epistemology or ontology, that Berkeley's doctrine, in brief, is absurd, is not in any way a novelty. All through the 18th century and well into the 19th century, thinkers of all sorts were convinced that Newton's cosmology had been scientifically proven, i.e., *epistēmē*. From which it follows that Berkeley's ontology is false; subjective. Hence Berkeley's epistemology is absurd.

Can matters rest there? What do we do when we find a counter-example to a proven established theorem, or a theorem which contradicts it? We have a choice: we can declare the counter-example or the counter-theorem false. Or we can declare the allegedly established theorem false. Examples exist in the history of mathematics which go hither and thither, and I shall do no more than direct the curious for details (and the details are as exciting as the work in which they appear), to Imre Lakatos's epoch-making 'Proofs and Refutations' in the *British Journal for the Philosophy of Science* of 1963–64. What Lakatos illustrates, likewise, is that we do not merely scrap the alleged proof of the alleged theorem or example, but we try to find the fault in the proof, the step that took us off the straight and narrow.

Whether this strategy is correct or not is hard to say. Intuitively we all feel the urge to be able to explain where a proof went wrong. In real life, however, and this must be a correction to Lakatos's admirable strategy, at times we simply cannot correct the error so easily as pinpoint the erroneous step in the deduction. It usually seems preferable to continue our studies knowing that we owe it to ourselves to pinpoint, even if we cannot correct, any error we find. I am doing no more than articulating Diderot's view of Berkeley's error.

Though I agree with Diderot's judgment that life must go on, I also think with him that it is risky to let an error lie long undetected. The reason for this is all too obvious: we may incorporate the error in other reasonings of ours, and so not only multiply errors, but also get into a bad habit of refusing to stand corrected even when someone does happen to pinpoint the mistake. But let me leave it at that and proceed with Berkeley's error.

Berkeley's error was only half-heartedly meant to be advocated as a scientific philosophy; the other half of his intention being a theologian's delight in reducing science to absurdity. And indeed, Berkeley half-believed his own philosophy, half-believed the more traditional Christian view of the world.

This is not an *ad hominem* argument meant to silence an opponent; it is an observation which explains some of Berkeley's tortured argumentation and makes it more feasible. What Berkeley seems to say is this. There is only one cosmology which has some *a priori* grounds, and it is Cartesianism. But Cartesianism is defective and scientists anyway reject it in favor of Newtonianism. Therefore, we must stick by empiricist epistemology. What can we establish by empirical means?

Here comes the strongest part of Berkeley's philosophy, and of Hume's too, and of Mach's and Russell's and others: we cannot establish by any empirical means anything objective: all empirical experience is subjective and therefore all it can possibly establish is subjective *eo ipso*.

I personally hold that this is logically true, and I know of no effort to refute it that has made even the slightest dent in it: empirically we can establish only our subjective experiences. More precisely, I can establish my experiences. At this point there appears in Berkeley's reasoning, somewhat implicitly, an added hypothesis, which I have already alluded to a few times in this essay. It is what Sir Karl Popper has christened the Doctrine of

Manifest Truth or of Truth as Manifest. The doctrine says that what in principle cannot be proven in principle cannot be true. More precisely, and following Descartes, what you cannot prove as yet, you must consider false, and what you can never prove surely is false. Descartes's rule is inconsistent: when I cannot prove a statement and I cannot prove its negation either, Descartes obliges me to declare both false, i.e., both true. And so, let us drop the counsel to declare false an unproven thesis. But even the rule, 'declare false what cannot in principle be proven', may run into trouble if both a statement and its negation are in principle unprovable. Take, then, the weakest version of the Doctrine of Manifest Truth: what cannot in principle be proven cannot be true. And if its negation also cannot in principle be proven, then neither it nor its negation is true, neither it nor its negation is false: it has no truth value. The latest modification of the principle that truth is manifest is the principle that the puzzle does not exist, the defunct verification principle.

Assume this principle, assume now also that only logical and empirical proof is possible, and subjectivism is here to stay—Berkeley's or (Young) Wittgenstein's. What does this mean?

Perhaps Berkeley and Wittgenstein have abolished reality. I will not discuss the merits and defects of nihilism. Perhaps it is true; it is certainly objectivist enough. Perhaps Berkeley and Wittgenstein claim that elements of subjective experience are objective parts of the objective world, whereas our own experience of them is really too subjective to take serious notice of. This is the neutral monism of Hume, Mach, Russell—as Schrödinger and Popper have observed. The real elements or atoms of which reality is constituted are sensa. One way of organizing sensa is physics, in its causal schemes and physical objects; another is psychology, in its causal schemes and mental objects—where objects are defined as classes of sensa. But the physical and mental objects are constructs, compound, not atomic, and so less real. This has been best elaborated by Russell and by Wittgenstein. It is crazy. It is a scholastic exercise. Nobody seriously conceives of the blackness of this blackboard as an atom, and not even of the blackness of a point of the blackboard. Wittgenstein wisely refrained from offering even a single instance of an atomic proposition to describe a single atomic fact of this kind. There are no such things.

Another possibility is that of the pre-established harmony. As C. I. Lewis put it, we may each of us sit in a private room and yet see the same movie—if we are tuned to the same channel for ever and ever. This will make our subjective experiences intersubjective and maybe even have objective truth too. Who knows?

This last doctrine is the most attractive one, need I tell you, as it enables us to hold on to our subjectivist epistemology and obtain an objective ontology too. And so you must by now smell a rat. The rat is, indeed, stinking, and on the surface for all to smell. We begin with manifest empirical truth even though it leads to subjectivism, yet add as an afterthought the theory that we all watch the same channel all the time—a wild speculation, and one refuted by empirical psychology and by comparative anthropology and by the history of science. There is an obvious inconsistency in adopting the anti-speculative, strictly empiricist, mood which lands us in subjectivism, and then extricating ourselves with the aid of any speculation, let alone an empirically refuted one. For, if we permit ourselves a speculation, why speculate on the nature of the connection between the mind and the world—the kind of speculation which Kant already declared the worst— when we can just as well and more parsimoniously speculate about the nature of reality?

3. SUBJECTIVISM VERSUS PROBABILITY

Consider the idea that all (synthetic) knowledge is empirical, then, except the idea that all knowledge is empirical. It has been presented by Bertrand Russell in his celebrated 'On the Limits of Empiricism'. To elaborate on this, he wanted some principle facilitating the evolution of empirical theoretical knowledge, which he realized as an *a priori* principle of induction. An *a priori* principle, of course, must be either proven analytically or not; in which latter case it is proven transcendentally. The transcendental proof rests on the observation that human theoretical knowledge exists. This observation, if valid, should lead to the observation of how human theoretical knowledge is provable: it is impossible to contend that knowledge can be perceived and proof not; since proof is the mark of knowledge. Yet no observation was ever made of an empirical proof, and so no transcendental proof is acceptable thus far.

But this is not all. Which principle of induction do we wish to accept? Which simplicity, which uniformity, which correlation between observed and predicated events—the so-called Carnap's lambda—shall we endorse? Any such endorsement is both epistemological and ontological, and it is cheaper to cut out the epistemological and stick to the ontological.

I think I am ready now for subjective probability or the Bayesian theory. It is based on the idea that a principle of induction is only operative after a few further specifications are added about initial probabilities and measures of dependence between evidence and forecasts. It is the suggestion that we can observe how people use these measures. If this were true, and if we could observe that the result is human knowledge, then we would have a transcendental proof on our hands—a transcendental proof which may not convince heretics like the author of this essay, but at least a consistent theory.

How can we observe knowledge? Or, to be less strict about that, how can we observe an increase in probability of the hypothesis thanks to observation? The answer cannot be, of course, that our merely subjective measures get modified on account of factual information; what is needed for this is the observation that our subjective expectations improve, have a better probability of being in accord with objective reality. We want to know, in other words, whether we can perceive that objective expectations of people's improved expectations improve. To repeat, we want an objective increase of the objective expectation that people's subjective expectations become better when they gather better information.

This is the crux of subjective probability. If it comes out all right then it is vindicated—it is vindicated by objective means, by reference to reality or truth. It becomes objectified, or objectivized, or gains objective basis. I like this idea very much. Regrettably it does not work, as Max Black has proven (by constructing a counter-example: a model in which it fails). Also there is the proof from the perfect inductive evidence: my subjective probability that a coin is unbiased will not change if evidence proves me right: both *a priori* and *a posteriori* the probability that the next throw is a head is one-half!

Alternatively my subjective expectation is that people's objective expectations improve. And my subjective expectation of all my subjective expectations improves with experience, including the fact that my subjective expectations improve with experience. Is this so, and is this analytic or synthetic? If analytic, is it so objectively as it is proven, or is it so for mere subjective reasons and so question-begging? These questions are all academic, because things are obviously not so.

Perhaps things are not so because people simply do not learn—most people do not, you know. Perhaps most people do not assess probabilities, and their not learning is no refutation of subjectivism. This is false: traditional Chinese, not to mention Sudanese (Azande) assess probabilities but do not learn. Ah, but they do not use the calculus of probability. This calculus, I suppose, is part of the objective vindication of probability. So let us look at people who follow the rules of subjective probability. Does everyone follow this rule? If not, does any special class of people, or anyone whose whim it is to do that?

We now come to a third sense of subjectivism. Something may depend on reality—let us call it primary; or also on humanity at large or intersubjectively—let us call it secondary; or also on the single individual—let us call it tertiary. When Galileo and Locke declared color secondary, they said it depended not on reality alone but also on the human observer. As Galileo put it, we may as well say that the tickle is in the feather. Now Robert Boyle wrote a study of colors in which he was anxious to encompass the phenomena within science, though they are secondary. He said, when I dream I can color my curtains any way I like, but not when I open my eyes. Subjectivity in this sense of tertiary quality is individual control. Fichte's theory is then subjective: the world is my dream and I fashion it the way I like. The world is all tertiary. As I have said, this is sheer megalomania.

I am very anxious to avoid ascribing to the Bayesians the Fichtean megalomania, and I do so by observing that in their view the subjective element of induction is rapidly diminished with the process of learning—I know of no other way of doing so. But the idea that the subjective element gets rapidly excluded is quite erroneous: it is a vain hope, a dream.

Let us try Olber's paradox, for example. Olber, you remember, says that in whatever direction we look at the sky there must be a star somewhere (in that direction) whose luminosity as well as solid angle both vary in the inverse square of the distance, so that its contribution to the lighting of our night sky is constant, so that in sum, the luminosity of our night sky should be the average luminosity of the stars—unless some stars are opaque. Now take any quality other than luminosity. Say, that there are intelligent beings in the universe, and the average chance that an intelligent being will be met if we go in any direction far enough depends solely on the average chance of there being an intelligent being in any portion of the universe. The same goes for any other quality. But these chances are *a priori* and vary subjectively from person to person. They alter with information and, it is hoped, the same information will lead all subjective estimates to converge toward the true estimates. When? How rapidly?

In a clear sense, then, the prior probability you ascribe to hypotheses—singular or universal—get out of the picture, you hope. They are arbitrary and irrefutable, but they will soon be modifed *a posteriori*, by experience, to converge toward everybody else's modified probabilities.

Subjective probability, then is a means of modifying our subjective expectations by trial and error to meet the true probability. It is really very similar to Popper's view of learning by trial and error; the question is, do we need the rules or probability? Is trial and error not a satisfactory theory without probability altogether? If we are so generous as to say: no matter what your initial probability measure and dependence measure, as long as we share experiences long enough, we come up with sufficiently similar expectations, then you can also say: as long as we confine ourselves to testable explanatory hypotheses and the experience of testing them, we come up with fairly similar expectations. Probability is then redundant.

REPLIES TO THREE SUBJECTIVISTS

how everything becomes a mirage

1. REPLY TO STEPHEN SPIELMAN

Stephen Spielman is right in saying that probability was endorsed by important apriorists, such as Leibniz, who advocated the theory of probability. But I am not discussing apriorism and its defects—I assume that would be quite redundant in this day and age. This is why the criticism of any inductivism that it is apriorist is fatal, whether Laplace's unconscious apriorism or Russell's conscious one ('The Limits of Empiricism', 1935). But to conclude that Laplace was an apriorist because unwittingly he smuggled into his theory an *a priori* principle (of indifference) is a bit odd.

Spielman poses the question "Is probabilistic information *worthy* of being used to appraise the merit of a scientific hypothesis, the goodness of explanations, or the desirability of performing this or that experiment?" And he admits that "the issues raised by these questions are tremendously knotty and far ranging". If so, then he has lost the battle before the first shot, since I can handle them with ease and with no knotty and far-ranging issues. I do not pose the questions thus. If I want to select a good explanation, I ask what are our criteria for the goodness of an explanation, and see whether any given explanation satisfes them. If I want to appraise the merit of a scientific theory, I ask for criteria of merit, etc. If I want an experiment performed, I ask 'what for?' etc. As to probabilistic information, I do not see how it comes in except on specific grounds. If I say I admire Kepler's theory as one of great merit, you may ask for 'probabilistic information' to examine it. Which? In Kepler's day there were no such data. In the 18th century, when such data were available, Kepler's theory was modified already and incorporated in Newton's. You would do better to ask me why I see merit in Kepler's theory; and why the astronomers after his death saw merit

Synthese, 30, 1975. Copyright 1975 by D. Reidel Publishing Company, Dordrecht, Holland.

in it; and you will receive two very different answers, none of which has to do with 'probabilistic data'. This would not be very damaging to Spielman's case were it not his claim, immediately following his previously quoted remark about knottiness, that "the main argument advanced by the subjectivists [whom he calls 'personalists'] for their view that probabilistic information is worthy of being used . . . is that it is *in fact* used by scientists in this way, and that all attempts to eliminate it have failed dismally. (Of course, personalists do not maintain that it is used in connection with the formal machinery of the probability calculus or that it is even quantified)." But "the manner mentioned" on the previous page speaks of "practical and scientific problems" that relate to such information as 'greater confidence that *p* is true than that *q* is true' and the like, none of which has much to do with the above-mentioned admiration of the merit of Kepler's hypotheses, their goodness as explanations, or the experiments he or anyone else has performed as the result of his positing them.

Spielman quotes Popper as a good example of failure to eliminate probabilistic information. Insofar as the aim Popper has in testing hypotheses is to see them refuted if they are false, Spielman's case does not hold water. Popper's theory is that of conjectures and refutations. Insofar as Popper can reduce other aspects of science (e.g., the content of scientific theories) to this (a high degree of content equals a high degree of refutability), still Spielman's case does not hold water; insofar as Popper fails to reduce all science to conjectures and refutations his program fails. Assume all programs have failed; does this vindicate subjectivism? Surely not. Assume, if you insist, that all programs except subjectivism have failed. Does this render subjectivism true? No: there may be unconsidered alternatives that will be imagined tomorrow; there may be no true alternative solution to the problem. Anyone who insists *a priori* on the existence of a true solution is a transcendentalist.

Spielman repeats that the task of developing a subjectivist methodology is difficult. Rather than outline it he offers easy examples. The subjectivists have a knack of illustrating their controversial views with quite uncontroversial examples. They have to be told that this will not do. If I contest the view that all swans are white it will not do to show me any old white swan; the least you can do is unmask or show how you intend to unmask at least one seemingly black swan as white at heart.

Spielman admits it is difficult to show how *a priori* probabilities can be revised in the light of evidence. Of course they can be revised, and it is easy to show how; but not for a subjectivist. For a subjectivist it is easy to show that this is impossible. Given any data, a follower of the subjectivist rules may, and often will, change the probability he assigns to a given hypothesis. The resultant new probability is *a posteriori*, since '*a posteriori*' means 'in the light of experience'. The *a priori* probability is prior to experience and therefore cannot be posterior to it. Spielman seems to me to be attempting to circumvent a logical point and perform a logically impossible task. I do not say that this is what he does, but since this is what he seems to be doing, I do not know what he really does.

2. REPLY TO BARRY LOEWER

The comments by Barry M. Loewer embarrass me. He says, "Bayesians are not committed to holding that personal probability distributions are immune to criticism." Now I do not know who is a Bayesian and who is committed to what. But I have alluded to Bruno de Finetti and Savage who say so, and I have alluded to Carnap who says the opposite. The de Finetti-Savage view seems dogmatic but I try to defend it against the charge of dogmatism by ascribing to them the view that no matter what our *a priori* probabilities may be, all of us will converge in our *a posteriori* probabilities, given abundance of shared data. Loewer has agreed on this. The trouble with this argument is that it is not valid, as Loewer notices, but it does exonerate the de Finetti-Savage view. Carnap's view is that our *a priori* probabilities, or rather our *a priori* dependence measures—throughout my essay I have taken *a priori* distributions and *a priori* measures of dependence together—can be viewed as conjectures to be replaced in the light of experience. If so, I ask: why not take physical conjectures that way and ignore altogether their *a priori* probabilities and *a priori* dependences? Loewer now says that we can be both Bayesians and Popperians, both subjectivists and objectivists. Granted. Assuming however that subjectivism came along to resolve a difficulty but failed, and objectivism then succeeded, why retain subjectivism?

Loewer reinterprets Savage's view that two people may have different *a priori* probabilities [but similar *a posteriori* ones] given the same data. He says this is due to ineffable information. If one believes in ineffable information, however, one may jettison both objectivism and subjectivism and say that it is the scientist's ineffable knowledge—tacit knowledge is what Polanyi calls it, the mystical is what Wittgenstein called it much earlier— that gets us over all possible difficulties. This I dismiss as quite irrational. A Bayesian, to quote Loewer, will "fleece" anyone who argues from ineffable information.

Loewer says that it is increasingly improbable that a true hypothesis will be less probable, given the accumulated experience, than a false one. Popper has proven this to be false even for hypotheses whose *a priori* probabilities are objectively determined and accepted (i.e., those of unbiassed gambling set-ups), let alone for hypotheses whose *a priori* probabilities are arbitrarily decided. Let us examine a variant of it which will suit Loewer's Bayesian style. We have an urn with infinitely many balls of different materials *a*, *b*, *c*, . . . and of different colors, *A*, *B*, *C*, ... Take the hypotheses all a's are A or B, all a's are A or B or C, all a's are B, etc. Take the hypothesis a's are x% A and y% B, etc. Take now any hypothesis which is very probable and undermine it by some given, fairly large set of data; take one of the less probable hypotheses which is *a posteriori* more probable given the same set of data than it was *a priori*. Here we have a possibility—we can calculate its probability given the conditions—that the first hypothesis which is empirically undermined is still *a posteriori* more probable than the second which is empirically sustained. Yet Loewer indicates that the hypothesis supported by the evidence is always more probable than the hypothesis undermined. The question is: given that the less probable hypothesis is true, and data drawn at random, will the increase in data render the true hypothesis more probable? How large has the sample to be before this becomes the case?

Loewer can solve the problem, provided our list of hypotheses is complete and provided the data are independent. "But this," he says, "has nothing to do with the subjectivity of the prior distributions." I am afraid he is in error: it is the very cause of the plunge into subjectivity. For, were this not an insurmountable difficulty, subjectivism would not be called for: Bayes's theorem would be applicable everywhere and solve the problem with ease, with no appeal to subjective beliefs. Indeed, when Loewer tries to show his view unproblematic he simply assumes such non-subjectivist characteristics of the system under investigation as randomness. But what is randomness to a subjectivist and how does it differ from *a priori* independence? It cannot differ from it: there is no room within one formalism for both an objectivist and a subjectivist interpretation of the formulas: if we want both we need two levels, one meaning objective distributions and one meaning subjective probabilities of the objective distributions.

Loewer ends with a new rule to exclude 'perverse' *a priori* probabilities, akin to the principle of insufficient reason. It is, he says, compatible with subjectivism. This is the way subjectivism becomes a chronic illness. It is first admitted in order to work out a solution, but then stays for dinner as unobtrusive. Yet one has to agree that it does not conflict with a better solution: it simply cannot conflict with anything since it turns everything into mere mirage.

3. REPLY TO I. J. GOOD

I. J. Good presents a solution to the difficulty I have presented, which, he says, I know, but which seems worthwhile to spell out. Almost any standard text on the topic presents the following view. There is the *a priori* probability of a hypothesis and the *a posteriori* one, and the accepted hypothesis is that with a high *a posteriori* probability. This view, and this view alone, is refuted by the case of a coin whose coming up heads has both *a priori* probability one-half and the *a posteriori* probability one-half after a large number of trials.

Good's comments are very brief, yet they offer two different solutions to the difficulty, a longer one which is to no avail, and a shorter one which is permitted in Good's own system but in no other system of subjective probability.

The first reply was already offered by C. S. Peirce and by John Maynard Keynes. It does not work. The subjective probability in the physical probability that the next throw is one-half is increased by the experience described above, they say. Now the *a priori* subjective probability that [the physical probability of the given coin coming up heads is one-half] is one-half, and the *a posteriori* probability that [the physical probability of the same coin coming up heads is over one-half] is likewise one-half. And so the difficulty remains. Moreover, Keynes and Jeffreys, as well as de Finetti and Savage, the acknowledged teachers of the subjectivist school, say that there is no physical probability (or relative frequency, or what have you). Sir Harold Jeffreys says that relative frequency is inconsistent unless founded on subjective probability! Jeffreys claims repeatedly to be the first who has managed to found physical probability or statistics on subjective probability, and his claim is endorsed by the other patron saint of subjectivism, Rudolf Carnap, in his subjectivist book, *The Logical Foundations of Probability* in which the major discovery is that there are two concepts of probability, the subjective and the objective, intensionally different but coextensive. Their coextension ensures the invalidity of Good's first reply as far as Carnap is concerned.

Good also outlines a different solution, for which his system makes allowance, but not those of the above-mentioned leaders or of most standard texts on the topic, since they speak of subjective probabilities, not of their distributions (regardless of what a subjectivist may mean by the *a priori* distribution of an *a priori* probability).

Shall we say that the standard versions, at least, have to be rejected, or shall we allow for a simplified standard esoteric version pierced with difficulties living side by side with a reinforced but complex and esoteric version fit only for the expert?

I am sorry to be so prolix in reply to Good's brief and graceful comments, but, to quote him, it "seems worthwhile to spell it out".

—14—

STAGNATION

a flood of words in a desert of ideas

The most interesting and critical paper in this collection is K. Zener's 'The Significance of the Experience of the Individual for the Science of Psychology'. It encourages the trend of research into conscious experience in spite of its being difficult to design repeatable experiments in this field and in spite of the highly interpretative character of the resulting observational reports. It is also the only paper which is too brief. Interesting examples are suppressed. Its critical thesis is that behaviorism, rightly searching for intersubjectively acceptable evidence, has aped the behavioral aspect of experimental physics but misunderstood its function in physics. In support of Zener's ideas I should like to add that his view of the experimenter's work as bold and creative is in no way alien to experimental physics even though some of its imitators were too impressed by its pedestrian side to notice its imaginative and exciting aspect. Indeed, by the behaviorist's standard all scientific experiments are equally significant, while few experiments equal those of Oersted, Hertz, Michelson, and Rutherford.

H. Feigl's 'The "Mental" and the "Physical" ' lacks a compact and systematic presentation. Its first two sections, however, are brief, clear, and interesting. Feigl's theory is that the mental process is a high-level physiological process. Transcending logical empiricism he explicitly recognizes his thesis as synthetic-yet-speculative. He also ends with a list of open problems. It is regrettable that he shoves off the main objection to his refined epiphenomenalism, namely, the dualism of facts and decisions, to another field, thus declaring it irrelevant rather than still unanswered (p. 418). He is slightly unfair once, when he criticizes dualistic interactionism on the ground that methodological monism (which requires us to try to formulate

This review of *Minnesota Studies in the Philosophy of Science*, Volume II: *Concepts, Theories, and the Mind-Body Problem*, edited by H. Feigl, M. Scriven, and G. Maxwell (Minneapolis: University of Minnesota Press, 1958) appeared in *Mind*, 68, 1959.

physicalist hypotheses to explain human behavior) has been successful. For methodological dualism has also been successful, and Feigl himself admits, *en passant* (p. 463), that methodological dualism is at present unavoidable. This admission invalidates the criticism on pp. 383–86. (Zener's paper forcefully advocates methodological dualism.)

The first paper, by P. Oppenheim and H. Putnam, on the unity of science, is a retreat to Comte's famous theory of the hierarchy of the sciences. Unfortunately it completely ignores Comte.

The second paper, by C. G. Hempel, poses the theory that hypotheses are 'economic systematizations' (p. 87) with no mention of Mach, Duhem, or Poincaré. It seems to me vague and unconvincing. He poses one problem, discusses another problem, and offers a solution to yet another problem, without discussing the relations between the three. (The problems are: Why do we assume occult entities to explain known ones? How do we know the meaning of terms which stand for these occult entities? and Why do we use explanations at all?) His chief problem is whether or not explanations are redundant. He calls his paper 'The Theoretician's Dilemma', but I would rather prefer the title 'The Half-hearted Theoretician's Dilemma'; for the theoretician wants mainly to find satisfactory explanations, and this aim leaves no room for Hempel's problem which, however, may exist for the instrumentalist whose aim is not explanation but prediction (for technological purposes). Hempel takes for granted the instrumentalist philosophy and he does not notice that the theoretician's prediction is not merely for the aid of technology but mainly and chiefly for the sake of testing his explanation.*

Next, M. Scriven asserts the conditional: *if* theories are redundant (for the purpose of describing the world), *then* theoretical terms are redundant (i.e., definable, at least in a wide sense of 'definition'). He devotes his paper to the contention that the consequent of this conditional is false, in order to conclude that its antecedent is false too.

A. Pap and W. Sellars add to the vast literature on dispositionals without telling the reader in simple words what is worrying them. In my

---

*This is Feigl's citicism if his 'factual reference' means what ordinarily 'truth or falsity' means. See page 427, passage commencing 'I remain unimpressed with Craig's theorem' (which concerns a method of elimination of theoretical concepts). Feigl seems to suggest that historically Craig's theorem is the cause of the 'theoretician's dilemma' yet that intellectually it is a false alarm. If so, it should be added, in order to avoid misunderstanding, that Craig himself tries (*Philosophical Review* 65 [1956], 38–55) to show that any elimination of a concept must be pointless, thus arguing that there is no 'theoretician's dilemma'. It is odd that Hempel does not try to answer Craig's arguments, or even state that in Craig's view there is no dilemma. He suggests, by hints too subtle to discuss here, that Craig is for eliminations, and that his theorem is of mere logical, but of no philosophical, significance. Craig himself does not overestimate his theorem (which is but a corollary of Kleene's theorem). And he uses it very competently as an argument against the philosophical view imputed to him by implication. And he uses himself, among other ideas, most of the criticisms which Hempel and Feigl appear to level against him. The interested reader should not rely on Hempel's report but read Craig's own presentation.

view dispositionals can worry only those who think that some observation-reports are *absolutely* certain. Against this Popper argued (1935) that every universal word ('glass') entails a dispositional ('breakable'), so that every statement employing it ('here is a glass of water') is further testable and therefore can never be certain. The attempt to discover statements of brute facts has swollen the literature on dispositions; how much the present papers contribute, either to the problem or to its solution, I cannot judge.

H. G. Alexander argues that the view of hypotheses as licences to infer one particular from another (Mill, Schlick) is misleading since it obscures the fact that our hypotheses may be false.

P. F. Strawson's discussion 'On Persons' ends with two points which he seems to think are identical. The one (p. 352) advocates 'the logical primitiveness of the concept of a person', the other (p. 353) defends 'the conceptual scheme we employ' in ordinary everyday discourse. I accept the second point which is, in intention at least, a refinement of the commonsense view on the matter, yet cannot see what 'logical primitiveness' has to do with common sense or with views. Which concept should be taken as primitive, or undefined, is of interest only in logic, where often such a question is shown to be partly arbitrarily decidable. If we use the term 'logical primitive' loosely, we should notice that common sense views persons (especially those with 'dual personality') as highly complex.

P. E. Meehl's is a disappointing paper apropos clinical psychology with the splendid title 'When Shall We Use our Heads Instead of the Formula?'.

The Appendix contains a correspondence between W. Sellars and Roderick M. Chisholm on the relation between the mind-body problem and intentionality in logic. I could not see its point.

The worst thing about the present volume is its editing; much could and a great deal should have been done by the editors to improve the volume. If the contemporary practice of publishing endless collections goes much further, ideas will be drowned in a frantic flood of words. 'Above all, my son, beware', said the Preacher, 'of the making of many books without end, and of much tiresome prattle. . . .'

—15—

WEIZENBAUM ON COMPUTERS

he really digs them

It is strange to begin a highly favorable review with savage criticism; yet this is precisely what I have to do here. For I started reading this book in a paranoid fit. It looked as if there were a conspiracy to make me write an unfavorable review.

The book came with a brochure telling me that the book is both very important and very original. So say, among others, Lewis Mumford, Noam Chomsky, and Victor Weisskopf; but the brochure asks me not to quote them. It may be pointless to discuss here the discourtesy of some publishers, but I must declare these three leading academics responsible for the abuse of their scholarly reputation. They ought to do something publicly against it. (Pp. 240-44 of the book include lengthy quotations from unnamed sources. This is less objectionable, but not in good taste either.)

The preface tells us that, after the introductory, somewhat technical chapters that can be read by patient, intelligent laymen, the book will argue that there is a difference between humans and computers and that certain tasks ought not to be relegated to computers. I think we all agree: we should not delegate our connubial duties to the robots. "There is nothing I say in this book that has not been said better, certainly more eloquently, by others," admits the author disarmingly. This raises interesting problems: what is the good of writing an unoriginal book? Is it better for an unoriginal book to be a mosaic of eloquent quotations or a flow of uneloquent restatement? Rather than deal with this intriguing matter, the author descends to a platitude: "As Lewis Mumford often remarked, it sometimes [when?] matters that a member of the scientific establishment [our author] say something that humanists have been shouting for ages."

This review of Joseph Weizenbaum's *Computer Power and Human Reason: From Judgment to Calculation* (San Francisco: Freeman, 1976) appeared in Technology and Culture, 17, 1976, and is reproduced here by permission of the Society for the History of Technology.

In other words, this book is written for those who tend to reject a thesis because it comes from humanists but who may readily endorse it when it comes from the scientific Establisment. I am not among those, and neither, I hope, are my readers.

But suppose we are intellectual snobs. What has Professor Weizenbaum to show to snobs that Norbert Wiener could not show? Perhaps, however, in addition to his advantageous membership in the same scientific establishment as the author, Wiener had the misfortune of counting as a humanist.

The introduction tells us how shocked the author was when people took seriously his program to make a computer play a caricature of the role of a Rogerian psychotherapist. He had tried a modest program, yet it was hailed as a breakthrough, signalling a future in which we shall delegate to our robots, perhaps not connubial duties, perhaps not even the whole of the task of psychotherapy, but . . . And it was really successful, in that it did establish contact with 'patients'.

I am afraid I am unimpressed. The robot as a psychotherapist is as old as the conjunction of science fiction and psychotherapy, and the idea that robots are better than people at some very human tasks is already to be found in Laplace's book on probability, in which he envisages computers as judges. As to the fact that a computer psychotherapist does something to some of us, this is just one of those things. Just look at how much simple porn or even mere nudity in photos or in verbal descriptions does to some people. Just as the person excited by porn is not misled, the one excited by the robotic psychiatrist is not misled. The author's surprise at the fact that even his secretary, who was well aware of his having programmed the robot, asked him to leave the room so as to converse with it is thus endearing but no more than others' surprise at people's notorious unwillingness to enjoy porn movies or nude photos in company—even that of the photographer. The author knows this. For he later describes—superbly—the compulsive programmer or the computer freak as the expert who obsessively interacts with his computer.

The introduction ends on a homiletic note: "The people only hunger for what is represented to them to be scientifically validated knowledge. They seek to satiate themselves at such scientific cafeterias as . . . popularized versions of the works of Masters and Johnson, or on scientology . . . . We count, but we are rapidly forgetting how to say what is worth counting and why." This homily is not to my taste.

So much for the first part of my program. To come briefly to the second, I do recommend the book. Here is a highly accurate and technical presentation of some computer business that any person can read, even one who has already forgotten the multiplication tables and who gets the shivers at the sight of a formula. From now on, nobody whose business it is to know about computers can hide behind technical ineptness. And this is but a pioneering work. Now experts can learn from this study too—both from its excellent technique of vulgarization and from its peculiar views and presentations which are of great interest. A computer, says the author, is an abstract entity, at times with physical embodiment. As such it can be a merciless critic. He says this repeatedly. I thought he meant by "merciless" no more than that it criticizes the slightest misprint or the minutest grammatical error with the same severity as it would criticize the worst error, except that I doubted it could criticize any error other than these. But it's not so simple. The programmer has to spell out correctly all his ideas, big and small, and he may err not only in his spelling but also in his oversight of a truism—and the truism, once stated, may be seen to be false! The rigidity usually associated with programming—reflected in science fiction from the very start (the BBC's *Black Cloud*?) by stilted language and stilted intonation—is easily overcome; as any box idiot can tell you, it is in any case quite easily absorbed through sheer habit. But the rigidity of programming as such cannot; it can only be absorbed by the memory banks of a well-oiled computer. But the criticism a computer makes of an inadequate formalization is hardly a "really deep criticism" (p. 109), though it may indeed occasion some.

The absence of an axiom is one thing; the surprising corollary to it is another. Thus (p. 164) Edward Feigenbaum's program, in which computer memory shows interference (of one association with another) which turned up unexpectedly (with neither an explicit sub-routine nor any foreknowledge or intention), genuinely surprised its designer. This is more like what we traditionally view as criticism.

I cannot spell out all the merits of this book or even all that I hope I have learned from it—despite my remaining impression that the philosophy the author here expresses is better expressed in Norbert Wiener's classic *God and Golem, Inc.* But if you have no time to read it all and you are a blasé expert, at least you should do yourself a favor and scan chapters 2 and 3 on the technicalities of computers, chapter 4 on the compulsive programmer, and parts of chapters 6 and 7 on artificial intelligence. This fellow really digs computers, and he pulls out all the stops. The knowledge of philosophy of science proper exhibited here is poor—it is just above average for the professional philosopher of science.

The author's revival of the 18th-century (inductivist) equation of superstition with madness has a touch of creativity, no doubt; but it lacks the thoroughness required.

The book is marred by inaccuracies, including ones I find surprising: for example, the author's ascription of Laplace's demon to Leibniz or his view of Einstein's relativity as that of all motions (Galileo's transformations and Lorentz's transformations) rather than of time (the latter only). But I shall not list more.

The book is oddly out of date. The author only touches on machine translations, where I think he could do better if he used Bar-Hillel's work, and on child psychology, where he could appeal to Piaget or even to Norbert Wiener. And when he discusses gambling, I wish he had presented the views of Luisa Howe; Church's thesis, those of Rohit Parikh; problem-solving, those of Popper and Lakatos; conceptual frameworks, those of E. A. Burtt, A. Koyré, or R. G. Collingwood, not to mention recent writers on the subject, including Bunge, Jarvie, and even myself; but above all I miss a better treatment of grand old Norbert Wiener. In an unquotable passage in the brochure, Mumford predicts that this book will stay serviceable for the next fifty years. This means the author should now be working on a second edition. I wish him luck.

The author's thesis comes at the end of the book. Computers belong to technology; humanity has both technology and culture; culture includes history, the arts, the fine arts, decision-making, responsibility, courage. Fine. But in order to be interesting—rather than hortatory—the author has to struggle with reductionism. He says nothing about it.

─ 16 ─

FEUER IN SEARCH
OF THE ZEITGEIST

insinuations instead of statements

I much recommend this highly scholarly piece of gossip. I confess that I would have enjoyed it just as much and have been less irked by it were I not reviewing it: it is a bit hard to live for days on a diet of fudge, treacle, and tarts, to say nothing of stones instead of bread, and no meat. And the thought of carefully analyzing a piece of chit-chat to show that it is no more than that is no fun either. What is a reviewer to do? Claims of wild distortion, great liberties with sources, of arbitrariness and of meagre results, cannot be made without proper substantiation, yet the attempt to substantiate them properly is a bore. I suppose a reviewer's duty is to read a text reasonably carefully, to write down (as an exercise) the substantiation of such claims—with all due caution and at all the necessary length—but to spare the reader such writing. The reviewer may then merely say why a poor book—and the present one exceptionally qualifies—deserves a review nonetheless, and report impressions of the poverty of the book not as a verdict—a verdict requires reasoned evidence—but as impressions that serve as no more than a warning to readers. Well, then: here are my impressions.

The book is exceptionally learned. Though, it is true, there is practically no physics at all in it, the author covers an enormously wide literature, and can quote scientific memoirs and political pamphlets, biographies, philosophy, a bit of sociology, Jewish chronicles and anything else. Yet if the reader is not very careful he may easily read in this book such stupid remarks—which are not there—as that Picasso was dadaist, de Broglie a Bergsonist, Heisenberg a metaphysician and a Platonist, Einstein a moderate Marxist; that Niels Bohr was a disciple of Kierkegaard and saw

---

This review of *Einstein and the Generations of Science*, by Lewis S. Feuer (New York: Basic Books, 1974) appeared in *Philosophy of the Social Sciences*, 5, 1975.

Heisenberg's argument present in Auguste Comte. I wish to state quite unequivocally that the book is full of such *insinuations*, and that the reader has
the choice of declaring it devoid of all thesis or ascribing to it some thesis
which the author no more than insinuates.

More about the book's scholarship. It relies on unreliable evidence such
as testimony by Heisenberg; it makes too much of passing incidents, even if
these are correctly described, such as Michelson's expression of regret about
his great experiment, and such as Bohr's flirtations with philosophy. It pays
no attention to incidents with opposite morals, such as Michelson's exhortation to study nature and follow her anywhere she leads us, or Bohr's
repeated confessions of positivism or near-positivism. The careless reader
may also have the impression that the author substantiates wild statements
of fact, such as that young Bertrand Russell was Establishment; this claim,
however, is made with no discussion or evidence, and in the midst of all
sorts of interesting and well-documented claims.

This is not the first book I have read with pages cluttered with references
and documented claims that serve no other purpose than to conceal the fact
that major theses presented there are unsupported. For my part I think it
does not much matter. This is not the first book I have read where major
theses are insinuated rather than stated: this was, after all, a regular feature
of scientific literature in the 18th century. This defect, too, does not matter
over much except that it is a bit tedious. This is not the first trite volume I
have read either: I like gossip, especially about great thinkers. But this is the
first book I have read that seems to be a concentration and concatenation of
all three defects, and this made reading it a bit difficult.

The book contains a sort of psychoanalysis and socioanalysis—it looks
to me to be Marx tempered by Freud and by some anti-Stalinism—an
analysis of all sorts of aspects of the personal lives of thinkers that relate to
their researches. Did you know that Heisenberg's high-school physics textbook had in it atoms hooked to each other? You should, if you know any
gossip about Heisenberg: it is one of his favorite stories. Did you know that
there is a sex-symbol lurking there? Did you know that it may also be linked
with Heisenberg's political sentiments? One day someone will write a
critical book on Heisenberg's politics. I will say nothing about it here
because I do not wish now to substantiate my view of it—which view cannot
go to press unsubstantiated. Professor Feuer has managed to avoid labelling
Heisenberg's youthful—and not so youthful—political sentiment with one
word; nevertheless he manages to offer a whiff of blood and soil. And he
does so without being too offensive—not too offensive to Heisenberg, that
is: he is too offensive to me when he compares and contrasts Einstein's
political sentiments and Heisenberg's.

Scientists have psyches, they have parents, they have political and artistic
tastes, they have philosophies, at times they fall in love, have friends, talk

about things, are even driven to suicide. That much I think we can safely adduce from this book. When the author suggests, if he does, that all scientists fight their fathers, then he is in trouble. Niels Bohr was on good terms with his father—he was a gentle rebel, we are told. And Heisenberg's rebellion was turned inside out when his father was wounded in the war. The same holds for the view that all scientists are scientific rebels. The author both admits and denies that Planck and Keynes were scientific rebels.

The leading thesis of the book, if it has one, is that the doctrine of relative truth is revolutionary, that statistics is relativistic, and that the two mark 20th-century science and philosophy and politics, and perhaps also psychology. The sub-thesis of the book, if it has one, is that a scientist's work develops on iso-emotional lines, on lines where sympathies run parallel: ideological, political, philosophic, emotional. Because of this parallelism, enormous powers concentrate and, with luck, lead to great discoveries.

In brief, the volume is a Hegelian hodge-podge, Marxist in spots or to some extent or other. It defeats itself with ease, by showing that such diverse political sentiments as Einstein's and Heisenberg's, such diverse personal temperaments as Bohr's and de Broglie's, such diverse philosophies as Einstein's Spinozism and Heisenberg's positivism, all go into science through a certain process of objectivization. The book contains a kernel of a better idea, when towards the end it endorses Boltzmann's idea that science develops in schools. But the idea comes too late.

And so I refuse to yield to the book's failure. Anti-Hegelian though I staunchly am, I am not so blind as to deny the existence of the Zeitgeist, not so insensitive as to cease to marvel at the co-operation between humanists and Nazi sympathizers for the greater glory of God. This book's failure is in part due to the vastness of the problems it purports to handle. If the book is a rather chirpy gossipy excursion, it at least penetrates where mighty investigation fears to tread, and therefore it qualifies as a trail-blazer. I would like my metaphor mixed a bit more, but I lack the talent.

A parting shot: the index of this volume is a veritable disaster. Even names are not properly cited, let alone subjects. Better luck in the next printing!

If there is a common tenor to all post-Renaissance philosophy and science and journalism and homiletics, it is the declaration that skepticism and dogmatism are both false. Which means that scientific proof—in a strong or a weak sense—exists for sure. There are two kinds of proof of the existence of scientific proof, *a priori* and inductive. The *a priori* proof is repeatedly claimed to exist, and believers in it are usually inductivists. The inductive proof is likewise repeatedly claimed to exist and believers in it are usually apriorists. (This strange inversion is unnoticed because of Kant's misnaming of his own peculiar—but neither first nor last—inductive proof as a transcendental proof.) In recent years a trend has evolved, which ascribes so strong a validity to the inductive proof that its followers eschew all discussion of the logic of scientific proof: scientific proof is any proof accepted by scientists. The clearest statement of this view belongs to Michael Polanyi. Thomas S. Kuhn and now Lewis Feuer follow suit.

Since Feuer is such an admirer of Einstein, I should like to draw his attention to the fact that Einstein found even Galileo's fight with the Church of Rome rather distasteful. What is it to a thinker, he wondered, whether he is believed or not? It is known that Einstein did not rush to open the telegram informing him that Eddington's observation supported his views. When he was asked why, he said he was fairly confident the outcome was positive. He used his metaphoric language, but it meant the same. I cannot help thinking he felt quite embarrassed at the thought that the success meant that the hoi polloi would now take him for their Pope.

Time and again we see in the social patterns of the scientific community ingredients reminiscent of a herd or a mob intermingle with ingredients exhibiting thoughtfulness, curiosity, readiness to reconsider. It is painful to read a book that takes these two kinds of ingredients with equal seriousness and purports thus to join the rank of the anti-dogmatic and anti-skeptical literature. It is time, I propose, to become skeptical at least about all this. There is a philosophical revolution going on, and Professor Feuer knows about it, as evidenced both by his general scholarship and by page 286 of the present volume, the one which compares in detail (the only page in the book with formulas and with careful analysis) Kepler's third law with Newton's version of it. But he prefers to follow the crowd and say the proper and reactionary thing (p. 283): "superseded classical theory is not so much [!] falsified as delimited in its domain of validity"—even though he notices at once that this takes the sting out of all scientific revolutions. It also makes his own epistemology rather funny.

Two points in the present volume impress me somewhat, brief as they are, and I wish to mention them. Both are presented as criticisms of views ascribed to Kuhn. Rightly or not, I shall let this ride. First the (Duhem—Evans-Pritchard—Polanyi) thesis of incommensurability of competing theories as two different languages is faulty: the two languages refer to the same world of fact and so the classes of facts they account for can be compared (in either of the two languages or in a third language). Second, the (Hegelian) view that revolutions are always responses to crises is not true: at times a rebel imposes a crisis on his peers.

Feuer scores on both these points, and by the force of logic alone. Regrettably, the logic of the rest of the present volume is not so good.

THE ZEITGEIST AND
PROFESSOR FEUER

valuable gossip

My review[1] of Lewis S. Feuer's recent book[2] could not have been very clear if in his rejoinder[3] he reads me as opposing the sociology of science when in fact I am addicted to it. He ends his rejoinder by admonishing me. "The inner tensions and turmoil in the unconscious" of a scientist, he intimates, "is something which no historian of science should aim to repress." I hasten to endorse this, and even to share his suggestion that this message may well deserve repetition. We are, essentially, in the same camp.

There is here a general difficulty which I have faced repeatedly in my long and varied reviewing career.[4] Members of oppositions tend to overlook differences between themselves when attacking the Establishment, and to ignore the Establishment and thus to exaggerate differences between themselves when engaged in quarrelling. My problem is, as ever, how we can sustain a sense of perspective, how both moods can be beneficially combined. I tried, but I have not yet succeeded. I have the impression that Feuer gives the impression that my review of his book is from the Establishment's viewpoint. It is not.

Feuer says I say his book is Hegelian and Marxist. I do not. I say it has Hegelian and Marxist qualities. He quotes another reviewer to say he is no Marxist, and he says of himself he is no Hegelian. I agree. Further, he says that I object to his saying that de Broglie had views with Bergosonian qualities. Heisenberg with Platonic qualities, Einstein with Marxist qualities, Bohr with Kierkegaardian ones. I do not object. It is important to notice that de Broglie was a Bergsonian at times, Einstein had Marxist friends and was a socialist, etc. Thus far I find Feuer's book valuable, and as a matter of fact I have commended it to this journal's readers. But I am very sorry that he has not found it necessary to tell his readers that Bohr and Heisenberg were mostly positivists and so opposed to Plato[5] and Kierkegaard; and that he overlooks many other facts that indicate he may be in error.

I am glad Feuer says openly that Heisenberg was a Nazi supporter, though he hides it in the sentence, "What Professor Agassi is saying with circumlocution is that because Heisenberg was a Nazi supporter his evidence is 'unreliable', and that I should not have discussed how Heisenberg's involvement in the German Youth Movement had affected his theorizing." Now the circumlocution is in origin Feuer's, not mine; but I am glad he now speaks straight. But not correctly: it is not because Heisenberg was a Nazi sympathizer that he is unreliable: Nazi sympathy and unreliability can be found both separately and jointly (and perhaps Speer is a reliable Nazi; I cannot say). My complaint is not that Feuer discusses the influence of Heisenberg's politics on his science, but that he does *not* do so. Nor *can* one do so without discussing Heisenberg's science. And he does not.

Professor Feuer tells us that in 1948 he helped bring food to besieged Jerusalem. I admire his courage, and, as a native of that city, I am deeply grateful to him. How did this fact, however, influence his own work? It did so, he says, by freeing him of the need to express his opposition to Naziism while discussing Heisenberg. Fine. No one need express opposition to Naziism today, anyway. Are we to reject, he continues, Duhem's work on the logic and history of science because he was an anti-Semite? No, he says. I agree. Yet Duhem's Anglophobia may have helped him oppose Maxwell[6] and to the extent that it did it may have contributed to his anti-Maxwellian contributions to the study of electricity that are now seldom noticed and always dismissed. If de Broglie was likewise influenced by anti-Semitism, as Feuer now tells us, I would like to know how; and how he allowed the Jew Bergson to influence him nonetheless. I am simply unclear about the logic of Feuer's argument. I think he leaves out too many details.

Generally, I ask again: does Feuer say that all scientists are rebels? How much opposition does one have to express, and how forcefully, before becoming a rebel? I am not clear. I find in his book suggestions and insinuations instead of hypotheses.

Nor am I happy about his facts. He says that young Bertrand Russell was Establishment. I say this is a wild statement. He now says that even knowledge of Russell's *Autobiography* should suffice to support the 'well known fact' that Russell was Establishment. For example, his first book, *German Social Democracy* of 1896, was written from an "orthodox liberal" standpoint; his early philosophy of mathematics was Platonist; his sexual morality was stoic.

I am dumfounded. "Young Russell" should refer to him roughly between his 18th or 21st and his 35th birthdays, between 1890 and 1907. At this period, as we find in his *Autobiography*, he was associated with the

Webbs and the early Fabians and lectured at the London School of Economics; on November 16, 1893, he was thanked for a generous cheque in support of a miners' strike; he married Alys against his people's wishes, and despite the enormous pressures they put on him, they got married in a Quaker ceremony, went to Germany, and were rejected by the Embassy there because they went to socialist meetings; in 1896, in Bryn Mawr, Alys spoke privately of free love and the two "were practically bounced out of the college"; "in 1901 I become pro-Boer"; in 1901 he also became a pacifist; in 1902 he spoke in defense of trade unionism; and in 1907 he stood in a by-election as a woman-suffragist. If there is any doubt about Russell's feelings, his *Autobiography* says explicitly that he had "ceased to be respectable" long before November 6, 1898, when he was 26 years old. So *there*.

As to Russell's mathematical philosophy, to call it Platonist will not do. Is Platonism Establishment? I do not think in the 1890s and in the 1900s it was. Is Logicism Platonist? Most logicians would not be so easily and cavalierly affirmative. It is still a tough question.

(Einstein's empiricism is more complex and I cannot take it up here. But I do wish to concede; the case merits more than the casual nod I—or Feuer—could give it.)

Was Michelson usually sorry he had made his famous experiment? I do not think so. He was an avowed aetherist and was highly strung, at one time even committed, says Feuer in his 'Rejoinder'; he suggests I overlook Michelson's "tensions and turmoil"; perhaps. For my part, I still say it is Feuer's book that overlooks them, and due to the theory of iso-emotional lines that it seems to purport.

Does Feuer present his book around questions? Does he offer explicit answers to them (e.g., the theory of iso-emotional lines)? Does his book pose explicit theses? Does he explicitly discuss seeming counter-examples to his theses? If any of these questions is to be answered in the affirmative, then I am in error. If I am, I wish to be corrected: by citing his questions, answers and/or his discussion of seeming counter-examples.

Contrary to Feuer's claim, I am not in the least against gossip. But gossip becomes sociology proper only with its explicit use in the raising of a problem or in a discussion of the merits and defects of given hypotheses, of given questions or answers.

The Zeitgeist does exist. Rationalist philosohers were quixotically all against it, and Romantic philosophers repeatedly used it as a ramrod to batter rationalism with. This must change. How I do not know.

SECOND REPLY TO PROFESSOR FEUER

This is, I suppose, the end of the exchange. [*Right. This discussion is now closed.*—Eds.] I should now say whether I endorse any of Professor Feuer's points. I do not. He says I should acknowledge his corrections; I do not. He says I have shifted my ground; I say he has shifted his. The interested readers can consult Feuer's entertaining but rather lightweight book and the previous installments of this exchange and judge for themselves. The issues do not warrant more space.

NOTES

1. 'Feuer in Search of the Zeitgeist', the previous chapter.

2. *Einstein and the Generations of Science* (New York: Basic Books, 1974).

3. 'Method in the Sociology of Science: Rejoinder to Professor Agassi', *Philosophy of the Social Sciences*, 6 (1976) 249–53.

4. See my 'The Present State of the Philosophy of Science', *Philosophica*, 15 (1975) 5–20, reprinted in my *Science and Society*, 1981.

5. Feuer cites an important letter from Heisenberg to him in his reply to me, page 250. The letter is evidence for my view, not for his.

6. See my 'Duhem versus Galileo', chapter 5 above and my *Towards an Historiography of Science* (The Hague, 1963. Facsimile reprint, Middletown, CT: Wesleyan University Press, 1967).

— 18 —

LISTENING IN THE LULL

a reflection of the general malaise

This volume requires much effort from the reader and offers little in return—unless perhaps it is excused as fairly typical of material in the field of the philosophy of the social sciences in the English-speaking world. It may well be typical in that it offers twelve chapters, each written by a different author, and each followed by comments and replies, thus reflecting views of 24 authors or more. It depends on how the contributors were chosen.

The editors put the accent on disagreement. The dust-jacket has the subtitle 'Confrontations'. As we shall see, debates are rare, and of questionable import. Had the editors chosen their commentators to ensure confrontations they could have made a better choice, as main contributors differ among themselves more than with their assigned commentators.

The topics of this volume vary, but reduction seems to be a major theme: of psychology to neurophysiology and physics, of sociology to psychology. But we also have papers on imperfect rationality, on relativism in the social sciences, on modern linguistics, and on psychoanalysis as a pseudo-science.

Methodology never quite counts as a topic for debate, though there is a skirmish here and there. Some writers are blatant inductivists, some are blatant anti-inductivists, mainly Popperian, frank or crypto (no conventionalists and/or instrumentalists), but there is no debate.

The most off-putting thing about the volume is its size and the haphazard way in which all sorts of odds and ends are stuffed in. The index contains well over 300 items, mostly incidental and from many fields and periods. In over 500 large pages on *Explanation in the Behavioral Sciences* we find only one reference each to Marx, Durkheim and Weber. Even

This review of R. Borger and F. Cioffi, *Explanation in the Behavioral Sciences* (Cambridge: Cambridge University Press, 1970) appeared in *Philosophy of the Social Sciences*, 2, 1972.

physics fares better, with many references to Newton, and a few to Brahe, Kepler, Galileo, Boyle, and Einstein. The most references in the social sciences go to Evans-Pritchard, Keynes, Freud, Skinner, von Neumann and Morgenstern; in philosophy to Descartes, Kant, Collingwood, Popper, Wittgenstein, and Gellner. Yet very few of these are treated decently; more often it is merely name-dropping, adequate and inadequate. With so many Popperians, frequent references to Popper were to be expected. Wittgenstein is a runner-up, but not a serious contender, not even in the work of Frank Cioffi, a Popperian with a Wittgensteinian record which he still tries to maintain in a pregnant enigmatic final footnote.

So much for an overview. But there is more to complain about. I shall discuss the essays and comments in the order they are printed, though for some reason the editors chose to put first some superfluous papers with no redeeming qualities.

The first paper is by Stephen Toulmin who uses rusty language analysis to establish the profound claim that purposeful and voluntary actions, as well as involuntary ones, do take place. Purposeful actions, he claims further, need not conflict with the possibility of causal explanations. He does not refer to Spinoza but he does find it useful to invoke Kant's distinction between reality and appearance. At one point, when revealing the significant truth that under exceptional circumstances blinking may be voluntary though it is usually autonomic, he tells us about a strange condition against which doctors recommend among other exercises regular blinking and which, he further tells us in a footnote, he has learned about from his wife who had personally suffered from it. I am sure we all hope that Mrs. Toulmin is now well and enjoying good health.

R. S. Peters is in sympathy with Toulmin's attempt to "retain and reconcile the dichotomy between reason and cause" (p. 27) where 'reason' is used in the sense of a purpose. That is, Peters shares his view that cause and purpose are compatible. He concludes (p. 28) that Toulmin's "account of justificatory discourse", i.e., his piece of language analysis of the use of "the reason I do so is", is "acceptable but incomplete", that "his account for reasons as causes . . . is ingenious but untenable", that "his account of the relationship between mental and physiological causes" is "true but irrelevant to the main point at issue". I do not know what is "the main point at issue" and I think it is finicky to ask whether Toulmin's "account of the relationship between mental and physiological causes" is or is not relevant "to the main point at issue", since any such account is bound to be most interesting, particularly if, as Peters alleges, it happens to be true. What is Toulmin's "account of the relationship between the mental and the physiological"? It turns out to be the hypothesis that even purposeful actions are caused. Alas! This is hardly an account. Toulmin ascribes it to some modern neurophysiologists—he claims no priority—and it surely is old hat. If a stone could think, said Spinoza, it would think that it wished to fall in a parabola.

Toulmin finds Peters's criticisms "wide of the mark"; I am glad he can find them at all. At the very end of his reply he modestly confesses he has "learned much from the work of Soviet psycholgoists" but he does not tell us what; he does not even show us how to find this out. Pity.

I have thus far skipped a lot of material, and even skipped entirely Toulmin's ideas about learning, which Peters comments on and which somehow tie in, Toulmin says, with what he has learned from the Russians. With all that skipping I have not yet covered ten per cent of the volume. At this rate my review of the 500 large and compact pages will be much too long and very disjointed. Let me then be more terse.

Charles Taylor thinks that mechanism is impossible—quite contary to Toulmin and Peters, I suppose. He begins with a view of scientific explanation. It "has two important properties", he says (p. 50), which he treats as *sine qua non*. First, explanation "gives the antecedent conditions [initial conditions] of the explicandum in terms of a set of factors which make evident its connection with others [other explicanda, or other initial conditions, or other sets of factors], which [connection] makes clear with some exactitude what [initial conditions] would need to be changed for other outcomes [other than our initial explicandum] to eventuate". What Professor Taylor means is that we need both the idea of a nomological deductive model—the so-called Popper-Hempel model—and, presumably a very strict kind of testability ensured by an idea of causality as necessary *and* sufficient—Aristotle, good old Aristotle. The other property of scientific explanation is that it is further explicable. I find this rather quaint. Moreover, the question arises: is this process endless or terminable? This point, so crucial for all discussion of reductionism, Professor Taylor dodges. Science is a "search for a conceptual framework". Conceptual frameworks in psychology exist, he adds, which compete with each other, one allowing for purposes, one not. And "a widespread belief among researchers in the field of academic psychology" is that the imputation of goals "is inherently nonempirical, that is, untestable" (p. 55). This is "ill-founded".

Behaviorism. Take Cartesian dualism, suppress the mind, and you have behaviorism (p. 61). But behaviorists are in error when claiming as self-evident "that the mental is unobservable" since I can see anger, for example, in others as well as in myself. Taylor does not mean that anger must be mental; since it may, he says, the question is open. Hence, the debate between behaviorism and psychoanalysis cannot be settled *a priori*; hence, it must be settled empirically (p. 62). Even if mechanism [behaviorism?] were true, continues Taylor, it is possible that the level of explanation we are now aiming at is not yet mechanistic and so the behaviorist's program is doubtful even if his metaphysics is true (p. 63).

I do feel that the last two sentences are in conflict. Also, I do not know where Taylor has found this idea of predetermined levels of explanation, the historicist version of the levels-of-explanation theory; he certainly does not introduce it: he uses it as a platitude in need of no introduction. This particularly puzzles me as he rejects this very idea at the very end of his paper.

The mark of Taylor's paper is its methodological bias: he uses ideas of levels of explanation, of testability, simplicity, and such. But he does not relate these to his initial presentation of his idea of scientific explanation, and he does not explain them. I am at a loss to find out how I can find out when he is applying a previously assumed general idea to a specific case and when he introduces a new one *ad hoc*. The same goes for his many references to much exciting neurophysiology. These will be a closed book to the untutored and a vexation to the tutored. In between, I stand perplexed.

Taylor concludes that we need more experiments and more thinking and that we cannot take for granted the behaviorist's [inductivist] assumption that we must start with the lowest level of science and go up slowly step by step. I confess I like the second point of Taylor's last paragraph very much, though it too comes as quite a surprise.

Comments on Taylor are by Robert Borger, the major editor of this volume, who contends that teleological and mechanistic explanations are no rivals—he seems to agree with Toulmin and Peters. He complains that Taylor presents a caricature of mechanism, or even of behaviorism. Taylor's teleology, he declares, is so flexible that it does not explain why a person performed some definite task rather than one slightly different. The inflexibility Taylor finds in mechanism is thus an explanatory virtue.

This looks like a real conflict. But it is not. We have Taylor's word for it in his reply (p. 89): he fully agrees with Borger (on his major points; but I skip all minor points in this review anyway). "For a causal explanation always has subjunctive and counterfactual implications." Now he tells us! The editors might—if I may add a subjunctive counter-factual part of my causal explanation of the quality of this volume—they might have returned Taylor's and Borger's papers for some serious re-writing.

Do we find here a disagreement? Does Taylor say Yes, causality and teleology are rivals, and does Borger say No? "The key step in the argument", says Taylor (p. 91), "is that which shows that these two accounts are necessarily rivals.[!] But above we saw that they were not rivals unless systematically coordinated." Do we find here a disagreement? On page 93 the answer seems a plain Yes; on page 89—I glance back to make sure—it still seems a plain No. The resolution is to be joyfully found on page 94: "My main point here, and in the paper, is that nobody knows now or can know" the future of science. Moreover "talk about a global mechanist theory tends to be a very far-fetched speculative kind, and is likely to remain such until we have much more knowledge . . . .' No. Definitely no disagreement. Just truisms.

N. S. Sutherland defends mechanism, but, it seems, tainted to this or that degree by the general-systems approach. As Sutherland is a professor of experimental psychology it behooves him to write a section entitled "empirical evidence" and a section entitled "invalidity of 'a priori' answers to the question"—provided the sections are properly labelled. Instead the section "empirical evidence" turns out to be a sermon on induction, intended to cajole us into accepting inconclusive evidence and arguments; the section "invalidity of 'a priori' etc." shows not invalidity but inconclusiveness. We had Taylor who argues from inconclusiveness to monism. Sutherland admits the existence of purposeful action; but purposeful actions are also caused. He does have a brush with Taylor (pp. 114–16), accusing him of vagueness which leads to inconclusiveness. Thus, there are two kinds of inconclusiveness: mine which acquits me and yours which condemns you.

Sutherland is capable of finding excellent sub-titles: one reads, "the possibility of finding negative evidence", i.e., the empirical refutability of his brand of mechanism. Here are the claims. First, "on a really close examination of a brain, we might find that the matter simply defies the laws obeyed elsewhere' (p. 120, line 10 from bottom). I find this almost incredible. Does Sutherland not know the law that all protein under ordinary well-specifiable conditions of temperature, humidity, and exposure to oxygen always gets putrid except when alive? Of course he knows that law, and of course he has merely overlooked that law when he formulated the above-quoted sentence. Since he does not discuss that sentence he fails to see the abysmal inadequacy of his formulation. Had he noticed the inadequacy and tried to make some improvements he might thereby also have learned to be less contemptuous of some of the classical philosophers whom he renounces. Second, clairvoyance may refute his mechanism. Clairvoyance, however, is non-inductive prediction, and so again the claim for refutability hinges on a highly questionable metaphysics to say the least. Moreover, clairvoyance will refute not only mechanism, but a number of our ideas about rationality: we really do not expect clairvoyants to succeed and we have barely worked out the implications of their conceivable success, including certain paradoxes which already puzzed the ancients, about the possibility of using a true prediction in order to make it false and such. So much from Sutherland. It is too much to expect an adequate comment on it. Nevertheless, here is a brief one: this is the first new idea in this volume, and it may show us how much more we may have to do in order to become clear about refutability.

Comments by J. H. Grundy. "Now there are strong grounds for thinking that Sutherland is right in saying that it is possible in principle to give physical explanations of actions" (p. 126). Grundy does find Sutherland's "treatment of action . . . inadequate" (p. 129) but only in that it handles the easiest examples of action.

Sutherland himself is embarrassed (p. 132) by Grundy's lack of disagreement. He concludes by saying that mechanists look for scientific explanations of things, dualists despair of explaining. They are like the Roman Catholic Church.

So much for my initial complaint. The volume could have been enormously improved and made cheaper to purchase, had it started on what is now page 139.

D. W. Hamlyn says that conditioning is bogus and a blind alley; not even Pavlov managed to illustrate it, and present-day conditionings are conditionings only by a long stretch which is preferably avoided altogether. It is, indeed, hardly a stretch: rather it is the piling of diverse meanings onto one label. Pages 140–50 are clear and delightful though they do only what little they claim to do: explain the differences between Pavlov, Watson, and Skinner. Briefly, Pavlov's theory is causal at least in tendency, but Skinner's is not (Watson's is a mess). Whether Hamlyn's analysis is true is another matter: surely, the Skinnerians do not know, to say the least, that they are rejecting the S–R theory. Hamlyn shows in parentheses (p. 150) that this has been noticed by someone already, to this or that extent. But noticed or not, the fact is that even Pavlov's dogs did not behave in accord with his S–R theory: they associated the bell with food not by the physiological law of association which then acted by making the bell physiologically cause them to salivate, but rather they recognized the bell as the sign of food, etc. Admittedly, we can have a purely physio-neurological case of Pavlovism or of anti-Pavlovism (p. 151). [Also W. Grey Walter has built a mechanical analogue of either.] This is neither here nor there, however, since its existing range of applicability is in fact very limited, whereas its range of applicability in principle is the very bone of contention between the mechanists and their opponents (pp. 151–52). This essay, then, is the first in this volume which I can commend.

Comments by A. J. Watson: he agrees with Hamlyn about conditioning, but finds him an anti-mechanist and this he finds dubious (p. 154). Hamlyn is pleased at this large measure of agreement (p. 163). In a note (p. 165) Hamlyn says he cannot believe that predictability is so important even for Skinner. I like that, though I regret I cannot endorse it.

With Watkins's 50-page essay we arrive at a new plateau. Apart from his elegance and polish, erudition and scope, he argues forcefully against widespread views, though he only exchanges pleasantries with Alan Donagan, his commentator and supposed critic. Watkins argues against the view (Collingwood's) that only success is explicable scientifically. Classical theory of choice (chiefly economics, of course) ignores risk: it assumes full knowledge of consequences of choosing this or that and centers on interactions between choices. The theory of expected utility says:

utility of expected event = utility of its outcome × probability of its outcome.

This is best viewed as an extension of the classical theory to relative frequency, when all is certain except which element of a series will turn out successful, which not. Game theory, by contrast, assumes expected utility (a) to apply even to unrepeatable events and (b) to represent the player's mental disposition to bet. Using known arguments Watkins dismisses that theory. Everyone knows that gambling all your fortune, or your life, essentially differs from gambling a marginal profit or even a substantial windfall. Watkins also criticizes and rejects Shackle's theory of indifference maps of gamblers. Taking a non-zero sum game with Popper-type instability—namely, instability caused by the prediction made by each player about each other's prediction about the other's conduct—Watkins short-circuits the idea that full knowledge precludes risk (pp. 197–98). This, next, Watkins extends to the zero-sum game known as the prisoners' paradox. In a devilishly clever analysis he shows how the paradox refutes a basic assumption of game theory by *creating* uncertainty through the strong interaction of the prediction of the two players of the outcome of each other's prediction of each other's next move (p. 206). His refutation seems final.

Watkins's game, incidentally, of two foes with no common authority, wishing for peace but unable to trust each other, sounds a remote Hobbesian thought-experiment, but is all too common in international relations. The deadlock can—I hope—be broken by international trade and such, i.e., by making the game not a two-player single game (*vide* the Sabine daughters' case). Watkins could have noticed this, and I am sorry he skipped it. But he does notice that as long as the game is a two-player single game (repeatable or not), guarantees and sanctions (by the Great Powers, in our case), are either part of the pay-off or irrelevant, in a strictly Hobbesian fashion, and so will not resolve the deadlock.

In actual decisions, says Watkins, any decision-schema employed is but a caricature of some theoretical preference images—a crude and barely articulated schema, with very few of the implications of the options ever noticed. Hence, it is easy to reconstruct the rationality of a failure by showing the discrepancy between the caricature and reality. The caricature itself is rational since decision problems are insoluble unless simplified—oversimplified. Watkins ends with a fascinating case-study of a strange and enigmatic failure which he explains as bungling due to over-schematization and, wouldn't you guess, due to Popper-type prediction-shortcircuits: two parties predicting each other's prediction of each other's conduct.

I do not know whether any of the arguments of Watkins is new—erudition, as usual, makes a writer seem to the less erudite rather dependent on a source for each of his steps. Even if not, however, as a closely knit argument the paper is highly significant. Readers may be indebted to him for his lucid presentation of game theory, and students of decision-making may hope that game theory will never be the same again.

With Jarvie and Winch swords clash, at long last. Jarvie begins with a lunge, an all-out lunge aimed at Winch's heart. Winch, he says, tries to avoid superiority when studying primitives, and he tries to avoid relativism too, by taking some universals—hatch, match, and dispatch—as common to all societies. This will not do, says Jarvie, since the question is: Does Winch endorse an absolutist or a relativist concept of truth and does he agree to compare primitive and Western beliefs on this or that? Winch is particularly indebted to E. E. Evans-Pritchard (we all are) who declared that the magically-minded can be critical of any particular element of their system but not of his system as a whole—as they have no tools to contemplate it except itself. (Evans-Pritchard, incidentally, does not wish to belittle the primitive, since he thinks his own religious system, as well as the Communist system, are likewise intellectual traps. Indeed, he says, his study of magic helped him understand the Moscow show-trials—in both there is an element of sincere confession of obviously false self-incrimination.) Polanyi used this to defend relativism, and Kuhn followed suit and said you cannot compare even Newtonianism and Einsteinianism. Not so, says Jarvie, since a culture may include the idea of its own self-appraisal as a whole, without demanding that the appraisal will always come up the same.

Winch is angry. Jarvie lunges against the wrong target, not even giving Winch the chance to parry. Winch declares allegiance to the absolutist or correspondence theory of truth (p. 254). Ergo, we can compare the views of some societies with those of ours, and, when in some disagreement, either re-examine and alter ours, or else declare theirs false. When they are a primitive society, we shall more often than not disagree and reject. This much Winch fully, though perhaps reluctantly, concedes to Jarvie. Had matters stood here we would be assured that Winch is the wrong target, perhaps not a target at all, since thus far he was only taking a stand at Jarvie's challenge, not having his own say.

What is Winch's say, then? It is (I am using his book *The Idea of a Social Science* (1958), as ancillary since I find his reply hard to follow) that different ways of talking indicate different modes of social intercourse. To understand social intercourse and to know with certainty that one's understanding is true, one needs to be able to participate in a language from within, and fully. The language will, Winch is willing to admit, include some truth-claims enmeshed in its fabric (institutionalized truth-claims endorsed by all members of a society), but what matters is not truth-claims as much as modes of behavior. For example, viewing magic as a poor predecessor of science is not refuted by data yet is erroneous in its misperception of the (institutionalized and largely verbalized) mode of behavior of the practitioners of magic. (The falsehood of the magician's views is insignificant.)

I find this view of Winch's no more than a teaser. It includes a defunct metaphysics of privileged access (I am certain about myself) and one of conduct fully reflectable in language (modes of conduct are fully reflected in conceptual schemes).

Jarvie's reply is a brilliant attempt to force Winch into relativism against his will. We do not progress by calling Negroes 'Blacks', nor by inventing any humanistic concept, but by deciding to treat them as equals come what may. Brilliant, but wasted on, oh!, so worthless a target.

One of Winch's points, however, is worth noticing. He argues, I understand, that when theorizing about the language and mode of thought of the magically-minded, Evans-Pritchard is using a very elaborate meta-theory. This is true; notice, for example, his comparison of the confession of a witch in a trial with the Moscow show trial. Winch is uneasy about this, and seems to claim that even the meager advantage of relativism (I shall not view my culture as superior to yours) is lost here (but my Malinowskian meta-culture is the final court of appeal). I think this point is valid and worth noticing.

As to Winch, the critique does not apply to him in the least; indeed, he seems to have hardly any meta-language or meta-theory, and Jarvie's attribution of relativism to him hurts him as an attribution of a meta-theory akin to that of Evans-Pritchard. He is thus understandably annoyed at Jarvie. Admittedly, for him the institutions of a society are reflected in its language; yet he takes no recourse to meta-language: he simply *points* at the fact (the fact *shows* itself?) that the conceptual system of the magic-minded differs from ours: he uses no elaborate meta-language to describe the different systems, much less to compare them. Here Winch, like many a Wittgensteinian (including the Old Master himself), thinks he follows Old Wittgenstein's *Philosophical Investigations* when he follows young Wittgenstein's *Tractatus*—on its claim for privileged access and its defunct claim for all power to the object-language and none to the meta-language; or almost none; or as little as my index finger (which *shows*).

J. O. Wisdom complains that Popper's social philosophy—his methodological individualism—seems reductionist, even in my own formulation. I do not know how Popperian my formulation is, but I will not recognize it as synonymous with 'institutions . . . consist of individual aims' (p. 272). On the contrary, I understood Popper to say only individuals and not institutions have aims, and institutions consist of existing inter-personal means of coordination (from conventions to rules of conduct to telephone directories). I do agree with Wisdom that Watkins's formulation of methodological indivudalism is reductionist, as Hayek's and Keynes's are. Popper himself, I now tend to agree with Gellner, is unclear about matters and so is free for all.

I do not mean to reaffirm the position I held in 1960, and I do not know whether today I will at all endorse methodological individualism. But since Wisdom rightly opposes reductionism of sociology to psychology, and since my 1960 view blocks that reduction, I find Wisdom's chief concern peculiarly out-of-date. I therefore prefer to see his chief point to be a critique of methodological individualism which does not allow institutions to have aims while recognizing the declared aim of the Royal Society for the Prevention of Cruelty to Animals (p. 274).

Wisdom presents a model of Britain, the British society that is, as a neurotic individual. Some Popperians have sneered at this model—which is a sure sign of a school dogmatism. For, it is a critic's privilege to construct a silly or ludicrous example. The sillier, indeed, the more damaging it is if it is legitimate by the theory thus criticized. Popper declares valuable every refutable model. Wisdom's model is highly refutable (p. 287). Wisdom's model ascribes to societies individual characteristics which may be read as institutionalized or otherwise shared (p. 291). Popper recommends looking for unintended consequences of modes of living and of actions, and Wisdom points these out in his model (pp. 291–92). Therefore, the more an orthodox Popperian, or Popper, ridicules Wisdom's model, the more he ridicules—unjustly, I think—Popper's social philosophy which has Wisdom's model as an unintended part.

Wisdom himself concludes, even further, that his model is true and requires a modification of Popper's social philosophy (p. 293). If this is so, then he offers Popper a way out; Popper may then reject Wisdom's model on the very ground that it requires a modification of Popper. Only if Popper's theory, or any other methodological individualism, is criticizable on the ground that we have a Royal Society for the Prevention of Cruelty to Animals, only then can Wisdom offer his model as one which modifies methodological individualism in order to allow for 'emergent' group-aims.

I salute Wisdom and his raising a point which requires logic much subtler than we have thus far used—all of us, Wisdom included.

Robert Brown does a masterful job of critical analysis. Of particular importance, I think, is his claim that we have no logic of emergence and so can hardly know what Wisdom is talking about. I feel Wisdom's reply is less adequate.

George Homans says (p. 324), "there is absolutely no general philosophical argument that will prove, or disprove" the reduction of all social science to psychology. Reductionists like Homans can offer examples and also "require . . . opponents to do as much on their side". Professor Homans can "require," to be sure; I think it is less than advisable to pay any attention to the Professor's requirement, especially since he permits himself to be so muddled and to adjudicate off-hand that "methodological individualism entails psychologism", brushing off Popper's denial (p. 325) with no discussion at all (as I said above, I do not defend Popper; I think nonetheless that to treat a point he controverts as uncontroversial is not a credential enabling one to "require" anything).

Homans makes an original point: social scientists oppose psychologism because they feel "insecure in their status". I think it positively unadvisable (as "insecure") for a social scientist to take up the cudgel here.

The commentator, Peter M. Blau, feels obliged to follow Homans's requirements. He "largely agrees with Homans's criticism of various

theoretical explanations in sociology" (p. 329). He then adds his own inadequate summary of the hypothetico-deductive model of explanation to that
of Homans. He then takes a sociological theory of his own to show it fulfills
Homans's requirement. What remains for him to do now is to check and
verify that his theory abides by the hypothetico-deductive model of explanation and let matters rest there. Instead he goes on in different directions.
The structure of his paper would be a sufficient reason to fail it, were it a
semester paper. But it is not, and I, for one, have no 'requirements'. "The
conclusion that empirical relationships between characteristics or [of?]
organized collectivities must be explained by sociological general propositions rather than by psychological ones requires the very conception of
scientific explanation Homans and I have adopted", says Blau, "whereas it
would be incompatible with some other conceptions of explanation" (p.
338). Not 'requires', but 'agrees with'. Professor Blau unnoticingly charges
Professor Homans with an inconsistency which he proves in one or two
pages, whereas all he tries to do is to answer Professor Homans's 'requirement' to offer an instance of a sociological explanation. I do think editors
might save authors such embarrassments.

In the opening of his reply Homans claims that Blau misunderstood his
'requirement'; I share Blau's misunderstanding and move on.

Boakes and Halliday advocate Skinnerism. Skinner rejects both
statements about mental states and statements about neurophysiology,
centering on statements about behavior and staunchly eschewing all theory
and all hypothesis (pp. 346–47). In this day and age. "His position is" they
add (on the same page) "essentially that there is no point in looking for explanations until it is quite clear what it is that needs to be explained". I do
not know if this is a theory or a hypothesis, but I know it is refutable since it
contradicts some fairly accepted statements from the history of science. Not
only Freud was unclear about "what it is that needs to be explained", which
is question-begging, but also Max Planck at the same period, as I have
shown in detail elsewhere (*Science*, 156 (1967), 30–37). Or, to take the
authors' example, no student of Galileo's experiment—rolling balls on inclined planes—thinks Galileo knew his data, and what was there "to be explained" (i.e., the rotation as well as the linear motion of the balls). "It is
now fairly generally agreed . . . . The rat . . . [in the maze] makes use of any
cues . . ." (pp. 347–48). Is this not a mentalistic explanation? Is this not the
result of asking whether Hull or Tolman is right? Not at all; it proves that
these "psychologists . . . ask largely irrelevant questions" (p. 347). "Irrelevant" to what? Or is it 'essentially' irrelevant? Critics of Skinner are summarily dismissed (p. 347): "the search for insight . . . based entirely on armchair reflection has produced neither agreement nor explanatory power". Is
this profundity an "insight . . . based entirely on armchair reflection"? Will
it "produce agreement or explanatory power"? Is this an intelligent way to

take criticism when trying to convince readers of the validity of Skinnerism while disowning "the sometimes dogmatic way in which it has been presented" and promising instead "to re-examine its basic content" (p. 345)?

For amusement, readers may search for responses to criticisms of Skinner voiced by Hamlyn elsewhere in the volume. They can recognize them, though only through the glass darkly. The one, that the word 'stimulus' is used to name the antecedent of the 'response' is dismissed as fruitless (p. 353). The other, that both 'stimulus' and 'response' should have meaning to the subject, is mentioned (on pp. 356 and 357) without noticing at all the 'mentalism' involved, not to mention the surreptitious theorizing. But all this is merely in fun. In earnest we move to the comments.

Comments, by Karl H. Pribram: ". . . what I have to say . . . may come as a surprise. In general I *agree*. . . . I do, however, object to some of the details . . ." (p. 375). The details are, "parochialism" (p. 376), "nonsense" (p. 377), "confusion" (p. 377), "confusion . . . compounded" (p. 378). "But I must say that the high point" of the criticism is the fact that the authors "openly and without shame displayed their scrubbed and sterilized conception with the comment 'Learning is a process about which Skinnerians have said little'! . . . they here do a grave disservice to Skinner (as many Freudians have to Freud, etc.)" I rush to the occasion to defend the Freudians. I have never heard of one who said "Sex is something about which Freudians have said little". On second thought, I might say so: with all his concern with the sex drive, its repression, sublimation, and whatever else, Freud had almost nothing to say about what D. H. Lawrence glorified as "an honest fuck". And the same, I suppose, holds for Skinner, whose invention of teaching machines is rooted in his observation of how rare an honest study is in any modern school. It is strange that the authors have not even mentioned the one contribution of Skinner of which many a non-Skinnerian or anti-Skinnerian may sing praise.

In their reply the authors begin by noticing that they are snubbed (p. 381), move to declaring it all to be "misunderstanding" (pp. 384, 386), and end up by saying that the commentator "read what he expected to find rather than" (p. 386). In between they chide the commentator for his oversight of their criticism of Chomsky, which they now try to elaborate. The editors could have asked them to incorporate this, if they saw it as improvement, into the text and let the commentator add a word of comment—or do something else. For my part I think it cheap to discuss the defects of a critic's own position. I think it cheap to admit in the reply that the authors agree with Chomsky about an "inadequacy in the Skinnerian position" and dismiss that inadequacy as "unimportant" (p. 382). I do think the mess is better ignored.

H. J. Eysenck restates the hypothetico-deductive model. He claims that the use of Bode's law in the discovery of Neptune, and Kepler's use of his theory of the music of the spheres in his astronomy are deviations from the hypothetico-deductive model. I do not see why. Nor do I see why he should remain faithful to a model which he thinks is untrue. (Incidentally, Bode's law has four parameters and applies to seven planets, so that its initial fit is almost entirely arbitrary, and what is surprising is its fit with one more planet—Ceres—before it was refuted by the next—Neptune. I do not know if Kepler's case is more striking or less.)

After this one may expect a defense of deviation from the rigid rules of science in psychology as well as in physics. For example, Eysenck may defend phrenology which is not much crazier than Kepler's music of the spheres. Instead he demands the introduction of personality factors to reduce the factor of error in psychological experiments. He introduces general theory of personality: "there is a very large body of evidence, based on questionnaire data, ratings, life histories, experimental tests, projective tests, physiological and constitutional measures, all of which support" it (p. 398). What all this barrage of inductivism has to do with hypothetico-deductivism is unclear to me.

Yet the hypothesis he offers is refutable and "as such deserving of critical attention" (p. 401). This is reasonable, yet unconvincing. At least I do not see here sufficient *specification* to make the refutability of Eysenck's hypothesis manifest. Eysenck also tries to offer causal explanations of his hypothesis. The hypothesis is that some people are more neurotic than others, some more extrovert. The explanation is that neurotics have lower thresholds than non-neurotics, and extroverts are more easily excitable and less easily inhibitable than introverts, where excitation is more or less Pavlovian. This explanation, we are told, is highly testable, and was confirmed (see p. 402); yet on page 403 we are told about difficulties of testing it. He also claims to be offering a reductive physiological explanation, but evidently (p. 405, line 15), he does not. He merely correlates psychological factors (arousal) with physiological ones (cortical excitation), again claiming both testability and confirmation (pp. 405ff.), too sketchily, however, to be convincing or unconvincing. "Insofar as falsification is clearly possible along empirical lines, we may perhaps say that even Popper would agree that in principle this is a scientific argument", he concludes. Perhaps 'should' is more appropriate than 'would', as Popper, in fact, erroneously declares all reductionism irrefutable. Bull's-eye for Eysenck. But then he makes the same error as Popper and declares his opponents essentially unscientific as their views are essentially irrefutable. I would love to propose that we all declare a truce and cease calling each other names. Maybe 'unscientific' is less of an insult than 'meaningless', but nevertheless.

Comments by D. Bannister. He scores a K.O. before the bell rings. "The aim of science is not prediction at any price", he says thus showing a serious defect of almost all hypothetico-deductivism, particularly Popper's where high degrees of falsifiability (by prediction, of course) is declared a paramount *desideratum*.

Bannister does not like Eysenck's static view of man (once a neurotic and/or an extrovert, it follows from Eysenck's theory, always a neurotic and/or an extrovert; which Eysenck himself notices, refuses to admit, and modifies *ad hoc*; p. 407, line 21). The static view forces experimenters to view character change as 'error'. Bannister's critique of reductionism is attractive, but I find it less conclusive than he does. Even his argument from reflexivity (the application of a psychological theory to the psychological theoretician may result in self-elimination: the explanation turns out itself to be certain neurophysiological moves and thus utterly meaningless), so intuitively cogent, is not clinching. Still, Bannister's comments are brief yet very clear, enjoyable, balanced, and thought-provoking. Eysenck's reply begins with acknowledging this fact. Yet he dismisses the comments as opposition not sufficiently reasoned. Pity.

But Eysenck knows how to make his point stick. Take memorizing. It baffled many experimenters. Because extroverts memorize badly, introverts well; so says Eysenck, but his experiments are far too complex, and his identifications of extroverts and introverts are dubious. I am sorry I cannot find his assertion credible. Whether extrovert or introvert, I can report a very selective memory, highly polarized to excellent memory for my cup of tea and terrible memory for names, dates, and bothersome details. I know, in his experiments Eysenck uses the usual nonsense series of syllables. That's just it. He was testing tolerance, not memory; he was also, I guess, using tolerance as a criterion of introversion. This is a mere hypothesis, of course. I shall be delighted to be refuted, since my bad memory does embarrass me so.

Eysenck claims (p. 422) to have given us "the promise of a unification of personality theory, experimental psychology, and physiological theory; one could hardly ask for more." More unification or more promise? Eh?

This is a good discussion. Each writer attacks the other, and sparks fly. I enjoyed reading both, and recommend a detailed discussion in seminars, since the texts can, and may profitably, be improved upon.

Noam Chomsky can be trusted to write well, lucidly, and interestingly—even if he has nothing new to say. Grammar is presented as explanatory theory which, going beyond the evidence, is well testable, particularly if the grammar is quite universal. Universal grammar, of course, deals with the very human intellect. "Linguistics, so characterized, is simply a subfield of psychology" (p. 429). This is Chomsky's thesis—not new in the least—and he offers, further, a progress report. "Obviously, any conclusions . . . must be tentative . . ." (p. 429).

Chomsky repeats concisely and elegantly the argument that we comprehend ambiguous surface structures by reference to deep structures. I dare say the deletion example is new to many, and the phonetic examples may be too difficult for most. I hope they will whet the appetite of readers and make them peruse Chomsky and Halle, *The Sound Pattern of English*. I am myself an enthusiast and quite willing to read any example; but I know the choice of each example is fairly arbitrary, and rich as their number is it is hard to evaluate them except as parts of the general system outlined here. It is no criticism of Chomsky to say he has not done that—it will take some time before anyone does—nor that he fails to return to his topic about universal grammar except for his last footnote. Rich as his essay is in references, that footnote is without any. (Perhaps he should have mentioned von Neumann. Chomsky's new hypothesis amounts to saying that the rules of translation are in a sense universal and so operate as a sort of 'short code' (or compiler); the hypothesis, then, is the same as the one offered in the last paragraph of von Neumann's posthumous *The Computer and the Brain* (New Haven, 1958). Both von Neumann and Chomsky are deeply aware of the accidental part of language and are in search of the universal—which must be inbuilt, they are convinced.) Speaking of grammar, essays have their grammars too, and there is a long tradition, I observe, of putting one's most darling speculation in a final footnote—a descendent, I conjecture, of Newton's *Scholium Generale* and/or *Queries*.

Max Black rightly ignores Chomsky's paper altogether and responds to his general theory. He declares Chomsky not an apriorist (the truth is known by contemplation) but a nativist (our speech forms depend on our genes), and he even prefers to replace nativism with a system of codification which is part of mathematics (axiomatics), dismissing (p. 458) the old dispute between nativists and empiricists as "quite without interest" since every one, human, machine, and even "a blank piece of paper" has some inborn, some acquired qualities. Admittedly, humans learn their mothertongue and no other animal can ever acquire speech qualities; the question still is: does a human learn grammar while using an inborn universal grammar, or while using a more general ability to discern speech patterns, or any patterns, without having a universal grammar? Universal grammar was construed as a minimum pattern shared by all languages. If so, the question is, does it exist at birth? In his last footnote Chomsky offers an alternative view of universal grammar, namely transformation rules between deep and surface structure of any given language. This is another version of nativism, again very interesting and different from empiricism. Black himself thinks that since we know so little physiology nativism is nowadays "a dead end" and he opts for empiricism (pp. 458–59). On one page Black both dismisses a dispute and participates in it!

Without going into details I should say that enjoyable as the Black-Chomsky exchange is, it hardly adds anything. Chomsky exhibits again his ambivalence about explanation versus codification, but otherwise easily wins the upper hand. Let me mention one odd fact. Black touches upon reflexivity. (See above; Chomsky argues as an empirical investigator that language is *a priori*, and this seems incoherent.) He uses a reflective argument which was invented by Russell (in his introduction to Wittgenstein's *Tractatus*): Chomsky's work suggests impossible rules, unnatural languages. These could be taught and thus refute Chomsky. Answer: it depends at what unnatural cost these languages could be acquired; in particular, could children pick them up, or would they render them natural?

Finally, Frank Cioffi—the junior editor of this volume—on Freud and pseudo-science. "A successful pseudo-science is a great intellectual achievement", he opens. On a clever passage by Mary Baker Eddy, he comments: "If Mrs. Eddy had always reasoned this well we should never have heard of her" (p. 473). Pseudo-science is manifest in its avoidance of refutation (p. 473) and in its presentation of interpretations of facts as facts (pp. 473–74). Thus a pseudo-scientific hypothesis causes an expectation that may, if confirmed, confirm it, but may not, if refuted, refute it (p. 474).

Then comes a study of Freud's way of taking liberty with evidence. I confess I don't like to see a hatchet job, but I agree: if you have to do it, you may as well do it in style. The story of the distortion of evidence in the case of little Hans's animal phobia (pp. 485–86), gave me a jolt, both because it is too crude even for Freud and because Freud makes so much of it in *Totem and Taboo* (*IV* (3)). (Those interested may find a fuller account of the case in H. J. Eysenck's *Fact and Fiction in Psychology*, London, 1965, ch. 3.) It is a pity, though, that Cioffi compares Freud to numerologists, even though reputed ones like Dante and Newton. After some discussion of Freud's techniques, Cioffi claims that we can rather easily make explicit the applications of these techniques and rectify Freud's reports, reconstruct them into "pseudo-soliloquies" (p. 497). Whatever happened to Cioffi's opening claim that "a successful pseudo-science is a great intellectual achievement"?

Comments by B. A. Farrell, one of the Freudian targets of Cioffi's paper. He scores here and there. I lose count. Though I share Cioffi's appraisals of Freud's techniques as dishonest—intellectually, Cioffi is not attacking Freud's person—I think of Freud as both an incredibly sensitive humanitarian and one of the greatest thinkers of the century. It may be ironical, but it may be just one of those things—Kepler and Newton were numerologists, Marx was a Hegelian, Max Weber was a Nietzschean, both Freud and Whorf had numerological phases, and so it goes. It may teach us not to preach too much intellectual hygiene, for all I know; or rather, hygienic as I choose to be, I should not be too eager to condemn those who do not apply my standards.

In line with this, I should not condemn the editors or authors of this volume. Yet I would not have read it all were I not reviewing it. How representative is it of the scope and calibre of work in the field?

It is interesting that quite a few contributors to this volume restate the hypothetico-deductive model, more or less poorly. It is interesting that inductivism is still widespread, explicit for the old-fashioned, implicit for some of the others. It is a fact that reductionism, also an old-fashioned issue, is still bothering many in spite of positivism: indeed, it was the way the positivists themselves could legitimately air a metaphysic. The logical trouble most writers suffered was, obviously, their inability to relate their views on reduction with their views on induction and/or the hypothetico-deductive model. For my part, I think that the hypothetico-deductive model has to be restricted to given metaphysical systems which can act as frameworks ("conceptual framework" is the expression used here), and the question how such frameworks are adopted and given up is still open. If this volume illustrates anything it is that hypothetico-deductivism cannot—at least as yet—itself decide the choice of frameworks without some further discussion. But this, of course, betrays my own bias in methodology. I am afraid I think the proper choice of framework at this stage will almost entirely dodge the problem of reductionism, which is the only one shared by quite a few of the authors and commentators. The question of choice of frameworks is not of much use if it leaves us stuck with the classical problem of reductionism. There must be more exciting and newer problems for frameworks to handle. And on these uneasy topics, I suppose, the volume reflects the general malaise in the field, one way or another. This is a period of lull, and so an occasion for anyone who has anything interesting to say to catch the public's ear.*

*For more details see my *Towards a Rational Philosophical Anthropology*, The Hague, 1977.

— 19 —

THE SCIENCE OF SCIENCE

reserving a seat on the bandwagon

I do not know how representative is Professor D. Mackay's and Professor J. D. Bernal's paper, which heralds the science of science and which I was kindly invited to comment upon—I do not know how representative it is of either its writers or the present epoch. One of the first jobs they assign to the science of science is the statistical study of science, which study might perhaps tell how characteristic their paper is. But the science of science, as the title of their paper ('Toward a Science of Science') indicates, is still nonexistent; it is still, one learns, in its pre-scientific stage, but at the point of a breakthrough.

How does one behave when seeing a new subject developing, a totally new bandwagon starting? One reserves a seat on it, to be sure; one secures one's right to the seat; one conjectures where the bandwagon is heading and stakes a claim at that future position. All this is not easy at all, especially since one may be so wrong. Still, a few simple rules may be safely adhered to.

One can always praise one leading pioneer, use the jargon of another pioneer, etc. The pioneers here are Derek J. de Solla Price, whose statistical studies of science are the true omens of the closeness of success in developing the new discipline, and Thomas S. Kuhn whose new word 'paradigm' is here used or misused (I cannot say which) a few times. But one should not identify too closely with the pioneer, since some movements are known to have devoured or rejected some of their pioneers. Perhaps Price is too statistical; obviously some statistical studies are carrying statistics too far—even in the science of science. But when in doubt, refrain; jumping on a bandwagon is enough of a risk, and you need not risk any more. In particular, do not say when statistics is fruitful, when not. Only assert your

---

This comment on the paper 'Toward a Science of Science', by D. Mackay and J. D. Bernal, appeared in Polish in *Zycie i Mysl*, 19, 1966.

sincere faith in statistics, and qualify it judiciously but most ambiguously. Details will be studied further by members of the next generation who may view their work as the filling of gaps in yours—if you are lucky. You also have to express faith in other good qualities of science—the science of science must be scientific, you know—such as criticism and experiment. You can recommend the starting of the project with the eclectic search for anything that has been done and can possibly be *post hoc* incorporated in the project. This technique was discovered by Francis Bacon three centuries ago, and has been used incessantly in recent years: this abundant use proves the technique to be safe enough. Another technique of Bacon's which has been often repeated: if you have no solution, appoint a committee to study the problem, appoint professors and investigators, etc., etc. Our authors bluntly recommend that chairs for the science of science be instituted. Presumably for next year.

Imagine yourself appointed first professor of the science of science. Naturally, you are ignorant of it; everybody is. It's a new subject, an embryo, remember. Now, you are equipped with statistical instruments (you have an assistant or two at your service); you know how to conduct experiments and observations (everybody). Problems abound, and our authors have alluded to hundreds of them. For my part, I suggest the following problem: do subjects or disciplines benefit or suffer from advance publicity, early chair-creations, etc.? So you study this problem; you conduct suitable observations, perform relevant experiments, use appropriate statistics. You soon come to the (all too obvious) solid conclusion that the results are negative. You follow your own conclusions, resign your job, and shut up. Of course.

Our authors are in dead earnest. They not only wish to see new chairs instituted at once, they are even willing to learn something from the Ur-Boy Scout, Lord Baden-Powell: they recommend the creation of clubs with quaint-sounding names for weekend outings, especially for historians (of science?) to study in nature's bosom the new science of science. And from the Ur-Zionist Theodor Herzl too: they are quite ready to approach the rich Sheikh of Kuwait for his support of the project.

*   *   *

What exactly has happened? There is no doubt that both writers are respectable and respected members of the academic community. Presumably they had an understandable lapse in offering their paper to the Eleventh International Congress for the History of Science. That their contribution is deemed so important, however, as to merit further symposium, is perhaps somewhat of an excess. But the question of whether this is so does not seem important enough to study. Rather I wish to make my own humble contribution to the science of science, such as it is, right now.

Throughout the history of science, bandwagons come and go, and people divining their time-tables and destinations also come and go. And some of these individuals even manage to hang on to some real wagon or another. And even make a minor contribution. This all matters very little. Also there is the tradition of prosecuting such pathetic diviners, of ridiculing them, of driving them out of town. This is not so nice, because those who do the ridiculing are usually well-established and are thus willy-nilly guarding not only the interests of science but their own interest as well, whereas the person who is ridiculed is usually poor and naive, and sometimes a real fighter, sometimes—however rarely—even for a worthy cause. It is amazing, come to think of it, how many of our respectable ideas were ridiculed once by some established professor.

Thus, by and large I am against ridiculing prophets of new trends and of new bandwagons. But I am not speaking from experience: perhaps experimenting will show that once we cease ridiculing pseudo-pre-science and fighting it by other means, it may swallow science. Still, as long as the need to be harsh is not proven, I prefer to be tolerant. Indeed, some of my best friends are pseudo-scientists—some of them even pseudo-pre-scientists. But I demand from my friends tolerance, too: when I think they are pseudo I may call them pseudo; and they may call me whatever name they like, of course. I am easy.

Normally I would not have commented on 'Toward a Science of Science'; normally I would not even have read it carefully. As Shaw once said, you need not eat the whole egg to know that it isn't exactly very fresh. But perhaps we should from time to time say fully what we think, especially when invited, especially when the pseudo-scientific work is not of a poor and naive person but of well-established people, and especially when their aberration is taken somewhat too seriously.

20

MARXISTS ON ANTHROPOLOGY

reconciling heroes

This book is evidently a trend-setter. Robert Ulin, its author, is a graduate of the New School of Social Research and a young but apparently already well-established member of its faculty. On the reasonable assumption that the School will stay as influential as it is, he is a coming man in the anti-establishment establishment. This makes a review of his first fruit a heavy burden for anyone with some idea which direction scholarship ought to take: a reasonable review of such an author may have an immense multiplier.

The book is an introduction to the current debate on rationality in the light of anthropological studies. For the choice of topic alone the author deserves warm praise. Also for the relative clarity. It has pages and pages obscure to me, let alone to the beginner, yet, on the whole, the book earns points for relative clarity. I recommend it (1) to the Marxist beginner, (2) to the beginner who can read critically, and skim, and move back and forth, and, particularly, (3) to the sociologist of science interested in Marxism as a significant social phenomenon.

My review proper begins after a few complaints, especially about the book's esotericism. Here are some general impressions about Marxian esoteric practices and their reflections in this book.

It is all too common to expect the class a of all those who admire a thinker and who admit his influence openly, and the class b of that thinker's followers, to be coextensive. Not so. We have in the case of Marx, to the contrary, members of a and not b, such as Karl Popper. We also have in that case members of b and not a. These are people who disregard the works published in Moscow as the Marx-Engels classics and center instead on

This review of *Understanding Cultures: Perspectives in Anthropology and Social Theory*, by Robert C. Ulin (Austin, TX: University of Texas Press, 1984) appeared in *Philosophy of the Social Sciences*, 1987.

Marx's youthful manuscripts posthumously published in Moscow in the thirties; who prefer to disregard *Das Kapital* and expand on choice paragraphs from an early, posthumously published draft of it; who cite from *Das Kapital*, in a pinch, utterly uncontroversial sentences, such as the claim that the poorest architect is superior to the cleverest bee on account of his having some foresight. Not all Marxists' writings conform to this description, of course. Ulin's bibliography and references to Marx do.

Who, then, is a Marxist? It is hard to characterize the Marxist's essence, but easy to describe his appearance: it is very easy to spot a Marxist, whether self-declared or closet—by his use of Marxian terminology, preferably the wrong way. The favorite term of misuse is 'praxis'. It is the term Marx invented to denote the unity, which he postulated, between theory and practice. This unity is obviously rejected by quite a few contemporary Marxists; they therefore have an idle term, 'praxis'; so they use it as a synonym for 'practice' (perhaps for intentional practice only, but lines are blurred here in diverse ways). Ulin does this throughout the present book. And he uses the word 'dialectically' in any way he likes except in that of Marx, and he falsely declares (p. 174, n5) that he uses it in a specific manner—one which I will not cite since it is peculiar to himself as far as I know. Marxists also like to mention facts about class-distinctions when they are irrelevant. Thus, referring to Azande magic, the standard example in the current dispute on rationality, Ulin observes that Zande commoners are forbidden to charge Zande aristocrats with magical ill practices, admitting (p. 39, lines 13 and 14) that this fact is irrelevant to the dispute. They also tend to quote other Marxists approvingly and non-Marxists disapprovingly, thus distorting all sense of proportion by insinuating that only Marxists agree with them on this and only non-Marxists disagree with them on that. (One gets the funny impression that one has to be a Marxist to admit that the silliest architect is cleverer than the cleverest bee.) Most of the seeming inconsistencies in this book, I suspect, are due to no more than this malpractice. At times Ulin is explicit: in one undocumented four-line note (p. 180, n16) he accuses Edmund Husserl of solipsism and praises Merleau-Ponty for having returned Husserl's doctrine to the fold of inter-subjectivity. It is clear that non-Marxists are at times treated with respect—perhaps because they are near-relatives. In the book at hand they are the inter-subjectivists who admit the socio-cultural matrix within which we all operate, and those who in one way or another oppose scientism. But this cannot be the case in every instance. At times non-Marxists are cited and harshly criticized—perhaps they have succeeded in penetrating the ranks. One had better ignore these aspects of the present book and give up on the question of how its author chose to cite approvingly and count as friends not only Marxists. Hans-Georg Gadamer and Paul Ricoeur, he more than insinuates (e.g., p. xv), are Marxists. Of course, he does not mean this: he is a victim of the careless Marxist style.

Not all misrepresentations here are stylistic, however. Ulin describes Peter Winch as "abdicating the categories of the anthropologist . . . thereby privileging the native's categories" so that he turns out to be "in the same abstract position as the natural scientist", i.e., he is left with faith in full verification. He also ascribes faith in full verification to I. C. Jarvie, a fetishism of science to Robin Horton (p. 62), a reliance on the authority of Marx vitiated by a "non-dialectical" understanding of his text to Steven Lukes (p. 77), and, even more astonishingly, the demand "to go beyond the informant's interpretation, so that ideology or false consciousness can be discovered where it is manifested", as well as an "insistence on the importance of causal description in social science as a logic of one unified science [which] contributes to the very condition of control that he wishes to identify and overcome" (p. 86) to Alasdair MacIntyre who is, as the last quoted words indicate, friend, not foe.

Such repeated misrepresentation is partly due to a terminology not uniformly fixed throughout the literature, but it is also partly sheer carelessness and partly a hefty dose of naiveté. Carelessness: For example, Jarvie's methodology is presented as strict verificationist, in as strict a sense as one can ascribe to anyone (p. 66, line 4 and the following lines), only to possess, later on (p. 88), "a tentative nature of truth assertions as exhibited in intersubjectively verified hypotheses". Naiveté: "For example, I am not well versed in the principles that enable astronauts to be sent to the moon. I do, however, have a clear understanding of what it means to spend federal funds on the escalation of the space race as opposed, for example, to community hospitals" (p. 62).

Ulin's self-appointed task seems to be that of reconciling the different New School of Social Research heroes. What has Dilthey in common with Marx? And, reconciling by finding the lowest common denominator may, indeed, mean going down quite far. Anyway, what has the technique—the hermeneutic technique of Dilthey—devised to comprehend ancient sacred texts—to do with anthropology? Both are attempts to comprehend people largely different from ourselves (p. 92). In the summary of his chapter on hermeneutics, he says (p. xv) of hermeneutics, "In Chapter 5 I show how this form of interpretation theory transcends the untenable dichotomy in the rationality debates between understanding and explanation by presenting all acts of human understanding as permeated by the social and historical contingencies of informants and anthropologists. I also illustrate that the meaning of human interactions and cultural products is not tied to the immediacy of context but, on the contrary, is capable of addressing all actual and potential speech communities. The encounter of the radical other, which typifies the fieldwork experience in anthropology, is portrayed [in this book] as an intercultural dialogue that leads us to grasp the native's social world while simultaneously deepening the understanding of our own social world." This is correct: we do have the "radical other" and the "intercultural dialogue"; we can, at times, cross barriers or frameworks; we do thereby learn both about others and ourselves. What has this to do with Marx, Habermas, Gadamer, or Ricoeur? Allegedly, they are the leading lights which have led Ulin to his conclusion. How?

Marx ascribed class-prejudice to everyone, declared one can opt for the most progressive class—the proletariat, of course—and implied that total rationality, i.e., freedom from all prejudice, will be the property of classless society alone. Gadamer defends prejudice. He is quoted (p. 94ff) as saying that the Enlightenment defended utter rationality thus eschewing all tradition; the Romantics went the other way round, but Gadamer (at least Gadamer à la Ulin) opts for both by simply denying that prejudice is the opposite of rationality: rather the two are complementary and mutually supportive. Ulin reports that Gadamer has opted for continuity as opposed to scientific radicalism (p. 94, lines 25-26). How can one more clearly contradict Marx? Ulin ignores Marx at this point, ascribing to Gadamer the view which is Popper's celebrated signature-tune (p. 96, lines 21-22): "Prejudices are [to be] neither suspended nor dogmatically maintained but are [to be] corrected . . . ." The additions I have made, in square brackets, are necessary in order to transform a trivially and palpably false statement into a sane recommendation. Yet the recommendation is not readily assimilable into Gadamer's hermeneutics, since most traditions are, as a matter of fact, dogmatic, irrationalist, etc. Ulin's text trails off to Collingwood who, admittedly at times (e.g., in his essay on Croce) saw historical studies as in constant need for improvement but, alas, all too often (e.g., in his *Autobiography*) declared his faith in finality. All is well, however, that ends well. The end of the Gadamer section has a paraphrase of Habermas's critique: Gadamer forgets all about "different forms of dominion as they are embodied in the normative institutional structures of various traditions": he is not friend but foe.

Ulin then tries to replace Gadamer by Ricoeur, admits failure to apply Ricoeur's early theory of metaphor to the Nuer view of twins as birds, moves to Ricoeur's late theory, loses it too, and never returns to the twins. He drops it all and moves to Marxism.

Should a Marxist be more esotericist than usual when introducing Marxism or less? More: he cannot offer a capsule version of Marx. He cannot even offer a capsule version of a leading Marxist. Ulin presents the views of Georg Lukacs and of Louis Althusser very lamely and briefly, calling them two traditions of Marxism and moving on to followers of Althusser.

How did any Marxist tradition gel? Why two? Why these two? No answer. Obviously, there are diverse political traditions sustained by political institutions: revisionist Marxism, Austro-Marxism, Marxism-Leninism, and Trotskyism, at the very least. How much did Stalin contribute to Marxism-Leninism and are his contributions still retained? These last are two questions uppermost when discussing Marxist traditions. Yet many Marxists will not touch them. The intellectual aspects of the political traditions, however, are still significant and silence will not drive them away. There is, in particular, the speech delivered to Soviet philosophers by Yuri Andropov just before his death, censuring them for their excessive obsequiousness to Western-style Marxism, and there are the Eastern-European sociologists of science whose views were well-received in the first international meeting of the Society of the Social Study of Science over a decade ago. There are traditions more within the intellectual than the political institutional framework, especially the young-Marx tradition begun with Georg Lukacs and Herbert Marcuse, to which the present book belongs; the Marxist branch of the small but interesting neo-Ricardian school of economics headed by Marxist Piero Sraffa; the Yugoslav tradition centered round the periodical *Praxis*; and lone wolves like Milovan Djilas. Ulin is a Marxist author who speaks briefly of two traditions as a prelude to his discussion of a few Althusserians, culminating with Maurice Godelier.

"Maurice Godelier, more than any of the other Marxist anthropologists, provides us with a perspective from which to draw the issues of the rationality debates into a fully[!] Marxist theoretical framework" (p. 138). "Although Godelier is critical of the methodological individualism of the empiricist tradition, there is a surprising convergence of his notion of theory with that of the neo-Popperians", namely to that of Jarvie, except that Godelier rejects verification (p. 139). Now it all becomes clear: Jarvie cannot be properly presented because he is not of the self-selected élite; Godelier is. Once the author's misstatement of Jarvie is corrected, and the views of Marxist Godelier coincide with the views of non-Marxist Jarvie on all essentials, then self-selection into the Marxist fold ceases to be a matter of ideas and becomes a sociological mystery.

Now we come to the beef. Are alien cultures rational? Is magic, in particular, in any sense rational? Sir James Frazer called it pseudo-science, since it does not deliver the goods. His contemporary, Émile Durkheim, declared religion the ritual that does deliver the goods of expressing and enhancing social unity, and magic an inferior version of it, less unified and less integrating in societies where division of labor is less detailed and less rigorously maintained. Bronislaw Malinowski followed Durkheim and deemed magic expressive rather than technological, so that he can equivocate about what goods it delivers, if any. Evans-Pritchard, who also followed Durkheim, declared magically-minded people rational in the sense that they can and do assess the efficacy of each individual magic-claim though not magic-as-a-whole, and rational in the sense in which magic-as-a-whole is an intellectual system within which they operate—a language system, so to speak. But Evans-Pritchard never concealed his own view that magic does not deliver the goods.

Out of Ludwig Wittgenstein's later philosophy Peter Winch developed an idea of the social sciences which extended the master's famous dictum of language as a form of life in two steps: first, a form of life is a way of life, so that each society has one; second, every way of life constitutes a language. This led him to an utterly relativistic theory of truth, and he criticized Evans-Pritchard as not relativist enough. It is clear that we have a dilemma here: absolutism and relativism are both uncomfortable, the one leading to dogmatism and the other to excessive tolerance, as Bertrand Russell repeatedly emphasized while frankly and plainly confessing inability to overcome it. There is only one proposed alternative to Russell's dilemma debated in the contemporary literature, which may be unsatisfactory and in need of reform, and it is that of Sir Karl Popper: the truth is an ideal; received opinions in diverse societies are all in need of criticism and improvement which will hopefully increase their proximity to the truth. Sociologists of science may examine the claim that all contemporary efforts to evade Russell's dilemma appeal to one or another variant of Popper's view (though, of course, many writers prefer the one or the other horn and feel comfortable enough with it).

Where should we place Marx? This question is anachronistic and so rather unfair. Marx seems to have been a relativist, though this is hard to pin down. Yet, even so, he refused to grant legitimacy to any opinion as relatively true; he seems to have linked legitimate theory to practice by his theory of praxis, and practice to inter-subjective stages of economic organization by his historical materialism, and inter-subjective stages of economic organization to objective stages of technological progress by his dialectical materialism. And as some self-styled Marxists protest that this is not at all Marx but Engels, let me concede and ascribe these views to either Marx or Engels, or both. Thus, if any theory can be viewed in retrospect as the reasonable predecesor to Popper's solution of Russell's dilemma, it may very well be the author of the praxis theory, namely either Marx or Engels, or both. Most Marxists who have met and struggled with Russell's dilemma, Robert Ulin in the present book in particular, seem to be plucking up their courage to state this point. And at the risk of irritating some Marxists and many Popperians, I agree with Ulin if and only if this is indeed what he means his reader to understand him to hint at.

The book at hand begins with Franz Boas, who does not belong. It also surveys the views of (1) Malinowski and Evans-Pritchard, (2) Winch, (3) Jarvie and Horton, (4) Lukes and MacIntyre, (5) the hermeneuticists Gadamer and Ricoeur, and (6) the Marxists. Lukes is an absolutist who hopes that comparative anthropology needs no presuppositions so that there is no need to fear that it is dogmatic. MacIntyre's position is too intricate for me to summarize—at least in a brief review. Ulin presents MacIntyre as an absolutist who, we remember, suffers the weaknesses of traditional absolutism—especially the lack of historical perspective and dogmatism. Gadamer is presented *de facto* as a variant of Popper, we remember; and Paul Ricoeur is declared inscrutable. The final and longest chapter is a survey of works by diverse followers of the Marxist-Althusserian tradition, including Marshall Sahlins, and culminating, we remember, with Godelier.

The index is extremely spotty. Even as an abbreviated name-index it fails. But the book is relatively readable and concerns itself with a genuine problem which increasingly forces itself on the philosophical agenda. Broadly speaking, any historical approach to rationality sooner or later will endorse Jarvie's view of it as historically determined in its social context and thus as a matter of degree. This is both in accord with Marx's spirit and transcends his letter. Call this fact 'dialectical'; pay Marx proper homage, and cease treating his works, published by him or by his successors, as an authority. Marx belongs to our history. We are all influenced by Marx as much as by many other thinkers; hence, declaring oneself a Marxist is a political act devoid of all intellectual meaning except for some faintly ludicrous and obstructive lip-service.

21

(NON-)PARTICIPANT-OBSERVERS OF SCIENCE

trading in absurdities

This book, by a rising star of the sociology of science, undertakes in a fast-paced manner to show us how working scientists 'manufacture' knowledge from esoteric rites, procedures, and traditions. Little attempt is made to disguise the site, which was a laboratory where her spouse, D. Knorr, was engaged. It is not a work of participant observation, since the author is no biologist; rather it is modelled on the ethnography of the police-court reporter, close to events but not taking them quite at face value.

In his admirably lucid preface Rom Harré places Professor Knorr-Cetina's work within the broad context of "the anthropological approach, as one might call it", where "laboratories are looked upon with the innocent eye of the traveller in exotic lands". Knorr-Cetina applies not only anthropology but also economics to her study of science; but this matters less than Harré's apt characterization of "the innocent eye" of the anthropologist who observes, he says "with the objective yet compassionate eye of the visitor from a quite other cultural milieu". The most surprising thing the innocent, objective, compassionate visitor sees is that induction, as well as "conjectures and empirical refutations of the logicist philosopher of science, is quickly refuted. Logic, it seems, is not among the 'idols of the tribe' ".

What one is to say to the logical refutation of logic, to the empirical refutation of all empiricism, etc., I will not discuss here. Rather, as a "logicist philosopher of science", I shall compare this refutation to

This review of *The Manufacture of Knowledge: An Essay on the Constructivist and Contextual Nature of Science*, by Karin D. Knorr-Cetina (Oxford: Pergamon, 1981) appeared in *Inquiry*, 26, 1983, under the title, 'The Cheapening of Science'.

another. Imagine the reverse position of an innocent, compassionate, objective visitor from a remote corner to a modern country. Imagine his surprise at finding that modern economy is no longer carried on with the use of money—rather, banknotes, checks, promissory notes, etc. are the order of the day. Moreover, ever so many promissory notes are worthless, he notes; ever so many credit cards are fake. All this has a trivial side—promissory notes promise money—and a non-trival side: is the legal tender money or promissory notes? It is not clear, especially since, when there is a gold standard, a banknote is clearly a promissory note, while when the gold standard is cancelled, who knows? In brief, the claim that science is not concerned with the truth about the facts but with consensus about them is the same as saying that someone does not care for money who accepts promissory notes instead.

The question is: what is the position of the sociologists of science described by Harré? Do they say: money is abolished as promissory notes and credit cards are currency? Or do they say: promissory notes and credit cards are substitute money but not a perfect substitute? The first thesis is bold and simple and rather silly. The second is timid and sophisticated and calls for much more research than the mere discovery that some credit cards are fake, some stolen, etc. Which of the two does Knorr-Cetina affirm? It is possible to quote her defending either. Hence, possibly she has not worked out her claim yet. Possibly, however, she is negotiating: she would like to manufacture the fact, i.e., convince us, that money does not exist. If so, she may have to settle for less—for the other alternative, that some credit cards are fake or stolen. She may, then, wish to haggle for a middle position. But there is no middle position, and for obvious logical reasons.

But this is said by a "logicist philosopher of science" who thinks logic forces us to deem refuted theories false. And this is question-begging for people like Harré who think logic seldom appears in science and "where it appears it is an insert in the pursuit of rhetorical advantage in the debate". Thus, Harré may waive my logic and seek rhetoric instead. Here then is my presentation repeated with more rhetoric, but with no less logic.

The intended value of a human artifact need not be the one attributed to it later: no matter why we value the head of Queen Nefertiti in the Berlin museum where it rests, we know it was not supposed by the sculptor to rest there but in the belly of a remote pyramid somewhere in the vast Egyptian sand dunes. Moreover, there are clearly unintended values, such as the value of a page from a text by Immanuel Kant for a teacher who wishes to put an impossible task to students engaged in the analysis of the grammar of lengthy and tortuous and opaque sentences.

The major purpose of intellectual activity is the intellectual love of God, the sheer delight in the pleasure of the participation in an intellectual trip. When one reads a book such as Erwin Schrödinger's *What Is Life?* then one may enjoy its exquisite ideas, presentation, language, etc. Anything else seems as secondary as putting the volume—it is a very thin volume—under the short leg of a table to prevent it from wobbling. Now, no doubt, the fun of reading a book and the use of it as a physical solid are two extremes. There are all sorts of in-between cases. Consider, for example, a student reading *What Is Life?* for an exam. The student's purpose is practical: getting a degree in order to get a job in order to get paid in order to afford a new table to replace this annoyingly wobbly thing. Yet, by some sort of transformation, by the Grace of God, really, one in ever so many students may see the light. Hey, he may mutter, by Golly! this is great fun! Fancy having such a lovely book to read for an exam! Incredible! I must tell my analyst about this! Incredible!, etc. etc.

But there are many other kinds of in-between cases. The teacher may value *What Is Life?* as a text he can examine his students about. But who will value the teacher? The trustees of the school and the city fathers, of course, who knows that graduates of their school get good jobs and acquire good homes and heavy solid furniture, so that they can pass the discarded pieces of furniture to succeeding generations of students along with the used volumes of Schrödinger's *What Is Life?* which may be used to stop the nagging wobble. Where, then, is the fun in such a system? The fun of a stray student who may be graced and enjoy reading the book can be ignored. Oh, he can tell his analyst about his experience, and even his close friends and associates. He will then learn that he sounds weird and keep his experiences to himself. What else? It is the fun of living ordinary pragmatic life in ordinary pragmatic society in our modern technological world.

Let us not put down the fun of ordinary life: we may regret that most people cannot enjoy reading a beautiful text as a beautiful text: but practical people who read that text for practical purposes are not in the least worse off than those who do not. And just as we can love and appreciate an honest illiterate peasant, so we can love and appreciate an honest literate modern farmer or an honest literate agronomist, no less because somewhere in his training he had to read Schrödinger's *What Is Life?* while enduring life in a remote urban college living for four-to-seven years in shabby rooms shabbily furnished before going back to the land and becoming again a useful, honest member of society.

Enter the sociologist of science. He too has to make a living; after all, he too has spent four-to-seven years in shabbily furnished shabby university housing reading whatever his professor has forced him to read. Worse still, he has spent his years reading thick volumes and has had to find something other than books to put under the leg of that damned wobbly table.

Enter the sociologist, I say. Not only has he read the thick volumes. He can hardly read the thin volume that is Schrödinger's *What Is Life?* He can hardly say whether this book is scientific or philosophical. He has no view of the education of our meanwhile-settled agronomist, and cannot even ask: Was that volume essential to that agronomist's education or was it mere ballast? And if ballast, would the agronomist—or the society he is now honorably serving—be better off or worse off without it? A professor of medicine in Boston University told me that the main thing about medical education is quantity, not quality: medical students must get used to being overburdened from the very start or else, etc. You see, doctors are not born stupid—they are trained to be stupid. Our agronomist has had his lean years, but he was lucky: he was also trained to be resourceful and find his own solutions to his problems from the very start, by improvising with unorthodox uses of all sorts of handy objects.

But we should not necessarily show less respect to the sociologist than to the illiterate peasant: both cannot read Schrödinger, after all, and this should count for something. Moreover, both have learned to survive by showing some respect for practical matters, and for those scholars who are good at practical matters. The agronomist is by now so reticent about the joy he had experienced one dreary day in his dreary university apartment that he himself has forgotten almost all about it; it appears to him from time to time, through a glass darkly, but he pushes on with practical matters, and for this he earns the respect of practical people, including both the peasant and the sociologist.

Except that the sociologist has to handle the situation of the agronomist, whereas the farmer may be satisfied with tidbits of useful results of the work of the agronomist. Now sociologists can study the density of agronomists, the interaction between children of agronomists and those of farmers, the difference between those who come from the city and settle in the country and those, like our hero, who come from the land, stay in college for a while, and return to the land to live happily ever after.

Or so they think. Because, sometimes disaster strikes, and for one reason or another the agronomist may have to wander and again find himself in the city. And his observer, the sociologist, may have to move with him and even change sub-profession from rural sociology to the sociology of science. Nature is still kinder to the agronomist than to the sociologist. The agronomist reads books and papers he understands and studies things he does not understand, like fertilization and its excesses, trying to make sense of them and control them for the betterment of the farmers and the consumers and the rest of mankind. And he may be studying such questions as how to make his conclusions comprehensible to the barely literate farmer, so that expected changes and improved controls may ensue. Our sociologist of science has to read materials he finds incomprehensible—whether statistics from Yale or myths from Edinburgh; moreover, he handles materials such as books and articles agronomists read and write, which he cannot possibly comprehend or else he would desert his low-prestige job at a drop of an invitation to become a life-scientist.

What is the sociologist to do? He looks at reading lists of agricultural science courses. *What Is Life?* is on them. Odd. Distinctly odd. Is this life-science or metaphysics? Let us see who wrote it: if a life-scientist wrote it, it is life-science; if a philosopher wrote it, it is metaphysics. Shucks! of course! Schrödinger was a physicist! Now, dare a physicist cross boundaries to life-science? It must be metaphysics, then. No, life-scientists say it is a must. It is something very special, then: it is a paradigm-forming text: the text became obligatory in the molecular biology field and has led to the rise of a new paradigm!

What is a paradigm? A book read by a group of scientists and declared obligatory for them. How can we test the gossip about Schrödinger's book? Can there be a pseudo-paradigm? Could there be a whole sub-specialty with a reading list which is more-or-less standard in the sub-profession, and with one item on the standard list redundant? Or the whole list perhaps?

I submit that only an expert from within can answer this kind of question.

I submit that almost no sociologist of science is an expert from within.

Things are getting warmer. Sociologists of science bluntly deny that one need study matters from within. We do not question the validity of a magic ritual when we study it; we do not study the validity of an item of common knowledge when we do the sociology of knowledge as conceived by Karl Mannheim; this was the idea that all knowledge other than science is as superstitious as magic, and should be studied from the outside with no reference to truth or validity. The sociologists of science are those who follow Robert K. Merton and apply the same techniques to scientific knowledge proper. Now this means either that science is neither more nor less superstitious than common knowledge, or that truth and validity have nothing to do with it. Sociologists of science take the second option. Since the anthropologists, and therefore also the sociologists of knowledge, study not any old superstition but institutionalized ones, so do sociologists of science.

As it happens, the most institutionalized superstition amongst scientists is that science is a body of demonstrated truths which are neither contested nor contestable. Now demonstration is an institutional matter, and so the sociologist of science must take notice of it; but scientific truth is, we remember, deemed irrelevant to the sociology of science, or even considered sheer myth. Hence the sociologist of science accepts half of the demonstration (= uncontested establishment of truth): he studies the rise of consensus, but as if it has nothing to do with the truth. The culmination of this ill-conceived compromise was a book which won instant consensus among the sociologists of science and so must count as scientific without the study of the question, Does that book tell the truth? It is a book by B. Latour and S. Woolgar, *Laboratory Life: The Social Construction of Scientific Facts* (Beverly Hills: Sage, 1979). It was praised and used by Dr. Knorr-Cetina, and her praise and use of that book makes what the book reports into a scientific fact, regardless of the fact that what Latour and Woolgar did was apply anthropological methods to the laboratory, that is to say, they studied the laboratory as if it were a desert island populated by magicians.

Dr. Knorr-Cetina, to do her justice, is not in total accord with Latour and Woolgar. She attempts to apply not only anthropology but also economic theory. When the guinea pigs whom Latour and Woolgar observe attempt to construct a scientific fact they try to convince people, i.e., to sell some commodity. To whom? In what market? Robert K. Merton has discovered the Matthew Effect: a well-published scientist will find it easier to be published again than a novice, and will publish in the better journals and command better consensus. Is this not an imperfect market? Economists call this statistical discrimination. Statistical discrimination is the reliance on signs rather than on knowledge, on the supposition that though signs are less efficient than knowledge, they may be more cost effective. Thus, though not all Armenians are good at business, rather than examine a candidate who is Armenian we may hire him in our business establishment at once and, if he is no good, fire him after one month. An error like this is costly, but so is examination and discrimination is economical if the result is less costly. Applying this to Merton's Matthew Effect, we can assume that the process of refering is both poor and costly, so that referees find it reasonable to recommend and editors find it reasonable to publish a paper by a famous scientist sight-unseen.

The assumption may be true or false, yet behind it stands the suspicion that some papers published in scientific periodicals were better rejected. Indeed, no one contests this. What is the criterion of acceptability? Truth? No: truth is the product of consensus. What creates consensus? This can be examined economically: who sells consensus and at what price for what commodity? Again we have here statistical discrimination: rather than test a commodity for quality we can trust the rubber stamp of the chief rabbi of the community. But sooner or later his rubber stamp, if it is too often misused, will lose its credibility. The long and the short of it is that it is too often misused. The long and the short of it is that we want quality commodities. What is quality? What makes some magic good, potent, desirable, and other magic only so-so? What magic does science sell?

Agronomists sell agricultural technology which is purchased when it gives a high economic yield. Now the economy is full of malpractice, and looking at science as economics includes malpractice in science. Selling toxins is one of the best-known economic malpractices, and many of these toxins are artifacts and all industrial and agricultural artifacts are these days linked with science. And so science includes malpractice.

Except that when the toxins were sold to the market there was scientific consensus that they were benign. And if scientific fact is created by consensus then the toxins were at the time not toxic at all. They became toxic when someone managed to sell the idea that they were. If you believe this you can believe everything. Yet this is what Dr. Knorr-Cetina has on her shelves for sale—at half-price.

Does Dr. Knorr-Cetina believe this? I do not think so. Do Latour and Woolgar? I do not think so either. Do Berger and Luckmann, the vulgarizers of the crazy idea that social facts are all in the mind? I do not think so. What are they all talking about? Why are they trying to convince us of these absurdities? I honestly do not know. As long as I am outside the consensus, it is my fault, of course. So be it: they do manage to sell. In the meantime I wish to conclude with what I think engages these sociologists of science.

First and foremost, the sociologists of science, especially Latour and Woolgar and Knorr-Cetina, have recorded a significant and hitherto unjustly and systematically neglected fact: negotiations do take place. And they are improperly conducted: they should be conducted, if at all, above board, so that science can maintain its claim to objectivity and its hard-earned dignity.

When the agronomist discovered undesirable side-effects in fertilizers, he thought all he needed do was to publish his results in one of the less prestigious agronomical journals and stay put. He discovered that editors of such journals have neither the courage nor the inclination to enter a dispute. He fought, he met with hidden threats and with promises, he resorted to counter-threats: he would publish in a foreign journal; he would appeal to the authorities, and more. His paper was reviewed by referees who took their time, returned it for checking and rechecking, and for dotting the i's and crossing the t's. All this gave other parties ample time to prepare themselves—to jump his bandwagon before it started rolling. But he knew he would win: he knew that the truth was on his side. Again and again he was asked, by his spouse, by friends, by colleagues: Are you quite sure? He was not, but he could not invalidate his empirical data, nor could his opponents; and he was determined to stand by this plain fact.

This story is, of course, a rhetorical representation from the viewpoint of the conjectures and refutations of "the logicist philosophy of science", to echo Rom Harré. Let me conclude the presentation of the sociology of science from the same viewpoint, in a less rhetorical fashion.

There are many myths about science, such as that it includes no mistakes. Sociologists of science are constantly battering this idea. There is also the myth of scientific unanimity of which many sociologists of science are victims. They are in a tough position, viewing science as unanimous yet viewing scientists as resourceful and even opportunistic. In the meantime there is the bandwagon effect noted by George Bernard Shaw: every bandwagon has its joiners, the rabble and the mixed multitude. Many professional scientists are ingenious, yet some are simply frauds who do not know what they are doing as scientists. These sociologists of science unknowingly expose them. Most professional scientists, however, are simply not very good. Those sociologists of science who know nothing about scientific standards simply deny their existence. Instead of seeking the standard they take the average to be the norm. This is an error even in the anthropology of simple folk; when applied to self-selected subcultures it is simply a joke—since self-selection itself, willy-nilly invokes some standards. It is true that, as anthropologists observe, standards proclaimed are often quite different from standards followed. Yet to say there are no standards is to make an obviously false statement. Thus their ethnographic debunking fails to explain the status ascribed to scientific work by society in general as well as the subculture of scientists in particular.

— 22 —

GERMAN PHILOSOPHY ENGLISHED

fatally delicate about the past

1. The Language Barrier

The phenomenon of the language barrier to the spread and growth of culture and knowledge has hardly been studied. Its existence is, of course, sufficiently evident to bring about the contrary phenomenon—the *lingua franca*. Though it is historically of supreme significance, scholars have still to grapple with the role of Hebrew as a *lingua franca* in the Middle Ages, especially in commerce between the Moslem and Christian worlds, which had Arabic and Latin as their own *linguae francae*. We know that it was crucial to the history of culture in general and of science in particular. Latin was the *lingua franca* of the modern world until the French Revolution and beyond. A symptom of this is Ben Franklin's observation, in his best-selling autobiography, that it is advisable to learn a modern Romance language before learning Latin: advice for an intending reader, not writer, of Latin. Winston Churchill's complaint, in his autobiography, that he was drilled in Latin the old way, is a complaint both concerning matter and concerning manner: he was maltreated by those who gave him a tool that was of no value to him. In the 18th century, French was a serious candidate for the position—with the blessing of the Royal Prussian Academy. In the 19th century, French was challenged by both German and English. French lost, and today the position of English as the *lingua franca* of the West is scarcely challenged.

If we narrow considerations to the sub-culture of a country, say, the intelligentsia, the problem gets more focussed and so better manageable. Still better, we may consider the avant-garde, and their ability to use innovations introduced in a foreign language. The physical sciences, the natural sciences

---

This review of *Modern German Philosophy* by Rüdiger Bubner (Cambridge: Cambridge University Press, 1981) and *Philosophy in Germany, 1831–1933* by Herbert Schädelbach (Cambridge: Cambridge University Press, 1984) has not been previously published.

in general, not to say the technologies roughly based on them, are little affected by language barriers, both because of the intense competitiveness of these fields and because in them problems are in focus on the public agenda. We find there, of course, different barriers than those of language. The spread of a scientific idea due to a heretic, such as Barbara McClintock in the United States, may be blocked for a longer time than the transfer of an acceptable idea presented by a member of a foreign scientific establishment. Indeed, at times a heretic wins notice at home only after having won notice abroad in a large way.

The impression, then, is that in the arts the language barriers are higher than in the natural sciences. This is not always so. The West has learned of cultural changes in foreign lands with immense rapidity, both in the Middle Ages and in modern times. A poet who gains an audience anywhere will quickly earn an international reputation—very small, no doubt, but we are now restricted to the avant-garde anyway. If one thinks of famous German or French poets, for example, then one can see that they were famous abroad as soon as they were famous at home. Nineteenth century American poets who had audiences at home were known to the avant-garde in Europe within amazingly short time-gaps, and American Edgar Allan Poe, perhaps, was given respectability by Frenchman Baudelaire.

Philosophy. How long does it take a philosopher to acquire a readership at home? This has to be determined before one can examine the effects of the language barrier. When was Kierkegaard established in Denmark and when was he established abroad? If we ignore the fact that he was not considered more than a local curiosity at home, then it seems that it took half-a-century or so before he crossed the language barrier. But this must be said very tentatively, as there are, to repeat, no studies of the situation.

The idea that philosophy suffers most from the language barrier is, if not very popular, at least one which gains assent within the philosophical community with little or no objection. (This is an empirical observation grounded in much and varied experience.) It is, however, rooted in the preconceived notion that philosophy is more characteristic of its home ground than science. Yet, no doubt, fairy-tales and poetry are much more characteristic of their native lands than philosophy, yet fairy-tales cross language barriers much faster than philosophy.

To come to modern times, Heidegger's 1927 *opus magnum* was noticed in England and France at once, and Sartre's *magnum opus* of 15 years later is generally acknowledged to be both profoundly Heideggerian and very French—whatever these epithets may mean. So what does a book on German philosophy signify? It may concern, like a book on German physics or mathematics, the activities and contributions of the overlap of the avant-garde international community of philosophers—or physicists or mathematicians—with the German-speaking people, or the German people. In such books the general situation must be considered as given, or briefly sketched, and the local situation surveyed in more detail than the general one. This is the same as in the study of national politics; one either takes the international scene as given, or describes the general items in brief and the national scene as if it were the center of the international scene, and this creates some presentational problems. Yet, at least the foreign reader concerned with Heidegger, for example, or even with Sartre, will be particularly interested in the detailed treatment of Heidegger both as an international figure and as a national one.

All this is true of philosophy the way it is true of physics or of mathematics. What is characteristic of philosophy, however, is the schools of philosophy. For those who say that physics and mathematics have no school, this differentiation is obvious. Yet even those who know that every field of inquiry has its schools will agree: in other fields, schools show respect for each other and do not overlook findings and interesting ideas which come from the competition. In philosophy things are somewhat different. How, then, can one report them from the outside and/or to the outsider?

These are not idle questions, and authors of books for foreigners, especially in philosophy, do struggle with them. This is particularly true of traditional German philosophy. The translation of German philosophy, especially Hegel's, into English, led to the rise of a new language, Hegelish, which enables one to move more easily from German Hegelish to English Hegelish, than from English Hegelish to analytic-English. And so the barrier is not linguistic but philosophic.

And so a book on German philosophy may be an attempt to tell the English reader about activity in Germany, or to the non-Hegelian reader about Hegelian activity in non-Hegelian English.

We have before us two important contributions to the study of current German philosophy published in a series devoted to the topic by one of the most respected scholarly houses—Cambridge University Press—one by Rüdiger Bubner, the other by Herbert Schnädelbach. Let us see what exactly they are doing, and how well they are doing it.

2. Bubner

Rüdiger Bubner, *Modern German Philosophy*, 1981, 220 pages, divided almost equally into three parts: phenomenology and hermeneutics, philosophy of language and of science, and the schools of Hegel and Marx. This, by itself, suggests that it is not just distinctly German philosophy, but philosophy now done in Germany—unless it is philosophy done in a distinctly German way. Ernest Gellner has observed that any popularizer of Hegel sooner or later tends to slip into Hegelish. Gellner also observes that in every state of the United States there is the local representative of each philosophic school, and that this fact renders all of them distinctly American. Is this the case also for American Thomists? Is this the case also for German philosophers?

Bubner's preface sees something of a scandal in the mere fact that philosophy has a history: philosophy must be more than a mere speculation or Weltanschauung: it must be demonstrated; and then it is the absolute truth, and the absolute truth cannot be swayed by the vagaries of history. If so, then physics, too, not to say mathematics, may not have any history! Is that the case? Does Bubner think this is the case? No answer.

Phenomenology. In ten compact and lucid pages the whole of Husserl's work and its impact are handled. It is an excellent presentation, in which Husserl's program is explained and dismissed and his influence is explained as the result of his instituting a distinctly philosophical method. In brief, Husserl had hoped that by excluding from the picture both the subject and the object of experience, and centering on the phenomenon experienced, and seeking its essence, we would find that a by-product of this search would be the bridge between the real subject and the real object. This, incidentally, fits well with the method of many detectives from the world of unreality who declare a story unreal because the details in it do not strongly coagulate. The unreal detectives finally succeed. Real Husserl failed. His method, says Bubner, is neither natural science nor mental science, as it has never reached the real object or subject. So the method is distinctly philosophic and so favored by philosophers. To what end? No answer.

Heidegger changed the question. What kind of world can inhabit humans? To answer this he coined new terms: being, being-there, being-in-the-world, and existence. His answer should overcome the dualities subject-object, phenomena-noumena; that is to say, he too wanted the bridge. To learn the answer we need to understand the terms, yet the terms are understood hermeneutically, namely when one is engaged in the interpretation of texts, yet the text is the being-there. How, then, is hermeneutics performed? I do not know.

Very roughly, being is an object, myself and my subjectivity included, being-there is myself, my subjectivity included; yet this cannot be meant quite literally, since we have thereby created an object and a subject yet no bridge. So let us go on and see where the bridge comes in. Being-in-the-world is any being-there dwelling in the midst of being and relating to being. Now this way the being-there achieves self-actualization. So the being-in-the-world is a self-actualized being-there, one that is bridged! Not so fast, though. Self-actualization involves risks, risks involve worry. One may avoid worry by recklessness, but Man's essence lies in the future, and so Man worries about the future. Worry destroys bridges and divides the world into subject and object, to phenomena and noumena. How is it, then, that nevertheless the world can accommodate us? Bubner says that both substance and appearance are—still according to Heidegger, of course—some sorts of manifestation (p. 27). Beyond that he does not go, but gives the contrary impression. "His idiosyncratic style has been the chief obstacle to the understanding of Heidegger in other countries" (p. 30). What about the understanding of Heidegger in Germany?

> The study of Heidegger's philosophy . . . kept the German academic world productively occupied in the 'forties and 'fifties . . . . there was also a fashion for adaptations in several neighbouring principles. [Why? Because] The need felt in the period after the Second World War for the secure return to the great masters did give Heidegger the status of a central figure.

Here, then, is the true basis for engagement with Heidegger, and it is not so much a German philosophy and not so much of anything, really, except for a sympathetic observation of the emptiness of life in Germany after its defeat, the appeal of talk about worry and self-actualization that struggle in a subject's heart, and also the need for a national hero. "Even Heidegger's short-lived but fatally mistaken attempt to create an alliance in educational policy with the powers-that-be" says Bubner (p. 22)—he could not put this more delicately—even this was an asset, presumably (Bubner does not explain) since it was so easy for ever so many compatriots to identify with him.

All's well that ends well. The emptiness of life, which gave rise, as we are told, in the post-war era, in the forties and fifties, to "the mindless cult of Heidegger" (p. 31), finally gave way to Marxism.

Back to Husserl. In his last work he gave up his optimistic view of philosophy as demonstrable unshakeable science. Rather "the life-world is the foundation of meaning for science" (p. 33), meaning, common sense, all that we usually take for granted and that Husserl initially proposed to eschew together with science in order to regain. Science itself is now presented as based on common sense. This, Bubner notes (p. 34), is American pragmatism. Except that common sense is now not postulated dogmatically, but is seen as given in its historical context (p. 35), but accepted only as soon as these historical roots get forgotten (p. 35) and not before.

It is hard to see where all this leads and what is gained through all the changes and modifications. Husserl insists to the end on the claim that philosophical method is distinct. So does Heidegger, even though he shifts from the view of philosophy as a science with its own method to a view of it as a poetry with its own method. Yet the method, hermeneutics, turns in the hands of Hans Georg Gadamer, a follower of both, to be a method distinct to all the human sciences, and one which transcends the methodological dispute between the explaining human philosophy which stresses universal law and the understanding human philosophy which stresses the individual: the disagreement is but a matter of emphasis and both methods "frequently or always intermesh"; there is but one method (pp. 52, 53): hermeneutics!

Hermeneutics contributes not only to scientific method but also, says Gadamer, to the study of the cost of using it, especially in "the glossing-over and abstractions it demands" (p. 54). "Hermeneutics does not only concede the relative legitimacy to science, it also contributes to its grounding'' (p. 54), an extra-scientific grounding, that is. Which? How? By "elucidating the genesis and structure of scientific knowledge'', presumably (p. 55). What, then, has hermeneutics taught us about science and how did it legitimize science within its bounds? Which bounds? First, we have truth not only in science but also in art (p. 55), whose level of understanding is the highest (p. 66), partly because it is not limited to a community, a specialization or a closed club (p. 57).

History is the natural ground for hermeneutics. Gadamer has a view of history similar to Collingwood's (p. 61), and in it the unity of subject (historian?) and object (of historical study: the nation?) in a frankly Hegelian fashion (p. 62). Bubner then tries to explain the disagreements Heidegger and Gadamer had with Hegel, in which effort Heidegger is simply unfair to Hegel who still dominates the scene. Most of those who dissent from Hegel turn out to exhibit very small, not to say merely verbal, differences from him. Finally, Bubner concedes (p. 64): "Hermeneutics, according to this objection, is in reality a disguised Hegelianism'', where, "this objection'' is that the historian does not look at his object—history—from the outside but from within his own limitations, which are historically given. This objection is, indeed, the most important chracteristic of the whole philosophy of Hegel and his followers. And, let me add, it is doubtless valid.

Bluntly, here is the central disagreement in modern philosophy: positivists, 17th-century and contemporary alike, deem a good thinker's judgment absolute and so outside history; irrationalist romantics declare all judgments limited to within some historical context. The increasingly popular viewpoint is critical realist: his limitations are often errors to be criticized and in part transcended, thus leading to improvement, to the elimination of some error and the approach to the unattainable total and absolute truth. It takes Bubner pages of devious obscure writing to hint at all this.

3. LANGUAGE AND SCIENCE

Wittgenstein first presented a positivist theory of one, a-historical, context-free, ideal language, and then turned to the view of limitations on language depending on context (p. 72). This, of course, is an application of the previous paragraph to language-as-a-tool-of-cognition. If, however, we list all contexts and modes in which language is context-dependent, then we move back to positivism—Husserl style, of course (p. 88). But we arrive at this by a lengthy discussion of the ideas of Karl-Otto Apel, one of the few German philosophers who is gaining reputation today in the English-speaking sector of the philosophical community, and even as an original thinker akin to Habermas and equal to him in stature.

Apel's innovation is this. Wittgenstein does not study empirically sets of specific, concrete language-games; rather he offers a concept of a language-game; this is an ideal; the ideal is of a communication community, however, not of all mankind, and what we study is the general conditions for the very possibility of there being any specific communication community. Here, obviously, we have a sane translation of the problem which Heidegger thought central: what kind of a world is it which accommodates humans? Even though Bubner keeps Heidegger in reserve for the discussion of the views of Ernst Tugendhat, the Wittgensteinian pupil of Heidegger (p. 93). Apel broadens the question to ask, what is the transcendental (i.e., the prior conditions necessary for) pragmatics (i.e., the theory of human affairs)? And transcendental pragmatics includes the conditions for language-games, for human communication. The rules of human communications constitute rationality (p. 77), especially the rules of argumentation. This idea is, I should add, an echo of Popper's theory of rationality as critical debate (p. 92). The necessary condition for humans to exist, then, is the very readiness to communicate in an exchange of ideas. How extraordinary! The only problem Bubner has with this extraordinary view is that, contrary to Apel (and Ronald Searle), the norms of rationality cannot be extracted from language through analysis (p. 79). This is truly amazing as well, since Apel claims for rationality the status of transcendental truths, not empirical ones! What is so unbelievable is Apel's overlooking of the fact that some societies forbid almost all dissent and no society tolerates all dissent. What are they talking about? When Popper describes rationality as openness to criticism, and the language of debate and criticism as a fourth level added to Karl Bühler's three, he never dreamt that the ability to argue would be declared essential to human communication: he accepted as obvious Bühler's claim that descriptive language is more basic than argumentative language, and that signalling is still more basic, and that human signals are better than those of lower animals. Bubner makes no mention of Bühler. Instead, he observes that no debate is isolated and played exactly by the rules, as Aristotle and Toulmin have informed us (p. 82)! Worse, still: Apel wants proof and certitude (pp. 84–85). His transcendental proof has to refer, however, to a community of communicators, and the community has to have both the transcendental conditions and proof of its having them. This is impossible: as Bubner reports, Apel is aware of the fact that "linguistic communities cannot reflect" (p. 88), so that even if one community existed whose members were all perfect communicators who can reflect perfectly, this would not be a sufficient condition for the community to have a proof, not to mention a transcendental proof (p. 90).

Ernst Tugendhat, the pupil of Heidegger, finds use for something he has picked up from Wittgenstein's work. He sees in Wittgenstein an infant Heidegger (the way Bar-Hillel sees in Husserl an infant Carnap, incidentally; see p. 14n). Tugendhat offers a Teutonic-style language analysis in his view of Alfred Tarski's definition of truth as "clarity . . . bought at the price of triviality" (p. 94). Tugendhat's alternative (p. 95) is profundity bought at the price of no clarity, culminating with a theory of truth as the "correct characterization of the objects of an assertion", namely, the predicate of a true statement does apply to the subject, just as Aristotle has said. Tugendhat's contribution is the analysis of the predicate "apply" here, an analysis which fuses rules of grammar with the truth-value of the result of applying them (pp. 96–97) and which invites an unfusing. For the sake of the unfusing, ontology is dragged in, on the excuse that the subject of the statement in question is an entity (p. 97). What is wrong with this kind of German philosophy is the disregard for all scholarship, already instituted in Heidegger's philology, of course.

What is wrong with German philosophy, Tugendhat is reported to say (p. 100), is not Hegelian idealism but terrible logic. Who will disagree that this applies to Tugendhat? Hegel, we are told, and I tend to agree, attempted to rehabilitate common sense, as so many did before and after him (p. 102). Hegel failed, yet, Bubner sneers, so did language analysis. In the final analysis, what we see here is an Anglo-German contest, and of the one-upmanship type. It is not wise to do a one-up on the English, though—in this kind of contest they doubtless always come up tops. I suspect I understand now the strange fact that the English editors of this book did not offer its author advice, even, not about some possible omissions.

Having exhausted the most recognizably German part of the book we come to more familiar territory, the theory of knowledge, or theory of science as Bubner prefers to call it. The Vienna Circle was anti-philosophical and its members "were compelled to emigrate"—how delicately put! Modern German philosophy of science consequently would only get going after the war. "The political situation in Germany" (still delicately put) "cut off native philosophy for almost a decade from international development", and the isolation continued even later due to "the phenomenological school and Heidegger's blatantly anti-scientific thought" (p. 104). The only originally German school of the philosophy of science is the Lorenzen school, yet both Carnap and Popper have followings there, with Stegmüller as an important thinker, chief follower of Carnap, and defender of his idol against Popper's challenge (still p. 104).

Let me skip Bubner's presentation of Karl Popper's position, except to observe that his presentation is not from a viewpoint acceptable to Popper fans like myself. Even his sensitive observation of the slow growth of the force of Popper's ideas is apologetic—it is a disguised attempt to conceal the reluctance of most philosophers to notice Popper's very existence between 1935 and about 1965. Nor will I discuss Bubner's presentation of Hans Albert, Popper's leading disciple and one of Germany's leading philosophers, since Bubner cannot possibly discern the differences between the two from the viewpoint he has chosen. His heavy hand—it would be wrong to consider it as typically German—spoils everything. He says, for example (p. 112), "A critique without a criterion would be an absurdity". Why? Were there no good critiques in history—in the (problematic) history of philosophy, for example—which were presented with no criterion? If a critic offers his critique with a criterion and one rejects the criterion, must one also reject the critique? Do we not have examples—especially in the (problematic) history of philosophy—of good critiques offered with poor criteria to justify them?

Bubner does take account of these questions. He answers them (p. 114). He fears, he says, the dogmatization of criticism. I do not understand. As a remedy to the dogmatization of criticism he offers the idea of self-criticism. Now, we have problems, solutions, criticisms. A criticism of a solution should be assessed on its own merit, not on whether both come from the same pen. Bubner thinks self-criticism is essential and an antidote to self-righteousness. Yet some contributions were made by self-righteous thinkers in a self-righteous effort to justify and enhance their self-righteousness. And they are welcome to it.

Bubner mentions the current debate in Germany between the intuitive school of the human sciences, the 'understanding' school, and the empirical or 'explanation' school. He notices that Popper invites intuition as a tool to forge explanations that can be tested empirically (p. 119). Rather than see this as exploding both sides of the dispute, Bubner writes with amazement that this strengthens both. Mildly amusing. The same holds for Bubner's discussion of the place of value in science and of the value of value-free social science, since Popper can operate with an open-minded attitude: he allows a free debate which assumes only the value of the truth (p. 123). The modern German Marxists, Adorno and Habermas, Bubner observes, see here a danger, a danger of "uncontrolled knowledge" (p. 124), and of the defense of the status-quo in politics masked as indifference to values (p. 125). Clearly, here we come to the heart of a debate which took part in Germany, which spilled over to debates in the English-speaking world yet died out fast there, but which is still very much alive in Germany. In particular I was fascinated by the fact that two of the leading German philosophers today, Karl-Otto Apel and Jürgen Habermas, have welded German (pseudo-) Marxism and Popper's critical philosophy by describing an ideal society where the ideal practiced is Popperian critical philosophy (p. 128). Bubner refuses to discuss this in detail but returns to it a couple of times (see below). This is a pity. It seems to me that here a powerful refutation of Popper's theory of rationality may be constructed perhaps.

Bubner moves on to present Thomas S. Kuhn and Paul K. Feyerabend as disciples of Popper, especially since they had much influence in Germany. Since he says nothing important about them and as I consider their influence to be ephemeral, I will skip all this except to say that in Germany attempts to popularize their ideas are great improvements over more traditionally German philosophical activities. The most significant rationalizing, positive influence in German philosophy and in German philosophical education, is Wolfgang Stegmüller, Rudolf Carnap's leading disciple today, who is the chief source in Germany of the tendency to be apalled by Hegelian, Heideggerian, and similar modes of speech and who demands that philosophers acquire some proficiency in logic. Stegmüller's own philosophy, hovering somewhere between Carnap, Popper, and Kuhn, invites as little notice as possible. The barrenness of his works may send some of his devoted and gifted followers to seek spiritual nourishment in the enemy's domain. Even Bubner, clearly a Stegmüller fan, finds it hard to defend or even describe his views, and the five pages he devotes to them are extremely inadequate—both ambiguous and ambivalent, not to say uninformative.

The only originally German philosophy of science—the Erlangen school of Hugo Dingler early in this century and his current successor Paul Lorenzen—is given the last ten pages of the chapter. These thinkers cling to the idea of scientific rigor and certitude. Lorenzen has developed a new system of (finitist) logic, and one which was noticed by mathematical logicians who have no interest in or sympathy with the philosophy of Lorenzen in general. Bubner does not even mention it and his pages on the Erlangen school are the most disappointing in the book: they are quite uninformative. Even the presentation of Lorenzen's application of his method to ethics is quite unsatisfactory; a book on German philosophy for foreigners should be informative on the Erlangen school.

The third part of Bubner's book (pp. 154-218) is devoted to Hegel and Marx, who are as popular in Germany as in North America, now more than ever. The specifically German contribution is from the well-known Frankfurt school, the negative dialectic school, of Theodor Adorno, Herbert Marcuse, and Jürgen Habermas, to name only three of its illustrious members. Since Marcuse published largely in English, since much of the writing of that school and about it are in English, there is hardly a language barrier here. Nonetheless, one could expect some illumination of the stage by reference to background material, to some specifically German side-scenes or stage-props. Bubner attempts to provide this by narrating the contribution to German neo-Marxism of the Hegel revival in Germany and of Georg Lukacs. He fails.

It is hard to summarize Hegel's philosophy in a few pages, not to mention the Hegel revival. Anyway, Bubner notices that Hegel was always popular in Germany and states his views very briefly, missing two items I deem very important.

The first is general, namely the Hegelian theory of the truth as culturally relative. One can accommodate this theory in an absolutist theory of truth as a theory of frames of reference, while admitting that, say, classical physics approximates modern physics and that discussing some classical problems, whether the three-body problem or some technological problems, within the framework of classical physics we may take that framework as true. Otherwise, Nature has followed classical physics until She got tired of it and then moved on. The second important idea of Hegel is that history is the high court of justice, that God reveals Himself on the battlefield, that Reason cunningly moves great men by endowing them with great passions so that they are compelled to do Her will. I heard Germans of all walks of life and of diverse levels of intellectual sophistication take the military defeat of the Nazis as a refutation of their doctrines. Stalinism, however, was not defeated. Nor was Hegelianism—at least not in Germany and not in Bubner's book.

Bubner writes (p. 163), rightly I think, of the Hegelian ancestry of the Frege-Popper theory of the third realm or world, the domain of ideas. He ignores the Popper critique of Hegelian dialectics as absurd; he defends it against the charge that it is unintelligible or meaningless though he reluctantly partly endorses it (p. 162). I cannot judge. Is the claim that the fruit is the negation of the flower unintelligible, meaningless, or absurd? My example is from Hegel, and so, by a dictum of Walter Kaufmann ('The Hegel Myth and Its Method') it may be unfair. Bubner offers no example at all.

After ten pages on Hegel, we have four on Lukacs—too brief to mention the fact that his life-work was the attempt to reconcile Marx with the criticisms of Marx launched by his teacher, Georg Simmel, as well as the innovations which Simmel introduced. Any serious history of ideas must refer to underground movements. Simmel is now coming back, partly because certain American sociologists (some of them German refugees) have managed to revive his ideas. But Simmel was easy to revive because his ideas, however distorted or misplaced, were repeatedly made public by writers who either did not mention him or mentioned him misleadingly, among them his disciples Max Weber, Georg Lukacs, and Erich Fromm. (Simmel is not mentioned in this book.)

Bubner summarizes the ideas of Lukacs's major work, *History and Class Consciousness*. He sees it as an *ad hoc* rescue of Marxism from its refutation. The first idea is that dialectic is the central Marxist idea to be rescued. This conflicts, by the way, with Lenin's idea (*Materialism and Empirio-criticism*, Conclusion) that realism is central, since we can use it to learn empirically how valid or invalid dialectics (or any other important idea) is. Lukacs, says Bubner, gave up the materialist basis of consciousness and became an idealist (pp. 167–68). Yet he is still a Marxist in believing in the proleterian revolution. This is not philosophy in any sense recognizable by Bubner (though I am myself less dogmatic about it), and I think he should say so. In a way he does. He accents not that revolution but the holistic late-Hegelian gloss which Lukacs put on it (p. 169).

Bubner's history of the Frankfurt school is based on an American work (p. 173n). Yet the chief thesis is Bubner's own:

The historical experience of fascism, but no less the deep disillusion which the Stalinist perversion induced in all progressively minded Marxists, and finally the isolated situation of the émigrés, brought them to the conviction that the illusion which leads society astray is in complete control, that reification has taken hold of all spheres of life.

This is a most remarkable quotation. It says, first, that illusion and reification are in complete control everywhere. This is either a metaphor or a reification of illusion and of reification. As a metaphor it is trite and has been asserted forcefully and with all solemnity by all preachers of enlightenment from Sir Francis Bacon to his contemporary successors in elementary schools all over the world. As a reification it is the worst sort of superstition; worse than the reification of capital. The contrast between fascism and "the Stalinist perversion" is remarkable too: is fascism not also a perversion of something better? The idea that what convinced the Frankfurt émigrés was their isolation makes them more egocentric and foolish than they would be—quite apart from the fact that they were not isolated, at least by comparison to some other exiles. (See Susan Buck-Morss, *The Origins of Negative Dialectics*, 1977, p. 152.) My point, however, is that any discussion beginning with such a reference to the control which illusion and reification has on all spheres of life can hardly be expected to be enlightening. Regrettably this expectation is all too easily coroborated by the reifications used throughout the presentation.

This is a pity, since some Frankfurt philosophers have been individualistic—for example Adorno refused to join the Communist party on account of his individualism, and he attacked Lukacs on aesthetics as authoritarian—and they have criticized Marxist progressivism as utopian. Admittedly, there is reference to that in Bubner's book (p. 179), but one not easy to follow, and one used to make them seem even more Hegelian than they were.

Bubner's expressions of the highest praise go to Jürgen Habermas who, we are told, unified the theory of science, hermeneutics, and communication theory. The description (pp. 183–86) is partly platitudinous, partly incomprehensible, partly evidently absurd. He says the interest of research is theoretical, pragmatic, and self-reflective—whatever this last item means. "Communication presupposes equal partners and freedom from external factors such as domination", says Bubner (p. 185, lines 3 and 2 from bottom) either meaning that commands are impossible to communicate, or that they are not communications, or that they are not really commands.

Yet his presentation of objections to Habermas (p. 186ff.) contains a hint: all three research activities are forms of Socratic dialogues. Now this sounds exciting, but not easy to work out in detail. One contemporary philosopher, Sir Karl Popper, has tried to execute something like this task, but I think he has not quite made it, that even with improvements offered by some of his critics-cum-disciples (myself included) the task is not yet accomplished. Now some of these, e.g., Albert, are Germans. The chief difference between Albert and Habermas (or Apel, for that matter; see above), if my reading of Bubner is right, is then chiefly a matter of style: Albert writes in the style of the British tradition, Habermas writes in the style known, since Schelling, Fichte, and Hegel, as German. Now this does not mean they agree; it does not even mean they disagree. It means Albert communicates, argues Socratically, attempts to advance knowledge. It is doubtful that Habermas communicates, and without proper communication there is no proper dialogue, and thus not much chance of progress. All this is the case only if I have understood Bubner correctly. But it is not for me to say that.

4. SCHNÄDELBACH

Herbert Schnädelbach's *Philosophy in Germany, 1831–1933*, 1984, 259 pages, has an admirable groundplan. Writing for the English-reading public, Schnädelbach assumes, he tells us, no prior knowledge of the material at hand. He attempts to rectify the standard misconception of the epoch. It is customary, he says, to overlook all 19th-century authors as either epigoni or precursors, and therefore unimportant, with the exception of Marx, Kierkegaard, and Nietzsche, who are usually misread by the very transfer of their ideas from the background against which they were conceived; Schnädelbach, however, attempts to study the history of philosophy as a history of problems. Finally, he offers his work as an attempt at a contribution to the current process of sifting the healthy elements in traditional German thinking from those which led to the breakdown of academic resistance to National Socialism. All this is just perfect. It deserves a review, regardless of its disappointing execution.

In the book's introduction we find a discussion of Hegel's idealism. The author complains that Hegel's identification of reality and rationality is erroneously taken as an apology for the political status quo, since 'reality' and 'rationality' mean for Hegel something else (p. 6). What? It turns out that not these terms but the term 'identity' is the source of the trouble, since Hegel speaks (wouldn't you have guessed?) of the identity of identity with non-identity. Reality is both the same and not the same as rationality, then. It seems that, as Schnädelbach suggests, the two converge. Hence, Hegel is both an apologist for the status quo and a champion of progress. This is true, and is the sole good argument known against the view that Hegel is an ultra-conservative. None of Hegel's defenders says why this argument makes him less of an ultra-conservative than, say, Stalin, or different from him in any significant political manner. They do differ, but not in the point at issue, it seems.

All this, however, is an interpretation of our interpretation. The text itself is in the standard non-English tradition: "Hegel identifies what truly is with the theoretical idea and the good with the practical Idea, and [he identifies] states [as things] in transition to the Absolute idea", adding a few lines from Hegel which begin with "The truth of the good is thereby posited, as the unity of the theoretical and the practical Idea". "This makes it clear" (p. 7). The word 'clear' is here meant in its German Philosophic Cognate.

In brief, Schnädelbach's good intentions aside, his book is not written for the English-speaking reader, unless that reader is already familiar with Hegelish. Thus, when he speaks of the German version of secularized Protestantism, the view of culture as personal redemption, he adds, "The reinterpretation of this process of cultivation in world-historical terms has, since Lessing and Herder, been the basic image of idealist philosophy in general" (p. 28). Now Lessing had the view of enlightenment as salvation, yet he was not an idealist, at least not in any of the senses used by Schnädelbach throughout his book; and Herder's view of culture was more tribalist than individualist; but what does the phrase "in world-historical terms" mean? And what does Droysen mean when he speaks of the "morphological character" of historical material (p. 53), and what does Dilthey mean when, contrary to Hegel, he says, "the spirit is embraced by life" rather than the other way around (p. 56)? What exactly is the "dynamization" of science, except for its "empiricization" and "temporalization", and what do these terms mean (pp. 81ff.)? And "theoretic structure of the Dasein" (p. 137)? How can I resist the final quote, which is presented with no explanation? Martin Heidegger, *On Humanism*, "The arrival of a being depends on the destiny of Being. . . . Man is the shepherd of Being. . . . Yet Being—what is Being? It is itself. To discover this and to say this is what future thinking must learn to do".

The book begins with idealism, old style: did Hegel dissent from it? Not really. It ends with contemporary philosophy: is it free of traditional Hegelian and post-Hegelian thought? Not really. Except that we have now relinquished the quest for certitude and self-validation and justification, which has led to either a-historical rationalism, or nihilistic relativism, or nihilistic gut-feeling epistemology. What is not clear from this book is: What is left of 19th-century philosophy if it has centered on issues which are lost on us?

The author is apologetic, especially about Hegel. His reactionary politics are declared to be marginal; his utter ignorance of natural science is denied outright with no discussion (p. 72); his attack on Newton is saved (p. 84) by elevation from the lowly plains of science to the height of metaphysics. The fact that Newton's greatest sin was that he stole his idea from Kepler, that in addition it was a sin of an Englishman against Hegel's fellow-countryman, are utterly unnoticed. Similarly, Goethe is praised as a precursor of Darwin, and on the authority of Hermann von Helmholtz (p. 241, n16) who was clearly ashamed of Goethe's scientific pretences. The author likewise cites approvingly Helmuth Plessner to say (p. 20) that while the old West established its nation-state in the 16th and 17th centuries and enjoyed the Golden Age of the Enlightenment, Germany was busy searching for its national identity. Now the Western nation-states were Britain and France, Sweden, and perhaps also Prussia. Neither Italy nor Austria had a nation-state until the *Risorgimento* and World War I, respectively, and Austria was prevented by the Allies from joining the German nation!

The quote from Plessner will not stand the slightest scrutiny, yet it seems pivotal for the book's political thesis—though it is hard to argue this case since that thesis is never explicitly stated in this book. A large portion of the book's argument is used to illustrate just how much overlap there was between diverse 19th-century schools of philosophy, even between opposing schools. But the author never explains the significance of any idea. He discusses history, especially historicism and the opposition to it; views of science and of reality, which are largely epistemological; views of the basis for the human sciences, again, largely epistemological, much of it about *Verstehen;* and, finally, the philosophies of Being and of Man. Since he is not clear about problems it is hard to question his choice to discuss at length one author and ignore another. It is also hard to understand why he is so unfair to Georg Simmel as to place him after Weber, to put in Weber's mouth mostly ideas Weber took from him, and introduce him briefly as "Also worthy of note" (p. 135)—faint praise, if there ever was any. The author seems to be a Weber fan, but I cannot be sure. And he seems to endorse, at least he does not repudiate, Weber's most repulsive claims. For example (p. 133):

"Rational certainty is achieved above all in the case of action in which the intended complex of meanings can be *intellectually* understood in its entirety and with complete clarity". Taken literally this is just as questionable as any claim for certainty, even when all the achievements of modern logic are utterly ignored. But it is not what Weber says here that matters. It is the tone which makes the music. That Max Weber was a liberal is unquestionable, though equally unquestionable is his Nietzscheanism, and he was repeatedly charged with irrationalism—a fact ignored here. If anything hints at the explanation of the timidity of German intellectuals in the face of a national disaster, in a period in which a newly appointed Kanzler willingly confessed to having murdered his own comrades in their silky pajamas by the dozens and added that history would justify him, it is here that a clue may be found. For more details one may turn to the bagatelle on Hegel that is Chapter 12 of Popper's *The Open Society and Its Enemies*.

4. GERMANY AND THE DREADFUL PAST

It is hard to distance philosophy from practical affairs. The Enlightenment movement did ignore as much that went on around it as was possible—but in protest, in radicalist rebellion. The only matter which it could not pass in silence was intolerance. But given tolerance, they felt, they were forging tools for a new and superstition-free society of free spirits. The Romantic movement was conservative and supported the status quo—not entirely, but enough to combat the Enlightenment. Karl Popper has shown that the word 'enlightenment' got, as a result, bad press even in Britain.

What we need today is a philosophy which can claim to avoid both radicalism and conservatism in all matters, from the loftiest philosophy to the most mundane matter. This, already, makes it political.

Nevertheless, I contend that philosophers may do useful work without showing that their works are relevant to daily political and social matters. When they do, however, it is better if they avoid radicalism and conservatism.

The dreadful past is philosophically pregnant. It shows us that humanity can sink to depths previously unimagined. The dreadful past showed us that the academy could co-operate in, or at least fail to resist, sinking to such depths. Even if the dreadful past has only forced us to take Job's complaint to God seriously, then we cannot ignore its philosophic import (Walter Kaufmann). And certainly any writer or German philosopher could relate to it at least by discussing Karl Jaspers, or at least his book on German guilt.

Is it incumbent on German philosophers to grapple with the past more seriously than their colleagues overseas? Is it incumbent on Israeli philosophers? I do not think so. But this I do think: it is hard for either German or Iraeli philosophers (myself included) to ignore the dreadful past. (I imagine the same holds equally forcefully for the Japanese, but I do not know enough about Japan. And it certainly holds even more forcefully for the Austrians.) And if we cannot ignore it we had better be frank about it. I propose that being delicate about it, as Bubner and Schnädelbach are, is deadly.

We all have our cultural backgrounds and they are all mixed bags. German culture is an enviable blessing and an unenviable burden. Throughout my comments on two German philosophers who made efforts to get a comprehensive picture, I took no cognizance of the burden, or rather I may have pushed the burden on them with regrettable insensitivity. I apologize. Were I more tactful I could convey my message more appreciatively. Let this apology of mine stand as an invitation and a challenge to anyone who wishes to follow in their footsteps and do better.

— 23 —

THE PRESENT STATE
OF ANALYTIC PHILOSOPHY

skeletons in the cupboard

INTRODUCTION

Universities pride themselves on being non-doctrinaire. In a serious university department, the teaching of a doctrine, for a conspicuous example, cannot be the exclusive property of the doctrinaire. We require of one who teaches the doctrine—religious, psychological, political, biological—to master the ideas, information, arguments; not to be a convert. Where only Freudians are allowed to teach Freud, only Marxists Marx, etc., things are amiss.

Can one teach modern analytic philosophy without being a convert to that philosophy? It seems to me a historical fact that most teachers of modern analytic philosophy are converts to it, and the same holds for continental philosophy, so-called. Things cannot go on like that as long as universities are non-doctrinaire. And so the need mounts to spell out doctrines in a non-doctrinaire manner. Recently attempts to meet it were made. Here is one.

Simon Blackburn's *Spreading the Word: Groundings in the Philosophy of Language* (Clarendon Press, Oxford, 1984), comprises a dense 350 pages plus brief but extremely revealing Glossary and Bibliography, both highly idiosyncratic. Yet the book purports to be the opposite of idiosyncratic: for better or worse, modern analytic philosophy concerns itself with language, and here is an ambitious work—both an introductory course and a high-powered survey-course—presenting a summary of the field: problems, methods, and some results. Yet the idiosyncracy is there from the start: paragraph one mentions a few heroes —"Frege, Russell, Tarski,

Previously unpublished.

Quine''—and the reader may be impressed by names conspicuous by their absence. To the index, then: Wittgenstein is referred to at least as often as they. Who else? M. Dummett, G. Evans, N. Goodman, D. Hume, I. Kant, S. Kripke, D. Lewis, J. Mackie, H. Putnam, and P. Strawson, all have more than one line each but R. Carnap, G. E. Moore and G. Ryle have fewer references even than N. Chomsky.

The reason for this becomes clear at once: the author presents problems, methods, results: philosophical problems are back in style. Is this not the end of analytic philosophy? In a sense, yes. The author does not approve of "the linguistic turn" (p. 6, line 1), (where the quotes, we are told (p. 5n) "are used for direct quotations from other writers, and to register deliberate .distancing from a particular phrasing")—'the linguistic turn' which robs philosophers like "Hume and Kant, or whoever was doing worthwhile philosophy" of almost anything they did; they are consequently forced into the linguistic mold and their views are thus grossly distorted.

There is something amiss here. Ordinary-language philosophers wrote histories of philosophy—recent, classical modern, even classical ancient—from a point of view which declared all philosophy either linguistic analysis or confusion, under the slogan, 'the puzzle does not exist'. Blackburn's survey ignores them all except for a couple of pages which harshly condemn popular (anonymous) readings of Hume's analyis of causation as meaning analysis. Bastions of linguistic history e.g., Stuart Hampshire on Spinoza, Geoffrey Warnock on Berkeley (both in Pelican editions), are not even alluded to. They may have lost all value, yet a survey need be a bit more explicit! The wrong, excessive, linguistic turn, as well as the anti-linguistic-turn must be assessed! Why was either popular? Did either bear any fruit?

Intellectual establishments baptise their new ideas with pomp and circumstance but never bury them with honors. Not having been buried properly, they can return and haunt us, of course. Yet establishments prefer to let corpses lie unburied and to hope that exorcism of ghosts, when necessary, will not be too costly. It is standard conduct, and standard error: the corpses become skeletons in the cupboard and so much energy is spent hiding them that none is left for the exorcism—indeed, it is a famous and true superstition that before exorcism can be effective skeletons must be brought out of the cupboard and properly laid to rest.

Let me spell all this out by scanning the example at hand, a recent textbook from a highly-placed young author and his position vis-à-vis language philosophy and its heroes for the last 80 years or so, and his quiet replacement of Moore and Ryle with Evans, Putnam, and Kripke, not to mention other kings-for-a-day.

The open agenda of Blackburn's book is simple, very straightforward, clearly presented and executed (except for the more technical material) and deserves high praise. The table of contents is rich, as the book is long and meant to be quite comprehensive: the shape of the problem, the very possibility of meaning, conventions, intentions and thoughts, realism, truth, semantics, and reference. Tremendous amounts of material are displayed, vast areas are shown from a birds-eye view, a comprehensive perspective is forged under the reader's scrutinizing eyes. It is impossible even to list all items, let alone discuss them, without running into trouble. Some of these are asides which may be ignored at this or that cost. To take the one aside nearest to my heart and further from the author's interest, in one page or so we get Karl Popper's demarcation of science (scientific theories are refutable), Imre Lakatos's [mock] critique (clear-cut refutations are extremely scarce) and the author's comment explaining why this [mock] critique is a veritable K.O. [Popper required refutability, not a clear-cut one in Lakatos's Duhemian sense of clear-cut.] Now since the linguistic philosophers upheld the positivist view of science (scientific theories are verifiable or refutable [in clear-cut ways]) which Blackburn rejects, and since he rejects Popper's view of science so lightly, he needs to say, even roughly, what his view of science is. He seems to be both anti-reductionist and anti-sensationalist. Good. But what is his view of science? He recognizes the problem of induction, though from the angle of Goodman's Paradox, which looms large in this book, as we shall presently see (cf. Index, Art. Goodman). But he offers hardly any view of science.

This, then, is the forte of the new agenda of analytic philosophy: it is not nearly as ambitious as the old language philosophy, and not nearly as comprehensive: you can do analytic philosophy while putting your philosophy of science on ice (or bracketing it). The sooner the reader notices this point, the greater his pleasure in reading this comparatively clear work; yet the changing of the agenda is itself a major item on the hidden agenda; the untrained reader may not notice it, especially since the hint about it, the center of the charming and seemingly very frank preface, is likely to mislead him; I was nearly taken in myself. I was saved by Blackburn's warm endorsement of Quintilian's adage: "write . . . so that you cannot be misunderstood!" My own aim is very much lower. I try to write as clearly as I can, but I dare not go beyond the hope that here and there we can overcome some of the colossal obstacles to communication and from time to time glean the lustre in each other's eyes. I find this rewarding enough.

Part I, Chapter One. How come we both speak the same language (p. 8)? Do we really (*loc. cit.*)? Can we ever (p. 9)? A living language is elastic (p. 10), so that improving a part of it, say arithmetic, though quite impressive (p. 14), raises new problems (p. 15ff.). In particular, it is not which word happens to denote which number that matters, but that such denotation is at all possible. Even this point is hard to articulate, as it has a psychological component which we may wish to ignore (p. 26) and the rules of denotation which we may wish to explore.

Gilbert Ryle's critique of Noam Chomsky's theory of language (p. 29) [allegedly] teaches us that we learn by comprehending the *point* of a rule. The word sequence 'if you catch no fish you may eat them', for example, is ungrammatical because it is pointless. Comment: I am at a loss. Has Blackburn forgotten his Lewis Carroll or does he think when Carroll plays with such instances he is merely as ungrammatical as when he warns us of the Jabberwocky? It seems to me clear that here the author slips and violates his own allegiance. He falls prey to old, introspective language analysis while proclaiming his opposition to introspection (p. 27). He also considers Chomsky anti-introspectionist, without saying that despite his endorsement of Ryle's critique of Chomsky he shares Chomsky's anti-introspectionism. What prevents clarity here? Enormous weight was given not so long ago to the frankly introspectionist response to Benson Mates's attack on linguistic philosophy made by one Stanley Cavell (absent here) and hordes of Cavell's followers. Blackburn could have done better had he addressed himself to this literature, had he asked, what and how much of it still stands, and which way may introspection be expected to help solve what kinds of problems? Meanwhile he has not caught his fish: we have here a general critique of classical linguistic philosophy which the author is utterly oblivious to: every rule, even the best, may be properly yet pointlessly applied, unless we have a rule forbidding pointless discourse! What, however, is pointless and what is to the point? Can the author say? No. No one can: it is too context-dependent.

Rules, meanwhile, govern the chapter to the end: when is a rule implicit, when absent? When speakers conform to an implicit rule are they thereby guided by it? How? Does one's 'semantic system' cause one to follow a rule? (Gellner's classic 'Maxims' is no more alluded to than his classic *Words and Things*: it makes no appearance in the book, which may explain other conspicuous absences, such as J. L. Austin's.) Still, we know that the command of a language includes the ability to compose sentences out of words. How? This leads us to

Chapter Two. Philosophical problems arise in a clear and pressing manner when we discover that our views of the world in general [= our metaphysics] clash with our specific judgments (p. 39). I do not know how to express my delight at this legitimization of philosophy and of philosophical problems and this ascription of a central role to the unrestrained critical attitude, to the advocacy of conjectures and refutations. I should observe, however, that in the view of Lakatos, say, we may ignore such problems: any excuse to smooth rough edges will do (p. 256), he said, in his [mock] refutation of Popper.

The dog-legged theory says, words have meanings by virtue of their being interpreted in some other medium (p. 40). Problems ensue when this view is criticized (*loc. cit.*). The medium may be ideas (Sec. 1), images (Sec. 2), innate representations (Sec. 3) or manifest meanings (Sec. 4)—which last

medium is presented in some variant of a Quinian or Davidsonian theory. I
had hoped that Blackburn's clear and decisive pen would provide me with
entry to these arcane ideas. I was disappointed. Blackburn notices that
meanings are shifty, and that claims (e.g., the radical untranslatability
thesis of [Duhem and] Quine) may be understood in a manner which makes
them trivially true (e.g., 'no translation is perfect') or trivially false (e.g.,
'no translation is possible'), and in a manner which makes them problematic (?) (p. 60). I fear that reading these authors I, for one, cannot hold
to one meaning without breakdown. And, indeed, when I can, I find Quine
superb, his transparency reaching heights last visited by Russell, e.g., in his
'Ontological Relativity' (regrettably not mentioned here) and his *Set Theory
and Its Logic*. Still, the author is quite right to say that Quine's system of
meaning is inherently behavioristic (p. 63)—yet Quine's arithmetic is
Platonic, of course. Whether the two are mutually exclusive is an open
question. Also, the author is right in agreeing with Dummett, that
behaviorism is one version of the doctrine that meaning is manifest in use.
Why the young Wittgenstein does not show up here I do not know; the
chapter ends with an odd remark: the attack on [all? some?] dog-legged
theories, both overt and disguised, was one of the central achievements of
the later Wittgenstein. But he had no alternative to them (pp. 66–67).

Chapter Three. The coasting on the runway is over. On page 70 we
prepare to take off. I am here deflected by scholarly considerations and by
the author's ascription of ideas to other authors who had published "more
or less simultaneously, and independently" (p. 69, lines 4 and 3 from bottom), with a qualification that is relegated to a note (p. 107) which mentions
Wittgenstein and is cast in such florid language that I suspect it possibly has
no meaning at all. Let us note this meaningless bow to the Master and let
scholarship and ascription ride for a while. We must now take off. "Three
Ways of Being Odd". They are, (a) users are making some [obvious?]
mistake, (b) a term is used while its speaker uses a different meaning than
listeners have presumed, and (c) a speaker uses a word without having
ascribed to it a meaning—like a parrot (p. 70). The author calls these three
options or hypotheses to explain odd uses of words, (a) the right rule view,
(b) the bent rule view, and (c) the no-rule view.

There is a sense of *déjà-vu*. When I read a philosophical text written in
the Moore-Wittgenstein style I feel the way Moore felt when he read any
philosophical text: he saw in the text no problem but found the text itself
problematic. The opening move in the book at hand, on p. 70, presents no
problem, yet I cannot follow the text without its raising a serious problem
for me.

The reason I see no problem is simple; when someone utters an odd
sentence and I find it difficult to decide whether that person utters that odd
sentence while following the normal rules, some bent rule, or no rule—and
this happens to me, though quite rarely—it either does not matter or I take

the trouble to find out which is which. Why should that not suffice? Too much hinges on the three ways of being odd, and the author should tell us why he studies them; why he studies the odd rather than the ordinary. Will he study and classify arithmetic errors or possible errors instead of arithmetics? Wittgenstein and Carnap and their friends and relations studied verbal oddities in order to illustrate the view that by clearing out verbal nonsense we do away with philosophy. Blackburn [tacitly] disagrees. Why, then, stick to a technique while rejecting the purpose of its use? What is the problem of odd sentences?

The reason I find the three ways presented here quite problematic is the typical verbal ambiguity on which so much philosophy hinges. We have to ask, right at the beginning of the discourse, before the three ways of being odd are explained: What is the author's intent? Is he saying that there are only "three ways of being odd"? All hints in the immediate context sound to me to say: Not necessarily; why should there be only these three? We shall see, however, that the broad context rests heavily on the view that there are only these three; that, in particular, a statement like the oriental saying that the world is but a dream, which is repeatedly asserted, say, in certain Japanese movies as not odd at all, yet which sounds to our Western ears as distinctly odd, must be seen as odd in one of the three ways just mentioned. From here the road is clear to the resting place of the ghosts of Wittgenstein's *Tractatus Logico-Philosophicus* 5.4733: "Every possible proposition is legitimately constructed, and if it has no sense this can only be because we have given no *meaning* to some of its constituent parts" and his *Philosophical Investigations*, Pt. I, 464: "My aim is to teach you to pass from a piece of disguised nonsense to something that is patent nonsense", and 401: "(Think for example of the question: 'Are sense-data the material of which the universe is made?')"—and you get caught in a time-warp.

Why do bent rules bother thinkers? Why does it matter that we may prefer the word 'grue' to the word 'green'? After all, not all words and rules in natural languages are as straight as we could imagine! For example, consider those assets which have small market-value until some change makes them highly valuable; we have no words for such assets. An emerald may be green to maturity and then turn blue; in which case we may well say it is grue! Of course, if someone says something which sounds odd, it is usually a fact that we either face an error or alternatively a person using a strange rule—children and foreign speakers do so regularly! What of it?

The picture and question will alter radically if we notice a fourth way of being odd—a way which has little to do with the choice between right rule and bent rule: innovation, whether in science or in art. When Einstein developed his theories he caused relatively few problems of comprehension; he was held to be saying false and even foolish oddities. He was then seen to only seem foolish, but to be quite interesting and provocative. But an Einstein is even more rare than one who changes meaning and rules without prior discussion. As the reader may check, we often hear people say something odd and seemingly foolish, yet they may provoke us to see that, be they right or not, they are no fools. True, this happens more often in science than in daily experience, since the fourth way is that of bold hypotheses. Yet it may regularly happen in the theatre if a provocative play is on show, such as one by George Bernard Shaw.

One of the chief authors in the bent-rule literature is Nelson Goodman. He is concerned with science. Science for him is not bold hypotheses but generalizations which are projections, where projections are constrained by unknown rules such as: Thou shalt not try to project odd qualities like grueness—where an emerald is grue if and only if it is green till maturity day and then turns blue, we remember. 'What characterizes grueness?' is Goodman's question. Since his concern is with scientific method and with the justification of the conclusions of science by empirical means, his work scarcely belongs to the present context. Wittgenstein may serve as a better candidate, except that his examples are bold-hypothesis examples. Thus, he asks (*Philosophical Investigations,* Pt. I, 146), "But couldn't we imagine that God suddenly gave a parrot understanding and it now speaks only to itself?—But here it is important that to this presentation we took recourse to a presentation of a deity" (my translation). Wittgenstein was far from suggesting that people follow bent rules; rather, he felt, they follow bold hypotheses and thus bend rules and thus they become dogmatic (*ibid.,* 131: "(The dogmatism into which we fall so easily in doing philosophy.)"). He saw no option but the dogmatic endorsement of some (pseudo-?) proposition and the dogmatic acceptance of the right rules (*ibid.,* 219: "When I obey a rule, I do not choose. I obey the rules *blindly.*"). Blackburn can describe Wittgenstein pretty much this way (pp. 82–83, p. 89) and yet he does not mention the fourth way of sounding odd. A footnote on page 83 dismisses Hegel's and T. H. Green's idea that "the infinite or absolute mind" lays down "standards for description", yet he calls Hegel "Kant". This is a bent rule for sure, unless it follows some quite bold hypothesis.

Though Blackburn does not discuss the creation of hypotheses, he discusses the creation of rules of meaning, for example the creation of paper money. Can Wittgenstein's theory of meanings as embedded in a way of life account for that, or is it a static theory (p. 86)? And can we embed meanings in a community's way of life without knowing the meaning of 'way of life' and the meanings a way of life embeds (*loc. cit.*)? Good questions. Blackburn assumes Wittgenstein's theory [of forms of life] was to be determinate enough to offer us an answer. It does not. The feeling one gets from reading Wittgenstein, as David Pole has noted (he is very regrettably absent here too), is that Wittgenstein was ultra-conservative. But is the conservative flavor personal or part and parcel of the theory?

A conservative theory of meaning is almost adequate: it holds for all societies except those which incorporate science into their way of life, and it incorporates these, too, for all times except for times of rapid change. The exceptions should not, however, be a cause for much concern for one not particularly interested in science, especially if one is willing to endorse Lakatos's permission to scientists to handle exceptions somewhat arbitrarily. Rather, Blackburn's concern lies elsewhere: is an idiolect a dialect (pp.90–92)? If that were the only question left open by Wittgenstein, he would be my hero too. And so I can leave the rest of Chapter 3, as I will not object to any solution it offers to this very marginal question: Is a private language possible?

Chapter Four. Speech rather than mere sound may be rooted in speakers' attempts to convince audiences of a proposition. Assume no language and some conduct by speaker meant to do that, characterize that conduct and see if you can identify that characterization with the meaning the proposition meant to convey. This, roughly, is the program of H. P. Grice of 1957. Now, 30 years later, do we still have to examine it in detail? Is it really so obvious that I want you to think proposition P, rather than that we both want to explore question Q? Whence this urge to convince? Is one-upmanship so vital in the eyes of Grice?

The question of communication is plain: we transmit only signals, never symbols, and hope that they are received as symbols, not signals devoid of meaning or invested with unknown meanings. Once some meanings are established, more meanings may be constructed with their aid. How do initial meanings happen? They are preverbal, of course: Grice is right at the parent-suckling level. Blackburn discusses a sexual communication with body language between strangers in a restaurant but not mother-child relations, on which a relevant literature has developed.

Conventions, verbal or not, are co-ordinations; these may evolve on the basis of other conventions or in a tradition of some groping. David K. Lewis, we are told, rehabilitated convention in a beautiful study (p. 119). What does Lewis add to the views of Hobbes, Burke, and Oakeshott? They take meaning, and even language as a whole, as given and as conducive to the creation of conventions, yet a vicious circle operates here. Oh, we know the circle need not have a decreasing radius—on the contrary it may grow. But when and how did the first verbal convention begin? A century ago Robertson Smith advanced a hypothesis; he is not mentioned here, as David Lewis does not need that hypothesis: any habitual pattern may be the seed of convention (p. 121).

Yet a problem lurks here (p. 122): "which kind of habits or regularities in our use of signs might be regarded as conventional?" Here the expression "might be regarded as" imposes a broad answer: any. Blackburn evidently rather means 'is'. This question thus reworded leads Blackburn straight to Robertson Smith's hypothesis, which he revives (p. 124), though in a less colorful variant than in the original. Analytic philosophy is finally catching up with 19th-century paleolinguistics.

Since Grice discusses the ontogenesis of meaning and Lewis its phylogenesis, we have a gap here. In a roundabout way (p. 127) we slowly arrive at this gap (p. 130). The gap is easy to close, however: children are deferential to convention and willingly endorse it (Sec. 6). True. And so we have a conjectural history of meaning—not yet a theory of meaning as invited in Chapter 1, Sec. 1.

Anyone familiar with the history of anthropological linguistics and psycholinguistics may find this chapter painfully naive and/or flat. This feeling disappears when the author returns to thought (Sec. 7). After all, meaning is concepts and ideas, and what these are neither anthropological linguistics nor psycholinguistics deign to discuss. Can we discuss the meaning of a proposition without a theory of the mind? Or vice-versa? [No, says Popper, and postulates World Three so as to have a theory of mind. Can this be done? Not his way.] A machine can utter a sentence without putting meaning into it. [We do not argue with a phonograph, observes Popper.] Can a machine ever utter a sentence and mean to put its meaning into it? Can a computer ever think? We do not know; we cannot as yet characterize well enough either computers or thinking. The author cites John Searle's convincing argument to show that apparent thinking need not be so (pp. 136–37); of course. Yet we assume Searle's own apparent thinking to be thinking. We may do the same with some sophisticated future computer, who knows? Popper even offers a criterion, which is strikingly simple. Had Searle found himself arguing with a computer, then, says Popper, we would say that he had made the assumption that the computer does think, and if the argument were productive, then Popper too would make this assumption. Searle and Blackburn, however, follow Grice and speak of knowledge, not of debate; and we all agree that some computers—even some books and records— know much but do not think. [Grice says, we speak as we want to convince; Searle says, we speak as we want to convey information; neither knows of Karl Bühler, who influenced both Wittgenstein and Popper.] Blackburn then seeks to link thought with comprehension and this with language, without which arithmetic ability, for example, is greatly constrained (p. 138). This is interesting but needs squaring with Einstein's seemingly different description of his own thinking as preverbal in a sense (*The Psychology of Invention in the Mathematical Field,* Jacques Hadamard, 1948) and with Russell's similar self-observation (*Autobiography*). Still, I find pages 139–40 worth examining in some detail. Does the author offer an answer to his questions (How is language possible? How is denotation possible?)? I do not know.

Part II. From Part I, 'Language and Ourselves', we move to the tacit rehabilitation of the very philosophy which was unjustly condemned by language philosophers [who followed Wittgenstein's famous edict, "the puzzle does not exist"], to Part II, 'Language and the World', which is longer than Part I by one-third.

Chapter Five. Realism and Variations. Scientific theory need not supply the truth about reality. Therefore, our views of science and of truth both enter the debate [!] (p. 145). These the author will debate both locally (ethics, mathematics) and globally [metaphysics], preferring the 'top-down' strategy, beginning with the nature of truth (p. 146). Blackburn begins with a difficulty. "In writing the history of science . . . we want to express what was right and wrong about particular doctrines" yet there is something amiss here. What? (p. 149). It seems clear to me, perhaps not to Blackburn, that he means by "wrong" false, and by the ascription of false ideas to past scientists a condemnation of them, and one which is often enough quite unjust. This is, indeed, troublesome. My own *Towards an Historiography of Science* of 1963 completely supersedes these two contentions—to Blackburn's satisfaction, I am sure, had he taken the trouble to glance at it: I say there that many old theories were intelligent and valuable mistakes. Reductionism (Sec. 3) is discussed in linguistic terms, though it is ontological. No progress here. The holistic objection to reductionism (Sec. 4) is thus put lengthily and clumsily while missing the ontological thrust of holism, and while committing the traditional positivistic error of confusing an ontology—the world consists of sensations [Mach]—with an epistemology—knowledge is based on sensation [sensationalism] (p. 100). It is thus no surprise that the next step concerns status and the question is of justification—by [only?] three possible modes (p. 165): by convention, by putative contingent-truth claims, and by transcendental proof. Of course, traditionally, and in Vienna till the end, epistemological reductionists claimed the status of empirical proof (or at least of empirical confirmation) for [allegedly] well-founded reduction theories; here the author omits this claim and blames [all? some? which?] 20th-century reductionists for neglect of the problem of status. Page 166 is already much better: "I think the problem of status raises profound difficulties for the enterprise of doing metaphysics by searching for reductions" (p. 166). How true; yet 20th-century reductionists find this a compliment, not a critique, and 20th-century non-justificationists will not care much for either status or reduction and openly advocate the free search for (intelligible) metaphysical theories. On pages 167–68 we have an interesting item: in the heyday of linguistic philosophy metaphysical views were translated into suggestions: say not 'X causes Y', say 'X is offered as an instrument for bringing Y about', etc. [Of course, this does not work at all: old age causes all sorts of undesirables, for example. Old age is no instrument for bringing wrinkles about.] Yet, the author rightly reports (p. 169), the purpose was to circumvent both metaphysical and epistemological pitfalls. The discussion here (up to p. 171) is tolerable but obscures the fact that the issue at hand is a program, not a full-fledged theory, not even a half-hatched one. Metaphors (Sec. 7). Are they Legitimate? Dead metaphors are all right (p. 172). (Rousseau argued convincingly that all language is metaphor, largely dead.) A good live metaphor is "an invitation to explore comparisons" (p. 174) (—and, still better, a bold hypothesis—like material waves in 20th-century physics). (And, since all language grows by exploration, Rousseau has won unless we know of another way in which language is explored.) The author edges in this direction (p. 176.) with an odd timidity. Clearly, he would be bolder had he acknowledged the explorer's (commonsensical) right to err. Is this too Popperian for analytic (Oxford) philosophy as yet? Time heals.

Chapter Six. Evaluation, Projections, and Quasi-Realism. Here the author introduces his technical apparatus. Until now I have overlooked the peculiar use of the word 'commitment' to denote a wide range of views in one's head—mused about, considered, entertained, employed, endorsed, believed, and even unshakeably believed. Now the author's frequent, vague use of the term begins to cause some concern. I do not comprehend the diagram on p. 181, which concerns commitment. Still, we have competing sorts of theories here, concerning the way we evaluate theories, particularly moral ones. A projective theory, for example, moral emotivism, "intends to ask no more from the world than what we know is there—the ordinary features of things on the basis of which we make [ordinary!] decisions about them, like or dislike them" etc., (p. 182). "By contrast a theory assimilating moral understanding to perceptions demands more of the world" (*loc. cit.*), namely that its furniture may have moral qualities. Projectivism is also preferred on metaphysical grounds: moral qualities are additional to natural ones (pp. 184ff) (the discussion of natural necessity here is both superfluous and erroneous; see my 'What is a Natural Law?' [reprinted in my *Science in Flux*, 1975]. The situation is tricky not only concerning ethics but also, of course, concerning science: can we imagine two distinct theories both in full agreement with all observable facts (p. 187)? The question tickles the language analysts who are bound to ask: Do the two theories have two distinct meanings? Charles Sanders Peirce wanted to construct a theory of meaning in which the negative answer to this question is demonstrable. There is no comprehensive theory of meaning as yet with which to approach this matter. Yet the discussion meant to lead us toward a theory of meaning began with Frege. Frege observed that a statement need not be asserted but may, say, appear as a part of a condition in a conditional, yet retain its meaning there; hence, meanings are independent of attitudes at least to some extent. Of course, Frege assumed a fully objectivist, metaphysical theory: laws of nature and of ethics and of other domains exist in a Platonic heaven and so our assertions in these domains correspond or do not correspond to Platonic facts and thus are true or false. Blackburn overlooks this theory for its want of a transcendental proof. He is thus a victim of the verificationist theory of meaning of his earliest predecessors, all his intentions to the contrary notwithstanding. Moreover, having endorsed this theory he has prejudged the issue. The projectivist is forced, by arguments of Frege as presented to the author by Peter Geach, to a position where he must use many *ad hoc* hypotheses (pp. 195–96). Why should Lakatos not be called to the rescue and permit such hypotheses?

Under what conditions is it objectionable to use *ad hoc* hypotheses? Why was Copernicus right to reject Ptolemy? Lakatos has an answer at variance with Blackburn's (p. 196), and where are we to turn for help? Blackburn has not worked out his endorsement of Lakatos: his attention is directed elsewhere. He says, projectivism "has the merit that it *protects* our ordinary thinking, in a way that mere reminders of the way we do actually proceed cannot do" (p. 196). Whatever this means, it is also what Lakatos calls a protective belt; it protects him from Russell's critique of the cult of ordinary usage (where what is judged ordinary is what is taken as ordinary in any Oxford college common-room, says Russell). Yet Blackburn is not too apologetic: he notices that projectivism, too, is not quite ordinary, as ordinarily we exhibit quite a realistic bent (p. 196). The rest of the book is a defense of a sort of commonsense realism—quasi-realism—which projectivists can endorse.

Page 197 seems to me to be crucial. In it we encounter the violent attack by Alasdair MacIntyre, himself a respected member of the Oxford analytic school, on emotivism as quite amoral and thus as unintentionally monstrously immoral. This attack is dismissed as "ridiculously beside the point". What does a reader do when what looks to him very forceful and to the point is brushed off? I suppose he may lay the book aside, or skip the chapter, or try to pretend to agree with the author as long as possible so as to proceed. Blackburn's reason for this dismissal, his reference to emotivists' own honorable moral attitudes, is as erroneous as the Oxford establishment's similar response to C. E. M. Joad's similar charge (*Positivism*, 1945). For the critics refer not to intentions, but to unintended consequences. Hence, the response, not the charge, is beside the point, and even "ridiculously" so. Yet, even allowing an emotivist his moral sentiment, discussion of emotivism then goes to the impasse between any two equally legitimate different emotive views, or rather sentiments—and in ethics as well as in aesthetics. Emotivists will have to allow both sentiments equal status, then. This is relativism, and it seems a consequence of emotivism (p. 201). [This argument is shared by all critics: relativists have no possible argument against the worst ethical system.]

The crux of the book's argument is complex. There is projectivism, the doctrine that "evaluative properties are projections of our sentiments (emotions, reactions, attitudes, condemnations)" (p. 180, n5.5). There are projective predicates which describe attitudes and moral commitments as if they were factual judgments, which judgments may be put in propositions, whose truth-value may be debated (p. 195; if I misconstrue this, let my reader blame the author). Furthermore, there is quasi-realism, the claim that projected predicates are not improper or 'sick' [in the sense in which Wittgenstein declared, *Philosophical Investigations*, P. I, 133, that all philosophical doctrines are sick, and that a philosophical method does not exist, only "methods, like different therapies"]. Assuming quasi-realism, then "the issue whether projectivism is correct is *not readily* decidable" (p.

210). What does all this mean? It means that perhaps goodness and beauty are, as A. J. Ayer has claimed, only in the eye of the beholder, but perhaps they are objective. It is funny that all this rests on the assumption that Ayer's doctrine is not 'sick' rather than on the assumption that, say, MacIntyre's doctrine is not 'sick'. Oxford philosophers, of course, never said Ayer's doctrine was 'sick'; rather, they said this of his metaphysical opponents, the predecessors of MacIntyre.

This oddity is in the author's way of rejecting Wittgenstein's idea that metaphysics is 'sick', especially on the ground of Wittgenstein's allegation that metaphysics is necessarily dogmatic. For, we remember, the best philosophic problems come from the recognition of the force of some criticism of our metaphysical 'commitment'. Here the bent use of the word 'commitment' to mean opinion pays a high dividend. For, it turns out, he does not really allow for metaphysical views as putative truths.

To illustrate his view, the author takes Hume's claim that causality is but a projection, and Hume's claim (the references offered are to one section in Hume's *Treatise* and one in his *Inquiry*: no discussion and no direct quote; the severity of the censure, see below, may require more scholarly treatment) that "the quasi-realist can again earn a right to the notion of the true causal structure of things", which together entail that he—Hume—"has been shamefully abused by commentators" (p. 211); commentators of the analytic school, we should remember (p. 6). Kant, too, is a quasi-realist, it seems (p. 212), just as much as those committed to the possible-worlds theory, where possible worlds are, of course, no more than mere projections. Everybody, then, may count as a quasi-realist. The puzzle fizzles out.

What, then, is the outcome? The metaphysician may say what he will; his claim for the reality of whatever he claims reality for, may be re-worked in a quasi-realist mode: this way his theory will remain intact, and even be defensible, but deprived of its objectivity. Quasi-realism, then is pseudo-realism, the very same realism which Bishop Berkeley insistently claimed for his idealism—as his claim was based on his (false) observation that his idealism did not contradict any commonsense judgments, only the metaphysical-realist view of the material world as constituting a genuine and indestructible material substance.

This is not so much Wittgenstein as Carnap—his principle of tolerance (not mentioned here): we may choose any system we like, but declare real only what is empirically verified to be as it is. Not in vain is Carnap here seen as a paradigm of a "hard-line empiricist" (p. 245).

The question is, then: How can there ever be an effective criticism of any philosophical 'commitment'? And remember, without criticism, no excellent philosophical problems! Alas!

Correction! The final section of Chapter 6 shows my reading in the last three paragraphs of the point at issue systematically erroneous. Projectivists do not say that goodness and beauty are in the eye of the beholder and they are not relativists, we are told (pp. 217–220). Rudeness is in the eye of the beholder—or rather that mode of conduct that is judged rude; rudeness as such is not, even for the projectivist. Idealists are projectivists, but they do not deny that objects exist. "This is extremely important" (p. 218). How, then, can two different projectivists—say an idealist and realist—at all attempt to criticize one another? This depends on what makes the projected qualities not in the eye of the beholder. I think there is no answer to this question: what makes real any projected quality? Indeed, as we all learned in introductory courses, when Berkeley, the best idealist ever, attempted to answer this question, he invoked *deus ex machina*: Berkeley said, the ordinary reality, as opposed to the substantial quality of ordinary objects, differs from dreams thanks to their being perceived by God [or projected by Him]. (Are dreams unknown to God?) Lakatos would approve, no doubt, of any excuse. And even I find Berkeley's excuse better—at least cleaner—than Blackburn's; but then I have missed his point; it is clear that the idealism of the projectivist kind is not Berkeleyan but Kantian. If so, then Blackburn's claim—that he is a quasi-realist on morals, yet not a subjectivist or a relativist (p. 219)—tacitly rests on transcendentalism. For an author who wishes to be explicit, this is astonishing. A note on this matter (p. 219) begins with the claim that the theory the author expounds is one which "Wittgenstein may have come close to" and ends with a cryptic remark on the status of '7 + 5 = 12'; this is a touch of old-fashioned scholarship; it tantalizes the reader with allusion to Kant and thus to Wittgenstein's possible quasi-Kantianism (as noted first by Feyerabend—he is also conspicuous by his absence).

A minor presentational complaint. The debate begins (p. 182) with "To ensure that a projective theory starts at reasonable odds", thus allowing the reader to expect its rejection sooner or later; it grows on us slowly, and I, for one, cannot say where it begins to be projected as the author's choice and where it turns out to be his central 'commitment'.

FINAL CHAPTERS

We are on page 224 now and have 125 pages to go—about a third. Yet from here on it is all coasting downhill, with two chapters on truth and one on reference. I will be less systematic from now on, and only cite points I wish to comment on with new material: I think my objections made thus far apply increasingly forcefully as we go along, but will not further weary my reader with this point. The final part concerns results, and one chief result, due to the application of Blackburn's quasi-realist technique, is to render Tarski's correspondence theory of truth, which is *prima facie* realist by virtue of its very idea of correspondence, into a quasi-realist theory.

There is the question: Does one say different things when saying that p is true than when saying that x, when 'p' is the name of the sentence which says that x? This question is important, especially since the view which constitutes the false answer to it—the "redundancy thesis" (Sec. 3 of Chapter 7) or the idea that we can do without the concept of truth—is still very popular. An informed author should say to his reader at once and unequivocally that this view is a gross error, rather than that it is "not entirely unproblematic" (p. 232). This is the poorest point in the book. Let the holder of the redundancy thesis try to assert that everything the Bible says is true in their own way and then continue the debate; moreover, let him try to assert that everything in the Bible, being the Word of God, is indubitably true. (I have heard important mathematicians sweepingly ascribe truth to all of the writings of Georg Friedrich Bernhard Riemann, on the strength of their profound admiration of his allegedly unfailing mathematical intuitions.) And, of course, Russell and Whitehead said something like that in each and every theorem of the *Principia Mathematica*—by their insertion of Frege's assertion-symbol before each of them. To omit the assertion symbol as redundant, as was done some time under the influence of Wittgenstein, is a howler: when an assertion-symbol stands before a conditional with the antecedent having the same shape as the consequent, for example, it means that any conditional statement is demonstrably true whose antecedent is identical with its consequent. Omitting the assertion-symbol, we have to replace this theorem by a countable list of statements, one informing us that if the snow is white then the snow is white, and another that if the snow is green then the snow is green, and so on *ad infinitum*.

To top all these trivialities, we have a non-trivial point. It may be a mere matter of convenience to reduce the bulky *Principia* to the size of Quine's *Math Logic* by putting all proofs in the meta-language. Yet it is a fact of cardinal importance that there are theorems not provable in *Principia* but provable in the meta-language—such as Gödel's famous Statement G. Not in vain did Wittgenstein, who tried to do away with the concept of truth, deny Gödel's theorem altogether. (Had the error discussed here not been endorsed by Wittgenstein, I think it would have been treated better in the book at hand.) The desire to do away with the concept of truth is patently positivist, as Carnap admits shamefacedly in the introduction to his classic *Introduction to Semantics*. Karl Popper, too, tried in 1935 to do away with the concept of truth; but at least only for science, and while observing that even in science we cannot do away with the concept of falsehood.

Of course the importance of Gödel's theorem is that it refuted Wittgenstein's thesis that we understand a theorem only if we can prove it. This is the verification principle for mathematics. The verification principle for empirical science is much more complex, since verification is at most local, whereas meaning is global. Blackburn tends to the view of meaning as global (see Index, Art. Holism), rather than endorse it as a demonstrated fact: the meaning of a concept in a system may alter when the system undergoes a natural extention, so-called. Thus, the meaning of the connective for the conditional is weaker in positive logic than for a logic with negation, such as standard logic. Also, the meaning of the Boolean class-membership symbol differs from that of the Cantorian one (which is the gambit of Quine's *Set Theory and Its Logic*). Hence meaning must precede empirical tests; which was initially Popper's cardinal argument against the Vienna Circle's verification principle.

I will not go over the author's study of semantics and all that. Let me only observe that, in line with his projectivism, he wishes to almost endorse the correspondence theory of truth.

He rightly asks: what does the phrase 'correspond to facts' mean (p. 226)? He also rightly observes that the correspondence theory of truth is attractive because it makes excellent sense of "the general maxim: that a good new [scientific] theory should be able to explain what was attractive about a superseded theory" (p. 246), though his wording is defective: Only the explanatory and predictive power of a past scientific theory has to be explained, not its other attractive features. Newton saw much that was attractive in Descartes' theory which he regretfully had to let go. Anyway, the author is right: a relativist, who can see no merit in this [not so] general maxim, may very well deny it, as Thomas S. Kuhn does. Does the author accept the correspondence theory of truth? If yes, he should explain what 'corresponds to facts' means, if not, he should tell us what he does with the maxim just cited. What is it to be? He offers an in-between position, with all the cost of both extremes and no benefit: There really is no correspondence theory of truth; "there is rather invitation to think of the relation between true belief [i.e., statement] and whatever it is in the world which makes it true" (p. 248). This sentence, first and foremost, does not make use of Tarski's discovery; it is Fregean. The expression 'corresponds to the facts' has two ambiguities: which fact? and what is the correspondence? (The structures of facts and of sentences cannot correspond as they are obviously divergent.) Frege said, as to the first: truth is correspondence to all the facts; and as to the second, to correspond is to denote. All statements in Frege's (and in Russell's) system have as their proper subject either everything or nothing (except for those whose subjects are proper names, perhaps). And the true and the false denote respectively 'the true', the total state of things as it really is, or nothing at all. Tarski had a different idea: the truth of a sentence depends on whether the facts it describes are as it describes. In other words, the sentence that says that x, is true iff x; since 'p is true iff x' is partly in the meta-language, partly in the object language, the demand for a hierarchy of languages and for the employment of one language in a sentence made him demand that x be first translated into the meta-language.

This demand is central for Tarski; it is also extremely troublesome. For example, when we discuss abstract set-theory, we need the whole of abstract set-theory also in the meta-language. With this we give up hope of employing Hilbert's sane program of using a finitist meta-language. Nor is the demand to use only one language in a sentence so very obvious, at least not to readers of the Marx-Engels correspondence. Nor is it reasonable to exclude French and English playing meta-language to each other. What is at stake, of course, is the expulsion of the Liar. But since the Liar, alas! is forgotten here, I will not expand. Let me only say that the complaint, seriously cited by the author, that Tarski's theory is trite, is quite the opposite of the truth, and quite obviously so. (All this has been extensively discussed by Karl Popper, incidentally.) Here is an additional argument for this.

The fact to which a truth corresponds is covered by Tarski by his explicit statement of each fact in the definition of each corresponding truth. Hence he defines the truth of each sentence one by one—his definition is a definition-schema, and if we agree that definitions are axiom-schemas this complicates things further. Yet the question still remains, What is correspondence? The definitions (in the plural), we saw, manage to evade the question, each by itself, but correspondence is what binds them. What is it? It cannot be reference, as in Frege's theory. Tarski says it is satisfaction. The axioms of satisfaction are given here in some (unsatisfactory) version. What satisfaction has to do with correspondence is not explained—nor is Frege's theory presented as an alternative solution, so that it naturally seems "highly doubtful" (p. 286) and a "curious doctrine" (p. 228). For, it turns out, satisfaction brings Frege in through the back door (Hattiangadi). The author travels into the fairly unknown terrain of possible worlds and there one must cling to the problems Kripke has attempted to solve (they are absent here) or else one could not possibly seriously entertain the doctrine: after all, in that doctrine a wild and far-reaching possibility like the snow being black may be entertained, but not the humble one of calling the snow the schmo.

CONCLUSION

And so this review fizzles out, because the reviewer has the questionable habit of reviewing books chapter by chapter. Let me then sum up the situation. The book's declared intention is met best at the beginning. The more it shows the author's familiarity with some up-to-date work or another, the less credible it appears that the book is a definitive restatement of a school's position. The author should have shown more sensitivity to the difficulty of recording the latest positive lasting achievements while avoiding ephemeral discussions.

Yet the book is clear, problem-oriented, tolerant to both metaphysics and the history of philosophy (alas! in intent only), and it records clearly certain sets of problems which may define the field of analytic philosophy so that even people not favorably disposed to Wittgenstein, Oxford and/or the Vienna Circle will be able to teach a course in it or contribute to it in a manner competent enough to let their heresies be forgiven. And, finally, the book hopefully heralds a new era, in which analytic philosophy will interact with logic, paleolinguistics, linguistic anthropology, psycholinguistics, and even cultural history. The future is open, and therefore things are beginning to look up.

PART II

POPPER AND HIS ENTOURAGE

INTRODUCTION TO PART II

Many observers have expressed pleasure at the fact that they were situated right in the middle of their own field of vision: it presented to them everything they deemed important. It was against these people that Mark Twain observed that he was fortunate not to like onions; otherwise he would have to eat that distasteful vegetable.

In the center of my field of vision, at least as far as the philosophy of science is concerned, stand Popper and his crowd. I felt this way when I first had the wonderful luck of meeting him in person, though then the learned profession scarcely referred to his work, and I feel so now; then I agreed with almost all he had to say, or so I thought; now I disagree with it. Yet his revolutionary ideas force every philosopher to take serious notice of his opinion or to stay behind. As W. W. Bartley III has often said, if Popper is even remotely on the right track, then almost everyone else in philosophy today is simply wasting their time. I still remember how moved Popper was when I first told him that Faraday's ideas were utterly ignored in his lifetime in preference to ideas which are now seldom mentioned even by historians of physics. This sounds like submitting to the judgment of history, despite history's notorious capriciousness. But it only means to say that physicists, too, could pretend to ignore certain advances in their field, but sooner or later they had to notice the force of these advances. In other words, the community of physicists also prefers, at times, politics to truthfulness, but only up to a limit. This may be the same for philosophy. And if so, then in time Popper's ideas will have to be noticed.

What causes the oversight is clear enough, since it is simply the preference of any immediate cause over the general cause of the advancement of learning. What, however, causes a reversal? Max Planck is reputed to have said what William Whewell, Joseph Lovering, S. P. Langley, and Florian Cajori had said long before, that holders of the old views die out and younger scholars come to the field with no preconceived notions and reconsider ideas on their own merits. This theory is empirical, and so it can be tested. It is easily refuted by very well-known facts. On the one hand there are the physicists who learn to take seriously ideas they had pooh-poohed very loudly only the previous year. On the other hand philosophers now raise a new generation of students who have no knowledge of Popper's ideas and who swallow distorted recent histories, including distorted versions of these ideas, such as distortions presented by Rudolf Carnap and by Carl Hempel.

How, then, do good ideas come to fore? It is not only Popper who is a case in point; so are other philosophers, such as R. G. Collingwood and Michael Polanyi. And so it is not the question of consent, since no one in his senses could agree with all three of these, but of appreciation. How is it that Collingwood was so painfully overlooked during his lifetime, indeed until recently? Why was it so hard for his peers to express appreciation of his ideas despite his popularity as the author of quite a few best-selling books? I really do not know.

Whatever the way towards the recognition of important ideas, one means to facilitate the process should be the technique of expressing dissenting recognition of interesting ideas, the technique of distinguishing respectful disagreement from disrespectful, the technique of overlooking expressions of agreement with leading figures concerning theses and claims which happen to be quite generally uncontested, and overlooking them as sheer acts of undesirable piety. It is time we trained our students to express impatience with those who take pious agreement as more important than respectful disagreement.

The first part of this collection focussed on the leading schools of philosophy, proposing that their members would do better if they took more cognizance of Popper and of his school. This part is devoted to the Popper circle and its present state. The first two contributions concern writers on Popper who belong to the leading schools of philosophy. The final contribution is my summary of the contributions of Karl Popper himself, of his works in general. I have asked some people whom I have criticized to add their comments to this book. Louis Feuer refused, as did Adolf Grünbaum and others. Paul Feyerabend has kindly permitted me to republish one of his two responses to my criticisms. Gunnar Andersson has kindly allowed me to publish his. I hope that co-operation of this kind will become customary.

Perhaps a word is in order here concerning humor, or rather concerning poking fun at another's ideas. It is enjoyable, but one's target may take offense, and the target's sympathizers may feel the same. This is why comedians are so favored who poke fun mainly at themselves. And, indeed, when Woody Allen began to use his humor also against others, his audiences and reviewers split and offered very different responses. I therefore wish to express here my appreciation for Mario Bunge's assurance to me in person that my poking fun at his expense (and mine) in the essay on his work here republished, did appeal to him. I hope readers take all my jokes, good, bad, or indifferent, in the same spirit. It signifies, after all, what social anthropologists call "joking relations": only those are allowed to poke fun at each other who do not take offense. Whatever may be thought of my style, I hope my intent is always deemed to be not the giving of offense but the raising of my reader's ability to take both criticism and friendly jibes in good part.

— 24 —

GRÜNBAUM ON
(POPPER AND) FREUD

the elusive neo-Baconian

1. BACKGROUND

Every review is a compliment: a highly critical reviewer should therefore explain why the book under review should be noticed. For, following the contrary view, that works which are not the most appreciated are always better ignored, would create a social vacuum in which only superior contributions would seem to have been produced. It would thus distort not only the background but also the substance of the superior contributions: thinking is a social phenomenon and as such it must be of varying quality; much of a thinker's product is willy-nilly a response to his or her environment, superior or inferior as that environment may be—the product of their thought must then be judged as responses to their environment and by reference to that environment.

Let me illustrate this with two examples of contributions which I consider superior, and which are also the subject matter of the book I wish to review in the course of the present essay—Sigmund Freud's psychoanalysis and Karl Popper's falsificationist philosophy of science. Both were taken by their immediate peers as of little significance and this colored their peculiar characteristics and are still causing problems as to what attitude one should take vis-à-vis each of them.

The major social event in Freud's life was the hostile response to his announcement of his theory of infant sexuality culminating with the Oedipus complex. It is not that Freud the individual did not expect or invite hostility; perhaps he even thrived on it; in his autobiography he puts down as not

Previously unpublished review of *The Foundations of Psychoanalysis: A Philosophical Critique, Pittsburgh Series in the Philosophy and History of Science* (Berkeley: University of California Press, 1984).

serious the Americans who had invited him and honored him—perhaps because he met no hostility in their country. But here we may ignore the personal aspect and stay with the social one even though the two do reinforce each other. There was a mutual reinforcement between this hostility and the development of the psychoanalytic closed society, and Freud became exceedingly intolerant of dissent and of criticism. Not only were leading members expelled; a high level of discipline was maintained and every member felt constantly under threat. Ernest Jones tells us in his life of the Master, which is a major work in many respects, that the Master nearly expelled him when he once expressed in print a highly qualified word of faint praise for Melanie Klein.

The isolation of the professional group led to its growth and final victory. The victory was much assisted by the success of psychoanalysis with the general educated public, where it was known and spread by various means, including Freud's masterful popular writings, the parlor games such as catching people making Freudian slips, the flood of psychological novels and thrillers, and the conversion to the doctrine which many socialites underwent during psychoanalytic treatment.

All this is background. Its influence on the doctrinal evolution of psychoanalysis was the inevitable distortion of doctrines under valid attacks, chiefly due to changes leading to ever-increasing levels of immunity to criticism. Freud could keep developing his ideas without allowing his associates to question the logical relations between the old and the new. When Freud introduced the pleasure principle, did he thereby expand on his idea that the only basic impulses are the desire for food and sex, or did he give it up? As the death-wish theory is in clear conflict with his early ideas, how radical is the change? Since only criticisms which Freud acknowledged were permitted, especially criticism he himself had generated, the picture needed clarification and reassessment, yet these were forbidden.

The worst was the result that the very relevance of evidence to the theory became very problematic—even though relevance is a logical category! When Freud developed his theory that dreaming is wishful thinking, he stressed that the existence of wish-fulfilling dreams is ancient knowledge, that the novelty of his theory is in its utter generality. This is strongly connected with psychoanalysis, which teaches us that the strong sexual impulse is usually repressed: in dreams, Freud said, as well as in day-dreaming and in free associations and in slips of the tongue, and so on, one is off one's guard and then the lid is lifted. And so Freud elicited much evidence to prove that all dreaming is wishful thinking. Later on he added that there is the wish for punishment which may also be expressed in dreams. This is not very contestable, yet methodologically disastrous. For it makes sense to argue that all dreams are pleasurable since it is contestable, yet it is quite pointless to seek empirical evidence in favor of the logical truth that every dream is either pleasurable or not. But the loss was bigger. At first, Freud explained the role of dreams as attempts to prolong sleep. Rather than wake up and go to the toilet, the bed-wetter dreams that he is already there; rather than wake up and go to the office, the obsessive procrastinator dreams that he is sitting at the desk. When the idea of punishment-wish was added, this idea was silently lost. This is very upsetting. Freud's dream theory is further changed by the theory of the structure of the soul. And a reassessment of its final version is called for, and is still awaited.

That Freud's (self-)critical acumen progressively dulled after 1900 can be documented in detail. His latest works were the least self-critical. For example, his *History of the Psychoanalytic Movement* explicitly dismisses the critics of his theory as sick, thereby making assent to it obligatory for any sane person. For another example, the preface to his posthumous and unfinished *Moses and Monotheism* is even more embarrassing in its exhibition of his readiness to be self-indulgent: reaffirming the taboo on wild speculations, he granted himself a dispensation from it. In the period prior to his discovery of his theory of infant sexuality and the Oedipus complex, he worked in the critical medical tradition inaugurated by Claude Bernard and J. M. Charcot, was open to criticism, and repeatedly invited criticisms from his friend Wilhelm Fliess with whom he had much in common, as a non-practicing Jew, a medical man, ambitious, and a fountainhead of both wild speculation and sharply scientific critical reasoning. Freud then developed his theories of infant sexuality and the Oedipus complex, and soon met with hostile responses—even from Fliess, who doubted the validity of Freud's empirical evidence for his new theories. Freud terminated all communication with him despite the obvious pain which this severance involved. He demanded endorsement of his views and thus added to his isolation.

Despite the isolation and its high cost, Freud won. The scientific Establishment is now ready to forgive itself its dismal pretense that Freud did not count. Had he lived, they might have by now granted him a Nobel prize in medicine. But he is dead, and honoring him must be done not by declaration but by rethinking. A few works are devoted to this rethinking, some of them, of course, from the psychoanalytic side, but some of them are from the intellectual or scholarly Establishment. I should mention one significant work by Frank Sulloway: *Freud, Biologist of the Mind*, 1979. It is a significant book, much to be commended for its historical scholarship and for its dispelling of many myths—most of them frankly attributed to Freud himself. Yet the thesis suggested by the very title of the book is not. Today psychiatry is divided into the biological or materialist school and the mentalist school, with the biological school ruling the Establishment and with the leading mentalists being descendants of Freud one way or another. Sulloway presents Freud as a member of the biological or materialist school, as a reasonable thinker, and as barely related to Fliess, who was undoubtedly in part highly critical and scientific, yet in part also quite superstitious.

The superstitious, especially the one with scientific aspirations, is one who seeks wondrous insights, who develops theories on the basis of wondrous clues—which Sir Francis Bacon approvingly described as Clandestine Instances: intriguing and meaningful phenomena. It was Galileo and Robert Boyle who managed to banish the wondrous from science. Scientific research, they said, seeks repeatable observations, and it seeks to explain them. Are there repeatable psychoanalytic observations? Freud put much emphasis on the success of psychoanalytic treatments in the scientific validation of his theories, and he admitted, indeed stressed, that we do not know under what conditions such treatment is successful. This seems to amount to a dismissal of a claim of psychoanalysis to scientific status. Whether this is so or not will be discussed further on.

I do not mean to single out Freud's theory. The claim that Freud belongs to the biological or materialist school of psychiatry will not change the situation much since this school—often known as the medical model—is equally superstitious, and for the same reasons, as well as for other reasons which vitiate the statistics it uses. These reasons are quite simple and straightforward: we have no characterizations—of neurosis, of psychosis, or of cure—which are open to standard test methods (sampling, comparing different samples, checking statistical results). And test methods are required before empirical statistical evidence may be deemed scientific. (For details see Y. Fried and J. Agassi, *Paranoia: A Study in Diagnosis*, 1976, and *Psychiatry as Medicine*, 1983.)

Thus the picture gets complicated. The question, 'What is the criterion for granting a theory its scientific status?' becomes increasingly urgent. The problem, often known as the problem of the demarcation of science, is these days ascribed to Karl Popper, though it is, of course, traditional and not in the least peculiar to him.

And so we come to my second example, Karl Popper. He worked in isolation; unlike Freud, he did not create a school in the traditional sense of the word. This was done for him by others—but thus far with little success. Popper has declared that schools are based on doctrines so that they have the poor choice between freezing their doctrines despite valid criticism, surreptitious changes, or splits. The Popper circle, as a result, though it has members who freeze and members who effect surreptitious changes, has no splits but quite a few members who rebel against the Master. Whether such a diverse circle can be called a school in the first place is a new question, which obtains no traditional answers. For my part, I would view it any way my reader chooses.

Nevertheless, Popper, like Freud, won despite the pretense of the intellectual or learned Establishment that he scarcely counted. He was repeatedly put down by the philosophic Establishment, especially the one in his home town—the reputed Vienna Circle—as a philosopher who had little new to say and who blew it up. This line of defense has failed, though it is still voiced (for example, in A. J. Ayer's autobiography). The difference between them and him now looms larger than ever. He gained his reputation slowly and by the sheer volume and import of his output. The general and the scientific audience acknowledged his import before the philosophic Establishment did. Finally he was elected Fellow of the Royal Society of London, and thus entered the scientific Establishment as a philosopher who was still put down by his peers. Two revolutions in the Royal Society took effect in the last century and rendered it a body of professional top-level scientists. This is why Bertrand Russell, the leading 20th-century philosopher, was elected a Fellow, not as a philosopher but on the pretext that he was a mathematician. The election of Popper was the first conspicuous violation of the rules.

This is not to rejoice in the grace and favor the scientific Establishment has bestowed on Popper. They did it for their own reasons. Their official philosophy of science, to the extent that they had one, was always anti-philosophical, pro-scientific, or anti-speculative-metaphysical, pro-empirical-facts—positivistic for short. This positivism is quite untenable, since science makes use of speculative or metaphysical ideas which Kant has labelled regulative, and which are now often known by the *pareve* titles of intellectual frameworks or paradigms. The Royal Society expressed its positivism in a stringent manner by endorsing the view of Sir Francis Bacon, who opposed all speculations and required that theories emerge slowly from facts. When the question, 'What does "emerge" mean exactly?' was asked, the authority of Sir Isaac Newton was invoked, his *hypotheses non fingo* echoed. (It was claimed—for example, by Sir John Herschel and by John Stuart Mill—that only generalizations from observed facts are acceptable as science proper.) This is a straightjacket, and Popper was invited to destroy it, without, however, giving way to metaphysics. Can this at all be done?

I do not think so, yet Popper does think so, and even claims to have accomplished that mission. Speculative thinking has to be allowed, he said, but for it to count as scientific it must be shown to be held in check: we have to show, before granting an idea scientific status, that we can imagine an experiment which will conceivably falsify it. For example, we can imagine a world with the planets perceived to be fixed in the sky, and in such a world all known astronomical theories will be falsified, except the primitive ones which, true or false, are not falsifiable.

Popper is, and always was, convinced that much of what Freud had said was true, and even significant. But he denied every theory of Freud scientific status—because no conceivable fact, he said, would falsify Freud's basic tenets. Thus, some speculations are unscientific, even if possibly true, others are scientific, though in the course of events they get falsified—for example Newtonian mechanics which is but an approximation to Einsteinian mechanics.

This should do as an exposition of Popper's ideas. The problem, however, lies elsewhere. How should he be treated? Should he be allowed into the philosophic Establishment? His isolation there is a serious source of trouble. He still high-handedly dismisses most of the teachings of his peers, so that their heirs, the Establishment of the philosophy of science, are facing the choice between the option of sticking to the claim that he barely counts and the option of having a revolution. In his isolation Popper has left a vast area of philosophic scholarship open, since he has ignored—not to say dismissed with no debate—most of the contributions of other philosophers. Should these be dismissed unexamined? How will the philosophic Establishment survive such a dismissal? Can they order a vast change in the curriculum of graduate studies? What should replace all the courses which Popper and his followers and semi-followers declare to be a sheer waste of time?

Enter Adolf Grünbaum. His self-selected task is to decide the fate of both Freud and Popper in the Establishment of the near future.

Grünbaum rejects Popper's philosophy as gravely erroneous; he claims that his own secret inductivist criterion—neo-Baconian, he calls it—is superior to Popper's falsificationist criterion in being more stringent than Popper's, even though it too is no straightjacket for the imagination. He claims that, quite contrary to Popper's own claim, psychoanalysis is scientific by Popper's falsificationist criterion, but not by Grünbaum's own neo-Baconian inductivist criterion. Yet, though psychoanalysis is not vindicated by Grünbaum, Freud himself is vindicated nonetheless. This is achieved by elevating Freud from the status of a (defunct) scientist (as Grünbaum would have it) to the status of a (significant) philosopher of science. He was, Grünbaum assures his reader, "as sophisticated scientific methodologist, far superior than is allowed by the appraisal of friendly critics . . . let alone by very severe critics. . . ." (p. 128): he is "the Freud who gave us the Tally Argument" (p. 141). Have you ever heard of the Tally Argument? Not unless you are familiar with Grünbaum's 1979 or later publication. For this Great Argument "seems to have hitherto gone entirely unnoticed" (p. 127). Now that we notice the Tally Argument and learn from Grünbaum that he considers it sophisticated and superior, we can appreciate Freud and welcome him, posthumously, to the community of scholars. But we should not admit psychoanalysis, since it rests on the Tally Argument, which is really great but which, alas, is "empirically untenable", due to "Evidence accumulated in the most recent decades" (p. 128, line 19); it is also, we learn, "aborted" (p. 129, line 4). (I returned the dish to you whole so that it must have been cracked later, and anyway it was already cracked before I borrowed it from you.) Until the Tally Argument is replaced, "there is woefully insufficient ground to vindicate the intra-clinical testability of the cardinal tenets of psychoanalysis" even if the patient's clinical responses are believed (p. 128).

What is the Tally Argument?

The newly-discovered Tally Argument, or its "bold law-like premise" (p. 127), amounts to the claim that the only way and the sure way for curing neurosis is the patient's discovery of the event which has caused it and whose memory he has repressed. This is a variant of the Breuer and Freud catharsis theory of 1893 which they themselves soon gave up. Since this theory was empirically undermined, psychoanalysis became untenable. This, I think, is Grünbaum's chief point concerning Freud: just when it could become respectable it lost all hope of ever receiving empirical backing.

All this is not very convincing, especially since we are not told what the new theory is which he labels 'neo-Baconianism', nor why the neglected Tally Argument is so very significant. To make things worse, it is hard for any philosopher, however authoritative, to adjudicate concerning scientific acceptability or unacceptability: philosophers either rubber-stamp scientific adjudication and their work is thus redundant, or they are in conflict with it and are at risk of censure by leading scientists. (This is the so-called paradox of analysis, usually ascribed to G. E. Moore.) Especially when Grünbaum's verdict is so sensitive, his status as a judge may be highly questionable. Moreover, as long as philosophy is not even unified, his authority may be questioned—and was questioned and challenged—even amongst the ranks of philosophers.

Grünbaum solves both problems at one go. His book attacks both philosophers who defend psychoanalysis and reject science (allegedly or in-truth)—the "scientophobes"—and philosophers who denigrate psycho-analysis as scientifically untestable. The first establishes Grünbaum as a *bona fide* scientophile (not to say an uncritical one); it also establishes Freud as a scientophile, which, no doubt he was (as he always eagerly coveted scientific status and recognition for psychoanalysis). The second stresses the difference between the standard view of psychoanalysis as un-scientific *tout court* and the utterly new view of it as would-be scientific, even if in fact it is not.

It is hard to find, through his massive attacks in all directions, precisely what points Grünbaum thinks important. The Epilogue, however, makes it clear that (1) psychoanalysis is untestable and has little likelihood of being tested; that (2) Freud's claim to scientific status rested on the Tally Argu-ment; and, finally, that (3) Popper's charge against psychoanalysis as un-falsifiable is a myth. This, then, is his major triple thesis. Freudian psychoanalysis, though falsifiable, is not testable because testing it should rest on the Tally Argument which is false.

With this elaborate discussion, I hope it is clear why I deem Grünbaum's book a major event and I hope I have prepared the ground somehow for reviewing it despite its being so complex, tortuous, and high-handed.

2. SUMMARY AND CONCLUSIONS

Adolf Grünbaum is a leading philosopher of science. In the United States his status is of the highest. Among philosophers of science there he is second only to C. G. Hempel in authority, and to none in displaying this authority—in professional meetings, in learned publications and behind the scenes. A *Festschrift* in honor of his sixtieth birthday was recently published in the celebrated *Boston Studies in the Philosophy of Science*. He is a professor of philosophy and a research professor of psychiatry in the University of Pittsburgh and chief editor of the *Pittsburgh Series in Philosophy and History of Science*, in which the volume at hand, *The Foundations of Psychoanalysis*, appeared. The message this volume presents is hardly surprising, particularly since it is a rework of a series of articles in book form (p. xiv). As the dust-jacket informs us, it has been hailed as a great event by some of the most celebrated intellectual leaders in the United States. Why? Amongst these are some leading psychoanalysts, which is quite impressive, given its highly critical verdict on their field. How strange! How come?

The book contains a 94-page introductory essay against "scientophobic" interpretations of Freud; Part I consists of 75 pages against the Freudian clinical method of research; Part II, 93 pages on the empirical basis of psychoanalytic theory, and a brief epilogue. The volume at hand is highly polemical; this is its great virtue. It has three defects. First defect: it contains no background material; this makes it barely readable even for the few who may boast the expertise it requires of them (in philosophy of science, psychoanalysis, psychiatry, and experimental psychology). Second defect: it includes barely a sentence of praise of, and a lot of expressions of impatience with the authors cited, not to mention downright unfriendliness. Since attacking all "scientophobic" defenses of psychoanalysis is more than a full-time job, obviously Grünbaum has to be selective; he does not tell us why he has selected Jürgen Habermas, Paul Ricoeur, and George Klein to attack. He does not even prove them all to be scientophobes. Would it not have been wiser, in particular, to attack the works of their respective mentors, Theodor Adorno and Jacques Lacan? Or does the scientophilia of these earlier authors disqualify them? And does Grünbaum discuss Freud because Freud's ideas have some intellectual merit, or only because he finds them so popular? Or only because they are a case in point of a controversy Grünbaum picks with Popper? And why Popper, of all the philosophers of science Grünbaum dissents from?

On this Grünbaum makes his attitude amply clear: Popper is a mythmaker, and his myths are spreading like an epidemic (p. 282). Nowhere in the book at hand is Popper shown as in any way intriguing or challenging—even though Grünbaum grudgingly admits that his critique of psychoanalysis is often correct and he tacitly endorses much of his methodology. The lack of background and clear outlines of positions and arguments in the book are not mere omissions—they constitute evasions. Even a neologism like "neo-Baconianism" is left hanging in mid-air: let the readers make sense of it as best they can. I will not play tit-for-tat and will not declare Grünbaum's influence a source of any epidemic. Rather, the book at hand is a symptom, not a cause, of the sad state of affairs in current philosophy of science.

The third and worst defect of the book is related to the previous two. Due to the lack of background material and due to the absence of criteria of choice, the reader does not know what weight an argument is given, and in different parts of the book the same argument seems to be given different degrees of significance or even to be used in opposite directions. This makes the Epilogue most important, as it is an attempt by the author to sum up his own argument. I shall therefore take great care not to omit any point presented as central in the Epilogue.

Grünbaum's book is exclusively devoted to the question, 'What is the scientific status of psychoanalysis?' To answer it one needs to decide what psychoanalysis is and what criterion of scientific status is used by the examiner. One may then dismiss the question for want of respect for either science or psychoanalysis or both (Introduction). Alternatively, one may dismiss the question as snobbish. One may, then, be enticed to take the question seriously only when told why it has more than a merely snobbish interest. Once the question is endorsed, however, what are the alternatives? A theory (Freud's) may not qualify for the examination (Popper), or it may qualify and receive the grade Fail (Grünbaum). The difference between these two cases is crucial. A theory, further, may receive one or another passing grade—a Pass grade for short—and it may receive an Incomplete grade, which means that a Pass grade is promised upon completion of some task (Epilogue).

A scientific theory, tradition says, has to be proven. When proof fails, a surrogate proof is traditionally called for, namely, empirical confirmation. Grünbaum concurs: a theory's claim to scientific status must be sustained by experience (p. 223), experience should underwrite it (p. 223), authenticate it (p. 224), certify it (pp. 226 and 228) and provide *cogent* reasons (p. 230), to pick a representative sample of Grünbaum's locutions. And, Grünbaum claims, the experience required does not exist since the little which does exist cannot carry the enormous burden of validating the whole of psychoanalysis (p. 256, point 1); unfortunately, he does not say what the evidence does validate. Does it validate a bit, a small section of psychoanalysis, or does it only validate the whole edifice, but slightly?

One cannot blame Grünbaum for this fuzziness, since the cleavage between a theory's being true and its being confirmed has troubled generations of philosophers and could easily claim a book all to itself. As Grünbaum knows, the most highly confirmed theory ever—Newton's theory of gravity—has been superseded and is at best an approximation to the truth, not quite the truth. I will not discuss here the cleavage between confirmation and truth, and I will explain the different theories of confirmation later on.

Popper, too, wants our theories to be true, but he does not demand that the truth be attained, nor even that our conjectures be confirmed; suffice it that science includes only conjectures that we can test—so that if they are false we have a chance of eliminating them. This is his celebrated requirement of falsifiability: he grants scientific status to all and only those conjectures which can be shown to satisfy this minimal requirement.

Popper thus offers scientific status to any theory which qualifies for a test. The result of the test itself, then, can never be a straight Fail according to Popper; strictly speaking, there is only Pass-with-Honors or Fail-with-Honors. And the paradigm case is the already-mentioned Newtonian theory of gravity, the paradigm case of a scientific theory, which for two centuries passed increasingly severe tests yet has now the grade of Fail-cum-Laude. To use Popper's metaphor, the falsified theory is buried with full military honors—buried, that is, in the domain of its successor.

We see now that a Popperian should be sensitive to the difference between Grünbaum's claim that Freud's Tally Argument was aborted, and his claim that it did not stand up to tests. If it was aborted it does not have the status of a once-successful and then superseded theory. Surely, Grünbaum must admit this difference! For we need no evidence for ascribing to him the view that the theories of Einstein and others have superseded Newtonian mechanics, as well as the view that Newtonian mechanics has not lost its respectability. Had Grünbaum denied this point of Popper's, he would thereby "saddle us with philosophic defiance of scientific practice and good sense" (p. 99), which he endorses—or should endorse—as the mark of the ultimate philosophic *faux pas*. Had Grünbaum explicitly affirmed his agreement with Popper on this point, he would have written a more balanced and more readable book. The nearest he comes to explicit agreement with Popper on this point is on the significant page 103, where he reports obliquely Popper's preference of the grade Fail to the *ab initio* disqualification from examination.

Since Popper requires that a scientific theory should be testable, and since Grünbaum requires that a scientific theory be (1) testable and (2) tested and (3) pass the test with success, it is clear that Grünbaum is quite right to claim that his own, traditional, requirement is more stringent than Popper's new one. This is so obviously true that one may wonder how at all Popper could have declared the opposite. And, let me stress, this is the target of Grünbaum's book as far as the philosophy of science is concerned (p. 105 and Epilogue). For Popper himself had chosen psychoanalysis (and Marxism) to illustrate his view that his standard is more stringent than the traditional empiricist standard (p. 105 and Epilogue).

The crux of the matter is, of course, the question of testability. Some traditional empiricist philosophers understand testability to constitute falsifiability and view a theory as scientific only if it survives tests; they hold a standard obviously more stringent than Popper's. These are William Whewell and Claude Bernard, as well as their few followers. Among empiricist philosophers they had almost no following at all, especially since the philosopher most influenced by them was Pierre Duhem, the leading conventionalist-instrumentalist modern philosopher of science, whose attack on empiricism is very well known. The philosophers of science who were contemporaries of Popper, the Vienna Circle and C. G. Hempel, considered instantiations of a theory to confirm it. Their standard is clearly more lax than Popper's, and he used psychoanalysis to prove this. There remain the majority, Bacon and his followers, who are neutral in this matter, since, according to Bacon, anyone who entertains a hypothesis, however tentatively, will no doubt confirm it come what may: the method of anticipation, he said, forces its user to see only confirming instances and overlook instances to the contrary, often by the use of frivolous distinctions.

Hence, Popper's verdict is correct for some inductivist standards but not for any inductivist standard. To quote Grünbaum, and in complete agreement with him, "the moral I draw is the following. Popper is seriously mistaken in claiming that IN THE ABSENCE OF NEGATIVE INSTANCES, all forms of inductivism are necessarily committed to the (probabilified) scientific credibility of a theory, merely because that theory can adduce numerous positive instances" (p. 106 lines 3–7), though it really would have been nice had Grünbaum said clearly that his Vienna Circle heroes, such as Hans Reichenbach, Rudolf Carnap, and Carl G. Hempel, not following Whewell, 'are necessarily committed', whereas Whewell is not committed, to the view of confirmation which Grünbaum's passage describes, and which is usually known as Hempel's Paradox.

3. THEORY, OBSERVATION, AND PRACTICE

The present section does not belong to the present essay; it is brought in so as to explain why I find almost all discussion of the scientific status of psychoanalysis, Freud's, Popper's, and Grünbaum's included, quite wide of the mark. The literature on psychoanalysis, as far as I know, does not discuss the standard of observation accepted in the scientific community on psychoanalysis. I take it that Grünbaum wishes to abide by the tradition of "scientific practice and good sense" as he charmingly puts it (p. 99); otherwise we should demand that he abide by "scientific practice and good sense". We may also wish him to tell us what this is, rather than to present it unexplained and incidentally, as "a lesson drawn" by a philosopher whose work he discusses in some detail. He would have done better to discuss what is "scientific practice and good sense" than the detail of this or that philosophic technicality. As to Popper, he does discuss the status of observation in science, and I will make some use of his discussion. Popper himself has never discussed the scientific status of observation within psychoanalysis. Grünbaum does, and extensively, but he ignores the traditional standard which I shall soon invoke.

The same holds for practical standards. Grünbaum is "dumbfounded" that George S. Klein could consider psychoanalytic free-association a mere research tool—scientific yet not practical (p. 186)—because, we may remember, he says (with no argument to support his claim) the following: were there any scientific status for psychoanalysis it would rest on the Tally Argument—on the claim that psychoanalysis is the only and the sure treatment of neuroses. He does not even explain this odd claim. He invokes standards of pragmatic efficacy, but says about them that they are statistical and comparative of samples, thus implicitly circumventing the Tally Argument. Let me, then, present what I deem is the public situation on these two matters.

The scientific status of this or that theory is often contested in the scientific community. For example, is natural selection scientific? I do not think Popper would have contested the majority view of the matter were it forbidden for philosophers to contest the status conferred on a theory by the scientific community. It is regrettable, even painful, to observe how biased Popper is: almost every argument Popper offers concerning Darwinism or concerning Freudianism can be applied to both, yet he praises the one and disdains the other. Even his claim that some facts agree with one theory or with another are quite parallel, except that within the Darwinian framework there are some scientific theories of natural selection; whereas it is not clear that there are scientific theories within the Freudian framework. Yet there is some justice to Popper's bias since many Freudians but no Darwinian would declare their critics sick.

In any case, the scientific tradition permits a controversy about the scientific status of a theory. It does not, however, tolerate controversy concerning the scientific status of observation. Why? Immanual Kant and William Whewell ascribed to generalized scientific observation the status of certitude, which would explain the lack of controversy about them—except that they also ascribed certainty to theories, yet concerning theories the same ascription did not prevent controversy. Sir Isaac Newton has observed (*Opticks*, last Query), that a generalization may be falsified, and it then needs to be reinstated with some qualification. To this Pierre Duhem has added that with the alteration of the theoretical framework the wording of a generalization of an observation may need restatement. And, finally, Popper has added that a generalized observation may be replaced by its empirical falsification. What is common to all of these thinkers are two points. First, we have their insistence that past observations are improved upon, not simply discarded. Second, we have their endorsement of the standards of observation reports proposed by Robert Boyle (*Certain Physiological Essays*, first two essays), endorsed at once by the Royal Society of London and accepted as standard by the scientific community ever since. An observation report is scientific, and its endorsement is obligatory until it is overturned, if and only if it can be reported as an eye-witness testimony in court, it is reported repeatedly and independently so, and it is claimed to be repeatable. An unrepeatable observation report, according to Boyle's proposal, is neither declared true nor declared false, but is scientifically overlooked. In line with this, parapsychological observations such as premonitions, are ignored. Sir Francis Bacon and Sigmund Freud have psychologically explained the occurrence of these observation reports: Some people tend to forget premonitions which did not come true and to remember those which have come true; and they then deem the latter confirmed. A better, and more Freudian, psychological explanation, is that some premonitions are projections of immoral wishes whose fulfillment lead to a sense of guilt. Yet these explanations of some specific premonitions do not explain, and are not, generalized observations; scientifically they may safely be ignored for the time being.

Since Popper explicitly declared single-observation reports—such as the 'protocol sentences' of the Vienna Circle at the time—unqualified as scientific unless generalizable, we can hardly disregard Grünbaum's complaint that Popper's criticism of psychoanalysis is barely evidence of familiarity with Freud's writings. For Freud repeatedly admitted that his central claims concerning psychoanalytic treatment are not repeatable and not universalizable, or else he qualified them in vague ways. Yet the claim that only repeatable, universalizable, eye-witness testimony is scientific observation, is less impressive than the claim that success is assured to the psychoanalyst who uses his theory as a means for an *ad hominem* dismissal of the person launching an attack on it. And this point is, as Grünbaum repeatedly and rightly observes, the standard technique of psychoanalysis which vitiates its claim to having been empirically confirmed.

Thus, not withstanding all the many derogatory claims in this book to the contrary, as far as psychoanalysis is concerned Grünbaum agrees with Popper: he concludes that Freud's major ideas, which Freud considered amply confirmed and which are still endorsed by most psychoanalysts, are unfalsifiable in Popper's own sense: Freud wrongly claimed certainty, he tells us (p. 271) "for the *clinically* inferred etiology of a patient's affliction, and then relied on that very etiology to: (1) *explain* therapeutic failure . . . and (2) justify dismissing the patient's dissent . . . as . . . the result of neurotic resistance. . . ." Grünbaum brings against Popper such arguments as that "in 1901, Freud broke with his longtime close friend Wilhelm Fliess when the latter objected that the psychoanalytic technique of free association was vitiated by inability to prevent the production of specious findings" (p. 283). This is the concluding part of the book.

I confess I find the whole thing rather distasteful. Consider the following popular joke:

—My tsadik is holier than thine.

—How do you know? Can you prove it?

—Yes I can: he converses with angels.

—And how do you know that for a fact?

—I heard him say so himself.

—And you take it, of course, that your tsadik is telling the truth?

—Do you presume that a person who converses with angels would lie? Since both Popper and Grünbaum ascribe this mode of arguing to Freud, I propose to call a truce and ask, instead, is there no more to Freud than that? Can we not forget the scientific status of psychoanalysis and see what, if anything, we should thank Freud's memory for? And, as far as scientific status proper is concerned, let us ask, first, has Freud discovered any general fact? Probably not. He has changed our ways of looking at facts; but he never succeeded in presenting us with a repeatable generalizable fact.

So much for facts. And now to practice, i.e., to technology. It is clear that technology develops its theories with a a certain disregard for the realism of science: it does not care whether matter is atomic or continuous, for example, and, unlike Einstein, space technologists are happy to amend Newton's theory of gravity quite *ad hoc* and use it as they find fit. Yet, whereas scientific theories may prove of enormous value if they are at all testable, technological theories have to undergo certain test procedures and pass them by some legally prescribed standards of success. To be precise, not the theories but the factual observations which may confirm them must be carefully tested. The test procedures may be defective, and when a defect makes a sufficient public stir (as in the case of thalidomide), test procedures are legally altered, and the alterations are at times partially successful, seldom practically fully successful. Yet we cannot do without test procedures which are legally prescribed.

We may make the following general point about technology. The purpose of tests is to fail the claims of innovators: the tester seeks adverse aspects (undesirable side-effects) or evidence that the proposed product is useless or at least no more useful than its older or cheaper alternative. And the search proceeds along lines prescribed by law and to the extent prescribed by law. Popper is utterly right in seeing tests as attempts to refute, and so is Grünbaum. Yet both ignore the institutional aspect of tests in technology and thus (con)fuse science and technology. Also, Grünbaum confuses tests with John Stuart Mill's similarities-and-differences and concludes that he differs from Popper on this point. Perhaps I am in error when I say that Grünbaum confuses tests with the procedures proposed by Mill; he calls his view neo-Baconian, and I have no sufficiently clear idea what that is. Let me, however, explain why tests with the aid of control groups are not identical with Millian similarities-and-differences. The statistical method may consider the independent measure of observability of cause, of observability of effect, and the likelihood of cause bringing the effect about. In different cases the likelihoods may easily go one way or another in that there may be a frequent link not frequently observable or the contrary, so that we may use an infrequently-seen event as evidence for a frequent event. This is why scientific observation methods have to be tested independently of the results of observations. They then may lead us to read the less-frequently-observed tendencies to be the more significant ones. Mill's method is too simplistic for that.

Incidentally, this validates the reluctance of psychoanalysts to accept seeming falsifications presented in the Kinsey Report: if Freud is to be believed, then the lack of inhibition which Kinsey's interviewees exhibited reduces the likelihood of their answers to questionnaires being true. Yet psychoanalysts, Grünbaum insists, refuse all statistics. Is this so? Are there no psychoanalysts who express hope for statistical tests? I do not know. Grünbaum also says the theory is not testable by statistical means, especially not on the couch, and he suspects, not even epidemiologically. He is open on that, but not hopeful. This is no clinching argument, and is not meant to be.

Now the absence of comparative statistics is no proof that other tests are impossible to find. What conceivable facts are there which may serve as tests of the theory in question? We must know this before we can decide on the scientific status of the theory, of course.

The first task one has before even contemplating a test, as Whewell has amply emphasized, is the wording of the theory precisely enough before deducing the test statement from it. In the case of psychoanalysis this is not so easy. Not only is it difficult to say what theory is labelled by the name of psychoanalysis, or what is the canonic form of Freud's own psychoanalytic theories (in the plural!); clearly, it is a group of theories which share as an intellectual framework some metaphysical (meta-psychological is a better word) assumptions, yet each of these theories claims scientific status on its own. Which theories, precisely, are we talking about? I do not know. Fortunately, however, it so happens that we need not insist on the specifications of these theories: their status may be settled without these specifications. Otherwise, of course, we may have to return to the question and try to specify the theories at hand.

From theories we move to the scientific status of observed facts. What are the facts in question? Are they scientific?

We are free to discuss the scientific status of psychoanalytic or Freudian theory, since the demarcation of the status of a theory is a matter both traditionally open to controversy and here controverted. We are not free to discuss the scientific status of observation, as this is determined strictly enough by tradition: It is a matter of "scientific practice and good sense". What, then, are the scientific observations at hand?

Scientific observations, let me repeat, are generalizations, telling under what observed conditions what observed events occur. There is no doubt that Freud was always aware of the need to offer generalizations, and was repeatedly in search of them, often formulating statements in search of generalizations, at times offering generalizations tentatively, and sometimes as if they were verified and beyond dispute. All this is neither here nor there when one seeks scientific observations. Despite his search for generalizations, Freud was not at all clear about the need to have factual observation reports generalized. Grünbaum quotes him as saying this. In 1917, while discussing the observed fact that sometimes treatment was utterly successful, Freud says, and Grünbaum quotes him as saying: "But the conditions determining such a favorable outcome remain unknown" (p. 156). Grünbaum himself takes issue and denies, it seems, that Freud had ever observed successful treatment. He may be right, but, we remember, the scientific tradition prefers to suspend judgment—until it is reported under what general conditions complete cure is regularly observed.

This is not to condemn therapy on account of its possibly not being scientific. Medicine suffers from the practical pressures of its task and cannot drop an accepted practice without having a better replacement for it unless it is truly falsified; this is precisely why the intelligent patient is advised to examine his complaint carefully and see whether the factual part of medicine pertaining to it is scientific or not. And in technology it is facts which have to be examined, hardly ever theories, and these are easier to ascertain the status of.

Philosophers are expert in their ability to "saddle us with philosophical defiance of scientific practice and good sense" (p. 99), at least in part because scientists and technologists do not always live by their own standards. Yet matters need not be complicated. Diagnosis, etiology, treatment, and prognosis are parts of medical technology [not science!], and as such they are almost exclusively factual, with the exception of some etiology—and the factual claims are subject to legal standards of tests.

Diagnosis, especially differential diagnosis, is not much different from examining a witness on the stand. The more intricate part, the evidence of signs elicited by some laboratory techniques, has the status of eye-witness testimony given by an expert witness. When an expert witness is cross-examined, a wise cross-examiner will always be alert to the distinction between his eye-witness testimony and his expert testimony. Since Perry Mason exhibited this alertness on a popular television show, I take this distinction to be fairly unproblematic and quite accessible to the general public.

Scientific research into diagnosis is no small matter, of course, since it is not a small matter to identify a disease in the absence of etiology. Yet once etiology is found, it is brought into the diagnostic process whenever possible.

Philosophers will complicate matters. The presence of a pneumonia-bug is neither a necessary nor sufficient condition for the presence of pneumonia, nor is the shooting of the victims for their death. Yet just as an eye-witness can testify that the accused shot the victim, so can a physician testify that the pneumococcus attacked the patient. This, however, is not to say that universalizability has been achieved. Diagnostics and etiology achieve universalization, and with the aid of statistics, with the aid of independent tests, with the aid of theory which itself is tested, and more. Yet, clearly, the diagnostic generalization differs from the etiological one, since the former speaks of all pneumonia patients infected by pneumococcus, yet the latter speaks separately of the effects of the pneumococcus and of the causes of pneumonia. This is why when etiology is better, so, generally, is diagnosis.

The most celebrated etiological hypothesis is Pasteur's theory of disease, often named the germ theory of disease. But it is or functions as a regulative idea and thus not falsifiable. Thus when Pasteur failed to discover the germ causing rabies he declared very small germs to exist nonetheless, and we call them viruses. He was proven correct on this. Today when so many diseases are deemed congenital, Pasteur's theory is superseded. Yet it, too, has the grade 'Fail with Honors'.

Freud's general theory of repression is a general theory akin to Pasteur's. But whereas Pasteur's theory obviously has many general facts conforming to it, perhaps Freud's has none.

4. THEORY AND FACT IN PSYCHOANALYSIS

The general theory of psychoanalysis includes two simple items and one problematic item. First, the Oedipus Complex, including infant sexuality and the allegedly psychosexual origins of all genuinely mental ills. Second, the illness as a patient's failed but obsessive effort at a self-cure by repression (akin to oedema or the swelling of the body's extremities which is the body's failed effort to overcome high blood pressure), of which the patient is unaware due to the repression itself—which is the (unconscious) reluctance to return to the scene of the original trauma. Their conjunction is the intellectual framework of psychoanalysis. It is only as unfalsifiable as Pasteur's theory, and for the same reason: one can always look and go on indefinitely looking for the cause of the illness, be it a germ as in Pasteur's case or a trauma as in Freud's case. Moreover one can always try to explain a trauma as a psychosexual one.

Freud's third point is terribly important and very problematic. It is the catharsis theory: the overcoming of the abovementioned resistance and the subsequent return to the scene of the trauma brings about an excitement which is easily visible, which according to the theory can only happen when there is no mistake in the identification of the trauma. This experience—this excitement—supposedly cures the patient. Hence the trauma is observable by the observation of the excitement and the memory which coincides with it—the memory of the (alleged) crucial trauma. The observation of the trauma, then, enables one to present the etiology as being just an observation of a fact (i.e., of the trauma), and in a universalizable fashion. (Diagnosis is a different matter altogether. We still lack any theory of diagnosis in general. Yet, ever since Charcot, no one contests the attitude exhibited when a diagnosis is offered of a specific illness in a properly repeated fashion.) It is very hard to resist comparison between the general theory of psychoanalysis and Pasteur's (germ) theory of somatic disease, as both blame an external cause for the disease and recommend that it be eliminated.

This makes Freud's excitement about the catharsis theory (as that of the elimination of the trauma) very understandable and likewise his subsequent inability to give it up though he himself declared it falsified. This sad fact is noticed by Grünbaum, and he places great stress on it (see Index: Art. Tally Argument). He also notices that without the catharsis theory the rationale for the standard psychoanalytic treatment—for free association (or for the couch, as it is known in the vernacular)—is lost; every time the value of this treatment is vindicated, Grünbaum observes, some version of the catharsis hypothesis is invoked (p. 142). This makes the catharsis hypothesis a psychoanalytic myth. (See Alexandre Kojève's contribution to the Leo Strauss *Festschrift* on the inconsistency inherent in myth.) Grünbaum complains (p. 116) about Popper calling Freud's theory a myth. On this point he loses, and by his own recognition of the myth-quality of the catharsis theory. But there is more to the facts of the matter. The catharsis theory relates both to self-knowledge and to the accompanying peculiar experience. The value of self-knowledge cannot be seriously questioned, even when it is accompanied with the license for regrettable self-indulgence.

Freud's view of the falsification of the catharsis theory, incidentally, is erroneous. There was no generalizable observation that he could report, we remember. We may, nevertheless, consider it an error and modify it. Though Freud compared psychoanalysis to a surgical operation, he never deemed post-operative care necessary. If we agree that mental patients are decidophobes (in the sense of Walter Kaufmann's *Without Guilt and Justice*, 1973), and that decision comes with training, then we may modify the catharsis theory by adding to it the following unscientific regulative idea. Post-operative care in the case of psychoanalysis is the training to decide. We may then explore the question, how can this idea be supplemented so as to render it scientific? We will thus be following Grünbaum's proposal to try to replace the Tally Argument with something better. This, perhaps, is the central paragraph of the present review.

Freud regularly distinguished his specific psychoanalytic theories from his general psychoanalytic theory as well as the two from his use of the couch. He was not aware of the difference between general observations and general theories, though he was aware of the need to generalize. To show how confused Freud was about generalizable observations we may consider the defunct seduction theory. A patient told Freud her father had molested her when she was a child. Freud first believed her and blamed her father for her troubles; he later disbelieved her. Is this in any way an empirical falsification? Of course, this depends on why Freud changed his mind. If he changed his mind because his view was in conflict with a repeatable observation of fact, then it was falsification; otherwise it was not. This, incidentally, renders irrelevant the fact that historians now believe the poor woman, and, for all I know, she told Freud the truth. For, if evidence is erroneously repeated, then it must be taken as scientific observation until overturned and then replaced by its improvement. There was, and still is, no repeatable observation going one way or another, except the repeatable observation of the high incidence of sexual abuse of children in the family. Grünbaum acknowledges the relevant facts in his usual elusive way. Speaking of Freud's seduction theory (where "seduction" is a [repressive?] euphemism for the terrible act of molestation of one's own child), he refrains from explicit mention of the contemporary alternative view that Freud's change of mind was an error. He likewise refrains from explicit mention of the fact that this is the reason which Jeffrey Masson offers for his proposal to return to that theory, and that this is why Masson's book was so "much publicized" (p. 50). Rather, he summarily dismisses both views as "etiologically unfounded," meaning, presumably, that they have no general fact to support them, "whatever the merit of the accusation [by Masson] of Freud's repudiation of his erstwhile seduction etiology as a fateful error, which grievously misdirected all subsequent theorizing" by Freud and his followers. In brief, Grünbaum says, and he is right in saying, that neither the seduction theory nor its rejection had any scientific basis, but he does not say, and he is in error in not saying, that scientific basis is generalizable observation report, and he is at fault in being so elusive.

Nothing so illustrates the arbitrariness and high-handedness of Freud as his view of women and of psychoses. Why, for example, should women suffer from penis-envy and men not suffer in the same way from breast-envy? Because Freud was convinced that women are quite inevitably inferior to men and he tried to explain this. The falsification of Freud's [or rather Marie Bonaparte's] views about vaginal versus clitoral orgasm, as Grünbaum rightly observes (p. 270), is dismissed by some psychoanalysts as a falsification of a hypothesis which has hardly any psychoanalytic point. Yet the role of the error was to stress the horrendous claim that a woman cannot be normal unless she recognizes her inferiority—and as inevitable! Even the pressure from women psychoanalysts and from the women's movement to discard this—official—doctrine has brought no relief. Under pressure Erik Erikson is now ready to change the term penis-envy to female masochism! (We have come a long way, Baby!) And from this to psychoses in general. The view of all pathogens as the same sort of sex-related trauma forced Freud to view all mental ills as different only in degree, not in kind. He therefore declared some of us utterly cured (Freud and his recognized followers, etc.), most of us mildly sick, others neurotic, and the worst of us psychotic, demented and catatonic. There is no doubt that all practicing psychiatrists know that there are severe cases of neurosis more severe than some mild cases of psychosis. (See Y. Fried and J. Agassi, *Paranoia: A*

Study in Diagnosis, 1976.) The question, how to remodel the psychoanalytic intellectual framework, however, is neither easy nor needed for the discussion of Grünbaum's book except to say the following. Grünbaum is anxious for psychoanalysis to rehabilitate itself by acquiring scientific status. To that effect he thinks it needs an alternative to the theory of catharsis to justify its practice. For my part, I think this calls for much more preparatory work, and for the time being we may well overlook the question of scientific status altogether. But this view is shared by neither Grünbaum nor Popper, both of whom still insist that the inquiry into scientific status is of great intellectual significance. So let us put my proposal aside for a while.

To the dispute, then.

Grünbaum claims that Freud's theory of latent homosexuality as the cause of psychosis was open to revision. He also claims that the relaxation of taboos against homosexuality should reduce the incidence of psychoses if Freud is right. It would be easy to concede to Grünbaum in Popper's name and admit (as John Watkins did) that psychoanalysis may become falsifiable after all. After all, nobody deems the *Genesis* story of creation scientific; nevertheless, taken literally, this story is falsified, and many think it is. This, if considered a falsification of Popper's view, is a much better and simpler one than Grünbaum's book-long exegesis on Freud. For, Grünbaum claims that, somehow, many years after its invention, psychoanalysis turned out to be falsifiable; he thus ignores the fact that Freud claimed scientific status for his successful psychotherapy—this is the celebrated Tally Argument discovered by Adolf Grünbaum himself—and that Freud claimed no success for the treatment of psychotics. Clearly, then, Freud claimed scientific status on the basis of a misconception—making his theory plainly a pseudo-science. The question of relaxation of standards, on the other hand, is, of course, much more complex than Grünbaum presents it. The question Grünbaum raises concerning psychosis may more easily be raised concerning neuroses. It was raised by Anna Freud in her famous centenary lecture of 1956—where she expressed disappointment at the fact that the popularity of Freudianism has not brought about the expected improvement in the general level of mental health of the population at large. The matter was also raised generally in Vienna early in the century, by the contention that Freud took the mores of his small circle to be universal ethics—thus precluding the question: How should the change of mores affect the general level of the mental health of the population at large? All this raises many very broad questions.

Back to the dispute, then.

5. FREUD VERSUS FREUDIANISM

Grünbaum has a fact which he repeatedly and emphatically presents as one major falsification of Popper's claim that psychoanalysis is unfalsifiable. It is that Freud was aware of the need for falsifiability, that he requested falsifications from Fliess, offered some of his ideas as falsifiable, and that he often changed his mind due to falsifications. Grünbaum is emphatic on this, and even scathing. "Even a casual perusal of the mere *titles* of Freud's papers and lectures in the *Standard Edition*" of Freud's works, he says (p. 108), "yields two examples of falsifiability". And, further, on Popper's charge that psychoanalysis is unfalsifiable "and/or that Freud was inhospitable to adverse evidence", he says (p. 117): "I see no escape from the conclusion that this charge ought never to have been levelled in the first place, or at least should not have been repeated by Popper".

I think it is true that Freud was "hospitable to adverse evidence" of a certain kind, and I do think that, properly worded, some psychoanalytic claims—generalizations of observation—are quite legitimate scientific claims by both Robert Boyle's standards and Karl Popper's. Yet this has nothing to do with Grünbaum's attack on Popper, which I now proceed to make light of.

Now, Popper said some harsh things about Freud; harsher things have been said by others about Freud's being "inhospitable" to criticism and dissent; Grünbaum is aware of evidence amply justifying these allegations, though he does not even allude to it. Grünbaum manages to convey an impression—which no mildly knowledgeable reader will entertain for a moment—that Popper simply picked on poor Freud; this impression simply permeates this book, a book concerning standards which fails by their application to itself.

Yet all this is neither here nor there, and on both general and specific grounds. As to the general grounds, let us observe that Sir Isaac Newton was nastier than Freud, less "hospitable" to criticism and to dissent, and to "adverse evidence" such as the one procured by the Astronomer Royal's lunar observations: Frank E. Mannel's *Portrait of Newton* portrays him quite systematically and consistently so. There is such a thing as a scientific character, and we want everyone, particularly an important thinker, to display it. But Newton did not, and he is not alone. Grünbaum compares the scientific status of Freudianism and Newtonianism (pp. 98, 115); he could also compare the scientific character of Newton and Freud. Neither was very pleasant. Moreover, as Laplace has observed, Newton covered his tracks and we may never know exactly how he arrived at ever so many of his great discoveries. Freud did not cover his tracks, though he is known to have tampered with some significant evidence (Little Hans is notorious). Yet he reports his changes of opinion in stages of deliberation. Like Newton, he wrote in an unpleasant majestic style and in a repulsive cantankerous style; like Newton, but more often than Newton, he wrote also in an exploratory style—and it is there that he is at his most enjoyable. Yet Grünbaum's claim that, since Freud at times altered his views, Popper is in error, is a *non-sequitur*; alterability is not Popper's criterion of scientific status (but, as far as I know, it is the exclusive property of Stephen

Toulmin). It is no accident that Grünbaum reports on Freud's style briefly and partly obliquely—by reference to others' books and to Freud's early personal correspondence with Fliess.

And now to Grünbaum's specific broadsides. To begin with, the two examples referred to in the mere *titles* of papers by Freud. The first is an example from a Charcot-style early somatic diagnosis of a mental complaint (p. 118). Freud's diagnosis was falsifiable and falsified. This is not in the least psychoanalytic, and, in any case, the controversy concerning psychoanalysis was never diagnostic (much to my regret: see the discussion above on Freud's diagnosis of psychoses). Closer to home is the second of Grünbaum's examples from the "mere *titles*" (why "*titles*"? will mere 'titles' not do?). It is concerning the etiology of paranoia. The diagnosis of paranoia is perhaps the only known repeatable observation about paranoia. Freud's change of mind is no Popperian falsification; yet it does show that Freud kept his views on psychoses fluid—because, he stressed, there still is no treatment for psychoses. This fact is only obliquely mentioned by Grünbaum (p. 114, last line, quoting Freud to say he had "never dreamt of trying to explain 'everything'"; Grünbaum uses this quote erroneously against Popper's correct claim that ascribing the appropriate motive to an actor enables one to harmonize every observed behavior with psychoanalysis).

Still closer to home, then, is Grünbaum's claim that Freud gave up the catharsis theory. For what really mattered to Freud was therapy—this is both admirable and questionable, of course. Except that, as we saw, as Grünbaum emphatically declares elsewhere in the book, Freud never quite gave it up. Nor could he find, as we saw, the conditions necessary to declare treatment success or failure, so that he had no empirical scientific observation at his disposal one way or the other.

A final specific broadside. Grünbaum cites (p. 125) a 1937 paper written by Freud, in which he ascribes to "a certain well-known man of science" the unjust claim that his theory is only confirmable but not falsifiable. Freud repudiates this by discussing the testability of conjectures made by an analyst about a patient during the clinical session. This reply is pathetic, as it confuses a theory (psychoanalysis) with a specific singular case. It is amusing to note, however, that the testability of such hypotheses (of a patient's complaint) was discussed by J. O. Wisdom in a well-known paper on falsifications within psychoanalytic sessions. Though Wisdom is a leading scholar of both Popper and Freud, he is not mentioned in the book at hand. Finally, as the point cited by Freud and by Grünbaum, to the effect that having a theory which is only confirmable but not refutable is not proper. It is obviously a Popperian point made to Freud in 1937, two years after the publication of Popper's *Logik der Forschung*, in the same city; this is an intriguing historical fact.

To prove that Popper is picking on Freud, Grünbaum asks (p. 113) what "*proof*"—he means proof—or even merely an "*argument*" (p. 113, last line)—meaning an argument—did Popper have "to convince himself" that psychoanalysis is not falsifiable? This is presented as Grünbaum's checkmate to Popper.

How can any theory be proven not falsifiable? This is a general question not pertaining to Freud. A theory has infinitely many consequences, and if any of them is falsifiable, so is the theory itself (p. 116). Hence, Grünbaum knows, Popper cannot prove any theory unfalsifiable. And he presses this point: it is his alleged checkmate. For, if we accuse someone of having offered an unfalsifiable theory, we may have to prove our accusation.

Yet, the question is, generally, on whom is the onus of proof of status? This is a snob question I do not care for. Yet since Popper says the onus of proof is on the claimant for scientific status, the boot is on the other foot. Of course, Popper here follows Wittgenstein and the Vienna Circle—even though he is, obviously, less stern and demanding than they. Grünbaum pretends to be more on their side than on Popper's. He is not. And, the *argument* by which Popper "convinces himself" that psychoanalysis is unfalsifiable is that it cannot specify, as we saw, under what conditions cure can be expected or how quickly. As we saw, Freud himself was aware of the fact; but, Freud or no Freud, it is a fact.

Grünbaum's vindication of Freud the individual is a central point of the book; he is presented up to the last sentence as critically-minded, fairminded, aware of the problem of methodology and innovative in that field. Grünbaum even quotes a passage from Freud, which indicates faint familiarity with the writings of the conventionalist philosopher Henri Poincaré, as evidence for Freud's greatness. He may even hint (p. 42, last two lines) that Freud was himself a conventionalist, but, despite the evidence, I refuse to ascribe this to Grünbaum, since he knows, of course, that Freud was a staunch inductivist, and since he knows that, adopting conventionalism is a "trivialization of Freud's entire clinical theory" which would be "nihilistic" and "frivolous"; the "radical hermeneuticians" who adopt this stance, we are told (p. 58), thus offer "the kiss of death for the legacy" of Freud. It seems clear from this, and from other passages in the book, that Grünbaum's rush to vindicate Freud the individual while slaughtering his "legacy" is a bit on the "frivolous" side.

6. Grünbaum on Induction

Since most of the volume at hand is about the scientific status of psychoanalysis, Grünbaum's job only begins when he disposes of Popper's view of it as unfalsifiable. "It is one central thesis of this essay", says Grünbaum (p. 124), "that the clinical psychoanalytic method and the causal (etiologic) inferences based upon it are fundamentally flawed epistemically, but for reasons other than non-falsifiability." The reasons are, by the way, the invalidity of the catharsis method and Freud's reliance on it despite his own disclaimer, and Grünbaum's view of Freud's theory of repression as central to psychoanalysis and as resting on the catharsis hypothesis (p. 178). Indeed, he takes the repression hypothesis to be the heart of psychoanalysis, the one "fundamentally flawed epistemically". (See Index: Art. Testability of psychoanalysis *qua* repression etiology.) In a chapter on the post-Freudians (Pt. II ch. 7) he argues that either they endorse Freud's "etiological, developmental and therapeutic tenets" and so are equally "fundamentally flawed epistemically" or they are not Freudians (p. 247). Indeed, he finally declares that the post-Freudians still believe in some variant of the catharsis theory (p. 239 line 2) as well as in its validation of psychoanalytic theory. It is clear, then, that what Grünbaum demands of psychoanalysis is that it be properly validated. To this end, he says (with proof?), a substitute for the catharsis theory is required. And, it seems, he thinks none can be found but he is willing to be surprised.

What then is proper validation? Grünbaum does not say outright, but he gives bits and pieces of hints. The most important hints come in the opening and conclusion of his attacks on Popper. In the first passage he recounts his earlier brushes with Popper and his defenders. His focus of attack, he informs us (p. 105), "was on the *comparative* stringency of the two demarcation criteria when I discussed Freud vis-à-vis Popper" and he "went on to assess the strictness of the inductivist criterion"; indeed, as we remember, he wishes to prove his inductivist criterion stricter than the falsificationist one. Grünbaum has "declared" the following two significant points. First: "the mere fact that inductivists try to use supportive evidence to 'probabilify' or credibilify hypotheses does NOT commit them to granting credible scientific status to a hypothesis *solely* on the strength of existing positive instances, however numerous." Second, "Popper was seriously mistaken in claiming that IN THE ABSENCE OF NEGATIVE INSTANCES, all forms of inductivism are necessarily committed to the (probabilified) scientific credibilty of a theory, merely because that theory can adduce numerous positive instances." And in his Epilogue he says (p. 280); "It is ironic that Popper should have pointed to psychoanalytic theory as a prime illustration of his thesis that inductively countenanced confirmations can easily be found for nearly every theory, if we look for them. . . . Freud's theory is challenged by neo-Baconian inductivism to furnish a collation of positive instances from *both* experimental and control groups, if they are to be inductively *supportive* instances. But . . . if such instances do exist, the retrospective psychoanalytic method would find it extraordinarily difficult, if not impossible to furnish them."

So much for text. Though the clearest on methodology in this, presumably methodological, book, it invites explanation, and one which might both show Grünbaum's charge against Popper to be valid and explain his elusiveness and hostility. Let me offer a very brief history of inductivism to replace Grünbaum's hints.

It all began when Sir Francis Bacon discovered the thesis Grünbaum ascribes to Popper: "inductively countenanced confirmations can easily be found for nearly every theory", to use Grünbaum's wording. Bacon believed that the search for confirmation is only natural since criticism breeds contempt. Now this thesis, criticism breeds contempt, may be well illustrated by Grünbaum's book, yet it is falsified by the falsification of Newton's optics, which has not led to any contempt for Newton. Bacon advised researchers to propose no hypotheses but to start with facts and let the facts lead to theories which are discovered as being certainly true. This idea, too, was falsified with the falsification of Newton's optics. We thus face the question, might not Newton's theory of gravity meet with the same fate?

William Whewell rose to this challenge. He said that confirmations may be just as cheap as Bacon said they always are, and then they are worthless; real confirmations, however, are failed severe tests which have genuinely risked falsification, and then they constitute proofs. (I am using Popper's terminology here for the sake of brevity.)

Popper was not aware of this idea of Whewell's, though at the time it was fairly familiar in scientific circles: Whewell's work was translated and Claude Bernard was influenced by it, as well as Oswald Külpe, whose assistant, Karl Bühler, became Popper's *Doktorvater*. The evidence is in Popper's autobiographic sketches, where he reports his effort to pin-point the difference between the confirmations of general relativity and those of psychoanalysis. He finally came up with the same view of differences in style of confirmation as Whewell though, of course, unlike Whewell, he saw in confirmation no necessary validation. Grünbaum, by contrast, sees here validation, but not to the full extent which Whewell had expected it to be. Yet, whereas Whewell's pre-Einsteinian position is clear enough, Grünbaum needs to offer some explanation. Instead, he pretends to be more different from Popper than he really is. His history is sketchy and garbled—perhaps because he does not wish to appear close to Popper, and perhaps because he refuses to admit that Popper characterizes correctly some inductivists: those who see confirmation as instantiation, a view which C. G. Hempel ascribes to Jean Nicod and which Hempel endorses. Hempel's celebrated paradox of confirmation is precisely what Grünbaum ascribes to Popper, namely "the thesis that inductively countenanced confirmations can easily be found for nearly every theory" and, more specifically, "that IN THE ABSENCE OF NEGATIVE INSTANCES, all forms of [instantiation] inductivism are necessarily committed to the (probabilified) scientific credibility of a theory, merely because that theory can adduce numerous positive instances"—except that, contrary to Popper, not all forms of modern inductivism are instantiationist: there is the falsificationist form as well.

Is Grünbaum a falsificationist inductivist? It is impossible to say, and it is possible to suspect that the book may be so complex, ponderous, and difficult in order to drown this central difficulty.

At times Grünbaum seems to say that psychoanalysis is falsifiable but not scientific because it never withstood an attempt at a falsification. This would make Grünbaum a falsificationist inductivist, a post-Einstein Whewellian of sorts (i.e., of confirmation, Whewell-Popper style, between Whewell's verification due to confirmation and Popper's denial that confirmation at all validates). At times Grünbaum says even that unfalsifiability makes confirmation impossible. At times he speaks of subjunctive confirmability: were Freud's Tally Argument, or rather "its bold law-like premise" confirmed, psychoanalysis might become confirmable. All this is highly Whewellian. Yet when he argues that we need not falsifiability but confirmation by agreement-and-difference *à la* John Stuart Mill, things look different.

Should we guess what Grünbaum's view of induction is, or ought he to tell us? All he says, cryptically, elusively, not explicitly, in the first of the two points made above in his name, is that he disagrees with Hempel, and in the second, that not all inductivists agree with Hempel. In the Epilogue he says that it is ironic that Popper declared psychoanalysis unfalsifiable, since today Grünbaum is challenging its adherents to have statistical tests and use control groups and come up with *supportive* instances, meaning, I suppose, confirmations Whewell-Popper failed-falsification style, even though Grünbaum knows that it is unfalsifiable. To paraphrase Grünbaum's closing remark, it is ironic that Popper should say in 1935 what Grünbaum endorses nowadays. It is.

This, to repeat, is not to endorse Popper's view on confirmation, since confirmation is required only in technology, and by law. In science, refutable explanations should suffice. We need only legislate tests to prove psychoanalytic practices not harmful, that is.

Finally, as to the demand for statistical tests of psychoanalysis, especially tests by making comparisons between the results of psychoanalytic treatment, of alternative treatments, and of no treatment. This demand was made decades ago, by Hans Eysenck and Joseph Wolpe if not earlier. The refusal to consider such tests is one of the *"arguments"* Popper used to "convince himself" that the confirmations psychoanalysts seek are not scientific. This is where things stand, apart from obfuscations and from programs for future research into avenues opened by Freud and still left not fully explored.

So much for my comments on points made in *The Foundations of Psychoanalysis*. The question raised in the beginning of this review can now be better answered. It is not only the force of the argument presented in a study that matters. What matters as well is the place of that study in the learned literature at large. Even a book is given to the vagaries of fortune, as the ancients observed, and fortune is at times a reflection of fashions, and fashions, at times, reflect the intellectual market-place better than some analyses, however valid. And this invites a writer to respond to the market. And if the giants in our intellectual milieu are not too haughty to respond to fashion, surely I should not be so haughty as to ignore it, at least not in the present case. The enormous enthusiasm which Grünbaum's book meets these days from people far more expert in the field than I, makes it clear that it is futile to list all the works which deal with the same issues, and more successfully, beginning with Paul E. Meehl's brief (149 pages) *Clinical Versus Statistical Prediction: A Theoretical Analysis and a Review of the Evidence* (Minneapolis: Minnesota University Press, 1955) and including many with more or fewer technicalities of statistics, of psychoanalysis, or both. Yet it is not the mere technical elusiveness of Grünbaum that I find so "amazing"—I am particularly "dumbfounded" at his not explaining his neologism "neo-Baconism" even once briefly—it is the enormously enthusiastic reception of the book, its wanting in "scientific judgement and good sense" notwithstanding. Yet, despite its shortcomings, if not even because of them, this book may succeed where other books have failed. And, quite possibly, the success of this book rests on the very fact that Grünbaum endorses Popper's criticism of psychoanalysis while pretending to reject it. For, why has Popper not succeeded even though, as Grünbaum hints, even Freud heard an echo of his criticism?

Popper's criticism was launched from an avant-garde philosophical position. And it was devastating. It is really too much to expect fashion to sway so wildly as to reject an accepted psychological theory and practice in favor of a way-out philosophy. At the very least the public may wish to see how well that new philosophy weathers critical attention by peers. And psychoanalysts could not suspect, in addition, that Popper's peers have been as unfair to Popper as Freud's peers were to Freud, and more. Yet Popper's criticism is also commonsense. (It is to stress this fact that the Jewish joke about circular reasoning was cited above.) And now Grünbaum brings this criticism as if it were balanced, rather than devastating, and as if it were mainstream philosophy of science. (This explains his intolerable evasiveness about his neo-Baconianism.) Yet, alas! we have to make an effort and adopt an avant-garde philosophy in order to judge psychoanalysis in a balanced way. Here is an example. Two decades ago, the proceedings of the tenth conference of the American Academy of Psychoanalysis were published—Jules H. Masserman, ed., *Sexuality of Women* (New York and London: Grune and Stratton, 1966)—which may illustrate more of scientific practice and good sense than exhibited by either Popper or Grünbaum on psychoanalysis. Judd Marmor, in his presidential address, observed that psychoanalysis was in a crisis due to petrification and sectarian isolation and in part he even blamed it on "Freud's own attitude". For, "the hostility of his contemporaries and the professional isolation that this imposed on him . . . drove him to equate theoretical disagreement on the part of others with personal hostility or disloyalty." Marmor saw the isolation of the psychoanalytic profession as a threat to its scientific character. The volume is devoted to a move from the Freudian hostile attitude to women to a more mature one, and to the integration of the professions of psychoanalysis and of psychiatry through attempts to integrate psychological theory so as to encompass various achievements from neurophysiology and psychopharmacology as well as from social psychology. The volume includes very interesting and balanced critical debates. Though it most regrettably makes no reference either to Alfred Adler or to Betty Friedan, it is a mature and sensible volume which should have made a greater difference than merely to help ego psychology replace to some extent the libido theory within the camp of the faithful. I do not know why the volume has failed. In part, possibly, its failure is rooted in its shortcomings, mainly in its naive and unself-conscious view of scientific method as that of empirical proof. The critical view of science as an ongoing debate, and of empirical evidence both as ammunition for criticism and as challenges, as material to be explained by new theories—whether this is Popper's view or a variant of it or an alternative to it—this view fits much better the commonsense, mature, and critical attitudes and intelligent perspectives of that book, not to mention its hard-hitting yet friendly criticisms. Yet the Masserman volume is all but forgotten. Can one stimulate public interest in it?

Perhaps Grünbaum's book will manage to sway the psychoanalytic movement out of its dogmatism and sectarian isolation, lamented by Judd Marmor two decades go. If it does anything of the sort, then I shall have to re-examine my criticism. And even if perfectly valid on each point—not a likely case—it will still prove deficient and in need of supplementation. We are all in great need to learn how we can best overcome dogmatism and sectarianism, since they are regular visitors in our midst. Any contribution in that direction deserves a warm welcome. If Grünbaum's book proves to be such a contribution, it certainly will have earned my sincere appreciation.

POPPER AND
THE HUMAN SCIENCES

no scores settled

This book is a landmark in offering critical yet quite appreciative studies of the philosophy of Karl Popper, by twelve authors most of whom are not his disciples. Yet it is hard to guess who will benefit from their careful study. Popper connoisseurs will find them full of misrepresentations and of criticisms which are mild or timid by comparison with those offered by some of his leading disciples; others, presumably, will hardly show much interest. The anecdote characterizing the situation at hand still is the (true) story of Ludwig Wittgenstein's invitation to Popper to come to the Cambridge sanctuary to recant and repent; of Popper defiantly accepting the invitation, and of the host storming out of the room in the middle of his guest's performance. I suppose the two schools of thought represented in the story upset each other because the very situation is a loud criticism of both. Popper and his followers are busy, creative in an activity declared impossible by mainstream Anglo-American philosophy, so-called. And this mainstream exhibits a form of rationality—Popper never allows himself to dismiss them as he dismisses mainstream Continental philosophy, so-called—which rationality has no room in Popper's views since its exponents flatly disregard his criticism and since he finds no valuable fruit of their labors.

Yet some change has occurred, and *Popper and the Human Sciences* is symptomatic of it. The process is one declared inevitable by Samuel Butler. The strongest example these days is the Marxist's respectful study of Trotsky as mainstream Marxist, along with the right-deviationists Kautsky,

This review of *Popper and the Human Sciences*, edited by Gregory Currie and Alan Musgrave (The Hague: Nijhoff, 1985), appeared in the *British Journal for the Philosophy of Science*, 38, 1987.

Bernstein, and Adler. Differences iron out with the gain of new perspectives and the passage of time. Yet, scores have to be settled even after the civilized burying of the hatchets, or else confusion reigns. Here, to my regret, no scores are settled, and perspectives hardly emerge, though civilized the book certainly is.

Indeed, the authors often find it difficult to co-ordinate, and the paucity of Popperian studies of other, mainstream philosophers is no help. At times a complaint to this effect is explicitly stated (pp. 107, 116, 148, 167). The Popperian disregard of so much that is going on is due to lack of interest. The disregard for Popper, however, is also quite often, yet distinctly not always, due to lack of interest. The fact is that some writers are quite interested in Popper's work yet will not admit it publicly. This had led Popper and others to a somewhat unphilosophic grudge—as if those who might or even would comment on Popperian thought owe some explanation to the public. They do not: they are rational, but the rationality they exhibit is not the one Popper describes when he discusses rationality as the institutions of learning fostering the critical approach. Michael Polanyi and Thomas S. Kuhn exaggerate the other way when they discuss rationality as the institutions imposing uniformity. The truth—alas!—is more complicated than either.

Ontology is the major topic of discussion here, for no reasons that anyone offers—the editors could, perhaps should, have said something about their selection. I do not know how one should discuss critically any modern ontology. Classical ontology rested on the polarization of the world to reality and appearances or nature and convention. This enabled one to examine competing ontologies for their relative merit. But it is now passé. Commonsense ontology is unproblematic and does not permit too much analysis, nor too much criticism. Moreover, common sense admits that concrete physical things, living things, human individuals, societies and nations, and even concepts, exist in different senses. Ontology goes further, but what makes a thing which by common sense really exists, an entity proper, what not? And why does it matter? One answer, cursory, I am afraid, can be found in Popper's works: if A and B are entities proper, then we may hope no satisfactory scientific hypothesis will ever be found reducing the laws governing A to laws governing B alone. This claim unbelievably confuses satisfactory explanation with true explanation.

The second and third themes of this volume are Popper's critique of the doctrine of historical inevitability, and his liberalism.

Let me, then, sum up the volume's content, except for the (unsatisfactory) editorial page and the (not representative) bibliography, in the order chosen (why?) by the editors, and add my comments in brackets.

    1. L. Jonathan Cohen. Popper's postulate of the existence of the third world—of objective spiritual entities—is an essential part of his theory of growth-of-knowledge, not a metaphor (no explana-

tion for this is offered). Yet it is a problematic world—it may be split into parts not in communication with one another and is clustered with contradictions which entail (objectively) all statements, including unknown corollaries to given theories. Popper's Darwinian analogy is anyway extremely objectionable. [This is correct, but only the last point scores.]

2. Frank Cioffi finds two criteria for pseudo-science: one is irrefutability, the other this plus pretense. He rejects the one and endorses the other—on behalf of Popper. [But Popper is ambivalent here. The most outrageous pseudo-science is a refutable, refuted theory presented as refutable and confirmed. By this standard, a variety of the doctrines of meaning-as-use, presented as scientific, are pseudo-scientific, presented as logical are pseudo-logical, and presented as rational are pseudo-rational. Yet Popper proposes that the empirical is the refutable, including the refuted: we learn from experience by admitting refutations.]

3. Roland Puccetti. Popper cleverly identifies epiphenomenalism, parallelism, and the identity theory, and settles for nothing less than interactionist dualism. What makes the mind a true entity, contrary to epiphenomenalism? [Parallelists may declare the mind a true entity proper. To deny this is to call everyone a heathen and an infidel who does not fully endorse one's own kind of religion.] Interactionist dualism is objectionable unless souls are mortal. Sir Karl Popper is a mortalist yet he shares his book with Sir John Eccles, the immortalist. This shows clearly that there are different interactionist theories. Eccles thinks that during sleep the brain, not the mind, is shut off. This theory is apologetic, and overlooks those states of sleep, where mental activity—mental, not just brain—still goes on. Popper and Eccles speak of the experience of brain-mind interaction, but Eccles, at least, overlooks the experience of mind-atrophy which need not accompany brain-atrophy. Puccetti presents an effort to render interactionism falsifiable by a thought-experiment in which links between two sense organs and their two respective centers are switched around. [The thought-experiment only shows him to be naive about brain centers.]

4. David Papineau ascribes to Popper the view that though souls do exist, societies do not. He defends this view. [Any similarity between Popper à la Papineau and Popper himself is merely unavoidable: all avoidable ones are assiduously avoided.]

5. A. F. Chalmers claims that Popper's version of methodological individualism is inconsistent. [He too gets Popper wrong, though at least he realizes the matter is problematic. Why is it so hard? The word 'methodological' is opposed, Popper says, to 'ontological':

ask not, 'Do societies exist?' and assume as a device for creating refutable theories that the societies and social institutions which individual actors find significant for their actions do affect their rational conduct. I once ascribed to Popper the view that institutions exist but possess no ends or purposes or goals. I do not know if I was right.] Chalmers thinks that Mill's denial of the existence of institutions differs from Popper's, in that Mill refers to human nature, but Popper does not. [Yet Popper has shown that the denial forces one to fall back on human nature (the methodological myth of the social contract, he calls this point).]

6. Alan Ryan. Popper's philosophy of science and his liberal philosophy are the same—more or less. Ryan fears Popper would be hostile to this thesis. [Popper states it in his conclusion to his *The Open Society*: social institutions are conjectures that can be refuted and reformed, just like scientific theories.] Ryan argues that liberalism can be constitutional—*à la* Kant—or fallibilist—*à la* Mill. Popper is a bit of both, but tending towards Kant. [This is intriguing. It also connects: science rests on institutions fostering criticism, yet institutions are fallible: we boost them, perhaps, by constitutions.] Constitutions, unlike laws, can be fallibilist! [For my part, I think nothing can replace the principle of toleration as a supreme principle.]

7. Jeremy Waldron. Popper's dualism of facts and decisions. It turns out that Popper believes in the entity called morality: he is a moral realist or objectivist. And his view of ethics is not very idiosyncratic. [True. What is idiosyncratic is his view that there are two moralities—collectivist (wrong) and individualist (right).]

8. Noretta Koertge opposes cultural relativism in a rather standard Popperian manner.

9. Peter Urbach seeks an argument against the doctrine of historical inevitability as giving rise to an objectionable approach to social science and thus polluting any item it gives rise to. If valid, such an argument will render *a priori* objectionable any hypothesis fitting its mold. [This is a very odd program, since it is condemned by the fact that some important already-refuted hypotheses were created to fit the doctrine of historical inevitability—most significant of which is Marx's theory of the capitalist trade cycle. Some of Urbach's criticisms of Popper's work, however, are valid, though far from new.]

10. W. A. Suchting admits much of Popper's critique of Marx and shows that some passages of Marx support the doctrine of historical inevitability, others are written in defiance of it. He opts for "a Marxism of sorts". [This is a far cry from E. H. Carr's influential *What Is History?* which opens by dismissing Pop-

per—and Sir Isaiah Berlin too—and from the epoch-making review of the second edition of *The Open Society* in *The British Journal for the Philosophy of Science* by J. D. Bernal, which denies all of Popper's charges and identifies Marx's position with one which most scholars would view as almost identical with Popper's—without Bernal admitting this to be the case, of course.]

11. Robert Ackerman's essay discusses Popper's position in Germany, where he had both a strong discipleship and a strongly hostile opposition which in time is becoming friendlier. The misuse of Popper's views in German politics hints at defects in them, especially in view of the blame Popper heaped on his predecessors as their views were susceptible, and sometimes put to misuse. [This is doubtful: in his *Open Society* Popper mentions the wrong accusation of Socrates on account of the fact that some of his disciples, notably Alcibiades, were tyrants. Ackerman's argument invites further examination.]

12. Richard Kraut presents an interesting and careful criticism of Popper's view of Socrates as a democrat, and replaces it with a modified view according to which Socrates's concern with ethics, not politics, led to a more complex position, though one on the whole favorable to democracy. As Kraut notices, this invites a solution to the Socratic problem more satisfactory than Popper's.

— 26 —

POPPER ON
LEARNING FROM ERROR

gems that look like snippets

Sir Karl Popper's *Logic of Scientific Discovery* presented the method of science as making conjectures and trying to refute them by experiment. His *Poverty of Historicism* offered the view that the doctrine of historical inevitability is not scientific in the above sense. His *Open Society* advocated a reformist social philosophy according to which we may try to criticize our social and political system and to improve it, criticize the improvements, and so on—in perfect analogy with the series of conjectures and refutations which, in his view, is science.

The present volume is a collection of essays, most of which were written after these three books. The essays seem—quite mistakenly no doubt—to consist of snippets, of details which somehow failed to find their way into the previous and more comprehensive volumes. The author perhaps reinforces this impression when he suggests in his preface that the unity of this collection is the general theme that runs through them: "*we can learn from our mistakes*". This thesis, as it stands here, is a platitude; and the author immediately adds that he wishes to incorporate it into a theory of rationality and of criticism. This is more interesting, but still not strikingly new. So he adds that he means to equate rationality with criticism, that there is no room within rationality for any finality in or justification of one's opinions. Here Sir Karl distinguishes himself from the majority of philosophers; but not from all of them, and thus far he does not differentiate this volume from his own previous works. This break is achieved when he adds the very controversial idea that all criticism is constructive: the elimination of error, in science and elsewhere, is in itself progress, a step

This review of *Conjectures and Refutations: The Growth of Scientific Knowledge*, Karl R. Popper (London: Routledge, 1962) appeared in the *Jewish Journal of Sociology*, 7, 1965.

nearer the truth. The preface does not herald this last idea as a recent achievement. But it really is.

The theory of stages of proximity to the truth, of the approach to the truth through series of theories which are false (though, obviously, they may contain a great number of true empirical statements), this kind of *scientia negativa*, is the culmination of the development of Popper's philosophy. It is certainly adumbrated in his previous writings, yet the idea is new, and very remote indeed from an original section of *Logic of Scientiic Discovery* published in 1935, in which the idea of truth is rejected altogether as redundant. The essays in this volume are "revised, augmented, and rewritten", but the spirit of the alterations is not indicated. In this period of rapid change the author's newest ideas may very soon penetrate the academy; if so, then we may look forward to a few doctoral dissertations in the near future discussing the revisions in these essays, distinguishing the stylistic ones from those, if any, necessitated by the author's intellectual development, and so on. All this, however, is secondary.

The essays in this volume are gems. They look like snippets, but, brief as they are, they are themselves great unifying themes. My first choice among them would be that on the three views concerning human knowledge: first, as knowledge of the nature of things; second, as the achievement of usefulness alone, but not truth; and third, as the progression towards truth, perhaps through an endless series of falsehoods. As second choice, one might take the essay in which the pre-Socratic philosophers are described as the forefathers of Western civilization on account of their invention of the dialectic method, namely the method of criticism, in a process of myths developing into bold conjectures which invite criticism. As third choice one might take the essay expounding the author's theory of traditions which, in line with his likening of institutions and their reforms to conjectures and refutations, depicts traditions and customs as more akin to myths than to conjectures. To make things more exciting, one might add the essay on public opinion, which presents *vox populi, vox dei* as a liberal myth which we should reject and thereby reform liberalism.

These and other essays have touches of classical serenity; they are delightful to read, thought-provoking, and very useful as tool-kits for philosophers, social philosophers, and sociologists. Also, they have a touch of the classical in being great in their serious defects. The author's theory of Western civilization is purely Greek: the Jewish element is totally ignored. A criticism of his view from a Jewish standpoint should be highly interesting. In previous works he portrays Judaism as a version of the doctrine of the Chosen People, which doctrine he sees as akin to Hegelianism. Consequently, one might expect his views on both tradition and liberalism to be utterly useless for, and irrelevant to the works of, Jewish sociologists and historians. Yet it seems to this reviewer that the author's theory of tradition is best exemplified by a better-informed and less-biased view of

Judaism and Jews, and that his view of liberalism and its history needs to be modified so as to allow for the historical fact that Judaism, as a tradition, includes some sort of liberalism as a sub-tradition (to say the least).

There is, then, great interest and challenge in this volume, both generally and from the viewpoint specific to readers concerned with Jewish affairs. Another quite intriguing aspect of it concerns the development of the author's own philosophy. The volume includes a charming and lively intellectual autobiography, which has immediately and rightly achieved the status of a minor classic. We are also offered a glimpse of a different side of the author's biography in the essay in which we are told about the changes of views of Rudolf Carnap—Popper's arch-opponent and the intellectual leader of the Vienna Circle—changes which came about partly because of our author's criticisms. Although this essay is of some biographical and historical significance, especially for those interested in positivism (scientism), it is of a much more limited interest than other essays, and has a polemical flavor that is very different from that exhibited in other essays. The wisdom of including it in this volume may be questioned. The topic of the essay is the demarcation of science. The author insists that, as usual, he is very ready to alter his views, but only in the light of valid criticism; and this he has failed to find. He demarcates science as series of conjectures and (presumably empirical) refutations. This, it seems, is the source of the title of the present volume. The volume is further divided into two parts, one entitled 'Conjectures', the other 'Refutations'. These titles seem to present nothing more than a playful idea, a pun: the book is obviously philosophical, and thus obviously not scientific. The thought comes as a shock that possibly the author means his titles literally, that perhaps he considers this volume as scientific: possibly, in spite of all his important arguments against the positivist identification of all (extra-logical) significant ideas as scientific, he is prone to equate all (extra-logical) criticism with empirical refutation, and thus to equate rationality with science, and consequently to view his own work as scientific. At least, this is the impression one may get.

POPPER'S HOPEFUL MONSTERS

a thicket of misconceptions

1. INTRODUCTION: PHILOSOPHY AND GOSSIP

Sir Karl Popper's recent collection of essays, *Objective Knowledge: An Evolutionary Approach*, 1972, is an important yet unpleasant volume. I must, in fairness to the reader, declare my intention at once: I intend to discuss the unpleasant garb of this volume no less than its philosophic content. I am thus readily opening myself to the charge that I lack a sense of proportion. My purpose, if I may explain myself, is to reduce the risk that what I consider to be some of the greatest ideas in the history of contemporary philosophy may be ignored by the learned world—ignored for the reason that by now they are buried under a thicket of misconceptions. Some of these misconceptions are due to the very author of these ideas (others I have discussed elsewhere).[1] And they are misconceptions which few will take the trouble to clear as long as they are so entangled with so much that is better ignored—being so unpleasant and embarrassing.

The thesis of the present essay, then, is that Popper has regrettably let pass the chance to erect his definitive philosophy; rather, that in his latest volume he has reduced whatever was great that he had erected before; that further, he seems to pursue a policy of arguing with the multitude of philosophers until they openly admit that all along he was right and not they, and until all his claims for priority are publicly recognized.

Let me begin my review, then, by asserting that the present volume projects clearly an image of its author—a personal image, that is. That image is in surprising agreement with the image one gets from philistine professional gossip. I say "surprisingly" because first, Popper strongly projects this image while, presumably, desperately attempting to refute it. Secondly, the

This review of *Objective Knowledge: An Evolutionary Approach*, by Karl R. Popper (Oxford: Oxford University Press, 1972) appeared in *Philosophia*, 4, 1974 under the title, 'Postscript: The Futility of Fighting the Philistines'.

image is, undoubtedly, quite false, indeed, grossly unfair. I am constrained to put it to paper in a sort of pen portrait, unfair though it is, and in the uneven, unsettling, perhaps jarring manner that long ago I heard it, and that recently reappeared in the pages of this volume. The pen portrait describes a forceful person, bursting with interesting ideas; a person at times wonderfully straightforward, yet at times infuriatingly cagy; a person at times immensely commonsensical, yet at times verging on the absurd; at times kindly and personally concerned, yet at times harsh and hostile; at times self-effacing, yet at times demanding unlimited attention and recognition; at times terribly rational and lucid and appealing, yet at times appallingly dogmatic and more than a bit bullying. Especially cruel to an occasional colleague, but always interesting, bursting with ideas, dominating, domineering. And capricious and dogmatic. And bursting with interesting ideas. There is sheer fascination for you, if you are strong enough to take it.

This is only part of the composite picture—the direct one, so to speak; the indirect one, concerning the author and his peers, is more germane and painful: he is constantly neglected by them, and constantly complaining about them. Again, the two parts of the indirect picture reinforce each other, as do the direct and indirect. Let me add to this that in my judgment, public recognition of Popper's work was systematically withheld. I think it is now otherwise, simply because Popper's philosophy is too important to be ignored. Whether the composite picture does justice to Popper or (as I think) not, it certainly does rightly depict his peers as less brave and outspoken than philosophers are traditionally expected to be. Let me mention a few instances. I have heard from a world-famous philosopher that when he first got hold of Popper's *Logik der Forschung* in 1935 or thereabouts he was most excited and sat up all night studying it. I am fairly familiar with that philosopher's many publications, and can report that for many years he did not mention Popper in them and when he finally came to mention him he did so in a not exactly complimentary manner. On another occasion a well-known philosopher told me he found no need to mention Popper's work except on a rare occasion simply because he is so far out. Yet another has told me that you do not need to read Popper as all he says can be found summed up in a nut-shell and refuted in Carnap's *Testability and Meaning*. One more anecdote: a rather famous and somewhat younger philosopher told me in his seminar that it is well known that one doesn't refer to a philosopher who calls Hempel a plagiarist in print.

So much for the gossip which, I think, both reinforces and is reinforced by the author's lengthy and rather complex complaints. And this vitiates his philosophy. And so I do not see how I can avoid reference to gossip when reviewing *Objective Knowledge*. I had hoped that no one would suggest that I review it. But I knew that once asked I would not refuse: I have been praising Sir Karl Popper's philosophy ever since I started publishing in the learned press, at times when doing so was no assurance that one's work would be accepted by editors, and I do not wish to pretend to my readers that I am as enthusiastic about Popper's recent writings as I used to be about his earlier. On the contrary, it is in defense of his earlier works that I feel obliged to be critical in detail of the unpleasant and seemingly incidental parts of this volume.

Also I hope to discuss critically some of the more important aspects of this volume in particular and of Popper's philosophy in general. I should warn my reader, however, that my view of Popper's philosophy, as well as my criticism of it, is fairly idiosyncratic.

In conclusion I should add this. I am at least pleased about the timing of this review, since in the last few years Popper has become increasingly acceptable in respected philosophic circles. For, as long as he was not, there was some force to the erroneous contention that any public criticism of him might be heard as support for the Establishment's disregard for him. But the conspiracy of silence has been over for about two to four years, and so the truth or falsity of that contention is of no practical significance here. At least the present volume is a big commercial success. Its first printing, both hard-cover and paperback, was sold-out in no time. So was its German translation. It won highly favorable reviews, some sincere, some bandwaggoning, and it was praised sky-high in Bryan Magee's highly laudatory and quite successful essay on Popper in the popular Fontana series. The present volume surely does deserve a critical review, on account of its intrinsic significance and on account of its popularity; and the critical review should be useful to the potential serious reader. To this end a preliminary study of the redundant part seems unavoidable.

2. POPPER STAKES A CLAIM

I shall begin with the worst, a one-sentence paragraph in the middle of page 282. It reads,

> I have always been interested in Goldschmidt's theories,[2] and I drew Goldschmidt's 'hopeful monsters' to the attention of I. Lakatos, who referred to them in his 'Proofs and Refutations'.[3]

This really gave me a jolt. What was the author's intention in publishing it I cannot say; what it sounds like to me I can report; to quote Heinrich Heine—a lovely writer and a profound philosopher who is slowly emerging and gaining the recognition he amply deserves—the arrow which has left the hunter's bow belongs to the hunter no longer.

Popper here is possibly claiming some right to recognition and possibly denying someone else's claims to the same. It was he who drew the attention of someone to some book. Now, is such a thing ever a matter of right to recognition? Is it a right? Is it important? Should someone have to acknowledge the fact that a book was brought to his attention by Popper?

Can someone claim the converse? What force can the converse claim have?

If Sir Karl has a right, then he deserves the recognition, and then, clearly, the someone in question should have made the acknowledgment: "This book" he should have said, "was brought to my attention by Sir Karl Popper." "Sir Peter Medawar," says he in a note on page 268, ". . . has drawn my attention to Waddington's paper." Lovely. Which book and which paper deserves such honorable mention, however? Any book? Let us say, an important book. Query: important to whom? To donor, to recipient, or to the public at large? Important generally or important in one given respect? I wish to answer these questions, but first I have a personal note in this connection.

I do not know how much I am indebted to Sir Karl Popper, except that but for my having been his student and research associate I would not be what I now am. I consider that fact my greatest fortune, but it may very well be his—small, I hope—misfortune. I have often made acknowledgments to Sir Karl, as my teacher in general and as one from whom I have learned this, that, or the other idea—the man is bursting with ideas, and sometimes I found a successful paper of mine based on or at least triggered by some casual remark of his, intended more as gossip than as a profundity. Yet I refuse to take it for granted that this testifies to the high quality of his work; it may more reasonably testify to the low quality of mine, if not simply to my ignorance of the literature. Were I to record with all clarity and precision Popper's contribution to my work, however, such an act would be very lengthy and complicated, as we shall soon see, and so it would lower the quality of my production much further. I wish to use this opportunity and record that for years on end I constantly had to struggle against editors' and referees' and readers' and friends' and colleagues' remarks about excessive acknowledgment to Popper, except for the inner circle which repeatedly made it clear to me that the truth goes the other way.

I do not know what are the major ingredients in my intellectual makeup. I find this question a bit narcissistic and yet fascinating. Many of my excursions into intellectual history were in search of influences which I had absorbed in childhood and early adolescence (when I still had fathersubstitutes). But I really do not know much about any of my intellectual ancestors, even though I published a few books and papers about some of them. Nor do I know how and to what extent this author or that has influenced me. Consider such writers as Hans Christian Andersen and Jules Verne, who, I do not doubt, left an everlasting impression on me. I cannot begin to analyze that impression. I do not know the names of the persons in whose debt I am for having brought these authors to my attention; I do not even know the names of the translators but for whose efforts I would have entered adult life without the moving experiences of an Andersen fairy-tale or a Verne adventure tale.

Not knowing my intellectual ancestry, and regularly being chided about making too few or too many acknowledgments, I showed more interest in the matter than others. I now think that today, as in the days of old, the person acknowledging is usually leaning on authority, that it is usually good for a scholar of good standing to mention the leading authorities on the topic he is writing about, particularly if his views sound a bit unorthodox. The ordinary scholar is all too often a philistine (who will now frequently mention Popper, if my theory is true, for the very same reason he refrained from mentioning him before. My theory is testable and so it is scientific!) For others, acknowledgment is mostly a public act, a public expression of gratitude for the innovator. It may also be historical—a hint for the scholar who wants more information. And these two are the same—except if we acknowledge a theory (say the inverse-square law of electric force) not to its originator (be it Franklin or Priestley) but to its careful student (Coulomb). But this need be no trouble one way or another, as long as we say whom we make an acknowledgment to, why, and what sort of. If, for example, we note that James Watt could not possibly know of the unit of energy-flow, the watt, then we do not violate any principle. If, for example, we think that Faraday's ideas were so obscure that Kelvin deserves mention if not praise for his advice to Maxwell to read Faraday, then we say so; and, indeed Joseph Larmor published the Kelvin-Maxwell correspondence with this idea—or a similar one—in mind.

But these are extreme cases. There is no scientific or scholarly honor to Hans Christian Andersen; he is honored otherwise, and quite nicely. And so his work is now public property. And so, anyone who draws anyone else's attention to him may be thereby doing a great favor, but a private or a personal one; we publicly consider such debt of gratitude private not public. Bringing this item of private knowledge to the attention of the public is an act which is akin to, or part of, an intellectual biography. It is not an acknowledgment in the sense discussed in the previous paragraph. I could well imagine Sir Karl writing the life of I. Lakatos, and saying, *en passant* "I always admired Goldschmidt's 'hopeful monsters', I naturally aroused the curiosity of young Lakatos in Goldschmidt's work, not knowing that this was the first step that Lakatos took on his long and arduous career of breeding hopeful monsters that ended with his celebrated monster-farm." I could likewise imagine an autobiography in which Sir Karl might say, "Sir Peter Medawar changed my views of the matter profoundly, and I never forgot his kindness to me." Facts go otherwise. Lakatos's classic *Proofs and Refutations* will be remembered for its being a pioneering effort of great consequence; its reference to Goldschmidt is another matter. And the above-quoted note on page 268 regarding Sir Peter's contribution is of no consequence either: "Originally," Sir Karl himself informs us, "I referred here" to another work, which he mentions and I will not, but "Sir Peter Medawar has drawn my attention to the fact that the reference is dubious in this context" and replaced the dubious reference with a better one: Sir Karl's debt to Sir Peter is merely for a better reference; in another place (p. 258) Sir Peter is mentioned because he corrects an omission of another reference; such things are really private affairs,[2] and one may wonder why here Sir Karl makes so much of them. When making the reference to Sir Peter, on p. 268, Sir Karl discusses Lamarckism and its status from a neo-Darwinian point of view. He mentions a few authors on the present status of Lamarckism, and the note to Sir Peter may convey the impression that Sir Karl had searched high and low, and in the process even acknowledged something to one who barely deserves it; an error corrected by Sir Peter. But if anyone gets this impression, then he is in error.[3] A conspicuous omission, for example, is E. B. Ford. Goldschmidt, too, in his heart-warming book which Popper once drew Lakatos's attention to, refers to Ford in this connection. So why the reference to Sir Peter? I do not know. And how comes Goldschmidt himself into the picture?

I do not mean to ask who told Sir Karl about Goldschmidt. Nor do I ask whether Sir Karl claims credit for having found Goldschmidt all by himself—a claim implicit in the very fact that he takes credit for Lakatos's knowledge of Goldschmidt without giving anyone credit for his own. Rather, I mean, how does Goldschmidt come into *Objective Knowledge* in the first place? The answer is disappointing: through the back door, in a 1972 Addendum (pp. 281-84) to a 1961 paper called 'Evolution and the Tree of Knowledge'. The Addendum says, "I am no expert" on evolutionism and mutation "and an expert discouraged me from publishing" that paper. Yet he could not suppress his feeling that a certain distinction of his is "an important contribution to a theory of evolution of the Darwinian type". Recording my amazement that (most uncharacteristically, and in a mode typical of his linguistic opponents) here Popper offers a distinction instead of a problem or a theory, and recording that I am unable to comprehend what I have just quoted, I proceed. "What I called 'genetic dualism' . . . seems to me to offer an explanation," a theory, and an explanatory theory at that! "of genetic trends. . ." I don't find such an explanatory theory anywhere in the book, on which more soon.

Popper was discouraged by an expert, but he thinks his distinction and theory are important. His theory, he adds, is an improvement on that of Goldschmidt.

I have thus far covered about half a page of Popper's Addendum, skipping a lot, wondering about a lot, and finally now I ask, why Goldschmidt, and why only in the Addendum? The old Darwinian theory postulated small mutations only, and this had led to big problems; Goldschmidt had the theory of occasional big mutations which he labelled, we are told, "hopeful monsters". That takes us one page further, and straight to the above-quoted passage about Goldschmidt, Popper and Lakatos.

One can hardly avoid at this stage the erroneous conclusion that, feeling uneasy about not having mentioned Goldschmidt in the body of the paper, Popper protests admiration for Goldschmidt and, to enhance it, by a contrast, seemingly less than admiration for Lakatos. Popper is not unaware of this, it seems, for he forestalls it: "But it was only a few days ago that I read" a certain book "that it struck me that it might be time to revive Goldschmidt's 'hopeful monsters' in a new form." Upon which Popper quickly shows, in the remaining two pages of the Addendum, the superiority of his variant of Goldschmidt over the original.

All this requires much clarification. I think, however, we are in position now to solve the initial mystery. In 1961, when the original paper was written, Popper did not mention Goldschmidt because he did not then think it was "time to revive Goldschmidt's" theory, but in 1972, when he wrote the Addendum, he did. Now someone may not believe this and say, He picked it up from Lakatos who, in 1963, shows knowledge of it—beforehand Popper was simply unaware of Goldschmidt's very existence. The very thought of this is so annoying, presumably, that Popper found it necessary to deny the possible allegation. It reads, of course, rather differently, as I have just indicated. It is, of course, a common failure of communication once one insists on small details of no public import. Let me say that Mach, Freud, and other Viennese scholars, have suffered similarly: they created the very misunderstandings they wished to evade. If anyone might deny that Popper knew of Goldschmidt's book before Lakatos wrote about it he will be in a better position to do so because Popper protests so much. As for myself, I think the absence of reference to Goldschmidt in the body of the paper makes the whole business quite worthless.

3. EVOLUTIONISM AND SCIENTIFIC METHOD

We have landed in compound presentational problems now. I have learned from Sir Karl, and I easily discern his teaching practiced in his early work, that for the best results one should (a) start with a problem, (b) present the past solutions to it as best one can, thus paying one's predecessors all the due they deserve—indeed, Popper used to go further and demand (I consider the demand excessive) that by the way one should try to improve past solutions as best one can—from these proceedings to (c) show the faults of past solutions; all of this prior to the effort—again, optional—to (d) present one's own solution. If one has a new solution, further, then for best results one should try (e) to show that one's own solution is immune to the criticism levelled against the previous solution. To this beautiful list I wish to add (f) if there are previous solutions not yet validly criticized, and one offers a new solution nevertheless, one is better off if one adds a discussion concerning the variance between them and its possible import. But I shall return to this later. Let me here apply Popper's canons to his own essay.

The first corollary is that either Goldschmidt should appear in the body of the paper, or not at all. The claim that "reading a new critical book" on

Darwinism made Popper think "that it might be time to revive Goldschmidt's 'hopeful monsters' " is both cryptic and irrelevant: did Goldschmidt offer a solution to the same problem Popper addresses? Yes. Is the solution significant? Yes. Hence, it should have its place in the body of the paper. The paper, being the 1961 Herbert Spencer lecture, was read before Lakatos published his classic 'Proofs and Refutations' in the *British Journal for the Philosophy of Science* in 1963–64. Had the paper contained reference to Goldschmidt, the paragraph which serves as text to the present commentary would not have been written at all, perhaps.

But what problem does the paper present? Let us quickly go through it. First there is a section on problems and the growth of knowledge: learning (scientific or otherwise) equals problem-solving; therefore, theory precedes observation, contrary to popular prejudice. Let us grant that without further ado on the ground that these days the opposition is popular prejudice, supported only by philistines (including such giants as Konrad Lorenz, I grant, who is a philistine in matters methodological nonetheless, and even worse than that in matters moral and political, by the way) and that it is better to ignore the philistine. Popper views the problem-solving theory as an analogue to Darwinism: the natural selection of hypotheses is the cause of scientific growth. Moreover, it connects the amoeba and Einstein as problem-solvers. This, incidentally, is the origin of the title of the essay: 'the tree of evolution' is a biological expression which Popper adopts when he offers the neologism 'the tree of knowledge'. This, also, is what gives the present volume its sub-title *An Evolutionary Approach*. The thing I like about the analogy is that the fittest, both in the tree of evolution and in the tree of knowledge, need not be very fit, and, indeed, may find it hard to compete with a newcomer who, being fitter, will drive it to extinction. The thing I dislike about the analogy is that the ecology of scientific ideas much differs from the ecology of species: defective species or even lineages of defective specimens (haemophiliacs, albinos), can survive when competition is lax, whereas in science a hypothesis refuted is knocked out *even if it has no competitor at all*. Rather, metaphysics, having a few perennial species, resembles biology more. But enough of that; thus far we have met no problem that Popper himself is attempting to solve; it is merely background knowledge.

In the second part of the paper "I propose to discuss briefly a number of problems concerning the methods of biology" (p. 264). The second part covers less than eight pages. I do not find there a single problem "concerning the methods of biology." Not knowing what to do about this, I shall continue my summary.

"I shall start with two general theses". First, no royal road to scientific success; second, there is no scientific method proper. Rather, there is only trial-and-error.

From here on I lose the thread completely. Darwin's theory, unlike

Newton's, is not a universal statement. Nevertheless, it had a wide influence, in that it showed that in principle we may be able to reduce
teleology to causality. In principle, since no evolution of a single species or
organ has yet been causally explained. On the contrary, Darwin showed that
we are free to use teleology and let others try, at some later date, to reduce
teleology to causality.

This point, to interrupt my summary, is of great import, both generally
and for Popper. It is clearly Popper's view that Darwin both started a reductive trend and allowed for the non-reductive one, contrary to the appearance that he loathed the latter. Thus, of course, there is room left by
Darwinism for trial-and-error as a part of the fight for survival. Yet, the
trial-and-error is only tolerated on a promise that sooner or later it will be
explained away!

To continue, Popper argues that thus Darwinism allows for Lamarckism. The Lamarckian hypothesis of members of species surviving
through will may be translated into the Darwinian theory of struggle for
survival.

I must interrupt my summary again—with incredulity, this time. There
is a logical error here, so trite that I am baffled. Darwin wanted to explain
all teleology as caused, but allows for teleology, *pro tem*, even when not yet
causally reduced. For example, the struggle for survival. The struggle is, of
course, Lamarckian, and Darwin permits it *pro tem*. But Popper views it as
Darwinian and claims that here Lamarckism can be reduced to this part of
Darwinism. I hope I am in error here. In any case, here comes Popper's
claim (p. 282, quoted above) that he has an explanatory theory. He has
none that I can see.

The fact of the matter may be a bit more complex, in the sense that a
process may be in part causally reduced and so be partly Darwinian, partly
not. Take, for example, our celebrated Goldschmidt; perhaps he makes the
same mistake as Popper—I cannot tell. He studies the struggle for survival
as Popper does, and offers more examples, especially from the study of
ecotypes, preadaptation of plants, and from industrial melanism. In
melanism, animals (moths and butterflies in particular) become black—
usually in industrial regions. Goldschmidt says, a few times, Harrison has
explained industrial melanism in a Lamarckian fashion but E. B. Ford has
explained it in a Darwinian fashion, referring to Ford's 'Problems of
Heredity in the Lepidoptera' (*Biological Reviews of Cambridge Philosophical Society*, vol. 12, 1937), where, on p. 499, in his summary, Ford says
(§15):

The various theories accounting for the recent spread of melanism in industrial
areas are considered. It is concluded that none of them are entirely satisfactory,
and a new view is advanced. It is held that the chief agent in this change is selection operating in favour of characters other than colour, produced by genes normally present as rarities. When, as already in some instances, these combine

melanin production with a physiological advantage, it is suggested that they cannot spread save in industrial areas, owing to counter-selection against black coloration. This theory is confirmed by the existence of melanic varieties hardier than the normal form which, however, they do not supplant in unpolluted country.

Ford also says, in the body of his paper (p. 487)

> In my opinion, melanic forms have spread in industrial areas owing, primarily, to selection for characters other than colour. The action of the genes producing melanism as one of their effects may sometimes give the organism a physiological advantage. That such favourable factors have not become widely established may be due to the handicap of black coloration which, in normal circumstances, would render some species very conspicuous. On the other hand, melanism, as such, may at least be no longer a drawback in the blackened countryside of many manufacturing districts, in which, furthermore, the number of predators may be reduced. Here, then, the insects may be able to avail themselves of the other benefits conferred by these genes.

Here we have the option: either the mutant insects "avail themselves" and so the theory on p. 487 is partly neo-Mendelian or neo-Darwinian but partly Lamarckian, or we have on p. 499 a purely Darwinian view where the mutants spread everywhere, are destroyed by predators everywhere, but not to extinction in industrial areas, where they 'exploit' the advantage of the mutation which also has turned them black (very much like in the case of plant preadaptation).

All this is very interesting, and though Popper is in error, he touches a significant central problem, handled by Ford, Goldschmidt, and others. But no problem thus far, certainly not of method, except: Can we explain causally seemingly purposive developments? At this juncture Popper mentions a problem, though not of method: the problem is known as the problem of correlation; it is ascribed by Goldschmidt to classical Darwinian theory though it surely is at least as old as evolutionism, and even has pre-evolutionist variants. Now in the classic Darwinian view all mutations are in small steps which only makes the problem of correlation all the harder: ever so many mutations have to be lined up; how could they be so nicely arranged? Moreover, clearly half way up the tree of evolution a mutant is more vulnerable than up or down, in its relatively stable evolutionary niches. How then does it pass the vulnerable phase? E. B. Ford has explained the survival of half-way mutants by a theory of fluctuation: when ecology is more propitious to a species it develops unstable mutants which disappear soon and their offspring mostly go back to the old niche, but possibly to a new one. Goldschmidt, rather, said there may be a 'hopeful monster' which is a multiple mutation leaping from one ecological niche to the next. The question, who is right, Ford or Goldschmidt, cannot be answered in general: it depends on historical facts: some species developed à la Ford, perhaps, some à la Goldschmidt.[4] Back to Popper.

Just here Popper mentions, quite appropriately, that Darwinism is not a universal hypothesis but a schema for historical hypotheses. To be precise, he says (p. 270) "To put it more precisely, Darwin's theory is a *generalized historical explanation*". I cannot call this precise: when *a* is a generalization of *b*, then it is also more testable: when *b* is refuted, so is *a*. But when one Darwinian hypothesis is refuted we may try another: Darwinism is a metaphysical theory and a research program. More on this later. Now I shall continue my summary.

Survival may be adaptation and it may be fecundity. Why is it the former and not the latter? Why is the struggle not so severe as to destroy all but the very fittest? Popper thinks (p. 271) the idea of Darwinism-cum-simulated Lamarckism solves these problems. In my opinion some species survive because of fecundity, some because of other causes; fecundity also depends on other characteristics,[5] and how fit a species should be to survive depends on an ecological niche: if animals destroy too many of the helpless plants they consume, then very soon they starve and the plants can recover from the devastation. This was known to Volterra and I feel that "the fashionable pursuit of mathematical exactness" which Popper is so justly skeptical about (pp. 270–71) is rooted in the enormous success of Volterra's equations.

Popper's section 3 is devoted to a hypothesis he calls 'genetic dualism'. Popper says, wherever a mutation complex includes both the evolution of a new organ and its control (one alone is of no value) the two may come together or in succession, and he feels, *à la* Lamarck, that the control comes first.

No doubt we have both organs we can't (naturally) control and controls with no (natural) organs. (This is evidenced by artificial controls, such as the pill; and artificial organs, such as pianos, bicycles, and even switches.) And so, in history, things went both this way and that. Popper's hypothesis seems to me rather puzzling. Not only is it obviously false, I do not even know what problem exactly it comes to solve and how it differs from other solutions.

In the Addendum Popper says Goldschmidt's hypothesis is quite inferior to his, since Goldschmidt's is more anatomical and physiological, Popper's more ecological. I cannot agree, since the general problem they all solve *is* ecological: how does a mutant move—or hope to move—from one eco-niche to another? I find it also hard to disagree as I am not quite clear about the problem-situation and I do not know what are the specific problems at hand.

I would love to commend Popper on yet another success in the face of experts. I am loath to agree with the expert.

4. A MIX-UP

So much, the reader may need reminding, on the important fact that Popper told Lakatos about Goldschmidt and about my not unrelated inability to comprehend Popper's picture of modern biology and its difference from that of Goldschmidt. My next choice is a shorter appendix, a 'Bibliographical Note' brief enough to quote in full. It can be found at the end of Chapter 5, which is a reprint of a revised version of Sir Karl's classic 'The Aims of Science', first published in *Ratio* in 1957 and originally a section of his *Postscript: After Twenty Years*, the book which remained unpublished and in galleys for over twenty years and was known only to members of a very small circle until it was brought out in 1983. The 'Bibliographical Note' (pp. 204–05) includes much information, some of which also appears in another note (p. 191).

BIBLIOGRAPHICAL NOTE
The idea here discussed that theories may *correct* an 'observational' or 'phenomenal' law which they are supposed to explain (such as, for example, Kepler's third law) was repeatedly expounded in my lectures. One of these lectures stimulated the correction of a supposed phenomenal law (see the 1941 paper referred to in my *Poverty of Historicism*, 1957, 1960, footnote on pp. 134f.). Another of these lectures was published in Simon Moser's volume *Gesetz und Wirklichkeit* (1948), 1949. The same idea of mine was also the 'starting point' (as he puts it on p. 92) of P. K. Feyerabend's paper "Explanation, Reduction and Empiricism" (in Herbert Feigl and Grover Maxwell, editors, *Minnesota Studies in the Philosophy of Science*, 3, 1962) whose reference 66 is to the present paper (as first published in *Ratio*, 1, 1957). Feyerabend's acknowledgement seems to have been overlooked by the authors of various papers on related subjects.

The substantive point Sir Karl makes here is dual. Assume that we try to explain a phenomenon p: we devise a theory t from which we hope to deduce it. Suppose what we deduce from t is not p but a close relative to it p^*. For example, Galileo's theory G says gravitational acceleration on the surface of the earth is constant, whereas Newton's theory N explains the fact G^* that gravitational acceleration on the surface of the earth is nearly constant. From this Popper deduces the conclusion that whereas N entails G^*, N is quite inconsistent with G. More generally, t entails p^* and contradicts p. This is a most important claim. Popper draws from this most important claim two important conclusions. First, that inductivism is false. Traditional philosophers of induction assumed that the principle of induction is a principle of inductive logic which has to be added to those of deductive logic; they would all have agreed that if inductive logic conflicts with deductive logic then it must go. This conclusion, then, which is already explicitly and clearly stated by Duhem, seems to me unquestionably valid. The second conclusion, which Duhem is less explicit and clear about, and so I would like to ascribe it to Duhem and Popper jointly, if not simply to Einstein, is this. There is a test of the new theory available, namely the crucial experiment between p and p^*. Indeed, by adjusting a pendulum clock at sea-level and then taking it up to the mountains, or even taking it down south (where sea-level is at a different distance from the center of the earth since the poles are nearer to the center than the equator) we get the clock to retard ever so slightly, and if it is a sufficiently accurate clock the retardation will be cumulative and show Newton's theory nearer to the facts than Galileo's. This experiment was indeed performed, and as a crucial experiment. (It was a variant of one proposed by Bacon as crucial between Galileo and Gilbert.) Einstein designed such crucial tests between his theories and those which preceeded them from the beginning of his career, and quite systematically.

So far so good. Except that from all this a third conclusion can be drawn and was drawn both by Feyerabend and by myself: Popper's theory of explanation is false. For, according to Popper's theory, expressed with great clarity in his *Logik der Forschung*, (causal) explanation is deduction. If *p* is a statement of fact a theory *t* explains *p* if and only if *t* entails *p*. But since *t* contradicts *p* it does not explain it. Moreover, since *p* is a general fact, i.e., is an empirically founded (general) statement of observable facts, any theory which contradicts it, such as *t*, must be rejected on empirical grounds until *p* is rejected. Thus, in the *Logik der Forschung t* is refuted from the very start, not at all the welcome member of the body of science as Popper has it in 'The Aims of Science'. Of course, already in his *Logik der Forschung* Popper enjoins us to try and refute *p* in spite of its high degree of empirical backing. And this is a magnificent idea which Popper's commentators for a generation or so noticed only when attempting to dismiss him. Now, as Lakatos has noted (and this he did regarding mathematics but we can easily translate it into physics with but a slight modification), if you find it hard to refute *p*, try to explain it. For, if your theory *t* fails even to explain *p* but instead entails *p**, the two failures together may yield a success. This is, then, a nice readjustment of Popper's theory of explanation to fit the general sentiment of his *magnum opus*. But it can only be performed after seeing that the story of *t*, *p*, and *p** refutes Popper's theory of explanation—the theory that *t* entails *p*.

All this has been stated at some length both by Feyerabend and by myself. I cannot put it any simpler and would like to know what, if anything, is wrong with it. I can barely imagine that Popper thinks it is so obviously erroneous as to deserve no comment—he has often commented on the silliest criticisms of his view anyway. And I can hardly imagine that he fails to see the point of this criticism. I greatly regret that he neither rebuts nor accepts it but avoids the issue. Perhaps the remark on Feyerabend's acknowledgment and the commentators who have missed it has priority. I am willing to wait for my turn, then.

The history of the topic is, of course, fairly complex. First, Popper accused Hempel of not making a proper acknowledgment, and we Popperians—I confess to the serious mistake—have implicitly or unknowingly endorsed the accusation: we insisted that 'the' explanation theory is Popper's. We thus led to the usage, accepted in some circles, of the oxymoronic name the Popper-Hempel-model—a name that indicates a confusion between an inductive and a deductive theory of satisfactory explanation.

Hempel requires confirmability or confirmation: whereas Popper requires testability, I think. The confusion grew when Popper introduced, in *Conjectures and Refutations*, what I deem a new idea and he calls a clarification of an old one (for the noticing of the need for which, alas! he thanks me) namely his requirement that a satisfactory explanation be not only testable but also tested and supported by experience before it be refuted. (The acknowledgment to me is an error: he introduced this idea alone in 1948; see below.) Also the label for empirical backing is, usually 'confirmation'; he changed it to 'corroboration', but since corroboration is a legal rather than a scientific procedure, I do not like it. Words, anyway, need not matter, as Popper repeatedly says, and I heartily agree.

Popper's attack on Hempel, thus, did not add to clarity. A few of Popper's admirers and former students of diverse kinds, myself included, used to stake claims and accuse each other of not recognizing these claims. (The existence of a book in galleys was an added strain.) And usually this involved some fantastic claims, which led to difficulties in seeing even what is new at all in what anyone ever said. In one of his famous papers, for example, Lakatos accused me of having taken from him the idea which he had implicitly (!) expressed before me, that metaphysics contributes to science something of great importance. Namely, regulative principles, to use Kant's idiom, or research programs to use a more modern and widespread expression. In another publication he accused me of having plagiarized the idea from Popper's unpublished book. (I felt I was in a position to write a fairy-tale about the king's new clothes, which were made, in this case, from rags found in the ancient ruins of the City of the Dead; but it is already told in the penultimate paragraph of J. M. Keynes's *General Theory*.) and Feyerabend, perhaps because of great sensitivity to such things, perhaps because of some deep aversion to the whole issue, came up with the idea that Popper never said anything new anyhow, at least not on the major problems of philosophy. And I found Feyerabend's claim sufficiently forceful to answer it in a paper, 'On the Novelty of Popper's Philosophy of Science' (republished in my *Science in Flux*, 1975). Yet I did not refer there to Feyerabend, or to anyone in particular, but to the fact that it is—as it certainly was only a few years ago—a standard game among the philistines to dismiss Popper as a non-innovator.

5. HISTORICAL INACCURACY

The Bibliographic Note quoted above contains a few errors, distortions, and diplomatic remarks which I shall now discuss. Popper says here he first invented in New Zealand (where he spent the war years) the idea that t explains not p but p^* thus offering an excellent test for t. To my knowledge, however, this idea was first conceived in a lecture early in the year 1953: I was present at that lecture, a part of his course on scientific method, and he told me afterwards at some length that it came to him during the lecture. I did not like that lecture and could not say why. I know now why: Popper presented the case of a test where p^* turned out to be true and as lending credibility to t. (He compared this to the credibility of a detective who, by the force of his reasoning, makes corrections of police reports, and the police, upon rechecking, concede the correction.) I never understood what credibility had to do with science; in my doctoral dissertation which I wrote soon afterwards under Popper's stimulating guidance I declared that the concern with credibility within science is a left-over from Catholicism as practised before the Scientific Revolution; I wrote a few papers arguing against the view that science related to credibility, and found encouragement in some passages of Popper and in clearer ones in the writings of George Bernard Shaw (especially in the prefaces to *Androcles, St. Joan, Doctor's Dilemma*, etc.).

I have looked up the 1941 paper referred to in Popper's Bibliographical Note. It is a paper written by a New Zealand colleague of his. I saw no connection between it and Popper's philosophy, except that it is taxonomic and so one which Popper might well disapprove of *in toto* as essentialist. The reference to "another of these lectures" is puzzling since that other lecture is of 1948 and serves as the Appendix to this volume. The opening of the Appendix includes a note which claims that "most of its ideas . . . go back to my New Zealand days. . . . This Appendix is especially closely related to Chapters 2 and 5 of the present volume"; the Bibliographic Note is appended to Chapter 5.

I may be dense but I cannot find the idea that t explains p^* rather than p anywhere in the Appendix. On the contrary, on pages 349–51 I find the explicit claim that t does explain p, and no mention at all of p^*. The story is told much too briefly, and in a note Popper refers his reader to his other publications where he expands upon it, including *Philosophy and Physics* (1972), a still-unpublished collection of essays (this is another questionable practice which he resorts to, i.e., publishing projected publication dates as if they were reported publication dates—in the sincere hope which then fails to materialize; a practice effectively borrowed by Lakatos and used by him quite extravagantly).

But I must carefully examine the Appendix before leaving it at that. On page 357 there Popper introduces "a good example from the history of science . . . to illustrate my analysis," namely "the transition from the theories of Kepler and Galileo to the theory of Newton." Yet, instead of illustrating his analysis, according to which N explains G and K, he claims N contradicts them, and then uses this claim against inductivism—a point acknowledged to Pierre Duhem on page 358 in a new note[6] where Popper shows at some length that "Duhem's analysis" could be improved upon—by Popper, of course. But what is the improvement of the argument? After all, both Duhem's argument and Popper's establish the point—that inductivism is false—and it is the point, not the analysis that matters. A reference also takes us to other publications of Popper for more detail, including Chapter 5 (to which we remember, the Bibliographic Note is appended). There is no mention there of the difference between G and G^*. There is no putting into use this difference in the form of a crucial test between them that is also a test of N.

There is, however, a very brief appearance of a close relative to all this, which is very exciting, right there on page 357: "Had Newton achieved no more than the union of" K and G, "it would have been only a *circular explanation* of these laws and therefore unsatisfactory as an explanation. Yet its power of illumination and its power of convincing people"—I shall not discuss credibility here—"consisted just in its power to throw light on the way to independent tests . . . ."

I was always told that Newton's theory of the tides proves that N is not just a conjunction of G and K; and, of course, it offers a way to test N. Also the difference between G and G^*; this, however, is not mentioned here—not that I could see. Perhaps I am a pedant, but important as I consider the idea of independent tests I cannot see that it is conditioned on t contradicting p; this contradiction is neither a sufficient nor a necessary condition, as Popper notices in Chapter 5, page 230, when discussing as yet another point, namely that depth of "illumination", adding that it, too, is not entirely conditioned on the contradiction between t and p. His example for a deduction proper, there, is Einstein's special relativity which includes Maxwell's equations (and so trivially entails them). It is no accident that this discussion is in Chapter 5 of 1957, not in the Appendix of 1948: you have to make the distinction between p and p^* in order to conduct it.

There are, then, a number of provocative ideas here, and it is not surprising that Popper may slide from one to another and so even contradict himself. Let me mention that, indeed, Popper's 1948 lecture is very exciting. We all want explanation and we all want independent tests. But there is a difficulty lurking here. Hermann Weyl's generalized relativity looked suspiciously like a conjunction of general relativity and (the convariant version of) Maxwell's equations. Now Einstein was aware of it and tried to build generalized relativity with an inbuilt factor which prevents the universal field from always splitting into gravity and electromagnetics. Hence, we can say, his new theory contradicts his older one yet again. Is this a general method? In retrospect it looks so. It certainly did not look so when Newton combined G and K, as he said both were literally true and yet another theory, of the tides, followed from N, offering an independent test. And so I do not see that all the points could be successfully put together before Popper noted that since t contradicts p it explains p^* and more clearly before Feyerabend and I noted that this refutes Popper's theory of explanation.

I suggest it is time, then, to leave the die-hard inductivists alone, and center on the issues at hand. Here is the center of action, and the interesting developments.

6. THE IMPORTANCE OF THE PHILOSOPHIC ISSUE

The philosophical heart of all this is no small matter. There is a classic problem lurking throughout the epistemological literature of all ages. If reality is true but appearances lie, and if reality deductively explains appearances, how, then, can truth yield falsehoods? Sir Francis Bacon's solution was ingenious: only true appearances are scientific and these are perceived by the eye unguided by conjecture. But Sir Francis is in error. Already Sir A. S. Eddington pressed this point: physics does not explain the smoothness of my desk: it denies it flatly! In his monumental 'Three Views' (*Conjectures and Refutations*). Sir Karl avidly quotes even Galileo against inductivism: I cannot fully express my admiration for Copernicus, said Galileo, who distrusted his senses and clung to his doctrine. Here comes Feyerabend and says, Hence Popper's theory of science as explanations and their refutations is in error too!

Which returns us to the classic problem. To repeat, how can truth explain error? The answer, I suggest, is that truth does not explain error, and its correction is no deductive explanation; rather, I suggest, truth explains how the error comes about. In other words, we only explain why the desk looks smooth, not why it is, since it is not. Also we do not explain Galileo's law, nor its correction. Rather, the theory, which yields deductively the correction, plus the claim that the error resembles the correction under certain conditions, plus the fact that Galileo lived under these conditions, all this put together solves the problem, How did Galileo err despite his precaution, and how was his error so well supported by experiment though it was an error? (See Einstein's preface to Stillman Drake's translation of Galileo's *Dialogue*.)

On this, too, Sir Karl will not comment. That makes his current work, the present volume in particular, quite outdated, though less so than works of the multitude. The discussion between him and them may continue. The burden of study of the problem has, I regret to admit, shifted to his critics and to their critics.

One last point. The acknowledgment to Duhem in the Appendix (page 358) is, I think, grudging, claiming that "we can . . . go beyond Duhem." This is neither relevant (since Duhem proves the point, i.e., of the contradiction between Newton and Kepler and its invalidation of Bacon's inductivism), nor an improvement (Popper shows that a theory intermediary between Kepler and Newton also contradicts Kepler). The alleged improvement upon Duhem is expanded in 'The Aims of Science.' The question, 'What is the improvement?', however, is ignored. Rather, we find here a note on Duhem (page 200), even less friendly than the one in the Appendix: "See, for example, P. Duhem", he says, reminding us of the Germanic philosopher who says, "Consider a rational being, a human for example." And adding puzzlement to pedantry, it seems, he says, "Duhem says more explicitly what is implicit in Newton's own statement." I find this bewildering.

How implicit is a statement before we may stake a claim on it? Since the matter is of a contradiction between theory N and theory K, can we say that the contradiction is implicit in the very juxtaposition of the theories? Surely in a clear and important sense this is trivially true. Not just true, but trivially so. Suppose we refuse to ascribe the recognition of a contradiction to one who is not aware of any pitfalls or any danger or any difference. Then, surely, since Newton was aware of it, and since he even noted that his theory N explains deviations from K (perturbations) he was aware of the contradiction. If so, then he was also aware of the fact that N explains not K but K^*, and so, by clear implication that a theory t designed to explain p may explain p^* instead, and, since he bragged about his success (the success of his perturbation theory), that this should offer a new way to raise the credibility of t!

What is sauce for the goose is sauce for the gander, and the way we can read Duhem in (into) Newton we can read Popper too. In fact, however, the contradiction was explicitly enough denied by Newton who claimed that both G and K are true. It was not even noticed by William Whewell, even though Whewell himself explicitly stated it. He did so while arguing against Hegel's charge of plagiarism (remember Heine's jovial laughter at these philosophers' stake-claiming and plagiary-charging in his classic *Religion and Philosophy in Germany*?). Hegel made the statement that Newton derived N from K after adding a merely terminological change. (Popper notes incidentally, on page 198, the importance of the new concept of force, not saying, however, that this is a point everyone conceded and stressed.) Whewell slowly and patiently proves that, after defining forces properly, N can be deduced from K only for a two-bodies system but otherwise N contradicts K. When he has done with Hegel this great philosopher and marvellously rational and clear thinker was left with a terrible result: two verified theories contradict each other! He dismisses this result in a cavalier manner, saying, that the difficulty is on another level! And so, though he asserts that N and K are contradictory, he also dismissed his own discovery, and so, I think, we will do better to ascribe it to Pierre Duhem who took the bold step and said: 'We have trouble on our hands here. Two scientific theories contradict each other! Something must give!'

Duhem was an instrumentalist. He resolved the contradiction by inventing the Kuhn-Feyerabend doctrine so-called, or the doctrine of incommensurability so-called. If you are an inductivist you are a realist and if you are a realist your science which contains N and K is inconsistent. Give up realism and you can say that N and K cannot be compared and found conflicting. Let us take this slowly: we need not deny realism to declare that two theories cannot be compared. Instead we may merely deny that they designate the same designata. For example, no one denies that economics and astrophysics cannot be compared—are incommensurable. Deny that scientific theory has any designata, i.e., become an instrumentalist, and you can claim incommensurability between K and N, or between N and Einstein's theory E. (Duhem went further than Kuhn and Feyerabend; see my essay 'Sensationalism' in *Mind*, vol. 75, 1966, reprinted in my *Science in Flux*, 1975).

The greatness of the ideas of Sir Karl is, as I see it, in his following the series of great methodologists which ends with Whewell and Duhem, and endorsing the one's realism, and the other's observation of the contradiction between K and N, admitting that both K and N have been refuted. This is no catastrophe for Popper, however, since he declares science to be refutability and not verifiability; K and N are refuted, hence they are refutable; hence they are scientific.

The discussion of explaining by t not p but p^* is encumbered greatly and quite unnecessarily. At one point Popper notes that calling K a phenomenon is rather wild (in his Appendix, unfair note on Duhem, page 358). "The term 'observational' applied here to the 'laws of Kepler' should be taken with a good grain of salt: Kepler's laws were wild conjectures . . . . they cannot be induced from Tycho's observations. . . ." Now why take such an inaccurate case as "a good example" (page 357) for a theory of explanation of facts? Were Tycho Brahe's facts corrected by Kepler? I do not know. Were they corrected by Newton, perhaps? Do we have any example, in which genuine facts are corrected? (Yes, and many of them. See my above-mentioned 'Sensationalism' and my 'Testing as a Bootstrap Operation in Physics', *Zeitschrift für Allgem. Wissenschaftstheorie*, 4, 1973, reprinted in my *Science in Flux*, 1975.)

Why does a new theory have to yield the old as an approximation and a special case? Clearly, it should explain the same facts or else the two are not competing (as an economic and an astrophysical theory would not compete). If they explain (not necessarily deductively) the same facts then this very fact makes them approximate. After all, what is an approximation is not very clear, especially since we have, in mathematics, domains of approximation, and we can define the domain of the explained facts as the domain of approximations. What we want from the new theory, however, is an assessment of the older one: why did it succeed, why did it fail? All this is admirably explained by Popper in his 'The Aims of Science', soon after he forgets his competition with Duhem. Now if a theory can explain the explanatory success of its predecessors, it can also explain why certain statements of fact were made, inaccurate though they are. This greatly deviates from Popper's theory of explanation: we do not explain facts but appearances, and what was yesterday a deep theory is today the appearance. All this goes well with Popper's spirit and he surely could develop it better than others. Instead, he claims that metaphysical—non-explanatory— theories may be approximations; which claim, as we can see, does not make good sense (as there is no explanatory success to explain).[7] And, instead of relating all this to Popper's older views on the problem of induction, his book opens with the claim that he has solved the problem of induction, that most philosophers deny this, that his first chapter "is an attempt to explain my view afresh, and in a way which contains a full answer to my critics" (page 2). He means old critics, or young ones who chew the cud of the old—he does not answer the new critics who take him seriously, who endorse his claim to have solved the problem, thus changing the scene radically, but who criticize his new solution all the same. Come to think of it, what does the above claim exactly mean? That he offered some solution no one denies; that his solution is the last and incontestable solution no one asserts. So where do we stand? Where do we disagree about his contribution? What does his complaint mean? I confess I do not know.

7. The Demarcation of Science from Metaphysics

Popper has denied in various of his publications that he ever was a logical positivist, a meaning-analyst, a language philosopher. To no avail. Those who read Popper seriously know this anyway, others would not accept it. If people today are less prone to misrepresent Popper's views of science than they previously were, then this is so merely due to the general discredit that is now accorded to logical positivism or meaning-analysis. In this sense, at least, the present volume is a relief. Using Jeremy Shearmur's excellent index we can find that Popper mentions logical positivism here only cursorily: once where he presents the equation of positivism with logical positivism as reasonable (page 321), and a few other times briefly, where positivism appears as one variant of that subjectivism, or as a theory tinged with that subjectivism, which is the outcome of an indiscriminate use of Ockham's razor.

Ah! But if we declare subjectivism an error, is this declaration not an invitation for realism? And if so, is not realism also metaphysical or non-scientific? Is not, to use Popper's own criterion, realism irrefutable?

This question reverts us to Popper's *Logik der Forschung* of 1935, which handles it quite deftly. This work is frankly anti-metaphysical, in the sense that it includes its author's frank and explicit plan to exclude and disallow metaphysics from the sharing of privileges with science as much as possible. In the literature of the period prior to the aberration of logical positivism, any anti-metaphysics pro-science attitude merited the label of positivism; and so the only reason that Popper's positivism has been, and still is, overlooked, is that he argued so much and so often against the vulgar and silly view of himself as a logical positivist. And so, Popper's protests in an attempt to rectify vulgar misconceptions not only failed but also acted as a distraction. Back to realism.

In his *Logik der Forschung* Popper admits his realist bias, but declared it private, on account of the fact that realism is irrefutable and hence metaphysical and unscientific. This view he still holds in the present volume, at least he is willing to concede the irrefutability of realism (see, however, page 39n), stressing even more that attempts to overcome metaphysical realism lands one in metaphysical idealism-subjectivism, which is much worse. But this is not all. Popper's realism is threefold. First, he thinks, the external world exists (i.e., things which I perceive, not only my perceptions of them, do exist). Second, theories exist, problems exist (in World 3, of which later). Third, scientific theories are true or false and stating a scientific theory is quite equivalent to the claim that it is true. This third point may be the same as essentialism, except that essentialists claim for their scientific theories the status of demonstrated truths whereas Popper claims that some scientific hypotheses are tentative and some are false (N): where the false ones are once-successful-but-now-refuted: and the refuted ones are first-approximations to the still successful ones. This may sound instrumentalistic since instrumentalism declares the validity of each theory within its domain of application unchallenged by further progress so that theories are in a sense never superseded. Popper denies that by comparing depths of theories; a more general theory (refuted or not) is deeper than its less general (refuted) predecessor, where 'depth' is touch with ultimate reality, namely the proximity to that famous elusive ideal, the truth, the whole truth, and nothing but the truth (page 202).

Here we have another sense of realism, then. We have a still different sense, and one which I found in Robert Boyle as a criterion of objectivity: I can imagine my curtains having this color or that, he said, but when I open my eyes I cannot convince myself that my curtains are not red. Hence their redness (contrary to Democritus and Galileo) is in some sense objective and hence the proper object of scientific inquiry. Towards the very end of this volume (page 360) in the Appendix (which is the earliest publication in this collection), Popper says in an italicized sentence: "It is through the falsification of our suppositions that we actually get in touch with 'reality'." As I prefer to put it: 'We err, ergo, the world exists.'

Is realism scientific or metaphysical? Is it refutable or the fact that something we 'get in touch' with is what makes science scientific in the first place? I am still not clear about this. The attitude to metaphysics throughout the *Logik der Forschung* is quite hostile, as I say. Whatever Popper needs of metaphysics there he converts from statements—which are untestable—to rules of method—which are fruitful or unfruitful (in some sense of the word). Example: instead of the law of causality, Popper presents the proposal, Let us search for causal explanation. This theory is highly positivistic, since it offers every satisfactory explanation as causal, whereas, throughout the history of the philosophy of science there was the famous distinction—still upheld as very significant even by William Whewell—between the causal and the accidental. (The words are 'causal definition' and 'accidental definition', of course; but Popper will be the first to view essentialism as attempts to view definitions as ultimate explanations; see above.) Indeed, Popper's own example from the explanation of a wire breaking due to the weight appended to it will be considered as accidental, and the causal explanation will have to refer to molecular forces, etc.

Moreover, causality so presented, or the principle of simplicity of Nature (translated into the rule: Search for the simplest explanation), are quite universal; what about competing metaphysical theories? For example, determinism and indeterminism. Here Popper is quite clear. Metaphysical determinism leaves him cold, but there exists a scientific version of determinism which he says he has refuted. This leaves him with indeterminism which, though metaphysical, is a precondition for all social sciences. Another example, monism, dualism, pluralism. Here Popper is averse to both metaphysical monism and dualism. The note on page 231 is worth quoting:

> ... I am almost a Cartesian ... I have no sympathy with the Cartesian talk of a mental *substance* or a thinking *substance* or extended *substance*. I am a Cartesian only in so far as I believe in the existence of both physical *states* and mental *states* (and, besides, in even more abstract things such as states of discussion).

The blunt positivistic hostility aside (I find quite redundant the derisive talk about "Cartesian talk"), I am lost. Was there ever any philosopher who denied the existence of material, mental, and other states, as such? Not to my knowledge. When Bishop Berkeley declared his philosophy common sense and more comprehensible to the common man than others, he was stressing the fact that he never denied the existence of material states, only of material substance. Admittedly, a joke, a rude and hostile joke, existed, about Dean Swift's refusal to open the door for Bishop Berkeley; it is quite clear from Popper's exposition of Berkeley's philosophy that he is no party to this rude joke: Berkeley never claimed that we can walk through doors, only that this is not due to doors comprising impenetrable substance. On this Berkeley and Popper are agreed. Where are we then?

Of course, Popper is no party to Berkeley's instrumentalism. Also he denies that different substances characterize the material states which belong to his material World 1, the mental states which belong to his mental World 2, and the rest of the states which belong to his World 3. But what, then, differentiates between Worlds 1, 2, and 3? Moreover, once deprived of substance, World 1 and World 2 have no trouble interacting any longer, no more than electricity and magnetism, to mention J. O. Wisdom's example. Now surely, even though nothing prevents the interaction of electricity and magnetism, we may nevertheless want a theory of it which is testable, or at least which explains some of the known interactions. Popper's 'Of Clouds and Clocks', Chapter 6 here, from which the above quote is taken, seems to offer here two new mind-body problems: how do minds and matter interact? and how can there be any interactions and coordination between people? But if he offers any testable theory or explanation here, then I have failed to find it. I declare I find that essay, Chapter 6 in the present collection, though beautifully written and full of new ideas, nevertheless on the central points it raises, quite pointless and most presumptuous. It may be my blindness, of course; no reviewer is perfect.

I confess in retrospect I find roots of this difficulty already in Popper's classic *Open Society* where he rejects reductionism and determinism as metaphysical but accepts dualism both as methodological and as true.

In his *Open Society* Popper expresses a more open hostility to metaphysics than in his *Logik der Forschung* (while attacking more fiercely the logical positivists whom he again considers positivists unqualified) and at the same time puts it to further use. Individualism, institutionalism, indeterminism, even nominalism, all of them classical metaphysical doctrines, are endorsed as methods, in line with the *Logik der Forschung*. In addition, conflicting metaphysical doctrines, e.g., human nature is good, and, human nature is evil, are put to work together, again as guiding ideas, as interpretations, as points of view: holding the view of the natural goodness of man we would write one history, extolling instances of human dedication, courage, and benevolence, and holding the other we would write the history of mankind stressing tyranny, slavery, and treachery. No views proper and no contradiction, and so no metaphysical doctrine proper and no metaphysical dispute. On the whole Popper suggests a bold and quite metaphysical hypothesis: the history of philosophy is the history of interpretations—of "isms". Shall we translate this hypothesis into a point of view? Is it a new interpretation of the history of philosophy?

And yet something has broadened. In the *Logik der Forschung* only empirical refutation played any role in the process of learning. In the *Open Society* something was added. When, looking at the result of our good intentions plus moral doctrines, we shudder, as the priest in Shaw's *St. Joan* does when he sees her burn at the stake, then we change our moral perceptions or intuitions or doctrines. Horizons somehow broaden. Further attempts to broaden the horizon can be found in *Conjectures and Refutations* where, in 'On the Status of Metaphysics' criteria are given for the adequacy and arguability of metaphysical doctrines (as reported in this volume on note to page 40). All this is promising, until we arrive at the present volume which reverts to the old positivism.

The metaphysical doctrines handled here (see index) are Darwinism, Lamarckism, and Bergsonism. Popper does not apply to them his criteria from *Conjectures and Refutations*: rather he declares two of these approximations to the best one—Darwinism (pp. 147, 269, text to note 13, 270). I do not understand this; I think it should be better explained before we can discuss it.[8] If we take simulation to be approximation, and we speak here of metaphysical theories, then, we have a lot of new approximations, since determinism simulates freedom of choice and vice versa; humans simulate machines and vice versa; institutions simulate individuals and vice versa. And, there is no doubt that at times Popper is quite aware of the fact that Darwinism is a metaphysical doctrine, interpretative of facts and generative of research programs—if I may be bold enough to use a different terminology here than Popper's (not, heaven forbid, that I claim priority here, whether of terminology or anything else). In particular, unless we admit this characteristic of Darwinism, it is hard to comprehend Popper's severe and just complaint that "some neo-Darwinists seem to be almost blind" to "the countless difficulties of Darwin's theory" (page 271n). Yet Popper does not call Darwinism "metaphysical", as far as my checking could show. He calls it (page 270) "*historical*". Or, "to put it more precisely, Darwin's theory is a *generalized* historical explanation." But I shall not go into this again. Popper complains again that Freud's theory is untestable (page 38n), saying nothing more about him in the whole volume. As if Wisdom's and Bartley's excellent dissent and criticisms had never existed. And when he fails to chastize Darwin for the same fault, he falls prey to it. It is not only that this is a double standard, but that also Popper pays the price. Freud erroneously claimed that some untestable ideas of his were confirmed; so did Darwin; at such points Freud was pseudo-scientific par excellence, perhaps more than Darwin, but who is free and clear of such things? Take, further, Popper's own hypothesis of plastic control. How does it differ from Darwin's? Is it metaphysical or is it testable? What status is claimed for it? Is it scientific? Does it include the claim that an insect's control is plastic (i.e., somewhat free), for example? Take Compton's switch-board model which Popper rejects. Is it scientific? (I think not.) Has Popper effectively criticized it? (I think not.) Take Popper's theory that all organisms from the amoeba to Einstein live by trial and error, only differing in that the amoeba's corrections are almost random whereas Einstein is critical and systematically tries and corrects. Does it apply to servo-mechanisms that can try and correct, like computers fed with approximation techniques, guided missiles, or Professor Grey Walter's artificial tortoises that teach themselves to circumvent obstacles on their way to the source of light which they use for energy? Does this not reduce Einstein's knowledge to a superlative proficiency unequalled by any other animal? Does Popper, finally, endorse T. H. Morgan's instinct-modification theory, and if so what does he do with Konrad Lorenz's claim that he has empirically refuted it? (Lorenz and Compton seem to agree, but I cannot tell.)

I confess ignorance. My questions are not rhetorical and no mere exercises for the reader; they are tough questions which indicate how far is Popper's target and how mistaken he is in presenting matters as simple. I confess I found all this very puzzling, and I think it has much to do with the brevity of his essays. But also, I feel, it might be claimed that all of Popper's claims that he has explained anything—on the interaction of body and mind or in evolutionism—is just as faulty as Freud's and Darwin's unjust claims for scientific status; but they, at least, could not benefit from Popper's insights; he could and seems to have refused. Further, his claims could be linked to areas of inquiry where he himself breaks new ground. Darwinism explains Lamarckism as an approximation. Does D entail L or L*? What is L* and how does it differ from L? Is Popper's theory a part of D or is it only vaguely Darwinian but different? It is "an important contribution to a theory of evolution of the Darwinian type'', we remember his claim (p. 281), not "a Darwinian theory''. Do we have a contribution to a theory which explains D* rather than D, I wonder? Or is Popper simply reluctant to say he is offering a metaphysical hypothesis or a vague historical hypothesis which is not testable?

Popper could easily say, in line with *Logik der Forschung* (Sec. 80), that he is offering a metaphysical theory that may be rendered scientific. But quoting from that passage he will also be able to quote from it objections to the method of proposing metaphysical hypotheses. Also, he could take recourse to his essay in *Conjectures and Refutations* on the status of metaphysical theories. He could apply the criteria of that essay to his present views.

The first criterion is: does the metaphysics in question come to solve a problem, and does it solve it? When I try to apply this criterion to Popper's views I am baffled: I do not see clearly enough what theory comes to solve exactly what problem.

This may be due to the fact that the problems are non-existent, or hidden, or unperceived by one individual with a peculiar blind spot. I cannot tell.

8. Induction and Negative Philosophy

Popper's philosophy can be viewed as philosophia negativa, in line with the classic theologia negativa. The more I think of this parallel the more I like it; theologia negativa was not despairing or defeatist, but considered God inaccessible yet approachable by the denial and criticism of diverse doctrines about Him. A corollary of this which negative theologians barely noticed but which is important nonetheless is this: We should try to create new positive theologies when we have finished destroying all the old ones, so as to have new ones to destroy. Take the formula *deus sive natura* any way you like, and science as natural theology becomes in Popper's hands science as negative natural theology.

I therefore found quite invalid the criticism levelled against Popper's *Open Society* that it is negative. For it offers a negative philosophy of society. Popper offers his positive views by the very act of criticizing others. But in order to make this possible he has to offer a problem, and defend earlier solutions to the problem, first as satisfactory solutions, and second as having attractive aspects. His criticism of these theories is then quite valuable; it is not the mere dismissal of any silly old idea.

Looking again at Popper's excursions into biology, I am amazed to find how much pointless though valid criticism it includes. Looking at his papers on the objective mind and on objective knowledge (which is not knowledge but objective, i.e., institutional, i.e., neither physical nor psychological and so in World 3), I am amazed to see that they start with attacks. No problems, no discussion of strength of valid solutions to be attacked. Just attacks: very negative in attitude and so quite contrary to the spirit of negative philosophy. Take from this book all that is out of character, namely the attacks on worthless errors, and little is left—but that little seems to me still to be exciting master strokes. All those opponents whom he appreciates such as the Dutch mathematician Brouwer and the English philosopher Collingwood, he discusses wonderfully. Perhaps also the more formal parts of the volume include something of great value—I am in no position to judge all of them.[9]

But I must hurry along. The point I wish to stress is one which I find, usually, hard to explain. I do agree with Popper's contention in his essays on the objective mind, or objective knowledge—that is to say, knowledge as public and as institutionalized. Popper calls physical states World 1, mental states World 2, and other, such as states of debates, or as libraries, and any other, World 3. No one will deny, as I say, that the three kinds of state do in fact exist. Some philosophers would grant the status of substance to only one or the other of these worlds; Popper himself believes in no substance. He, then, must concede that his distinction is trite. The question is, as I shall now explain, what question does he answer?

The forte of Popper's solution to the problem of induction (I shall specify it soon) is in its very triteness. The more we agree about the triteness of the view that we learn from our mistakes and that in science hypotheses compete at times and survive attempts at refutations at times—whole or mutilated—the more we should admire it as a solution to an awesome problem: it is like purchasing the Hope Diamond for a nickel! And so the very triteness of Sir Karl's arguments may have a depth that eludes me.

A question well put, we are told, is half the answer. Yet volumes about the problem of induction have passed my hand in which the problem is not even stated. I should think that half a volume in the presentation of the problem would be reasonable since putting it well is half a solution. But most writers do not even bother to state the problem and even Popper's *Logik der Forschung* only states the problem of induction very casually. This is much improved upon in the present volume, in the first chapter—as well as in Chapter 5 on the aims of science which I shall leave now—on the problem of induction, and its echoes in the second. Yet the chapter opens in a most off-putting manner which may well conceal this asset from the reader. Popper starts with the claim that he has solved the problem of induction, and that few will admit this, so he repeats himself so as to confute the critics (pp. 1–2). On page 9 Popper comes across the view that all statements of science are hypothetical or conjectural. "This view is by now fairly popular. . . ." Good; we can push on, then. Oh, no! "but it took quite a time to reach this stage"— namely time and effort on the part of a certain pioneer (p. 9). For example, in 1937 Ryle argues that it is an error to view the statements of science as 'mere hypotheses', meaning merely hypothetical or conjectural. Rather Ryle thinks some hypotheses get 'established' and are elevated to the status of 'laws'.

If there is one thing the world wants to know about Popper it is this: does he think Einstein's theory, or Dirac's equation, are mere hypotheses? Granted, they are uncertain, we cannot prove them, ergo they are hypotheses; but are they just any old hypotheses? Are they in any way distinguished from any other educated guess?

The most obvious answer, and one least discussed in the literature, is that scientific theories are refutable, whereas unscientific ones are not; hence, science is not 'mere hypotheses' but refutable ones.

There are a few reasons why the above characterization of science was not taken seriously. It is considered obvious (a) that scientific theories are refutable, (b) that not all refutable theories are of equal merit, and (c) that there must be more to a theory than its mere refutability, something more positive. At times Bertrand Russell (the great teacher of us all) ascribed to Popper the view that current scientific theory has some positive attribute, and this attribute can be called probability, and the theory describing it a theory of induction, so that Popper is but an inductivist of a different color. Popper, from whom I have heard this, corrected Russell's impression. Later on, in the 1961 preface to Nicod's classic book on induction and probability, Russell views Popper's theory as somewhat desperate. No *philosophia negativa* for Bertrand Russell.

Popper has spent so much time arguing that the positive side of current science is no probability in the current mathematical sense of "probability" that matters get more and more obscure. At least I myself found it hard to pin matters down. Now I think I have it. In his *Logik der Forschung* of 1935 Popper claims causal explanation to be deductive. It seems clear enough, but more careful study may suggest that a causal explanation, to be satisfactory, must be testable. Certainly in his *Conjectures and Refutations* Popper makes that claim. But already in 1948, in the already quoted Appendix to this volume, page 352, he offers the view that A is a causal explanation of B iff A entails B, and is not only testable but also tested and passed the test. This is questionable, since it makes Newton's theory a causal explanation until it was replaced by Einstein, upon which event it ceased to be so. But right or not, the view here recorded seems to vindicate Russell's impression. This does not in the least invalidate Popper's critique of other views on the matter; it only makes one wonder, assuming other views are given up, what is his view. But it is of no avail to keep attacking his opponents on the pretext that they do not concede that he has solved the problem of induction.

Am I ready to concede this? I honestly do not know yet. I think *philosophia negativa* does satisfactorily solve the problem of induction and I have learned from Popper that it does. This is no small matter. There is little doubt that Darwin himself was deeply concerned both with the problem of induction and with the problem, where does our intellectual apparatus come from? (see M. T. Ghiselin, 'Darwin and Evolutionary Psychology', *Science*, 179, 9 March 1973, pp. 964–68); that some Darwinian theories of the growth of knowledge were popular before Popper was born; yet neither Darwin nor his successors saw in the survival of the fittest theory—whatever exactly this may mean—the route to a solution of the problem of induction. [10] This oversight is due to the lack of appreciation of *philosophia negativa*. When Popper practices it, I grant his solution; when he demands positive evidence, he is, for me, just another inductivist: it all depends what is the problem of induction.

I use here somewhat strong language, when I say Popper on corroboration is just another inductivist. In a recent debate in Germany Hans Albert, in defense of Popper, discusses what he says Agassi calls Popper's whiff of inductivism. I must disown this charming epithet and, for all I know, ascribe it to Popper himself. One person's whiff, to coin a phrase, is another person's mouthful.

The problem of induction is presented in Popper's *Logik der Forschung* briefly, how do we conclude from singular (observation) statements regarding (theoretical) universal ones? He answers, by the modus tollens. Or, how do we acquire theoretical knowledge from observation? Answer: by refuting our theories and thus transcending them. But when the problem is, how do we choose hypotheses, which Bar Hillel, for example, views as *the* problem of induction, indeed *THE* problem, Popper's solution is at best ambiguous. [11]

Here is my own reply to the problem of choice of hypothesis. I have tried to show that the question is vague, containing choice of hypotheses to believe in and choice of hypotheses for the purpose of technical application in practice. Now every matter of belief is a matter of conscience, and is thus private and its privacy is protected by every democratic constitution. Not so in matters of practice: for practice we have social institutions, such as bureaux of standards, food and drug administrations, aviation control, etc. etc. Now in western countries tests often are severe; and only when claims—hardly theories—for effectiveness are corroborated, may they be employed. May, not should. And the standards of severity and broadness (a concept untouched by Popper, but significant nonetheless especially where side effects—medical or ecological—are expected) vary from country to country, and are at times vague enough to call for further legislation, inquests, and litigation. Here, then, corroboration, as an institution, belongs to World 3. So much for my view of choice as applicability.

On page 22, in Chapter 1, Popper discusses applicability and equates it with degree of corroboration. Unlike Popper, I do not mind that he ignores my criticism and my view; but I cannot pretend to appreciate his repetition of an old view, nor can I ignore this fact when engaged (reluctantly) in a review of his latest book.

What I do appreciate in Chapter 1, however, is its presentation of the traditional problem of induction in diverse ways (page 27). Priority may go to Mario Bunge, but I like everyone to do it, and I think Popper's way is enlightening: had he done it more thoroughly he would have gone further.

9. CONCLUSION: THE NOVELTY OF POPPER'S VIEWS

The modern scientific tradition is permeated with inductivism. And inductivism is the admonition to avoid jumping to conclusions, i.e., to avoid the invention of bold conjectures. How deeply permeated this was is illustrated by the indignant remark made by Jules Verne when his science fiction was compared to that of H. G. Wells: *he invents*! said Verne contemptuously.

The view that science is bold conjecture is not Popper's. If we must ascribe it to one philosopher, then my choice is the early nineteenth-century genius William Whewell. But Whewell demanded the boldness to be prescientific: what makes a bold conjecture scientific, he claimed, was its verification. This is a large step from Laplace's effort to present scientific theories as "natural" but it still takes the boldness away by the very finality of the verification. When verification was later replaced by probability, things were not improved. But what happens to one who boldly invents but never confirms?

The conventionalists dispensed with confirmation, and asked only for simplicity. Does simplicity as they understood it square with boldness? It is hard to say, and all one can say is that they hardly noticed the question, and bold Einstein was not exactly their favorite.

Popper's theory of trial and error is realistic: it values even false bold conjectures, as way stations on the road to truth. It expresses philosophically Einstein's idea of scientific theories as successions of approximations (to the truth).

Popper's view of testability as the hallmark of realism seems to me to be a false theory. When we offer a testable hypothesis in hydrodynamics, aerodynamics, or two-phase flow theory, which conforms to the continuum theory, we do not consider it realistic, regardless of refutation and/or confirmation, unless we *reinterpret* it in the light of our more atomistic views. We view as more realistic a barely testable and quite inadequate theory of nuclear forces. And so realism seems to me to demand more than mere conjectures and refutations. But boldness was introduced by Popper as a respectable quality, with no further qualification. And this was both bold and admirable.

The idea of boldness, then, when sufficiently developed, ousts both inductivism and conventionalism as the idea of daring to be mistaken. Now Popper translates this to the engagement in the development of bold (a) explanatory conjectures, (b) conjectures, and (c) solutions to given problems.

He seems to identify the three, or at least ignore my refutation of this identification and the problems this refutation obviously engenders. Instead, he tried to show that problem solving is evolutionary, and the bolder the better by evolutionary standards. That may be so. But this volume seems to go further. It equates problem solving with the (Popperian) offering of refutable explanatory conjectures, as well as with the (Darwinian) struggle for survival. But this is an error. Struggle for survival is not fully causal and so not orthodox Darwinian. And problem solving and explanation merely overlap but are far from being the same. Also, this volume claims an objective status to problem-solving. This has been elaborated more in other works, of the same author and of previous ones.[12] It is not devoid of its problems which are not even mentioned here.[13] And so this volume seems to present views which their author could vastly improve on with ease had he not distracted himself by attacking the philistines.

To wind up, I should now sketch a contrast between the erroneous composite portrait of Popper with which I have started and the one I hope emerges from this conclusion. Popper, first and foremost, is a person who struggles with problems and who offers bold ideas. This fact is conspicuously absent from the composite image, and for the obvious reason that it is drawn by philistines. It is when Popper pays the philistines the courtesy of noticing what they say or do not say or might say that he unwittingly lends force to their picture. And he pays them this courtesy each time he stakes a claim.

Why do people stake claims and insist on them? Is it merely a psychological need for recognition? We may learn from Heine that there was a German tradition of claim staking. And the biographies of giants like Mach and Boltzmann and Freud and Planck illustrate similar conduct. But let us not think this is a matter of psychology or of tradition alone. There is a clear situational logic here: a pioneer who opens new vistas depends on followers if he or she is to be remembered as a pioneer rather than as a visionary forerunner. And so consequently a pioneer may well overestimate the importance of his or her being noted or not, and if yes, whether critically or not. Somehow, I feel, there is an optical illusion shared by many pioneers who made too strenuous an effort to secure a following or at least to perceive whether they have any. We cannot know these things. In particular, when criticism was still equated with disapproval, a much criticized pioneer was often too unjustly dismissed as a bad influence. Nowadays, thanks to Popper, we know better.

NOTES

1. See the following chapter.
2. Private acknowledgements are usually put in general terms in one note in a

paper, more often than not in the first note. Review essays, traditionally, do not contain such acknowledgements—in order to avoid embarrassment, I presume. (See also the acknowledgements on p. xi above.)

3. According to G. Révész, *The Origins and Prehistory of Language*, New York 1956, the first to deny the Darwinian theory of continuity is Hugo de Vries, *Species and Varieties*, Chicago, 1905, and *Die Mutationen in der Erblichkeitslehre*, Berlin, 1912. The important question, of course, is how integrated is continuity within Darwinism. That is to say, does a deviation from continuity require deviations from other Darwinian views? Popper does not raise this question. On the contrary, he has lumped together Erwin Schrödinger, the renowned Schopenhauerian and so of Lamarckian bias, with the leading militant anti-Lamarckians such as James M. Baldwin. (The label 'Baldwin's effect' for phenomena that seem Lamarckian but, neo-Darwinians insist, are not, need not have impressed Popper so. It is really a misuse of a tradition of naming a factual discovery after its finder, akin to the label 'Tyndall's effect' for the dust particles glittering in a beam of sunlight. In both cases the inventors of the label felt the person in question deserves the honor even though he made no distinct discovery to name after him.) In fact, Schrödinger claims that Darwinism, even when it explains all it claims to explain, leaves open to the will of the members of a new species to exploit or not to exploit their given new characteristic. The neo-Darwinians explain things causally (where cause is strict or statistical but not final) by saying, every new characteristic is sooner or later exploited—at times to advantage at times not—simply by the law of large numbers. Thus, not that a thickly furred animal travels to cold places, but that it sooner or later travels in all directions and benefits in cold places.

The crux of the question is, indeed, as Popper puts it, can all final causes be reduced to causal ones (strict or statistical)? And, as his answer is no, he is no orthodox Darwinian and this is the end of that. This does not make him a Lamarckian, any more than Schrödinger's view makes him: for, as Lamarck spoke of the inheritance of some acquired characteristics, and what Schrödinger and Popper seem to say is that we are in control of the stock of our inheritance though we cannot add voluntarily to that stock. Thus, Schrödinger and Popper can be called neo-neo-Lamarckians.

4. To readers familiar with R. Goldschmidt's *The Material Basis of Evolution*, Yale, 1940, I should add this: he calls microevolution changes brought about (a) by small steps and (b) by gene-reordering in the chromosomes. Here I am speaking only of (a); as to (b) he may well have a disagreement with E. B Ford, as he views all (b) as "evolutionary blind alleys" and Ford not. Cf. E. B. Ford, *Mendelism and Evolution*, 2nd ed., London, 1934. Goldschmidt is not terribly clear as to whether all changes due to chromosomal (rather than gene) mutations are called macroevolution, or whether all such changes lead to great departures of offspring from parent, or what.

5. The criticism that struggle for survival may only increase fecundity is hardly significant, since fecundity and speciation are most deeply linked: but for interspecies infertility there would be no species and no speciation. Darwin postulated the impact of speciation on (further) sexual selection, and G. J. Romanes suggested the other way around. Clearly, both trends are possible.

In addition to all this R. A. Fisher suggested that for some characteristics the heterozygote allele may be more fertile than the (dominant) homozygote. This suggestion, too, was applied to diverse cases.

6. The note on Duhem in the Appendix, p. 358, is added in the translation. Here one finds no explanation for Popper's belated revival of Duhem's hopeful contradiction, and so one may wonder if its absence from the text is not simply due to the fact—assuming it to be a fact—that in 1948 Popper was hardly familiar with

Duhem's opus. If so, one may wonder, how did Popper chance upon Duhem later on? Did he discover Duhem all by himself, or was Duhem brought to his attention by someone else? My own conjecture is that here acknowledgment may very well go to P. P. Wiener, the translator of Duhem's celebrated *Aim and Structure*. Translators receive acknowledgment by the very mention of their translation as theirs. Nevertheless, I feel, Wiener's translation of this book deserves special mention as epoch-making. Many of Duhem's ideas were disseminated in the English-speaking world by writers like J. B. Conant, who neither properly presented not properly acknowledged their own source. And so when the source itself became available it had a great impact as something fairly well recognized yet better than could be expected. (A similar case is that of the belated appearance of the English translation of Popper's first vintage where the ground was prepared chiefly by the same author.)

7. Admittedly, the Darwinists explain away seemingly Lamarckian phenomena as due to natural selection; also natural selection can be explained away as willed. Thus, in the preface to his *Back to Methuselah* Shaw says, all appearances to the contrary notwithstanding, the sick or the wounded wishes to die; and, in the end of his *A Black Girl* he says, one who wishes to live finds in himself unimagined abilities. I should call this the Shaw effect, or the inverse Baldwin effect. I should ask Popper whether this makes Darwinism a first-approximation akin to its inverse, and if not why not.

8. See note 7, above.

Popper's theory of verisimilitude has been meanwhile refuted by David Miller. Nevertheless, I feel the theory plus its refutation are very important. The theory may be relativized to fields of known facts and thus offer a better function than Popper's corroboration as conjectured degree of approximation to the truth and with no connection with corroboration as applicability.

9.   Popper's note on Tarski's theory of truth has not been reviewed by the logicians, and I, for one, cannot assess its correctness and worth.

The best page in this volume seems to me to be page 285, a poetic page on alienation, which stands all alone yet is very satisfying all the same—even though I cannot swear that I know what problem(s) it comes to solve and even though I cannot see its connection with anything else in this volume. The worst seems to me to be page 190 where Popper insists on misreading Bacon's demand that the philosopher be chaste as the demand that he be modest. Quite apart from his quaint reliance on Ellis's translation (which is very inadequate on all points where Bacon alludes to the cabalistic and hermetic traditions); apart from the high-handed demand that an interpretation fit the problem situation—presumably of interpreted author—(a long line of interpreters of Bacon claim that Bacon's texts to a large extent are hardly responses to problems and, more often than not, rather mere transcriptions); and apart from the unjust rebuke of someone who (with Ellis and many others) views the preface to Bacon's non-existent *Instauratio Magna* simply as a fancy preface to Bacon's *Novum Organum*; on top of all these injustices he really overdoes it when he rubs his rebuke in by saying the mistranslation is of a "simple Latin text"—after he himself notes that his translation of "caste et perpetuo" into "modestly and devoutedly" is "a free translation", especially since he (perhaps correctly) reads modesty here as the quality of not jumping to conclusions.

Is this reading correct? Bacon's requirement of moral rectitude all round is a remnant of the older tradition of cabalistic magic, going back to Plotinus, if not to Plato himself. The practical cabalist could bring the Messiah, on condition that he be absolutely faultless; and so all-round purity was the end of lengthy preparations, and failure to bring the Messiah was explained away as the outcome of a fault in the preparation. And so, chastity and modesty were both required among other virtues, by the tradition of the Cabalah that Bacon was following. All he added was, indeed, that jumping to conclusions was sinful. But he denied that timidity alone will prevent the jump: he insisted that all other traditional virtues plus the worship of nature were necessary. Jumping to conclusions was, however, the rape of Nature (as well as other sins, such as the forcing of Nature into chains); and so we may indeed use 'chaste' and read it metaphorically. (See notes to my 'Unity and Diversity in Science' *Boston Studies in the Philosophy of Science*, vol. 4, 1969, reprinted in my *Science in Flux*, 1975.) And so we do not need a free translation, and we can read Bacon to require chastity in a metaphorical sense. In this way we can rescue both the translator whom Popper censures like a schoolboy *and* Popper. What all this shows is that the insult, namely that a celebrated historian and student of interpretation mistranslates a simple text, is quite a boomerang: the text is not that simple.

10. It is an interesting historical fact that practically all those who spoke of the natural selection of hypotheses were instrumentalists of varying shades, some were inductivists, and, of course, there were, one cannot say how many, those who mixed the two convictions in varying proportions. Of the few who were genuinely not at all justificationists George Bernard Shaw stood out. But he, of course, was no Darwinist. For Shaw, see the final section of my 'Sociologism in the Philosophy of Science', *Metaphilosophy*, 3, 1972, reprinted in my *Science and Society*, 1981.

11. Popper claims explicitly that corroboration may serve as a rational degree of belief. I have discussed at length the ambiguity and the inadequacy of this claim in my 'Testing as a Bootstrap Operation in Physics' *Zeitschrift für Allgem. Wissenschaftstheorie*, 4, 1973, and in my 'Imperfect Knowledge', *Philos. and Phenom. Res.*, 32, 1972, both reprinted in my *Science in Flux*, 1975.

12. Problem-solving is objective in two ways, as Popper makes amply clear. One is the way in which mathematics is. This is the idea of axiology of the Polish school of philosophy, expounded already by Ludwig von Mises. The second is the institutional aspect, and the objectivity of institutions is long standing; Popper has expounded on it in his *Open Society*, chapter on the autonomy of sociology. Hegel, incidentally, identified the two in his philosophy of identity, poked fun at in that book. See references there, Ch. 12, nn35ff.

13. The objectivity of mathematical theorems was viewed by Leibniz as proof of their eternity and thus of the existence of an eternal receptacle for them and thus, somehow, of God. Popper will not have a substance, and no eternal receptacle, or Platonic heaven. When, then, comes a theorem into existence? By being institutionalized? That will be too Hegelian. Never? That will be too Platonic. When it was invented? That will be too Lockean. When, then? It seems to me that in different works Popper tends toward a different alternative. This seems to me to be a very important issue.

— 28 —

KUHN AND HIS CRITICS
rational reconstruction of the ant heap

Tristram Shandy is a novel of an order of magnitude and interest which defies any quick summary. Ostensibly concerning everyday life in provincial 18th-century England, it is an ebullient, irresistible, outrageous, good-natured satire. It attacks, amongst other things, contemporary philosophy, contemporary philosophy of science, and contemporary biology. The famous Tristram Shandy Paradox derives from a chapter in which the author notes that here he is, in the middle of his book, struggling to cope with the events leading up to his birth, and concludes that as long as the in-stallments of his books are purchased by the public this is fine by him, as it ensures that he will not run out of writing material. The Tristram Shandy Paradox is, in brief, the claim that it takes Shandy longer to record history than to live it.

Without knowledge of the philosophy of science of the time one might take this as a mere witticism. The philosophy of science of the time, however, makes this a very forceful critique. Francis Bacon was the philosopher whose standing at the time, as Paul Hazard notes in his *European Thought in the 18th Century*, was that of "reason incarnate". Bacon was the only man, says Hazard, who could be mentioned with Newton in one breath without insult to Newton. Bacon taught that science is the elimination of prejudice and the collection of enough facts to let theoretical truths emerge from them. Nowadays philosophers do not mention Bacon's theory of prejudice, only his theory of collecting facts. Yet Bacon said that without eliminating prejudices facts only tend to make us worse people than we are, because we all tend to confirm our prejudices with our facts. For an example I invite you to study Tristram Shandy's own father. Mr. Shandy was an undoubtedly positive character. He was kind, even to his incompe-tent, inept, bungling helpers; he was patient, indeed his patience was of

---

This review of *Criticism and the Growth of Knowledge: Proceedings of the International Colloquium in the Philosophy of Science, London 1965*, edited by I. Lakatos and A. Musgrave, (London and Boston: Cambridge University Press, 1970) appeared in *Inquiry*, 14, 1971 under the title of 'Tristram Shandy, Pierre Menard, and All That'.

steel, for otherwise Mrs. Shandy and Uncle Toby would have killed him by their endless pesterings; and he was enlightened. Yet Mr. Shandy was not a flawless character. He had two prejudices: he believed in the theories that good names are good omens and that long noses are signs of virility. Lawrence Sterne, the author of the book, offers us a glimpse into the world of an enlightened man with a quirky opinion, and (with Dr. Johnson of the *Rasselas*) can thus be classed as a pioneering psychologist. Incidentally, the main running joke of the story is to explain how Tristram Shandy was saddled with a silly name and an almost noseless face.

One fundamental corollary to Bacon's doctrine of prejudice is that facts must be indiscriminately observed, since selecting facts is either willful or based on some reason, and that reason is a prejudice since it precedes the collection of facts. Though writers today do not explain Bacon's excellent rationale for his injunction to collect facts indiscriminately, the injunction itself has been noted. Jacob Bronowski, Paul Feyerabend, and Imre Lakatos report Popper's fables against this injunction, the one about a man who made observations all his life and recorded them, and in the eve of his life bequeathed all his records to the Royal Society so that the learned Fellows of that august body could distill science from them; or the story of the teacher of science who, for an exercise, told his students to observe and record what they were observing, there and then. They were paralyzed, we are told, by bewilderment: they didn't know what to observe.

The miracle of Laurence Sterne's novel is that it is seemingly an unending stream of minute observations, infuriating in its endless flow of details all going nowhere; in one place the book even dips, hilariously, into free-association; and yet, at the same time it is a devilishly clever satire on the period. Its subtlety is easy to overlook; Dr. Johnson plainly hated it. It could not be so penetrating a satire if it did not undermine the foundation of the philosophy of the age. By the very execution of the Baconian exercise (record everything!), Sterne showed its futility, and by the very conveyance of the sense of futility, Sterne gave his reader a taste of the slow pace and impotence of English provincial life. It is no accident that Sterne centers on philosophy, rather than religion, say, in *Shandy*. He clearly tried to take religion to task in his other novel, excellent for other reasons, but as comment it never got off the ground.

I will not dwell on other aspects of 18th-century philosophy of science, but urge you to compare Paul Hazard's book with Sterne's, in the exhibition of that century's inductivist love of detail as the epitome of science. Today we would hardly consider the amateurish collecting of butterflies or mushrooms a serious scientific activity. But if, as historians of science, we insist on the dogma that collections of butterflies are not science, we shall come no closer to the sense of the 18th century. I know of some historians of 18th-century science who have not read *Tristram Shandy*. I cannot for the life of me see how *they* can rationally reconstruct any significant part of the 18th century, its science least of all.

I am now moving to rational reconstruction. Let me first say I have not as yet succeeded in conveying to my satisfaction my feelings about induction and inductivism. A while ago I talked to the history-of-science group in Oxford, and the chairman started the discussion by saying, more or less, "We all know of the fatal blow you have dealt to Bacon, Duhem, *et al.*, and of your just contempt for them. But what is your positive proposal?" I protested; I said, "I have no contempt but deep admiration for Bacon *et al.* I have written a eulogy on an inductivist history of physics—that is, on the historical chapter in Laplace's *System of the World*—and now you tell me I have contempt for Bacon *et al.*" Yes, yes, said my learned host impatiently, we know all that; and he repeated his question. Obviously he took what I said to be partly lip-service, partly homage to the dead past; what he wanted to know was what comes next, in my opinion. It strikes me as somewhat incongruous that even historians rush to where the action is, doing all they can to keep up-to-date. I am afraid this will not do. I am afraid nothing short of satire will get my point across: it was inductivism which equated error with sin and thus criticism with condemnation. But inductivism is an error. Error, far from being sin, can be delightful, interesting, and instructive. As such, inductivism, which is indeed an inseparable part of what is strong in our tradition—no less than Homer, the Bible, or Newton—is to be criticized but not condemned.

Of course, this is the point of rational reconstruction: for error to be delightful and interesting it must be fresh and innocent; it must therefore be reconstructed afresh. Adam Smith was a genius; a student discovering Smith's ideas for himself is bright; a professor of economics who discovers Smith's economic model, or who plagiarizes it, and then tries to publish it in the current economic literature, is a jackass. But one can reconstruct it as an historian of economic thought. Likewise, contemporary inductivist historians of science are jackasses, but Laplace was great. This is the principle of historical reconstruction: apply no hindsight.

The greatest fault of inductivist historians is that they apply hindsight all the time. They cannot study phlogistonism but through the knowledge that it was overthrown—and is thus an error and thus a sin. But I shall not repeat myself on this point.

It may look as if the principle of rational reconstruction supersedes inductivism and with it the need to record indiscriminately—and so, it seems, Tristram Shandy's spirit may at last rest in peace, as he no longer poses a problem for us. But, instead, it has transmigrated into the body of Pierre Menard, the author of the *Quixote*, whose problem is all the sharper.

Jorge Luis Borges, the creator of Pierre Menard, belongs to the same long tradition as Lawrence Sterne. One of the fascinations of this tradition is the peculiar role it plays as a coupler between the arts and the sciences. The thought-experiments this literature conducts have intellectual thrust only because they are not devoid of literary merit. Thus, when, in Samuel Butler's works, we feel what is wrong with Darwinism, it is not merely because he has extended the theory of natural selection to machines; it is not even in his logical conclusion that any reductionist biological theory may extend beyond its intended limits. The eerie atmosphere which Butler's description exudes is an argument—it feels wrong! So to speak. We know that the choice of atmosphere is important. Butler's first work in this genre, his *Fair Haven*, was unsuccessful as a mock-Christian document, because its style, its atmosphere, was too naturalistic. Clergymen read it from the pulpit with voice trembling and choked with tears. Butler learned his lesson and later added the air of mischief and satire, which is so evident in Sterne, and occasionally of sarcasm, as in Swift. There is no doubt, sarcasm is essential if there is too much to criticize which is also too familiar. Bacon's doctrine of prejudice is particularly justified when applied to scholasticism, which should not be criticized so much as shoved off. I do not think Bacon could have succeeded but for the sarcasm which came before and after, in the works of Erasmus and Molière.

So there need not be a rational reconstruction of everything. But we can rationally reconstruct any idea rightly or deliberately wrongly, or rightly in order to blow up some errors. I find the story of Borges called 'Funes the Memorious' most wonderful in this respect. It is an attempt to describe a man who has a Lockean mind: who has sensations and who correlates them by association, etc., who has, of course, total recall because Locke forgot all about forgetting and saw no problem in regard to information retrieval.

But rather than go on to reconstruct a variety of such cases, let us center only on interesting ones. Now Borges created a man who did one such job—Pierre Menard. The man was very able. Borges offers us as evidence this man's list of publications, with some comments, and we can see at once that he is a gentleman and a scholar. It is incredible that Borges should have condensed a series of books that he might have written into a brief annotated bibliography; this must be the most condensed piece of literature in history. The greatness of Menard, we are told, is not his many books but that he wrote the *Quixote*. This, you understand, is an exercise in rational reconstruction. But let me exlain it anyway, being the verbose philosopher I am.

The principle of rational reconstruction is sometimes known as the rationality principle, and is not confined to history alone, since it is applied in the generalizing social sciences too, sociology, political science, etc. The idea is that if you assume an actor's aim and circumstances, you can deduce from your assumption, plus the principle—false, no doubt—that he is rational, that he does, or did, or would do, whatever action you set out to explain or predict, as the case may be. This, taken to the extreme—which is the technique of Sterne, Butler, or Borges—yields the idea that, assuming some propositions about Cervantes, you can explain his having written a page as he did. If you are a true scientist you could, like Pierre Menard, refuse to read that page but deduce it from your rational reconstruction!

Actually, says Borges, Menard managed to rewrite only two passages of Cervantes; but this suffices to bestow upon him the honorific title 'Author of the *Quixote*', with the definite article in the title referring, of course, to Cervantes's book.

Menard did only a small fraction of the job. He also created a new work of art. Borges gives an example. He quotes a sentence from Cervantes's *Quixote* which is racy and written very much in the vernacular of the day; he quotes the same sentence from Menard's *Quixote*, and shows that it is archaic, elegantly and interestingly so, yet archaic all the same. Moreover, Menard achieved his feat by an endless series of trials and errors. Unfortunately for us, he burnt all his manuscripts, and the only way we can know what they contained is to apply that same principle of rational reconstruction which he has applied to the *Quixote* to his own early manuscripts.

All this puts Tristram Shandy in the shade as a mere poor uncle. The magnitude of a historian's task has now reached new powers of infinity, no doubt.

Nothing is easier than to dismiss such flights of fancy as I am parading for you. It is easy, come to think of it, to dismiss any criticism, or even avoid criticizability altogether. I do not doubt that many people become historians in order to become archivists and librarians so that they can sink easily into a knowledge of details which no one would care to criticize. I wonder what would happen if I offered the reader streams of data about the works of the Hon. Robert Boyle, including the publication dates of his *Seraphick Love* and *Spring of the Air*. It is a respectable occupation, and, like it or not, you would be forced to approve of me, however mildly. Instead, let me tell you that there is a list of publication dates of Boyle's *Seraphick Love*, which is published in Fulton's celebrated Boyle Bibliography, and which serves no purpose except to show that the work was once immensely popular. I do not know if people ever read it, since many books are bought and not read. But I do know that no modern commentator has read it. All that the modern commentators say is that *Seraphick Love* is a theological work; which is for me evidence enough that they have not read it. It is easy to reconstruct the fact that they have not read it. It is written in the florid style of the period, ornamented with quotations—Biblical and classical—in the sermon style of the writing of the period. But it is still a puzzle to me. We know of one reader of *Seraphick Love*, one John Evelyn, gentleman and diarist. Evelyn was a Baconian who wanted Boyle to give money to found a non-religious college in which fellows would practice scientific research. Boyle gave Evelyn the manuscript instead of a check; Evelyn was moved to tears, and from here to there things moved. Wilkins was asked to call the founding meeting of the Society and the rest is history. Now, how was all this related? What is the Royal Society to a non-religious college endowed by rich men, and what is this to a theological tract called *Seraphick Love*?

I have mentioned only a few facts relating to the rational reconstruction which may be made both of the rise of the Royal Society and of the history of the incredible, seemingly nonsensical, talk about it—in the Dictionary of National Biography, in histories of the Royal Society and of science, in biographies, etc. You may think that the history of the history of science is too much. I doubt it. I find it very interesting. I find the history of science without the history of the history of science as defective as today's science without today's history of science—too defective for words. I find Pierre Menard very hard to ignore.

What I have said thus far is but an expression of a problem, and an elaborate one at that. The problem is one which may be felt as a sinking in quicksand, or expressed as, What should I study next, and why? It is as old as scholarship. It may be insoluble, or soluble only partially. Einstein said in his scientific autobiography that he had considered entering mathematics, but felt he could not solve this problem for himself as far as mathematics was concerned, and so he gave up becoming a mathematician.

What has prompted this effort to convey the feel of an intellectual quicksand is a sense of despair which has accompanied me ever since I undertook to review the Kuhn volume edited by Lakatos and Musgrave.

The volume contains two items. One is Kuhn, the other is Lakatos. Lakatos's paper, of over 100 pages, is a longer version of an essay already twice printed[1] and soon to come out once again, as a book.[2]

Lakatos has a problem on his hands, though I do not think he presents it anywhere. So here is my rational reconstruction of it. He wants to know how best to reconcile Popper's theory with the view that metaphysical theories may offer scientific research programs. This view is an interesting one. It was advocated by Descartes and many of his followers and successors, up to and including Kant. It was expressed clearly by William Whewell a century and more ago when he showed that Kepler was executing Plato's program, and, in this century, by Koyré who did the same in much more detail in regard to Galileo. Indeed it is a fairly popularly known view, since its paradigm is Greek atomism which was metaphysical and its metamorphosis has been into 19th-century chemical atomism. This paradigm also occurs in Popper's *Logik der Forschung* of 1935 as a prime argument against the positivist view of metaphysics as always opposed to science. Popper also thinks that Franklin's theory of the electron is a metaphysical theory which adumbrates the present-day scientific theory of the electron. This example may be somewhat debatable historically, but it is good enough as a hypothetical instance of metaphysics influencing science.

Though Popper endorses the theory of metaphysical research programs, it is an idea quite marginal to the main theme of his logic of scientific research. It also contradicts at least one other idea, if not more, expressed in Popper's *Logik der Forschung* at some length. Popper says in that book that we should always choose the most highly testable hypothesis, that we should not reject an empirically corroborated hypothesis unless we have a more testable substitute, and that we should not rescue a hypothesis by *ad hoc* amendments since these reduce its testability, except perhaps as a temporary stop-gap when there is no better (i.e., more testable) hypothesis. I have argued abstractly as well as historically that when a hypothesis is out of line with our metaphysics, e.g., when a hypothesis is of a continuum rather than atomistic type, no degree of testability and no amount of corroboration will induce scientists to take it seriously, that metaphysical objections such as those against action at a distance may make a scientist like Faraday reject the most corroborated theory ever, such as Newtonian mechanics. Faraday kept modifying his refuted hypotheses—and many of them maintained a low content and low degrees of testability throughout their modifications—because he stuck to his field metaphysics. And so, if we are to take the idea of metaphysical research programs more seriously than the casual remarks on it in Popper's book warrant, and if we follow it methodically, we will be more careful than Popper and have to reject, at the very least, his unqualified requirement for high testability and high regard for corroboration.

Yet, I confess, there is something more intriguing than the question of how much we should modify Popper's theory, or even of whether we should be *allowed* to modify a theory which looks askance at modifications. There is some deeper incongruity here, between two tendencies both of which I find very interesting, between soft focus and hard focus, as I shall call them. Popper's theory is of hard focus: every modified hypothesis, however slight the modification, is a new hypothesis and is to be examined on its own merit completely afresh. I find hard focus, whether in Galileo, Whewell, or Popper, delightful in its very sharpness and clarity. But I also like the soft focus which takes a law of gravity with a third-order correction to be a variant of a theory with a second-order correction, unless there is strong reason to suppose that the third-order anyway will lump the corrected version with some other theory along some broad lines. For example, Einstein's general relativity can, under simplified conditions, offer a correction to Newton's theory, yet it is better seen as a version of field metaphysics than of Newton's theory of gravity (*pace* Sir Harold Jeffreys). The theory of the body alpha, which should come up with testable results similar to some of Einstein's, is still a variant of Newtonianism. As I say, I like both hard and soft focus, and see no difficulty in appreciating some scientific ideas as hard, some as soft: I do not endorse Popper's idea of assessing the value of all scientific hypotheses by one and only one criterion; indeed I cannot even find one criterion by which to admire Galileo, Boyle, Faraday, and Planck—so different do they seem in their strong points and in the kinds of strength they exhibit. I do not see why we cannot enjoy two good photos of the same scene, one hard and one soft.

But I am talking of Lakatos. He follows Sylvain Bromberger[3] (though without reference) in maintaining that there are two kinds of acceptance of a scientific hypothesis. According to Bromberger, acceptability₁ is credibility—which, incidentally, should be hard if you go for such things as beliefs in science (I would leave belief to religion)—and acceptibility₂ is readiness to examine a hypothesis—and which, incidentally, is at times better hard but more often is better soft. Lakatos, I say, accepts this splitting of the concept of acceptability into two. He further splits the concept of refutability in three, in varying degrees of hardness and softness, and calls the hard type of refutability, which I ascribe to Popper and like very much, naive. Lakatos splits Popper himself in three ways. Since he has done it four times we now have twelve or so versions of Popper, different from each other to varying degrees. It is reminiscent of Borges's garden of forking paths. I find that Lakatos's own maze defies rational reconstruction and therefore also critical examination; it really wants a sarcastic Erasmus to do away with it all. In particular, I do not see in what sense Lakatos claims that he is a disciple of Popper and I do not know who cares. Allow me, in lieu of Erasmian sarcasm, to quote a note from the end of Lakatos's long and scholarly study (p. 182). "If the reader is in doubt about the authenticity of my reformulation of Popper's demarcation criterion, he should re-read"—I must draw attention to the tone: "If the reader is in doubt about the authenticity of my reformulation . . . he should re-read", we are told, in a rather authoritarian style, "the relevant parts of Popper [1934]"—I interrupt my quotation again to observe that it is an idiosyncracy of Popper's devotees, authentic or otherwise, to refer to his *Logik der Forschung* (1935) as a work published in 1934, at his insistence. But since we customarily refer to the *Annals of Science* or the *Journal of Symbolic Logic*, for example, with the fictitious dates imprinted on them, I think we can refer to Popper's work as '1935'. Anyway, those who doubt Lakatos's authenticity should re-read Popper [1934], if I may continue—"with Musgrave [1968] as a guide. Musgrave wrote . . . against Bartley who . . . mistakenly attributed to Popper" the criterion of demarcation which I have called hard-focussed and which Lakatos calls hard-lined, and which Watkins (p. 30), Bartley, and I ascribe to Popper and which Lakatos and Musgrave do not.

In case you are exasperated by this dreadful pedantry and detail, let me tell you that in this manner I am taking revenge for Lakatos's declaration, in the Kuhn volume, that I follow Otto Neurath, the positivist, and that I endorse an illogical theory of metaphysics which he calls the syntactic theory, and which I shall let lie.

Lakatos's excuse for bringing his maze into a Kuhn volume is this. Kuhn speaks of paradigms. In this volume Kuhn's sharpest critic is Margaret Masterman, who incidentally, although she pretends to be an admirer of his, makes mince-meat of him. She shows that he uses the word 'paradigm' in 21 different senses, that he allows for pre-paradigm and bi-paradigm science, etc. With 21 paradigms at hand, Kuhn can afford to use one of them as metaphysical research program, even if he is not very congenial to metaphysics in general. This will come easily if you agree that Popper's theory of refutability is hard-focussed, and both Lakatos and Kuhn now dislike hard focus. Kuhn himself views himself as a split-Kuhn, a Kuhn₁ and a Kuhn₂ which differ from each other, he insists, no more than the duck from the rabbit in the famous duck-or-rabbit picture. This enables him, he seems to think, to be loved both by the Popperian ducks and the non-Popperian rabbits. As we shall see, it is important that he be believed, since otherwise he is inconsistent. Toulmin finds an Ur-Kuhn, a Kuhn₀; but Kuhn corrects his dates: it is only a Kuhn₁.₅.

Jokes and profusion of scholarly nonsense aside, I do not know what to do with this wretched volume. It has an opening and closing paper by Kuhn of, respectively, 20 and 40 pages, and it has papers by Feyerabend, Lakatos, Masterman, Popper, Toulmin, Watkins, and Pearce Williams. I do not even know what problems all these papers are facing, and I have many interesting details to quote from the various papers which may or may not give an image similar to Sterne's detailed and chaotic but rather charming picture of inept provincial life.

Just to illustrate this haplessness with two points. First, Kuhn's over-concern to be sincere obliges him to mention every difference between himself and Popper—menacing or innocuous: he even compares tastes in choice of word (he dislikes the word 'refutation' as too hard). Yet he mentions, quite *en passant*, that science is "our surest example of sound knowledge". I suppose an attempt to show him on this point to be not exactly like Popper would be easy enough—but may well be dismissed as carping at a casual remark. Is there a procedure by which to decide what remark is casual? For my part, I think not. We can take problems, solutions to them, criticism of these solutions, and apply to these the time-honored rules of rational debate, Platonic, parliamentary, courtroom, perhaps even scholarly—or any other—rules which we can agree upon. Such sets of rules do include procedures concerning significance; but when it is not a case of problems, solutions, and criticisms, I know of no rules or procedures.

Secondly, let us note attitudes to criticism as displayed in this volume. Kuhn criticizes Popper. Popper recognizes Kuhn's criticism with incredible graciousness. He opens his essay by saying, "Professor Kuhn's criticism of my view about science is the most interesting one I have so far come across" (p. 51). After a page of complaints about misunderstandings of Popper's texts that even Professor Kuhn harbors in his breast, which Popper summarily dismisses as "minor", he returns to praise: "Kuhn understands me very well—better, I think, than most critics of mine I know of" (p. 52). If anyone says I envy Kuhn, I will not deny it. Kuhn has two criticisms, says Popper. First, he criticizes Popper for overlooking 'normal science' which is routine, rather dull, attempts to answer fairly minor questions. Incidentally, contributors to this volume agree that most scientists today spend their working lives entirely on 'normal science'. Popper has noticed normal science, he assures us; he was told by Phillip Frank about the unwillingness of Frank's engineering students in 1933 to think about big questions, only to be told the truth about big questions and concentrate on small ones. Yes, says Popper, today many are normal scientists, and this is an important fact. But they are bad scientists and their work is scientifically redundant: normal science is dangerous.

And thus, Kuhn's first criticism seems less than "most interesting". Nor does it show such a deep understanding—of Popper, or of anything else. Anyway, Popper rejects it—flatly and lightly. Or does he? On page 55 we read "I have always stressed the need for some dogmatism: the dogmatic scientist has an important role to play. If we give in to criticism too easily, we shall never find out where the real power of our theories lies". This couple of sentences seems to me to concede fully to Kuhn that normal science is valuable, since normal science, as Popper explains, is the most that the dogmatic scientist can allow himself to engage in. Popper anticipates my simplicity: "But this kind of dogmatism is not what Kuhn wants", he continues. And so Kuhn's criticism, as well as Popper's parry and riposte, degenerate to a comparison and a contrast of views.

Let us move, then, to Kuhn's second criticism. Popper never comes to it. There is always a first, it seems, and here is Popper's first sloppy paper; perhaps for once he does not wish his contribution to stand out too far above the level of the volume in which it appears, Instead, Popper launches a counterattack. Kuhn, he says, is an historical relativist. "No, this is not the way", he finally (p. 58) shakes his head. What a sad affair!

Kuhn's reply to Popper, incidentally, is humiliating, and I wish I knew how to rebut him, but I do not know the rules of 'compare and contrast'. Also, Kuhn repeats a point or two of criticism of Popper's endorsement of the view of metaphysics as containing scientific research programs. We can compare the verisimilitudes of Newtonian and of Einsteinian theories of gravitation, as the one is an approximation to the other; but we do not know how to compare Newtonian and Einsteinian metaphysics. (This paraphrase of the critique is mine, not Kuhn's.) I find this challenge which Kuhn repeats very interesting. But I shall not discuss metaphysics apropos of Kuhn's passing remark. I have discussed it elsewhere.[4]

Normal science is one where many scientists work in concert on many small and manageable tasks. Clearly the concert is achieved here not without some authority and some measure of repression. Does Kuhn like all this?, asks Feyerabend, who, in this volume, is Trotskyite of all things. Kuhn does not dare say so openly, says Feyerabend, but he hints that he does. Lakatos says similar things. Rubbish, says Kuhn; he loves normal science and says so out loud. Rebels cannot exist by themselves; to be a rebel you must live in a society which keeps up with the Joneses. To say that everyone is a rebel is absurd; there are revolutions, and they are delicious; but science is hard work and not all pie.

This is important to Kuhn. He does not know what he means by 'paradigm'; he does not know what a paradigm is; he does not much care whether there is a paradigm in the first place. A paradigm, anyway, is only that which holds normal science together. There are myriads of small problems and myriads of modes of attacking them. Allow for diversity and you get chaos. Hence we must have authority imposing unanimity. If you love science you cannot love only the greats, from Archimedes to Zermelo; you must see that science is an ant-heap and love every contributor to every small learned journal, including the *Journal of Fluid Mechanics for Normal Range Temperatures and Viscosities*.

To a large extent Lakatos agrees with this. He points out, against the hard-focus view, that historians of science omit a lot and apply a lot of hindsight in order to get "instant rationality". I like his point and his expression. Did you know that Michelson viewed his experiment as a crucial experiment between Fizeau and Stokes and thought Stokes's idea had been verified? Did you know that he therefore expected an ether drift on a mountain, failed to find it, and was nonplussed? Did you know that Dirac believed that beta-decay refutes the law of conservation of energy and confirms the Bohr-Kramers-Slater theory of statistical conservation of energy? Did you know that Bohr put his authority against this and in defense of the neutrino? Lakatos tells all this and much more in racy snippets, much of which is exciting and some of which is true. It will take too much to explain why his story of the neutrino is more interesting, though in need of further and more careful rational reconstruction, than his story of Michelson. Anyway, let me say, I find his snippets tantalizing and deserving of expansion. (I have expanded one of them myself in *Mind*, vol. 76, 1966.)[5]

Lakatos seems to agree with Kuhn who seems to disagree with Popper, but they both say that Lakatos goes with Popper against Kuhn. We can now worry about reconstructions not only of facts but also of disagreement concerning them. Pierre Menard already belongs to history, but he is also already out-of-date. I am going to write a Biblical play called 'The Trials and Tribulations of Eldad and Meidad, Scribes', to illustrate how much work can be put into a disagreement about whether and where a disagreement has taken place to begin with. Did Pharaoh really ever disagree with Moses? What was the real issue between them? Come and see.

Unlike Tristram Shandy and Pierre Menard, Eldad and Meidad may hopefully remain fictitious characters. We may hope to stick to our guns and say this: Dear friends, unless we and you agree to differ, and agree reasonably clearly about what it is that we differ about, let's forget it all. In particular, let's not take 'compare and contrast' exercises too seriously. When Watkins accuses Kuhn of not contrasting Popper's hard-focusing with Kuhn's soft-focusing, and when Lakatos blames Bartley for his attribution of hard-focusing to Popper (following Popper's lamentable *ad hominem* reply to Bartley, I suppose)[6], one may only ask if it is not sweeter to exegetize on Biblical texts than on Popper's. The Talmudic lore tells us moving stories about bitter quarrels between exegetes, and of subsequent calming of the spirits, and the resultant learning to enjoy sharp exchanges for the greater glory of God. Will the Popperian lore of the future have such a happy ending too? Or will it happily come to an end?

Back to Kuhn, who merely strayed into a family to-do in which someone had the brilliant idea that he could bring unanimity. Watkins has shown (p. 26), in the most mature paper in this volume, that Kuhn views science as a closed society, that according to Kuhn himself today's science much resembles medieval theology (p. 33)—not modern theology, where disagreement is so common. (As if closed societies have no rifts.) Feyerabend shows (p. 200) in the least Teutonic paper he has ever written, that even safecracking is a normal science with its normal jobs, crises due to tightening security measures, and revolutions which are inventions of new techniques. I have mentioned Popper's point, which may be read as the criticism that technical college students like normal science more than normal research scientists. Kuhn takes all this very lightly. I think he has lost a great opportunity to give up a false view.

It was very hard for me to take sides in the matter at hand, and it was only with difficulty, and aided by a stimulating argument with Charles M. Sawyer, Jr., that I found out why. There are various components to normal science. First, there is a healthy aspect to it, and I wish to sing its praise. Anyone will understand this who has observed the misery of the worker doomed to a routine job, and the relief that by comparison is felt by the skilled worker able to exhibit pride in work. I cannot here distinguish between the skilled worker without a college degree, with an engineering degree, or a B.Sc.—who is the paradigm of Kuhn's normal scientist. I am opposed to Frank's and Popper's sense of superiority to these fellows, though, of course, Frank was at liberty to teach them or to go to America as he wished. There is, further, a rather distasteful but not objectionable aspect to normal science, the desire to keep up with the Joneses, to be like the other family. And there is also the objectionable side of it, the repressive measures which, though to an extent permitted in a democratic society, insofar as they are used in such clubs as the professional societies, colleges, etc. are at least in spirit always very antidemocratic.

How does Kuhn know that there is agreement in science? How does he know that it is desirable? Ben Franklin said, Faraday said, Oliver Heaviside said, Boltzmann said, Professors Tom Jones and Dick Smith here say, disagreement in science is very important. These are scientists, abnormal, normal, and super-normal. Daniel Bell has noted in Holton's best-selling *Science and Culture* that in society at large scientists were not Establishment until recently and rather tended to be anti-Establishment. Only lately has this changed—since World War II—and it worries Bell very much. Is it possible that the latest aberration is what Kuhn finds normal? What is the normal historian of science? Is he a scientist? Is he following a paradigm? Is Kuhn's *Structure of Scientific Revolutions* a paradigm for historians of science to follow? Is Kuhn, then, as the leader in the field, permitted to make a revolution and impose it on his authority and say-so? Do we then have to believe him that there must be unanimity because he authoritatively says so, or does he say so because it is true? (Incidentally, he says he is not an absolutist about truth, and so he cannot say his view of unanimity is absolutely true.) Where does he observe unanimity and how does he measure its degree? I think this is all poppycock and the one and only foundation stone of his philosophy (and of Polanyi's). I think he would do well to revise it drastically and make a small revolution in his own backyard before he launches one on us.

When all is said and done, there remains the quicksand on which science is built. There are too many facts to observe, too many questions to ask, too many explorations to approach from too many angles, and reconstructions of all we did and reconstructed. There are too many seeming agreements and seeming disagreements to reconstruct, past and present. What are we to do? First, in a true democratic spirit, we should say that everyone can pick and choose his own study and his own mode of attack. True, it happens that we want to share our meager knowledge, and this entails the desirability of some co-ordination. But the co-ordination can be democratic, it need not be authoritarian. For this we need a steering committee for science: what topic is agenda? There is only one answer: that on which you make more people follow you becomes more agenda. They may follow it like sheep or like interested parties: there is no authority in science as in the Catholic Church; science is either a democracy or a herd; Kuhn may yet be our fearless leader. Metaphysical research programs, too, become agenda either when the herd follows them—or, democratically, if and when they stir the public imagination. But they are rare and problematic in any case. The agenda for today in philosophy, I feel, or I suggest, is the agenda itself: how do we select problems to study? Kuhn and Lakatos answer this problem, but all too poorly. We have to try again. Historians of science, too, may wonder how they pick a problem to study. This is an interesting question, and a vital one for those who are soon to choose a thesis-topic.

NOTES

1. Imre Lakatos, 'Criticism and the Methodology of Scientific Research Programmes', *Proceedings of the Aristotelian Society*, 1968-69, pp. 149-86, and 'Changes in the Problem of Inductive Logic' in Imre Lakatos and Alan Musgrave (eds.), *Problems of Inductive Logic. Proceedings of the International Colloquium in the Philosophy of Science*, London 1965, vol. 2. Amsterdam: North Holland Publishing Co., 1968, pp. 315-417.

2. The much-lamented early demise of Professor Imre Lakatos precludes the completion of this project. Though announced as completed, it seems not to have begun.

3. Sylvain Bromberger, 'A Theory about the Theory of Theory and about the Theory of Theories,' in B. Baumrin (ed.), *Philosophy of Science. The Delaware Seminar*, vol. 2, New York and London 1963, pp. 79–105, esp. 104–05.

4. See my 'The Nature of Scientific Problems and their Roots in Metaphysics', in Mario A. Bunge (ed.), *The Critical Approach to Science and Philosophy: In Honor of Karl R. Popper*, Glencoe, IL: Free Press, Collier-Macmillan, London 1964, pp. 189–211, reprinted in my *Science in Flux*, 1975.

5. See my 'Sensationalism', *Mind*, 76, 1966, 1–24, reprinted in my *Science in Flux*, 1975.

6. K. R. Popper, 'Remarks on the Problems of Demarcation and Rationality', in Imre Lakatos and Alan Musgrave (eds.), *Problems in the Philosophy of Science. Proceedings of the International Colloquium in the Philosophy of Science*, London 1965, vol. 3. Amsterdam: North Holland Publishing Co., 1968, pp. 88–102.

— 29 —

AFTER LAKATOS
the end of an era

1. THE MAN WHO WOULD BE A PHILOSOPHER KING

Imre Lakatos fled Hungary in 1956, where he had had a stormy political career and began a humble mathematical career. He worked in Cambridge toward his Ph.D. until 1959, and moved to the philosophy department of the London School of Economics. He stayed there till his untimely death in 1974. His writings, republished posthumously in three volumes, and the four volumes of proceedings of the celebrated 1965 London Conference which he edited together with Alan Musgrave, are more or less his whole output, but his career was meteoric. Two conferences were organized for the study of his philosophy and led to two volumes of proceedings each. The *Boston Studies in the Philosophy of Science* series includes a volume of essays in his memory.

The present situation regarding the philosophy of Lakatos is probably best reflected in the first volume of the proceedings of the second conference, Gerard Radnitzky and Gunnar Andersson, editors, *Progress and Rationality in Science*. It is a volume bound to remain noticed, as it signifies the end of an era, the era of the Lakatos school of philosophy: he founded it in 1965 and it died a few years after his death.

In 1965 Lakatos convened in London a star-studded conference on modern philosophy of mathematics and science. I was not privileged to attend, yet heard much about it and discussed it with Lakatos himself in quite some detail both before and after the event. The picture that emerges is myth-like so that the truth of its detail cannot be guaranteed—especially

---

This essay in response to *Progress and Rationality in Science*, edited by Gerard Radnitzky and Gunnar Andersson (*Boston Studies in the Philosophy of Science*, 59, 1979), appeared in *Philosophia*, 16, 1986 under the title 'God Saves Us From Our Friends: Enemies We Have No More'.

since the chief informant was not averse to trying his hand at the gentle art of prevarication. Nevertheless, the myth is potent and significant, and the following version is a true ethnography of myth. It is said that a few significant events occurred in that conference. Rudolf Carnap and Karl Popper, the old antagonists, went arm-in-arm into the lecture hall to debate their differences. Lakatos read a detailed and scholarly paper on the controversy between the two, pretending that he deemed Carnap a serious and able thinker. Thomas S. Kuhn had a philosophically significant debate with Popper and his disciples. A quarrel between Popper and his close disciple and friend W. W. Bartley, III, began and led to a big rift. Waves of excitement followed; it was the talk of the philosophical community for quite some time. End of myth.

The myth contains truths (Lakatos loved to explain why he held Carnap in contempt) as well as falsehoods (the debate with Kuhn, he agreed in a sober moment, was not serious). It is a myth of origin: the founding of a school of thought. A school sprang into being, with a history, an opposition, an apostate, and a place in the sun. It is scarcely credible that the whole complex process was conceived, designed, and executed by one man; yet this is how it looks in the light of many conversations with Lakatos before and after the event, in the light of many details that are better forgotten, and viewing the Lakatos phenomenon as a whole.

The Lakatos era is over; the volume at hand is sufficient testimony to that. Not that the contributors to the volume admit it: schools seldom officially close down. The surviving members usually go on teaching the gospel until a better alternative appears; or until they die out. There is absolutely no moral objection to the mere teaching of defunct doctrines; otherwise all histories of ideas would be immoral. It is not morally or intellectually wrong to doubt the force of new criticism or to hope to see it answered, or at least met by a minor doctrinal face-lift. In fairness toward those who misjudge deadly criticism as harmless, we may notice that we are all prone to be mistaken in this way, especially since most new criticism is indeed harmless, and that historical perspective always helps assess the force of criticism by altering situational logic: when the position from which a criticism is launched is made clear and developed, it is much easier to accept the alternative plus the criticism it contains than it was to assess the criticism by itself. Moreover, since good criticism is rare, it is dangerous to declare any new criticism good before it has gained public acceptance. It is thus quite proper to overlook current criticism prior to its public acceptance; this is why we appreciate those who take such criticism seriously early in the day and why we appreciate all the more the trail-blazing critic of an accepted doctrine—for example, Lakatos.

Thus, we need neither admire nor condemn the mental inertia of the adherents to popular doctrines. Nevertheless, it is admittedly not very truthful to recognize the validity, or even the mere possible validity, of a given piece of criticism and yet remain silent about it. There are two reasons, observes Popper, for not doing this. First, concealing a difficulty prevents people who may be able to overcome it from making a contribution. Second, not acknowledging a criticism while effecting a doctrinal face-lift in order to meet it, one makes the doctrinal change silently or surreptitiously, especially when it is small. Surreptitious change is usually effected among the members of the school's inner circle, and this makes the school into a closed society. Surreptitious change may also lead anyone to confuse the original doctrine with the face-lifted variant of it.

To conclude this point, those who invent criticism and who freely accept criticism are admirable. We should not censure those who accept only constructive criticism, therefore, since this would be to condemn mediocrity. The demand for constructive criticism, however, is evil as the demand to be mediocre as well as the legitimation of public denial of privately admitted criticism, a denial which is both dishonest and conducive to surreptitious changes. We therefore may argue against the demand for constructive criticism but not against the practice of it; and we may likewise expose surreptitious changes but not as necessarily immoral.

It is not pleasant, nonetheless, to say of anyone that he has effected a surreptitious change since it sounds like saying that he has acted irresponsibly. When Popper presented Plato's works as a major surreptitious change, he did not charge him with irresponsibility and even expressed his highest admiration for both his motives and ideas; yet he was taken to be a debunker of Plato, both intellectually and morally. Sir Karl Popper's doctrine may be summed up thus: criticism is both a mark of understanding of and a tribute to the criticized; therefore, criticism ought always to be sought and whenever possible welcomed. By contradistinction, Lakatos's doctrine is: criticism is, in itself, useless, and when neat should be discarded: only constructive criticism does and ever should count.

These are two doctrines in their barest forms. Details obscure them and help effect surreptitious changes. The volume at hand is, briefly, the legitimation Watkins gave to a series of surreptitious changes, some of which are due to Popper, some due to Lakatos, some of his own making; yet I do not wish to declare him, or Popper, irresponsible. If any of them acted irresponsibly, it was Imre Lakatos; and irresponsibly by his own lights. He flirted with pre-Popperian ideas, and was extolling good old inductivism in a Popperian garb. But he did so with too much fanfare—as a mere crowd-pleaser. He intimated to me that, once in a position of power, he intended to compensate W. W. Bartley, III and other victims of his charades. (Quite possibly he planned to effect a surreptitious change away from inductivism once he had consolidated his power. But there is no telling: he died too young.)

The image of Lakatos presented here is, of course, controversial; but in factual detail it is supportable by much documentation—including his private files (which should be opened to the public one day).

2. IMRE LAKATOS SAT ON A FENCE

Popper declares that traditional philosophy of science answers two cardinal problems: the problem of the demarcation of science from metaphysics and pseudo-science (What theory is scientific?), and the problem of induction (How do we gain theoretical knowledge from experience?). The solution to the problem of induction is also the solution to the problem of demarcation. Let us accept this tentatively.

Let us first take learning from experience. The inductivists consider it to be endorsing the theory best supported by empirical information. They therefore look for a criterion of empirical support. By contrast, Popper proposes the view that not support but refutation is the process of learning from experience. But there is no need to search for a criterion of refutation: it is already offered by formal logic proper: an observation report refutes a theory if and only if it contradicts it. Let us take, then, the demarcation of science. Those who believe in support demarcate science as the body of supportable (or of supported) theory; in parallel, Popper demarcates science as the body of refutable (and of refuted) theory.

Popper uses the logical asymmetry between the ability of negative instances to refute and the inability of positive instances to verify as an argument in favor of the view that theoretical learning from experience is through negative instances as against the view that theoretical learning from experience is through positive instances. He thus invites the criticism that negative evidence is problematic too. This is the most obvious move. It was made by Popper's contemporaries in 1935, soon after publication of his classic *Logik der Forschung*, and it was Lakatos's parting shot. In his posthumous contribution to Paul Arthur Schilpp's *The Philosophy of Karl Popper*,[1] and in a posthumous discussion note (originally a radio talk, 'Science and Pseudo-science', *Conceptus*, 24 [1974], 5–9), he stressed that Popper is in fundamental error, simply because refutation is no more conclusive than verification, that only constructive criticism ever counts.

Let it be so. Let us assume that Popper's solution is based on an invalid argument. Nevertheless, the situation remains clear: the inductivists recommend that a scientific theory be supported, and that its value be assessed by the empirical support it has attained; Popper recommends that it be refuted, and that its value be assessed by its refutation. According to inductivists and according to Popper, the value of a theory is in its inviting the search for the discovery of its confirmation and of its refutation respectively. This holds regardless of the relative merit of inductivism and of refutationism.

What seems confusing is Popper's view of refuting instances. Had he said that all refuting instances are unproblematic and final he would be clear, and clearly in error. He said, however, that refuting evidence is problematic and tentative. Since observation reports are scientific, and since in his view scientific theories are tentative, any observation report that is theory-laden must also be problematic and tentative, not final. And all observation reports, says Popper, are theory-laden. Why, then, should the problematic character of observations make positive evidence problematic and not negative evidence? Because, says Bartley, the inductivist must reject any solution that is not final as insufficient justification, but Popper is under no such obligation.

Enter Lakatos. Lakatos did not care about symmetry or asymmetry, about whether empirical evidence is questionable or not. He was excited by the idea of learning from criticism and found in his mathematical background ample opportunity to exemplify the thesis that we learn from criticism without permitting the doubtfulness of empirical evidence to arise: mathematical criticism is not at all empirical. For this Lakatos had to change some of his views, and endorse Popper's view of logic. He thereby made Popper withdraw his own logicism, with results that have yet to be assessed. It is clear that for his *Proofs and Refutations* and his 'Infinite Regress in the Foundations of Mathematics' posterity owes Lakatos a debt of gratitude: he changed the scene irretrievably and by handling a matter no less vexing than the problem of empirical evidence, namely the problem of mathematical or scientific rigor.

For, rigor is in mathematics what evidence is in physics: justification; the ground for validation. That rigor has an intuitive appeal is obvious to anyone who has read about Kepler's struggle with eight minutes of an arc of a difference between conclusions from theory and from observations, or about Russell's dissatisfaction with his Cambridge mathematical education and his admiration for the Continental views on the foundations of analysis. Yet the question is: why is rigor such a benefit? Kant said: rigor is proof. Scientific experience, for example, differs from everyday experience in being cast in a mathematical language. William Whewell used rigor as a means of verification. He said, unless we deduce our test statement rigorously from theory and then compare it with fact, the test will be unable to overthrow a false theory and therefore it will likewise fail to verify a true one. Some philosophers of mathematics went further and saw in mathematical rigor not only the means of validation, but the sole criterion of merit.

Popper's theory not only explains the value of rigor in science, but also its limit. Thus Popper is the first to explain the known phenomenon of the negative value of excessive rigor. Rigor is solely a means for testing a theory and both deduction and experiment should be made rigorous enough to be made to clash in case the theory is false, but no more. Lakatos cannot use this idea, yet by replacing test with criticism, the idea becomes useful for his Popperian philosophy of mathematics. This is an enormous triumph because excess rigor is a worse and commoner pest in mathematics than in science; also, it is justified by the leading school of the philosophy of mathematics which values rigor as such. For Lakatos, proper rigor increases with mathematical growth, with the improvement of both criticism and theory.

Lakatos's *bêtes noires* were those who admired rigor as such, the formalists. Yet he was savage in his *Proofs and Refutations* against those who reduced rigor in order to escape criticism.

There is for Lakatos a problem parallel to the problem raised against Popper: Just as Popper was attacked with the question, 'Is empirical refutation clinching?' so could Lakatos be attacked about mathematical criticism. Both Popper and Lakatos were unmoved. Both said: either you admit the criticism and thus are forced by logic to reject the theory it clashes with, or you reject the criticism. Popper made a rule: do not reject criticism. He then said: you may temporarily reject it at times. This is a confusion, yet we can replace it with Popper's rule of simplicity: accept criticism and refutation when and only when it is simpler to do so. Lakatos had a parallel and more general strategy. He called the rejection of criticism "monster-barring" and noticed that doing so is at times progressive, at times degenerative. He also noted that the tendency towards excessive rigor is degenerative. And a progressive problem-shift, he seems to have suggested, is intuitively easily distinguishable from a degenerative one. Clearly, Lakatos launched with one stroke a few brand-new solutions and raised a few new problems in their wake. Again, some will view this with favor, others with chagrin, and still others, the justificationists, will have to view his contribution plainly unfavorably.

Lakatos was aware of the problems his work raised. He intended to work on them. But he moved in the meantime to the philosophy of science, where his work met instant and stupendous success: it won the esteem of members of a large and heterogeneous group who shared the following attitude towards Popper's philosophy: they (a) rejected it, (b) appreciated it, and (c) could not bring themselves to publicly express their appreciation. Lakatos evidently touched a nerve: he was a wise Popperian who knew that criticism is so very important. Yet he was even wiser: he knew that negative results do not suffice. And riding the waves of popularity, Lakatos finally went all the way and declared that criticism is never clinching and so refutation is impossible, that when refutation is accepted it is accepted only because it is backed by a better alternative to the idea criticized, so that it is always the positive, not the negative, that does the clinching. He rejected Popper's falsificationism as naive and extolled his own total rejection of falsificationism as if it were a sophisticated falsificationism.

Lakatos changed his opinions about many issues, especially regarding criticism. He had a way of stressing the continuity in his work and slurring over the discontinuities. Unfortunately we have a short-circuit here, since the main change that occurred in the philosophy of Lakatos concerns criticism and continuity. By the standard defended by the later Lakatos it is proper to stress continuity even at the cost of toning down criticism; by the standards of early Lakatos's *magnum opus*, *Proofs and Refutations*, the opposite holds. Can we introduce theories of continuities without toning down criticism? Let us postpone this question for one paragraph. What matters in this paragraph is that Lakatos never repudiated his *Proofs and Refutations*, though he knew that the differences between his earlier and his later work were conspicuous. He told me he was eager to return to the philosophy of mathematics, but he felt that the time was not ripe—meaning either, uncharitably, that he wanted to be better-established first, or, charitably, that he felt his philosophy of science was still too defective; probably he just lost perspective and could not decide.

3. IMRE LAKATOS HAD A BIG PROBLEM-SHIFT

Lakatos modelled his first and most significant work, his *Proofs and Refutations*, after Popper's philosophy of science; even his title alludes to Popper's *Conjectures and Refutations*. His work, not surprisingly, has thus absorbed some of the weaknesses of Popper's philosophy, especially his refusal to see trends in the growth of science, much less account for them. This was rooted in Popper's staunch critical attitude, in his refusal to see one theory as a mere modification of its predecessor, in his strict demand that every variant of a theory stand on its own feet and submit to tests afresh. Of course, there is no contradiction between the claim that a theory is but a minor variant of another and the claim that it does not inherit any of its predecessor's credit and must be assessed afresh. Nevertheless, those who have stressed the lack of inheritance, Whewell and Popper in particular, refused to notice continuity, and those who saw continuity, Duhem in particular, refused to see discontinuity and denied that criticism is ever clinching. The scene changed somewhat recently, with some authors allowing the history of science both continuities and discontinuities, especially Michael Polanyi and, following him, Thomas S. Kuhn. They belong to the uncritical camp, or the post-critical, as Polanyi calls it. It is embarrassing to side with the irrationalists on this point. Popper tacitly and surreptitiously vacillates these days between his old, critical position and a view more favorable to the admission of continuities and the existence of trends in the process of the growth of science. And indeed the theory of trends in the history of science need not be irrationalist.

Popper's initial refusal to take account of trends was not premised on a denial of their existence; it was not a mistake but an oversight. The penalty for an oversight is that those concerned with the problems overlooked by an author may find him uninteresting; if they still find him interesting, they simply notice that one cannot handle all problems together. This is the most obvious fact about such matters: we are interested in the classic authors (in different fields) despite their obvious ignorance of today's problems.

Hence, the logic of discovering counter-examples to, or of criticism of, or of disagreement with a theory fundamentally differs from the logic of finding its limits, or of showing its failure to handle or solve a pertinent problem. Yet, incredible as it sounds, the first author to stress this point and to elaborate on it and on its significance is the author of *Proofs and Refutations*, the self-same Imre Lakatos who later confused the issue he was a pioneer in clarifying, by pretending that Popper's omission, the absence of a discussion of trends in his early classic work, by itself invalidates Popper's views and amounts to their refutation. He even went so far as to attack Popper in this way while overlooking the obvious fact that his own early classic work suffers from the very oversight, and even hinting that it does not so suffer.

Theories of trends in the history of science should explain why some pairs of scientific theories are variants of each other, others not; why some resemblances between theories are superficial, others deep. The traditional idea is that significantly similar theories belong to the same trend when their similarity constitutes the sharing of an intellectual framework, a framework that constitutes, largely, a system of metaphysical presuppositions. This, to repeat, is a traditional idea; Lakatos has claimed that it is adumbrated[2] in his *Proofs and Refutations* and that I have picked it up from there. In this way he admitted that he had noticed that the center of action was here, and that he was joining the game. He combined the traditional idea of the development of science within metaphysical frameworks with Popper's idea that, whereas science is refutable, metaphysics is confirmable. If so, and if we can lump together a series of variants of a scientific theory and identify them all with their metaphysical framework, then, perhaps, we can declare the framework to be the real scientific theory unfolding itself in that series and conclude that science is confirmable rather than refutable. This, really, is the sum total of the Lakatos insight and contribution to the field. It does not work, of course, and on many counts. Its merit is that it brought inductivism into the Popperian camp; it is the merit of any Trojan horse. Perhaps it has also the merit of synthesizing inductivism with Hegelianism. Amazing.

The shift Lakatos has attempted to effect on Popperian philosophy was not a mere name-shift, though that is how it started, as W. W. Bartley, III, has observed. Lakatos's real shift was from intellectual to political problems. For, once the name-shift had to be defended as an intellectual achievement, the role of criticism had to be played down, the significance of constructive criticism had to be exaggerated by endorsing the silly proposal to reject valid criticism until an alternative to the criticized theory could be found: Lakatos simply denied that any scientific theory could ever be refuted plain and simple. In the history of science a great number of scientific theories have been presented to the world, tested, refuted, and at once deemed false by the students of the problems they came to solve. The latest such example, perhaps, is to be found in last year's scientific literature. Those who want an outstanding example may prefer the Bohr-Kramers-Slater theory of 1924. But the Lakatosians need not be moved by my refutation. After all, they deny that refutation is at all possible.

The idea that there is no refutation in science is very common today, and is often presented by the mere use of the word "disconfirmation". This move is pointless. It makes the contrast between the inductivists and Popper only slightly different: they recommend seeking confirmations and he recommends seeking disconfirmations. Also, this is plainly illogical, since the admission of any number of positive instances does not in itself verify a hypothesis, whereas the admission of contrary instances does refute it, so that when in debate a contrary instance is introduced, at the very least the party refusing to admit it as evidence is obliged by logic to seek an excuse. Pierre Duhem said that an excuse could always be found, and he may have been right. But he never said that therefore criticism could be dismissed; in order to tone down criticism in general he proposed to empty science of all its informative content except for the content of empirical observations. Lakatos wanted to tone down criticism too, yet he decidedly refrained from the move proposed by Duhem. The question is, by what means did he propose to tone down criticism? Nothing. Nor could he declare that criticism does not ever in itself succeed because we can always refuse to accept it, that it does not exist because we can destroy it. All that Lakatos said was: it is unreasonable to admit that a theory is false unless it can be replaced. Hence, the admission that the theory of Bohr, Kramers, and Slater was refuted was then unreasonable; which is absurd. For, the honest search for the truth, be the truth pleasant or not, includes the unqualified readiness to accept any criticism if and when it seems valid (*Phaedo*, *Gorgias*), not before, and not when it ceases to seem valid. Naive refutationism is for lovers of the truth, then, and sophisticated refutationism is but opium for the intellectuals.

End of background information; next comes a review of *Progress and Rationality in Science*.

4. ALL THE LONDON SCHOOL OF ECONOMICS HORSE

The London School of Economics group cannot remain loyal to Popper, young and old, and to Lakatos too, without some thorough and wide-scope reappraisal. They do not do this; in the volume at hand they play down the inconsistencies like loyal members of any other school. Were Popper and Lakatos not such great philosophers, and were their maneuvers not a threat that their great contributions be forgotten, perhaps we could ignore the volume at hand.

Without a framework to decide which items to report and discuss it is impossible to review such a book. Here is an example. Of the 400 pages, a two-line point plus a footnote out of Noretta Koertge's important paper already call for much commentary.

Koertge says, "Popper believed that most statements found in science lay in the falsifiable category" (p. 271), adding in a note that Watkins has found exceptions, such as "every metal has a melting point." She is familiar enough with elementary science to be able to choose good examples. Presumably she knows that the example she cites is falsified by experience: a metal may sublimate rather than melt, and thus have no fixed melting point. Now, such a metal exists, and is usually known as calcium. Certainly she can conclude that a falsified hypothesis is falsifiable. Hence, a little attention to detail would have prevented this slip. Moreover, she could easily take another example, such as, "there exists a particle, identical with the electron in all but one property: it has only one hundredth or one thousandth of the electron's mass or charge." Since good examples are easy to find, it is hard to explain her ascription of a bad one to Watkins with no reference. Let me apologize for the pedantry of noting that the alternative example presented here comes from the reply Watkins gave to Hempel in the late 1950s in his response to Hempel's criticism of Watkins's view regarding the existential claims that science is full of. It is easy to convince the reader that any testable theory is equivalent to a set of statements each of which is untestable in isolation: very few examples come to mind of statements testable in isolation, in any sense of the expression, even if one tries hard.

The interest of all this is clear: Lakatos said we can always blame an auxiliary hypothesis for the failure of our predictions to come true. Koertge therefore asks, can there be a theory testable with no need for an auxiliary hypothesis? But if she found any, Lakatos would have simply used another kind of excuse: he said, every theory had a hard core and a protective belt; hence he had a ready excuse for every refutation conceived. Hence, Koertge's strategy is not well devised.

What is a reviewer to do in such a situation? He cannot overlook sloppiness, he cannot and should not make an issue of it either. He has to warn the reader, and even suggest that the work be rewritten if he thinks it worthwhile, so as to free it from its bugs. But how many bugs can be tolerated? When can a work be saved and when is it worth while to try and save it, or at least an insight it might contain? A reviewer can only make suggestions, mention what may be worthwhile insights, or recommend or promise another try.

These are my rules. I will try to follow them. But the above example already shows a little more. Anyone who has participated in an informal and fluid debate knows that a statement uttered in the heat of the moment can be almost at once placed in the right framework and sound plausible, or the converse. This freedom is at times very enjoyable, when the purpose is heuristic, when a half-baked idea pops up and we are willing to spend some time on it and try to fit it this way or that, to this frame or that, at this cost or that—all in order to see what can come of it. This same freedom is at times also most frustrating, when the debate is a game of one-upmanship. Now, in the volume at hand Watkins blames Feyerabend for playing the frustrating game of one-upmanship. Feyerabend scowls and protests that he plays the game of heuristic. Since science never is a finished product, he adds, it always is heuristic anyway. Rather odd though this is, one cannot deny it is provocative: though almost no formulation is final (except in a post-mortem of a theory; Feyerabend forgets this), we must ask: how final should a formulation be before heuristic exits and criticism enters? Oh, yes, Feyerabend will say, they coexist; and he will be significantly right in some context. But in the context of a reviewer wondering what poor formulation to make a fuss about and what to correct silently, this question is a good one, and Feyerabend forces me to articulate it so as to make me skip his many silly points and obvious mistakes that seem deliberately planted in order to distract.

In what follows the search for a framework within which statements make good sense will precede the task of critically examining them. The search may fail regularly, or some part of the book under review or all of it may pass the initial test, opening the road to the next test, to the examination of the correctness of the sensible points in it. The most obvious candidate for a framework for the Radnitzky-Andersson volume may very well be the London School of Economics school of philosophy.

This school of philosophy, or this name for it, is new. Who belongs to this school? Present members of the philosophy department of the London School of Economics? This excludes Popper and Lakatos. Past members too? This includes myself and Bartley. Both options, then, are absurd. What remains? An intensional definition? For this we need a definite school doctrine, and the conflict between Popper and Lakatos prevents the school from having a definite doctrine. Extensional? For this we need a list of members. In a pinch, ostensive, perhaps? Ostensive definitions are troublesome in any case, but at least we normally can use our intellectual framework to help us point at something; hence, this device will not help to specify an intellectual framework. Unless a school's doctrine crystallizes soon, it will have to disintegrate. We have in the volume at hand four position papers, in which this task ought to be performed.

Position papers can be written within a framework, on the supposition that the framework is accepted by all parties to a dispute. Political position papers often enough declare by name the intellectual frameworks within which they are written in order to exclude certain opponents from a given dispute; and quite legitimately so, of course. Philosophers too can do so; a position paper can be written within the analytic school or within the phenomenological school, or amongst Marxists, etc. Are these position papers within a given framework? To say that they are or are not within the Popper framework would be to prejudge the issue. This need not matter: the intellectual framework need not be a philosophy of a given school, or else there would be none for inter-school debates. In this volume there clearly is a debate between people who are not all members of one school. Yet it is hard to say on internal evidence that Koertge still belongs or Ernan McMullin still does not belong to the London School. For the sake of "thematic unity" the editors have delegated all papers dealing with "the philosophical presuppositions, the limits and implications of scientific theorizing" to the second volume (p. x). And so, all that the editors have left for this volume is the said "thematic unity".

We may take recourse, then, to the editors' introduction. The introduction is, no doubt, crafty and very carefully written. It offers some background material, including the following claim—which is becoming increasingly easy to endorse, incidentally: "Popper's criticism of inductivism," and of conventionalism too, we may add, "and his proposal of falsificationism as a basic method of science, has generated one of the main intellectual confrontations in 20th century philosophy of science" (p. 4). They also seem to endorse Popper's view (see, e.g., the clause in the introduction's last sentence), though it is by now outdated or confused. As background material they also offer a bit of classical justificationism, especially inductivism, a bit of Thomas S. Kuhn, a bit of Imre Lakatos, and a conjecture about Kuhn's influence on Lakatos. (This conjecture seems plausible enough, but is hard to examine, since Lakatos's views did not congeal enough to justify the study of their origins in critical detail.) The editors do what is expected of good editors: they introduce the papers of the volume while giving a preview of their content with emphasis on the strong points of the papers and on the "thematic unity" of the book. They use Watkins's own idiosyncratic way of introducing classical justificationism as the background to their introduction of Popper, and this as the background to the volume, which is all excellent. They also present problems of refutationism, as they phrase it, and differences of opinion as they appear to them. The introduction is so seductive that it looks like an excellent overview and so a model review. And so it is very easy to miss at first the strange fact that the introduction skips introducing the two leading position papers.

This is no criticism; on the contrary, it is praise: the editors discovered an elegant way out of a predicament. But this way out is not open to a reviewer in the same predicament. They were able to avoid the task of summarizing the position papers since they reproduce them. A reviewer must try to sum up if he can. I expect to fail, and let no one complain that the devil's advocate is biassed, since biassed he should indeed try to be, though fair. Readers can check how fair a reviewer is, and when in doubt look up the volume under review, and even auxiliary material, especially the chief writings of the *dramatis personae*.

5. ALL THE LONDON SCHOOL OF ECONOMICS MEN

"The Popperian tradition"—so begins Watkins's presentation—"is opposed to *criterion philosophies*." What a strange sentence! The subject denotes an entity that is either non-existent, or embryonic, or diffuse, and at least problematic. The descriptive phrase in italics that is its object is a neologism. But the verb is clear. Presumably the statement implies that Popper dislikes offering criteria. Yet he has offered a criterion of demarcation of science as a solution to one of the two *Grundprobleme* in the field, as well as a criterion or criteria to distinguish valuable metaphysical systems, and a possible criterion of rational belief (not possibly a criterion, but a possible criterion). A footnote by Watkins explains by offering a reference to and a quote from a work by Popper: "I do not propose any 'criterion' for the choice of scientific hypotheses." Why is the word designating any criterion used in quotes in Popper's passage? Does not Popper propose in his *Logik der Forschung* of 1935 the rule that science choose the most highly falsifiable extant hypothesis? Did he ever explicitly withdraw his proposal? It is all a mystery to me. Still, perhaps a criterion philosophy is the claim that criteria are required so as to prevent misconduct. But then Popper explicitly says this when he introduces a criterion for rejecting observation reports: not offering a criterion to that end, he says, invites dogmatism, heaven forbid. Leaving Popper aside, we may note that the lead position paper opens with a declaration supported by a quote that repudiates the search for criteria, though it is the only theme of the book that may offer it the alleged "thematic unity". This is not to reject the search for criteria in general. On the contrary, philosophy is but the critical search for criteria. As to criteria for choice of hypotheses, the choice depends on the purpose it serves. We can choose to study, examine, compare, apply, teach, derive morals from, believe, admire, or do other things with, any hypothesis. And we may choose simultaneously different hypotheses to different ends. Yet this volume leaves the choice between these different kinds of choice undetermined. It is therefore, as a whole, barely comprehensible.

Here is a summary of Watkins's position paper.

One: Let us give up the plausibly desirable but unattainable classical ideal of science while keeping as much of it as possible. Let us keep precision and universality of deductive explanation (rather than probability and such), with truth as a regulative idea.

Two: Corroboration is introduced as relative. First, a theory is initially (prior to experience) better corroborable than another (which the reader may take to be its predecessor) when it answers more questions or with more precision and competes with it. Second, it should win the competition by empirical tests (which the reader may take to be crucial experiments). At times one theory is initially better corroborable than its two or more competitors (which the reader may take to be empirically corroborated predecessors). It then also exhibits increased depth. Also, depth is increased when the untestable residue (constructed with the aid of the Ramsey method) of the new theory differs from that of its competitors (which the reader may take to be shared by all predecessors). To justify this odd idea Watkins says nothing beyond calling the residue metaphysical. Finally, the better-corroborated theory may be judged preferable, he says, yet only in the sense that it is better corroborated.

Three: Popper's theory of corroboration is not hit by the paradoxes of confirmation, Hempelian or Goodmanian. These are troublesome for inductivists because they are obliged to consider all possible explanations, and there are too many of these, mostly silly. Nor can inductivists select *a priori* the simple among them. Popper prefers simplicity, since it is the same as falsifiability.

To conclude this brief summary of an already condensed position paper, Watkins mentions two difficulties: first, what to do with corroborating evidence that is not new, and, second, the assumption that the better corroborated theory is nearer to the truth (more verisimilar) is troublesome since Popper's theory of verisimilitude is refuted. The first problem was solved by Zahar, the second is taken up by Worrall in the second position paper. End of summary.

The position outlined above is not Popper's, whose solution to the problem of induction says that learning from experience is by refutations. His theory of corroboration is both a descriptive theory of what counts in science as positive support plus his (erroneous) claim that corroborations must also occur in science, so as to prevent frustration and to give a sense of progress towards the truth. By contrast, Watkins offers Popper's theory of corroboration as cutting classical philosophy of science down to size. Also, Popper did not speak of depth until the 1950s, and then he confessed that his theory of corroboration is wanting in capturing both depth and the sincerity and severity of tests. Watkins is more confident than Popper. He indicates that the degree of corroboration which a theory has attained is also the measure of the degree to which it is a precise testable explanation, and has attained depth and verisimilitude. He also mentions corroboration (p. 36, lines 5 and 6) as a possible or more than possible "guide in the making of ratational choice among competing scientific theories": he says Popper's theory "can . . . serve as a guide".

The last quote is ambiguous. Does Watkins take corroboration as a guide or does he not? The answer to this question should guide our assessment of his discussion of the paradoxes of confirmation. The paradoxes concern the theory of science and of learning from experience as the theory of choice of the theory best empirically supported from among a given set of theories is an object of belief. If Watkins endorses this theory of science and merely tries to avoid the paradoxes that bedevil it by equating empirical support with the survival of severe tests, then he is an inductivist of the Whewell school; if he does not endorse this theory of science, the paradoxes never arise for him in the first place. Popperians who try to solve these paradoxes—young Feyerabend and Bartley have done so in print —puzzle me no end. But perhaps they take it for granted that empirical support—Popper prefers the word "corroboration"—does play some role in science, and they therefore wish to divide positive evidence or corroboration proper from other evidence that the paradoxes marshall as positive. What role, then, does this corroboration or empirical support or positive evidence play in science?

No one denies that corroboration is useful as increased explanation. This alone suffices to explain the worth of the corroboration of a refuted theory (e.g., Bohr's atom) despite Popper's denial of any such worth. Popper claims that corroboration is necessary as encouragement and as Nature's hint that we progress on the right lines. This is problematic since we need not and often do not assume that a highly corroborated theory is true or on the road to the truth. We explain the fact that one theory is better corroborated than another, or explains more than another by the conjecture that it is nearer to the truth or by some other conjecture. Popper cannot account for this fact as he wants to prove both his theory of positive evidence as that of survival of severe tests (his theory of corroboration) and his theory of science as a series of approximations to the truth (his theory of verisimilitude). But the attempted proof has failed, and Watkins engages in a rescue operation, when a glance at the rationale of the enterprise should indicate the aim of the choice of hypotheses, and thus should suffice to elucidate the role of corroboration. In science the general requirement (for testable explanation) suggests the view of corroboration as increased explanation (at times, observes Popper, with decreased testability, and thus making things unsatisfactory!). In technology the general requirement (for the responsible avoidance of obvious errors prior to the implementation of an innovation) suggests the view of corroboration as evidence of a responsible attempt to avoid obvious errors (by some varying standards of severity). In controversy, corroborations are refutations of, or at least challenges to, the opposite side. In education it has other roles.

Finally, metaphysics. Watkins has devised a new method for isolating the untestable residue of a testable theory. This makes his paper a personal progress report, not a position paper, much less a position paper regarding Popper, who says that the untestable residue of a theory is better eliminated, since thereby the theory's degree of testability and simplicity increase. Watkins is (rightly) interested in the metaphysical import of a theory that can claim scientific status, namely its import to ontology (p. 35, lines 11 and 12). But then he cannot identify the untestable residue of a theory and its ontological import; his calling them both "metaphysical" merely invites a paralogism. He is right in observing that a revolutionary theory repudiates and by-passes some or all of the ontology of the old theory: ontology, however, does not dwell in untestable residues, but sweeps whole vistas. Watkins offers a sweeping proposal here: whenever one can invent a metaphysics (ontology) and reinterpret existing scientific theories in its light, then each and every reinterpretation will constitute a progressive problem-shift, to use Lakatos's terminology. Popper, however, would prefer us to increase the degree of testability of a theory rather than change its untestable residue; as to depth, Popper repeatedly confessed inability to define it. There is no reference to this fact in Watkins's allegedly Popperian position paper.

6. COULD NOT PUT LAKATOS

John Worrall's paper is embarrassing, since, whereas viewed as a paper by a young aspirant it is promising, viewed as a position paper it is a failure. We see how wrong Feyerabend was (in his response to Watkins) not to distinguish between a position statement and heuristic deliberations. Since the paper concerns heuristic, a subject both difficult and neglected, I would love the reader to grant Worrall all possible leeway; he deserves it. To this end it is better dismissed as a position paper on a technical consideration, so as to be presentable as praiseworthy by more appropriate criteria.

Worrall begins by declaring that he will overlook the history of Popper's theory and take it as presented in its final version by Watkins, compare it with another view, and argue for the latter's superiority (p. 45, lines 3 and 5 of second paragraph). He promises to confine his discussion to the different answers Popper-à-la-Watkins and he give to two specific questions: "when does a fact provide genuine support for a theory? And when do the facts support one theory better than another?" He is after a criterion to decide when "one scientific theory is better than another" on the supposition that it is "better . . . if it is better supported by the facts." He falls back at once on public opinion—thus defining, we remember, the audience to his position paper—saying, "most recent attempts to provide an objective and generally applicable criterion of scientific merit have started from these two assumptions," i.e., that scientific merit equals empirical support and that the more the better. But as a criterion of demarcation of empirical character Popper has offered refutability, not corroboration. Admittedly, there is a difference surreptitiously introduced in the very concern with the matter at hand. Popper speaks of refutability as scientific character, and Worrall speaks of corroboration as scientific merit. Moreover, Worrall at times speaks of scientific merit, at times of heuristic merit and seems to equate them. But ideas which have little or no scientific merit, ideas that were never scientific, much less corroborated, had enormous heuristic value. Popper regularly mentions as a standard example the heuristic value neo-Platonic metaphysics had for the Copernicans. Clearly, then, Popper does not equate heuristic and scientific merit. Does Lakatos equate the two?

Worrall promises a comparison of views; to that end they need be well formulated, put in canonic form, so that one canon should clash with another. Popper is alive and so canonizing his view is somewhat premature, which is not the case with Imre Lakatos whose early demise is much regretted. One need not complain about Watkins's premature canonization of Popper's view, but surely one may expect something approaching a canonic wording of Lakatos's view, especially in view of the fact that his work was very fluid and he kept rewriting it and changing his mind on large matters and small. Instead, Worrall appends a footnote to his second paragraph, saying (note 1), "I should add that the answers proposed . . . have also developed over time. The answers I shall give are not those given in Lakatos (1970).[4] The idea that heuristic considerations have to be imported into theory-appraisal was developed in discussion between Lakatos, myself, and Elie Zahar, who was in this respect the prime mover." Watkins's paper is a preamble to that of Worrall, who was primarily moved to write it by Elie Zahar, the dark horse of the contingent and its once and future mentor. The position paper is of Zahar's position primarily, as developed in discussions.

Here is a summary of Worrall's paper, interspersed with critical comments.

Contrary to the declared intention of endorsing Watkins's formulation, we have here a new presentation of corroboration as a three-, not two-, place predicate, relating theory, test, and background-knowledge. "Simplified slightly," evidence corroborates a theory when it follows from that theory but not from background-knowledge. This view is neither Popper's nor Lakatos's: the latter viewed background-knowledge as inconsistent, thus making Worrall's formula cancel corroborations. As to Popper, his view is given to misinterpretations. In Worrall's view, background-knowledge is for Popper what "we accept (tentatively) as unproblematic while we are testing the theory." "We" may mean here an idealized group of Popperians who endorse the conventions defining the game of science which he proposes. Worrall makes a tiny but amply rewarding shift. "We" is for him "the scientific community" and "while we are testing" becomes "at the time of the test." This small shift makes Karl Popper endorse the views of Michael Polanyi, as expressed in his famous 'Critique of Doubt' in *Personal Knowledge*. The difference is enormous, and as follows.

Popper's view is critical. He wants a crucial experiment between new and established views; he wants new experiments to shoot through as many levels of generalization and force as wide-scale a revision as possible. Polanyi is post-critical. He wants science to be taken upon faith and a problem judiciously isolated and studied while all else rests assured. Yet a small shift of emphasis suffices to move from the one to the other.

Popper was not the first, of course, to demand rigorous tests by new experiments; William Whewell already argued that tests must be rigorous and new since the alternative to this is the license to adjust theory to existing evidence, and thereby confirm the theory by already-discovered evidence with no risk of overthrow. And this procedure is not *kosher*, he said. (Worrall calls Whewell by another name, p. 46, last paragraph, and note 9.)

But Whewell—and with him, Popper (not to mention Watkins; see above)—may run into trouble, Worrall argues: the perihelion of Mercury was known prior to Einstein's discovery of general relativity yet he (Einstein) felt encouraged by it. Whewell and Popper will not allow for that. Hence, Worrall argues, the background-knowledge of which a thinker is personally ignorant while constructing his theory may be used as empirical support (p. 48). This is preposterous: Einstein was not ignorant: in any case, ignorance should never count as a necessary condition for a bonus in science. Yet "it is precisely this suggestion that the methodology" Worrall advocates "incorporates" (p. 48, lines 4 and 3 from bottom). So much the worse for Worrall.

Worrall's discussion has nonetheless the merit of taking the dilemma by its horns: taking into account the path of the growth of knowledge, we may arrive by different paths at different appraisals of one theory on the basis of the same set of factual reports. Alan Musgrave (like John Maynard Keynes) has taken this to be a *reductio*, yet we must choose between a unique theory-appraisal (given the facts), that thus makes history irrelevant (Keynes), and allowing history to play a part, thus permitting two histories to allot different statuses to the same theory (on the same facts) (Popper). (A theory loses all the empirical support it ever had, to take the tritest Popperian example, once it enters the background.) Lovely. (Why not admit that we use both horns, each for a different purpose, one for historical assessments, one for policy planning?) Worrall sees the dilemma thus: if history is allowed to enter considerations, as he wants, we may have to give a bonus for ignorance, as he does not want to do. To put it in Worrall's language, "does it not . . . make empirical support a 'person-relative' affair?" (p. 51). No, he says; "it is not a person-relative but a heuristic-relative affair." It is not the question Worrall was posing in the opening of his position paper about the scientific merit of corroboration, then; rather, it is the question of the heuristic merit of corroboration. But heuristic has no rules. It is marvellous that Einstein felt encouraged by it to continue with his work, and that Faraday or Dirac refused to be discouraged by its absence. Koertge takes up this point ably, not bothering about scientific and heuristic merit simultaneously.

We may, perhaps, view Lakatos as the source of the confusion of questions of scientific merit with questions of the viability of a heuristic policy. What is rational and advisable to do, however, is to ask, in each case, what is the purpose at hand? If we want corroboration, what do we think it is good for? It may be good for different ends at different times. The methodology of Lakatos, we learn, had a public aim; in Worrall's words, (p. 52, line 11 from bottom), it "transfers the methodological spotlight away from refutations and focusses it on verifications of excess content."

The citadel has fallen to the hands of the inductivists. But that does not matter. What matters is that Lakatos has claimed to explain thereby the growth of science along given lines, along given research programs. But, as Feyerabend observes (p. 153), he gave no explanation: he merely called the wise choice progressive and the unwise regressive.

Since Popper did not discuss heuristic in his classic works, since he discusses all the aspects of Worrall's discussion not related to heuristic, Worrall makes no case against Popper. He does not even argue that what Popper says about corroboration should help heuristic, nor that what Zahar says does. Confusing no answer with mistaken answer, Worrall manages to miss everybody's point.

7. TOGETHER AGAIN

We have passed less than a quarter of the volume, but from now on the reviewer's task is all down-hill, though we have still two position papers to go.

Elie Zahar offers an elegant analysis of the logic of an experiment that at the time seemed crucial but never was. This shows, of course, how important crucial experiments are, and how difficult can be the deduction that goes into their appraisal and that methodologists take as given. Zahar thinks his case-study throws light on the Popper-Lakatos disagreement, but he does not even outline, let alone analyze, the logic of his case-study as a crucial experiment between Popper and Lakatos.

Peter Urbach, in the last of the position papers, contrasts the Bacon-Descartes view of the method of discovery with the Whewell-Popper view of its denial. Both, of course, preclude heuristic; yet one explicitly, one by default. Is there heuristic in science? And if yes, what does it consist of? A few writers have said yes, and illustrated the answer. Urbach unifies them into one mythical Prometheus. What does it consist of? Urbach doesn't say. Rather, he wants to define a measure for the objective promise of a program. This wish goes far ahead of even the wildest dreams of any Prometheus. Since the rest of the essay, allegedly preparatory to this great discovery, contains fragments of interesting ideas, the curious reader is advised to consult the relevant part, pages 107–111, as very stimulating and worthwhile heuristic material.

End of position papers.

Adolf Grünbaum attacks inductivist relics in Popper. He is generally right, except when he thinks he attacks Popper's central thesis. He also says that Bacon too spoke of refutations. The editors say: so much the better. But Bacon says refutations are not enough, we need demonstrations in order to positively learn from experience. Only Popper says that refutations already constitute positive learning from experience. Bacon thus gives rise to the problem of induction that Popper overcomes. Right or wrong, this is simple enough. But it is Popper *à-la*-Agassi, not Popper *à-la*-Watkins. Will the real Popper please stand up?

Paul Feyerabend's marvellous anti-inductivist quotations from Goethe achieve a weird effect, due to his suppression of both the problems Popper studied and Goethe's inductivism. He defends Aristotle, common sense, and a small, reasonable measure of certainty, silently equating the three though they are distinct enough. Though he defends logic (in science, he says "exact agreement is not necessary. The logical demands, however, must be strictly satisfied," (p. 155, lines 17 to 15 from bottom), he insists "that science often violates those laws of logic which our critical rationalists regard as a *conditio sine qua non* of rationality" (p. 156, lines 18 to 16 from bottom). Watkins sharply quarrels with him on this point (pp. 341ff. and 387ff.), but the absence of a framework makes it questionable whether they disagree. He need not write a treatise to offer the framework, but a few clear sentences may help a lot. It is ironical that this advocate of the lovely and peaceful doctrine of pluralism aggressively denies Popperians a place in his pluralist heaven. The excuse that there is no room there for anti-pluralists will not do as he will not permit a pluralist variant of Popper, yet tolerates anti-pluralists. He attacks Popperianism as "content-increase"; is content increase anti-pluralist? A content-increase-yet-pluralist-philosopher is Hans Albert, as his contribution to the volume at hand illustrates.

Feyerabend's verbal assault on his erstwhile hero, John von Neumann, swells all the time. As the Marquise of O— said to her man, if you did not look to me like an angel at first, you would not look to me like a devil later on.

Alan Musgrave promises the mild criticisms of a sympathizer (p. 181). He begins by affirming the obvious falsehood that to deny the merit of evidential support "is to deny that empirical evidence matters in science": the title of Popper's *Conjectures and Refutations* already suffices to indicate at least a possibility of valuing empirical evidence, yet not as support. One may value evidence as (1) explicanda and (2) refutations. Musgrave's paper ignores both. Even his section labelled 'Falsification' discusses support and the evasion of falsification, not the possible value of refutations and the scientific success they open the road to. He then discusses Lakatos as an anarchist and a pluralist, indeed as an anti-empiricist.

Hans Albert has a comprehensive position paper in the guise of a comment on the official position papers with which, he oddly says, he is in fundamental agreement. To be precise, he says he is in "fundamental agreement" only "with the general thrust of the position paper," and without indicating which one of the four. Anyway, he forgets them all. His position is of "consistent fallibilism, a methodical rationalism, and a critical realism," combined into "critical rationalism." No mention of the position papers or their authors. Nor of their mentors, except for Popper in the end (and

Lakatos in a footnote on mathematics). It is at least in part a historical survey, and one attempting to do justice to Popper's predecessors. Highly recommended.

Ernan McMullin offers a new and intriguing taxonomy of philosophies of science. Here is not the place to discuss it. His essay signifies here only in that he uses the occasion and gives Popper and Lakatos a larger share of the essay than its inner logic demands. He also complains that Popper and Lakatos confuse a conventionalist description of the behavior of a scientist with the behavior of a conventionalist scientist (note 19). I am glad to defend Lakatos for once: he thought that the conventionalist scientist is a poor scientist who hardly counts anyhow. As to Popper, he has not given any ground for this complaint, as he has never discussed the way one's philosophy of science interacts with one's scientific research.

Noretta Koertge's paper is the *pièce de résistance*. Just as Albert's is comprehensive, hers is exploratory. She takes her cue from a humble manual, *Zen and the Art of Motorcycle Maintenance*, in a poetic opening page which is just terrific. Yet she could simplify matters. Koertge takes for granted that when Mendeleev rejected an empirical statement, he rejected some auxiliary hypothesis. He did not; what he explicitly rejected was some observation-reports that contradicted his theory. When trying to explain the error of the reports he rejected, he conjectured about some experimental errors; he did not speak about any auxiliary hypothesis. The question, moreover, is not whether Mendeleev fixed his belief on the proper object of belief or not; but whether he considered enough options and deliberated on them in a way that we find enlightening, fruitful, 'progressive'.

Koertge's note 12 is interesting. Taking the utility of a hypothesis to be, as usual, its probability times its expected benefit, taking its expected benefit to be its content, and its content to be its inverse probability, makes all hypotheses have the same utility! Popper did endorse inverse probability as a possible measure of content once—in his third note on degree of confirmation (see Appendix star-nine of his *Logic of Scientific Discovery*). But usually he sticks to his original suggestion that the measure of content is improbability. This suggestion makes utility the product of a probability and its complement, and the maximum utility then goes to hypotheses equally as probable as their negations (in the abstract or under given specified conditions). Hence, this utility approach, recommended by R. B. Braithwaite, incidentally, may be the compromise between Popper and the inductivists that falls between the stools.

Kurt Hübner's paper is brief yet extremely ambitious. He presents a sweeping attack on "Falsificationism (which is only another word for Popperianism)" London School of Economics style, "(largely identical with Lakatos' ideas)" and outlines his own alternative philosophy. Unfortunately, he presents a series of variants on Popperianism as if they were one consistent theory. He also chooses for each of his attacks the Popperian variant that is the easiest target for it. This is not very scholarly, even when supported by quotations, much less when presented in easy-going paraphrase. As to his own—composite or eclectic—philosophy, it is a variant of relativism; Hübner opposes the absolutist criterion of truth on the ground that the absolute truth is a mere regulative idea and so cannot be meaningfully posited (p. 281, line 16 from bottom). This last point invokes the worst variant of verificationism, namely the defunct verificationist theory of meaning.

Nevertheless, much that Hübner's paper refers to is serious criticism, too briefly outlined and mixed with unserious stuff, yet criticism that should excite the interest of every criticism-seeking Popperian.

Gunnar Andersson's careful essay on verisimilitude shows that Popper's quantitative measure of verisimilitude is objectionable and perhaps irreparable. It is technical, though very readable; it is useless to go into its detail unless one reads it all. Andersson is careful not to conclude that the intuitive idea of verisimilitude is in error.

Heinz Post attacks relativism and postulates truth as an ideal of objectivity, adding, somewhat to my surprise, that I disagree. In response perhaps I should call him an inductivist, except that his claim is based on no evidence. His problem is: By what criteria should we decide to prefer one theory over another? Presumably, 'prefer' means here: consider the most verisimilar. Post opts for Popper's preference for high empirical content. Yet as a physicist Post prefers any barely empirical elementary particle theory to many highly empirical specialized theories which industrial and shipping and aviation engineers develop and test regularly. Post seems to suggest (p. 316, lines 16 to 9 from bottom) that engineers only apply existing hypotheses to new cases, not invent and test new ones. He knows, however, that they do invent hypotheses; he dismisses these as mere *ad hoc* auxiliary hypotheses. This claim of his (lines 9 to 7 from bottom) is an *ad hoc* excuse. Nor does the excuse help: the engineers' hypotheses have to be excluded by his criterion, yet they are not.

The rest of the volume is replies and rejoinders.

John Worrall's reply achieves an increased confusion between the corroboration of a theory and the success of a research program (see his note 9). He regrettably uses a new unexplained oxymoronic expression, "the corroboration of a research programme".

John Watkins analyses Feyerabend's reply to Gellner's review of Feyerabend's book and exposes it as a piece of demagoguery. He also responds to Grünbaum's and Hübner's attacks on the seemingly justificationist element in his position. Much effort is required in order to decide whether Watkins is a systematic non-justificationist or not. If he is, he could parry the attacks with much more ease and clarity than he does. When he is clearly non-justificationist (pp. 346–47), he defends falsification, not any general rule of policy for the choice of a hypothesis. (To infer from the rejection of all but one of the known competitors the acceptance of the remaining competitor is questionable, possibly justificationist, and leaves no room for any heuristic.) When citing Wesley Salmon's excellent (though mistaken) dictum, 'Corroboration is either empty or inductivist', in a section called 'Does Corroboration Matter?', Watkins regrettably trails off. Popper says that corroboration matters as encouragement. Alas! it matters differently when different aims are served by it. Watkins says it is a measure of comparative goodness. Goodness for what end?

Watkins's reply contains an impressive, technical, compact, 20-page paper on the comparison of theories. It is hard to discuss it for want of a framework within which to present it, except that this time the difficulty is part and parcel of the traditional problem. As long as science was verified the problem was trivially solved. Pierre Duhem, denying verification, asserted the principle that since each theory is its own intellectual framework, no comparison between theories is possible. This principle was rediscovered by Sir Edward Evans-Pritchard and by Michael Polanyi. It was given currency in the inferior variants of Kuhn and Feyerabend. Watkins wants to supersede Duhem's principle by offering a rule of comparison, the kind of which it forbids. This policy is extravagant. Suffice it to notice that the principle rests on the proposal to take a theory as its own framework: in so doing, obviously, we take a theory together with much of its background. Let that be so. Then, on the one hand Judaism and Catholicism are incomparable, since each recommends itself under any condition; but on the other hand Newtonianism, by its own light, gave way to Einsteinianism. It is a fact that these four, taken as their own frameworks, are of the two kinds—recommending themselves under all conditions and offering criteria for choice, respectively. And it is likewise a fact that Newtonianism did give way to Einsteinianism but not Judaism to Catholicism. We can now see the defect of Duhem's view: he said theories were their own frameworks and so not comparable; yet, he also offered a framework and one which contains two criteria for choice—comparative simplicity and comparative utility. Hence Duhem's principle is confused and needs no rebuttal.

Back to Watkins, who begins with Popper and Grünbaum. Popper said: prefer the theory that answers more questions; in criticism, Grünbaum presents questions answered by Newton but not by Einstein (what force will give a body the velocity twice that of light?). Watkins protests: Grünbaum's questions, though not answered by Einstein, are pseudo-answered by him—to use the terminology of the logic of question—i.e., answered by denying the question's presupposition. None of the three discussants present the logic of questions as a framework for their all-too-prematurely too technical debate.

The volume at hand ends with two parting shots, by Feyerabend and by Hübner. Interminable debates may be exciting and useful; it is regrettable that such examples as the ones at hand give them a bad name. Feyerabend says that his critics do not read his works, and explains this as the result of their perversity. Kurt Hübner begins his reply to Watkins by quoting Watkins as asking " 'Does Popper's purely conventionalist view of basic statements render falsifications "practically" meaningless?' " (page 393, first sentence) without giving any reference, and one should not take it on faith that Watkins could ask such a stupid question. Popper stressed in his early *Logik der Forschung* the fact that since science is verbal it is impregnated with conventions; he presented it to be his concern to overcome the conventional element in science, never fully, but as much as possible, and by instituting conventions to encourage, foster, and enhance falsification. One of the cleverest moves in that work is the suggestion that the conventional element in a given observation report is easier to surmount than the conventional element in a given theory.

The department of philosophy of the London School of Economics is not dead. It still has enormous assets. It has a great tradition and excellent connections that may come back to life after some housecleaning. It has excellent minds from Watkins down to the latest junior recruit, not to mention powerful Gellner who for some time joined it, and others in other departments. May we all be fortunate enough to have our best contributions remembered. Let us hope to see some London School of Economics position papers on mathematics. That will put the great Lakatos together again.

NOTES

1. *The Philosophy of Karl Popper*, Library of Living Philosophers series, Paul Schilpp (ed.) (La Salle, IL: Open Court Publishing Co., 1974).

2. In his eagerness to claim priority for the (commonplace) idea about intellectual frameworks, Lakatos tried to see its "implicit" presence in his early work. To this end he conflated problem-shifts between and within intellectual frameworks. These two kinds of problem-shift raise different kinds of problems.

3. I.e., 'Falsification and the Methodology of Research Programmes', in I. Lakatos and A. Musgrave (eds.), *Criticism and the Growth of Knowledge*, Cambridge University Press, Cambridge, 1970, pp. 91–196.

LAKATOS AND *PROGRESS AND RATIONALITY IN SCIENCE*: REPLY TO AGASSI

by Gunnar Andersson

The main thesis of Agassi's review of *Progress and Rationality in Science* is that Lakatos's methodology of scientific research programmes (MSRP) ended with defeat final and complete. As one of the editors of the volume I agree: In his discussion of science Lakatos did not succeed in solving the problems he wanted to solve. I will return to this point later.

First I want to discuss some minor points of disagreement. Agassi finds "sloppiness" and even "bugs" in Noretta Koertge's contribution, and he goes so far as to ask "how many bugs can be tolerated?". The main "bug" is the following one found in "a two-line point plus a footnote" in Koertge's paper. There Koertge writes that statements like "every metal has a melting point" are unfalsifiable. [1] Agassi thinks that this is wrong, because "the example she cites is falsified by experience: a metal may sublimate rather than melt, and such a metal exists, and is usually known as calcium". However, when Koertge writes about unfalsifiable statements, she uses 'unfalsifiable' in the same sense as Popper, namely as unfalsifiable by basic statements *alone*. According to Popper basic statements should have the logical form of singular there-is-statements. [2] Such basic statements cannot falsify the hypothesis that every metal has a melting point. This hypothesis has the logical form of an all-some-statement (for all metals x there is some point of temperature y such that y is the melting point of x). It is a logical matter of fact that such all-some-statements cannot be falsified or contradicted by a singular statement, and thus cannot be falsified by any basic statement alone. Hence, the singular statement alone that a particular piece of calcium has sublimated at a certain point of temperature cannot falsify the hypothesis that all metals have a melting point. For a falsification we need an auxiliary hypothesis, e.g., the hypothesis that sublimating metals do not have a melting point. With such an auxiliary hypothesis a falsification is possible, and that is what Agassi means by "falsified by experience". But falsification by basic statements together with auxiliary hypotheses is something else than falsification by basic statements alone. Agassi uses 'falsified' in the first sense. Koertge and Popper use 'falsified' in the second sense. Since Koertge discusses Popper's view, it is natural that she uses 'falsified' in the same sense as Popper, not in the new sense suggested by Agassi. Thus Agassi's criticism on this point is purely verbal.

Agassi thinks that Koertge ascribes the discussed hypothesis that all metals have a melting point to Watkins "with no reference". However, in note 16 (p. 277) Koertge refers to "Watkins (1958)", and in the bibliography (p. 278) we find: "Watkins, J. W. N.: 'Confirmable and Influential Metaphysics', *Mind 67*, 344-65 (1958)." Thus there is a reference satisfying all criteria of scientific honesty.

With these remarks I hope to have saved the honour of the one and only female contributor to the volume. There are no "bugs" in her contribution.

Now I come to the points on which I agree with Agassi. In the volume the editors have used expressions like "the LSE position" and "the LSE reply" as titles for different parts of the book. 'LSE' stands for the London School of Economics. Agassi asks if there is such a thing as the London School of Economics school of philosophy and if so, "who belongs to this school?" With the benefit of hindsight I must admit that these titles and expressions were not well chosen. There is no such thing as the "LSE position" in the philosophy of science. What is called so in the volume is Lakatos's MSRP as presented by Worrall, Zahar, and Urbach and "The Popperian Approach to Scientific Knowledge" as presented by Watkins. Thus the "LSE position" as discussed in the volume is mainly Lakatos's position in the philosophy of science plus Watkins's "Popperian Approach". But Watkins's two contributions to the volume are also more or less influenced by Lakatos's ideas and problems, especially his contribution on corroboration and content-comparison in the "LSE reply". There Watkins writes: "Without the possibility of content-comparisons between logically incompatible theories, this [the Popperian] philosophy of science would be in total disarray." (p. 366.) This is true for Lakatos's MSRP, in which comparison of contents is essential but not necessarily for Popper's philosophy of science.

Agassi's main thesis is that Lakatos's MSRP is a failure. According to Agassi this is the main lesson to be learnt from the volume. This is a controversial view and a view that is not admitted in the volume, at least not explicitly, but it is a view which I think is right. Agassi concludes that "the Lakatos era is over", at least in the philosophy of science, and that "the volume is bound to remain noticed, as it signifies the end of an era."

In the rest of this reply I will explain why I think that Agassi's main thesis is well-taken. In so doing I will work out some points which are only suggested in the introduction to the volume written by Radnitzky and myself. In our introduction we refer to Alan Musgrave's important criticism of MSRP (p. 7). MSRP ends with a dilemma. Lakatos has to choose between epistemological anarchism and inductivism. Feyerabend dedicated his *Against Method* to Lakatos as a "fellow-anarchist"—not without reasons, as can be seen in Feyerabend's book. The other horn of the dilemma has been presented by Herbert Feigl, who has argued that Lakatos "cannot help being a second level inductivist".[3] Depending on how MSRP is worked out, adherents of this position have to choose between "the frying pan of anarchism" and "the hell-fire of inductivism", as Musgrave puts it.[4] Musgrave suggests charitably how his former teacher Lakatos might avoid this dilemma by very substantial changes in MSRP, changes so substantial that they require that all the main ideas of MSRP be given up. Probably Musgrave did not want to present such a devastating criticism of MSRP explicitly in the Lakatos memorial volume. Therefore he gives what Radnitzky and I called "a rational reconstruction" of MSRP. But in reality the dilemma between epistemological anarchism and inductivism shows that MSRP is beyond repair.

Musgrave's "rational reconstruction" of MSRP is highly problematic. According to Musgrave a "progressing research programme throws up more unsolved but solvable problems than a degenerating one", and "science ought to devote more energy to investigate unsolved but solvable problems".[5] But how can you know that a problem is solvable before you have solved it? You cannot assume that research programmes which have thrown up unsolved but solvable problems in the past will continue to do so in the future, because "at this point those with a keen nose for such things will smell an inductivist rat".[6] Especially you cannot assume that problems will continue to be solvable. The next unsolved problem might be unsolvable and fatal. Thus Musgrave's attempt to save MSRP does not succeed.

This is in agreement with Agassi's main thesis. I suppose that Agassi can accept much of the criticism of MSRP indicated above, at least the inductivist horn of the dilemma, because he writes that Lakatos "flirted with pre-Popperian ideas, and was extolling good old inductivism in a Popperian garb". Inductivism in a Popperian garb? I would prefer to say that Lakatos presented "good old inductivism" in a Lakatosian garb. What is wrong with "good old inductivism"? Not only that Lakatos presented it "with too much fanfare—as a mere crowd-pleaser" as Agassi writes. Whether it pleases the crowd or not, inductivism is untenable. After Hume and Popper it is a "mortal sin of the first order".[7]

Agassi is right that MSRP is presented in a Popperian garb. But beside the garb there is nothing Popperian about it: it is either anarchism in disguise or inductivism. In MSRP falsifications (in the logical sense) do not play any role whatsoever. From Kuhn Lakatos has learnt that all theories have their "anomalies". Lakatos thinks that this shows that all theories as a matter of fact are falsified. (Since Kuhn uses "anomaly" in a psychological rather than in a logical sense, I do not think that this interpretation of Kuhn is correct.) For this reason Lakatos thinks that falsifications are unimportant. Important is instead "verification" of excess content, that is a kind of empirical support. After this "problem-shift" we soon arrive at "second-level inductivism", as is to be expected when you flirt with the pre-Popperian idea of empirical support. Nevertheless Lakatos continued to speak about "falsifications" of theories. He says that a theory is "falsified" if it is eliminated by a better theory. This is a curious way of speaking, because theories can be "eliminated" by better theories without being false, and thus they can be "falsified" in Lakatos's sense while still being true in the normal sense of the word. This is an example of what Agassi calls "surreptitious change".

Agassi does not think that Lakatos's debate with Kuhn was "serious". As indicated above I think it was. Lakatos's central methodological problems were posed by Kuhn's investigations in the history of science. I think that Lakatos seriously believed that Kuhn had shown that the history of science shows that falsificationism is untenable. For this reason Lakatos abandons falsificationism and develops his MSRP. Agassi calls this "a conjecture about Kuhn's influence on Lakatos" and says that it is "plausible enough, but . . . hard to examine". I think that this "conjecture" can be examined by the study of Lakatos's published papers, and that it is corroborated by such a study.

University of Trier
Trier
Federal Republic of Germany

NOTES

1. Noretta Koertge, 'Towards a New Theory of Scientific Inquiry,' in *Progress and Rationality in Science*, ed. by G. Radnitzky and G. Andersson, vol. 58 of *Boston Studies in the Philosophy of Science* (Dordrecht: Reidel 1978), p. 271 and n16, p. 277.

2. Karl R. Popper, *The Logic of Scientific Discovery* (London: Hutchinson 1969) §28.

3. Herbert Feigl, 'Research Programmes and Induction,' in *In Memory of Rudolf Carnap*, ed. by R. Buck and R. S. Cohen, vol. 8 of *Boston Studies in the Philosophy of Science* (Dordrecht: Reidel 1971), p. 146.

4. Alan Musgrave, 'Method or Madness?' in *Essays in Memory of Imre Lakatos*, ed. by R. S. Cohen, P. K. Feyerabend and M. W. Wartofsky, vol. 39 of *Boston Studies in the Philosophy of Science* (Dordrecht: Reidel 1976), p. 480.

5. Ibid., p. 482.

6. Ibid., p. 480.

7. Cf. ibid., p. 480.

— 31 —

REFUTATION *À LA* POPPER:
A REJOINDER TO ANDERSSON

a changing universe of discourse

Dr. Andersson honors me with his friendly response, thereby putting to shame my regrettable manners. It was arbitrary of me to pick as an instance of a confusion, typical of the Lakatos legacy, a point from the excellent contribution of Noretta Koertge to the volume of Lakatosiana edited by Gerard Radnitzky and Gunnar Andersson and reviewed by me in the pages preceding the latter's comments on it. Yet his comments do not help dispel the regrettable confusion.

The focus of controversy here is a statement, *Exhibit A* for short, "All metals have melting points". Koertge says it is not refutable; I say it is. Refutable *à la* Popper, that is. Andersson says it is not refutable *à la* Popper, and he says *she* says it is not refutable *à la* Popper. Well, then, either Popper is so vague we'd better forget his proposal, at least its details, or Andersson is clearly in error. He is. I refer now to the same classic discussion in Popper's *Logik der Forschung* (1935) to which he refers.

Popper does not discuss *Exhibit A*. (Nor does Watkins, incidentally.) Popper takes another example, *Exhibit B* for short: "All planets move in ellipses". Consider five space-time co-ordinates of any given planet. (Since four points determine an ellipse uniquely, we do need five.) We call all five together, or their conjunction, a potential falsifier; and when actually reported by an astronomer, we call the conjunction a basic statement. Clearly, the said potential falsifiers are likely to be logically inconsistent with *Exhibit B*. Popper was somewhat concerned with the fact that basic statements do not reflect the astronomer's act of perception, but not in the usual manner: the usual concern is that of one who tries to make sure, and who thinks only when the report of an observer reflects his perception is it (the report) quite sure. For, says Popper, no basic statement is ever sure, and, on the contrary, to be scientific it must be refutable. Yet, Popper offers as a convention the rule: until a basic statement is refuted the hypothesis it conflicts with should be viewed as refuted.

Take now *Exhibit A*. Consider the potential falsifier reporting a piece of metal beginning to melt at two different temperatures on two different occasions or beginning and ending to melt at different temperatures, *et voilà!*

Be Popper in error or be he right, Koertge's discussion is not *à la* Popper. End of my rejoinder.

Let me attempt to criticize my rejoinder. Popper overlooked the fact that at times refutation led to a major revision, says Lakatos, at times to minor revisions. Indeed, Popper says, explicitly, every revision, however minor, should be viewed as the positing of an utterly new hypothesis to be tested on its own with no regard to its ancestry. This well accords with our intuition of severe testing but conflicts with our intuition of sameness of all variants of one guiding idea. And in his concern for heuristic Lakatos accepted the latter and rejected the former. He ended up saying, strictly speaking, there is no such thing as refutation.

Considering Lakatos a variant of Popper with no debate, then, we have to take Koertge's Lakatosian discussion of *Exhibit A* Popperian *à la* Lakatos and non-Popperian *à la* Popper. Hence, my claim that her discussion of *Exhibit A* as non-Popperian is biassed. (I was oft called more Popperian than Popper, but now Andersson says I am plainly idiosyncratic!) Is this critique of my critique valid?

We need not go into all this: Lakatos was in plain error. The two intuitions are not a contradiction, especially when taken heuristically: only statements are contradictory, and only strict rules are in conflict; heuristic is too vague for that.

Yet Popper is in error: a basic statement which is truly singular in his sense—confined to a space-time point or small region—is irrefutable: only its universalization is. And, in any case, demanding, as he does, to view accepted basic statements as repeatable, amounts to the demand to endorse only universalizations. Popper's other example, "here is a glass of water", is too vague for his own purpose: "Here-now is a glass of water", is irrefutable, until somehow universalized, and it is hard to know how to universalize it, since it is an everyday instance presented out of any scientific context. Moreover, it is not at all clear how any scientific observation is universalized—say, the potential falsifier of *Exhibit B*, concerning the position of an observed planet. It was Kant who noted, however vaguely, and in passing, that the very universalization of the test-statements for Kepler's laws are Kepler's laws themselves! For Kant this is a *tour de force*; for Popper it is a problem, and a subtle one! He even notices it in passing in the penultimate footnote to his *Objective Knowledge*, but does not stop to see a difficulty here.

Also, Popper is in error when he says that we will be in danger of dogmatism unless we endorse his rule and always reject a refuted hypothesis with unrefuted refutations. I have often discussed this rule—Boyle's Rule—and will not continue until challenged.

I do not know if we need a substitute for Popper's theory of refutability. This hinges on whether we still deem the problem of demarcation of scientific theories important, and this depends on the context of our discourse. We are in an exciting, rapidly developing state. The price we must pay is to repeatedly delineate our universe of discourse, since it keeps changing. I do not mean to censure Noretta Koertge, but to notice that her discourse is hard to follow for want of clear context for it.

32

LAKATOSIANS ON ECONOMICS

the research program that does not exist

Let me start with the background to the book[1] I intend to review, before I express my negative view of it. Imre Lakatos escaped from Hungary in 1956, graduated from Cambridge in 1959, then joined the London School of Economics and stayed there till his premature death in 1974. He organized an international colloquium in the philosophy of science in 1965 in which Rudolf Carnap and Karl Popper met as friends after decades of estrangement. He thus launched Popper into the limelight, inaugurated the Popper philosophical school, and acted as its major-domo; soon he took over its leadership. He gained ever more international reputation and notoriety, then departed the scene abruptly. He left behind a *magnum opus* on the philosophy of mathematics, his *Proofs and Refutations* of 1963–64, recently republished in book form (the work is in essence his Cambridge doctoral dissertation); and a series of papers on the philosophy of science in which he purported to offer a striking new philosophy of "the methodology of scientific research programs", as he labelled this non-existent theory; and even the label he declared his own registered trademark. In addition there are the four volumes of the proceedings of the London International Colloquium, already mentioned, especially the already-classic Kuhn volume, *Criticism and the Growth of Knowledge*, edited by Lakatos and Musgrave, the Boston Colloquium *Essays in Memory of Imre Lakatos*, and now, finally, two volumes of proceedings of a conference on the Greek Island of Napfilion, which Lakatos organized but did not live to participate in, on the methodology of research appraisal in economics, edited by Spiro J. Latsis, and on the methodology of research programs in physics, edited by Colin Howson.

This review of *Method and Appraisal in Economics*, edited by Spiro J. Latsis (Cambridge: Cambridge University Press, 1978), appeared in *Philosophy of the Social Sciences*, 9, 1979 under the title 'The Legacy of Lakatos'.

I have expressed in the Lakatos Memorial Volume my deep appreciation of his trail-blazing ideas concerning mathematics and mathematical education. I shall always remember with gratitude the pleasure of my encounter with his ideas on these subjects. I have also expressed my view of Lakatos's publications concerning empirical science (in my review of the Kuhn volume—chapter 28 in this book) as deserving no more than a humorous comment. The two volumes out of the Lakatos Napfilion conference seem to be a living monument to the fruitfulness of his ideas on scientific method and thus a refutation of my low esteem of them. Or are they? I take the opportunity to check the content of the economics volume; the physics volume I am too biased to review: I have run out of humor.

Introduction (by the editor, Spiro Latsis): "The central problem that binds together the contributions to this volume is the problem of theory-appraisals in economics. When is one theory better than another? Are there objective criteria for assessing the cognitive value of theories and what is the status of such criteria? Are there pragmatic temporary criteria? Or are there no articulable criteria at all?" Hicks, we are told, holds the view that criteria are pragmatic and transient; Hutchison holds the view that the criterion of falsifiability is timeless. Latsis, Coats, de Marchi, and Blaug, are four followers of Lakatos and his "new and provocative methodology of scientific research programmes". What Lakatos's view may be, the editor tells us only scantily. He says it "insists that the recognition of 'goodness' in a theory is a complex matter and that no single criterion is capable of demarcating good from bad theories". Moreover, among the list of criteria is the one concerning the role a theory plays in a series of theories lumped together by a common presupposition known as 'the hard core': is the theory the result of a 'progressive' or 'degenerative' move? As to refutability, Lakatos, I remember well, jovially pooh-poohed it, and had quite a tiff with Popper about it in the Popper volumes of Schilpp's Library of Living Philosophers. The present volume, with the exception of Hutchison's excellent critical study, offers us another Lakatos: the editor insists that Lakatos's criteria "supplement the usual logical and empirical criteria"; and the Lakatosian essays, all four or five of them, take "the usual" to read Popperism, falsificationist, refutationist.

"Although several of the papers in this volume are suggestive of the power of the approach [of Lakatos] in one social science, the desirability that more work should be done is evident". Not to me. Lakatos insisted, the editor adds, that the study of a program should be retrospective, not prospective; "we should be careful to demarcate *appraisal* from *advice* . . . the proper domain of philosophy of science is the appraisal of past science and not the rendering of heuristic advice". No sooner does the editor offer advice (to apply Lakatos's program) than he tells us that following Lakatos he is against giving advice. But then perhaps giving advice is simply not "the proper domain of philosophy of science", and then we may simply conclude that the editor's preface does not belong to "the proper domain of philosophy of science". To which domain does it belong, though? Science? Metaphysics? Social philosophy? Caprice? I am dumbfounded, especially since the advice is so 'evident' and yet I cannot even place it in any framework, as is demanded by the Master.

Simon and Leijonhufvud are the two contributors left to the end of the introduction, as their contributions "include forward-looking elements". Since they "include forward-looking elements", their recommendations for future programs do not belong to "the proper domain of philosophy of science". Where then do they belong? Where do they all come from?

I will try to take the introduction's description of Lakatos's philosophy as correct when possible and I will show in what follows that every description of the contributions cited thus far is plainly false. The problems posed in the volume are genuine enough, and exciting enough; at first glance this volume looks terrific: interestingly written, scholarly, and a proper mixture of glamorous names and new ideas—I recognize the Lakatos touch. But it is the last gleanings.

Spiro J. Latsis: 'A Research Programme in Economics'. A criterion for a good economic theory must yield both good and bad examples, so as to avoid being too lax and too stringent. Why? Will Latsis apply this to ornithology, theology, astrology, exobiology? No matter. "A priorism is too lax, while falsificationism is too restrictive". In Latsis's opinion, it follows, no known economic theory is empirically refutable. But since quite a few economic theories have been empirically refuted, they might be refutable and so Latsis is in error. A refuted theory, though no longer proposed as a putative truth, must remain a good falsifiable theory for ever and a day. Hence, falsificationism is not "too restrictive" and the only need that Latsis claims his Lakatosian views come to satisfy is a false need.

Moreover, Latsis applies the idea of Lakatos not as is, but in a few modifications. He should discuss the question whether his modification is progressive or apologetic and regressive. Instead, he consigns it to a mere footnote on page 2. Rather than demanding *à la* Lakatos the assessment of one program relative to another, in that mere footnote Latsis kindly permits assessment in isolation. He also requires that a theory should be "empirically progressive" (I do not know why he puts the words in quotes, nor what they are meant to convey). The other modifications he does not even bother to state. To me he seems to be a heretic wearing the guise of orthodoxy. Erosions like this happen in the best schools, but usually not at conception or even birth; they usually happen both past maturity and past the period of growth, not merely past the period of growth.

An important idea: social science can have a research program based not on a theory of society but on a theory of science and of method. Of course, this idea too is quite anti-Lakatosian, since Lakatos demanded a theory that can be served as a hard core, not a mere methodology. Yet it is a true and important idea despite its conflict with Lakatos. (I have discussed it in 'Methodological Individualism', *British Journal of Sociology*, 1960, reprinted in J. Agassi and I. C. Jarvie, *Rationality*, Dordrecht, 1987; I suppose the idea belongs to Gellner: 'Time and Theory in Social Anthropology', *Mind*, 1958, reprinted in his *Cause and Meaning in the Social Sciences*, London, 1973; see also discussions of it in I. C. Jarvie, *The Revolution in Anthropology*, London, 1964, and in my *Towards a Rational Philosophical Anthropology*, The Hague, 1977).

Latsis's paper is hard to follow; it is, anyway, but a sketch. If one cleans the paper of the Lakatosian irrelevancies and the idiosyncratic terminology of Lakatos and Latsis, then one may find in it something which can be developed. Whether it is worth the effort is the next question.

A. W. Coats: 'Economics and Psychology: the Death and Resurrection of a Research Programme', its author tells us, is a rewrite of a 1974 paper on an early Lakatosian paper by Latsis, written at Lakatos's invitation when he was the editor of the *British Journal for the Philosophy of Science*, which 1974 paper is a rewrite of the author's 1953 Ph.D. thesis. This seems to be the early swallow of Lakatos as a (Kuhnian) paradigm for philosophy of science: every established philosopher of science is now invited, I suppose, to rewrite his doctoral dissertation in Lakatosese and to claim, like our author, to be making "a constructive contribution to the collective effort" (how Kuhnian can one get?) "to assess the value of MSRP", i.e., of the views of Lakatos on the Methodology of Scientific Research Programs, "as a research tool" (p. 43). Anyway, Lakatos offers a better paradigm for a historian than Kuhn, we are told, "largely owing to the vagueness of such key terms as 'paradigm', 'crisis', 'revolution', and 'normal science' " (p. 44). Admittedly, the key terms of Lakatos are vague too (p. 44, line 14), "yet, paradoxically enough. . . ."

Coats's case study is the history of American economics, particularly of the debate about "the psychological foundations of economic theory". The debate was epistemological and methodological. Hence, again, its study is not very relevant to Lakatos's theory of the methodology of scientific research programs, his celebrated MSRP, which has to do with the central metaphysical presuppositions of the researchers, not at all with their methodology. Like Duhem and Polanyi and Kuhn, Lakatos felt that the proper approach to the history of science requires that its practitioners ignore the epistemological and methodological views of the historical figures whose works are under examination; Lakatos even advised researchers to ascribe his own views on these matters to the scientists of the past—a procedure that is justified, as he said in his seminar when I visited it just before he died, by Hegel's doctrine of the Cunning of Reason. This seems to be noticed even by our author, who confesses, "Viewed from the perspective of MSRP, this miscellaneous ragbag of assertions does not amount to much". "Nevertheless, and with some stretch of the imagination", he continues unabashedly (p. 49). Generally, Coats is incredibly cavalier about his own main points (see, e.g., pp. 54-55, 59-61), and he thus invites disregard.

Yet Coats's story is fascinating, and makes one wish his doctoral dissertation were being prepared for publication. I cannot possibly do it justice here beyond suggesting that the reader enjoy it with its Lakatosian irrelevancies. Like Coats, I am an admirer of Frank Knight who is oddly respected yet ignored as an alleged mere predecessor to Friedman. Yet the author misses his own opportunity: he refuses to discuss Knight's fallibilism which he misinterprets as the view "that scientific knowledge was ultimately inferior to knowledge derived from intuition, emotion and commonsense" (p. 51, note); while boldly and in flagrant violation of the truth considering both George Stigler and Jacob Viner as refutationists. He does this (p. 56) in two steps. First, he correctly ascribes to them the view that science requires testability, and, second, he presents testability in its 'usual' (i.e., Popperian) reading: "testability, i.e., capacity to generate falsifiable predictions". In this way it is easy to make almost any scientist look Popperian, also Whewellian and also Duhemian. I am at a loss when I read such loosely constructed arguments, and can only say that with such logic one can get from anywhere to anywhere else.

Neil De Marchi: 'Anomaly and Development of Economics: The Case of the Leontief Paradox', starts on the wrong foot: it delcares Milton Friedman a falsificationist. I need not refer him to Klappholz and Agassi, 'Methodological Prescriptions in Economics' (*Economica*, 1959): he should know his Friedman and his falsificationism better without it. De Marchi's quotation from Lakatos on "the naive falsificationist's disconnected chains of conjectures and refutations", fits Lakatos of the celebrated *Proofs and Refutations* so much better than it fits Friedman. Characteristically senescent, the members of the embryonic Lakatosian school treat the early Lakatos the way Marxists once used to treat early Marx, and so by analogy there is still hope that the Lakatosians will one day discover early Lakatos and rehabilitate his naive falsificationism, despite its defective presentation of the history of mathematics as "disconnected chains of conjectures and refutations". But, to repeat, I do not wish to declare Lakatos quite as important and quite as durable as Marx; for, this is—or had better be—the last hurrah of the Lakatos school.

De Marchi praises Lakatos's idea as leading to novelty and endorses in a footnote a theory of novelty which is supposedly Elie Zahar's and supposedly Lakatosian. It happens to be mine and I suppose it is Popperian. No, on reflection I must correct myself: it appears in Bacon's *Novum Organum*, I, Aph. 109, though Bacon's presentation suffers from the mistaken confusion of the unexpected with the counter-expected, a confusion which the Lakatosians share and which I have observed and analyzed in *Towards an Historiography of Science* (facsimile reprint, Wesleyan University Press, 1967) and in my essay on novelty (reprinted in my *Science in Flux*, Reidel,

1975) where I define the new *à la* Popper, as the counter-expected.

A country tends to export goods which are cheap at home and expensive abroad, and *vice versa*. When the portion of a cheaper factor in a product increases, the tendency to export it increases too. Now, Leontief has claimed, on the basis of some empirical data that he has analyzed, that American exports tend to increase when the portion of labor-cost in the exported product goes up relative to capital investment. Hence, paradoxically (since contrary to first impressions), the United States seems to be more labor-abundant than capital-abundant. Perhaps, he says, this is indeed so because the American worker is so effective. So much for Leontief. What can one say in response?

Some doubted the findings; some tried to check the limits of validity of the theory that leads to the seemingly false conclusions; others designed alternatives to that theory; yet most students of the topic simply ignored Leontief. De Marchi groups those who ignored Leontief in one research program. I think it is too little for a research program since the Master says that a research program has to have a 'hard core'. De Marchi uses Lakatos only twice, and then only his idiosyncratic terminology. Nevertheless, he says, Lakatos "fits remarkably well" the historical facts he describes (p. 123). What of it? After all, De Marchi admits that Lakatos's view is "not necessarily the only one" to deliver the goods (p. 124). He should therefore refuse to conclude that either the Lakatosian research program in methodology or the one in economics which ignored Leontief altogether, "is a paradigm of virtuous . . . research" (p. 124). Instead, he concludes so only regarding the economic one. For my part, I think Don Patinkin has summed up well the general state of empirical economic research in a statement that is by now classic, and is cited in this volume by Hutchison (p. 203): all facts cited by economists fit too well only the doctrines of the schools in which they had been trained. It is easy to ignore such facts.

Mark Blaug: 'Kuhn versus Lakatos or Pradigms versus Research Programs in the History of Economics'. "In the 1950s and the 1960s economists learned their methodology from Popper". Blaug explains: he means not Popper but Friedman, who is, indeed, popular; except that, anyway, "Friedman is Popper-with-a-twist applied to economics". Let me remind Blaug that he contradicts the Master: Hutchison quotes Lakatos's view about economists' "reluctance" to accept Popper (pp. 200–01). That might trouble him more than his violation of the rules of civilized presentation and debate. Alternatively, not only Friedman, but also Lakatos is Popper-with-a-twist. But what a twist!

Now "particular theories" cannot be appraised "without invoking the wider, metaphysical framework in which they are embedded", we are told. Being myself known as something of an advocate of the idea of appraising metaphysical frameworks and of theories within them, I am embarrassed: God protect us from our friends. So let me now refute Blaug's careless exaggeration. A scientific theory, to begin with, may be very important just because it fits no known metaphysics; think of all the poor theories of radioactivity prior to Rutherford's, which do fit the 'progressive' framework of their time, and think of the shock caused by the statistical but not causal, refutable—indeed refuted—radiation theory. Or think of Malthus's theory which can be embedded, if at all, only within some ecology or another, though the first ecologist was his follower Darwin. Darwin refuted Malthus by sheer ecological considerations: human populations grow geometrically, but food grows arithmetically, said Malthus; but food is a population too, retorted Darwin. Hence when a framework to assess Malthus's theory came into being, the theory was already thereby superseded. This paragraph may serve as an instance of the travails of a critic: though the reviewed essay is obviously in error, refuting one sentence from it may take a whole paragraph and deserve much less. I therefore chose instances which refute not only Blaug, but also Lakatos, who postulated the dogmatic 'hard core' theory because he overlooked Popper's great insight on the theoretical import of the refutation of an interesting theory. Had Lakatos learned his Popper better, we would not have the Lakatosian school on our hands. Ignorance is bliss.

Blaug wishes to discuss the question, who is better, Lakatos or Kuhn? "The task is not an easy one. Lakatos is a difficult author to pin down. His tendency to make vital points in footnotes, to proliferate labels for different intellectual positions, and to refer back and forth to his own writings", are all qualities that make life hard for his poor disciples. Also, on this matter I should add, his disciples emulate him in this volume, though to a lesser degree: they lack his wit and vital energy.

Popper's theory, taken descriptively, is in error, we are told, because natural scientists never endorsed Popper's proposal to reject a theory after one refutation. (Did any ever endorse Lakatos?) Kuhn is in error because revolutions do not occur overnight, but take ages to be completed. I am flabbergasted. The refutation of the Bohr-Kramers-Slater theory of 1924 led to the new quantum theory of 1926, thus refuting Blaug on both Kuhn and Lakatos in one blow. This is very annoying, I think, but I must proceed. In Blaug's opinion (p. 154) Kuhn confuses prescriptions and descriptions. This, of course, is one of the few charges made against Kuhn that cannot stick: he is explicitly describing facts as he sees them and he explicitly says he likes them. But let this too ride for now. Lakatos's position is 'softer' than Popper's but a great deal 'harder' than Kuhn's, we are told. It is both prescriptive and descriptive—with or without a confusion?—and the descriptive aspect of it is "perfectly refutable" (p. 155). Perfectly. Is it "perfectly refutable" in a hard sense or in a soft sense? Does it require only one good counter-example or do we need a series of Lakatosian theories so as to be able to evaluate each of them as 'progressive' or not? I confess I am at sea. And so I have been asking questions on the possible refutability of Lakatos's alleged views of science ever since I began commenting on his obscure essays on science. Lakatos hinted he was aware of the trouble here.

He said (PSA Boston Meeting, *Boston Studies*, vol. 8) that my own—Popperian—hard-refutationism was refuted, but not in the hard sense of refutation, since in this sense refutations do not exist since my hard refutationism is refuted; he did not live to say in which sense my refutationism was refuted. Myself, I see no point in adhering to one and only one mode, and see in history delightful cases and silly cases of both hard and soft attitudes to putative refutations; the Lakatos gang simply cares too much about the proclamations of the Master about history and too little about history itself. When two parties disagree, they often try to refute each other. When their views of the force of refutation disagree, then perhaps there is a communication barrier. Communication barriers often lead to charges of relativism and/or dogmatism. Since neither Lakatos nor I can be viewed as relativists, had he lived longer we might very well have ended up calling each other a dogmatic philosopher of science. Except that in order to earn the title of a dogmatic philosopher of science he would have had to produce more ideas concerning science than his early demise permitted.

All this, however, is way above the head of poor Blaug who presents Lakatos's criterion of the goodness of a theory in two mutually exclusive variants without noticing this fact. Variant one: a program must be progressive or perish. Variant two: a program must be more progressive than all its competitors.

So much for Blaug the methodologist. Blaug the historian says (p. 161), "Keynes went still further [than whom?] in tampering with the 'hard core' that had been handed down since the time of Adam Smith". To me this seems a deviation from the pure doctrine: the theory of tampering tampers with the theory of Lakatos, for whom 'hard cores' are perfectly solid. Hence, if Lakatos is "perfectly refutable", then perhaps Blaug has perfectly refuted him. Perfect.

How did Keynes tamper with the 'hard core'? First of all, he departed from the principle of 'methodological individualism'. But Smith was not a methodological individualist—he was an individualist proper, of course, an ontological one. And I remember Watkins, in his celebrated paper on Weber's two ideal types, quoting Keynes on the psychological nature of liquidity-preference so as to make him a good methodological individualist. Our author seems to be alluding to Watkins while dismissing him: "To be sure, he [Keynes] felt impelled by tradition to speak of a 'fundamental psychological law' but he was merely paying lip service to the bankrupt tradition". Blaug likewise takes unusual liberties with Smith and Ricardo. He seems very pleased with his tampering with historical facts, and I shall not spoil his fun. But he gets very greedy when, for a grand finale, he undertakes an attempt to "appraise the whole of neoclassical economics with the aid of Lakatos's methodology" (p. 171), which attempt can only be undertaken in retrospect, we remember, and so it cannot be done today, since neo-classical economics is—justly or not—still so much alive and kicking.

To conclude, I consider the alleged Lakatosian essays failures, more teasing than substantive, and manifestly deviating from Lakatos all the way. The failure, however, regarding Blaug, is the editor's acceptance of his diatribe for publication. Anyway, our editor, we remember, makes his case rest on the four Lakatosian papers. With this then, my case can rest: the research program doesn't exist.

Axel Leijonhufvud: 'Schools, "Revolutions", and Research Programmes in Economic Theory'. One day Lakatos, knowing neither economics nor the author, met him and demanded that he rewrite his celebrated book on the Keynesian Revolution as a test case between Kuhn and Lakatos. The author decided to comply, and the result is a discussion "of the problems in the way of applying recent Growth of Knowledge Theories [i.e., Kuhn and/or Lakatos] to the history of economics" and "concrete illustrations of these problems". Very appetizing indeed. Except that, incredible though it seems, it is clear that he thinks he is both a Lakatosian and a Kuhnian (see note on pp. 83–87). This volume really is a bit aggravating: after Lakatos put so much stress on his divergence from Kuhn, a Lakatosian tells us nonchalantly the opposite.

In a footnote early in his paper the author compares old-fashioned normative methodologists to peddling knife-grinders who press their services and wish to sharpen even adequate knives to make them capable of splitting hairs; "some farmers, it was said, would set their dogs on people like that. Some philosophers of science may, of course, feel that without the grindstone always in evidence charges of vagrancy without means of support are inevitable" (p. 66).

How is a reviewer supposed to respond to what is an obviously intentional and outright insult? Perhaps overlook it; perhaps also criticize the factual distortion. Well, then, I offer here an empirical observation: philosophers hardly ever pester scientists; most of them usually adore them; most of the rest ignore scientists; most of the rest bark at scientists at a safe distance; philosophers who criticize scientists (as scientists) hardly exist, alas! Scientists, by contrast, often tell philosophers all about scientific method and pester them and call them lazy and set metaphorical dogs at them.

Not that it matters to our author that philosophers of science prescribe: Kuhn and Lakatos prescribe too, yet he loves them both (p. 66). It is not even that the philosophers of science mix descriptions and prescriptions: so do both Kuhn and Lakatos too (p. 66)—but in the way economists do (p. 66). But the author means something extremely simple here: Kuhn describes the activities of scientists approvingly; so does Lakatos (not true; see discussion of Hutchison's paper below; but let this ride); and, after all, economists describe the entrepreneur's activities approvingly too (again, not true; but so what?).

The history of economics is a history of schools and of revolutions. This bothers our author since it is "not structured in accordance with any explicit Growth of Knowledge theory". Too bad for the facts. Moreover, the author says, schools and revolutions are different in the physical sciences from the social sciences. How? Why? Does it matter? If so, how? No reply.

Like the other contributors thus far, our author only thinks he is a Lakatosian. I do not mean to criticize him, as the editor does, for being future-oriented as against the Master's injunction: in this, we have seen, he is not alone; and excesses can anyway simply be trimmed. The author notices two kinds of hard-cores, of irrefutable centers of refutable theorizing that allegedly bind clusters of theories into programs; the one is the presuppositions, the other is the formal move or a part of it (p. 72). This, of course, is conventionalism, not methodology of scientific research programs Lakatos style—no MSRP. Also, whereas MSRP is "severely internalist"—"in clear line of descent from the Vienna Circle via Popper" (p. 73n)—economics is forced into 'externalism' by what Popper has called the Oedipus Effect and Robert Merton has called the Self-Fulfilling Prophecy. So again no MSRP for our author.

There are clever *aperçus* here and there in the text and in the notes, but I do not know what to do with them. In particular, the author does notice that Lakatos's idea of progressiveness stands on its own and is interesting, which is refreshing, though it is but a step short of the return to early Lakatos, who fathered the idea with no RP at all. He also notices that Lakatos suffers from what Lakatos has derisively labelled 'instant rationality' (p. 79 and note); still without having his faith in Kuhn and Lakatos shaken. He even notices that the conventionalist protection of a model as mathematically true is in conflict with early Lakatos who is thus more relevant to pure economics (p. 81). Here is a very good insight: Lakatos is here prescriptive and critical; indeed a really lovely knife-grinder. I cannot avoid quoting the last blow the author delivers to Lakatos at the end of his methodological part (p. 81): "The development of the language convention, without which 'strictly irrefutable' hard-core propositions are impossible, poses a problem in applying Lakatos's theory in that the process will resemble that of degeneration". Resemble! It is truly amazing how much the Lakatosian degeneration resembles degeneration despite its so very early onset.

The second part of Leijonhufvud's essay is on the history of economics. He discusses the book he had written prior to the momentous meeting with Lakatos, and so was not cast in the language of KLMSRP. He tells us (p. 85) that the book "was concerned with the problems and conundrums resulting from the collision of Keynesianism with the, by then stronger, 'neoclassical' program" (p. 85). *Mirabile visu*: the job Lakatos assigned the author had been completed even before their historic encounter, and all the author had to do in order to comply with the assignment he received from Lakatos was to let it surface and really look the instance of LMSRPDQ that at heart it always was. This seems to me too facile: *ex post facto*.

The modern debate between the schools of economists finally led to the question of "why the . . . system fails to absorb unemployment", a question our author alone thinks is the wrong question. Can this deviation be justified by "the modern Growth of Knowlege theories"? Certainly not, since both Kuhn and Lakatos are staunchly authoritarian, and so anti-deviationists, we may remember. Our author admits that he is "not able to make it of direct relevance to Lakatos's or Kuhn's theory. A philosophical problem would seem to be involved but, if so, it is a problem on which the Growth of Knowledge literature . . . has little to say" (pp. 88–89). If this literature—that concerns itself almost exclusively with agenda for research—has nothing to say on the question of which questions are high up on the research economists' agenda then obviously it has nothing to say to them. (See my 'Logic of Questions and Metaphysics', reprinted in my *Science in Flux*.)

Though seemingly a confused and ignorant philosopher, our author is an astute historian of recent economic thought whose allegedly Lakatosian-before-Lakatos book has won some acclaim. For my part, I love his attempt to develop his views on the history of economic thought around the question of choice of questions.

Herbert A. Simon: 'From Substantive to Procedural Rationality' is one more paper in a distinguished series by a distinguished author. The references to the Lakatos literature were added as an after-thought to make it possible to re-read it at the Lakatos Greek Island Conference (note on p. 129). He does so by claiming that the Lakatosian terminology is a new dress for a familiar old lady—and an old Rose by any other name fades as fast as any. I need not say that I am unconvinced; it is no old lady but an old junk-heap of all sorts of flotsam and jetsam.

Simon has interesting observations about economics and psychology. The cost-plus theory, for example, was offered by psychologists as an alternative to marginalism (p. 137). I am unimpressed: the marginalists are quite right in dismissing this as a minor detail. They say that the mark-up, or how much an entrepreneur adds to the production-cost of a commodity so as to fix his sales price, is determined not psychologically but by the market: the margin is raised or lowered (and at times is made negative), depending on the market mechanism, and only in equilibrium is the mark-up fixed as the income the entrepreneur could gain by other means. More interesting observations are made about operational research: whereas economic theory attempts at methods determining uniquely answers to given questions, operational researchers are trained at a trial-and-error method (pp. 139–40). Lovely, though hardly psychology, and so, I am afraid, beside Simon's declared point.

Simon is presenting and advocating a problem-shift in the field of the interface of economics and psychology. He does not convince me, but I am grateful for his thought-provoking ideas. They are challenging to anyone concerned with the general theory of shifts of intellectual frameworks; he is not: he has been trying now for years to effect one specific shift, along his own specific research program.

T. W. Hutchison: 'On the History and Philosophy of Science and Economics' is a masterly survey, studded with incredible quotations, of the views of Popper, Kuhn, Rawls (where have you been till now?), and Lakatos (treating Latsis, our editor, as a mouthpiece for Lakatos) on the methodology and status of economic theory. It is brief, succinct, critical. I highly recommend it: it is both civilized and hard-hitting.

"According to Lakatos: 'While Polanyite academic autonomy should be defended for departments of theoretical physics, it must not be tolerated, say. . . .' (p. 197)." Once a Stalinist always a Stalinist? 'Must not be tolerated', I think, must not be tolerated. But perhaps there is no cause for any real worry: as it happens Lakatos does not explicitly forbid 'Polanyite academic autonomy' for any known standard department of a standard university. Hutchison, however, reads him to forbid autonomy for all social scientists. And he goes on citing Lakatos's injunction to philosophers of science to impose the proper standards. So much for Lakatos's injunction to appraise only in retrospect. But perhaps I am too rash: there may be no inconsistency here. To the past Lakatos offers appraisal without imposition; to the future, imposition without appraisal. Somehow this does not sound quite right.

Sir John Hicks offers the *pièce de résistance* of the volume, ' "Revolutions" in Economics'. It presents economics as a historical study and hence a tradition, very much the way Sir Edward Evans-Pritchard used to present social anthropology. It is very well written and most enjoyable. Its only connection with Lakatos is on page 215 where Hicks's adamant and continued un-Keynesian attitude is also translated into Lakatosese.

Finally, the *Index* by Barbara Lowe. It is one of the brightest I have seen; still, it is too incomplete and uncritical to be satisfactory: it hides major differences between the contributors.

Epilogue: I hope the picture that emerges raises in the reader a few questions. In particular, why is it that a few Lakatosians, hand-picked by the Master himself, cannot agree on fundamentals, cannot produce one work of value, and bungle things so? I first met Lakatos in fall, 1957, in the Oxford meeting of the British Society for the Philosophy of Science. At a gathering between sessions he said that the later Wittgenstein could pass for a serious philosopher until his enemies (meaning his literary executors) began to publish his stuff. His words still ring in my ears, and the laughter they provoked too. I think what happened to the later Wittgenstein may now be happening to the later Lakatos.

Perhaps there is a moral to this comparison. Both individuals were strong, imposing, engaging, charismatic, glamorous, scintillating—IT for short. IT, however, is hard to keep alive beyond the grave: how many people can warm up to the 'once most glamorous but now-dead movie star'?

Memory of IT is something else; nostalgia, sentimentality, regrets, perhaps even history; not IT. Intellectually, moreover, IT is the worst. When an actor with IT seems to be talking to every member of a huge audience and seems to tell each of them how to overcome all difficulties with little effort, no one will call him a false prophet. If the actor occupies an intellectual position, then the picture may, but need not, radically change. I do not wish to blame Latsis *et al.* for trying to keep alive the memory of their IT mentor. But no one can do it; IT is most transient anyhow, and as intellectual food for thought it comes dangerously close to being sham. And so, I suggest, let things be. Let Lakatos remain the trail-blazing author of *Proofs and Refutations*, and let his ruminations on empirical science remain what they are, an endeavor unfinished, or even hardly begun.

In conclusion I wish to tender an apology to both my readers and the editor of the present volume on the economic part of the Lakatos Greek Island conference. My review is longer than the book itself warrants—only good books deserve reviews, really—and not long enough, considering the circumstances. I think I have shown that the editor's preface is very misleading on each particular point of his introduction of the papers (whereas on the general point of the introduction, we remember, he is inconsistent in requiring us to look forward to the evolution of a backward-looking program). Indeed, he can hardly avoid all the difficulties present, since all his contributors are inevitably forward-looking one way or another; Hicks is un-Lakatosian in pushing forward his unorthodox program and his reliance on Lakatos here is spurious, whereas Leijonhufvud is, of course, as self-declared a Lakatosian as his colleagues; and so it goes. Hence, the editor had an impossible task, and my catching him cheating a bit in his introduction is really too fussy and a bit unfair. So much for the apology. And now for the circumstances that have put me on this sticky wicket.

Imre Lakatos was no ordinary mortal. He could and did take liberties he knew he should not, in the hope that he would live long enough to rectify them and compensate the injured parties (I have this from the horse's mouth). He was thus unusually ill-prepared for his lamentably early demise. Ordinarily, when a scholar dies we let the dust settle and the good tower over the bad. In some cases this is excluded by the scholar's high-handedness. In our case there is also Lakatos's importation of the East European style of political intrigue into the western commonwealth of learning. And so, much discretion is required, more than can be reasonably expected of one review—if Lakatos is not simply to be forgotten by all but his cronies. Yet for what it is worth here are two points which I deem central.

The worst in Lakatos was his demand to look backward (a confession of one's inability to be sufficiently forward-looking is so much better for the same ends; except that humility never had any appeal to Lakatos, even when it would have been very becoming). To say, with Hegel and with

Lakatos, that the owl of Minerva flies at dusk, is to say: you cannot test my ideas by attempts to implement them, and you are not competent to judge me before my death anyway. So be it. The dusk has come and the night is dark; for better or worse the sun of Lakatos has set. We must now judge his backward gaze as backward. But I wish to plead that it be noted and remembered that there is more to Lakatos than that. Not only are his philosophy of mathematics, his critical heuristic, a significant breakthrough and a trail-blazing adventure, they also have broad implications, the most significant of which is his idea of forward-looking and backward-looking problem-shifts. It excites me so because it offers a schema for efforts to explain rationally the historically recurrent fact that problems evolve, alter, take alternating roots, and ever so often end up neglected in the middle of the investigations concerning them; they lead to better problems, they become too tedious to study, their study remains valid with a 'ghost intellectual framework'.

This is why economists can find Lakatos exciting and useful and forward-looking. Are the monetarists living within a ghost intellectual framework or are they living in a viable one? It all depends on how forward-looking their researches are. Are perhaps the Keynesians the ones who retained an outdated program even though a younger one? Hicks has got this point, and at times even Leijonhufvud. Though I find Hutchison's scathing critique just, I wish to end on an encouraging note. Let us see the fruitful ideas of Lakatos stand out and survive his idiosyncracies. I hear his ghost approving of this as quite a progressive problem-shift.

NOTES

1. For more details, see p. 353ff above.

33

THE LAKATOSIAN REVOLUTION

how not to pull rabbits out of hats

1. LAKATOS AS A TEACHER

Lakatos's classic *Proofs and Refutations* (Cambridge University Press, 1976) reports the goings-on in a classroom in Utopia. Lakatos himself tried out the Utopian experiment in a real class early in the day—it was in Popper's seminar, and while he was writing his doctoral dissertation which includes an early draft of his masterpiece. Not surprisingly, then, he was acidly critical of some aspects of the accepted modes of mathematical teaching (to be discussed below). Nonetheless, I know of no discussion of his educational philosophy—printed, manuscript, or orally presented.

Perhaps this reticence, thus far, relates to the fact that Lakatos took an active part in the student revolt affair, and the definitely wrong part. There was, I am of the opinion, no right part, at least no obviously right part, to the students' revolts of the 1960s anywhere in evidence (except, I think, for the initial demands of the French students, the rejection of which sparked off their revolt); but there were greater or lesser degrees of wrong. The students at times demanded the wrong things, and usually in the wrong way. But this is not to condemn them out of hand, much less to take a reactionary stand in the name of the preservation of all that deserves preserving, refuse to yield on any point, and recommend non-negotiation. Lakatos did take such a stand.

Perhaps the reticence, thus far, is due to the fact that Lakatos evolved into a highly successful university lecturer of the old style and was highly censorious of those colleagues of his who, he felt, did not live up to the obligations of a university lecturer as he understood them, failed to prepare for each lecture elaborate lecture-notes, failed to cover much informative

This essay first appeared in *Essays in Memory of Imre Lakatos, Boston Studies in the Philosophy of Science*, 21, 1976. Copyright Reidel Publishing Company, Dordrecht, Holland.

material in each lecture, and so on. I am too averse to the old-fashioned view to do it justice, but I think the reader may be familiar enough with it, even if he is not familiar with its Central-European, rich, and thick, and learned, and emotionally charged, and witty, and sweeping variants. I assure the reader that all these epithets fit Professor Lakatos's later performances as a university lecturer in his lecture courses in the London School of Economics; that he would have taken this ascription of them to him as a high compliment; that I for one do not see anything to praise in the tradition or mold he was so proud to belong to; and that his Utopian lectures, in *Proofs and Refutations* as well as in his earliest performances in the London School of Economics as a guest speaker in Professor Popper's seminar on scientific method, which I so admire, had as little to do with that tradition as is at all conceivable.

We once used to wonder about the fact that makers and starters of revolutions so often stayed behind. T. S. Eliot has changed this with his deep insight in *Journey of the Magi*.

2. SCHOOLS AND SCHOLARSHIP

Inasmuch as schools supposedly convey in a condensed manner all that is worth preserving in our heritage, it may just as well be an excellent representation of it. Even when what schools pass on to the vast population that passes through them is not the very best, nevertheless it often is representative. I have found from experience that some puzzlements about a foreign culture may be resolved by even a superficial perusal of the curriculum, the set texts, and similar educational materials.

I suppose it is very customary still, in the curricula and syllabi of many university departments around the globe, to claim that students are offered there not only materials but also the means of acquisition of more materials. These means are software and hardware, with instruments and libraries as hardware and techniques of using them as software. The software is often carried in the student's—or researcher's—head or notebooks, and known by the embracing name of methods or methodology. Schools often claim to be teaching methods and/or methodology. They do not.

An exception, noted by Lakatos any number of times, is this. Whereas most teachers claim that they teach methods, some of the most high-powered mathematics teachers openly deny that they teach methods. They think that the acquisition of large doses of mathematical knowledge in itself develops in the student a high level of mathematical sophistication which enables one to resolve old puzzles one's teacher has chosen to leave unsolved and to develop the necessary skills to continue in one's predecessor's footsteps investigating new areas of knowledge.

What Lakatos briefly suggested is that this is a mere excuse; that, in other words, the puzzles a teacher leaves unsolved he cannot solve—at the early stage in which they arise or even at any other stage—and that the methods he does not teach he does not know. A fish, Lakatos was fond of saying, may well be able to swim with not the slightest knowledge of hydrodynamics. Lakatos never explained.

Now let us be open-minded about this. Popper's philosophy, which influenced Lakatos at the time he was writing his drafts, starts with the assertion that there is no scientific method. And, Lakatos is right in claiming that the view that there exists scientific method in the sense in which Popper combats it—the Baconian sense of a sausage-making machine with a sure output as long as input keeps flowing—thanks to Popper "at least among philosophers of science Baconian method is now only taken seriously by the most provincial and illiterate" (*The Philosophy of Karl Popper*, ed. P. A. Schilpp, Open Court, 1974, p. 259). Inductivism, Lakatos thought, was definitely out. I am not even quite happy about that since I read Konrad Lorenz's and Nikolaas Tinbergen's Nobel Lectures that are fairly Baconian; philosophers of science are still not ready to dismiss as insignificant the views of such big fish. Anyway, at least in the present essay we can take it for granted that no Baconian method exists. It is clear that Popper—and Lakatos too—assumes that in other senses methods do exist, however vague this statement is; for example, it is left open whether the more general method of testing in science or more specific methods, more peculiar to given ages and fields, like the mathematical methods in theoretical physics, the empirical methods common in ever so many contemporary laboratories, etc. can be taught. Are laboratory manuals of much use, and, even if they are, should one read them rather than consult them on occasion?

I speak of the teaching of mathematical methods because, I think, Lakatos was right: mathematicians did not teach them because they were ignorant of them. I shall claim that the only excuse teachers have for teaching is ignorance—their own; their students' is taken for granted, of course. If so, then teachers will do better to study rather than teach, since the more they will know the less they will wish to teach, which is all to the good. This is particularly true concerning methods. We all know that foreign aid in the form of consumers' goods is only good for emergencies and as a stand-by, that the important goods foreign aid can transmit are means of producing consumers' goods—both hardware and soft. What is true of underdeveloped countries is true of underdeveloped individuals.

3. THE PROBLEM OF THE MAGIC OF MATHEMATICS AND LAKATOS'S SOLUTION

Consider the observation of a magician pulling a rabbit out of a top-hat. He can do so spontaneously, or after he is requested to do so by members of his audience. It is in a sense less surprising—namely, expected—in a sense more surprising—that he can do so upon request. The second sense of surprise, not the first, concerns a mathematics student. For, in the first sense surprise is momentary and can be cushioned by the preparation of anticipation; in the second sense surprise can be retained until alleviated by explanation, and so is a kind of puzzlement. (This is why some magicians like it this way, some that way. Those who like it this way keep talking to avoid interruption; those who like it that way plant people in their audience who make the proper request.) Now observing a magician we are puzzled and are meant to be puzzled; not to understand. But when a mathematics teacher pulls rabbits out of a top-hat we are meant to comprehend, yet we are puzzled. How can we both comprehend and remain puzzled?

There is no doubt that mathematics teachers do pull the rabbits of exciting theorems from the top-hats of all sorts of axioms and definitions. Whether they do so apologetically—sorry to be unable to relieve the puzzlement as any magician does for his apprentices—or with a vengeance—defying his students as any magician defies his audience, especially if the audience is rather presumptuous—is not a matter I shall go into. I do accept Lakatos's observation: they cannot resolve the puzzlement, at least not as yet. Perhaps later on they can explain the puzzlement to a budding colleague, after he or she has acquired much more insight into the working of the mathematical method. All right, says Lakatos, let us spell out to ourselves what is this working of mathematical method and how the puzzlement is to be resolved by it. It turns out to be no mean matter: very few studies exist on mathematical methods, whether written by working mathematicians or not, and their whole product is quite meager.

Before Lakatos came to make his mark, a few ideas were extant on the matter. The simplest idea, one which is still not rare in mathematics departments, one which he felt compelled to fight time and time again—though now it is somewhat less popular, and so toward the end of his life he felt he could ignore it—is the sausage-machine idea. Essentially, the view goes, you choose a set of axioms, try to avoid inconsistency, and feed them into any old deduction-machine which will start churning out theorems, mostly worthless and uninteresting, but some useful, some interesting, some both. If so, then mathematicians are simply finding needles in haystacks and have no idea which haystack—axioms—to choose or how to increase the frequency of finding needles—interesting or useful theorems—in the haystack. In that case the puzzle is unresolvable, and all a budding mathematician can hope for is better luck and a better intuition for short-cuts. But that's all. The promise which the mathematics professor makes to students, of a better understanding in maturity, then, is quite pointless: he does not have it himself.

Another theory, which I have heard from Popper in his lectures but I think is not unknown, looks the very opposite of the above idea, but in a surprising manner turns out to be a variant of it. We start not with axioms but with problems (so runs the variant), where problems are theorems to be proved. The rest is a matter of intuition and luck: you choose your axioms or you have them given, and you wade through innumerably possible deductive routes, looking for the one which leads you from your axioms to your theorem. If you succeed, you have to tell your students that you can deduce the theorem (or its negation, or its independence), but not why this route was successful, whereas other routes lead not to the same destination. (Nor can you tell whether an open case is decidable, or which way.) This method is a variant, since it only adds lucky short-cuts.

There is a lot to this variant: the student is told what should be understood—namely, each single step in the deduction—and what remains a puzzle—namely, how a specific deductive route was chosen; one can see how the few attempts which have failed have failed, and that the successful one succeeds. The strong evidence in support of this explanation, of the success of the short-cut as lucky, is also mentioned by Popper (in Schilpp's Popper volumes, p. 1077): once a proof is discovered, "almost invariably it can be simplified." That is to say, even when the needle is found, it is part needle, part hay to be removed; yet the very removal of the hay shows the existence of a proof-idea, an idea to be hit upon by trial-and-error. It is this proof-idea, incidentally, that allegedly the mathematical students learn to appreciate when they acquire an ever-increasing number of proofs. If so, says George Polya, we can teach from the start both proof-ideas and the method of trial-and-error by which one may learn to hit upon a successful proof-idea oneself—first a known one, as a true apprentice rather than a passive student, and then a new one, as a novice.

Suppose all this is true. Can we, then, explain the method of mathematics, so as to make a success more understandable than drawing a rabbit out of a hat? Not quite. We may, perhaps, explain one proof-idea but each proof has a different one. And so, Polya's idea of letting students discover proofs for themselves is too hard to execute, though his intentions are perfect.

Such was the state of the understanding of methods of mathematics when Lakatos came on stage, with a bow and an expression of gratitude to Polya, while adapting Popper's philosophy to his end; he achieved his end and threw things into a state of havoc.

The relation between Polya and Lakatos is the same as between Whewell and Popper (even though none of the other three knew of Whewell; likewise Lakatos learned about Popper only after his work was begun). All four believe in trial-and-error, in deductive explanation, in starting with problems, with the search for explanations. Yet, whereas Whewell and Polya believe in verification, and see the corpus of (scientific or mathematical) knowledge as the set of successful trials, of verified explanations, Popper and Lakatos are fallibilists and view refuted theories as part and parcel of our heritage.[1]

Lakatos's masterpiece deals with mathematics, not physics. So his refutations are not physical; they are potential counter-examples; at times, but rarely and gratuitously, they are even actual. The task is to look for them; proofs facilitate refutations as they specify conditions which we may violate in our search for counter-examples. This makes us able to stretch and shrink concepts, as well as to criticize theorems as at times too narrow—not covering all cases of the theorem—and at other times as too wide—covering counter-examples (whereas actual counter-examples in physics only prove a theorem too wide; its being too narrow only leads to a quest for a further or a better explanation). In a manner not quite clear to Lakatos's readers, a theorem's transformation and transfiguration may end up in formalization. In a sense formal systems are end-products. But only in a sense; formalization does not end the process of proofs and refutations since we can always ask, is the formal system the same as the pre-formal one, or does it have an unintended model?

So much for Lakatos's standpoint. He claims that he is the first to provide a theory about the role of proof in mathematical research. Before him people saw a proof as closing an issue; he saw it as a part of the process of the growth of mathematics. Anyone who reads his masterpiece must notice that the very fact that the proof procedure is a long process of fumbling, of trying again and again, makes the growth of a proof-idea reasonable, especially intriguing and human—as opposed to being an act of magic—in that it is far from perfect and we poke holes in it and see in its strong points and in its weak points matters of great insight and an increased interest. It is the claim that proof-ideas are essentially correct, even if they need a correction or a simplification, that leads to the attempt to offer a simplified condensed version, and thus, further, according to Lakatos, to an appearance of magic. Only if we appreciate errors enough to incorporate some obvious errors into the dynamic growth of a proof-idea do we offer our audiences those details of the making of the act which makes a magician utterly unable to be surprised when he sees a colleague use tricks he himself knows so well and draws rabbits out of top-hats galore.

4. CAN LAKATOS'S METHOD BE APPLIED?

If I were a mathematics teacher asked whether I should emulate the Lakatos method of Utopian teaching, I should hesitate. I would not hesitate if I were asked to teach mathematics to non-mathematicians, or if I were to teach whatever I do teach (since in fact I exhort my students to break the equestrian and asinine habit of hard work and passivity in preference for intelligent work—and the two only seldom overlap). As a mathematics teacher of, say, topology, I should have to cover the material which Lakatos discusses in his *Proofs and Refutations* in the space of a fraction of one lecture. I would have no time at all for his details. Oh, I would gladly advise my students to read Lakatos on a weekend or during a vacation or as relaxing bedtime reading. Still better, if my mathematics students can take credits in either the history of mathematics or in the philosophy of mathematics, then I would gladly propose Lakatos as their major text. But the cruel fact is that Lakatos's very lengthy discussion ends more or less where the modern textbook of topology begins, to wit with Poincaré's algebraic version of the Descartes-Euler Theorem. What shall we do about advanced topology? Can I present it *à la* Lakatos? Do I have the time to do it within a prescribed semester course? Do I know how?

Let us not be finicky. Let us assume that in a small seminar of advanced mathematics, where we are going over raw new material, we can make better use of the deliberation and fumbling of recent students of the field in order to see how they work and not be puzzled to see them pull rabbits out of hats. Let us also agree that if we do not have to move quickly and cover a lot of ground, we can, indeed, use the Lakatos method at leisure. Let us also observe, as a matter of fact, that Lakatos did succeed in making non-mathematicians participate in his Utopian mathematical discussions and reproduce historical cases—with the aid of the teacher, of course.

This last point signifies much. It shows that students' interruptions need not be any impediment; that, erroneous as they are, they help dispel the impression that mathematicians draw rabbits out of top-hats.

Let me stress all this. The general view of the matter is that students' participation is of low quality and so at best a necessary evil. And the minority view—the view known as the discovery-method of teaching—is that students' participation is or should be of high quality, the highest indeed, if only certain conditions are met. But, no doubt, the discovery method is an unrealizable dream: students cannot possibly be systematically so good as to emulate the best minds and the best results in a given field, no matter what that field is. In any case, I insist, whether students are of high quality or low quality matters little, since we want to help them raise their quality such as it is—indeed we should worry more about the low-quality ones. The fallibilist view that the students' interruptions, however low-quality, can be used in class—this view is thrilling because it makes the question of quality superfluous. It assumes that students do fail, and do need help to learn what to do about their failure, how to improve performance, where to find some solution which they have overlooked, and how to try to assess these and perhaps even transcend them. There is one hard question: can we assume that we can pursue such a line of activity for a whole university course? I do not think so.

Let me also concede that at certain junctures even small doses of the Lakatos technique may be added to traditional courses with some excellent results. Let me take a different example of Lakatos's. The foundation of the calculus taught in a rough-and-ready manner to uncomprehending students is very hard. It is much better to tell them something about the early calculus, say Newton's; Berkeley's criticisms; attempts by diverse writers to answer him, culminating with Weierstrass. This can be even read into

Bell's most conventional and wrong-headed history. But, says Lakatos, there is much more to it. Let us look closely at Cauchy. You take a Cauchy series, and you prove that it converges. You have a criticism: that it converges assumes a convergence-point to converge into: is there one for every Cauchy series? Comes Weierstrass and says, yes if we identify the series with the point. I need not explain how revealing this example is, especially of the historical proximity of Cauchy and Weierstrass.

Can we, however, do this for a whole course of mathematics; present a body of mathematical knowledge as a series of proofs and refutations? Is Lakatos right? In other words, is Lakatos's view of mathematics comprehensive?

I think not.

5. MATHEMATICAL SYSTEMS AND SUB-SYSTEMS

Lakatos himself was aware of the fact that his own researches presented not a total view of mathematics and its development, but first and foremost a criticism of all prevalent views—since these were invariably verificationist of one kind or another—and second, a tentative view of mathematics which, when viewed as comprehensive is found wanting exactly in the way that Popper's view of physics is.

I do not think Lakatos ever developed a comprehensive view of mathematics and of its history. I do not think he even had an idea that satisfied him about the way comprehensive views of mathematics have interacted with the growth of mathematics. He wanted to rewrite his 'Proofs and Refutations' in a manner that would include a comprehensive view. He never did.

Let me take an example. Lakatos enthusiastically endorsed Russell's thesis (*Foundations of Geometry*) that 19th-century mathematics is largely the outcome of a response to Kant's comprehensive view of mathematics. I have myself commented on this point elsewhere and shall not go into it now, except to say that Lakatos wanted to incorporate such facts as significant factors in his view of mathematics as a whole, yet he never did. In some place he even declared that formalism, his pet enemy, had a role to play in the history of mathematics. But he never put this into a comprehensive framework.

But let me touch upon less comprehensive instances. I am loath to take cases of any established mathematical truths—seemingly or in truth—as I remember how Lakatos fought like a lion when presented with these. He either disproved them, or claimed that his interlocutor was offering the latest modification of a theorem, designed to overcome a recent refutation. But one example, I think, he did concede and had to concede.

The example is the field of ordinary differential equations. You can, of course, say that it is not so much pure mathematics as applied mathematics.

This will raise a host of important questions—more questions that Lakatos's early demise prevented him from taking up as he intended to do. So let us not go into that.

As a student I found this field particularly irksome. I suppose—though I could not articulate it then—a book will be found irksome if each of its paragraphs makes sense but as a whole it makes none (e.g., a book by L. Wittgenstein). But putting it into its context, offering its problems and methods, makes the field of differential equations eminently lucid and sensible.

Differential equations are puzzles or riddles. We cannot find answers to the puzzles, but we can guess them, try each guess and refute or, on occasion, verify it. This makes the field eminently in accord with Whewell and with Polya. It does not accord with Lakatos, since refutations of blind guesses in this field lead nowhere, but verifications are true successes. To prove this perhaps we need proofs of existence theorems and of uniqueness or generality of solutions or of forms of solutions (uniqueness up to a constant, or up to the product or sum or such of some function or another). Yet, whether existence and uniqueness theorems are above criticism or not, clearly, when we solve a problem set by a differential equation by guessing what the function may be, differentiating and substituting, and arrive at the set equation, then we have solved the problem even though perhaps not uniquely or generally enough. That much, but not much more, Lakatos did concede. Moreover, we are taught a few useful tricks, such as guessing a transformation of the variable(s), which just might transform an unsolved equation to a solved one; and of such tricks we can say we do not know why they work but many people tried many tricks and some were indeed successful. All this is as plain as your nose and quite outside Lakatos's concept of mathematics; his concept is too narrow. Moreover, the idea of transforming differential equations has very wide extensions in modern mathematics, which have axiomatic systems based on similar general ideas though within them the Lakatos method may well be very useful and enlightening.

This includes category theory. Indeed, the natural way to introduce both category theory and a specific category (with respect to a specific composition rule) is axiomatic. On the whole, since mathematicians these days all too often introduce abstract entities axiomatically prior to investigating them, the role of axiomatics has radically changed. It is well-known, of course, that in the 19th-century axioms ceased to be self-evident and competing axiom-systems for geometry and the different geometries were studied. But these geometries were seen as having their own characteristics, depicted axiomatically or otherwise—especially since Klein showed embedding to be a general way of presenting geometries. When Hilbert introduced his meta-mathematics and theorems became objects of a different kind, and deduction became an operation that took its own quality rather than the way to show—in a way developed by Hilbert himself!—that the characteristics of a geometry are indeed successfully depicted by the axioms. Nowadays the axioms do not depict the characteristics of a geometry (a category, an algebra, a space with a topology, etc.) but, in abstract cases of some sorts, the axioms generate the system. We have here, in this short outline, quite a few views of axiomatics and these need much further study. Lakatos merely repudiated the Hilbertian one.

What Lakatos had to say about the choice of axioms, of such systems or of geometry, was largely negative. We start not with axioms but with problems, theorems, proofs, refutations, he said. We axiomatize a system only after its concepts are quite sufficiently knocked into shape—he gave no criterion—and often systems are not axiomatized or only quasi-axiomatized. Yet the fact is that often a new field springs into being, nearly axiomatized almost from the start, not struggling toward its axioms as the calculus or as the theory of probability did.

Let this be. How do we get axioms (choose axioms or move toward them)? By trial and error, of course. But what do we aim at? There proofs and refutations systems do not make. We have peculiarities of systems, and Lakatos says nothing about them.

Take a trite example that also troubled me as a student. In the calculus we postulate the existence of divergence of functions, and we allow our variable(s) to vary from minus to plus infinity. Yet we postulate one point at infinity. In affine geometry we postulate a line at infinity. This is puzzling. It is more puzzling if we know that measure theory postulates two points of infinity for each variable, but I did not know that then. I asked my math professor why there was this difference between the calculus and affine geometry. He said: the one projects a sphere on the plane, the other a semisphere. I asked why, and never got an answer.

I subsequently asked a few mathematicians the same question. They all knew the answer but many could not articulate it. The answer is this. The calculus is concerned with well-behaved functions and tends to lump together unpleasant and bothersome exceptions; in affine geometry we are concerned with directions (i.e., complete sets of parallel lines) and each point at infinity corresponds exactly to one direction.

Speaking as conventionalists, mathematicians are bound to view their choices as arbitrary, and so not explain them; speaking as naturalists they feel an urge to prove the correctness of their choices. Lakatos quite rightly rejected both of these philosophies and wanted problem-orientation or the dialectical view to take over. But he showed no way to explain overall concerns and overall or global problems of mathematical subfields.

Work in this direction should well suit his general attitude, and it has already started—but is not yet at a stage where we can fully apply the Lakatos method.

6. THE ONGOING REVOLUTION

The feeling that mathematicians, and teachers of mathematics, are pulling rabbits out of hats is rightly disturbing—at least to an apprentice who wishes to know how the master does it and how to emulate him.

We cannot fully explain this, as there is no systematic way for inventing mathematical ideas—there is no algorism of discovery. Yet much can be done. First, the aim of a given exercise can be explained. Second, attempts to accomplish the aim that look fairly obvious may be presented and criticized. These two kinds of steps take much of the mystery away and explain to some extent the given discovery, thereby they also offer partial algorisms of sorts, as I have explained elsewhere when examining the parallel situation in empirical science. In mathematics, but not in empirical science, often the partial algorisms play a significant role in that they become subject to investigation in attempts to complete them, making them into algorisms proper.

Lakatos has shown that the formalist view is erroneous. Those sets of problems for the solution of which we do have algorisms we do not much care about; where the action is matters are fluid and criticism is the daily routine. Nevertheless, here is a complete and unbridgeable break within the system: whereas in physics we have nothing but conjecture and test and no algorism, in mathematics algorisms are an important and an ever-increasing sedimentation.

All this requires much more study. And the more we cover in the spirit of Lakatos, the more we can teach by a dialectical method, as practiced in Lakatos's lovely utopian class.

NOTE

1. In his contribution to the Schilpp Popper volumes Lakatos ridicules this view and opts for a more inductivist philosophy of science. I have expressed my view on his philosophy of science elsewhere; here we come to praise him, not to bury him. Let me just mention one fact that sharply exhibits the overall change in Lakatos's philosophy when he permitted a bit of inductivism in. His later works repeatedly—three times—attack the Popperian view (he quotes me on this) that empirical learning from experience is the discovery of counter-examples. This very idea, implicit in Popper, was explicitly stated in Lakatos's own classic, *Proofs and Refutations* as an anti-inductivist stand.

34

LAKATOS ON PROOFS
AND ON MATHEMATICS

no fallibility, no progress

I

Hugh Lehman has masterfully presented 'An Examination of Imre Lakatos's Philosophy of Mathematics' (*Philosophical Forum*, 12 [1980], 33–48). Since Lakatos was a skeptic, he asks, why should he have bothered with proofs at all? Lehman answers this question for Lakatos: skepticism was traditionally deemed to be the despair of reason, and Lakatos wanted to present a rationalistic skeptical view of mathematics—which made him study the role of proofs as something other than dispelling all doubt. Moreover, according to Lakatos, Lehman notices, the boot is on the other foot: the anti-skeptics cannot offer a good theory of the role of proof in mathematical reasoning, since dispelling doubt is not mathematical progress.

Lehman is thus led to the view Lakatos offers of the nature of proof— his theory of proof-analysis and of counter-example—and to its examination. He concludes that Lakatos partly describes the tradition in mathematics, but partly proposes a reform of that tradition. Let me repeat here my observation that this is not unique to either Lakatos or to the theory of mathematics: a new theory of science, of art, of religion, of economics, etc., will of necessity come up against the same situation: new explanation implies reform in all spheres of human action as long as the action is an ongoing concern.

Lehman examines critically the view implicit in Lakatos concerning acceptance or rejection of this or of that mathematical theorem. For my part, I agree with Lakatos that acceptance of objects of belief is never an issue:

Part I of this essay appeared in *Logique et Analyse*, 24, 1981. Part II has not been previously published.

what an investigator believes or disbelieves is his private affair. Lakatos endorsed Sylvain Bromberger's distinction between acceptance of an object of belief and acceptance of an object for investigation. For my part, I think acceptance can be for a plethora of purposes. But I need not elaborate this point here. Lehman's reference to Peggy Marchi—Lakatos's former student and leading exponent—and her presentation of theorems as explicanda suffice here, since Lehman shows that proof-analysis Lakatos-style is a form of explanation in a number of senses. So much for a brief abstract.

Lehman's contribution is important, and in a way rather overlooked by him. It can be stated in two brief sentences. *Lakatos's theory of proofs is designed to solve a problem for the rationalistic skeptic. It is thus not meant to be a comprehensive theory of mathematics.*

When I first met Lakatos, he told me of his ambition to view mathematics as a whole in the light of developments from Frege and Russell through Skolem and Löwenheim to Gödel and Church. Only fragments of his early view are extant. He had divided already then the whole field of mathematics into the pre-formal, the formal, and the post-formal. He noticed that definitions are often used as a means for escaping valid criticism, and he wondered when such escapes are regressive ('monster-barring'), when progressive (the axiomatization or the formalization of significant, crystallized systems). He agreed that fully axiomatized—purely formal—systems are immune to criticism, and was willing to relinquish all skepticism regarding them. But he declared them outside mathematics proper in the sense that they deserve the research efforts of robots, not of humans. Paradoxical though this thesis sounds, if not perhaps perverse, no mathematician will disagree with it, though the above presentation of it is unorthodox and even, to speak empirically, quite annoying for some anti-skeptical mathematicians. Yet, to be clear, though purely formal studies are for the robots, the formal systems are themselves of great interest for mathematicians proper; especially, said Lakatos, since their interpretations are conjectures.

All this was clear, to repeat, in Lakatos's earliest stage, and in his first exposition of his views I heard he made it clear that he was aware of the significance and explosiveness of his ideas. Yet he was driven to study the problem Lehman so masterfully presents, and never returned to his overall view. He died young. In his last years, he moved from the philosophy of mathematics to other activities. And, to conclude, he was then fully aware of the deficiency of the views he had presented in his masterpiece, *Proofs and Refutations*, which he intended to rewrite and correct. The defect was already studied by Peggy Marchi in her doctoral dissertation written while she was a student in the London School of Economics with Lakatos as her supervisor: he took as his initial framework Popper's classic *Logik der Forschung*, considering a theorem as a given and the task of the mathematician that of providing a proof, i.e., an explanation (to put it in Marchi's way). Yet the question (a) 'Why pay attention to one fact or theorem and not to another?' is not sufficiently examined by either, nor the question (b) 'How do conjectures evolve?'

As to question (a), the facts that call our attention are often the counter-examples to earlier conjectures. But this will not suffice: some ventures go on—a series of conjectures and refutations—then are aborted, then taken up again with renewed interest. There are trends or fashions in the history of ideas, and this fact calls for more explanations of intellectual trends by reference to changing metaphysical frameworks. As to question (b), certainly Popper and Lakatos were right to ascribe an important role to intuition as opposed to the view of science as developed without intuition, algoristically, by a kind of sausage-making machine. They both referred to Henri Bergson with approval (in spite of his not being a skeptic at all, and hardly a rationalist). Nevertheless, there is more to the matter at hand since, as I think Russell Norwood Hanson was the first to suggest in this context, between algorism for research and no guideline at all there are partial alogorisms. These, I have ventured to show, are partially generated by metaphysical systems.

To conclude, Lakatos did not demarcate mathematics, did not explain axiomatization or formalization, did not demarcate premature axiomatization or formalization from proper axiomatization, did not discuss the impact of general mathematical or even extra-mathematical ideas on research projects. He 'only' presented a rational skeptical theory of mathematical proof. This makes his work seminal and highly future-oriented. He thus generated a new research program in the philosophy of mathematics which (being a rationalistic sort of skeptic myself) I hope will soon become the paradigm.

II

Mark Steiner's 'The Philosophy of Mathematics of Imre Lakatos' (*Journal of Philosophy*, 80 (1983), 502–21) opens with its declared aim: it "attempts a balanced assessment of Lakatos's contribution to the philosophy of mathematics." Taking so high an aim, one must not be over-critical if the work falls somewhat short of the mark. For example, Steiner refers to Peano's continuous curve which fills a square as a counter-example, very much in the spirit of Lakatos's opinion, yet as "the result of a formal proof, not informal mathematics or direct inspection—a case which Lakatos seems to have overlooked". Yet Steiner has no discussion in his paper of what constitutes a formal proof, nor what proof Lakatos would have considered as formal. It is here that Lakatos does follow the philosophers he attacks and deems as formal only what is formal in the strictest sense—and also as certain, he concedes. Peano's proof is not that formal, and Peano himself presented it as a refutation, though only of the mathematics of his sloppy contemporaries, not of *any* mathematics. What Lakatos says is: they all refute all the time, but have an ideal of irrefutability; it is time to see the facts of proving and refuting and see if these do not come closer to a different ideal, one which explains progress!

There is room for exegesis here, since Lakatos wrote mainly a dialogue, and died young. But perhaps we can avoid details and go on investigating the possibility of a fallibilist progressive philosophy of mathematics. For Lakatos had one and only one major complaint: the history of mathematics is full of refutations; searches for infallible mathematics ended in failure everywhere except for fully formal, utterly uninterpreted systems. (Even the identification of numbers with Peano numbers he deemed a—refuted— mere hypothesis.)[1]

Nevertheless, Steiner does score a very valuable point: he says, following Lakatos, one can extend a theorem and refute the extension even if one fails to refute the original. For example, extend the Pythagoras Theorem to any triangle and refute the extension. (The refutation is elementary since the extension implies that all sides of all triangles have zero lengths.) He then argues that at times Lakatos does that and thereby claims to have refuted the original rather than the extended theorem. This point is often moot since, unless fully formalized, or unless historically satisfactorily documented, the intended range of applicability of a theorem is vague, and even when fully formalized it may easily have unintended models for which the range may be problematic. Nevertheless, clearly, there exist cases that go Lakatos's way and cases that go Steiner's way. To re-establish infallibilism a proof is required that a certain mode of mathematizing will go only Steiner's way. Such mathematics demonstrably will exclude all possible error, yet will not be limited to petrified systems only. Steiner has no such proof.

Steiner concludes his important essay with an erroneous claim. We can have progress without fallibilism, he declares with no proof. Instead he offers an illustration. The illustration is a continuation of the story told by Lakatos in his *Proofs and Refutations* concerning Euler's Theorem, by offering the "post-Poincaréan treatment" of Euler's Theorem. The word 'post' would have doubtless delighted Lakatos, who would have requested from Steiner the refutation of the "Poincaréan treatments" before he would take up the "post-Poincaréan", and would then have tried to refute Steiner's latest formulation. It is, of course, a fairly well-prescribed sort of exercise: one need but list the lemmas Steiner offers, and go on from there as outlined in Lakatos's *Proofs and Refutations*. If one were to succeed, one would then be—rightly—chided for taking a bare outline from a journal of philosophy, and one would be, instead, directed towards a canonic text. What is a canonic text for a "post-Poincaréan treatment" of Euler's Theorem? Steiner uses one letter of the alphabet to concede that there is none—and we should not complain, since his paper is very short (18 pages): he speaks of the post-Poincaréan treatments in the plural. Lakatos would have found all the near-canonic treatments, including the book mentioned by Steiner, and he would have contrasted them in search of a counter-example. Steiner would welcome this—as any lover of mathematics would—and would claim this as a step towards certainty, so that we could have "progress without fallibilism". Lakatos would have observed that such progress is through detection of error, and that if the end-product of that progress were a purely formal system, then the certainty of that system would block further progress unless some new uncertainty were introduced, say, by the offering of an interpretation of the system.

But Steiner's expression, "progress without fallibilism", is just right: Lakatos does admit mathematics without fallibilism—but not mathematical progress without fallibilism.

NOTE

1. A detailed discussion of formalization is to be found in Philip J. Davis and Reuben Hersh, *The Mathematical Experience* (Boston: Birkhäuser, 1981). The relevance of this to the philosophy of Lakatos, and the vindication of his view on this matter can be found on pages 355–57.

35

FEYERABEND'S DEFENSE OF VOODOO

how to get away with murder

> It is a common subterfuge of those who deceive
> the gullible with *magic* arts, or at least
> who want to render such people credulous in general,
> to appeal to the scientists' confession of their *ignorance*.
>
> —Kant, *Religion Within the Limits
> of Reason Alone, Book II,* final note
> (italics Kant's).

How do you read a book which extols lies? Do you at least admire its author for his excessive honesty and take literally what he says? Or do you consider him a mere con-man? Con-man, I am afraid, is what our author thinks Galileo was, different words though he uses—he does call Galileo a mountebank (p. 106n), to wit, and a charlatan—and he does mock at the advocates of full truthfulness in preference to thrilling cheating; the choice between these two might pose a serious difficulty, I must admit (except that I find cheating such a bore). Our author quotes a license from the Philosophers' Pope Himself, Immanuel Kant the First, no less, a blank permission to knowingly use poor arguments in defense of a good cause. And he expressed the—sincere?—wish to be remembered—not as a Prussian philosopher failing at a game of clowning by being too serious—but as a light-footed charmer; "flippant" is his word. He wants, of course, to charm Philosophy—Newton said she was a harsh mistress, you remember—and make her reveal her charms. Though he cannot carry out his design to the end, he declares that some of his imitators might. This is how he cons his readers with false promises.

This review of *Against Method: Outlines of an Anarchistic Theory of Knowledge* by Paul K. Feyerabend (London: New Left Books, 1975) appeared in *Philosophia*, 6, 1976.

I confess all this is my bias. I confess I was incensed by the disregard of Galileo's conscientious devotion, good faith, and high standards (indeed his very creation of the high standard of no mumbo-jumbo (opening of his first 'Dialogue'; no wonder Feyerabend cheats just here). Yet Feyerabend's cheap story of Galileo has marvellous material and an excellent moral. Clearly, on this Feyerabend is right: had Galileo tried to record and discuss all the difficulties which Feyerabend mock-accuses him of having concealed, he would have been impotent forever. Does this mean, as Feyerabend suggests, that Galileo worried about none of the difficulties? Is the choice only between the happy-go-lucky and the no-go?

This is the crux of the matter. Feyerabend is against all rules and all regulations, against law-and-order of any sort. Anything goes, he says. He sounds super-revolutionary, in politics as well as in methodology; he also practically equates the two and makes Lenin the greatest methodologist of them all (p. 17n and elsewhere). He means Herbert Marcuse, of course, but he says Lenin. For my part, I wish to make my stand clear at the outset. We, the true revolutionaries in matters scientific, should beware of ultra-revolutionaries (left-wing deviants, in Lenin's jargon) no less than of compromisers (muddleheads and right-wing deviants, in Lenin's jargon), because the very excessive demands of the ultra-revolutionist can easily render the endeavor quite impotent and thus allow the *status quo ante* to stay *quo ante*: if the revolution means to bring back Voodoo—see below—then perhaps the *status quo* is not so bad. Feyerabend only plays the clown; he is not the clown; what he really is I cannot say; he may just happen to be a defender of the Established Order.

Feyerabend is against all method and for as much and as complete liberty as possible, he says. I shall later argue that this is not the fact, but let us accept what he says as true for the time being. He has predecessors in aesthetics (John Cage) and in politics (Danny the Red), but scarcely in the philosophy of science. I say scarcely, since he hints that he may have one, and he mentions one. The hint concerns Ludwig Boltzmann, who has allegedly anticipated Sir Karl Popper; and this anticipation is perhaps a Good Thing, perhaps a Bad Thing. I do not see how anyone can decide the matter before Feyerabend himself makes up his mind and decides whether his admiration or his loathing for Sir Karl Popper has the upper hand. The predecessor mentioned is John Stuart Mill. Lest this upset the reader, who is bound to be at least remotely familiar with Mill's staunch defense of a method, indeed of the inductive method itself, I should at once stress that all inductivists are Bad Guys but the Mill of *On Liberty* is decidedly a Good Guy. And the reader may wonder, at least so it seems to me, what Feyerabend does with Mill's *Logic* while talking of his *On Liberty*. Feyerabend hints: *Logic* is the fruit of Mill's own labors, and *On Liberty* really belongs to the influence which Harriet Taylor had on him. The hint, of course, will not do at all. There is no reason to think that the lady ever swayed his opinion radically. Did Harriet convince him, one might ask, that inductivism is an error and intellectual anarchism is correct? What exactly did he or she say on scientific method in this most remarkable and first manifesto of anarchistic methodology and how come this was overlooked?

The thesis of Mill's—or Harriet Taylor's, if Feyerabend would insist—*On Liberty* is bluntly declared in Chapter 1. It is political: no interference is allowed except in self-protection. As we shall see, Feyerabend's ideal is totalitarian China, and so he obviously rejects this thesis. In Chapter 2, Mill or Taylor recommends freedom of thought on the ground of fallibilism. This, to continue the report, may be contested on the ground that one opinion may be certain enough. Certain enough an opinion indeed may be, admits Mill, but only because attempts at refuting it have failed, whereas forbidding opposition may be the prevention of tests and thus the weakening of the very ground for the certainty that is used against the opposition. And he offers an example. "If even the Newtonian philosophy were not permitted to be questioned, mankind could not feel as complete assurance of its truth as they now do."

I do not quite know how to proceed. I feel that the above quotation makes it amply clear that Mill's *On Liberty* was not so very out of line with his *Logic*, yet I refuse to declare victory over Feyerabend because I do myself feel that there is a difference, be it even of a mere nuance, between these two books; and I feel that the difference is precious. Query: could this difference be due to the influence which Harriet had on Mill? Perhaps, but not necessarily so. We have a complete parallel here with at least one other—indeed many, but let me stick to one—great inductivist liberal, David Hume, who likewise showed no sensitivity to the discrepancy between inductive authority and liberalism. Of Hume's inductivism I need not say much. Suffice it if I remind the reader that though he found induction unfounded, he refused to deny it its authority even though this authority remained but the tyranny of habit. Yet in his admirable essay 'Of the Rise and Progress of the Arts and Sciences' Hume expresses practically the same views and sentiments as cited above from Mill's *On Liberty*. And, as we all know, there was no Harriet Taylor in Hume's life.

But I still refuse to declare a victory. Fallibilism is not enough. Perhaps the magic word is not fallibilism but proliferation. Or, as Feyerabend says, anything goes; for, he says, this is his thesis. And though Hume's already mentioned essay praises proliferation (as well as his 'Of Civil Liberty' which, however, is only economic and political and so not exactly on our topic, which is methodology), we may wonder if this was not a mere aside with him. But we have, just made to order, a better example, namely that of William James, and one which has been elaborated enough in Ralph Barton Perry's impressive life of James. For Perry was struck by the tragic quality of the conflict between James's strictest inductivism and his ardent liberal plea for proliferation—much more liberal than Hume or Mill, incidentally.

And, as we all know, there was no Harriet Taylor in William James's life either.

So much for Feyerabend's ascription of his world-shaking thesis to the influence of Harriet Taylor. But I am not done yet with Feyerabend's nonsense about John Stuart Mill. Feyerabend does not even raise the question I have discussed, namely, how come that Mill, the severe author of *Logic*, the defender of law and order, also wrote friendly anarchistic *On Liberty*; and so, *a fortiori*, he does not answer it; and so, *a fortiori*, he does not answer it by ascribing the benefits of *On Liberty* to the influence of Harriet Taylor. What he does is append a note (p. 48) to his claim that the separations between history, philosophy, science, and non-science all vanish, saying "An account and a truly humanitarian defence of this position can be found in J. S. Mill's *On Liberty*. Popper's philosophy . . . is but a pale reflection of Mill's." The reader who is familiar with either author may gasp: neither ever defended "this position", insisting as they did, each in his own way, on the importance of demarcating science from superstition, for example, quite contrary to our voodoo-enthusiast author. But our author proceeds in a mood indulgent towards Popper immediately after exposing the inferiority of his philosophy as compared with Mill's: "We can understand its peculiarities when we consider (a) the background of logical positivism"—here we may notice for once that Feyerabend does not think Popper's is the very worst 20th-century philosophy—"(b) the unrelenting puritanism of its author (and most of his followers)"—I am gratified to see in this volume a hint at the fact that I exist; but for the word 'most' just quoted I would have begun to doubt my own existence; the reader, however, will be less sensitive to Feyerabend's near-oversight of my existence than to Feyerabend's near-oversight of Mill's puritanism which is quite legendary, of course, but Feyerabend is prepared for him with the last consideration—"and when [(c)] we remember the influence of Harriet Taylor on Mill's life and his philosophy. There is no Harriet Taylor in Popper's life." Really, I do not know if this last sentence is a censure of Lady Popper, whose hospitality he and I enjoyed together more than once; it really may be nothing more than a mere confession of failure on the part of our author who may feel he could but did not free his erstwhile teacher of puritanism and other constraints. "The foregoing argument should have made it clear", continues Feyerabend, "that I regard proliferation not just as an 'external catalyst' of progress . . . but as an essential part of it."

So much in repsonse to a few lines on page 48, where Mill's liberalism is so forcefully praised; yet on page 47 I read, "nor is political interference rejected", meaning the Chinese Communist imposition of acupuncture on the modern hospitals in China. Feyerabend speaks (p. 50) of "the revival of traditional medicine in Communist China" and I shall do him the courtesy of assuming that he does not know that in most of the vast Chinese countryside traditional medicine never died and modern medicine was hardly heard of and its practitioners suffered from the Communist take-over more than other portions of the population (being largely foreign and/or missionary, of course).

If anything goes, then, of course tyranny goes too, and then there is an end to anarchism. The author takes up the political matter later on, and the reference to Chinese state intervention is here a mere preparation. Here he studies the question intellectually: is there any idea which is passé? No, says he. And he quotes Mary B. Hesse's criticism of his view. She says that she can hardly imagine he would recommend a preference for Aristotle or for Voodoo over modern science. The reader will forgive me if I skip Aristotle. Voodoo, says Feyerabend, (p. 50), is Dr. Hesse's *pièce de résistance*, but "nobody knows it . . . Voodoo has a firm though still not sufficiently understood material basis, and a study of its manifestations can be used to enrich, and perhaps even to revise, our knowledge of physiology." I do not know whether his treatment of Hesse is cheaper than his treatment of Popper. She says he will not recommend Voodoo. He says: we know little of its "material basis". This is a piece of Voodoo—see motto to this essay. Feyerabend adds a footnote with a few references: two to Lévi-Strauss who never advocated the return to Voodoo and who has nothing to say of the "material basis" of Voodoo, except perhaps in the sense that Voodoo does exist and does have a material aspect and a social aspect and so on and so forth. Lévi-Strauss, of course, concerns hmself with the intellectual aspect of every social phenomenon, Voodoo included, but he never declares "the science of the concrete", i.e., primitive thinking, comparable to science and so he is no stick to beat Hesse with. Our author's other three references are, indeed, to physiology, two to Voodoo physiology, and one to one phenomenon called Voodoo death, even though not in the least peculiar to Voodoo. It is the fact or alleged fact that a coupling of strong fear and deep sense of despair may, and reportedly indeed once did, cause death. How this relates to Hesse's criticism I cannot imagine.

I go back to *On Liberty* as Feyerabend advises his reader to do in the end of Chapter 8. The pamphlet, as I say, is political, not methodological. It only touches on science when attacking the illiberal who uses science as a justification of political oppression, and in this, to repeat, it belongs to a long and venerable tradition—from Spinoza to Russell, I suppose, but I should also mention Polanyi and Popper here. I wish to quote one sentence from Mill. "As mankind improves, the number of doctrines which are no longer disputed or doubted will be constantly on the increase: and the well-being of mankind may almost be measured by the number and gravity of the truths which have reached the point of being uncontested." This seems to me sufficient evidence that were Mill the judge between the Feyerabends and the Hesses, then the Hesses would have the day—as they still do. How Feyerabend can prefer this old-fashioned inductivism (while siding with Voodoo!) over Popper's refutationism would puzzle one, until one remembers that in Feyerabend's view anything goes, including total anarchy and including disguising an inductivist like Mill to make him look hostile to Hesse.

Anything goes, and now we go to pages 146–47, where we find a note on Marx, Lenin, Trotsky, and Mao. The note is too hilarious for a full analysis, but let me mention something about this most remarkable note. The note is appended to this text: "Many of the conflicts and contradictions which occur in science are due to this heterogeneity of the material, to this 'unevenness' of the historical development, as a Marxist would say, and they have no immediate theoretical significance." What is at stake here is a plethora of topics and problems. Contradictions indeed occur in science between new ideas and old ones, and something has got to give. For an example, Feyerabend mentions the fact that Copernicanism conflicted with older views of inertia and Galileo had to remedy the situation. Indeed, I find admirable his discussion of what Kuhn calls, somewhat metaphorically, the Gestalt-switch that is a scientific revolution; Feyerabend does bring the switch so much to life and he makes us admire Galileo's boldness all the more. But why this pooh-pooh? Why has this "no immediate theoretical significance"? Answer: In Marxism there are primary processes and secondary ones that depend on them and are also at times out of phase (i.e., secondary effects can precede their primary causes), yet without thereby refuting Marxism. This, of course, is a cheap transition from contradiction between theories, old and new, to the interplay between primary and secondary processes in Marxist philosophy. Moreover, these primary and secondary processes may be conflicts, and the word in Marxism for conflicts is 'contradictions'; in the text just quoted Feyerabend speaks of "the conflicts and contradictions which occur in science" meaning contradictions proper; but just as some social conflicts are of little theoretical concern for Marxists so some contradictions are declared by Feyerabend to be of "no immediate theoretical significance"; such as Galileo's worry about squaring Copernicanism with inertia.

The note quotes Marx to say that he permits the material base and the socio-cultural superstructure to be out of phase somewhat. Trotsky is quoted to repeat this, Marx's Phase Law. Why quote Trotsky though he adds nothing here? In order to let you know that he is a Good Guy or in order to show that a Good Guy says so? I do not know. And "See also Lenin", who also endorsed Marx's Phase Law, I presume, "concerning the fact that multiple causes of an event may be out of phase and have an effect only when they occur together." And see also, I should add, Descartes' remark to the effect that two plus two equal four, and Danny the Red's claim that fun is fun. The link between all this and Marx's Law evades me. The European bourgeoisie, quotes Feyerabend from Lenin, are backward. Tut, tut. "But all young Asia grows a mighty democratic movement, spreading and gaining in strength." In or out of phase? When? "All young

Asia"! Ban-zai! "For this very interesting situation, which deserves to be exploited for the philosophy of science," says unabashed Feyerabend, see Meyer on Lenin and Althusser on Marx. I do not think that all the years of my personal and professional contact with him, and all my detailed familiarity with his detailed writings to boot, could prepare me for the fact that in his books Althusser is a Good Guy rather than a Bad Guy. Why? Where have I failed? "The philosophical background is splendidly explained in Mao Tse-Tung's essay *On Contradiction* (. . . especially section IV)." The "especially" is a gentle coaxing to read the whole of the brilliant essay of the Philosopher King—or should I say, the Poet Chairman?—which has nothing to do with the discussion of things being in or out of phase. Section IV, however, does. It says,—oh, yes! I am going to tell you, and if you do not much care about it you are at liberty to skip this paragraph, or the whole of this essay; I promise I shall take no offence at all; feeling a slight obligation to tell you something about Feyerabend's scholarship, I shall ruefully do it as best as I know how, and please forgive my heavy-handedness—there are major contradictions and minor ones, and these differ from the esential and apparent ones. Thus, essential is the contradiction between capitalist and worker, but, say, under an imperialist attack local forces may join and consequently the major contradiction will be between colonizer and colonized. At each phase, says Mao's Law, one conflict plays the leading role. I do not deny that Mao's Law does not conflict with Marxism-Leninism; but it does not follow from it; nor does it help us predict when which of the existing contradictions will become major. Back to Mao, and only those familiar with the very specific peculiarities of Chinese Communist propaganda for internal consumption, especially of the older days, will take this in their stride: there are contradictions, says Mao, between little knowledge of Marx's texts and the much knowledge of them which is to be achieved through much commendable labor of love. And now comes, at last, Feyerabend's point, Marx's Law. Some people think that the changeability of phase between base and superstructure refutes dialectical materialism; but it refutes only mechanistic materialism. When we notice what is principal in a conflict, says Mao, the problem vanishes. What connects Marx's Phase Law with Mao's Law, Mao does not tell. And this is how "the philosophical background is splendidly explained." Let a thousand flowers bloom!

Feyerabend's thesis is: anything goes. His proof is easy: I say that you must agree that I may be right or else you are a bloody dogmatist; if you say I may be right, then, since all I say is that Voodoo may be right, Voodoo may be right. (The possibly possible is possible!) And so you have conceded my point. On the other hand, you may be wrong; hence you are. Q.E.D.

Check! What remains as a loose end in this splendid proof is the bloody dogmatist. This is why politics must enter the picture, I suppose. Even some of Feyerabend's best friends are bloody dogmatists. This volume is dedicated to, and was planned to be written in collaboration with, Imre Lakatos who was, alas! a mafioso (p. 210) and a sheer terrorist (pp. 181, 200). Parenthetically, I really do not know whether this was meant as a compliment or as censure; nor do I know whether Lakatos took this as a censure, perhaps as a censure which made him decide, as he did, to disengage: he loved to be called a terrorist, but strictly in private: in public he greatly chafed when he was called names that he did not think helped the cause. Anyway, as we have seen, Chairman Mao's terror was not rejected. Is science dogmatic and terroristic or not? Yes, says Feyerabend, and refers his readers to Thomas S. Kuhn (p. 298). Does he like it? Is primitive thought better? It seems not: the same development as that which can be seen in J. von Neumann's bullying work on quantum mechanics, we are told explicitly, also occurs in Nupe sand divination and other allegedly primitive modes of thought. Do not believe me: read note 23 to Chapter 5 on pages 64–65. See also pages 296–97. And so, science is a dogmatic venture and its regulars are terrorized by the von Neumanns. And I am glad to hear that the spell von Neumann had cast on Feyerabend is broken. But Voodoo is a dogmatic venture, too, I presume, where its regulars can even be terrorised to Voodoo death, i.e., killed by psychological means, by some Voodoo big chief. Where is the little guy to go? Two answers. First,—or last: last two pages—anyone can go anywhere they like, but no coercion, please! Second, and this is the theme of the last chapter, when state and science collude there is too much terror, but when the Chinese government forced science to use acupuncture, there were excellent results (pp. 305–06). Similarly, it is excellent to have both Catholicism and Protestantism, and anyone who does not like the former can leave and join the latter "instead of ruining it by such inane changes as Mass in the vernacular" (p. 308, final paragraph of the book!). Become a Protestant in Communist China? Not on your life! But this does not matter. Feyerabend can live without Chinese Catholics or Chinese Protestants. The limit to what even a Feyerabend can tolerate is, however, Catholic Mass in the vernacular, flat-footed rationalism (p. 277n), contemporary philosophy of science which is "essentially unscientific and sterile since ahistorical" (p. 146n), and so on. Not bad for "a dadaist [who] would not hurt a fly" (p. 21n). On the whole, I must admit, the hate blasts are at times a bit too much.

Perhaps the book should be dismissed as a bad joke. After all, it both claims that you cannot understand anything separately and explains things separately; it claims that two competing theories, whether both scientific or one scientific, one not, are both in a contradiction with each other and incommensurable; it claims that no empirical evidence would have made Einstein change his views without ever examining his repeated and persistent confessions of empiricism; finally it is a book *Against Method* which says, on p. 252, "that the anthropological method is the correct method for studying the structure of science (and, for that matter, of any other form of life)" (meaning by "the anthropological method", if anything at all, something akin to the classical British method, long ago exploded by I. C. Jarvie).

Yet the book is provocative. It contains all that the author can say in favor of non-scientific knowledge, it tries to criticize much popular mythology about science and some practices that should not occur. It is annoying but full of delights too. It looks as if the author tries to be impish and get away with anything. I confess my sympathy is with the author, and this review is simply an expression of regret over the loss of an ally to the forces of irresponsibility and irrationalism.

The book contains references and allusions to any kind of field of study possible (within the limits of the author's field of knowledge and erudition, of course, but the field is quite broad), to all sorts of social sciences and artistic and historical events; but there is no reference to Naziism, Fascism, or even to the Spanish Civil War, not to mention racism. He does say that it is not the state interference but the totalitarian state interference that was objectionable in the case of Lysenko (p. 306). (He does not explain how Communist China is different from Russia, but let this ride.) And he does speak of one who advocates (enlightened) self-interest as "a modern Frankenstein" (p. 188n). And he calls Lakatos a law-and-order philosopher. But how can one say 'anything goes' without a single reference to theories of racial supremacy? Of course, Feyerabend may protest that he "would not hurt a fly", but as he defends the Voodoo witches because they bloody well would cause Voodoo death, why not defend, say, the genteel racism of the learned Dr. Jensen, or of the sophisticated Enoch Powell, or the witty anti-Semitism of crafty Wilhelm Busch? Perhaps because anti-Semitism and racism may go too far and reach Dachau and Buchenwald? But then anything goes only if it goes not too far. And who can tell? The scientists? The Nupe sand-diviner? Paul K. Feyerabend? What a pity. What a real loss. The only true cause, the cause of all liberty, including the liberty to search for truth despite all silly rules and regulations, has lost a brilliant champion and the cause of Voodoo has won a champion for whom it has no use.

There is no doubt that Feyerabend still has the master's touch. His Chapter 10 is a masterpiece. Partly it is so thanks to Vasco Ronchi who evidently moved him greatly—in this case he even breaks his own rule and makes a friendly and generous acknowledgment (p. 125n). Yet the chapter goes far beyond Ronchi—it also shows great erudition, clarity, and the absence of teutonic humor. One page is particularly moving—p. 126, where all the difficulties of telescopy, physical, psychological, and philosophical, collude. "I still remember my disappointment when, having a reflector with an alleged linear magnification of about 150, I found the moon was only about five times enlarged, and situated quite close to the ocular (1937)." I find this confession very moving. I do not know how old he was in 1937, but I know he was still a minor when he joined the German army in World War

II; in 1937 Austria was no kind place for a lonely youth whose scientific escapades met, one might imagine, with little or no understanding for his disappointments—not even from high-school science teachers whose minds were elsewhere anyway. All this might explain a lot of the feeling shown in the present exposé of the view of science as pretty-pretty. I wonder if it is a mere accident that the same page on which we have the confession is also the (seemingly?) most erudite, including, as it does, reference to a manuscript letter, in the Gregorian University in Rome, by the very gentleman who received a telescope from Galileo and gave it to Kepler. Also, the page contains a scathing attack on the Jesuits who succumbed to Galileo too quickly—Galileo promised magnification of about 30; but he could not provide even that much—as well as an attack on the modern Catholic scholar who approves of them. To endorse Galileo's observations as factual only because of "their regularity and their intersubjectivity" is to forget all about mirages and rainbows and microscopic sense illusions and "the phenomena of witchcraft (*every* woman reported an incubus to have an ice-cold member)". "Every *woman*"? "*Every* woman"? Which witch reported an encounter with an incubus and which did not? Even the regularity of rainbows made them more real, and mirages likewise became more real when and only when they became regular: we can now specify and reproduce the conditions under which rainbows or mirages occur. But we could never do so with conditions under which a woman will report an encounter with an incubus, let alone the fine details. Or is this a teutonic private joke that I am missing?

I must grant that much: it is hard to ignore the nonsense and center on the valuable material in this book. Yet valuable material is there to enjoy and really benefit from. What a mess any scientific situation really is when seen from close quarters is hard to believe not only because of the pretty-pretty reports. I think any study of selenology before and after the first moon landing, any study made from close-quarters, that is, will show an even bigger mess; and this will make us admire the venture all the more. And Feyerabend suggests—or do I read too much into his text?—that a Gestalt-switch often occurs when the normal and the anomalous switch places. I think this is true. My instance (*Towards an Historiography of Science*, p. 43) is very easy to state: whereas for Stahl the normal combustion was of charcoal, which left almost no ashes, for Lavoisier the normal was of metal, whose ashes are heavier than the original metal; whereas the one was troubled by the other's instance, the other was troubled by the former's—and overcame his trouble! But Feyerabend's example—end of Chapter 12— from Galileo is more intricate, interesting, valuable. His conclusion is that the great thinkers of the past were right to conceal—if conceal is what they did—difficulties; this may be a challenge; he recommends that we go on doing so; this is just absurd. But again I chafe instead of ending with praise. I think I should say that we are now mature enough to be able to try not to sweep our difficulties under the carpet, and this will make us more accommodating to young bright experimentors who come to us with some obscure disappointments. This, I think, should appeal to Feyerabend when he is in his friendly humanitarian mood.

The heart of the book is Galileo's astronomy. From then on it is both mopping-up and redundancies, including the discussion with Lakatos, which is less comprehensible than Lakatos himself, and a defence of Chinese totalitarianism and more. Yet till the end the volume contains nice tid-bits. I should mention one item more.

Chapter 17, which is quite remarkable, has no reference or allusion to Galileo and studies perception theory and its application to art appreciation, notices that much of one's picture of the world, or rules of seeing, cannot be conscious except after a long study, and that one of these rules is the rule of irrelevance (p. 237). This sheds much light on Galileo's supposed acts of deception and brings art and science much closer together than hitherto owned. It should much delight Feyerabend himself, but regrettably he does not make the connection.

Lest this might sound as if I too follow Lakatos and Feyerabend to Polanyi's fashionable reactionary camp, let me say this. Not only do I deny what they all affirm, namely that science is a church like any, or worse, or better; also I deny, this time with Feyerabend, that there is such a thing as personal knowledge, or that learning the visual language required for empirical science renders scientific knowledge personal knowledge. For, personal knowledge is supposedly that expert knowledge that artists cannot articulate, yet they transmit it to apprentices; it is thus distinct from the foreign language, dead or alive, which one can learn in evening classes, by correspondence, etc. And, I suggest, visual language, and even the language of art, and any other, need not be as elitist as Polanyi or Kuhn or Lakatos suggests. But all this is an aside, as is Feyerabend's attack on esotericism. Indeed, were he of the opinion that Galileo could not explain his personal knowledge, he would hardly have been in position to call him a mountebank. Yet is Voodoo not esoteric?

In addition to quite a few interesting and uninteresting things which do and do not fall into pattern, what does this book say? That at times we all cheat, that we all say silly things now and then, etc. True enough. That therefore even the stupidest liar may say something worthwhile. True enough. So what? Should we all listen to any stupid liar? Should we aim to be stupid liars? Should we commend Voodoo? Should the U.S. Federal Government emulate the wise government of the People's Republic of China and impose folk medicine on government hospitals and sponsor Voodoo sessions in Federal City University? Should state colleges and universities teach astrology? If Feyerabend says Yes, he is a knave and a fool. If he says No, then he repudiates much that makes this book what it is. I do have the suspicion that he will waffle, that he merely cons his reader into a cheap fantasy, where science and Voodoo are both legit, and where all dreams come true, even horror dreams, but all ends well.

What is my verdict? Does Feyerabend get away with murder? I think, yes. This is why I wanted to review *Against Method* and this is why I have decided to publish this review despite all my vacillations and misgivings and dislike of his violence and vulgarity: I find enough in the book deserving the reader's attention. Feyerabend hints he is not going to continue on a similar venture. Perhaps he had to get so much rubbish out of his system so as to be able to start afresh. I hope he can now become the benign, flippant, exciting scholar that he so much wants to be.

My very best wishes to him, then.

36

REPLY TO AGASSI

by Paul Feyerabend

Berkeley, July 15, 1975

Dear Joske,

There are three things which never fail to amaze me when reading reviews of my book: the disregard for argument, the violence of the reaction, the general impression I seem to make on my readers, and especially on 'rationalists'.

As I see it, my book is a longwinded and rather pedestrian attempt to criticise certain ideas about science and rationality, to reveal the idols behind the ideas, and to put them in their proper place. Not being as blinded by slogans as my rationalist critics seem to be I *investigate*, and I report the results of my investigation. My investigation is far from comprehensive. The most important problem of the relation between reason and *faith* is not even touched upon. What I do is this. I compare three idols: Truth, Honesty, Knowledge (or Rationality), and their methodological ramifications with a fourth idol, Science. I find that they conflict, and I conclude that it is time to take a fresh look at all of them. At any rate, neither science, nor rationalism have now sufficient authority to exclude myth, or 'primitive' thought, or the cosmologies behind the various religious creeds. Any claim to such authority is illegal and must be rejected, if necessary, by political means. I would say that my book contains 85% exposition and argument, 10% conjecture, and 5% rhetorics. There are long passages devoted to the description of fact and procedure.

Now the strange thing is that hardly any review I have read deals with this material. The only passages the reviewers seem to perceive are places where, with a sigh of relief, I stop reasoning and engage in a little rhetorics. [1]

Philosophia, 6, 1976.

This means either that rationalists do not recognise an argument when they see one, or that they regard rhetorics as more important than argument, or else that something in my book so jars their thought and confounds their perception that dreams and hallucinations replace the reality in front of them. Your article, my dear Joske, is a perfect example of what I mean. I am very grateful that you are so deeply concerned about my book and that you have put so much time, energy, and especially imagination into the review. But, alas, I hardly recognized myself in the terrible portrait that glared at me from its pages. For you my book seems to be a mixture of *Die Räuber* and *Ubu Roi*, combining the "hate blasts" of the first with the cheerful nonsense of the second. Of course, you are very good, you almost succeeded in convincing me that I was a "super revolutionary, in politics as well as in methodology"—but the illusion did not last very long. A look at my book, and I saw that I was mistaken and that you were mistaken. How did this mistake arise? And, having realised it, how can I prevent you and my future readers from repeating it? How can I wake you up, make you open your eyes so that you see what I have written and do not at once wander off into a dream world of your own? I do not know the recipe, but I shall try. And I ask your and the reader's indulgence when in the attempt to make myself understood I shall often be longwinded and tediously repetitive.

According to you I am a "super revolutionary, in politics as well as in-methodology" and my "ideal is totalitarian China".

The first sentence of my book reads (page 17, text of the Introduction): "The following essay is written in the conviction that *anarchism*, while perhaps not the most attractive *political* philosophy, is certainly excellent medicine for *epistemology* and for the *philosophy of science.*"

Now I admit—one does not always read first sentences very carefully; one passes them over, one wants to go on to the more important parts of the book and see what surprises the author has hidden there. I also admit that people less pedantic than I do not turn every sentence into a package stuffed with information, they give the reader some leeway and permit him to get slowly acquainted with their style. So, I should perhaps be grateful to you for reading me as if I were a better and more elegant writer than I actually am. But, alas, at the present moment my gratitude is almost overwhelmed by my wish to be understood, and so the reader must bear with me when I explain the sentence in somewhat greater detail.

What does it say?

It says that I regard anarchism as "excellent medicine for epistemology and the philosophy of science".

Note the careful qualification. I do not say that epistemology should become anarchic, or that the philosophy of science should become anarchic, I say that both disciplines should receive anarchism *as a medicine.*

Epistemology is sick, it must be cured, and the medicine is anarchy. Now medicine is not something one takes all the time. One takes it for a certain period of time, *and then one stops.* To make sure that this is the way in which I shall be understood I repeat the restriction at the end of the Introduction. In the last but one sentence I say: "There may, of course, come a time when it will be necessary to give reason a temporary advantage and when it will be wise to defend *its* rules to the exclusion of everything else". And then I continue: "I do not think that we are living in such a time today". *Today* epistemology is sick and in need of a medicine. The medicine is anarchism. Anarchism, I say, will heal epistemology and *then* we may return to a more enlightened and more liberal form of rationality. So far the first qualification that is contained in the first sentence of my book.

There are two more qualifications.

I say that anarchism is "perhaps not the most attractive *political* philosophy". Qualification one: I intend to discuss the role of anarchism in epistemology and in the philosophy of science, I am not too enthusiastic about political anarchism. Qualification two: however, I may be mistaken in my lack of enthusiasm (anarchism, "while *perhaps* not . . ."). So far the first sentence of my book. Does it not sound very different from the picture of a "super revolutionary, in politics as well as in methodology"?

How does the difference arise? The answer is fairly simple. When reading my book you omit qualifications which I either imply, or state explicitly. These qualifications are quite important. They are the essence of what I want to say. I think that there is very little we can say 'in general', that the observations we make, the advice we give must take a specific (historical, social, psychological, physical etc.) situation into account, that we cannot proceed unless we have studied this situation in detail. (This, incidentally, is the rationale behind the slogan 'anything goes': if you want advice that remains valid, no matter what, then the advice will have to be as empty and indefinite as 'anything goes'.) Any statement I make has this *specific* character, the qualifications being either implicit in the context, or contained in the statement itself. You show no such discretion. Moving nimbly from page to page you notice only the phrases which shock you and you overlook the qualifications and the arguments that might have alleviated the shock. Let me mention another example to elucidate this procedure of selective reading.

In Chapter 4 I look favourably upon a certain episode in the relation between Party and Experts in the Communist China of the Fifties and I advise the democratic bodies of today to act in a similar manner. I think that *on that occasion* the Party acted reasonably and I suggest that democracies combat the chauvinism of their own experts in exactly the same manner. In your review this limited and concrete suggestion becomes "Feyerabend's ideal is totalitarian China". ("Chairman Mao's terror was not rejected" you write a little later. Of course it was not rejected; and why not? Because this was not the topic of my argument.[2])

However—you don't limit yourself to oversights. You not only omit, you also add, and in a most imaginative manner.

In my book I quote Lenin as a person well acquainted with the complexities of what some people call 'methodology'. I call him an "intelligent and thoughtful observer" and I add in a footnote that he "can give useful advice to everyone, philosophers of science included". Let me pass over the fact that in your review this becomes "Lenin is the greatest methodologist of them all"—for such a change of emphasis is still within the limits of poetic licence as practised by you and noted above. But you continue: "He means Marcuse, of course, but he says Lenin". I must confess, I was absolutely flabbergasted to read this remark. I mean Marcuse, and "of course"? How on earth did Marcuse get into the discussion? Do I mention him anywhere in my book? I look up the index, yes, I do, in a footnote, on page 27. I turn to page 27, for I have already forgotten how and why I mention him. On page 27, I find, I quote from a rather good introduction to Hegel which Marcuse wrote some time ago—and that is all. Did I mention Marcuse in other writings? Yes, I did, in the *essay* 'Against Method' which precedes the book, but in a severely critical manner. Besides, why should I "of course" mean a university professor and third-rate intellectual when speaking about a first-rate thinker, writer, and politician? Especially in view of the fact that I prefer people who are aware of the complex connexions between different fields to those who are content with simple-minded models?[3]

There is an even more amusing example of your tendency to let your mind wander when reading a book, and it occurs in connexion with an autobiographical remark of mine. I write (page 126, end of footnote 19): "I still remember my disappointment when, having built a reflector with an alleged linear magnification of about 150, I found the moon only about five times enlarged, and situated quite close to the ocular". This was to illustrate the difference between the predictions of *geometrical* optics and what one actually *sees* when looking into a telescope. You write: "in 1937 (the date when I started my observations) Austria was no kind place for a lonely youth whose scientific escapades met, one might imagine, with little or no understanding for his disappointment—not even from high-school teachers whose minds were elsewhere anyway. This possibility might explain a lot of the feeling shown in the present exposé of the view of science as pretty-pretty . . . ." It is very nice of you, dear Joske Agassi, to give such a moving account of my childhood and such a generous explanation of the "hate blasts" you seem to encounter in my book. But you again give me credit where credit is not due. Far from "meeting with little or no understanding", my "scientific escapades" were *caused* by an excellent physics teacher in high school who inspired us all to build meridian instruments, sundials, telescopes and who made me an official observer for the Swiss Center for Solar Activity at the tender age of 14 (it was at his lecture course at the university that I gave my very first public lecture on my thirteenth birthday). Now remember: it is one thing to write a fictional account of somebody's life and ideas for entertainment, or in order to direct attention to achievements which would otherwise remain unnoticed. But it is quite a different thing to make such an account (Lenin meaning "of course" Marcuse; Chinese totalitarianism as a political ideal; all this fostered by youthful astronomical frustrations) the basis of a review. *I* can afford such extravaganzas, at least the I you seem to perceive in my book can—but you, my dear Joske cannot, for you are a rationalist, and tied to more severe standards.

So much about your failings as a reader and reviewer. There is another item I want to discuss before proceeding to more substantial issues, and it is this.

Many readers, and you, too, are disturbed by my way of saying things. "I think *what* you say is all right; but I think *how* you say it is wrong" writes our common friend Henryk Skolimowski in a letter I just received. You speak of my "hate blasts" and of my "scathing attacks". You do not identify the former, but you give a page number for the latter, so I again turn to the book and read. And I am again amazed at the difference between your perception and mine. For the page to which you refer contains a very *mild* (though concisely formulated) criticism of Clavius, Grienberger, and Father McMullin, another common friend of ours. We obviously look at things in a very different way.

The reason, I think, is that we have different ideas about *style*. *You* (and many other readers) are fond of a perhaps lively, vigorous, but still *scholarly* style. *I* find such a style with its neat innuendos and its civilised strangulation of the opponent too desiccated and also too dishonest (strange word for me to use—eh?) for my taste. Even the style of scholars has changed in a way not altogether advantagious. In the 19th century scholars from the *Geisteswissenschaften* jumped at each other with a vigour which would shake even a really nasty contemporary, and they did this out of exuberance, not out of a desire to hurt. Dictionaries of remote languages, such as Mediaeval-Latin/English dictionaries gave racy equivalents in English—and so on. Then, slowly, a more measured tone started to insinuate itself, and became the rule. I do not like the change, and I try to restore older ways of writing. In this attempt my guides have been poets such as Brecht (his superbly written theatrical criticism of his youth, not the more weighty notes of his later years), Shaw, Alfred Kerr or, to move back to even earlier times, humanists such as Erasmus and Ulrich von Hutten (not to mention Luther who once called Erasmus *flatus diaboli*—and this was quite in line with the good manners of the time). I have no argument for this preference of mine, I just state it as an idiosyncracy. I state it because the emotion behind a sentence ("loathing" for example, or the absence of it) can be judged correctly only if one first knows the style in which the sentence is written.

Now we finally come to some differences *in substance* that exist between you and me. What are these differences?

To answer the question, I shall quote a footnote from an earlier version of *Against Method* that was published in Vol. iv of the *Minnesota Studies for the Philosophy of Science* (Minneapolis, 1970). I omitted the footnote (and other material such as a chapter on Mill and Hegel) from the book in order to make room for Imre Lakatos's reply (which now, unfortunately, will never be published). I write:

"The possibilities of Mill's liberalism can be seen from the fact that it provides room for any human desire, and for any human vice. There are no general principles apart from the principle of minimal interference with the lives of individuals, or groups of individuals who have decided to pursue a common aim. For example, *there is no attempt to make the sanctity of human life a principle that would be binding for all.* Those among us who can realise themselves only by killing their fellow human beings and who feel fully alive only when in mortal danger are permitted to form a subsociety of their own where human targets are selected for the hunt, and are hunted down mercilessly, either by a single individual, or by specially trained groups (for a vivid account of such forms of life see the film *The Tenth Victim* which, however, turns the whole affair into a battle between the sexes). So, whoever wants to lead a dangerous life, whoever wants to taste human blood will be permitted to do so within the domain of his own subsociety. *But he will not be permitted to implicate others who are not willing to go his way*; for example, he will not be permitted to force others to participate in a 'war of national honour', or what have you. He will not be permitted to cover up whatever guilt he may feel by making a potential murderer out of everyone. It is strange to see how the *general* idea of the sanctity of human life that would object to the formation of subsocieties such as the one just described and that frowns upon simple, innocent, and rational murders such as the murder of a nagging wife by a henpecked husband does not object to the murder of people one has not seen and with whom one has no quarrel. Let us admit that we have different tastes; let those who want to wallow in blood receive the opportunity to do so without giving them the power to make 'heroes' of the rest of society. As far as I am concerned, a world in which a louse can live happily is a better world, a more instructive world, a more mature world than a world in which a louse must be wiped out. (For this point of view see the work of Carl Sternheim; for a brief account of Sternheim's philosophy, see Wilhelm Emrich's preface to C. Sternheim, *Aus dem Buergerlichen Heldenleben* [Neuwied: Hermann Luchterhand 1969, pp. 5–19]). Mill's essay is the first step in the direction of building such a world.

It also seems to me that the United States is very close to a cultural laboratory in the sense of Mill where different forms of life are developed and different modes of human existence tested. There are still many cruel and irrelevant restrictions, and excesses of so-called lawfulness threaten the possibilities which this country contains. However, these restrictions, these excesses, these brutalities occur in the *brains* of human beings; they are not found in the *constitution*. They can be removed by propaganda, enlightenment, special bills, personal effort (Ralph Nader!) and numerous other legal means. Of course, if such enlightenment is regarded as superfluous, if one regards it as irrelevant, if one assumes from the very beginning that the existing possibilities for change are either insufficient, or condemned to failure, if one is determined to use 'revolutionary' methods (methods, incidentally, which real revolutionaries such as Lenin have regarded as utterly infantile—see his 'Left Wing Radicalism, an Infantile Disease'—and which must increase the resistance of the opposition rather than removing it), then the 'system' will appear much harder than it really is. It will appear harder, *because one has hardened it oneself*, and the blame falls back on the bigmouth who calls himself a critic of society. It is depressing to see how a system that has much inherent elasticity is increasingly made less responsive by fascists on the Right and extremists on the Left until democracy disappears without having ever had a chance. My criticism, and my plea for anarchism is therefore directed *both* against the traditional puritanism in science and society *and* against the 'new', but actually age-old, antediluvian, primitive Puritanism of the 'new' left which is always based on anger, on frustration, on the urge for revenge, but never on imagination. Restrictions, demands, moral arias, generalised violence everywhere. A plague on both your houses!" So far part of footnote 49 of my essay of 1970 (remember that the Vietnam War and the Student 'Protests' were then still very much in existence).

I think you will admit that the society described in this passage has little in common with "totalitarian China". Even during the period of the Hundred Flowers the freedom achieved in China was but a fraction of what I think is possible and desirable. Note also, that there is no complete licence. Not all actions are permitted, and a strong police force prevents the various subsocieties from interfering with each other. But as regards the nature of these societies, 'anything goes', especially in the field of education. And with this I now come to a very substantial disagreement between you and me. *I* say that the educational institutions of a democracy should in principle teach any subject, *you* say that only "a knave and a fool" would suggest to introduce Voodoo and astrology to "state colleges and universities". So, let us take a closer look at the matter.

As far as I am concerned, the situation is childishly simple.

"State colleges and universities" are financed by taxpayers. They are therefore subjected to the judgement of the taxpayers *and not* to the judgement of the many intellectual parasites who live off public money.[4] If the taxpayers of California want their universities to teach Voodoo, folk medicine, astrology, rain dance ceremonies, then this is what the universities will have to teach (the *State* universities; private universities such as Stanford University may still continue teaching Popper and von Neumann).

Would taxpayers perhaps be better advised to accept the judgement of experts? They would not, and for obvious reasons.

First, experts have a vested interest in their own playpens, and so they will quite naturally argue that 'education' is impossible without them (can you imagine an Oxford philosopher, or an elementary particle physicist arguing himself out of good money?).

Secondly, scientific experts hardly ever examine the alternatives that might come up in the discussion with the care they take for granted when a problem in their own field is at stake. They agonize over different scientific approaches to the problems of space and time but the idea that the Hopi Genesis might have to add something to cosmology is at once rejected out of hand. Here scientists and, for that matter, all rationalists act very much like the Roman Church acted before them: they denounce unusual and extraordinary views as Pagan superstitions, they deny them every right to make a contribution to the One True Religion.[5] Given power, they will suppress Pagan ideas *as a matter of course* and replace them by their own 'enlightened' philosophy.

Thirdly, the use of experts would be all right if they were only taken from the proper field. Scientists would laugh their heads off (or, to be more realistic: they would be very indignant) if one asked a faith healer and not a surgeon about the details of an operation: obviously the faith healer is the wrong person to ask. But they take it for granted that an astronomer and not an astrologist should be asked about the merits of astrology, or that a Western physician and not a student of the *Nei Ching* should decide about the fate of acupuncture. Now—and with this I come to the fourth point, such a procedure would be unobjectionable if the astronomer, or the Western physician could be assumed to know more about astrology, or acupuncture than the astrologist, or the traditional Chinese doctor. *Unfortunately, this is only rarely the case.* Ignorant and conceited people are permitted to condemn views of which they have only the foggiest notion and with arguments they would not tolerate for a second in their own field. Acupuncture, for example, was condemned not because anyone had examined it, but simply because some vague idea of it did not fit into the general ideology of medical science or, to call things by their proper name, because it was a 'Pagan' subject (the hope for financial rewards has in the meantime led to a considerable change of attitude, however).

What is the effect of this procedure?

The effect is that scientists and 'liberal' rationalists have created one of the most unfortunate embarrassments of democracy. Democracies *as conceived by liberals* are always embarrassed by their joint commitment to 'rationality'—and this today means mostly: science—and the freedom of thought and association. Their way out of the embarrassment is an abrogation of democratic principles where they matter most: in the domain of education. Freedom of thought, it is said, is OK for grownups who have already been trained to 'think rationally'. It cannot be granted to every and any member of society and especially the educational institutions must be run in accordance with rational principles. In school one must learn what is the case and that means: Western oriented history, Western oriented cosmology, i.e., science. Thus democracy *as conceived by its present intellectual champions* will never permit the complete survival of special cultures. A liberal-rational democracy cannot contain a Hopi culture in the full sense of the word. It cannot contain a black culture in the full sense of the word. It cannot contain a Jewish culture in the full sense of the word. It can contain these cultures only as secondary grafts on a basic structure that is constituted by an unholy alliance between science, rationalism, and capitalism. This is how a small gang of so-called 'humanitarians' has succeeded in shaping society in their image and in weeding out almost all earlier forms of life.[6] Now this would have been a laudable undertaking if the beliefs constituting these forms of life had been examined with care, and with due respect to those holding the beliefs, and if it had been found that they are a hindrance to the free development of humanity. *No such examination has ever been carried out* and the few individuals who have started taking a closer look at the matter have come to a very different conclusion. What remains in the end behind all the humanitarian verbiage is the white man's assumption of his own intellectual superiority. It is this high handed procedure, this inhumane suppression of views one does not like, this use of 'education' as a club for beating people into submission which has prompted my contempt for science, rationalism, and all the pretty phrases that go with it ('search for truth'; 'intellectual honesty' etc. etc.: intellectual honesty, my foot!) and not a mythical astronomical disappointment at an early age as you, dear Joske, seem to believe. And I do not see why I should be polite to tyrants who slobber of humanitarianism and think only of their own petty interests.

There are many more things I would like to say, but a review is short, and the review of a review is even shorter. So, let me conclude with a personal story. For the past half year I have been losing weight, about 50 pounds by now, I got double vision, stomach cramps, I fainted in the streets of London and felt generally miserable. Naturally, I went to a doctor. The general practitioners (this was in England) did not do me much good. I went to specialists. For three weeks I was subjected to a battery of tests; I was given X-rays, emetics, enemas and each examination made me feel worse than ever. Result: negative (this is a nice paradox: you are sick; you go to a doctor; he makes you feel worse, but he says that you are well). As far as science is concerned, I am as fit as a fiddle. Not being restricted by an undying loyalty to science I started looking for other kinds of healers and I found there are lots of them. Herbalists. Faith healers. Acupuncturists. Masseurs.

Hypnotists. All quacks, according to the established medical opinion. The first thing that caught my attention was their method of diagnosis. No painful interference with the organism. Many of these people had developed efficient methods of diagnosing from pulse, colour of eye, of tongue, from gait, and so on. (Later on, when reading the *Nei Ching* which develops the philosophy behind acupuncture, I found that in China this was intentional: the human body must be treated with respect which means one has to find methods of diagnosis that do not violate its dignity.) I was lucky. The second man I consulted told me I had been severely ill for a long time (and that is true: for the past 20 years I wavered between long periods of health and other periods when I was hardly able to totter along, but without any scientifically detectable signs of illness), that he was going to treat me twice in order to see whether I responded and that he might take me on if I did. After the first treatment I *felt* better than I had felt for a long time and there were *physical* improvements as well, a long lasting dysentery stopped and my urine cleared up. None of my 'scientific' doctors had been able to achieve that. What did he do? A simple massage which, as I found later, stimulated the acupuncture points of liver and stomach. Here in Berkeley I have a faith healer and an acupuncturist, and I am now slowly recovering.

So, what I discovered was this: there exists a vast amount of valuable medical knowledge that is frowned upon and treated with contempt by the medical profession. We also know, from more recent anthropological work, that 'primitive' tribes possess analogous knowledge not only in the field of medicine, but in botanics, zoology, general biology, archaeologists have discovered the remnants of a highly sophisticated Stone Age astronomy with observatories, experts, application in exploratory voyages which was accepted across cultural lines, throughout the European continent. Myths, properly interpreted, have turned out to be repositories of knowledge unsuspected by science (but confirmable by scientific research, once the matter is taken up) and occasionally in conflict with it. *There is much we can learn and have to learn from our ancient ancestors, and our 'primitive' fellow men.* In view of this situation, must we not say, that our educational policies, including your own, dear Joske, are very ill conceived and narrow minded, to say the least? They are *totalitarian*, for they make the ideology of a small gang of intellectuals the measure of everything. And they are *shortsighted*, because this ideology is severely limited; it is a hindrance to harmony and progress. Let us become more modest; let us admit that Western rationalism is but one of many myths, not necessarily the best, let us adapt our education, and our society as a whole to this modesty and, maybe, we shall be able to return to a paradise which was once our own but which now seems to have been lost in noise, smog, greed, and rationalistic conceit.

All the best,
Paul

NOTES

1. An example is Professor Rossi's article 'Hermeticism and Rationality in the Scientific Revolution' published in Bonelli-O'Shea, eds. *Reason, Experiment and Mysticism in the Scientific Revolution*, New York 1975, 247–273. Professor Rossi carries on an unhappy love affair with rationalism. There is much love, there is little understanding. The philosophers and historians whom Rossi criticises have produced many and detailed arguments to support their point of view. Their papers contain these arguments, the results of the arguments, and a sometimes rather colourful summation of the results. Professor Rossi recognises the colourful summaries but he does not seem to have the ability to recognise an argument. Moreover, he rejects the summaries not because he possesses arguments of his own, but because he does not like them, or does not *seem* to like them, for even in the domain of *liking* he is not quite sure which way to go. On page 266 he speaks of the 'Neoromantic Revolt against science' and clearly disapproves of it. But on page 247 he complains about the fact that my interpretation of Galileo has been received 'enthusiastically' '*even* in Italy' implying that a 20th-century Italian is better equipped to understand the Spirit of Galileo than a 20th-century Viennese—a typically Romantic idea.

2. Elsewhere you say: 'there is no reference to Nazism, Fascism, even to the Spanish Civil War, not to mention racism'. True. And I did not mention burlesque either. And why not? Because there was not enough room, and because the items have hardly anything to do with my main topic which is: *epistemological* anarchism. Of course, you believe that irrationalism and anarchism *are bound to* lead to all these things (even to Auschwitz, as you said in a talk in Germany—really, Joske!), you expect that an author who recommends anarchistic moves is aware of such dangers, and so you think he has an obligation to comment on them. This would be acceptable reasoning if one could be sure that rationalism is free from dangers of this kind. *But it is not.* Quite the contrary. *The unrelenting driving force of reason is much more likely to stay with an antihumanitarian idea once it has been conceived than the quickly-moving procedure of the anarchist.* Robespierre was a rationalist, not an anarchist; the inquisitors of the 16th and 17th centuries who burned tens of thousands of victims were rationalists, not anarchists; Urbach, who has found some very sophisticated arguments in favour of a very refined racism is a rationalist, even a critical rationalist, not an anarchist; the trouble with the Spanish Civil War was not the presence of anarchists but the fact that despite the majority they possessed they refused to form a government and so left the stage to more 'rational' politicians; and don't forget that the word 'god *fearing*' arose in Greece only after Xenophanes had replaced the Homeric gods by a more rational account of Being which was a forerunner of Parmenides' monstrous One and this change of attitude towards God was a direct consequence of the increase of rationalism. If I had your talent for generalization I would say that rationalists are much more likely to build an Auschwitz than anarchists who, after all, want to remove all kinds of repression, repression by reason included. It is not rationalism, it is not law and order which prevents cruelty, but "the unreasoning impulse of human kindness" as George Lincoln Burr said in a letter to A. D. White who tried to explain the disappearance of the witchcraft mania by the rise of rationalism. But kindness is an *irrational force*.

3. The reader should not be misled, as you obviously are, by my frequent praise of leftist politicians. I praise them not because they are on the left but because they are thinkers *as well as* politicians, theoreticians *as well as* men of action, and because their experience with this world has made their philosophy realistic and flexible. It is not my fault that there are no comparable figures on the right, or in the center and that intellectuals, with the sole exception of Hegel, have been content with admiring, or destroying each other's castles in the air. Considering my reasons for choice I

might also have chosen great religious figures such as Church Fathers in my examples—and I did so in some earlier writings of mine where I praised St. Irenaeus, Tertullian (superb intellect!), St. Augustine, St. Athanasius, and others. Even a Bossuet is preferable by far to the professional scribblers of today who extol 'ideas' but have very little to say about the fears and the needs of soul and body.

4. I welcome most enthusiastically the Baumann amendment which recommends congressional veto power over the 14,000 odd grants the National Science Foundation awards every year. Scientists were very upset by the fact that the amendment was passed by the House of Representatives and the director of the National Academy spoke darkly of totalitarian tendencies. The gentleman does not seem to realise that totalitarianism means direction of the many by the few while the Baumann amendment goes exactly in the opposite direction: it suggests examining what the few are doing with the millions of public money that are put at their disposal in the vain hope that the public will eventually profit from such generosity. Considering the narcissistic chauvinsim of science such an examination would seem to be more than reasonable. Of course, it should be extended beyond the narrow limits of supervision of the NSF: every department at a state university must be carefully supervised lest its members use public money for working out their private fantasies under the heading of philosophical, psychological, sociological 'research'.

5. Such an attitude is frequently found in Galileo. He argues with his fellow mathematicians, he has only contempt for the mathematically uneducated "rabble" (his own word).

6. The history of the American Indians is a case in point. The first wave of invaders came to enslave them and to "teach them Christian manners" as it reads in Alexander VI's bull on the new islands and the new continent. The second wave of invaders came to enslave them and to teach them Christian manners of a different kind. By now they have been robbed of all material possessions and their culture has almost disappeared—"and rightly so" say the rationalists, "for it was irrational superstition".

REJOINDER

August 28, 1975

Dear Paul,

I am grateful for your response to my review of your *Against Method*. It is always an honor to be noticed, no matter how critically.

I have a problem of procedure on my hands. It is customary to have, in any single exchange, an odd number of entries. Now, if we begin with your book, your response should close this exchange; if we begin with my review, I should be the last contributor. Since the book is the major cause of the exchange, I feel you should have the last word. But the editor, concerned as he is with future reviews, and with the good will of reviewers to suffer a counter-criticism, wants the reviewer to have the last word. And I concede his point.

Further, I am told that I should take your response seriously and answer it. I grant that my readiness to let you have the last shot may sound too cavalier. So I shall compromise and offer a brief answer. Anyway, we both agree, taking an opponent point by point may be a catastrophic expansion. Let me, then, take what seems to me to emerge as central to our dispute.

Let me concede that atrocities are and were committed in the name of every possible—and impossible—cause. I even concede that rationalism may lead to the fanaticism displayed by Robespierre. I am not here to defend his version of rationalism, or anyone else's. Whatever rationalism is, or should be, what I think we need agree on, is that responsible citizens should use their brains to avoid making obviously harmful suggestions. I think your advice to Jews to become *really* Jews, to Indians to become *really* Indians, etc., is dangerous. If there is such a thing as *really* a Jew, then he resides in the old city of Jerusalem and in Williamsburg, Brooklyn, and he is cruel to his children in the name of the Lord. But I also think the really Jewish temperament is also progressive, a trait ignored by these Jews. In brief a *real* Jew cannot really exist in the modern world; nor a *real* Indian. Rain-dances before the American Invasion, the destruction of the prairie, and the extinction of the buffalo, cannot be revived. The rain-dance you defend is but a folly and a defense of the most reactionary attitude to Indians today.

But how can one recommend that a Jew and an Indian become *real* Jews and Indians in a merely therapeutic mood? If the therapy takes, then the Jew is back in the Middle Ages and the Indian is back on the prairie. Who will bring them back to modernity when the therapy session is over?

Moreover, who decides about the diagnosis or the therapy or the prognosis? I mention Dachau and Buchenwald in order to refute the 'anything goes' thesis: anything short of these, of course, and we need a method to decide how to decide what may lead to Dachau and what not: hence your objection to all method is dangerous—even as mere therapy.

Peace,
Joske

37

AS YOU LIKE IT

hate is never justified

PRELUDE

This is a continuation, I hope a conclusion, of a debate with Professor Paul Feyerabend that began with my review of his *Against Method*. I say I hope a conclusion because—alas!—I have to concede to him.

In my review I urged him to repudiate his assumed role, because he was mistaken in thinking himself to be a flippant light-hearted clown. The mistake was mine. First, it turns out, he has type-cast himself so well that it would be harder for him to change than it was for Hedy Lamarr. Secondly, though neither flippant nor light-hearted, as I shall explain later, he still is the clown in the silent-movie tradition of acrobatic clowns who delight the kids, the tradition culminating with Laurel and Hardy, especially Hardy. Feyerabend says things he knows will not fool his readers, who know he is no fool: he is an iconoclast of the clowning sort, a pluralist who therefore has his heart in the right (left) place, who relentlessly harasses the best rationalists in town by pointing to their worst weakness. The best rationalists are the Popperians, and their worst weakness is the obsession with demarcation, a concealed moralism, the demarcation of the Good Guys from the Bad. And he either poses as a Bad Guy in order to make a point or he is a daredevil—who knows?

All this is far from being to my taste. Yet I do concede: even the most lenient philosophers of the rationalist school preach standards that are much too high, and in the name of an Almighty Science which they appropriate for themselves and in whose name they oppress the vivacious young. Unfortunately, however, the excessive reaction of Feyerabend, like the reaction of all those who flip out or recommend that we flip out, is merely a palliative, a momentary escape, from which sooner or later one comes

---

This appeared in German in *Versuchungen: Aufsatze zur Philosophie Paul Feyerabends*, edited by Hans-Peter Duerr (Frankfurt: Suhrkamp, 1980).

back to normal. The slogan 'anything goes', that is now Feyerabend's trademark, means that the present-day moralists who advocate high standards in the name of rationalism are right, and so we had better give up rationalism altogether. In his reply to Helmut Spinner he says, he refuses to cut off his nose just because the Führer of the Third Reich had a nose, yet he cuts off his reason because the moralists claim a monopoly over it and he denounces science because the moralists claim a monopoly over it. But I say the moralists are in error and to let them keep the monopoly over rationality and science should not be Feyerabend's general policy.

FIRST ACT

Helmut Spinner has ascribed to me the idiotic view that there is agreement between the public views of Feyerabend and the Führer of the Third Reich. He, Spinner, first opposed this idiotic view, and then, incredibly, endorsed it. Obviously, there can be hardly a greater disparity between two views: the one is a fanatic monism, the other is a sloppy pluralism; the one says: nothing goes except on my say-so, the other says: anything goes. How, then, can anyone ever arrive at such a strange idea as the comparison of these two? Perhaps Feyerabend himself permits this comparison, since he permits any idea, any suggestion whatsoever: if anything goes, perhaps equating his views with the Führer's goes too. But I am not discussing here the license Feyerabend kindly offers his disciples, nor his reasons for rejecting some of them, including Spinner's. How should non-Feyerabendians respond to such an equation? Perhaps they will be ready to accept it on the ground that all ideas they consign to the dust-bin are equal. I am afraid this readiness is rather too cavalier: there are considerations other than intellectual to take into account now and then. Whenever an idea becomes a social or political pollutant, not to say an intellectual pollutant, we are obliged to consider it seriously, even if we would prefer not to have to. It is always a tribute to criticize, at the very least the tribute to an author who, as a sufficiently significant pollutant, manages to impose his work on our attention. This tribute I am paying Feyerabend again: he always pollutes his own best products.

Nevertheless, I have not said as yet why I think it an error to equate all utterly unacceptable views, or utterly worthless ones, etc. The reason is that different pollutants have to be neutralized differently. I do not expect present-day pollutants to demand so much effort to eradicate as the ones which spread so rapidly in the twenties and thirties. But one never knows; we may have to analyze them in detail and try to understand why they find markets. What urges and needs do consumers expect them to satisfy and how can we find better substitutes for them that might oust them and how can prospective consumers learn to compare them and improve their tastes, etc.? We have here a complex of uninteresting and unpleasant practical problems, political as well as educational, that we may be forced to study in sheer self-defense.

Can we at all say that the Führer of the Third Reich has satisfied some urges and needs? Certainly. Most of them were emotional needs and I will try to avoid these. Can one speak of some intellectual problems, intellectual needs, some worthwhile arguments that the Führer has supplied? I do not think so: when we descend to the level where his arguments start to look good we find there as many competitors (to them) as one might wish.

I am well aware of the fact that the old chauvinist arguments in favor of hate still have some currency—in Germany as well as in Israel. Yet I think those who are still using arguments to incite hatred—Leftists or Rightists—they know very well that they are using weak arguments and they use them nevertheless; the way Professor Feyerabend uses some of his arguments, incidentally. And people who use poor arguments knowing that they are poor are often successful in the task that they undertake which makes them use poor arguments knowingly. Being successful they deem themselves very clever instead of seeing this as proof that the tasks they undertake are not worthy. And this makes their folly quite disastrous, since they are unaware of their folly, being so successful, until it is too late. But clearly, whatever the task they undertake, the people they convince by poor arguments are either poor thinkers or people who willingly accept poor arguments despite their ability to do better. They do so either because they feel that what they gain by poor arguments is worthier than their intellects, or because they are tired of their own intellects anyway. In either case they are anti-intellectuals, irrational, obscurantists. And there is, no doubt, a constant demand for obscurantism by all those who feel burdened by the intellectual and moral standards of their environments.

Obscurantism is a quality of all sorts of writers. The most important difference between different obscurantists seems to me to be the difference between the pacific and the sadistic, for example between the old Tolstoy and Georges Sorel. And the most important question about an intellectual polluter we try to neutralize is: Is he for or against violence? Is he a sadist or a pacifist? The answer may sometimes be obvious, but not always so, since the sadistic polluter may choose to appear as a pacifist. For example, the militarism of Israeli clericalists of the new style is what makes them of the sadistic variety despite the pacifist wording of traditional Judaism which is seemingly still accepted by them.

I do not think we can study the appeal of a given brand of obscurantism without knowing whether it is pacific or sadistic.

INTERLUDE

My review of Professor Feyerabend's *Against Method* contrasts unfavorably with Ernest Gellner's review of the same work. I assumed it to be pacific, but Gellner knew better. Oh, the passage in that book where Feyerabend preaches violence as a means of overcoming one's scruples and discovering one's strength had not escaped me, but I wanted to believe him when he said he was a kind of pacifist who would not hurt a fly. Addressing him as pacific I argued—mistakenly, as I know now—against his obscurantism with the classic argument against all obscurantism and in favor of reason: it is reason that enables us to distinguish between good and evil, as ancient mythology put it. As I put it, one cannot accept his slogan, 'anything goes', because it may mean anything including Naziism, and Naziism should not be permitted, since it leads to Dachau and Buchenwald. But I was in error: Feyerabend's obscurantism is not of the pacific kind. And so he could easily dismiss my criticism, as he has done in a later publication, saying 'anything goes', including the most beastly Nazi. He even gave an argument to support his claim: he had wished to write a play describing a revolting Nazi who, in the second act or so becomes more and more appealing, to end up as revolting as at the start. There are such plays written, I hasten to add, at least one of them quite impressive. (It portrays the commander of Auschwitz.) If such a poor argument suffices to convince one to take Nazis seriously, then it might also suffice to convince one to take Feyerabend seriously. I therefore would like to try out a sketch of such a play to advocate the taking seriously: a stronger argument I no longer have at my disposal, I regret to confess.

Second Act

Young Paul Feyerabend, an Austrian citizen under the *Anschluss*, volunteered for the German army and served with it as an officer. He tried to ignore the ideological and political aspects of the war, World War II, that is, not to mention the moral problems it raised for him whether as a soldier, or as a solider of one side rather than the other. Instead, he tried to busy himself by reading philosophy. He was wounded at the very end of the war and spent much time in hospital. After leaving hospital and after trying a few things he finally ended up studying philosophy, but still trying to avoid politics and all that. Rather, he tried to concentrate on the tougher and more technical side of philosophy. Nevertheless, somehow he got converted to Trotskyism, from which he was never freed (though he managed to put it aside and, while a disciple of Popper, even expounded rather anti-Trotskyite views). The centers of his concern were the tough questions of philosophy, especially the philosophy of science, in particular questions relating to quantum theory. He thus came to meet both Niels Bohr and Karl Popper. He became a student and a disciple of Popper's. (Oh, I know that he is in the habit of denying this claim of mine. One of us is obviously a liar, and it must be myself, since, as Feyerabend says, I extol science because the capitalists pay me and flatter me for doing so. Nice.) He became a passionate defender of science and of rationality as he understood them, preaching logic, quantum mechanics, and, above all, the philosophy of Karl Popper.

I met Feyerabend first in January, 1953. It was in the London School of Economics and Political Science, in the celebrated seminar of Professor Karl Popper. We were both young, noisy, gregarious, and argumentative, in that seminar and out; yet we did not talk with each other. Young Israelis at that time usually avoided the company of Germans, and hardly knew the difference between Germans and Austrians. The reason is simple: we did not want to befriend ex-Nazis or Nazis or ex-Concentration-camp personnel, and we did not want to examine the credentials of people who might have been in such positions. It was best and easiest simply to avoid the problem. When it was unavoidable and we found ourselves talking with young Germans, the discussion invariably came to the painful topic. One young German we met in the London School of Economics was Ralf Dahrendorf, who already then was, what he is so very well known now for, namely a liberal social thinker. With him, too, the discussion centered around Naziism and it was not very easy either. But he understood, I think. With Feyerabend the same conversation was postponed by a few years, which was a sad mistake on my part.

The way it came about is this. Popper was conducting with each of us discussions about metaphysics and physics; indeed he later acknowledged to both of us simultaneously that our joint enthusiasm was very helpful to his return to the topic he had left because of the unenthusiastic response of his colleagues. I need not explain how flattered we were by the interest our idol showed in our cogitations. And the flattery was marked from the start. Anyway, Popper wanted to meet us together in private, and so he did many a time. But before that he had to bring us together: without being told, he noticed my attitude toward Feyerabend and he understood. He told me that Feyerabend had regretted his earlier career, even with tears. And he simply instructed me to befriend Feyerabend, which I did with no hesitation.

I learned about my mistake a year or two later, yet remained on friendly and even, in a way, on close terms with him, chiefly because we were engaged in advanced philosophical debates. But by then he had admitted to me that he had hardly any moral sense. When I pressed he admitted that were "they"—"they"!—to return to the extermination of the Jews he would stand up and shout, "that is too much!", but he could not say what was so special about this. I let it go: he produced little on moral or political philosophy, anyway, and the little he did was of very little significance, since it was, to repeat, a rehash of Popper.

THIRD ACT

Things changed after the student revolution, so-called. From that time on, and increasingly, Feyerabend preached his odd slogan (I do not know if I quite find it comprehensible), 'anything goes'. It sounded like a joke in poor taste to hear that he recommended to African students and to students of African descent—as the rumor went—that they practice magic and eschew science. It was clear to me at once that the move was political, not intellectual, and I could see its allure, but also its dangers: in order to become equal, the discriminated-against Africans had to fight against discrimination, not to retreat to tribal customs and culture that were hardly useful to them in their difficult situation. It was hard enough for them without seeking lost pride in fake and lost roots. Moreover, what should one say about magic that is cannibalistic? But sooner or later Feyerabend came out in print, and the rumors were now facts. What the rumors did was prepare the ground; what they omitted was supplemented. The increased volume of Feyerabend's new philosophy illustrates this.

The early phase of Feyerabend's researches showed him as eager to find the toughest problems, the strongest arguments, the answers that were as near final as possible. The later phase is the opposite. If the strongest cannot be defended well enough to bring conviction and satisfaction, at least the weakest can be defended by some arguments that are not that bad, and with time we can learn to live with ever poorer arguments, provided we supplement them from time to time with really brilliant ideas to show that we say these silly things not out of stupidity. And it worked. Example: we defend Aristotle's physics which is reputed to be not really good; yet there are some very intriguing arguments in its favor. A worse example: we defend magic and superstition and pseudo-science. They interest the learned occultists, the anthropologists, and so on. Some systems of superstition are quite sophisticated; others may, at times even do, include some interesting item overlooked by the best of modern Western science and medicine. Hence, they should be studied. Hence they are serious contenders for the status of knowledge. Hence they are not inferior to the best of science. Hence science is wrong to condemn them. Hence science is inferior. (Do not expect Professor Feyerabend to correct my criticism of all this; he prefers not to, since he does not accept my method of arguing in preference to his. He is against method.) The worst example possible: he defends Naziism too, and merely because it may be interesting and intrigue the best of us. Hence it too is a contender, etc. The Nazi, too, can have a human quality now and then. And so we can take the beast as just one other animal in our zoo and shed no tear, especially no tear about our past: no one is perfect, not the Führer who hated the Jews but also not the Jews who now, except for Hannah Arendt, make such fuss about matters as if they were perfect. Violence, Feyerabend thinks, also has its good side, so that should count for something too. The popularity that Feyerabend has in the Federal Republic of Germany (I have no information as to how well he fares in the German Democratic Republic) would sound to me dangerous were it not pathetic.

Epilogue

Professor Feyerabend, we remember, has argued against my criticism of his views. He says: 'anything goes'; I say: not anything, not brutality, for example, not Auschwitz. He retorts: a well-written play may make us sympathize for a fleeting moment even with a Nazi brute. I concede; *a fortiori*, then, a play may make us sympathize for a fleeting moment also with Feyerabend. If a fleeting moment of sympathy suffices as a defense then, indeed, anything goes. But it does not. It does not justify brutality, and consequently it does justify preachers of the Gospel of Hate. For, it is a sad fact that Feyerabend is just another recruit to the army of its preachers. The question they often raise and discuss is: Whom should we hate and under what conditions? And the main consensus between those who preach the Gospel of Hate is that it is the Gospel of Unreason: Do hate Reason! And Feyerabend identifies Reason and Popper, and says: Hate Popper!

Beware of the Gospel of Hate. Beware of the question, whom should we hate? In Israel Naziism is taken very seriously, and as an object of legitimate hate, of course. Some Israelis argue against the preachers of hate on the terms these preachers like; they say, the Nazis are now too weak to be taken seriously. There is a smashing argument against this: in the early thirties many Jews thought so, and they were mistaken and paid with their lives for this mistake. What this amounts to of course is: better be on the safe side; better hate even when in doubt, or at the very least, sometimes hate is very important in the battle for survival. I have also met the Gospel of Hate in the universities, in the heyday of the Student Revolution, so-called: the New-Left preachers preached the Gospel of Hate. They justified hate by arguments from oppression: white men oppressed black men, imperialists oppressed the colonies, America oppressed the world, etc. All evil deeds, it was tacitly assumed, justify hate, especially hate of the big evil-doers. The New Left still preaches all this, especially in Germany, and the New Right too, especially in Israel; not to mention the New Islam in Iran.

I am a follower of Spinoza: I hold that hate is never justified, never to be recommended. The wise man, said Spinoza, does not hate his enemy, does not hate the confused multitudes, but rather sympathizes with them and regrets their shortcomings. All this, he said, is a simple matter of wisdom and of self-interest: hate is an expensive sentiment, giving in to it is self-destructive.

Exeunt omnes

Curtain

— 38 —

AGASSI'S ALLEGED ARBITRARINESS

philosophical bias of a historian of science

The present essay is a response to T. A. Beckman's 'On the Use of Historical Examples in Agassi's "Sensationalism" '. Section 1 is a point-by-point response to all of Beckman's concrete allegations. Section 2 is a response to his opening paragraph, perhaps to his general complaint as well. The Appendix further clarifies the logic of the situation.

1. BECKMAN'S DETAILED ALLEGATIONS

The statements which are the center of the controversy are three, and I shall give them names for the sake of brevity. I propose the following names:

Tom: All chemical elements except hydrogen are compounds of sorts of hydrogen.

Dick: The atomic weights of all elements are whole numbers (when that of hydrogen is chosen as the unit).

Harry: The atomic weight of chlorine is 35.5.

Clearly, Tom entails Dick and either of them contradicts Harry (see Appendix). Beckman begins (p. 294) with Harry. Harry, he reports in my name, was once true and is now false. I disclaim this attribution and declare this report false—as I assume truth to be absolute. Beckman goes on to deny that Harry is false, using an argument which an absolutist must reject *a priori*: he says that chemists still employ Harry, and so it is largely true. In this context he explains that we should not confuse Harry with another statement which I shall now present as:

Studies in the History and Philosophy of Science, 2, 1971.

Son of Harry: The average terrestrial atomic weight of chlorine is 35.5.

Let me add that in my 'Sensationalism' I also discuss:

Grandson of Harry: The atomic weight of chlorine is 35 or 37.

Whereas, for all I know, Son of Harry is true, Grandson of Harry is not; both, however, are on good terms with both Tom and Dick.

I find it hard to be told that I confuse Harry with Son of Harry: "Agassi has misrepresented the situation by oversimplifying it; one cannot just propose that [Harry] was mistaken", says Beckman (p. 295). Beckman's censure notwithstanding, I retain my position.

Professor Beckman makes the transition from Harry to Son of Harry by construing the words 'atomic weight' as having two meanings, one the original 19th-century meaning (according to which Harry is false), and one the meaning 'the average terrestrial atomic weight' which gives a new meaning to Harry—the same as that of Son of Harry. This kind of exercise is called by Popper 'the conventionalist twist'; it is obviously a verbal trick. To be more precise, Beckman makes the transition in two steps, adding first 'average' and then 'terrestrial'; and it takes him almost a page plus a footnote—and fairly complicated ones at that—ending with the assertion that I oversimplify. I feel I have not honestly earned the compliment: I think rather he overcomplicates; he has worked harder. Moreover, I do not see why he should use the same words to mean both Harry and Son of Harry and then warn us against confusing the two. My practice of using different sentences to mean different propositions seems to me less extravagant than his, especially since, for all we know, the one denotes a falsity and the other denotes a truth.

Beckman seems to add the following. Harry is a statement not declared false by scientists. Even if it were declared false, this need not matter for philosophers, since all philosophers can view with equanimity the overthrow of this or that hypothesis (p. 296). Moreover, even if Harry were false, and if its falsehood could be shown relevant, it would conceivably have to be refuted in the last century to be relevant—and, says Beckman (pp. 297-99), it was not. This is the way I read Beckman's rather involved argument. (First, the bowl is hardly cracked; second, it was cracked before I borrowed it; third, it cracked after I returned it. Each argument might do, perhaps, but no two of them go together.)

I do not know what Beckman wants. He does not deny that methods of precipitation exist which separate the two chlorine isotopes (chlorine-35 and chlorine-37), methods which were known in the 19th century. He does not deny that precipitation was used in the chemical experiments performed in the 19th century to determine the atomic weight of chlorine. Yet he says (p. 298) "it is not possible, as Agassi claims, simply to vary the circumstances [of these 19th-century experiments] (certainly not the chemical circumstances) so as to obtain" Grandson of Harry. I find his parenthetic phrase quite pathetic, though true (since precipitation methods are physical, not chemical); but in any case, why could 19th-century chemists not obtain Grandson of Harry? Is it perhaps that they had not conceived of him? As Beckman himself notices elsewhere (p. 304), they had.

Why was Grandson of Harry not discovered? Clearly the possibility was not taken seriously enough, and we follow only a small fraction of the possibilities we conceive. If there were one person able enough and intent enough, it was Jean Servais Stas, who loved Tom and accepted Harry only very reluctantly. I may be in error, but I think Stas said clearly enough that one must abide by the verdict of the facts. He took it for granted that sooner or later conflicting empirical evidence must oust a hypothesis, or else excuses will always exist to enable us to reconcile any hypothesis with any empirical findings. Clearly, allowing ourselves always to go against empirical evidence will be the end of science.

Here is the moral of the story for the discussion of my 'Sensationalism' (*Mind*, 75 [1966], 1-24). I agree that we can always circumvent empirical evidence. I find the rule (Boyle's Rule), which recommends never to circumvent empirical evidence, both almost universally recommended—the last to advocate it was Popper in his *Logic of Scientific Discovery* of 1959—and too stringent. It is enough, I say, if we require that we have a good reason to circumvent a given piece of empirical evidence, so as to exclude the permission to circumvent arbitrarily any piece of empirical evidence.[1] Now, what we think constitutes a good reason here depends on our general view of reason in science. Popper views testability as a good reason, perhaps as the best reason, not to say the only really good one. If so, then in the case of Stas it should be permissible to circumvent Harry and replace him by Son of Harry on the ground that Grandson of Harry is right; for this move is quite testable, and so Popper would have to approve of it—quite contrary to Boyle's Rule which he erroneously advocates. (Erroneously by his own lights, that is.)

This, need I say, is no criticism of Stas but of Popper. In case one should say it is a hypothetical case—were Stas to reject Boyle's Rule he would have done well—I add the case of William Prout who presented to the world both Tom and Dick, in spite of their divergence from other people's empirical evidence, and without offering any empirical evidence of his own.

The whole case-history used in my 'Sensationalism' has been repeated in the previous three paragraphs. This is not much history, to be sure. Though Beckman is appalled by the paucity of my historical details (p. 97, his first sentence and his exclamation mark), I still find no need for more history there. Is my history correct, and is it relevant to my discussion?

"Contrary to Agassi's statement some of [Prout's] information was Prout's own" (p. 300). I am glad to be corrected, and upon reflection I am willing to consider the correction as quite significant (see Appendix). The fact remains, however, that there was ample evidence which went against

Prout and which Prout and Stas tried to eliminate—quite unsuccessfully, we know.

"Agassi does seem over-enthusiastic about Prout's boldness in advancing hypotheses, particularly since the author's first anonymous remark is: 'The author of the following essay submits it to the public with the greatest diffidence' " (p. 301). I wonder whether my seeming "over-enthusiastic" is subject to criticism, but let us suppose it is. Why the diffidence and the anonymity if Prout did not feel that the publication was a fairly bold step? I have myself been involved in the publication of an anonymous paper of a friend of mine, and I remember that the anonymity of the author was occasioned by the boldness of the paper. This may not be the same for Prout, but Beckman is not at all clear about matters.

Beckman objects (p. 302) to my using such phrases as "fell in love" to describe Stas's early attitude towards Tom. I cannot take this criticism seriously, I cannot see how it is strengthened by his quotation of a passage from Stas in a more sober style, and I do not know how Beckman, who is such a historical scholar, has overlooked the fact that I was merely paraphrasing another passage by Stas, who himself said that in his youth he fell in love with Tom and so on.[2]

"It is very important to see that there was no question of either accepting or rejecting Prout's hypothesis when it was proposed. Prout himself avoided giving it strong recommendation and simply expressed the hope that its importance will be seen, and that someone will undertake to examine it, and thus verify or refute its conclusions." Prout's hypothesis is either Tom or Dick. Beckman and I think each other confused on this matter (see Appendix). Also, whereas I think that a verified hypothesis must be accepted and a refuted one must be rejected, Beckman thinks that Prout himself in proposing the hypothesis for verification or refutation saw "no question of either accepting or rejecting" it. Moreover, whereas (following Popper) I contrast the readiness to examine a hypothesis, and verify or refute it, with the recommendation to see it as a mere verbal tool for describing facts, Beckman says (p. 300) that Prout suggested Tom both for possible verification or refutation and in addition to this "as a device, a *façon de parler*". All this, however, is a philosphical disagreement, not a historical correction or a claim for the philosophical irrelevance of a piece of historical information. And so, on Beckman's criterion and fortunately for him, it is neither here nor there.

"If Agassi's philosophical objectives are to be served by the example of Prout's hypothesis, this hypothesis must be accepted today", says Beckman (p. 305). Why? Why can I not praise Prout's boldness even if I think his ideas false? Why can I not say: though it is false, had Stas declared it true in the face of his information he could have discovered Grandson of Harry? I think Beckman's conditional statement quoted in this paragraph quite extravagant. He spends a paragraph to show its consequent false, so as to refute me with a *modus tollens*, but he omits explaining why on earth he takes the conditional itself to be true. For my part, I find the servility to today's science which it expresses a bit too much; I have labelled it elsewhere[3] as up-to-date-science-textbook-worship.

Finally, Beckman objects to some of the emotional overtones of my paper, including some which he finds in my paper and which I do not. Let me pick a few examples. I adore Prout's speculative bent, and he does not. Let it be. He asks rhetorically (p. 302), "How can we possibly condemn Stas for refusing 'to stick to the hypothesis in the face of known facts in the hope that the facts will adjust themselves to theory', when it was Stas himself who had laboured so hard to produce facts which would be reliable and not susceptible to further adjustment." Beckman seems to take it for granted that I condemn Stas. I do not condemn Stas but (unlike Beckman) I do regret that he "laboured so hard" looking for the impossible, that is, for "facts which would be reliable and not susceptible to further adjustment". Beckman even goes further and suggests (p. 299, lines 5–11) that I view the 19th-century quantitative analysts, the likes of Stas, as unreasonable. I do not. He ascribes to me the view that Boyle's Rule, which I think needs modification, is "naive and, occasionally, dangerous dogmatism" (p. 299), and that it "has been damaging, or that it has the potential for being damaging" (p. 306). To this I offer an unqualified disclaimer. In its historical context the Rule has worked wonders. But it is invalid, it has been repeatedly broken, and it can profitably be reformed. It all boils down to the same point: Beckman sees every expression of disagreement on my part as an expression of contempt. He has not heard yet of such an attitude as a respectful disagreement, or, if he has, he is careful to hide the fact.

2. BECKMAN'S COMPLAINT

Beckman offers a very brief explanation of his having picked a bone with me. He speaks of the "increasingly widespread practice of using historical examples to serve philosophical purposes" and says that he chose my 'Sensationalism' as "a case study", wishing to "emphasize the need for reasonable standards of historical scholarship in those cases where historical examples are proposed as instances of philosophical generalizations". This is all Beckman says (in his opening paragraph) about his choice. I ask for the reader's further indulgence while I discuss all this in detail in the next paragraph.

First, my 'Sensationalism' is not a case of using "historical instances of philosophical generalizations", since that paper is rather critical of the generalizations of others, not a defense of mine. For that, if Beckman had to choose a work of mine, he could take my *Towards an Historiography of Science*, which abounds with historical examples, and, to my regret, is not free from historical errors. Or, he could choose my 'The Nature of Scientific Problems and Their Roots in Metaphysics', in Mario Bunge's Popper *Festschrift*. Or, he could choose more prominent Popperian examples of the use of historical examples, such as Popper's own 'Back to the Pre-Socratics', Imre Lakatos's 'Proofs and Refutations', or John Watkins's *Hobbes*. But he need not confine himself to my own habitat either, and he could choose the most prominent and important use of historical example—Koyré's study of the case of Galileo. Come to think of it, what is this "increasingly widespread practice of using historical examples'? Are there many philosophers who have managed to avoid using historical examples? One might defend Beckman here and say that though everyone has been using historical examples, the tendency is on the increase. For example, only in recent years Carl Hempel has undertaken a detailed analysis of a case history—his delightful study of the case of Semmelweis. But then my 'Sensationalism' is disqualified because the example in it is brief and marginal. Why did Beckman not take Hempel's example as a 'case study'? Is it because Hempel is precise and he wanted an imprecise example? But then, does the literature, any literature, not always contain some inexact cases? What do we gain from exposing an inexact case? Does one inexact case prove any "increasingly widespread" tendency?

Flattered as I am to see my name in the title of a paper in a learned periodical, I somehow feel that the honor is not well earned, and I wonder why Beckman has picked on a paper of mine, which he has no good word to say for, and which is so poor an example for his main theme. Why does he choose an example of a paper which uses little history, only to complain that it scarcely uses history? ('You have changed, Tom!' 'I am not Tom but Dick.' 'My, you have changed your name as well'.)

Beckman claims, allegedly in opposition to myself, that it is "naive to discuss science in the hard-and-fast terms of rejecting, or accepting, hypotheses" (p. 306). This is an advanced philosophical thesis, actually advanced by some of Popper's former students. Beckman sincerely thinks that he can illustrate the correctness of this new thesis by showing that the conduct of 19th-century chemists conforms to it.

With Davy's rejection of Dalton's hypothesis, with Dalton's rejection of Prout's (Tom), with the widespread acceptance of Tom reported by Stas, with the battle over rejecting or accepting atomism spilling over into the present century—with all these facts glaring against him, Beckman quixotically hopes to find his advanced philosophical thesis illustrated in 19th-century chemistry. Just like Lakatos. Here I much prefer Bartley's mode of advocating that thesis, which has to do not with how people used to approach hypotheses but rather with how best we might approach them. Moreover, Boyle's Rule, which I recommend that we modify, is a hard-and-fast rejection rule, still advocated by Popper in 1959, though not in Popper's 'The Aims of Science' of 1957, as I explain in my 'Sensationalism' in detail. How is it that Beckman does not even see the trend here?

APPENDIX

Tom entails Dick on the assumption of the law of conservation of mass. They are independent on the law of conservation of mass-energy, but this may be remedied by introducing Son of Dick which adds to Dick the qualifier, "minus the binding energy of each element".

It is interesting to note that Dalton accepted Dick implicitly when he rounded atomic weights. Yet he opposed Prout. Did he reject Tom or did he mean to say it was rash to publish Tom? This is an open question, posed in my *Towards an Historiography of Science*. I found the question particularly engaging since Prout himself presented Tom as an idea which was not unpopular in his own time. Is it possible that we ascribe it to Prout because he was bold enough to publish it, and was Dalton's point that what was needed was not boldness but facts?

I had overlooked, then, the fact that in his first paper, Prout did report some experiments of his. I must have viewed them as repetitions of others' experiments, since Prout himself is deliberately vague on this point. The explicit point of his paper was, of course, the presentation of a method of calculation by which experiment and reasoning may help us bring facts into better accord with hypotheses. This method required more new experiments and more new calculation, as Prout amply illustrates. The new method is, as Beckman notices, based on Gay-Lussac's theory (which, we know, Dalton rejected). This was applicable to iron, say, only by imagining cases of iron gas, as Prout did. How much all this was supported by the more precise repetitions which Prout performed on other people's experiments is an interesting question which is raised by Beckman.

It is still possible that Prout's greatest contribution, and the one which has put Tom on the map, was Prout's decision to fix the atomic weight of oxygen at 16 instead of 8—thereby giving water two atoms of hydrogen and thus at one stroke resolving most of the empirical difficulties related to Tom. It may be noted that raising the atomic weight of oxygen again—to 32—was not out of the question, and even Stas would have agreed, had he found the atomic weight of chlorine to be exactly enough 35.5, yet his result was 35.46 (not to mention similar deviations for other elements).

Be all this as it may, clearly, Prout, Dalton, and all other *dramatis personae* agreed that Tom entails Dick, as they took the law of conservation of mass as given.

Similarly Son of Dick was historically linked with Son of Tom. There are only two elementary particles, protons and electrons. Son of Dick meanwhile has become Grandson of Dick with protons, neutrons and electrons, as well as binding energies, replacing hydrogen atoms. Though thereby rendered much more complex, Grandson of Dick or its variant is here to stay, it appears, as an elaborate explanation of atomic weights. It has lost, however, all link with Tom; for Tom was once linked with ancient metaphysics, as Prout notes, and by now Tom or its cognate has lost this exciting link. By now the metaphysical problem has gone to the field of elementary particles, of course, which is the latest replacement of Son of Tom through a long line of descent.

While declaring that Tom was rejected, Beckman says (note 25) that Tom is completely false because atoms include both protons and neutrons. This is so if neutrons are particles different from protons, but not if neutrons are deemed excited protons. Here we see that Beckman has a relativist version of the thesis of the up-to-date-textbook-worshipper according to which a principle is partly true if and only if it has a fairly near descendant in the up-to-date textbook. The vagaries of the textbook, however, still plague up-to-date-textbook-worship, even in its relativist garb.

NOTES

1. Today even this weaker version of Boyle's Rule seems too strong to me. I say now that, wherever we can do interesting research while circumventing the facts, we are at liberty to do so—as long as we do not conceal the facts, of course. But this is all in parenthesis; I shall not pursue it here.

2. The passage is reprinted, not in the *Alembic Club Reprint*, no 20, which Beckman quotes, but in J. Kendall's 'The Adventures of an Hypothesis', *Proceedings of the Royal Society of Edinburgh*, 63 (1950), 4. These two sources would do for the present debate.

3. *Towards an Historiography of Science*, facsimile reprint (Wesleyan University Press, 1967).

WILLIAMS DODGES
AGASSI'S CRITICISM

using unbiassed history to illustrate a philosophy

The 1975 fall issue of the *British Journal for the Philosophy of Science*, (26: 241–53) includes a paper by L. Pearce Williams, allegedly reviewing my *Faraday as a Natural Philosopher* and W. K. Berkson's *Fields of Force*, under the title 'Should Philosophers be Allowed to Write History?' Leaving the part on Berkson as none of my business, I wish to respond thrice to Williams's review: in the next sentence, in the first section of this reply, and in the rest of this reply. Williams corrects some minor 'errors of transcription' of mine, for which I am grateful; he foolishly pretends that historians can be and should be immune from such errors; he claims that my thesis is erroneous and unfounded whereas I have ample evidence, especially to refute his alleged refutation of it; and he preaches a preposterous self-refuting view which is summed up in 'a resounding "No"' to his question. End of my reply, shortest version.

(1) Does Williams allow historians to write philosophy? Does he allow members of academic profession *x* to write in academic discipline *y*? I say "academic" since in the market place a few practices are confined by law to professionals, but not in the academies; not yet, at least. How Williams wants to ban intrusion—by law, by guild by-law, by editorial policy, or by reviewers' threat of a scowl—I would not know.

Should members of one academic profession be allowed to participate in another?

Suppose Williams says NO. He thus advocates professionalism. Whose domain is the discussion on professionalism? Sociologists'? Philosophers' of science? Surely not historians'.

Suppose Williams only says NO to philosophers' meddling in others' affairs. Again, surely discussion of this prohibition is not a historian's domain.

Suppose Williams only says NO to meddlers in history. Anything peculiar to history? YES: philosophers care for ideas, not their origins; scientists offer conjectures and their attempted refutations. Only history is inductive and so both comprehensive and entirely founded on (all the available) evidence.

By the inductive historian's canons Williams is very much at fault in saying what I report him to say: Rather than generalise from one or two instances he ought, by his own lights (not by mine), to write a comprehensive history of scientists' and philosophers' writings on history. He could then find many excellent histories written by non-historians; he could likewise discover anti-inductivist excellent historians; he could then find no instance of an infallible historian. Some of our best friends, he and I know, are fallible, anti-inductivist, excellent historians, some of them strictly amateurs.

And so Williams refutes his thesis when he defends it, and it is a thesis that demands that it be defended. (This is known amongst philosophers as a pragmatic paradox.) Instead he should, like a good historian, explain why he still thinks Boscovich held a theory of space filled with forces when I tried to refute it by arguing that forces acting at a distance do not fill space and that Boscovich claimed that forces act at a distance. He could also explain how come so many of Faraday's correspondents whom I quote were Boscovichian anti-Faradayans. In his review he simply reiterates that Boscovich's and Faraday's views on force are the same; and honestly, I do not know what to do about this stubbornness.

End of second version.

(2) The gist of Williams's first paragraph is this: "Both Agassi and Berkson overtly make it clear at the beginning that they are using Faraday, in Agassi's words, 'to illustrate a philosophy' and that philosophy is the one associated with Popper's name. This review will be directed at the question, what kind of history is written when it is 'to illustrate a philosophy?' " (This is incorrect; see my reference to Emile Meyerson below.) Williams then discusses our "errors of transcription" which, he admits, have nothing to do with his question. He then illustrates his question: he quotes a description of mine which "serves Agassi's philosophical prejudices perfectly" but which is "totally at variance with the facts". After exposing a few more of my alleged errors, he says this: "I have spent an inordinate amount of space pointing out these errors because Agassi has thrown out a challenge to scholarship that I think cannot be allowed to pass unanswered. Berkson seems to have followed Agassi and before their usage can swell into a trend, it must, I believe, be firmly blocked." Now I do not know what the "challenge to scholarship" is, how I threw it out, why it must be answered,

and what usage of mine and Berkson's can "swell into a trend". But if he means merely to say that we have committed historical errors or, to be more precise, made some errors of transcription and some conjectures that Williams thinks are false or in need of better proof than we have for them, then now is the time to mention that Williams quotes my book in his motto to say I do not aspire so highly, and those who find my aspiration too low may read my book as a historical novel of sorts. Certainly, he cannot demand that if I cannot write an infallible inductive history I should write no history and not even a historical novel; surely he can concede that my book is at least a historical novel for infallibilists though perhaps history for fallibilists? Even that may be too extravagant: even Williams's hero, the infallibilist Collingwood, could never bring himself to call fallible and erroneous histories no histories at all and worse than nothing.

(3) Williams agrees with Collingwood, who "is to be interpreted as meaning that the historian and especially the biographer must attempt, in so far as possible, to put himself literally in his subject's place." Should we take "literally" here literally? Otherwise, it simply means that a historian or biographer should empathize with his subject. Williams declares that I have not done so. He proves this by referring to my own admission that my story of Faraday is used to illustrate my philosophy and by (allegedly) showing me in error on various issues. His concluding paragraph makes it clearer: empathy allows no specific viewpoint: it is comprehensive and infallible.

This is all well and good, except that Collingwood has come to the wrong party: it is common knowledge that he thought comprehensive history is impossible since empathy brings certainty only to success stories, not to failures (of which Faraday's life was full) and since philosophic presuppositions are unavoidable, and even hypotheses are essential to research. Moreover, what should one—historian or not—do if one disagrees with both Williams and Collingwood? It is common knowledge that Collingwood never won public assent; how come he now appears to Williams as the right counsel and authority on history?

The penultimate paragraph of Williams's review explains his proposal to prohibit history from philosophers' pens: "Philosophers tend to be interested in ideas . . . They do not seem to find it very interesting to ask where ideas came from, how they developed", etc. ". . . as we have seen, they are at their worst when trying to account for the evolution of one . . . they cannot really follow Collingwood's advice . . . ." And he concludes by saying that science can develop on Popperian lines, where one author offers conjectures and another offers refutations, but not history: "History is an inductive science. There are a finite number of facts that pertain to Faraday available to the historian . . . any attempt to understand Faraday and discover him, in Collingwood's sense, . . . *must* take the whole body of historical facts on Faraday into consideration. The historian is not free to pick and choose those facts that suit his thesis . . . . Nor is it legitimate to make statements for which there is no evidence whatsoever . . . . If one does, the result is not falsifiability and progress, but falsehood and bad scholarship." End of review.

Does Williams say that he has considered correctly all the facts on Faraday when he wrote his book on Faraday? That he had made no conjecture there? Any reader who thinks that perhaps the answer is in the affirmative is invited to look up my book and Berkson's and easily check our comments on Williams. Does Williams think that his view is the same as Collingwood's? If anyone thinks that perhaps the answer is in the affirmative, they might easily learn that it is not so by any reasonable checking. Indeed, why do we need empathy at all if we have evidence to prove all that we say about our heroes?

(4) One section I wish to devote to Faraday as a natural philosopher. I do not know if Emile Meyerson, whom I follow, was a historian or a philosopher, but he has noted that though Faraday said he was following Boscovich, he was not, since for Boscovich matter centered in point atoms interacting at a distance, whereas Faraday denied such action. I have discussed this at great length in my book. I explained that Laplacian fields of force are no more than mathematical devices because Laplace and all other Newtonians thought that outside atoms space is strictly empty and action between them does not occupy the intervening space. I explained why Faraday insisted that the fields are real and why forces travel in intervening space in time, that Faraday distinguished between real fields and representational fields that may turn out later to be real or fictitious. I explained why the Boscovichian de la Rive, Faraday's best friend, considered him an idealist: he thought the view of fields of force as more fundamental than the atoms of matter seemed dangerously idealistic. I quoted Faraday's responses to some private letters on the controversy in which he expressed his wish to see the debate made public; his responses to the conspiracy of silence of the learned world regarding fields and concerning his rekindled interest and revived memory when fields were finally discussed. Now Williams says that I am in error when I differentiate Boscovich and Faraday, that a glance at Boscovich's diagram should have corrected my error, that I have no evidence regarding my psychological characterization of Faraday as vacillating between high hopes and deep despair, and that my story is sheer romantic fancy since (admittedly) Faraday was a member of the Establishment.

(5) Some of Williams's corrections of my errors—especially one or two of transcription—are accepted and welcome; with gratitude. I am sure my second edition should include an acknowledgment to that effect.

One last point. In his opening he has a note expressing unease about seeming to put down my book on Faraday so as to boost his: he protests he tried to be objective. Had he consulted me about this unease I would have recommended an easy remedy after criticizing his remedy: I would have told him he could not put aside ('bracket' as philosophers say) the fact that he had written a book, quite apart from his own demand that a historian be comprehensive; I would have advised him to do the opposite of putting it aside. I would have advised him to respond, one way or another, to corrections to his book in mine (and to his book and to mine in Berkson's!). In any case, my parting shot is this. People who live in intellectual glass houses should certainly be given all encouragement to throw intellectual stones; but their pretense that they are living in shatterproof, airtight, crystal-clear, comprehensive, faultless domes can be viewed as somewhat exaggerated.

Of the many mis-representations by Williams not central to our debate I pick up one: the course of Faraday's senility. Before Williams published his *Faraday* he told me he suspected Faraday suffered from mercury poisoning. I told him this was at best *ad hoc*, since many chemists worked on mercury and evaded senility; and, moreover, I had evidence against that idea: Faraday told Tyndall in a letter published in his official biography that seeing two papers that had made mention of his lines of force he found his memory refreshed and his ability to think revived, and he even decided, he added, to write a new paper or two. In his *Faraday* Williams does not discuss the causes of Faraday's senility. In his review of my *Faraday as a Natural Philosopher* he presents his old idea without referring to his book and without mentioning the evidence in mine.

I do not recommend censorship against one who violates a minimal standard—the standard that we should notice criticisms of our own views—and who preaches censorship in the name of the protection of a maximal standard—the standard that we should take account of every detail available. I understand that if he had everyone do things exactly in his way, he would feel very happy; and that it matters little to him that others might then feel less happy. But I suppose he can understand that some of us have our doubts.

— 40 —

BUNGE ON
BACKGROUND KNOWLEDGE

harsh but perceptive

I

I recommend this book[1] both as an important work in philosophy and as the experimental venture that it is meant to be. I confess, though, the experiment is more of an educator's dream than a plan; and I wish to complain that I had a hard time reading all the nearly 900 pages of the two volumes, tables of contents, bibliographies, problems and all. Much of the author's work is condensed into the problems (which are really abstracts of brief essays and bibliographies reminiscent of Borges's admirable 'Pierre Menard, Author of The Quixote'); it is hard to read the volumes without looking repeatedly at the general outline, bibliographies, and such additional indications as the author has found necessary to insert. My main technical complaint is that the volumes constitute a strange hybrid of the textbook and the treatise, of the handbook and the systematic work. The handbook may be used sporadically, as its reader need no more than delve into a chosen chapter or section; whereas the whole layout of the systematic text has to be grasped for its central message and argumentation to fully emerge. The general views Bunge has of science, of philosophy, and of scientific method are stated in a few final chapters; they can be fully absorbed only by going through his various problems for the student and other partial treatments of various topics, and after assimilating the general tenor of the two volumes. In addition one may be aided by an occasional glance at other of his prolific writings (by now, we can say, Bunge has

This review of Mario Bunge, *Scientific Research, I: The Search for System; II: The Search for Truth; Studies in the Foundations, Methodology, and Philosophy of Science*, volumes 3/I and 3II (Berlin: Springer, 1968) appeared in *Synthese*, 19, 1968–69 under the title 'Changing Our Background Knowledge'. Copyright Reidel.

created a body of his philosophic works)—some of which he refers to in his problems. When one takes into account, in addition to all that, Professor Bunge's intention to use this book as means to educate both professor and student and to initiate them into the various sciences (physics, biology and psychology, in particular), and their philosophies—one may then get the sense of how quixotic his venture is; perhaps even quixotic enough to be successful. Who knows?

The first of Bunge's messages may, in any case, get across fairly quickly: Bunge does not mince words about his *bêtes noires*, all irrationalism and hyper-rationalism in all its variants; the latter leads to infallibilism which inevitably fails to deliver the goods and, failing to recognize its failure, leads to the cul-de-sac of subjectivism. Versions of hyper-rationalism thus dismissed are, dataism, inductivism, operationism, pragmatism, neo-Kantianism, and conventionalism. Infallibilism finally comes down on the side of intellectual timidity: the less one says, the less chance one has to reveal one's own fallibility. Thus, the major lesson from Popper is hammered in persistently but is not argued at any length or in any great detail; rather, the argument is left to the student conscientious enough to work through the problems; Bunge merely hints at long lines of argument and supplies lengthy bibliographies, hoping that the readers who care will find the arguments for themselves. For Bunge's *bêtes noires* are the lazy thinkers; they are not to be taken seriously enough except as a social factor—as perpetuators of incompetence; one combats them, therefore, not by argument but by the training of new cadres. Now, I think this is not very fair of him. He writes as if industrious and competent philosophers hardly exist. Competence should never be stressed so much, as such overstress easily masks the fact that competence always is a mere tool. He poses to his students some formidable problems: an exercise that easily occupies half-a-semester's specialized graduate seminar can be found here in one-half-page or less, left to the reader to complete. In some problems Bunge tries to direct his reader to write an attack on a very distinguished contemporary scientist; "(Hint: take courage!)", he adds. At another time he is more brief: "(Hint: courage!)". He adds to the problem containing a suggestion to axiomatize a minor scientific theory, "(Hint: ask for a grant!)". Great fun; but a bit bewildering, perhaps somewhat too bizarre, even. Or is the similarity between Borges and Bunge something which cuts deep? Is this the new style of *avant-garde* philosophy? As long as it is possible, however, let me take Bunge's disapprovals and cavalier rejections for granted and translate Bunge's own message into the somewhat outmoded style of a square. Here, then, is Bunge's chief message in my reading.

II

Bunge's two chief philosophical ideas are not new, but new—as far as I can tell—as chief ideas. He takes background-knowledge as the final criterion of seriousness (the scientist must be well-informed, all-round, even); and he takes problem-orientation as the final criterion of significance (the scientist must pose or solve a good problem). Everything else must remain ancillary. Confirmation Bunge thinks is rather important; but even 'spooky' theories can be confirmed. Mathematical methods are even more important; but he offers a mathematical description of the behavior of ghosts. Measurement is almost a *sine qua non*; but he defines a fictitious unit of measurement, the milifarce, based on a farcical theory of bluff. What really counts, he says, is background-knowlege, the problems it gives rise to, the grounding it offers to possible solutions to such problems, the assessment of the force of originality, of depth, and of confirmation, which it offers. Spooks do not merge into a modern scientific outlook. If a simple knife fails to cut the steak, either the one or the other is to blame, and we perform an additional test (cut a crumb of bread, bite the steak). And when we perform such tests we use our background knowledge. Had background-knowledge been unproblematic and of one piece, our procedures would be circular, our outlook be perfected, and science would, indeed, come to an end. This is what happened to Mediaeval thought and to various pseudo-sciences. But civilized, enlightened people—these two adjectives play a very central role in Bunge's thought—can hardly avoid questioning bits of their background-knowledge while relying (practically of necessity) on other bits: we always have to rely on the stablest parts of our knowledge in order to attack the weakest; fortunately this procedure does not lead to any closure: on the contrary, this procedure, though a bootstrap operation, turns things around constantly. For example, Planck relied on the most reliable background-knowledge he had, and he needed one small extra *ad hoc* hypothesis—of quantization. This hypothesis became the most stable part of a new background, round which the old background crumbled as the new background developed. When Einstein presented the world with the hypothesis that Planck's quanta are light corpuscles, which are emitted in the photoelectric effect, Planck's quanta became more reasonable and less *ad hoc*, since Einstein had thus solved an important problem (why do sparks form more easily in light than in the dark?). In this way quanta badly clashed with well-grounded background-knowledge—Maxwell's theory and its electromagnetic waves. And so quanta were viewed with great suspicion, at first, even by Einstein. Either quanta had to be modified to integrate into the existing physical background-knowledge, or the whole background of physics had to be altered to accommodate the Planck-Einstein-Bohr set of ideas. And so it goes. Problems, therefore, must be raised as against a firm background, and attempts to solve them should, to begin with, be conservative: the harder the question, the more the conservative attacks on it are doomed to fail; and the harder it is, the more important its solution is; if a radical solution can be stabilized it thereby alters the scene radically.

Thus, for Bunge, *science consists of two polar procedures: grounding and upsetting; every step in science is a mixture of both; thus, the confirma-*

tion or any other stabilization of even a new minor hypothesis is a (minor) *revolution of sorts, and even the greatest scientific revolution is not total* (ii, 342): *science is a tradition, a part and parcel of a critical tradition, aiming at the increase of the truth-value of our traditional* (background) *knowledge; and so it must remain an aspect of civilized enlightened conduct: it can never be relegated to computers* (ii, 359). This is the core of Bunge's doctrine. The rest is a smorgasbord. Let me briefly give some of the tid-bits honorary mention.

Bunge uses his very intriguing black-box theory quite ably. Briefly, he says that every old theory appears more and more black-boxish, and is in need of a hypothesis concerning a mechanism in the box; soon the new mechanism gets tired and looks like a bunch of black-boxes. This, it seems, is an elaboration of the theory of approximation to truth. Bunge's theory of truth looks more novel than it is; he speaks in places of two truths—the imputed truth-value and the true truth-value, the one being the intersubjective and the other the absolute; and he speaks of the degrees of absolute truth of the putative truths. This is perhaps a mode of speech which may be more agreeable to (Duhemian) physicists than the theory of approximating by many false theories to the one (absolute) truth in stages; the two, however, do not differ in substance. What Bunge calls a higher degree of truth is what others, e.g. Popper, call a better approximation to the truth. Bunge utilizes a theory of verisimilitude very similar to Popper's (and published about the same time); he adds to Popper's proofs that verisimilitude does not follow the calculus of probability (is not additive); and he makes a few suggestions as to how to develop further the theory of verisimilitude. For myself, I do not know why we need the further development; I even saw little value in Popper's original formulas for verisimilitude until I read A. J. Ayer's review of Popper and noted that the formulas had incurred his wrath. For, Ayer was angry n times before, and in each case what he viewed as a trite old error turned out to be a quite revolutionary and significant novelty; and so, by induction. Bunge employs a few principles of induction. Somehow, either they are wild inductions or they are tame inductions which happen to yield wild conclusions. He may be too slick for his own good, but he is at times entertaining, and he keeps his inductivist reader on guard. Take any induction, change the background against which it was made, and see for yourself. What presuppositions enhance (this verb is one of Bunge's many endearing terminological idiosyncrasies) my induction concerning Ayer's judgment? Can they be rendered intersubjective? How is induction related to verisimilitude? To probability? And so it goes. Nobody can accuse Bunge of neatly tying all his loose ends. He certainly does leave to his reader a few problems concerning induction, verisimilitude, probability and the rest. One can hardly call him an orthodox Popperian. Considering how easy it is to accept Popper's conclusion while adjusting it to inductivist terminology; considering, that is, how easy it is to be orthodox Popperian while looking different; and considering that examples of such cases include such thinkers as R. B. Braithwaite, J. G. Kemeny, John Passmore, and J. J. C. Smart; considering all this, it is refreshing to find one who dismisses inductive logic out of hand as a chimera (pace Hintikka) which barely deserves criticism (pace Lakatos), and who still accepts induction with such ease (pace Watkins). Induction, all that Bunge cares to tell us, is O.K. if and to the extent that it is well-grounded (in existing background-knowledge). He leaves the elaboration to his reader.

The chief argument against Bunge's theory would be the Duhem-Quine argument—which he handles very deftly, I think. Cavalier as ever, he leaves his treatment of this topic brief and curt; which, in such a bulky work, may sound surprising. But there are quite a few more hits in these volumes, and surprisingly few misses. Similarly, Bunge handles Craig's Theorem very deftly (only he really should have said that Craig is not a subjectivist-dataist what-have-you); and he pokes barbed fun at the theoretician's dilemma. So much for examples of brief brilliant hits. His treatment of the paradox of confirmation, however, is easily amiss. You can look it all up if you care enough about these various topics—I no longer do; I have already dealt with them at some length elsewhere. Others will soon say more about them, I feel fairly sure, and analyze the details of Bunge's suggestions more than I can or would do here.

III

My chief dissatisfaction with Bunge's doctrine is rooted in his not having offered as yet a theory of background-knowledge. In particular, I do not even know whether his theory is going to be more descriptive or more prescriptive. Let me elaborate.

Background-knowledge is a mixed bag of working hypotheses and rules of thumb, of scientific theories of varieties of levels and metaphysical doctrines, religion, superstition, and whatnot. The scientific process, we are told, unites our background-knowledge, brings its parts together, eliminates some of the grossest inconsistencies and variations and fragmentations and superstitions. The process is endless and so development or progress is a mere matter of degree. But we do not have a theory of degrees of integration of background-knowledge, or even a developed feel for integration in general—though we do have partially rather obvious instances: studying results of attempts to integrate background-knowledge, such as may appear in works of Kepler, Galileo, and Descartes, may well help one to develop a feel for such partial instances of development; but these things are not easy to come by. Even reading Freud or Malinowski, especially when comparing the early and the late writings of either, does provide a sense of improved integration. But what gives this sense is hard to say, especially if we agree with

Bunge that it is not always a proper one (in psychology he sides with the 'hard' schools as against the 'soft' ones). I have elsewhere expounded a view that the chief ingredient of partial integration is metaphysics. Bunge, it seems, does not wish to disagree; but I think he will have to if and when he goes on to detailed exposition.

One trouble with much good contemporary methodology, Bunge's not excluded, is that it refuses to be either descriptive or prescriptive. When Bacon prescribed he had no such problem, nor did Descartes: they could both view the past achievements of science as negligible—at least by comparison with what they promised. So they either had no details to discuss or they had to invent their own—or so they thought. Now that we start from the given achievements we first have to say why we appreciate what we find; we thus present our predilections as filters for sifting what we would describe as genuine science from the rest: if you like Maxwell equations you call them scientific and if you do not like his models you pass them silently by; if, on the contrary, you do not like equations without models, you speak first and foremost of his models. Some historians of science adopt one of these two attitudes, some adopt others: they all view Maxwell as they view science and they all pay little heed to Maxwell himself, to his Cartesian convictions, and to his hopes of reconciling Faraday and Descartes—all too often they ignore his disappointments and difficulties and even blunders (this, under the influence of Koyré, is now changing).

I do not like methodology because it idealizes, yet I am a methodologist and I idealize too. I idealize metaphysics and its role as a unifier, because I feel for metaphysics and because I feel metaphysics is unjustly ignored and neglected and even abused by all and sundry. Also, I feel for the struggle that great metaphysicians of different persuasions, Kant, Boscovich, Oersted, Faraday, Maxwell, Schrödinger, have to undergo when they adjust to the community of scientists. For 20 years Oersted struggled alone and was nearly ostracized, and then he won fame which only altered his discomfort, I suppose, not eliminated it. I can see him sitting in the front row of that early meeting of the British Association—as a guest of honor no less—being the subject of the presidential address of Sir John Herschel. Look at Oersted, boomed Herschel; here is a scientist for you; a fellow who staunchly refused to speculate but for decades just looked at the facts, and patiently waited for the facts to reveal themselves rather than jump to conclusions. Oersted must have felt somewhat comforted by the fact that he had written a paper for the Edinburgh *Encyclopedia* claiming the opposite. But even this makes little difference; now that we know how successful Oersted was, of course we know he had every right to speculate! In short, you cannot cure cowardice by examples of boldness and imagination.

Bunge's books preach and argue for boldness and imagination. Hundreds of such examples are supposed to make it clear to his reader that he is contemptuous of people who ideologize cowardice and dullness. He encourages his reader to do likewise in all sorts of exercises he sets for his reader, easy, hard (Hint, says he: courage!), or impossible (Hint: ask for a grant!). Yet, clearly, the very abundance of Bunge's instances defeat his viewpoint. The average scientist and the average good scientist and the greatest majority of scientists since the foundation of the Royal Society to date are people like Herschel—stodgy, solid, responsible, good citizens, conservative even when they vote radical (Lord Snow idealizes them wildly, except perhaps when he compares them to other social groups: perhaps they are the best after all, though this is a rather gloomy thought). Bunge likes people to stick their necks out, to be bold, imaginative, deep, and original. So he sees science, like Popper, as the epitome of boldness and imaginative originality. As if Popper and Bunge had never visited any department of chemistry in the Midwest, as if they had never read any scientific literature except for excerpts of the best. Bunge, apart from being a physicist himself, shows he has read more, and more diversely, than almost anyone alive; but he thinks most of the junk that goes by the name of science plainly does not count. Maybe. But how does he know? Here his views on backgrounds and his conduct as against the background of his own severe judgments clash violently.

IV

We all idealize, I have said, and we are all ambiguous as to how much and to what end. Bunge, I think, has reached the peak. When he speaks of judging a new contribution to science by the use of existing background-knowledge, he idealizes more than anyone before: he wants the judge to be both bold and judicious, both poetic and erudite. Now, there are few bold people anyway. How many bold and how many judicious people have you ever met? Are these all scientists? Of standing in the scientific community? How many leading scientists, bold and judicious, poetic and learned, are there around? It is really too much to hope that Bunge's view is a true description. True, he does not say that all scientists are bold and judicious over the whole range of science; but who is? Sometimes someone bold and judicious becomes the leader of a specialism—I have Niels Bohr in mind—and then he is so idolized that it makes Bunge mad; yet Bunge will not admit that idolizing is a part of the traditions of science any more than anyone will ever admit having idolized Niels Bohr.

This is not to say that Bunge is now devoid of his familiar strong sense of realism. He notices all too well the ills of the scientific community. He even sees nothing good in psychoanalysis and he thinks that behind the pseudo-humanistic fear of the application of mathematics, harsh logic, and stringent test-techniques to social phenomena, there is nothing short of contempt for human lives (which could be saved by the rigorous application of scientific method). Now there is nothing wrong in principle for a very realistic person—i.e., one who naturally tends in his appraisal towards pessimism—to find something noble in human affairs and call it science, or by any other name, and place it on a pedestal (Hint: take courage!). But I suspect that Bunge's theory of science forbids the use of the pedestal.

It is artificial to isolate science from all other cultural and intellectual activities and to characterize it by a criterion which makes it all good; but is this artificiality harmful? Whatever one's criterion of the goodness of science is, and however satisfactorily it separates, say, Newton the scientist from Newton the theologian, will it separate Copernicus the scientist from Copernicus the theologian? However much it will separate Pasteur the critically-minded from Pasteur the uncritical chauvinist, will it separate Newton the scientist from Newton who neurotically suppressed any criticism? These are very tough questions; but perhaps someone can answer them. Not Bunge, though: if one insists, as he does, that science has a background, and that the process of scientific development is the process of improving our background, then one is forced to take not only Copernicus's theology but even Newton's; not only Newton's neurotic narrow-mindedness but even Pasteur's chauvinism, as relevant parts of the process. Bunge daringly accepts even Hegel's theory of the *Zeitgeist*, though with some modifications which he does not specify (i, 254), as relevant to the philosophy of science. Very good, but then science cannot be so idealized as to be barely related to the *Zeitgeist*.

Bunge's aim in writing the present book—so much more sprawling than other works of his—is intended to alter the existing background-knowledge of philosophers and to make it more congenial to his scientifically oriented philosophy. And if this does not indicate that his philosophy is a mixture of description and prescription, I do not know what might. But, the question is: Is his effort to alter the background-knowledge consistent with his philosophy? He draws attention to the fact that hypotheses which do not fit background-knowledge, such as Einstein's about quanta, are viewed with suspicion. The fact is, however, that Einstein's hypothesis was sooner or later accepted. In other words, Bunge is right in demanding grounding, but he suggests that if we fail to ground a hypothesis it is the fault of the hypothesis, not of the background—unless we succeed in altering the background accordingly. We have options then: shall we try to alter our background-knowledge every time it clashes with some hypothesis? If not, when? What source can answer such a question when the whole of our background is questioned by it? Strictly logically, only logic might, and it will not. This variant of the Duhem-Quine argument Bunge cannot dismiss.[2]

Now what does actually happen when a hypothesis, such as Einstein's or a less well-known one, clashes with our whole background-knowledge? The body of scientists stick to the background-knowledge and reject the ungrounded hypothesis out of hand and rather dogmatically. The rebel either has a rudiment of a new background-knowledge—a new metaphysics—or he is in search of it. Bunge tries to compromise these two tendencies, of the majority and of the rebel. This compromise is Bunge's hallmark. Popper, 'on the right', would rather see the tension stay and provide the inner dynamics, the dialectic, of the growth of science. Feyerabend and I, 'on the left', recommend as much rebellion, and as much freedom, and as many competing alternative systems of background-knowledge, as at all possible. Bunge claims that he is in the middle between Popper and the majority (ii, 325); no doubt this is but a sign of modesty, sincere though it surely is.

V

Whether Bunge's book may serve as an instrument for the reduction of timidity, ignorance, and incompetence—among philosophers or scientists—I would not say. As a monograph, it is perhaps the first monograph devoted to background-knowledge; only it was not written as a monograph.

C. S. Peirce is cited usually as the first writer to have introduced the demand to employ one's total stock of knowledge; one must use all one's information, he said, when judging the degree of confirmation of any hypothesis. Otherwise, he reasoned, we may select only the favorable evidence, and thus cheat. Keynes, Carnap, and cohorts of others, fully approve—emphatically, as one always does, like it or not, when one assents to a morally significant but intellectually rather trite point. Not trite, thunders Sir Karl, but *ad hoc*: there is no other reason to endorse Peirce's dictum than the one he has offered. Sir Karl himself has introduced something akin to total knowledge, namely background-knowledge. If my memory misleads me not, he first did so in 1954, when he wrote his classic 'Degree of Confirmation' (now published in his *Logic of Scientific Discovery* [1959], Star Appendix ix). I do not remember that he gave any reason at all for doing this, so I do not know if it is *ad hoc* or entirely capricious. But his theory of degree of testability soon proved rather inadequate on more than one count. In his *Logic of Scientific Discovery*, Star Appendix viii, he uses background-knowledge in a new effort to define the dimension of a theory and thus its degree of testability. He later used it for his formulas for verisimilitude. Later I myself argued, in my paper in Bunge's volume in honor of Sir Karl, that often a given system of metaphysics leads scientists to prefer a poorly testable theory, not to say an outright *ad hoc* theory, over a theory which is highly testable, but metaphysically unacceptable.

I do not know enough about verisimilitude, but I contend that background-knowledge cannot possibly all go into its formulas; that, on the contrary, only as much background-knowledge can be taken into account as can hang together by one metaphysical system. Those who assert more may try first to specify what exactly they have in mind when speaking of background-knowledge. Lakatos has claimed that he has a theory of background-knowledge which differs from Sir Karl's: in Sir Karl's system, he says, background-knowledge is consistent, in Lakatos's system it is not. And so Lakatos cannot accept Popper's theory of verisimilitude as it stands. Bunge and I seem to agree there is a constant struggle to render background-knowledge less inconsistent than it used to be. I am perhaps the only one to say that we cannot possibly operate with a concept of total or near-total background-knowledge.

There is a lot of intriguing work to be done here (Hint: ask for a grant!), and I should expect much of the study in the near future to go this way, at least among the Popperians, and so I think Bunge's present volume is hardly to be skipped by the curious. For it is the tenor of the Popperian school nowadays, I think, to go beyond Popper's classic works, away from a theory of handling theories in the direction of the theory of handling problems, as Bunge does. Whereas Popper in his isolation had to fight for the rights of problems to be recognized, now surrounded by disciples he faces a certain *embarras de richesses*: which problems do—or is it should?—we select to study? And why? This, I think, is today's agenda, and the reason why Popper and his disciples are catching the interest of the philosophical public. So Bunge is a bit harsh when dismissing philosophers as lazy, but perceptive when stating the following as the main moral of this story: there are publicly recognizable agendas in the commonwealth of learning, and this calls for the formation of a steering committee.

NOTE

1. The present form of the Duhem-Quine argument is, I think, due to M. Polanyi, and presented at length in Chapter 9 of his *Personal Knowledge* (1958). His own view is irrationalist—he says that taking a good hypothesis and rejecting the background-knowledge is a gamble which takes commitment. A risk surely is involved—as the number of possibilities to exploit is enormous and only a few of those are expectably fruitful. But we can reduce the risk by developing a rationale for the action—which is a kind of a metaphysics.

See Polanyi, *op. cit.*, p. 266: "No intelligence, however critical or original, can operate outside such a fiduciary framework"; p. 277: "as there is no rule to tell us at the moment of deciding what is the next step in research, what is truly bold and what merely reckless, there is none either for distinguishing between doubt which will curb recklessness and thus qualify as true caution, and doubt which cripples boldness and will stand condemned as unimaginative dogmatism"; p. 292: "Secured by its circularity and defended further by its epicyclical reserves, science may deny, or at least cast aside as of no scientific interest, whole ranges of experience. . . ."; pp. 309-10: "The active scientific investigator stakes bit by bit his whole professional life on a series of such decisions and this day to day gamble represents his most responsible activity."

ALBERT'S TWO TREATISES

posing as a mere popularizer

1. DEPTH IN ITSELF IS NO VIRTUE

The most painful and disturbing aspect of the empiricist philosophy of science—which has been by far the most dominant ever since the founding of the Royal Society of London—is that it is manic-depressive, though intellectually rather than psychologically, of course. On the one hand its faith in science, in its enormous potentialities both as knowledge and as power, is robust and naive in the extreme. On the other hand it recognizes the tremendous weight of all the evidence against trusting humanity in any sense whatsoever. We may take as an example Sigmund Freud, whose faith in empiricism was always the most basic aspect of all of his activities. His profound and moving *Civilization and its Discontent* lays great stress on this aspect of empiricism. The book begins with an extreme and robustly optimistic view of science: science has made us creative and thus Godlike: almost divine, indeed. Yet the book ends with an empirically-founded unredeemed malaise.

This extremely polarized view, the trust in science and the distrust of humanity, has led to a modern attitude which, I must confess, however reluctantly, has been to some extent vindicated by modern Western history. Not only the masses of the illiterate uncivilized parts of the world, but even the most educated and well-behaved parts of mankind are successfully treated by empiricists because of this manic-depressive stance. Realizing how difficult it is even to train the medical profession in the civilized world, for example, or even merely to improve its diagnostic procedures, medical researchers devise increasingly better diagnostic techniques to improve the diagnostic procedures of the average incompetent physicians, who still use procedures and standards centuries-old almost unchanged. Modern society,

Partly published in *Soziologische Revue*, 2, 1979.

having pushed this aspect to the limit, has tremendous power over the non-human environment but almost no control over the human one—thus intensifying the manic-depressive stance of empiricism. As Bertrand Russell repeatedly declared in the last years of his life, we have the choice between hell on earth and a near-Utopia which surpasses all dreams of the past. The choice is ours. This prospect led C. P. Snow to censure the artists as depressive conservative Luddites, at least as compared with the 'future-oriented' optimistic scientists. Among natural scientists Sir Fred Hoyle is an important social and political authority whose famous science-fiction novel advocates the dismantling of democracy in favor of technocracy.

What we need is new techniques, not techniques pertaining to our non-human environment—a new and scientific social technology—beginning with our educational system and our self-education; especially our self-education.

It is no accident that education is so highly conservative, so resistant to any innovations. B. F. Skinner, for example, invented teaching-machines because he could program them to encourage pupils and he knew that no amount of rational argument will sway teachers from their supreme misanthropy: come what may they will refuse to teach pupils proper rational self-assessment. Teachers base their misanthropy on millenia of experience which inform us that it is best to inculcate self-distrust and the dependence on the proper authority which will direct conduct as much as humanly possible towards the good of both individuals and their society.

One expression, one minor expression, of the distrust of teachers in their charges, is the constant exhortation by teachers for their better pupils and colleagues to avoid superficiality. The human beast is lazy and laziness trains one to make do with the least necessary, and intellectual activity, being very seldom urgent, is thus the first victim of laziness. And so on. My experience shows that the easiest, quickest and most explosive way I know to arouse incredulity is to sing the praise of superficiality.

The reason is obvious: if you allow superficiality, you recommend, it seems, utter thoughtlessness. Ernst Mach recommended intellectual economy. He saw in science as a whole nothing but an exercise in economizing thought. The most forceful argument against this was offered by Max Born in his provocative *Natural Philosophy of Cause and Chance*: one economizes best when not thinking at all. Born endorsed the standard medieval distrust of students, so common among educators. He was a true empiricist, a disciple of puritanical Sir Francis Bacon: he thought the disposition to prefer metaphysics to physics was rooted in laziness, and he said that only when one's working day is over, when one retires, preferably only in old age, may one shift from physics to metaphysics.

Mach's theory of science as economical or parsimonious is not new and the objection to his philosophy is not to his idea of economy or parsimony, but to the view that theories tell us nothing new—no more than the facts they explain; in explaining them, they are merely economically useful. Consider any intellectual task whatsoever—Mach's, his opponents', and others'—and seek the solution most adequate to it; clearly, we want the easiest, most economic solution.

The most superficial idea, deep enough for the task it is employed to fulfill, is, then, the very best. And for many obvious reasons.

When the task at hand is criticism, however, there is a bonus for the most superficial performance adequate to do the job: it forces the opponent to give up the criticized idea on the pain of explaining how they can deny such a superficial point as the critic makes: the more superficial the point, the harder it is to parry it!

This is not to say that it is easy to come up with a superficial *and* valid criticism. The history of thought shows how valid parries of valid criticism have operated to chisel away from the criticism every redundant bit and to present it so that its inconsistency with the criticised view stands out.

This, then, is the ideal critique: explain the problem at hand, and its solution in a manner as easily comprehensible as possible, and offer the most superficial and obvious objections to it; you may then stay on the surface and block all efforts to overcome the criticism.

Easier said than done, this conjures up in memory the happy few who managed such feats: David Hume; Bertrand Russell.

Hans Albert is very ambitious in his effort to follow in the footsteps of the great masters of the English-language style of philosophizing, even while discussing the most abstruse, complex, perhaps profound German-language-style philosophizing. His comprehensive effort in this direction is his *Treatise on Critical Reason*, originally published in German, 1967, 1968, 1970, and 1980, and now in English (Princeton University Press, 1985). The text is as much on the surface as possible, with the scholarly material tucked into the footnotes, many of which refer to his other writings (since he is a voluminous and successful author) where further details can be found.

The overall impression one receives from this volume, then, is of a daring stunt-man water-skiing on his bare feet with tremendous speed all over a vast lake, carrying an enormous torch with which he regularly illuminates different objects in the depth of the lake, but without stopping till he reaches the safe shore. One can see at once that Albert is very familiar with the situation in depth, that his staying on the surface is deliberate: it comes to accentuate Albert's chief idea. This is also the chief idea of the book: the best criticism of all dogmatism is the defense of the critical philosophy itself; this he defends more or less as Karl Popper did earlier in the century, though with modifications of his philosophy offered by his different disciples, which change it from a monistic positivist philosophy to a more liberal, tolerant, pluralist variant. Yet, for a more positive attitude, for a more detailed elaboration, one has also to consult his mature work, *Traktat über Rationale Praxis* (Mohr: Tübingen, 1978), which I hope will quickly find an English translation. In it he attempts to do for Popper what Peter Winch attempted to do for Wittgenstein in his *Idea of a Social Science.* Winch tried to present his mentor's philosophy as a system of, or a framework for, social science at large. Though he failed, his effort won much attention, and deservedly so: were Wittgenstein's philosophy so presentable, its importance would be quite unquestionable. Moreover, Winch's generally-recognized failure is no proof of impossibility, even though this is the thrust of Ernest Gellner's convincing claim that all Wittgensteinians are doing nothing but poor and old-style armchair social science. What is the case of Albert? To my mind Albert succeeds in presenting a workable framework, except that the philosophy is Popperian not in the sense that Popper has expounded it, and possibly even in a way that the master himself finds unpalatable.

2. ALBERT AND POPPER

It is hard to discuss Albert's confessed Popperianism without some view of Popper himself, and preferably from a German viewpoint. For it is quite significantly different from the English viewpoint. Though these days his position as a leading philosopher is quite generally acknowledged, it was not so from the start, and though his writings in political philosophy won him his knighthood, his first mark of recognition as an outstanding philosopher, these are still not as much noticed in the English-speaking world as in the German-speaking world, particularly Germany, where political philosophers are more often and more closely aligned with political parties than in any other Western country (except Italy, perhaps), and where all three leading parties acknowledge him as their ideologist. Why?

To begin with, Popper advocated the Anglo-American traditions—in politics, in political philosophy, in philosophy. To English-speaking philosophers who are in the tradition he praises, this is but a pleasant compliment; and to the others it is one more irritation. For German-speaking philosophers who are trying to advocate the tradition he praises, the picture looks quite different: to them he is a powerful ally.

There may be some philosophic substance to this difference, not only the language barrier, but also the difference in philosophic tradition and temperament which the language barrier helps retain. Whereas the English-language tradition makes light of any philosophy, metaphysics, principles, systems, etc., the German tradition takes these very seriously. And Sir Karl Popper seriously defends here the English as against the German. In a kind of a *reductio ad absurdum*, or in a kind of a synthesis?

This question is very important. The classical rationalistic philosophy demanded proof. The irrationalist response to it, the *tu quoque* argument, says: rationalism demands proofs but this demand cannot itself be proven without circularity, and so is taken upon faith; but then any principle can be taken on faith. Moreover, once we see that rationalism has failed because the demand for proof cannot be satisfied without some presupposition, then the only rational thing to do is to irrationally accept some principle. This attitude can be seen as the irrationalist refutation of rationalism, the reduction of rationalism *ad absurdum*. Or it can be a synthesis between irrationalism and rationalism: take your principles prior to logic, but take logic then as your guide in developing and applying them—perhaps also in replacing them if need be.

How can we decide between the two readings? According to Popper, and more so according to his disciple, W. W. Bartley, III, if the principles accepted prior to logic are accepted as dogmas then the reading of the move as irrationalism is correct; otherwise the compromise is the right reading and, indeed, it even makes rationalism all the better for it.

In complete parallel (if not more) one can say: the thoroughgoing systematic critique of the German political tradition may be a reduction and it may be a synthesis. Bertrand Russell, the paragon of the English tradition in the 20th century, was opposed to (German-style) system-building. In his book on the German Social Democrats at the end of the last century, and his report on them in his book about his philosophical development in the middle of this century, he said that when a doctrine recommends measures that happen to be cruel, he prefers the inconsistency that allows for compassion to the consistency that imposes cruelty. It is not clear whether Popper could leave it at that. He would say, as he did, that the cruelty of the recommendation which follows from a system should teach us to overthrow that system, as it has thus proven to be not good enough. Russell would not object, of course, yet he did not go that far—perhaps on the basis of some politically realistic assessment, perhaps from not wanting to delve into the deep.

We see, then, how interesting and significant is the question: Does Popper combine the English- and German-language traditions of political philosophy or combat the latter in favor of the former? Yet, it seems, the question is open. In particular, a few English-language commentators have said that Popper goes too far in his intellectual distinctions and disquisitions, just as a few German-language writers (as well as a few English-language writers of the German tradition) have declared him too shallow. Too shallow for what? The fact that he is attacked from both sides may suggest that he offers more of a synthesis, though not clearly enough so. And I think this is an intriguing point.

This, then, is the secret charm of the leading German political philosopher, Hans Albert, who humbly poses as no more than a vulgarizer of Popper, and who writes voluminously, successfully, and very influentially. It is clear that his strength is meant to manifest itself not in this or that argument—the specific points he makes are meant to be neither original nor striking—but in the overall effect, the effect that he strives for and evidently achieves significantly often. He has an enormous sense of proportion, he tries to stay reasonable and commonsensical—that is to say, those who accuse the English philosophers of superficiality will see him as English. Nevertheless, he does achieve some depth of overall view: he strikes the deepest metaphysical roots of all political philosophy. Since his effect is largely a matter of overall achievement, it is of little use to cite details of his works, and any detail cited can serve as illustration only, not as evidence of strength or of weakness.

The problems Albert raises in his two treatises are simple. In the first treatise, on critical reason, he asks: How can a philosopher with [merely] tentative first principles have a commitment to the life of reason? In the second treatise, on rational practice, he asks: How can a philosophy with tentative first principles have a pragmatic component and what should such a component be?

Let me repeat, it is not that Albert's philosophy is new; only its development is. Already Salomon Maimon said: Kant's philosophy is either proven about the human mind and not about the world itself, or else it is but a hypothesis. And he, Maimon, accepted it as a hypothesis. Kant had no response, and in a private letter commentng on Maimon, this great philosopher of the Enlightenment took recourse to a personal response (and even to an anti-Jewish one). Popper has an excuse for Kant: the success of Newtonianism convinced Kant of the certitude of natural science and made him aim to explain that certitude. But already Salomon Maimon, in his superb autobiography, showed that certitude is not to be ascribed to Newtonian physics on account of its being a partial explanation. To this, too, Kant had no reply. He was too set on his grand system to pay attention to minor criticism. And this, the English always felt, was the danger: the tragedy of a beautiful edifice, as T. H. Huxley mused, upset by a small nasty fact. Hans Albert, I say, tries to meet just this point: Can we build vast unifying systems yet stay critical and attend sympathetically to a small fact? Politically, we have the odd parallel: Can we attend to the political system as a collective, as a unifying whole, yet not ignore the individual's personal views and intentions and liberties?

Young Popper, in his *Logik der Forschung* of 1935, was clearly anti-metaphysical. Though he refused to brand metaphysics as meaningless, he declared it private. He accepted what he labelled Heisenberg's program of purifying science of metaphysical elements. He even claimed that he did better than Heisenberg at purifying quantum mechanics of the metaphysical element it had inherited. In later editions of his book he withdrew that claim, but not his endorsement of the program. In his *Open Society* of 1945 he dismissed determinism and logical positivism alike as metaphysical, endorsing indeterminism and methodological dualism as common sense. He ridiculed metaphysics (ch. 24). Still, he allowed for criticism less clear-cut than scientific experiments, thereby making it possible for some systems, notably history and ethics, to be quasi-scientific. In his *Conjectures and*

Refutations of 1963 there is a chapter on how to criticize a metaphysics, to which Albert refers here (178n). But Popper never offered in print anything like Albert's corpus of publications, or even his present two treatises, where the rationality of thought and practical life are subsumed under both a broad unifying metaphysical system and ordinary, everyday common sense. Popperian, yes; Popper, definitely not.

The novelty of Albert's system, then, is in its being a system, and a commonsensical one to boot. The question of assessing it, hinges first not so much on the interest or success of a detail, but on its possible interest and success as a whole. This preliminary already poses a problem. If we decide that it is true and altogether successful, we have a new final system, German style. If only details need correction, the system can still hold with a minor facelift. Very German and very un-English. If, however, we see the system as transient, as the author repeatedly enjoins us to do, how then will it be judged? It should be judged, to take the criterion Popper has recommended, by asking: 1. Does it fulfill the aims it tries to fulfill? 2. Better than its predecessors? And then: 3. Does it overcome the obvious criticisms one might launch against it? This is good enough as a beginning, perhaps.

The aim of Albert's system is to unify fallibilism, realism, and rationalism into critical rationalism—this can already be found in Popper's works—which encompasses a unifying philosophy in Kant's sense, yet is common sense. In particular, he wants here to outline the place of human thought and action in such a philosophy. His first treatise is dedicated to Popper, the leading fallibilist philosopher. In the first place he contrasts his views of reason with those of the old-style rationalists who require proof, and of the irrationalists who, despairing of proof, require commitment anyway—who "retreat to commitment", to use Bartley's apt phrase. In the second place he discusses his Popperian theory of reason as opposed to other leading ideas on the topic. And the same holds for his second treatise. His second treatise is dedicated to Adam Smith and Max Weber, the saints of individualistic social philosophy and science. Here he contrasts his views of action with those of the old-style rationalists and of the irrationalists. Then he discusses his theory of rational practice as opposed to other leading ideas on the topic. And from the start he takes the structuring of a system to be a rational practice; unlike the classical philosophers, he offers not only the complete prepared dish, but also the recipe, and a discussion of the recipe. Indeed, it is hard to decide where the one ends and the other begins. This, again, has a political parallel. In politics we also have procedures as well as contents of discussion. Yet the content of democracy is largely the democratic process itself.

3. CRITICAL REASON AS GENUINE OPEN-ENDEDNESS

Open-endedness is often used by philosophers as the last resort: when language, or science, or rationality, or anything else human is characterized as fully as possible, with the intent of offering a full characterization and with a performance that falls short of the intent, then an author can always appeal to open-endedness. This amounts to a tacit modification: the intent, in view of the failure to provide a full characterization, is now the mere achievement of the limit of possible characterization. This sounds eminently reasonable, since one cannot demand the performance of the impossible. Yet it is not in the least reasonable. Time and again attempts are made at a full characterization, and then the full characterization is replaced with something else, which is proposed at the last moment and is therefore not examined. The pious hope is expressed that efforts continue, that more ground will be gained. The idea is not expressed that the best way to ensure further conquest is to ensure further efforts to reach a full characterization. The atmosphere is pervaded with the idea that admitting defeat too early is discouragement and thus betrayal. The idea, by its very nature, cannot be articulated without self-betrayal. And so the idea is never examined.

Science triumphant thus continues to behave as science militant. It becomes as nasty as any victor who forgets to lay down weapons and declare peace. (This is the correct part of the otherwise anti-scientific irrationalist philosophy of Paul Feyerabend.)

Albert's *Treatise on Critical Reason* is relatively short—running up to 229 pages plus some prefatory material and index—divided into seven chapters and subdivided into 28 sections of a few pages each. Here is an abstract, with comments in square brackets.

I. 1. Classical theory of rationality is the problem of foundation, or of the Archimedean point, of a theoretical monism (p. 15).

2. Yet any proof is question-begging, leading to infinite regress, circularity, or arbitrariness.

3. The only alternative is to say that the truth reveals herself. Yet this only shifts the problem: Do we understand the revealed truth correctly (p. 23)? Admittedly the revelation of the truth through sensation (Bacon) or through reason (Descartes) is democratizing (p. 28), but is still authoritarian. [It was not viewed as such as long as revealed truths seemed quite unproblematic.]

4. This involved empirical data or some axiom as given. Yet empiricists underestimate speculations (p. 35), especially those which are counter-intuitive, as the intellectualists overlook counter-intuitive hypotheses (p. 36).

II. 5. The very idea that rationality equals proof is a dogma, and one which tends to inhibit scientific advancement (p. 40): the search for truth differs from the search for certitude (p. 44), because the road to the truth is that of criticism: infallibilism must give way to fallibilism (p. 47).

6. It is customary to distinguish the context of discovery from the context of justification (Reichenbach [it was William Whewell who did that, a century earlier]). But once justification is given up as a bad job, and thereby both methodological naturalism and methodological formalism are overcome (p. 53), the road is opened to the study of heuristic (pp. 50–51). [In 1935 Popper declared heuristic to be of no concern to methodology.]

7. Critical examination is the search for inconsistencies (p. 55). Logic is the organ of criticism (p. 56). The logic of critical rationalism is Socratic and pre-Socratic, not Hegelian (p. 57). Instead of justifications, seek refutations (p. 58)!

8. Though science seeks the truth which is one, scientific pluralism is thus made possible. Different avenues of theorizing may simultaneously be critically explored (p. 64), each resting on a different metaphysics (p. 65): science is the alternation of construction and criticism (p. 70).

III.   9. Existentialism leaves decisions free but unrelated to science, and irrational positivism goes the opposite way (p. 75). A critical attitude to values is more realistic.

10. Max Weber's idea of value-free science depends on the view of the value of science as the search for the truth (p. 83): it is a regulative idea to secure as much objectivity, i.e., openness to criticism, as possible (p. 84).

11. The search for the justification of values leads to the search for final values dogmatically held (Weber) (p. 90).

12. Replacing the status of final values as dogma with that of hypotheses inviting criticism opens up new vistas (p. 96).

IV.   13. The problem of ideology, that is to say, of the demarcation of ideology from science, is the same as that of the demarcation of metaphysics from science: the aspect of illegitimacy and the possibility that when one takes an ideology as legitimate one thereby accepts certain values, both vanish with the open-minded critical attitude, and ideology becomes a part of a social-scientific explanation (p. 106). The problem of demarcation is not thereby solved, but becomes a question not of the essence of ideology but of its causal import, as a possible tool of social technology (p. 109). [Here Albert minimizes the problem of the demarcation of science, which Popper says is the central philosophical problem.]

14. Instead of attempting—in vain—to establish any given ideology, we may then ask, how we can criticize it (p. 113).

15. Dogmatic rationalization is a way in which one relates one's thinkng to one's social circumstances; yet so is critical thinking, which is also healthier (pp. 121–23).

16. Indoctrination, the installation of a dogma and the defamation of alternatives to it (p. 123), is behind the practice of dogmatic rationalization (p. 124), common to both religious and secular dogmatic ideologies, are means of political control (p. 124): they lead to blind obedience (p. 126) by arousing anxiety (p. 127). They are supposed to bring about social and political stability yet we know empirically that the reverse is true (p. 130). [I wish I could endorse all that; it was Plato who claimed the opposite: free thought causes instability and has fatal consequences. The fatal consequences (p. 13) of Naziism are often blamed on the weakness and confusion that ruled Weimar Germany. I wish I could say this argument is baseless.]

V. 17. Theology presents the idea of a double truth, but the relevance of the secular and the religious domains to each other destroys this idea (p. 136).

18. The doctrine of demythologization is the opposite of what its name suggests: it allows any new myth on condition that religious obedience is unshaken (p. 145).

19. Protestant theology is on the brink of atheism (p. 151), from which it escapes by confusion or by epistemological naivety (p. 153).

20. Modern German theologians oppose freedom of speech (p. 155), oppose research which deviates from simple beliefs (p. 156n), and demand indoctrination in accord with the interests of their churches. Albert recognizes (p. 158) the legitimate functions of churches and even the authoritarian hierarchy of the Catholic church: the Catholics have an easier task than those Protestants fascinated with apologetic-dogmatic methods which do not hold water. [I really disagree: apologetics has its place in Catholicism no less than in Protestantism, and liberation theology is not much different from demythologization. But the whole issue is complex. All we need here is the defense of religious pluralism.]

VI. 21. The problem of meaning looms large in German philosophy; the hermeneutic school of thought claims that in the social sciences, unlike the natural sciences, we need not explanation but understanding, which is a culturally oriented grasp of meaning of diverse human phenomena (p. 168). In brief, just as in the natural sciences theories are justified by given empirical facts of observation, so in the human sciences the given are the empirical facts of meaning (p. 169). [This last sentence is extremely helpful for outsiders like myself to comprehend much of the hermeneutic tendency to take meanings so seriously. Or, at least, it makes that fact no more strange than the empiricism of the sense-data variety.]

22. Comprehending meanings, then, is just like seeing, and both are authorities like revelation.

23. Wittgenstein's language-games theory legitimizes both science and theology as different games (p. 181). It justifies, likewise, any existing set: it is hyper-conservative and high-handed. Language analysis, like phenomenological hermeneutics, merely restates the obvious in an esoteric manner and leaves things as they are. They are both immune to criticism (p. 184) yet their conservatism is objectionable (p. 185).

24. Meaning is regrettably ignored by the positivists, yet those who attend to it become irrationalists. It is easy to attend to it from a critical point of view: however intuitive our readings of meanings are, they are hypotheses in need of examination (p. 190). Any general theory of meaning will then be taken as a framework for a methodology of the social sciences. The question, 'How is understanding possible?', which looms large in German philosophy and is given the status of a transcendental question, is cut down to size (p. 196). Then hermeneutics ceases to be a political theology and may become a part of a rational study of history (p. 178).

VII. 25. Marx was right to examine the political import of philosophy, (p. 199), and even of the cosmologies of cultures which are sufficiently simple-minded (p. 200), Christianity included (p. 201). Yet critical philosophy has no trouble handling these matters commonsensically.

26. Philosophies opposed to the current political system and its accompanying political theology, may develop eschatologic and catastrophic ones. They are equally obsolete.

27. Democracy needs no intellectual authority, though the appeal to broad-based interests led to the replacement of earlier political theologies with a new one—*vox populi, vox dei* (p. 207). Whereas the earlier political theologies were quasi-deductive, the new one is quasi-inductive (p. 208). [This is an intriguing historical hypothesis of Albert's, well worth investigation. It may, indeed, explain the dogmatic adherence to induction in the more liberal democratic societies, despite the fact that inductivism is not harmonious with the bare existence of scientific schools and political parties.] The quasi-inductive quasi-democratic political theology was translated into the new political arithmetics of the neo-classical economic theory or welfare economic theory. This theory is a failure quite apart from its intent as a justification of the social system as an inductive machine to translate individual interests to public ones (p. 215).

28. Democracy needs no justification. It is the institutionalization

of pluralism and of criticism. Utopias play the role in politics akin to metaphysical frameworks in research. [Popper rejected metaphysics in his *The Open Society* (ch. 24), and utopianism (ch. 9). Albert is more tolerant and much more flexible.]

4. PRACTICAL REASON AS GENUINELY EXPERIMENTAL

The final pages of Albert's first *Treatise* are largely pragmatic, thus adumbrating his second *Treatise*. I wonder whether this emulates Kant's practice, when he ended his first *Critique* on a practical note anticipating his second *Critique*. In any case, clearly, Albert cannot follow Kant's schema closely, since Kant sought justification more than criticism. Consequently, not only is Albert less concerned with disputes within the physical sciences than Kant; he takes views and values together as unjustifiable yet subject to scientific study and so he treats them already in his first *Treatise*. Yet his second is devoted to practical reason in a closer parallel to Kant's second *Critique*. It is no accident that the second *Treatise* singles out Kant as a target for both appreciation (pp. 3, 13, 19, 140, 143) for his attempts to unify theory and practice, and criticism (pp. 16, 19, 141, 177) for his failure to execute his project because of his justificationism.

Let me then summarize Albert's *Treatise on Rational Practice*, which is shorter than its predecessor—running up to 186 pages plus some preferatory material and indices—divided into eight chapters and subdivided into 28 sections, of a few pages each. Here is an abstract, with comments in square brackets.

I.   1. Having overcome the classical theory of rationality as proof, without falling into subjectivism and irrationalism, we view science as a process, as both problem-solving and decision-making: it is the most plausible way (p. 10), the way of equating rationality with criticism. This has both philosophical and political implications.

   2. Fallibilistic metaphysics needs no transcendental deductions, as its starting-point is frankly a hypothesis, as Schopenhauer already knew (pp. 14–15). [Maimon both knew and followed this suggestion.] This constitutes a normative approach to knowledge (p. 19).

   3. The meaning of a problem—or of anything else—is context-dependent. Tradition is the context and storehouse of problems and solutions, theoretical and practical (p. 24), including matters of decision under uncertainty (pp. 25–26).

   4. Thus social science may be viewed as methodology, of science or of economics (p. 28); as trial-and-error progressing towards given ends (p. 29).

II.   5. For reasonable trials and errors we may want norms; and these too are achieved by trial-and-error on the assumption of the ideal objective norms: truth, justice, etc. (p. 34).

6. Popper's theory of natural science as aiming at a true cosmology fits this very well (pp. 38–39). [Not quite: he does not leave room for the growth of scientific norms nor will he allow an Albertian positive theory of the norms and regulative ideas of science akin to positive economics. Similarly, Popper never withdrew his opposition to metaphysics (*Logik der Forschung*, last section). According to Albert, but not according to Popper, trial-and-error in metaphysics as regulative ideas has a natural role. See my *Science in Flux*.]

7. Ends, regulative ideas, and norms of methods ought to harmonize, but often they do not, and so they need regular reform. In the natural sciences, norms of method may be viewed as the technology of research (p. 46). In all cases Albert sees action, action as tested by mastery; in research mastery is explanation of facts, in technology it is control (p. 48). This view we owe to Oswald Külpe, teacher of Bühler, teacher of Popper. Norms, then, are practical maxims that can be tested in their application, improved, or replaced (p. 50). Hence, though there is no total universal scientific method *à la* Francis Bacon or René Descartes, there are partial ones, or rational heuristic (p. 50). [Popper has viewed this idea of partial algorisms as a heresy.]

8. The social embedding of science is into a capitalistic market-mechanism of sorts, yet one where the public domain is better defined than by ownership (p. 55). There is also a middle ground between the private and the public—the institutions of learning, schools, accepted methods, etc. Loyalty to them may clash with the loyalty to the tradition of research as critical (pp. 56–57). [Popper, however, published his demand for loyalty toward one's teacher!] In economics there is little study of institutions, but the same may apply in that field (A. O. Hirschman, *Exit, Voice, and Loyalty*) (p. 57n). There are different reasons for conformity, and costs and benefit of conforming may be individually assessed: there is no general rule to this and no guarantees (pp. 58–59).

III.   9. In society at large, the norms in question are the laws of the land. The task of harmonizing social and moral codes thus achieves centrality, as it does in the writing of H. L. A. Hart (p. 61n).

10. This takes dogmatism out of jurisprudence, giving rationality to the famous flexibility of the law (p. 68), as a part of social rational technology (p. 69), and this without denying the presence of a metaphysical component in the law, of course, any more than the factual, the normative, and the technological (pp. 71, 73, 74).

11. Social norms thus have a positive role, not only the watchman role of traditional liberalism, yet we remain fast in the liberal tradition, since the positive role of steering society is understood as operating on and within the horizon of expectations of the individual in society (p. 75), where the individual is invited to take an active part in the steering (p. 76).

12. Political economy, then, finds its most natural place within the system of rational jurisprudence. Systems need not operate well in order to count as rational; for this they need to be open to improvement (through harmonization between ends, regulative ideas, methods, etc.). This defines the natural place for research, within economics, regarding economic institutions of diverse kinds and their interaction with the market mechanism. [Albert thinks better than I do of the economic literature concerned with property-rights (p. 81n).] Clearly, this makes economic studies a part of political studies, in the tradition of the political economy of Smith and Bentham.

IV. 13. Violence and war are the enemies of rationality: Albert endorses S. Andresky's claim [and here for once I disagree—cf. p. 106]: all wars were conducted for illusory ends (p. 87n). The state evolved out of, and as an attempt to control, violence and conquest. The idea of the state is the very idea of exploitation, despotism, and war (p. 88), the normal lot of all human high cultures, except for Western-type industrial society.

14. This exception is partly due to an ideologial change as expressed in the utopian literature (p. 92), that first envisaged a divinely justified and hence absolutely just state (p. 93), thereby and with the aid of developing natural science (p. 94) eroding the accepted systems (pp. 94–95), leading to anarchism of diverse sorts, including the Marxist doctrine of the state withering away (p. 96) and of the rise of the anarchic mode of production (pp. 97–99). This makes socialism a version of capitalism, slightly modifed, and yet unworkable (pp. 97–99). No state without violence is conceivable (p. 100) nor a stateless civil society (p. 100n). [Albert finds a positive historical role for utopianism in general as well as for anarchism; Popper does not.]

15. The social technological approach will recommend securing the peace-keeping function of the state. This still leaves international relations in poor shape. Viewing the modern state as an improvement over feudalism (pp. 102–03) suggests the next step: world government as a peace-keeping force. Yet, just as a weak modern state may experience civil war, so may a weak world government. And, a despotic world government may be a regression from the liberal state (p. 104). Disarmament, however, is no security; nor is

any balance of powers. International concords are hard to impose without world government (p. 105). War is not an expression of instinctive aggressiveness but a political instrument (Clausewitz) (p. 105n); we can learn whose interests it might serve (p. 106), and try to change the interest of that party so as to keep the peace, particularly when considerations of social stability are taken into account (p. 106).

16. True, the state takes an interest of its own, admits Albert (pp. 108–09), adding in a note (p. 109n) that this should not be taken as a hypostatization that would not harmonize with methodological individualism. We know in the meanwhile, he adds, how such holistic-sounding expressions should mean as abbreviations within the individualistic system. [I am loath to disagree, especially with a side remark. I have explained in detail in my 'Methodological Individualism' *British Journal of Sociology*, 1960, how institutional individualism can be viewed as reductionist about claims of interests of institutions but not about claims about their very existence and modes of operation. But I am far from being convinced that this is so, much less that it represents the views of Hayek, Popper, or Watkins, though it does represent Gellner; see my 'Institutional Individualism', *ibid.*, 1975.] Viewing the state as a tool, we can see its having a dynamic of its own (p. 109). An end, then, especially the state's end of peace-keeping, is a mere regulative idea (p. 220). The question remains, how it works as a norm and how regulative ideas affect social and political norms.

V. 17. The authorities cannot ignore the economy, as it plays a role in the application of force. Marx got this the wrong way around. The problem of welfare economics is how and when the state should intervene in the economy as a means for maintaining the social order (p. 113). The communist version of welfare economics centers on a fictitious entity, the social product (p. 114), for which we must postulate the existence of society as a collective, i.e., as a super-individum (p. 115). [We can oppose collectivist politics, I think, while conceding the existence of collectives.]

18. The main concern of welfare economics is with external effects, i.e., the effects a transaction has on a third party, since that party may require compensation yet be quite anonymous (p. 122). This leads us to the study of public goods or public utility, positive and negative (p. 123), a study that must continue, since social complexity increases (p. 125), so as to optimally internalize all externalities (Albert, *Marktsoziologie und Entscheidungslogik*, 1967), thus making room for all sorts of possible government-intervention philosophies between the two extremes of no intervention (anarchism, pure capitalism) and of full-intervention (socialism) (p.

126). (The interventions should be effected by individual citizens.)
19. Welfare economics in its traditional Pareto form with social welfare functions is too limited (pp. 127, 132),
20. being developed within the erroneous neo-classic purely capitalistic economic theory (p. 133), which avoids decision problems by ignoring uncertainty (Frank Knight) (p. 133n). Albert has no objection to neo-classical theory as idealization, of course, which might then be a regulative idea and a norm for developing possibly adequate decision theories; he objects to it as a decision theory since when it is applied this way it leaves too little room for decisions.

VI. 21. Property is the range of economic decision secured for the individual (p. 138). The property system, then, is an alternative to systems without property, whether feudalism or socialism, where this range is defined differently and more narrowly (Richard Pipes) (pp. 138–39n). The choice between alternatives, between realistic, imperfect economic systems, is the choice of a legal framework (p. 140). We have here norms, regulative ideas and decision procedures galore, and the need to harmonize them, particularly the traditional problems of choice between freedom and justice as well as between freedom and security, whether internal or external. Here enters a crucial new idea: approximation to an ideal (p. 144).
22. The idea of distributive justice makes the penal system protective. This is problematic, but the best we have (p. 146). The best distributive economy is that of a free market regulated by government intervention (p. 148), yet it, too, is very problematic (pp. 149–150).
23. Short-term *ad hoc* decisions are unavoidable, often involving institutional changes that are quite long-term. These must be countered by long-term political planning, not long-term in the utopian sense, but in the sense of more adequate, i.e., scientific, problem-solving (p. 151), more closely knit with regulative ideas (p. 152), and enabling legislators to present partial ends to approximate by piecemeal methods. [Here Albert embeds Popper's view of piecemeal social engineering in a broader context. He thus puts a limitation on it; yet he does not do so openly (p. 152).] This is a requirement for flexibility that should make political revolutions unnecessary (p. 153). Legislation, then, is subject to heuristic considerations, much like science (Hayek) (p. 154n).
24. Freedom is a matter of degree (p. 156), and the criterion of choice between alternative legal systems (Mill) (p. 157n). A system geared to securing freedom should evolve techniques of guidance by means of sets of incentives—positive and negative (p. 158)—intended to direct individual interests in institutionalized channels (p. 159), in an effort to better harmonize diverse efforts.

The channels in question may be markets or organizations, and their interplay also needs steering, with the usual aim of securing a broad spectrum of decisions open to the individual (p. 163).

VII. 25. What is wrong with political messianism? Its fanaticism (Russell) (p. 168n), couched in an erroneous methodology (Popper) (p. 168n). Worse, it offers no alternative ideas of rational practice (p. 169).

26. Political problems are not given to once-and-for-all solutions messianistic style, but to solutions that are strongly context-dependent (pp. 171–72), especially since far-reaching solutions at once alter the incentive system and thus the mechanisms of social controls (p. 173). This drives the new messianists towards favoring technocratic solutions to social problems, which are naturally undemocratic, dogmatic, and totalitarian (pp. 173–74). What is wrong with technocracy is its poor theory of social technology (p. 175).

27. The philosophy of freedom and democracy is that of the individual's intellectual and moral autonomy (Kant) (p. 177), and this goes well not with Kant's total justification of his system, but with a fallibilist philosophy, particularly because we do not have even a sufficiently good and consistent picture of any society that we may want to justify (pp. 179–180). This is why any dogma is liable to be an impediment to progress (p. 181) and the very legitimation of any social order is worst in this very respect (p. 182).

28. The last section recapitulates some of the chief ideas of the book, returning to the interplay between *ad hoc* legislation and legislating regulative ideas for society—which interplay, too, should be revisable.

I hope that the favorable reception of the English version of Albert's *Treatise on Critical Reason* will bring about the speedy translation of his more detailed *Treatise on Rational Practice*. I hope my summaries and comments may serve that end. I hope, too, that the reader can see the two treatises as parts of a whole. It is clear that the second *Treatise* is more detailed because of its more constructive concern. And it is always very hard to decide how deep to go and how involved to get in details: quite generally, the Scylla and Charibdis of a book that is programmatic are, as Aristotle already noticed in his critique of Plato's *Republic*, that it is too detailed or too sketchy (or both). By what criterion? By the criterion a programmatic book sets itself: it should help and goad and inspire and excite its reader. Details the reader can construct for himself are redundant at best, outlines that are too vague or too uninteresting will not be filled with details. This is very much like sheet music for improvisers: if they improvise better without the sheets, or if they cannot easily improvise even while looking at them, then the sheets contain too much or too little.

I cannot, therefore, judge this book as well as the reader might. I have found, for example, the critique of Marxism rather redundant, even though it takes a small part of this book. But then it was written for the author's countrymen, many of whom are still, in my view, caught in the web of Marxist casuistics. I find the book strongest on economics and weakest on social anthropology, but this is no criticism, of course. Politically, I am a bit more emphatically for participatory democracy than Albert is but this is mere nuance. As to Albert's general ideas as expressed in the two *Treatises*, whether of democracy or of scientific method, since I share most of them, I am not qualified to judge them. I hope the reader finds them useful. North American philosophers who engage in the study of German-style metaphysics, theology, and political philosophy may read Albert carefully in order to examine his claim that much of these literatures is a sheer waste of time. For, whether he is right or not, picking up his gauntlet has to be both instructive and sheer fun.

— 42 —

WATKINS ON SCIENCE
AND SKEPTICISM

cricket all the way

1. A JUSTLY IMMODEST BOOK

John Watkins, Popper's successor in the London School of Economics, a parsimonious author, has now published a sizable volume comprehensively presenting his version of Popper's philosophy of science. Many readers would want no recommendations and no explanation of the background but would proceed to devour this book. Yet the book is written not for fans only; it is written not for experts only; it is as self-contained as any comparable book can ever be, yet it is also as high-level as any.

The book is a symphony. Whatever I think of the ideas it contains, I cannot but praise the execution in almost every respect. I say 'almost' to exclude some technicalities. Yet even of these technicalities I should say that my reservations on them are qualified: read as English philosophy they are top-drawer, even if as mathematical logic they do leave much to be desired. But then, this book is about science, not about logic.

The book's lucid style and friendly tone of its polemics are no accident. It is a really clean book: it is cricket all the way. One can hardly catch the slightest deviation from the rules anywhere in this book and none of these, I propose, affect the outcome. It is also in one innings: the book opens with one claim, and the one claim is sustained throughout and to the very last page. There is one item badly missing here: it is the philosophy of science of William Whewell, of which this volume may be considered a variation; indeed, the best way to characterize the philosophy of John Watkins is that it is firmly planted between rationalism and common sense,

---

This review of *Science and Skepticism* by John Watkins (Princeton: Princeton University Press, 1984) appeared in *Philosophia*, 15, 1985 under the title 'Popper in Basic English'.

as well as between William Whewell and Karl Popper. Whewell himself, we remember, was much influenced by Immanuel Kant. His view of science as finality made his job harder than had he given finality up, but finality made his argument simpler. Now that finality is given up anyway, what Watkins shows is, really, how to use Popper's achievement to resurrect as much of Whewell's rationalistic philosophy as possible.

The book is a pleasure to read because its outline is clear and one can easily see how the parts are going to fit together, so that while the author constructs the part, the reader can see both what goes into it and into what it goes; the resulting sensation is the pleasure one gets when reading an intelligent detective novel. The sheer elegance with which the parts fall into place is something to experience. The conclusions of each part are given in advance, so that the reader is never led by the nose and is allowed to skip any part he wishes to skip, especially the technical parts, which he is encouraged to skip with the author's aid and blessing in case he is not up to it.

All this is regardless of philosophic convictions. A reader who has invested some effort in phenomenology, for example, and who has developed some respect for Edmund Husserl, may take offense at Watkins's dismissal of him as an idealist in a brief page or less. Yet no offense is meant: this book's concern is so remote from that of phenomenology, that the omission of that page or so would hardly have made a difference; the reason Husserl is brought in in the first place, it seems, is that Watkins shared his verdict on Descartes's failure.

"Immodestly stated, my purpose is to succeed where Descartes failed," opens the preface: the rescue of science from the worst skeptic assault. "More modestly stated, my purpose is to provide a neo-Popperian account of human knowledge, and especially scientific knowlege," he adds, explaining the 'neo-' at once: it is more Popperian than neo-, yet it is neo- in strictly avoiding all inductivism, having no verisimilitude, and differing from the master about the empirical basis of science.

I should say at once that most of the criticism which the book contains is deft and convincing. Whether it is decisive will remain in dispute, yet at least in part this hinges on the perceived success or failure of the positive part of the book. For, no matter how objectionable all extant variants of inductivism are, if science somehow requires induction, then the quest for new versions of induction will continue. And quite rightly by Watkins's own book! For, the idea that science requires induction, yet induction is impossible, leads to irrationalism—pro-science irrationalism or anti-science irrationalism. Watkins wishes a plague on both. He passionately wants to rescue rationalism—scientific rationalism and commonsense rationalism and any other kind of rationalism that ever was for sale. So he wishes to declare science neither in need of induction nor compatible with induction— not even a Popperian whiff of it.

What, then? Synthetic *a priori* knowledge? Not in England, not in this day and age. Anyone hoping to rehabilitate synthetic *a priori* knowledge is advised simply not to read the book (p. 10).

Ordinary-language philosophy, perhaps? Hardly. G. E. Moore is dismissed with even less fuss than Husserl; gentle fun is poked at L. Wittgenstein; John Austin is exposed as one who has violated the commonest of sense; A. J. Ayer, Norman Malcolm and Peter Strawson are treated a bit more carefully, but their cases are utterly demolished. Common sense all the way, with tremendous respect for the British commonsense tradition, Watkins deems ordinary-language philosophers not commonsense at all; they are not very rationalistic either.

Watkins's defense of rationalism and of science is a *tour de force*: all those who belittle or go round Hume's skeptical argument end up irrationalists of one kind or another. Can one fully admit Hume's criticism, give up induction, synthetic *a priori* knowledge, confirmation, and all that, and still rescue rationality? The irrational defense of science—Michael Polanyi's—is shown to be poor: Paul Feyerabend has convincingly redirected it against science. The unscientific defense of rationality is simply excluded: when Husserl's projected science is seen as not science in the usual sense and reference, but as something utterly new, then he is out of the picture. What, then, is left for a philosopher to use?

Science and Skepticism has all the marks of a well-written book: the reader feels the tension between the wish to savor the page he is reading and the wish to get to the end of the road; nor is there any need to skim through it so as to get the structure. The structure is clearly exposed and an arrow 'you are here' keeps moving while the reader strolls from one chapter to the next. At the end he is bound to realize that the very wording of page one contains the seeds of the solution to the riddle. And then the reader may wonder, had page one altered, slightly, would the verdict of the high court of reason thereby alter as well?

This question is the book's victory. A reader who tries to vary the book's presuppositions so as to see if its conclusions remain, is a reader who has learned a valuable lesson from the book. Myself, I do not know; I have not tried it; I can enjoy observing cricket, but cricket is not my own game. Before elaborating on this, let me outline some of the book's content.

The starting point[1] is Humean skepticism which allows my knowledge of all of my experiences, but no induction and no causation, so that it allows no knowledge of either the external world or of other minds. We dismiss, then, all efforts to resurrect induction by appeal to probability, to utility, or to naturalistic arguments. We wish, however, to overcome relativism, fideism and other forms of irrationalism. This brings us to the end of the excellent Part I (pp. 3–119), which concludes with two proposals: First, experience is not the source of truth but the means for eliminating falsehood, and it is more rational to hold the best explanatory hypothesis—provided it is not eliminated by experience; these proposals are elaborated and defended in Part II (pp. 123–355).

The Bacon-Descartes ideal is of certain knowledge which deductively explains all facts. Barring it, the ideal is (A) to progress towards certainty, and (B) to progress towards the ultimate explanation, unification, predictive power, and depth (p. 130). It is hard to quarrel with this as a weakening, but still only making explicit, of the same historical ideal. Somehow, the choice is scarcely argued for. In particular, it is not in the least clear *a priori* that the choice is coherent. Well, it is not. (A) and (B) are in conflict.

This is very lovely; it is Watkins's generalization of Popper's thesis that probability-increase and explanatory-power-increase go in opposite directions.

Equally lovely is Watkins's Popperian idea that (B) is coherent, that explanation, unification, prediction, and depth increase together. Only it is untrue, to my regret. We can just think of all technology, which has no depth yet much predictive power. But let us press on.[2] What we may expect the book to argue on the basis of what is said thus far is that, giving up certitude and all of its surrogates, we are able to draw a significant conclusion about the choice of the best explanatory theory (not in conflict with the extant evidence). Let us call this the ruling scientific theory. Its choice, we should conclude, furthers the aim of science (B), of progress. This is not to be, as I shall argue.

2. WATKINS'S LINE OF ARGUMENT

The argument evolves slowly. First there are those who not only prefer (A) to (B), but who simply reject (B) or parts of it regardless of (A). Yet (B) is a proper desideratum, it conflicts with (A), so (A) should go; we wish to have no certainty (and no certainty-surrogates). Well and good. Shall we, then, give up (A) altogether and stick to (B) alone? No, says Watkins; we want science to somehow "involve the idea of truth" (p. 124). In line with Watkins's idea of softening the Bacon-Descartes ideal until it gets manageable, I suggest changing (A) from the demand that progress should be towards certainty to the demand that progress should be towards the truth, the whole truth, and nothing but the truth. What, however, should this mean? First, that the thories of science are viewed as putative truths, to be rejected when refuted. This goes well with (B). Could we demand more? Yes, we could demand progress toward the truth as Popperian verisimilitude-increase, in the sense of Einsteinian increase of approximation. According to Einstein the older, superseded theories should be special cases of and approximations to their successors. If we assume a series or a succession of such theories, then none of them except perhaps the last one can be the absolute and unqualified truth; if the last one is, then all the rest have increasing degrees of verisimilitude; if the last one is the final unification of all past science, then verisimilitude-increase to the whole truth is possible. Yet there is no reason to suppose that human language is capable of expressing the whole truth and nothing but the truth. Bertrand Russell even claimed (*Mysticism and Logic*) that it is trivially true that language is limited. Yet not to assert the possibility of the ultimate comprehensive truth is not to deny the possibility of an ever-growing verisimilitude of science.

Why then does Watkins shun verisimilitude? It may be because Popper had proposed a measure of verisimilitude-increase which was amply refuted. But that measure never represented the scientific concept adequately; it was a boo-boo, and every author has the right to a few of those. No problem. Watkins's criticism is so general, he need not even mention Popper's specific boo-boo. Hume's criticism, taken in this book as basic, tells us we cannot infer anything about the future from past experience. Hence, Watkins is very appreciative of the fact that the past success of a theory, its measure of corroboration, to use Popper's term, has no predictive force: today's best-corroborated theory may tomorrow be falsified by new facts. Popper himself says so, but overlooks Watkins's conclusion from this very point. Assume that the better-corroborated hypothesis is probably nearer the truth. Then its chances of coming up better than its competitors in tomorrow's crucial experiment are high. Which is contrary to Hume's criticism (pp. 284–85). Hence, verisimilitude must go.

This is a lovely argument, and if it does not force Sir Karl Popper to publish a response, nothing will but his own free will: if he plays by the rules he must. But now we are concerned with Watkins's gaming style, not Popper's.

Now in Watkins's discussion of all the possible ways of taking account of Hume's criticism rationally, one option remains quite possible: a principle of induction held (neither as *a priori* given nor as empirically based, but) as entirely conjectural. And the question might then be: How should we formulate the conjectural principle of induction? The reasonable answer is offered clearly by Imre Lakatos (p. 283, line 5): if a theory yields its predecessors as special cases and first approximations, and if it wins in crucial experiments against them, it is likely to win all possible crucial experiments against them.

I have no idea whether this conjecture is true. I do know, however, that it is not yet criticizable by any argument offered by Watkins except that this conjecture "cannot be under any genuine critical control" (p. 287). It yields, however the conclusion which is a reasonable softening of (A) in the Bacon-Descartes ideal, Watkins-style. Indeed, another way of formulating the conjectural principle of inductions is: Science progresses towards the truth—which is evidently not a tautology and therefore must be a conjecture about science and reality or about science being neither fiction nor the final truth but the progress toward the truth (Karl Popper, 'Three Views Concerning Human Knowledge').

But the strategy of proposing this conjecture is contrary to the one consistently adopted in the present book. Here the skeptic is given full rein, and he destroys all philosophic predictions like the one offered here, while allowing science all of its predictions, and the question is: will the skeptic destroy the predictions of science as well, and thus science itself, or can science be rescued from the destructive force of skepticism without skepticism being ousted?[3]

The title of the book, *Science and Skepticism*, all of a sudden gains enormous significance. This is exactly Watkins's strategy: he wants science and he wants skepticism too. Can that be granted without violating logic? Lakatos said no (p. 283, line 8), and sought for the statement that corroboration-increase is a verisimilitude-increase, the status of a statement which lies somewhere between that of synthetic *a priori* knowledge and that of mere conjecture; Lakatos, too, could make a boo-boo. Watkins wants the skeptic to have the last word in philosophy: we cannot project any past success, including the past success of science, into the future, but he wants science, and science full-blooded, realistic, with its theories putatively true, and its predictions acceptable and accepted. Thus, Watkins's "immodestly stated" purpose of executing an attenuated Cartesian program, namely his "modestly stated" purpose of attaining a Popperian account of science which is one-hundred-percent cricket, is no joke: no projection in philosophy, yet rationally endorsing science, thus attaining projection via science. This is English on many levels; but the English—or should I say British?—rationale is Lockean sensationalism, and this Watkins will not entertain for one moment. So why have conjectures which are projective only in science and not in philosophy? Because, to repeat, he wishes his conjectures with which he executes his Cartesian project to be "under . . . genuine critical control" (p. 287, line 14), quite in the way Popper presented science.

The final result is thus not very surprising: by all means accept the ruling scientific theories as true (as long as they satisfy certain conditions and are in check; accept the ruling scientific theories as long as science is cricket). The question is: can Watkins show this to be the rational choice without the use of a rule of induction and without postulating any *a priori* principle? Without, that is, even a conjectural rule of induction? Since between the *a priori* certainty and the merely conjectural all options are covered, Watkins seems doomed to failure. Yet this is a misperception: there are desiderata for a rational attitude, the attenuated conditions of the Bacon-Descartes program, we remember: we want progress of science in the matter of explanatory power going in depth-and-breadth and in unity and in the matter of predictive power. Moreover, we want to optimize this within available means. This, then, is what Watkins takes as a basis.

3. WHY ACCEPT?

My own difficulty with this program is very, very preliminary: how will my humble acceptance of the ruling theories of science contribute to this wonderful cause? What, to begin with, is acceptance? How do I effect it and what am I obliged to do?[4]

This question is handled in section 4.51 of the book (pp. 156–59). If I were to single out the poorest part of the book, I would choose this, though Watkins has violated no rule here; he is misled by Imre Lakatos, who has. It is always difficult to steal an idea without violating it, because one is tempted to tamper with it so as to integrate it into one's act, yet if the tampering is an improvement then it is more tempting to make a proper acknowledgment to the original author of the improved idea. The question, to repeat, is: What does the acceptance of a theory mean or entail in practice? The inductivist standard answer is to declare that theory to be true and use it for forecasts. The instrumentalist answer rejects the former and endorses the latter; even falsehoods are sometimes good for prediction. Lakatos persuaded Watkins, however, that there is an error here (p. 339): "whenever a theory or hypothesis that is believed to be false is acted upon, this is because there is . . . a . . . theory or hypothesis . . . that endorses and controls reliance" on the one believed to be false, which itself is believed to be true. In other words, faith entails endorsement of forecast, endorsement of forecast entails faith—not necessarily in the forecaster, but faith nonetheless.

Perhaps "faith" is a crude word and I am a bit unfair. Rather than having faith in a theory, we can "go on" it (p. 340, line 22), and the question is, why "go on" the most corroborated theory rather than on tradition, astrology, the latest fashion?

What, however, is "go on" and how can my acceptance of, as going on, the ruling scientific theory help progress? It is here that Sylvain Bromberger, an inductivist of just repute, has noticed that the public may accept the finished products of science, whereas the researcher may have to commit years of productive career to the finishing of a crude product in the sheer hope that it could be prepared for acceptability. When this aim is achieved, the finished product becomes acceptable; hence, prior acceptance of, and investment of life assets in, the object of potential acceptance, is not yet proper, and perhaps will never be!

I am moved by Bromberger's point and by his sensitivity to the plight of the inductivist researcher who takes such a gamble with his life. Yet, not being an inductivist, I do not share Bromberger's standpoint. In particular, I do not think assent to the ruling scientific theory matters at all, and I do not think their researchers improve chances to contribute to human knowledge by accepting any ruling, even the ruling of his whole community of researchers. Following Popper, I think a researcher accepts the ruling scientific hypothesis as a challenge, as a target of attack. He therefore will not devise a new crucial test between it and its predecessor, since he wants it to lose and not to win and since he thinks it likely to succeed in further competition with the same defunct predecessor. He may thus win Watkins's reprimand, but at least here Watkins and the imagined contributor to progress view the situation differently. Rather the researcher begins by finding faults with the best we have. The plight of the researcher begins with this fault-finding: the researcher is often worse off than Bromberger fears, since he suffers unjust peer pressure.

Lakatos could not endorse Bromberger's inductivist idea as it is, nor the Popperian idea presented here, since he wanted a little inductivism—a little pregnancy; Watkins's whole book is an attempt to avoid being even minutely pregnant (p. 317). Lakatos accepted Bromberger's sense of 'accept' to mean 'work on', yet 'work on' in the inductive sense differs from 'work on' in Lakatos's sense, which includes the wildest heuristic. This wildest heuristic elicits nothing but my deepest and sincerest admiration; not the mess that he introduced to Bromberger's discussion. For, using the lesson he taught Watkins—which is sheer *ad hominem* on my part, since I would have nothing to do with this argument—I shall collapse 'work on' to 'accept' as follows: when we act on a false theory we believe another. If we do not 'accept' one theory but merely intend to 'work on' it, then it is because we do 'accept' another theory as true; and it is another theory which, of course, predicts that our 'work on' the one theory will be blessed and then the new theory too will be 'accepted'.

And so, Watkins clears up Lakatos's mess by telling us he does not enter the complexity of why and how a researcher decides to 'work on' a theory: he may work on an inconsistent theory in an effort to rid it of its contradiction, for all we know, so that we have no rules of acceptance of a theory to work on, only rules of acceptance of a theory to believe in (pp. 157–58). "So it is hardly surprising," adds Watkins wryly (p. 159), "that Feyerabend hailed" Lakatos's proposed "methodology as in accord with his own supreme maxim, *anything goes*, or as an 'anarchism in disguise'." There are, then, rules of research, and there are rules of acceptance of the ruling scientific theories. I understand that the rules of research are meant to make their adherents contribute to progress. One of them is, of course, for anyone even mildly influenced by Popper: Try to refute a ruling scientific theory if you can! Does this not conflict with acceptance in the sense of adoption or preference (p. 156, line 6)? What is adoption? Is preference absolute or relative to a given goal?

A person stands on a desert island. He sees footprints. He follows them, and is led to the scientist's hut. In the hut there is a small, hand-cranked, short-wave receiver; pre-war. The scientist motions the visitor to crank the dynamo while he himself fiddles with the resonating oscillator. A message: "science has come up with a new hypothesis H_{n+1} in the field F, which succeeds both H_n and G_n and even a hypothesis H'_n, from the field F'; the crucial experiment aroused much interest. The press came to hear the announcement of the empirical result. Hurray! H_{n+1} won!'' Interference destroys their ability to hear the end of the broadcast. The visitor is dumfounded. He turns out to be an intelligent layman; it took him great effort to comprehend H_n; he has less of a grasp on G_n, and knows, to his regret, much too little about the field F' though he always has hopes. The scientist is not busy. Indeed, he is all too glad to have a captive audience. He explains. As the visitor understands, he believes.

My apologies to Watkins. I could proceed with my review and discuss his idea of fields of potential falsifiers and show he should not take it as statically as he does (in which he follows Popper's *Logik der Forschung* of 1935, in which Popper made a magnificent point which fully suited his purposes then; but did not in the 'fifties!); I could discuss Watkins's idea of axiomatized scientific theory and show it to be barely ever applicable, not to mention his overlooking of the vagueness of theories on the frontiers of science (does he already believe in quarks and interferons?); I could attack his version of Ramsey-sentences or any other version (not to mention the troubles with second-order logic); I could attack his—and Popper's—views on simplicity (why has he ignored Mario Bunge so?); I could propose that axiomatizing the regulative ideas of science, which he presumes, is not only a mere regulative idea, but also a dangerous one (already Lakatos spoke against premature formalization; do we wish to be guided by ideas with fixed meanings?); that his flattering reference to myself is irrelevant (since my concern was different; but he might have referred to some of the ideas of other Popperians, strict, neo- or ex-); that his view that corroboration matters because the ability of a theory to explain, etc. is enhanced by being corroborated accords with my view of corroboration, not with Popper's (see pp. 288–89); that his idea of the organicity of an axiom system is troublesome (since he begins with axioms of physics, not of mathematics; and he does not mention Popper on this topic; why?). All these are minor matters. I think the reader should not be finicky about such matters and should read the book with indulgence toward its technical parts: they are sufficiently well-suited for their purpose. The major problem remains: does Watkins deliver the goods? Does he reconcile skepticism and science in a rational manner? I cannot say what the discerning reader's final verdict will be, but he or she will find the book both a pleasure and an education. Perhaps the reader will decide that this is the peak of contemporary English philosophy.[5] If he or she is English, they might then wish to move on. If so, I wish them good luck.

NOTES

1. Watkins emphasizes that Hume's skepticism is a derivative of Cartesian doubt. The first-person-singular in Descartes's famous dictum presumably bothered

Spinoza already, as he deemed everything in Descartes preceding his ontological proof mere scaffolding. Husserl attacked Descartes's very notion of abstract first-person-singular. Throughout his book Watkins accepts it, though as a little more concrete. Indeed, he conjures an ideal person, John Wideawake, who is nicely situated in between the abstract and the concrete first-person-singular of the author. I am amused but not impressed. I prefer Popper's notion of objective knowledge here.

2. I am still waiting for Popper or any of his followers to comment on the many counter-examples I have presented to the claim, made in his *Logik der Forschung* and never withdrawn, that degrees of falsifiability, explanatory power, confirmability, simplicity, predictive power, and more, all increase together. This silence is of the kind Popper found highly objectionable when he presented counter-examples to the equation of empirical support or confirmation with probability.

3. The traditional British program of wanting science and only science to have legitimate predictive power was endorsed by Karl Popper in his *Logik der Forschung*. It invites discussion, to say the least, rather than immediate endorsement.

4. I have argued repeatedly that acceptance for different ends or choice for different ends may lead to different outcomes, and that acceptance in the sense of endorsement of a belief is impossible since beliefs are not given to manipulation, as was observed by Robert Boyle, Baruch Spinoza, and even (in a letter to William James) by Charles Sanders Peirce. This point, I think, makes much of the philosophy of science of questionable value.

5. This is not to assert that the tradition of British philosophy is coextensive with philosophy as practiced by Britons, of course. Nor can I characterize British philosophy beyond observing its strong support of common sense and of science, perhaps also its identification of the two within some (rather unspecified) constraints. The identification of common sense with empiricism is due to (the perhaps not so very British) Edmund Burke; and the identification of empiricism with sensationalism is, of course, very old; within the present discussion it is due to John Locke. Fortunately, Watkins is not a sensationalist. Unfortunately, Watkins is not clear as to how much force he allows metaphysics above and beyond its ability to influence research within science. Fortunately, he tends to identify common sense and rationality. Unfortunately, he is concerned with the theory of rational belief, which has become increasingly identified with both the philosophy of science and with Anglo-American philosophy. Popper allows for a shift from the problem of rational belief to that of rational disbelief, but there is too little meat in this. Will someone comment on my proposal to shift the discussion from the problem of demarcation of the rationality of beliefs to the problem of demarcation of the rationality of both agreement and disagreement between any two or more parties to a debate?

SIR KARL POPPER IN RETROSPECT

the positive power of negative thinking

> Popperian *critical fallibilism* . . . The new
> central question, *How do you improve your
> guesses*? will give enough work for
> philosophers for centuries; and how to live,
> act, fight, die when one is left with guesses
> only, will give more than enough work for
> future political philosophers and
> educationalists.
>
> —Imre Lakatos

1. THE ARTISTIC METAPHOR

The concept of a retrospect is borrowed from museology: a museum or a gallery presents a retrospective exhibition of the lifework of an artist, a group, even a movement, to help the public develop an overview and an idea of the pilgrim's progress. What is thus gained is not fully articulated. We should take it for granted anyway, that though prose exceeds the language of art in some ways, the converse is also true. Traditionally prose was identified with the intellectual and the rest with the artistic. Immanuel Kant already disagreed, yet only in our own century was this dissent elaborated upon, when, in order to legitimate his elitist view of science, Michael Polanyi applied the artistic metaphor to scientific research: masters, apprentices, and connoisseurs are the élite, he said, who make art and science grow; great contributors emerge from great workshops. In short, Polanyi supported his conservative-liberal democratic politics by viewing all art and science as products of workshops while he deemed workshops to be closed societies—free but not open. Following Popper, I try to view both Western art and science as products of the open society.

Most of this is previously unpublished. Section 1 appeared in *Sonus*, 6, 1985.

Retrospectives invite the public to take stock: rethink, reassess and open up their emotional responses to new experiences. They challenge. The challenge is both to rethink and refeel. Is an intellectual retrospective also a challenge to our emotions? I think so; I will try to make this essay such a challenge. This is why intellectual and artistic autobiographies and biographies can be powerful challenges on both fronts. For, indeed, autobiographies and biographies are often retrospectives of sorts. I do not mean to sketch here an intellectual biography of Sir Karl Popper, but I begin with observations concerning his autobiography, *Unended Quest*, which is justly a bestseller. I shall ignore that which is not strictly retrospective in that work, including the lovely asides about the history of music and such, and make allowance for the fact that every retrospective is to a large extent, of necessity, mere repetition. Two facts stick out as unusual in Popper's autobiography, one concerning his ancestry and the other concerning his progress.

First, ancestry. Popper tells us he had no master, was no apprentice to any workshop. True, he had a Vienna Ph.D. in psychology; Karl Bühler was the newly arrived master there. Towards the end of his career Popper even repeated an idea of Bühler's about levels of language which he has accepted with his own modification, drawing fire from Noam Chomsky. But on the whole he disowned his own psychological training: he never looked at his doctoral dissertation again, he tells us. A recent study of his transformation from psychologist to methodologist while tenaciously holding to the problem, How do we learn?, appreciative and complimentary as it is, evoked from him only profound displeasure and considerable ire. Yet his earliest work, written in the early 'thirties and published in the late 'seventies, indicates a fascination with the parallel between psychology of learning and methodology: both say we can learn from trial-and-error. In his second Herbert Spencer Lecture Popper finally came out with a grand speculation about trial-and-error encompassing methodology, psychology, and life in general. In a sweeping metaphysical mood he divided the world between the inside and the outside of each living thing—beginning with the primeval DNA molecules which appeared one day in the primeval slime. The inside makes a move and the outside reacts; the first is trial, conjecture, usually error; the second is test, usually refutation. This metaphysics, vaguely reminiscent of Hegelian dialectic squared with logic and Socratic dialectic, is intriguing. When did he develop it? After he was an apprentice psychologist? As an apprentice psychologist or as an apprentice cabinet-maker? For Popper is a master cabinet-maker, and his autobiography begins with an acknowledgment of intellectual indebtedness to his master in that craft. Let no one say Popper acknowledges no master! This may sound nasty, but I know nastier tales. Thus, in his fragmentary autobiography Martin Buber tells us he caught the first glimmering of his I-Thou philosophy [not from reading Ludwig Feuerbach, but] from an encounter with a horse in his father's stable, from whom he was seeking consolation as a terribly lonely child deeply wounded by his mother's sudden desertion.

Popper emphatically acknowledges some intellectual debts, though; to Immanuel Kant and to Albert Einstein. What Kant was to Newton, Popper is to Einstein. This acknowledgment is like the one Newton makes when (quoting Fulbert of Chartres) he humbly explains his ability to see far horizons by the fact that he stands on the shoulders of giants. This also makes Popper much much more nimble than Kant. Kant began his Newtonian career—had his critical turn, as the jargon has it—only in his inaugural lecture of 1770 when he was in his mid-forties. Popper had his great insights, his solutions to the problem of demarcation and of induction, early in 1920, in adolescence, barely three years after general relativity was launched, and within a year of the publication of Eddington's observation which so greatly impressed Popper and the rest of the world: it hit the headlines of the London *Times* as the victory of Einstein over Newton, we remember.

In this light, Popper appears not like Einstein, Picasso, or Stravinsky, but like Newton, Leonardo, or Mozart: not a fox but a hedgehog, to use the ancient Greek metaphor.

Retrospects easily separate the fox from the hedgehog. The fox may move fast, oblivious of crowds or sweeping them with him as a tornado, but one way or another he is too busy to pay much attention. A hedgehog may hog his public or he may hog his hedge and wait for the public to come around to it. Otherwise he may complain. Leonardo kept complaining of ill-luck, Newton of the wickedness of his colleagues. And at times he would suppress his complaint: Faraday felt very bitter but kept a stiff upper lip. Popper complains regularly, yet his autobiography is almost free of complaints. This is as it should be: retrospects are meant to rectify oversights and disregard; they redress complaints and leave them behind. For they give the public the opportunity to reassess by offering them a new overview of old works as against a new background. The meanings of the same old works change with the change of backgrounds or contexts. This is a great philosophical thesis.

A famous and straightforward example for this important philosophic thesis is the setting which Rembrandt's painting 'The Night Watch' has in the Rijksmuseum in Amsterdam. It is set in a room full of contemporary night watch paintings. In that room one is able to rid oneself at a glance of the still popular fanciful stories about the allegedly unusual pose of the people depicted in it and their alleged displeasure at this alleged fact, which still find their way into books on art history and aesthetics. That the stories die hard indicates that retrospects can only offer correction, not impose it. Indeed, we may criticize the correction a retrospect offers. In a few retrospects Paul Gauguin was presented against the symbolist art of some of his immediate predecessors, yet I saw there more contrast than continuity.

Not that contrast is out of place in retrospect. For example, E. H. Gombrich elicits appreciation of Braque and Picasso by contrasting early cubism with some famous contemporary chocolate-box art. Now this is useful but problematic: (a) each age has its chocolate-box art; (b) much art is sweet yet not chocolate-box, such as early Rembrandt and most of Peter-Paul Rubens; and finally (c) some chocolate-box art may be of genuine value, such as Modigliani and Chaplin. Thus, when contrasting cubism with chocolate-box art one has to be more specific.

Still, contrasts are at times most instructive—a point we owe to Gombrich—because critical reaction is at times a positive creative ingredient—a point we owe to Popper; of course his main and central thesis is just that.

Popper received in this way the unexpected, exciting ancestry of the Austro-Marxist and Freudian ideas current in Vienna during his early adolescence. Special mention goes to Alfred Adler who supervised young Karl's voluntary social-work and whose cheap verificationism, the story goes, was dismissed off-hand by our adolescent philosopher. Contrasting this cheap verification of Adler with the hard-earned one of Einstein helped him develop his insight. (Though this insight was the cornerstone of the philosophy of William Whewell a century and a half ago, it was not known in the Vienna of Popper's youth.)

All this matter of negative ancestry is from a Popperian-Gombrichian viewpoint, not from the received Baconian-positivist viewpoint. Popper's own theory of ancestry, however, is not the Popperian but the Baconian. Only when remembering this do we see the justice of his complaints. Let me offer a very clear example. As a physics student, prior to my acquaintance with Popper and his ideas, I was puzzled by the way modern physics was introduced. Classical physics had been presented uncritically—whether inductively or axiomatically or, naturally, as a messy mixture of both. Yet the transition to the modern was presented to my class critically. Later on, while a student of Popper's, I learned the amazing fact that this was always so: modern theories were normally introduced critically, but with the flow of time the memory of the older theories got distorted to smooth the transition. Thus, to say that I noticed the importance of scientific criticism before I met Popper is a half-truth, just as to say that Buber learned about encounter from a horse he encountered as a lonely child in an hour of distress is only a half-truth. All of Popper's autobiographical self-observations are, I think, self-deceptions anchored in such half-truths, they are early truths read against a late background: in brief, his memory contains anachronisms and retrojections instead of self-critical retrospects. And Baconian views on priority are almost all based on retrojections of this kind (see my *Towards an Historiography of Science*).

All retrospects are also retrojections, so let me check up on myself—in retrojecting my own experiences I mentioned the critical presentation of the physics of 1900, 1905, and 1913, which I met as a student; I could have avoided this, since a pre-Popperian physics-student-turned-philosopher would look at things differently: most of my class-mates do. Similarly, Popper himself retrojects whether he likes it or not; but he does not make allowance for this fact, which is quite un-Popperian of him. In his unfinished book of the early 1930s, he still wrote as a half-psychologist half-methodologist, but in his published masterpiece, his *Logik der Forschung* of 1935, in which he destroys the doctrines of the logical positivists as illogical, he appears as a super-positivist and outdoes both Mach's and Rudolf Carnap's indifference to all metaphysics. In parallel with Carnap's well-known *Scheinprobleme*, but without the linguistic nonsense in it, Popper shows that his doctrine is neutral in all metaphysical controversy, especially between realism and idealism, between deism and atheism, as well as between the relativist and the absolutist theories of truth. Now in *Unended Quest* he forgets his own transition from psychology to methodology and his switch from positivistic indifference regarding truth to absolutism, and he systematically overlooks his change from the positive demand that science distance itself from metaphysics—still clearly expressed at the end of his 1938 'What is Dialectics?'—to the haughty toleration of metaphysics in his *Open Society* of 1945, and from there to the proposal that metaphysics offers regulative ideas and is thus a useful heuristic for science on a more-or-less regular basis.[1] He even claims, and in his latest book hints, that I have stolen this idea from him. In truth I stole it from Kant; Popper first rejected it and now he claims priority for it. (Kant at least confessed ambivalence toward metaphysics—the mistress to whom he said he would always return after a quarrel.)

Are these changes, confessed or concealed, not parts of Popper's pilgrim's progress? No. Here artists fare better than theoreticians: we may disregard what either says, though not off-hand; and so the confusion a thinker causes may be more damaging both to his public and to his own creative self. Surreptitious change, says Popper, even for the better, is no improvement.

Popper's confusion regarding psychology need not harm the public too much, especially as long as psychology is entangled in its own problems. Popper's past positivism may be ignored, as all positivism may, logical and traditional. What he says about his own past attitudes to truth is really neither here nor there. But his surreptitious change enhances the confusion between method and heuristic, and this is a great pity. The method which Bacon promised and Popper denies is (almost) algoristic. The heuristic part Popper never denied to be a possibility, like the proposal to drink strong black coffee to jog one's mind, and like following a metaphysical idea and beefing it up so as to make it scientific. (The one, he felt, may harm the body and the other may harm the soul; but this is a different matter.) When Popper admits later in life the—quite traditional—idea that metaphysics can function as a regulative principle for science on a regular basis, perhaps he makes metaphysics a rule of method of sorts. This, for example, seems to be Koyré's view: Galileo and Kepler had a method of sorts: they regularly followed Plato. Koyré is not naive: not every follower of Plato is a Kepler or a Galileo, he knew all too well. Hence, having or not having a method may very well be a matter of degree. Hence the difference between a method proper, which is strictly a routine, an artisan's technique, the skill acquired by training in high-level mathematical physics (which is mathematics, not physics), a set of standard rules of thumb which are often but not always useful, and a heuristic proper. The difference, except where fully formalized or absolutely routinized methods are concerned, between a method and a heuristic is but of degree. There is room thus for dull routine work, for fairly routine work, for a creative touch added to fairly routine work, for craft, for art, and for the Midas touch. Ahh!

Profound differences remain, of course, among Bacon's assertion at one extreme, that dull, only and exclusively dull, collections of experiments can lead to great discoveries; so that anyone can be a scientist; Kuhn's compromise assertion that only an élite of well-trained high-powered researchers, but also each of these, can do fairly dull work and be assured of making useful and interesting discoveries; and Popper's opposite extreme that no method exists, his claim that even Kuhn's description never applies to science proper.

This clarifies one puzzle of the many that Popper's *Logik der Forschung* of 1935 raises. Popper denies categorically that any method of creating a theory exists and he appeals to Henri Bergson's view of the creative genius. He also presents there refutations as theoretical lessons from empirical facts. In part this lesson is a lesson in a negative sense, in the way in which saying what God is not is a theology: Popper has offered here a *scientia negativa* in parallel to *theologia negativa*. But also, he says, as Gerd Fleischmann stresses, criticizing the old opens the road to the new. Unlike John Stuart Mill, who saw in refutations a proper method, and rather like Dr. William Whewell, who saw in refutations a mere heuristic, Popper sees in refutations and efforts at their assessment a heuristic of sorts, a way towards new ideas, and a very important one. But to see this we must hold fast to his idea that refutation is, in itself, theoretical learning from experience, as well as to the distinction between method and heuristic, and admit that this is a matter of degree. In his response to Kuhn, Popper nearly makes this distinction, perhaps, but he is never clear enough about the distinction between total and partial method, which is so vital for the comprehension of these delicate matters.[2]

2. THE POLITICAL METAPHOR

Retrospectives are misleading in their very success—in the very retrojection they offer. Seeing the past in the light of the present involves picking up the triumphant aspect of past struggles, and neglecting other aspects, as well as the struggle itself, the very dynamics of progress. A retrospect is most impressive when it is most misleading. When great creative work is unjustly ignored by peers, by other masters, so that their apprentices are ignorant of it until they go to the retrospective exhibition, then the novelty of the great work strikes them all the more freshly just because of the injustice now being quietly corrected and while overlooking that injustice altogether.

This is only possible because our intellectual Establishment—artistic, scientific, philosophic, cultural—our Establishment acts as a gang of bouncers rather than as brokers and auctioneers of ideas, still less as great patrons. (As a polite euphemism for 'bouncer' sociologists, following Robert Merton, have employed the term 'gatekeeper', and I shall do the same.) The theory of gatekeeping is known as 'the philosophy of': the philosophy of art, of science, of culture. The last great theoretician of gatekeeping is Karl Popper. My opposition to his gatekeeping is my opposition to gatekeeping as such. It is total. The temple of truth is no nightclub and those trying to get in are not bums.

It is hard to know how much Popper intended, initially, to be a gatekeeper rather than to utilize and replace the rule of gatekeeping endorsed by his peers; certainly in his old age he spoke vigorously against gatekeeping—yet in a way which, unfortunately, made him a worse gatekeeper. The ultimate rule of gatekeeping (one attributed to Aristotle in the Middle Ages) is: *contra principes non est disputandum*: proper debate can take place only between parties agreeing on principles. This makes rational debate marginal and subsidiary to the irrational choice of principle. Popper rightly criticized this rule. Popper also endorsed the very opposite stance: there need be no common ground among parties engaged in proper and fruitful debate. Why, then, is this so scarce? Because of no interest, no will to engage in debate. Why, then, are some efforts of this kind frustrated? Well, we need not only will, but also good will, says Popper. Hence, every time Popper fails to engage in rational debate despite his own good will, he can conclude that the opposite party lacks it. This is how, for example, he concluded that I, the person reporting all this, lack good will. For my part I think there are always some contingent obstacles to debate, such as the mistake made by Popper and reported here, and that parties to debate need time, patience, intelligence, and even luck in order to overcome obstacles. Indeed, the deeper the disagreement the harder it is to engage in a debate on it—but also the more profitable by far.

Gatekeeping becomes vicious when paid gatekeepers pretend to be patrons acting justly. They do not tell anyone how to behave or not to behave, whom to appreciate or not to appreciate. The gatekeepers seemingly speak for themselves, apparently they even speak *to* themselves, musing aloud, or rather mumbling half-audibly: you have to listen carefully in order to hear them. But listen you do, because they are gatekeepers and you know they are: their names are ordinary—just Austin or Lakatos or Rorty —but they strike terror so you listen.

The gatekeepers pretend to muse about credibility. They ask what criteria of endorsement are—of a work of philosophy, art, or science—and which item in the gallery shall be purchased. But in fact they are as honest as when they advertise for a university position, and make sure it will go to the greatest flatterer. Gatekeeper, too, are flatters. Big gatekeepers flatter only the greats: Einstein, Bohr, and Feynman; Rembrandt, Picasso and Pollock; Bach, Webern, and Carter; Tolstoy, Eliot, and Borges; Heidegger, Carnap, and Raquel Welch. Your typical gatekeeper may scarcely know Einstein from Bohr, can barely identify the most famous Picasso, and, truth to tell, may be a bit tone-deaf. Regrettably he has little time for poetry. But, being a philosopher, he knows all the gossip-columns by heart. Recently, a leading brilliant young star of the philosophy of science, Larry Laudan by name, put the problem of demarcation of science thus: how do I know that I can trust my colleague the physicist when that colleague swears by Einstein—or by whomever he happens to swear by today? This is the philosophy of the gatekeeper: he is paid to say why he believes what his colleague the physicist believes he has to model himself on the public relations officer, picking up enough of the jargon to sound learned. Laudan might not have had the courage to admit this craven desire to be a gatekeeper on behalf of established experts were gatekeeping not the official doctrine of analytic philosophy of 'philosophy of'.

Let us repudiate this gatekeeping. It may turn out to be impossible. But it is a beautiful thought, worth exploring, at least for a couple of hours. Let us do so now. What then? Most people do not comprehend Einstein or Picasso or Eliot or Carter. But those who do, how do they endorse them? This is the question, I say, which keeps the gatekeeper busy at the door. Can we change the question? It is very easy: if we ignore public relations then people can decide for themselves. Yet we can still ask, how do people decide? And by people, let us be clear, we do not mean Laudan and Rorty; let us now speak of people who can decide for themselves, a handful though they surely are, even amongst our colleagues the physicists and art critics—not to mention philosophers or culture vultures. How then? We do not know. Perhaps Einstein rejected his own general relativity and the received views about quanta simply because in all his majestic serenity he was a restless spirit. Following the modern discussion, at the very least we should modify the question: not 'How are initial decisions made?', since these are either too problematic or too unproblematic, but 'How are decisions reversed?'

Max Planck said that professors never change their minds. They die out and young ones make new decisions, which are usually unproblematic as they are still open-minded for a while. Hence, concludes Derek J. de Solla Price, rather bravely, prolonging life implies slowing down progress. Perhaps we should all have our say at our peak—they tell us it is before the age of 30—and raise a new cadre for a decade or so, and perish at 40. Or, as Isaac Barlow did, resign our chairs so as to let our star pupils take over—or resign as having failed to produce star pupils.

The Israeli Defense Force has a mandatory early retirement age for all of its members: they do not want the very antiquated military leadership which most countries have. When one remembers the fate of Billy Mitchell, who was penalized by the U.S. Navy because he foresaw the surprise attack on Pearl Harbor, then we must admit that the Israeli Defense Force has a point.

Here then is the clue. The question is not to mimic the greats and the not-so-greats, the rights and the less-than-rights. It is to build an intellectual and artistic and cultural Establishment that will act as broker and auctioneer of ideas rather than as gatekeepers keeping the temple pure.

Put it this way. Imagine a thought-experiment. Suppose we track down any professor who dares oust an idea instead of letting it circulate, and suppose we force him to resign. Wouldn't you think that then no professor would dare be a gatekeeper and act as a censor of ideas?

To clarify this delicious thought-experiment let us stress that we are speaking here of fairness, not of conviction. Gustav Mahler and Claude Debussy remained unconvinced; Walter Nernst and Hendrick Antoon Lorentz remained unconvinced; yet they were admirable in their fairness and openness to serialism and to polytonality, to quanta and to relativity.

It is easy to refute empirically Planck's complaint that older professors do not change their minds but are replaced by younger, more open-minded ones: in his ripe old mid-forties, Established Max Planck discovered Albert Einstein: the one was an editor the other a provincial contributor. The rest is history. But this refutation is futile. Michael Polanyi claimed that quite regularly recognition cannot but be delayed. And he cites his own case, his theory of adsorption published early in the century, ignored, independently rediscovered and endorsed a full half-a-century later! He did not complain, gentle soul.

The worst is yet to come. Thomas S. Kuhn endorsed Planck's claim. People will not change their minds, so rational argument is futile. But they may follow the leader, he says, and switch allegiance with the leader, as was the custom when a German prince changed from Catholic to Protestant or vice versa. And Kuhn is clear about the system. The Establishment monitors allegiance because it trades convictions for real goods: money, jobs, prestige, power.

The alternative is liberalism. Being liberal the Establishment may allow Polanyi to publish his odd idea and let it be. The idea did not catch. Who is to blame? No one, I think. The right to ignore a good idea is part of liberalism. There was no active suppression of his ideas. He says: because he was lucky; I say: because the scientific community is rather liberal.

The right to ignore a good idea, like any right, may be limited. For example, military leaders have the duty to familiarize themselves with the best military ideas, at least those pertaining to national defense. Can they do that? Up to a point. What point? It is hard to answer: the point shifts, and the more the military is alert to possible innovations and has the resources to test them, the better they and the national security fare. The same may hold for a producer on the open market, who has the responsibility—to share-holders and employees—not to fall behind and go bankrupt. Thus standards of excellence exist in the various fields of technology. They change. In view of the impending ecological and nuclear apocalypse, the population explosion, and the rift between poor and rich nations we can say for sure that the extant standards of excellence are not nearly good enough. We have to trade not only ideas but also problems, and as the Western military mobilized physicists and chemists in World War II in the face of that apocalypse, so we may need now a new mobilization. But while respecting the right of people to believe or not to believe, to appreciate or to fail to appreciate. This *is* the problem.

The problem is most tricky when it comes to education. Polanyi says, though it turned out he was right, he had to teach his students current dogmas, or else the gatekeepers would have caused them trouble. He was in error. First, even if descriptively correct, it is the wrong prescription: even if gatekeepers justify dogmatism, this fact should not justify the gatekeepers: we should be rid of them. True, some supervision of education has to exist, but it does and should allow us to teach our students many ideas, orthodox and heterodox. Second, Polanyi is also descriptively in error: educators may have to teach orthodox views but they also may teach unorthodox ones; furthermore the educators' task is not to teach students but to help them develop autonomy—the ability to choose for themselves. The worst is yet to come: Thomas S. Kuhn says that our students are not autonomous; we cannot hope that they will be autonomous; we cannot teach them many ideas and autonomy too, since there is no teaching-time for all that; last-but-not-least, he objects to widespread autonomy: it leads to anarchy.

Karl Popper, the last of the great gatekeepers, does not endorse all that: he is liberal and believes in liberty and in the importance of autonomy for the advancement of learning. He was permitted to publish his ideas—*Logik der Forschung* was published in the Vienna Circle's Springer series (which, he says, explains the attribution to him of membership in that Circle despite his repeated denials: it was a private club, he reports in his autobiography, and it would have been an honor to receive an invitation; but an invitation was never tendered). Yet he repeatedly complains. On what ground?

Plagiarism and distortion. Now these two charges seem to me to cancel each other: when an idea is both plagiarized and distorted then perhaps it is a different idea. Even in technology there is a way known as going around the patent, and Thomas Alva Edison's verdict on his opponents was that they did not even know how to steal a patent and get away with it. But stealing patents at least is a matter that ought to be settled in court. Plagiarism of ideas is practically unheard of, and to be penalized for it one must be a persistent plagiarist of the worst kind employed as a researcher in a field common to both university and industry. Even cases of flagrant plagiarism are usually hushed up: matters are quietly settled in closed clubs, while the gatekeepers watch every door and window.

This is not to dismiss out of hand all of Popper's charges—it is merely to belittle them. The clearest and perhaps worst is against Rudolf Carnap's *Testability and Meaning* of 1936, now scarcely noticed but the staple diet for apprentices to analytic philosophy in the 1940s and 1950s: Carnap presented there Popper's demarcation of science as a variant of logical positivism, Vienna style: as a theory of meaning. Is there a case here? No. Carnap evidently thought he was putting Popper's idea in a better perspective than Popper had done. It was admittedly improper both as poor scholarship and as lack of respect: Carnap should not have suppressed the fact that he modified an idea and overruled its author's intention while reporting it. But this is a minor matter—at least by comparison with the fact that *Testability and Meaning* was treated as a classic. One may ask, then, who is to blame for the fact that schools taught as a classic a book with poor scholarship? This, too, is a minor matter—at least by comparison with the fact that the book is a silly book. In that book Carnap attempted to answer Popper's criticism of the claim that simple observations are certain and final: even the sentence, 'Here is a glass of water', Popper says in *Logik der Forschung*, is not a mere report of facts since the nouns in it are dispositional terms and so it entails predictions that may be tested and perhaps refuted: a statement that entails predictions clearly is no pure observation report. Carnap did not present Popper's criticism but tried to answer it by his theory of reduction sentences. Consequently, a confused version of this criticism was made popular; hundreds and hundreds of papers appeared in the 1940s and 1950s—even the 1960s—on the ailing dispositionals and on Carnap's proposed cure for them, which has since left the scene with no trace. All this industry was in vain. Who is to blame? No one. All we can learn from this is that most philosophers lack judgment and/or autonomy. This calls for a plan of action, not for a complaint.

The learned world is, alas, not quite an open society. Kuhn is right: all too often one does have to declare faith in the right doctrine in order to gain entry. Popper's proposal that we ban refuted faith but not be forced to endorse confirmed faith is better, but it is not good enough: scholarship is in no way a matter of faith. Rather, the true scholar has the ability to appreciate in the manner of the true art connoisseur and of the true lover of culture. With no scientific and cultural gatekeepers the problem of credence disappears and is taken over by the problem of how to train ourselves to improve our ability to discriminate and to appreciate. We need incentives for appreciation. Popper speaks—rightly—of the need for institutions which foster criticism. He forgets that we also need institutions which foster appreciation and encouragement.

The politics of learning is problematic because learning is becoming increasingly elitist. Some say that this is inevitable, and for the following plain reason. Democracy invites democratic control, yet who can control the expert except another expert? Leaving the control of experts to experts creates expert clubs as a matter of course. Hence, says Polanyi, the best control of science is internal. Now, again, as a description Polanyi's claim has a significant truth to it. Control within clubs does exist, but it is not sufficient because club unity tends to have top priority at the expense of the public. Polanyi concedes this, but defends the clubs anyway. Clubs are maintained even in democracy—sustained by law and by educational monopolies. Medical associations and schools are paradigms. And so Polanyi opts for clubs and democracy. But clubs tend to turn democracy into technocracy!

This is the argument for technocracy: there is no way to alter the situation; though it is far from the ideal, it is the best. Michael Polanyi admitted that much; he admitted regrettable cases of abuse of power but defended the clubs all the same. The worst is yet to come: Kuhn's ideas are now very popular and he thinks we are not only tops but even ideal. He is empirically in error. Clubs are at times forced by outsiders to improve: at times democracy works and breaks club unity. We can learn how this happens and systematize it and systematically democratize our intellectual élites and our educational system. I will not here discuss how, but make a contribution: we must resist gatekeepers and force the leadership to act as the brokers and auctioneers of ideas. Einstein began this when praising old-fashioned Walter Nernst and, more so, Hendrik Antoon Lorentz, for their fairness. Planck, then, was in error: it is not that people should change their minds but that, like Lorentz and Nernst, and like Planck himself, they should learn to be appreciative of new ideas even while—particularly while—thinking them wild. Planck did think Einstein was too wild, and said so outright, but with all due respect.

Why do people fear wild ideas? Why does Larry Laudan want to know which physicist to trust? These are important questions.

3. THE RELIGIOUS METAPHOR

Gatekeepers, according to Popper, are the hall-mark of closed clubs, whether churches, political movements, or intellectual movements such as the psychoanalytic one, which ousted, we remember, Adler, Jung, and Lacan, among others. Popper also explains this. The open society, he says, welcomes heterodoxy and criticism; the closed society abhors them since it is based on the authority of the pure doctrine and so must keep the doctrine pure. Of course, things soon enough get more complex than that. Thus Martin Luther criticized Rome on the very ground that it did not keep the doctrine pure. The pure doctrine, he said, is what binds; not Rome. In brief, even the question, 'What is the pure doctrine that we should keep pure?' is contestable. There is no way to deter criticism, then, except by expulsion. Hence, the need for gatekeepers is inherent in the intellectual system of the closed society.

Popper says that science is open, and yet he knows that science has its gatekeepers who ousted Einstein himself, however gently, and other heretics as well. Even Popper felt exasperated when he learned from the horse's mouth that it might take decades before Einstein's generalized relativity could find its empirical test! Popper's demarcation of science is an idea of exclusion—of gatekeeping. He says clearly that science must have rules that positively prevent dogmatism. When most scientists you know are dogmatists, what is there to say to this? It is plainly dogmatic.

The parallel between religion and science is disturbing and it goes much too far for comfort. Religious leaders, for example, do not like retrospects. And one cannot blame them. Retrospects are critical histories, and critical histories were invented as tools against established religion, whether Spinoza's *Tractatus Theologico-Politicus* or Ranke's *History of the Popes*. Ever so many theologians insinuate that on essentials St. Paul, St. Augustine and St. Thomas fully agreed. Did they? What are the alleged essentials? And what is the case of the inessentials? The Catholic Church has a set of dogmas, orthodox Judaism has the 13 Maimonidean principles of the faith. Yet open-minded Catholics insist that the meanings of the dogmas are open to private interpretations and some orthodox Jews say: Judaism is purely ritual, not in the least a matter of faith! Even declaring one's faith, they say, is mere ritual!

I confess my shortcoming. I do not know how to respond to all this. I scarcely know what is official doctrine when speaking of a political party or of a government; but then, at least, a party or a government can change views openly and frankly and I do not know if there is here a parallel between political and religious doctrine. The Church of Rome has abandoned the inquisition method, and has changed from the Latin mass to the vernacular mass, and has even changed its verdict on eating fish on Friday. But the unchangeable, pure doctrine is mystery to me: it seems to me that it is either a matter of institutional arrangement, and this can change too, or else it is a pious wish.

The pious wish to have something not alterable is clear to me, and it can be the sight of a procession we wish to persist, the Latin incantation, or an official opinion. But how does one keep one's opinion unchanged? By not listening to critics and by prayer. This is not sufficiently safe. The pious wish for the safety of immunity to change is not that immune: at times criticism is found irresistible!

The pious hope that science offers us just the safety of doctrinal immutability was held, with some degree of reasonableness, says Popper, until Eddington's observation. It was George Bernard Shaw who said in his 1930 toast to Einstein: Ptolemy lasted two thousand years, Newton 200; I hate to tell you how long Einstein will last. They all laughed. Popper offered the same toast, not as a joke. Is he right? I think he pushed too hard, like an ambitious Jewish father. Still worse is the view of Thomas S. Kuhn. He says that we want change, but we want it at the right pace: we have to control the population of revolutions and each subject should give birth to only one in several decades—or else we will be swamped. How does he know? Is his knowledge empirical or *a priori*? It is religious dogma. But then perhaps frank dogmatism is not the very worst: shiftiness is.

Stephen Toulmin, in what seems a desperate effort to incorporate Popper's doctrine into his own tradition by a slight shift and without mentioning Popper, said: religion makes no official doctrinal change, science does. This is not good enough. He probably would have said, had he been braver and more philosophical or less political: official church doctrines alter surreptitiously, and official scientific doctrines alter openly. He might even have said so explicitly had he known that Henri Poincaré had already held this opinion—long before Popper.

By Poincaré's criterion, however, philosophy—at least the philosophy of 20th-century positivists—turns out to be a religion, especially the philosophy of science. Otherwise they must officially behave better—admit explicitly: We once overlooked Popper but now endorse his views; we said that no iota of scientific doctrine may alter because scientific doctrine is verifiable (and verified prior to its being established), and now we say science is modifiable since it is empirically refutable as he says.

By Poincaré's criterion even, much of science itself turns out to be religion. Science once officially endorsed phlogistonism and then, rather than officially admit error, the scientific Establishment declared those who ever held that allegedly ridiculous doctrine to be pseudo-scientific and superstitious (just as Popper declares Kuhnian 'normal scientists' non-scientists). Science officially presents Maxwell's equations as if they were Maxwell's electromagnetic theory. Science presents Mendel's laws of inheritence as if they were true even in textbooks in which refutations of Mendel's laws are presented side-by-side with Mendel's laws. Science suppresses the fact that only yesterday noble gases were deemed noble because it was believed on the best scientific authority that they could not enter chemical combinations, that likewise coherent light from different sources was too unlikely ever to occur, that we could not possibly circumvent Heisenberg's inequalities by repetition and statistics. This makes science still too much of a church: too many of the scientific changes I have witnessed in my own lifetime have been implemented surreptitiously.

Why are modifications and reversals of opinions in science made surreptitiously? Because the scientific Establishment pretends to hold a monopoly over ideas instead of acting as brokers and as auctioneers and consumers of ideas. Who wants the authority of science and why?

The first candidates are the positivists: those who need a religion, who make science and religion deadly competitors, and who take science as a substitute religion. They are the heirs of the giants of the Enlightenment. Once St. Robert, Cardinal Bellarmine, was concerned with the hegemony of the Church of Rome in matters intellectual and so looked for an excuse to give orders to Galileo Galilei; he said to him: Either prove to me that your doctrine is true, or else tell us that it is no doctrine at all, but a mere instrument of prediction, and that its presentation as a doctrine is a mere *façon de parler*. Galileo protested, but the challenge was accepted—even by Galileo, in part. Under the influence of Sir Francis Bacon, one of the greatest philosophers of all time, the idea that science equals finality was endorsed, and Newton's claim to have offered science proper (and the enormous success of Newton) did the rest. Science became substitute religion, better religion than Established Religion!

But all this is past history. Where in contemporary human affairs do science and faith compete? In politics, where radicalists, right and left, claim scientific status for their ideology, where all sorts of political ideologists claim scientific status for their political ideology as rooted in scientific certitudes of all sorts. For they compete with religious political parties and pressure-groups. And nowhere is the dispute sharper than in education, where scientific religionists demand that science textbooks offer as gospel truth whatever is received opinion among scientists today, and where religious scientists demand that the ancient myth of creation should be placed in competition with Darwinism in science textbooks in schools.

This is a shameful dispute, and it came before an American court, where Popper's doctrine was dragged in as an instrument to defend scientific dogma on the ground that it is refutable and dismiss religious dogma on the ground that it is not. What the logic of all this may be defies imagination. For my part, I find the dogmatism of the creationists who hold an irrefutable religion less objectionable than the dogmatism which rests on the claim that Darwinism is refutable science!

I do not wish to complain. Karl Popper has not studied the myths extant within the scientific community. Perhaps he took his cue from much-admired George Bernard Shaw who said, in the unforgettable passage, 'A Lesson to the Churches from Science', in the unforgettable preface to his *St. Joan*: science too has its myths, but they are not taken seriously there and so do little harm. By comparison, I agree: but only by comparison. Once churches have learned their lesson and the Church of Rome has made the Maid of Orléans a Saint and is going to beatify Galileo (I suppose), the comparison may well be altering.

What Popper did say is rather that scientific theories are refutable, and are put to severe tests which might very well refute them, and that they gain credibility at most when they pass such tests. He added that the scientific community has institutions which foster and encourage criticism. He put this in contrast to pseudo-science, and by extension also to metaphysics and, by further extension, also to theology. This part of his theory is clearly in accord with the views of the leading members of the Vienna Circle. He took it back, but only surreptitiously. Pity.

Never mind what theory is scientific. Never mind what views are endorsed by the monopolists of science today, yesterday, or tomorrow. We should not teach any textbook in schools—not creationist, not evolutionist.

The technical part of instruction should be frankly confined to handbooks, the intellectual part should comprise the history of ideas: biblical creationism, Lyell's creationism, Agassiz's creationism; Erasmus Darwin's evolutionism, Lamarck's evolutionism, Wallace's evolutionism, Darwin's evolutionism, and neo-Darwinist evolutionism. And always show of each known answer to a given question that it contradicts any other answer to the same question. And if a pupil asks: 'Whom should I believe?', offer him Galileo's answer: Make up your own mind!

The question is political: how can we kill the science textbook? This will be the Popperian revolution, the killing of the textbook, not the killing of logical positivism and not the pious declaration that science is our open society when science produces science textbooks. The worst of it is that the science textbook is called a paradigm, and declared *sine qua non*.

The secular revolution was the biggest revolution in the West not because it undermined religion: contrary to all forecast it did not. Nor did it even undermine theology. It undermined tyranny—in particular it undermined tyranny in the name of religion. But we still have tyranny, and some, though by far not the worst, is exercised in the name of the best in science. We now need to undermine the tyranny in the name of science. Popper himself says so, and even emphatically. But, alas! not consistently. Nor is it easy to find out the techniques of intellectual tyranny—in religion or science—especially in education, and to design means of countering them.

With this I have exhausted the political and the religious metaphors. For my part, I think science is a religion, and a good one; but its politics stinks as does the politics of every closed established faith.[3]

4. HEURISTIC VERSUS DOGMA

I have evaded my self-appointed task too long: I have given three preliminaries to my Popper-retrospect and have not begun it yet, though this discourse is rapidly coming to a close. I suppose the reason is clear: I am really not qualified; I have a strong appreciation of some of the things Popper has done, a strong distaste for other things that he has done, especially his cover-ups, and clearly my view of him is biased, at least in that, unlike an art critic or a museum curator, I am a philosopher too, and so willy-nilly may count as a competitor. Moreover, what he deems important in his writings, especially about science, is his demarcation of science from pseudo-science, which I think is limited and at times extremely useful but not very interesting, and his solution to the problem of induction, which I understand in a different way from him and which I deem as limited too, as it says nothing about applied science, technology, and practical affairs. For my part I wish to present Popper's philosophy, the important core of his writings, not as a thesis but as an attitude, even as a feel. I am afraid I have to say, and even emphatically, that he not only resents this, but finds it an attempt to belittle his contribution—and even an expression of a lack of respect for the truth on my part. Indeed, though he finds it hardly worth his public's while to know his strictures on me, he has kindly offered me admonition in a few conversations and personal communications. He has made it quite clear to me that he deems my critique of his views a reflection not of intellectual exercise but of an exercise of will—of my own corrupt character. This is meant as neither complaint nor gossip but as warning. The following is my view of Popper, my latest corrupt misunderstanding of him; with this caveat I may begin.

Let me point at a few items in the Popper retrospective, beginning with a general comment on them. Popper's output is large, almost invariably of high quality, and covering an extremely wide range over scholarly and academic fields—from classics to the natural sciences—always delivered in a clear, lively and thought-provoking manner. Delivery may be of secondary importance, perhaps, yet let me observe that the standard excuse concerning intentionally and systematically overlooked contributors, namely that they are not easily accessible, does not hold in the present case. On the contrary, Popper did aim at non-philosophers and caught their attention. It is a blemish on the philosophical establishment and its scholarship that Popper first caught the attention of the general public and forced his peers' attention only by interesting some intellectual and political idols; only then did his peers admit their familiarity with, and some appreciation of, his many writings. (Compare remarks on Popper by Sir Alfred Ayer in his autobiography with his attitude to him expressed, sometimes obliquely, in the rest of his output; or see Hempel's latest, in the Adolf Grünbaum *Festschrift*, and elsewhere in his writing, concerning expressed attitudes to Popper.) To Popper's output, then.

Popper's earliest is his unpublished doctoral dissertation which will doubtless be published one day, even though he expressly repudiates it, so as to place his *Die Beiden Grundprobleme* between his doctorate and his *Logik der Forschung* of 1935. His teachers' college dissertation seems to me insignificant. His *Die Beiden Grundprobleme* of 1932 or thereabouts appeared in 1979 and will soon come out in translation. John Wettersten's review of it argues that the additional material distorts the picture so as to bring the two books into conformity, whereas the earlier book was written prior to Popper's development of his trail-blazing skeptical realism (= realism without evidence for it) which is the moving spirit of his classic *Logik der Forschung*, despite the positivist mold into which it was cast: though Popper confesses there that his realism is a personal conviction, and he presents his methodology as quite neutral to all traditional philosophical controversy, particularly idealism and realism, its skeptical realism shines through its empiricist pages (to echo Einstein's review of Russell's *Inquiry*; see Einstein's contribution to P. A. Schilpp, *The Philosophy of Bertrand Russell*). The book solves the problem of demarcation of science by demarcating it as the body of refutable sets of statements (theories) and the problem of induction by the view that we gain theoretical knowledge from experience by trial-and-error, by refutation. He then takes up criticisms of his views and alternatives to those views and responds to them. Science, others allege, is verifiable, or probable, or confirmed; its theories are explanatory, based on facts, simple, abstract, quantitative, informative; moreover, theories about distributions (probability theories) are irrefutable and quantum theory puts a limit to experimental accuracy. Of all of Popper's responses, none is so important and by now so widespread (and unacknowledged) as the claim that informative content equals improbability. Yet, by and large, many of the criticisms I have just mentioned seem to me to be valid. The book is a mistake, but a magnificent mistake. And it gives us, for the first time, the theoretical background to the common and correct practice of appreciating some grand mistakes even more than some minor correct successes.

Popper's *Open Society* and *Poverty of Historicism* made the impact that the similar writings of the magnificent Georg Simmel failed to make, though neither of these authors has yet been properly assessed. Popper's influence on Greek historians, on Plato scholars, on political philosophers and scientists, all ought to be studied. Ernest Gellner tells us that the irrationalism of the student movements is rooted in Popper's having robbed Marxism of its rationality but not the movement of its Marxism. I cannot say. I wonder how this can be checked.

Popper's *Conjectures and Refutations*, his first collection of essays, contains his first intellectual autobiography, also his majestic 'Three Views Concerning Human Knowledge' and 'Back to the Pre-Socratics'; it marks a clear shift towards a view of science as revealing successive layers of reality—by explaining one layer we try to reach another—and thus as frankly realistic. The second collection, his *Objective Knowledge* of a decade later, won him acclaim and notoriety. Its follow-up, *The Self and Its Brain*, co-authored with Sir John Eccles, seems poor enough to be praised by some super-gatekeepers of the Establishment. Both books advocate a realistic view of the products of the human intellect, a view which is in a sense trivially true, in a sense invites many questions which Popper simply pretends do not exist. Skipping his autobiography, let me mention his recent three-volume *Postscript*. The first volume covers old ground in an effort to present a comprehensive philosophy, and the two others defend indeterminism in the most comprehensive way thus far, arguing from logic, from mathematics, from physics, and from ethics.

I cannot conclude without mention of his axioms of probability and his papers on natural deduction. Anyone who thinks I exaggerate in my description of Popper as intentionally and systematically overlooked by his peers should compare his achievement with those of his contemporaries and examine some popular surveys and anthologies of the epoch. The exercise here outlined is rather easy and not too time-consuming—especially in view of the extant *Journal of Symbolic Logic* bibliography. The exercise will lead anyone who performs it to one's own view on the matter. One may thereby gain insight into the Establishment and its gatekeepers. They will seem, then, I suspect, rather pathetic.

Science is a party of high prestige these days, and prestige invites gate-crashers, and popular wisdom has it, alas!, that gate-crashers have to be stopped by gatekeepers. Popper has appointed himself one. His critique of the Vienna Circle is not that they are gatekeepers, but that they are crazy ones: they admit gate-crashers and bounce the legitimate participants. I think Popper's critique of the Vienna Circle valid; I think the last remnants of the Circle and heirs to it, for example C. G. Hempel and W. V. Quine and A. Grünbaum, accept this; I think that were they not Establishment, concerned with other matters which they deem more important than sheer history, they would frankly admit it.[3] But I think this is a side-show. The real action lies elsewhere. Ideas, said Shaw and Borges, are created in the dark, not in the limelight.

This is a metaphor. God knows where ideas are made and under what conditions and due to what stimulation. Were there a simple straight answer to this, says Popper, we would have algorisms for the creation of both art and science. Life would be ever so dull.

We have arrived at the feel—religious, political and/or artistic. The feel of some thinkers is anchored in a sense of security. We are going to win, solemnly declares the candidate in a political campaign, because we are right, and because justice must win. Poor sod! He knows justice never wins, only, by the grace of God, at times some of the most intolerable injustices are put to rest. But he wants assurance, not the thrill of the adventure. Others want the thrill of the gamble: they want insecurity, not security, but they equally abhor adventure: let the spinning wheel decide my fate; I can be no party to it.

What is this sense of adventure which neither certainty nor chance can offer? I do not really know, but the English have an expression for it: a sporting chance.

Popper has freed science from the fetters of certainty, and fought like a lion all his life to prevent it from falling into the pit of chance. For him science has a sporting chance to progress.

Popper has fervently denied, in his *Logik der Forschung* as well as in all his lecture courses, that there is scientific method, since method is certain to succeed. (Even if the chance of method to succeed were only one in one hundred, turning the handle of the science-making machine a hundred times more diligently would ensure success.)

And yet, the whole importance of the refutation of received opinion, or of the best scientific opinion or idea or proposal, is just this: refutation opens the road to innovation. Nothing is a more potent heuristic than refutation. Nothing is more conducive to progress than criticism of the current situation, nothing more likely to herald the new than discontent with the old. Criticism is liberation.

The positive power of negative thinking.

Nor is this all. We can criticize science by attempting to empirically refute its doctrines; we can criticize pseudo-science by exposing its pretense; we can criticize metaphysics by showing its poverty; we can criticize a research program by finding and criticizing the comprehensive system—the metaphysics—behind it. And criticism opens the way to the introduction of an alternative to whatever was criticized, and vice versa.

But here we have criticism as a tool for heuristic, not a method. Heuristic prods, intrigues, insinuates; it promises nothing. It is worse than being irrefutable; it is elusive, ineffable. Yet we can institutionalize it as the means of democratic control and reform and legislation.

It is no surprise that Popper's most brilliant follower, Imre Lakatos, followed Polanyi before the end of his life: he was concerned with heuristic (it was his one true love) and so he was much taken by Polanyi's—it really is Dostoevski's—idea that some important ideas are regularly on the tip of one's tongue yet never come out.

Popper's stance as a gatekeeper is very harmful for his cause. He wants things clear-cut, new ideas, quick moves to put them to test, tangible progress. Lakatos felt that Polanyi had the better feel and Popper the better articulation. If he could only synthesize them!

But Lakatos was too corrupt and he died too young. He first tried to be a super-gatekeeper, and promised that once his worldly ambition to be super-established was satisfied, he would both compensate everyone in retrospect and perform valuable intellectual work. And he soon died. Yet in intellectual matters he hated gatekeeping, "*gendarmerie*", as he called it, and he found Popper's philosophy so wonderful because it was totally intellectually free: no *gendarmes*! It is a pity that this aspect of his philosophy was lost due to his temporary and tactical endorsement of Feyerabend's view of science as inherently intolerant.[4]

The game of science as Popper describes it is ideal. It is ideal both in the sense that it is an idealization *à la* Galileo: no friction; and in the sense that it is idealization *à la* Bacon and Descartes and Spinoza: no friction. Love is all you need, as the Beatles sang; the love of the truth, that is. *Amor dei*.

Assume the game played by lovers of the truth. Then we need no policemen; people who cheat at chess play no chess but quite another game. In chess one enjoys the game, not the scoring of a victory over an opponent. Proof: to score one needs a poor opponent, or, still better, a poor opponent who is reputed to be a good player, whereas to play with pleasure one needs an opponent equal to one's own self, or, still better, an opponent a little stronger, challenging, offering a sporting chance of success.

Consider chess as part of a way of life. A victory here or there matters little. What does matter is that in one sense each game has a beginning and an end, in another sense it is a link in an endless chain. To be precise it is not endless, both because the number of options is finite and because life is finite. But my life too can be a link in a chain. The finiteness of chess is, however, more theoretical than that of human life: to the end of life the game will not be exhausted. New gambits, new moves, new strategies will be invented without end.

Fallibilism ensures that science is literally endless: we can always seek errors in our past successes. The sporting chance, however, is not promised. It is assumed by Popper in his *Open Society*, Chapter 24. What if this assumption is an error? Popper says: I take it as an irrefutable dogma. W. W. Bartley, III, his official heir apparent, says: it is a criticizable view which I may alter. Popper then pretended he had no dispute with Bartley. But I, at least, dispute both. The sporting chance, I say, is a hope; losing it due to some valid criticism may mean a search for a new hope and it may mean a disaster for myself and for the scientific culture, perhaps. We do not really know, and when a new valid criticism appears, the picture will then alter.

5. CONCLUSION: AN IMAGE OF THE INTELLECTUAL VENTURE

Assume that science is the unending quest for the truth, the whole truth, and nothing but. What remains, then, says Popper, is attempts to present refutable conjectures and attempts to refute conjectures. To this one can add, first and foremost, the desire to have a comprehensive explanatory theory; this desire is never fulfilled, but we approach it by offering comprehensive theories, which are overall metaphysical suppositions, by offering explanatory theories, and by trying to bring the two together in efforts to use the metaphysics as a source of a heuristic strategy. By offering tests of empirical hypotheses, and debates on metaphysical issues, and more, we express our unending quest for the truth. If truth is unattainable, there is no proof that we progress and we can only find that we have more options of pictures of the world, of solutions to problems, and of objections to proposed theories.

To clarify the feel I have in mind, let me dwell on a very popular theory which, I think, has the opposite feel: the possible-worlds theory. Logicians tackled possible worlds out of diverse motives, the first of which is that the probability of a given outcome is a measure of possibility, or the ratio, roughly speaking, between the measure of the possible cases with the given ('favorable') outcome and the measure of all the possible cases relative to which it is assessed. And most philosophers of science look for certitude or for good chance, we remember, But also the modern theory of inference speaks of validity and invalidity of an inference as the impossibility or possibility of its having a false conclusion and yet true premises; and this possibility or impossibility, ever since Leibniz, may take us to possible worlds.

The theory of possible worlds which contemporary logicians handle may have its roots also in fallibilism. But, if so, then they seem to be trying hard to ignore this. Their possible-worlds system is semantic: they ensure that each thing has a name—indeed the same name in each world in which it exists—and each possible situation has a given statement describing it—so that the statement is true in possible worlds in which that situation occurs. Perhaps possible-worlds semantics helps solve a problem in logic which, despite all my efforts, I have overlooked. Here I am talking of a feel. The love of the possible-worlds semantics comes from the hope that even our wildest imagination is bound by today's semantic system. This may be so, but to love it is to me unimaginable.

Some Vienna-Circle philosophers developed the concept of open-ended concepts—especially C. G. Hempel. It is clear that they did not like it but learned to live with it. Kurt Gödel was a member of the Vienna Circle and his Proof shattered their deepest dogma, the verification principle—and thus brought an end to their venture. Gödel's Proof and its results are still open to debate. What I wish to mention is that Ludwig Wittgenstein, the spiritual father of the Vienna Circle, found it otiose, whereas Popper found it a liberator.

Can we think of all of our concepts as inherently open-ended? Can we imagine that perhaps all the wonderful ideas humans have ever created fall short of our ideals—of truth, beauty, or goodness? And finally, the key question: Is this idea disturbing to you?

I think this is the central point. If you say yes, such an all-round openness is disturbing to me, your heart is with the positivists, with their delight in verification, with finality—from the great Bacon and Descartes and Kant to the Vienna Circle and beyond. If you say no, I like it this way, you are with Einstein, with Russell's 'Free Man's Worship', with Shaw, with Popper. Remember the last words of Plato's *Symposium*. The best we can ever hope for, Socrates says, is to be in the twilight zone between knowledge and ignorance, where the views we hold will happen to be true, but we shall not be able to know that this is so. Today more than ever, it is evident that even the twilight zone is but an unreachable ideal, though an ideal well worth holding on to.

NOTES

1. Some changes in the opinions of Popper and some allowance for some possible changes are recorded in his *The Logic of Scientific Discovery*, star-footnotes and star-appendices, as well as in his *Conjectures and Refutations*, Chapter 10. Regrettably they are not straightforward and do not go nearly far enough.

2. Imre Lakatos, who was incredibly sensitive to opportunity, has spotted the ambiguity that had evaded Popper and systematically confused heuristic and method, labelling the concoction 'the methodology of scientific research programs'.

This fusing of Kantian ideals or regulative ideas with the inductivist canons was bound to deliver him the popular success he so much craved, since his ambiguity fits the popular ambivalence concerning scientific creativity.

3. The philosophy of Quine is enjoying these days a remarkable public retrospect, partly in an effort to ascribe to him some of the recent developments in philosophy that I tend to ascribe to Popper. Priority matters aside, no doubt Quine commands the respect of the philosophic crowds much more than Popper, and thus does deserve the credit, even though his agreements with Popper are not always as clearly expressed as they might be. In one way he is clearly in one party with Popper, even though he says he is in general heir to the Vienna Circle (for details see my 'Ixmann and the Gavagai', *Zeitschr. f. allgem. Wissenschaftsth.*): he stands out as distinct from the majority of the philosophers of science as they hanker after an inductive sausage-making machine and when not careful they even assert that the machine is there. These philosophers of science are doing no more than rotating the prayer wheel.

4. The view of scientific education here presented is not very different in thrust from that of Feyerabend. Yet, agreeing with Kuhn, Feyerabend says science is but a dogmatic religion and he recommends as an antidote to it the idea that it should be in a fair competition with religions, ideologies and superstitions proper. In this he appeals to democracy; see his contribution to this volume. His campaign is doomed to fail: he disregards the fact that the competition he recommends cannot possibly be fair: in the most democratic courts the creationists cannot win against the Darwinists, even though they cheat and dogmatize. Yet the representatives of science in the recent court case on scientific education cheated and dogmatized too, and this should not be tolerated. Feyerabend's proposal to support voodoo as a merely temporary cure for the ills of science is doubtful, especially since we should fight the dogmatism of science with no recourse to voodoo and then the chances of victory would be improved and its gains then could be institutionalized.

NAME INDEX

SUBJECT INDEX